W9-ARE-484

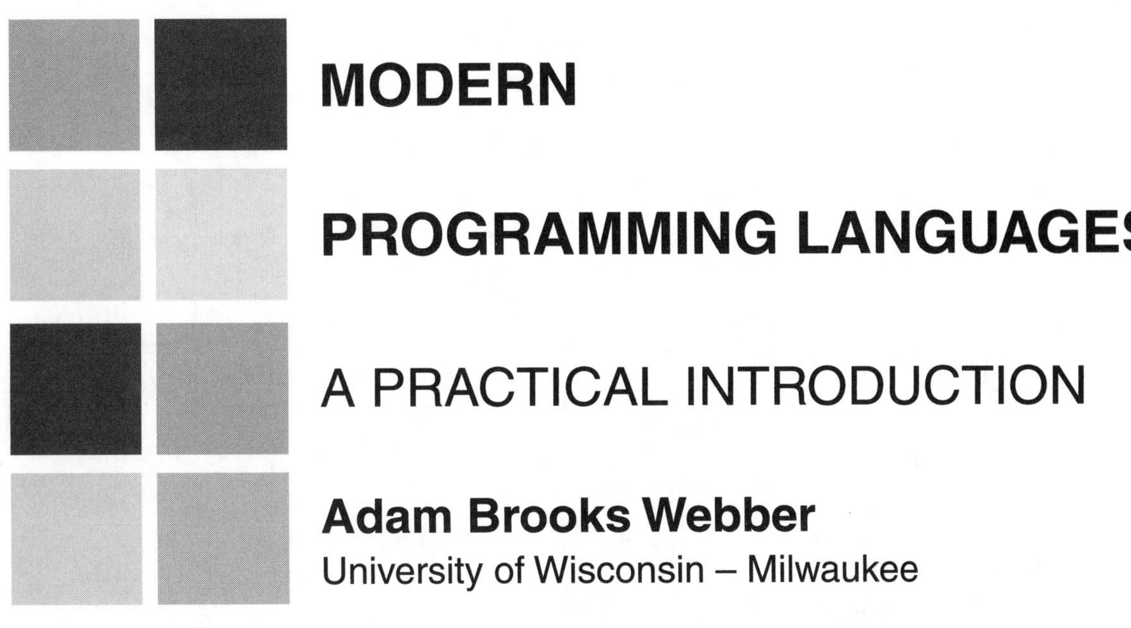

MODERN PROGRAMMING LANGUAGES

A PRACTICAL INTRODUCTION

Adam Brooks Webber
University of Wisconsin – Milwaukee

Franklin, Beedle & Associates, Inc.
8536 SW St. Helens Drive, Suite D
Wilsonville, Oregon 97070
(503) 682-7668
www.fbeedle.com

President and Publisher	Jim Leisy (jimleisy@fbeedle.com)
Production	Stephanie Welch
	Tom Sumner
Proofreader	Dean Lake
Cover	Ian Shadburne
Marketing	Christine Collier
Order Processing	Krista Brown

Printed in the U.S.A.

Library of Congress Cataloging-in-Publication Data

Webber, Adam.
Modern programming languages : a practical introduction / Adam Webber.
p. cm.
Includes bibliographical references and index.
ISBN 1-887902-76-7
1. Programming languages (Electronic computers) I. Title.

QA76.7 .W42 2002
005.13--dc21

2002029840

To

John Galloway McCubbin
1931–2000

Contents

Preface

This book is intended for the introductory programming languages concepts course taken by undergraduate computer science and computer engineering majors. It is suitable for a course that introduces the concepts of diverse programming languages for students who have already mastered basic programming in at least one language. It treats all the knowledge units in the area of programming languages that appear in the proposed ACM Computing Curricula 2001 report (Steelman draft) and introduces the core units thoroughly.

The book is organized to motivate today's students. The traditional approach is to present the history of the major programming languages and then to explore them, following a concept-driven or paradigm-driven sequence. Most computer science majors are not fully prepared to appreciate evolutionary details, unmotivated abstraction, and categorization. Typical undergraduate computer science and computer engineering majors have a practical orientation: they study computing because they like programming and are good at it. Other students study computing because they like theoretical computer science and are good at it. The challenge for a course in programming language concepts is to help all students understand programming languages at an unaccustomed level of abstraction. To help meet this challenge, the book includes enough hands-on programming exercises and examples to motivate students whose primary interest in computing is practical. It does not assume the reader has a high level of mathematical maturity. It is designed to lead students to think about abstract programming language concepts, starting from a foundation of simple programming exercises.

The book has two distinct kinds of chapters: practical and philosophical. The practical chapters are self-contained primers in three programming languages, developing a level of competence that will allow the student to complete simple programming exercises. It is important for students to experience programming in several different language families. Introductions to programming in three languages are provided—ML, Java, and Prolog—at least two of which will be new languages for almost all students at this level. (There are excellent free implementations of all these languages available on a variety of platforms, including Windows, Unix, and Macintosh; the book's Web site at **http://www.webber-labs.com/mpl.html** has instructions on how to get them.) The practical chapters give students a quick introduction to the linguistically unique parts of each language. They do not cover APIs, so they will enable the student to solve programming exercises but not to develop full-scale applications.

The philosophical chapters present the theoretical side: the underlying principles of programming languages. They are interleaved with the practical chapters in an order that allows ideas to be illustrated using examples in the newly learned languages and allows theoretical topics to be covered when their relevance to programming practice will be most evident. For example, Chapter 23 deals with formal semantics by starting with simple interpreters written in Prolog. These interpreters lead naturally to language definitions using big-step operational semantics. That is why formal semantics occurs so late in the book: only at the end of the Prolog tutorial are students ready to be led from Prolog exercises to this related, abstract topic.

The book is written at an introductory level. It is meant to be comprehensible and interesting for most students who have completed a basic CS1 / CS2 sequence using any language. A common defect in existing books on this subject is that they assume too much: more computing background, more mathematical maturity, and more native interest in abstraction and categorization than most students in the target audience actually have. It is very tempting to make such assumptions, since many interesting parts of programming language theory are not accessible to students at this level. But it does not serve the majority of the students well. There is more than enough material for a semester, without resorting to topics that require a knowledge of computer architecture, operating systems, formal languages and automata, mathematical logic, or inductive proof techniques. A course using this book need not be placed at the end of a long chain of prerequisites. This makes it more useful in a wider variety of CS / CE curricula.

Because of its narrative, tutorial-based organization, the book is easy to teach from when followed in order, as far as time allows. If students already know one of the languages (most likely Java), several of the tutorial chapters may be skipped or skimmed, making room for more in-depth coverage of others or for the introduction of additional material. If additional chapters must be skipped, the most important chapter dependencies are, roughly, as shown in the following table:

Chapter	Chapters It Depends On
1: Programming Languages	
2: Defining Program Syntax	
3: Where Syntax Meets Semantics	2
4: Language Systems	
5: A First Look at ML	2, 3
6: Types	4
7: A Second Look at ML	2, 3, 5
8: Polymorphism	4, 6
9: A Third Look at ML	2, 3, 5, 7
10: Scope	4
11: A Fourth Look at ML	2, 3, 5, 7, 8, 9
12: Memory Locations for Variables	4, 5, 7, 9
13: A First Look at Java	2, 3
14: Memory Management	2, 3, 13
15: A Second Look at Java	2, 3, 13
16: Object Orientation	2, 3, 5, 7, 9, 13, 15
17: A Third Look at Java	2, 3, 13, 15
18: Parameters	2, 3, 13
19: A First Look at Prolog	2, 3
20: A Second Look at Prolog	2, 3, 19
21: Cost Models	2, 3, 4, 5, 13, 19, 20
22: A Third Look at Prolog	2, 3, 19, 20
23: Formal Semantics	2, 3, 4, 5, 7, 9, 10, 12
24: The History of Programming Languages	Miscellaneous

In particular, Chapters 11, 14, 21, and 22 can be skipped without much damage to the others. If time presses at the end of a semester, it would be better to skip Chapters 21 and 22 rather than Chapter 23 or 24. Chapter 23 revisits and illuminates many important ideas from earlier chapters. Chapter 24 is at the end not because the history of programming languages is unimportant, but because it is more interesting when students understand some of the concepts whose history is being related.

The Web site for the book is at **http://www.webber-labs.com/mpl.html**. Materials there include a full set of slides for each chapter, useful links for downloading and installing free language systems, and all the larger code examples from the text and exercises. There are also instructions for contacting the author to report defects and for accessing additional instructors-only materials.

Acknowledgments

My family has been very supportive during the writing of this book, especially my wife Kelly and my children, Fern and Fox. Just one example: my little Fox, only just two years old, opened the door of my office one day while I was writing, said "Give hug," did so, and then left again, closing the door behind him. They have all been very generous about leaving me lots of time to work on the book. Thanks, dear ones.

In the early 1980s I was involved with an amazing group of programmers: the students and staff of the Kiewit Computation Center at Dartmouth College. I owe a debt to Dartmouth's peculiar tradition of student-authored system software. My mentor at Kiewit was Philip D. L. Koch, the author of an extraordinarily beautiful collection of programs including a mainframe operating system and a fine PL/I compiler. That was the start of my interest in programming languages.

I am grateful to my students at the University of Wisconsin – Milwaukee and at Western Illinois University, who endured my well-meaning experimentation and helped me, over a number of years, develop the course on which this book is based.

My thanks to Stephanie Welch at Franklin, Beedle & Associates, my production editor, who edited and laid out this book.

Many people helped by reading and commenting on early drafts of the book: John Tang Boyland of the University of Wisconsin – Milwaukee; Daniel Canas of Wake Forest University; Frank Friedman of Temple University; Assaf Khoury of Boston University; Shui Lam of California State University, Long Beach; Ernst Leiss of the University of Houston; Mike Morton; Robert Roos of Allegheny College; Randy Smith of Covenant College; and K. Vairavan of the University of Wisconsin – Milwaukee. Special thanks to Randy Smith, who used an early draft in his classes at Covenant College and gave me much helpful feedback.

The remaining defects are, of course, entirely my own fault.

Chapter 1 **Programming Languages**

1.1 Introduction

Computer programs are practical magic. To craft a program is to construct a complex and beautiful incantation; to run a program is to discover with delight that *the magic actually works!* Even if the program does not do exactly what you intended, it does something, which is more than can be said of most other kinds of incantations. The delight of practical magic draws many beginners to computer programming and continues to reward experienced programmers. The author, at least, has not found this pleasure to diminish after 20 years of programming practice.

This book is about programming languages. It gives tutorial introductions to three languages: ML, Java, and Prolog.[1] These languages are very different from each other. Knowing a little about them gives you three widely

1. The published definitions of the oldest languages usually gave their names in all upper case: FORTRAN, COBOL, and BASIC. Newer definitions, even for dialects of the older languages, usually give the names in mixed case: Fortran. This book follows the convention of using mixed case for names that are pronounced as words (such as Java and Prolog) and all capital letters only for names that are pronounced as sequences of letters (such as ML, which is pronounced "em ell").

separated points from which to triangulate the principles of programming languages. There are good, free implementations of these three languages on a variety of platforms, so you can enjoy tinkering with them. Interleaved with the tutorial chapters are philosophical chapters that discuss important concepts of programming languages more abstractly. Although these chapters are abstract, they are not particularly mathematical. Programming languages have, to be sure, an interesting and elegant mathematics, but there is plenty to appreciate about programming languages without going in that direction, where not all readers can follow or care to follow.

Before you read further, be warned: this book assumes that you already know at least one programming language well—at the level normally achieved by a college student after two semesters of study. It does not matter which language you know. But if you have not programmed before, this is not the right place to start learning how.

The rest of this chapter explains what makes programming languages such an interesting subject: the amazing variety, the odd controversies, the intriguing evolution, and the many connections to other branches of computing.

1.2 The Amazing Variety

One of the things that makes programming languages so fascinating is their diversity. Here is a quick glance at four very different kinds of languages, including the three core languages of this book.

Imperative Languages

Here is an example in C, an imperative language. This is a function that computes the factorial of a non-negative integer.

```
int fact(int n) {
  int sofar = 1;
  while (n > 0) sofar *= n--;
  return sofar;
}
```

This example shows two of the hallmarks of an imperative language: assignment and iteration. The C statement `sofar *= n--;` is an assignment to the variable `sofar`. The variable has a current value that is changed each time an assignment is made. The statement also affects `n`, reducing its current value by one. The `while` loop repeats the statement over and over. Eventually, `n`'s current value should become zero and the loop will stop. Because the values of variables change over time, the order in which the statements of the program are executed is critical.

To most C programmers, these ideas are so elementary that they go unexamined. Of course the order of execution is critical; of course variables have current values that can be changed by assignment. But there are many languages that have no such ideas; no assignment statement, no iteration, and no concept of a changeable "current value" of a variable.

Functional Languages

Here is the same function implemented in the language ML:

```
fun fact x =
  if x <= 0 then 1 else x * fact(x - 1);
```

This shows two of the hallmarks of functional programs: recursion and single-valued variables. Recursion is as natural to ML programmers as iteration is to C programmers.

Here is the same function in another functional language, Lisp:

```
(defun fact (x)
  (if (<= x 0) 1 (* x (fact (- x 1)))))
```

As you can see, Lisp has a unique syntax. This syntactic difference is superficial. Deep down, the Lisp `fact` function and the ML `fact` function are much more closely related to each other than they are to the C `fact` function: they are both written in a functional style, without assignment or iteration.

These examples look elegant compared with the C version, but the comparison is not really fair. The factorial function is exactly the sort of thing that functional languages do most naturally. There are other kinds of operations (for instance, matrix multiplication) that would show imperative languages to better advantage.

Logic Programming Languages

If the factorial function is most natural for ML, it is perhaps least natural for Prolog. Nevertheless, here it is in Prolog:

```
fact(X,1) :-
  X =:= 1.
fact(X,Fact) :-
  X > 1,
  NewX is X - 1,
  fact(NewX,NF),
  Fact is X * NF.
```

The first two lines give a rule that allows the Prolog system to conclude that the factorial of `X` is 1 whenever `X` is equal to 1. The remaining five lines give a more general way to conclude that the factorial of `X` is some value `Fact`. They say, "To prove that the factorial of `X` is `Fact`, you must do the following things: prove that `X` is greater than one, prove that `NewX` is one less than `X`, prove that the factorial of `NewX` is `NF`, and prove that `Fact` is `X` times `NF`." Expressing a program in terms of rules about logical inference is the hallmark of logic programming. It is not particularly well suited to computing mathematical functions, but there are problem domains where it really shines, as you will see starting in Chapter 19.

Object-Oriented Languages

In Java, the factorial function looks almost the same as in C. But Java is an object-oriented language, which means that in addition to being imperative, it also makes it easier to solve programming problems using objects. An object is a little bundle of data that knows how to do things to itself. For example, this is a Java definition for objects that hold an integer value and know how to report both that value and its factorial:

```
public class MyInt {
  private int value;
  public MyInt(int value) {
    this.value = value;
  }
  public int getValue() {
    return value;
  }
  public MyInt getFact() {
    return new MyInt(fact(value));
  }
  private int fact(int n) {
    int sofar = 1;
    while (n > 1) sofar *= n--;
    return sofar;
  }
}
```

This object-oriented example looks wordy in comparison with the others, but again, the comparison is not really fair. The object-oriented style helps keep large programs organized; it does not show to advantage on very small examples.

You have now seen examples from four language families: imperative languages (like C), functional languages (like ML), logic programming languages (like Prolog), and object-oriented languages (like Java). With a little effort, you can fit any language into one of these four categories. But these four categories are not well defined, and the best way to categorize a language is not always clear. There are plenty of languages that straddle the boundaries. There are, in fact, many categories of languages, not just these four. Languages have been variously categorized as applicative, concurrent, constraint, declarative, definitional, procedural, scripting, single-assignment, and so forth.

Some programming languages are so unique that assigning them to a language family would be pointless. Take Forth, for example. Here is a factorial function in Forth:

```
: FACTORIAL
   1 SWAP BEGIN ?DUP WHILE TUCK * SWAP 1- REPEAT ;
```

Forth is a stack-oriented language, similar to the page-oriented graphical language PostScript. The Forth word `SWAP` exchanges the two top elements of the stack. Forth could be called an imperative language, but it has little in common with most other imperative languages.

Consider APL. Here is an APL expression to compute the factorial of `X`:

```
× / ι X
```

APL is famous for using a large character set that includes many symbols not present on ordinary keyboards. The expression above works by expanding `X` into the vector of the numbers 1 through `X` and then multiplying them all together. (In practice, you would not write the expression that way in APL, since you could just write `! X` for the factorial of `X`.) APL could be called a functional language, but it has little in common with most other functional languages.

1.3 The Odd Controversies

There are some fields of study that seem inherently controversial. Evolution, the big bang, human sexuality—any subject that makes regular appearances in the Science section of the *New York Times* is bound to stir up an argument. But programming languages? Our field of study rarely makes it into the popular press, and comparatively few people know or care about it. Nevertheless, and oddly enough, the study of programming languages is full of heated debates.

First of all, there are partisans for every language, eagerly defending the virtues of their favorite against all others. Some partisans of ML are at daggers drawn with partisans of Haskell. Partisans of Forth will be sorry, but not surprised, to find they are holding yet another book that neglects their favorite language. Some partisans of Prolog cannot understand why logic programming has not been universally adopted. Some partisans of Fortran are confident that theirs is the not only the first but also the most important high-level language.

Among the proponents of a particular language are heated debates of another sort. The standards for programming languages are often developed by international committees. Who are the stakeholders, and who gets to participate in such decisions? What will and will not be in the next official version of the language? The development of language standards can be astonishingly slow, complicated, and rancorous.

Of more interest to us is the frequent disagreement about basic definitions. We have already used at least one heavily debated term: *object oriented*. Exactly what are the properties a language must have to be considered object oriented? This book dodges the question, giving only an informal description of object-oriented languages. It generally avoids giving strict definitions for such terms for two reasons. First, it would not be completely honest to pretend there is a definition, when in fact there are many competing and conflicting definitions. Second, strict definitions wouldn't be useful; the only use for a strict definition of "object oriented" is fueling partisan debates (my language *is* and your language *isn't*!). In the case of this book, informal descriptions are more useful. Some languages are more object oriented than others; such things are left to the reader's judgment.[2]

1.4 The Intriguing Evolution

People invent new languages all the time. Well, perhaps not *completely* new—language designers build on ideas from languages that have come before. But the designer of a new language has a free hand, since there are no issues of compatibility with existing code. Some new languages are widely used, while others languish. Used or unused, new languages can provide the ideas from which the next generation of languages develops.

A good deal of language invention is slow and incremental. Almost all languages, even relatively new ones, evolve multiple dialects. The venerable language Fortran is mentioned above; in fact, there is no such thing as Fortran. There are the initial designs and implementations of Fortran at IBM, which date from the mid-

2. In mathematical circles, a rancorous yet obscure argument is sometimes called a "frog-mouse battle." Albert Einstein famously referred to a hot debate on the foundations of mathematics, involving the mathematicians David Hilbert and L. E. J. Brouwer, as a "Frosch-Mäuse-Krieg" (that is, frog-mouse battle). The term comes from an ancient and often-retold fable; it appears in the Hellenistic parody of *The Iliad* called *Batrachomyomachy* (again, frog-mouse battle). The odd controversies surrounding programming languages often have a frog-mouse-battle quality.

1950s. There is a sequence of standards: Fortran II, Fortran III, Fortran IV, Fortran 66, Fortran 77, Fortran 90, Fortran 95, and, perhaps, Fortran 2000.[3] New standards supplant old ones slowly, if ever; many Fortran programmers still work in Fortran 77. For each dialect, different platforms may have different implementations, each interpreting the standard for that dialect differently. In addition, there are many special-purpose dialects. There are, for example, a dozen or more dialects of Fortran that add constructs for parallel programming.

Whether suddenly or gradually, *programming languages change*. They change quickly compared with natural languages. If you continue to program computers, you will almost certainly have to repeatedly learn new dialects and new languages. It would be easier to have just one favorite programming language forever, as comfortable as old clothes. Since that is not feasible, at least we can enjoy watching the story of programming languages unfold.

1.5 The Many Connections

This book is about languages, not about how to write beautiful programs. However, it will often have to address questions of programming style, because languages are never neutral on the subject. Each language favors a programming style—a particular approach to algorithmic problem-solving. The connection between programming languages and programming practice affects them both.

In one direction, languages guide programmers toward particular programming styles. Object-oriented languages like Java guide programmers toward a style that uses objects; functional languages like ML guide programmers toward a style that uses many small functions; logic languages like Prolog guide programmers toward a style that expresses problems as searches in a logically defined space of solutions. Writing in a style that is unnatural for the language you are using is always possible, but rarely a good idea. You can write imperative programs with loops and assignment in ML (although this book will not show you how!). You can write Java programs that do not create any objects and just pack a lot of ordinary imperative code into a single, large class definition. In Java, or any language that supports recursion, you can write function-oriented programs that avoid iteration and assignment. It isn't natural, and it isn't usually wise, but it can be done. These are exceptions that prove the rule. When you code in a style that is unnatural for the

3. Standards committees usually name standards optimistically. The Fortran 90 standard was revised as Fortran 82, 8X, and 88, before being released as Fortran 90 (in 1991!).

language, when you fight the paradigm, you can feel the language working against you.

In the other direction, programming practice often guides programmers toward new programming-language ideas. For example, recursion and conditional expressions were introduced in Lisp because Lisp's designer, John McCarthy, found that he needed them in the artificial intelligence applications he was developing. Classes and objects were introduced in Simula because Simula's designers, Kristen Nygaard and Ole-Johan Dahl, needed them for the large simulations they were implementing. Chapter 24 has more of these kinds of stories from the history of programming languages.

Programming languages are connected not just to programming practice, but also to many other branches of computer science. Language evolution drives and is driven by hardware evolution. The theory of formal languages and automata, one of the more mathematical parts of computer science, has many applications in the definition and implementation of programming languages. Operating systems interact closely with language systems. Every application area—artificial intelligence, networking, database management, business applications, numeric processing, and so forth—contributes its own point of view to the problem of programming-language design.

1.6 A Word about Application Programming Interfaces

Today's commercial programming languages are supported by large standardized libraries of predefined code. Such a library is called an API (Application Programming Interface). An API might include code to implement basic data structures (stacks, queues, hash tables, and so on), two-dimensional and three-dimensional graphics, graphical user interfaces, network and file input/output, encryption and security, and many other services. Understanding what is in an API and how to use it can be a big part of a working programmer's expertise. The printed specification of a language often takes up much less space on a shelf than the documentation of its API.

We mention APIs here in order to dismiss them. They are very important, but they are not the subject of this book. The tutorial chapters of this book present basic ML, Java, and Prolog programming—enough to enable you to solve simple exercises. But to develop full-scale applications, you would need a knowledge of the APIs as well. That, this book does not cover.

1.7 Conclusion

This chapter explained some of the reasons the author loves programming languages. Many people skip the introductory chapter of a book such as this one, expecting that it will be vague and boring—full of generalizations about a subject of which they do not yet know the particulars. This one was no exception, but at least it had the virtue of being short.

This chapter also introduced the organization of the book: a mixture of tutorial and theoretical chapters. All the chapters of this book, except the first one and the last one, have exercises at the end. Many have a section that suggests further reading. This chapter does not. The next chapter is the first theoretical chapter. It discusses the definition of programming-language syntax. (The tutorial chapters begin with ML in Chapter 5.)

Chapter 2 **Defining Program Syntax**

2.1 Introduction

The simplest questions about a programming language are often questions of form. What does an expression, a statement, or a function definition look like? How are comments delimited? Where do the semicolons go? Questions like these are questions of programming-language *syntax*.

> The *syntax* of a programming language is the part of the language definition that says how programs look: their form and structure.

The more difficult questions are often questions of behavior. What does a given expression, statement, or function do? How does it work? What can go wrong when it runs? Questions like these are questions of programming-language *semantics*.

> The *semantics* of a programming language is the part of the language definition that says what programs do: their behavior and meaning.

This chapter introduces the formal grammar used to define programming-language syntax. (One of the formal techniques for defining programming-language semantics is introduced in Chapter 23.) By the end of the chapter, you should be able to understand these grammars and to write simple ones for yourself.

2.2 A Grammar Example for English

Let's start with an example of a grammar for a familiar language: English. An *article* can be the word `a` or `the`. We use the symbol <*A*> for *article* and express our definition this way:

```
<A> ::= a | the
```

A *noun* can be the word `dog`, `cat`, or `rat`:

```
<N> ::= dog | cat | rat
```

A *noun phrase* is an article followed by a noun:

```
<NP> ::= <A> <N>
```

A *verb* can be the word `loves`, `hates`, or `eats`:

```
<V> ::= loves | hates | eats
```

A *sentence* is a noun phrase, followed by a verb, followed by another noun phrase:

```
<S> ::= <NP> <V> <NP>
```

Put them all together and you have a grammar that defines a small subset of unpunctuated English:

```
<S> ::= <NP> <V> <NP>
<NP> ::= <A> <N>
<V> ::= loves | hates | eats
<N> ::= dog | cat | rat
<A> ::= a | the
```

How does such a grammar define a language? Think of the grammar as a set of rules that say how to build a tree. Put <*S*> at the root of the tree, and the grammar tells how children can be added at any point (node) in the tree. Such a tree is called a *parse tree*. It is a convention that parse trees are drawn growing downward, with the root at the top, like this:

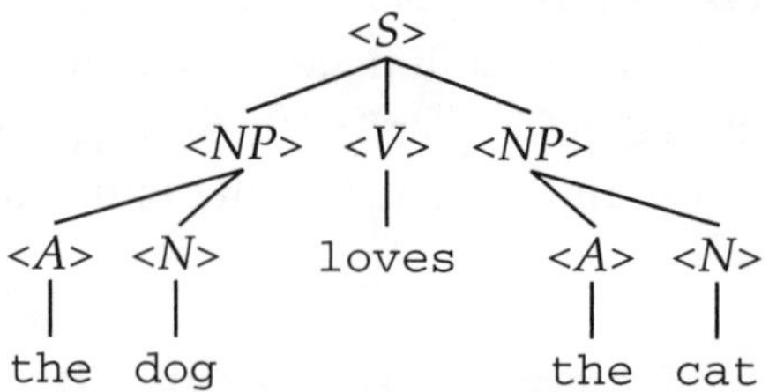

The children of each node in a parse tree must follow the forms specifically allowed by the grammar. For example, an *<NP>* node must have the children *<A>* and *<N>*, because the grammar includes only one rule for *<NP>*, namely *<NP>* `::=` *<A>* *<N>*. Check the tree above; you will see that every node with a child or children follows one of the rules of the grammar.

By reading the fringe of the tree from left to right, you get a sentence in the language defined by the grammar. For the parse tree above, it is the sentence "`the dog loves the cat`." Here is a different parse tree following the same grammar. The sentence "`a cat eats the rat`" is also in the language.

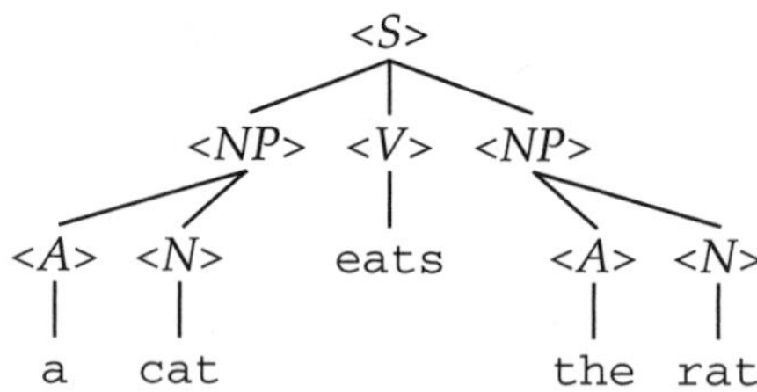

The language defined by a grammar is the set of all strings that can be formed as the fringes of parse trees generated by the grammar.

2.3 A Grammar Example for a Programming Language

Here is an example of a grammar for a simple language of expressions with three variables.

<exp> `::=` *<exp>* `+` *<exp>* `|` *<exp>* `*` *<exp>* `|` `(` *<exp>* `)` `|` `a` `|` `b` `|` `c`

The grammar says that an expression can be the sum of two expressions, the product of two expressions, an expression enclosed in parentheses, or one of the variables `a`, `b`, or `c`. Thus, our language includes expressions such as these:

```
a
a + b
a + b * c
((a + b) * c)
```

Here is a parse tree for that last expression, `((a + b) * c)`:

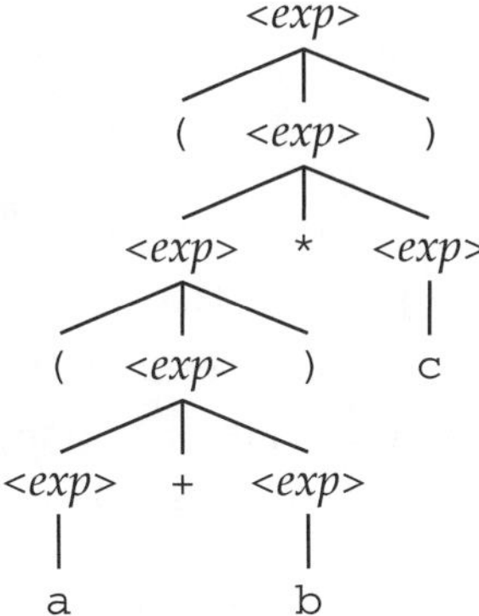

Unlike our first grammar, this one defines an infinite language; expressions can be arbitrarily long. It is a recursive grammar—an *<exp>* node can occur as the descendant of another *<exp>* node in the parse tree.

Finding a parse tree for a given string (with respect to a given grammar) is called *parsing* the string. Language systems must parse every program they run. There are many interesting algorithms for efficient parsing, but we will not go into them here. Sometimes a grammar allows several different parse trees for the same string. In Chapter 3 we will see why this is a problem and what to do about it. For now, our goal is simply to define the language. As long as the grammar generates at least one parse tree for a given string of tokens, that string is in the language.

2.4 A Definition of Grammars: Backus-Naur Form

Now that you have seen two concrete examples, let's go back and define all the parts of a grammar. A grammar has four important parts: the set of *tokens*, the set of *non-terminal symbols*, the set of *productions*, and a particular non-terminal symbol called the *start symbol*. Here are the four parts in our English language grammar:

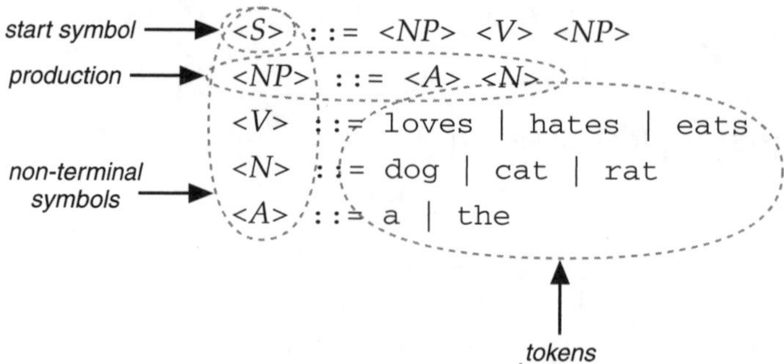

The *tokens* are the smallest units of syntax. They are the strings and symbols that we choose not to think of as consisting of smaller parts. In our example we choose to think of the word `cat` as a single token, just as in programming languages one chooses to think of keywords (like `if`), names (like `fred`), and operators (like `!=`) as single tokens.

The *non-terminal symbols* are strings enclosed in angle brackets, such as *<NP>*. The non-terminal symbols of a grammar often correspond to different kinds of language constructs. English has constructs like sentences and noun phrases; programming languages have constructs like statements and expressions. The grammar designates one of the non-terminal symbols as the root of the parse tree: the *start symbol*.

A *production* consists of a left-hand side, the separator `::=`, and a right-hand side. The left-hand side of a production is a single non-terminal symbol; the right-hand side is a sequence of one or more things, each of which can be either a token or a non-terminal symbol. A production gives one possible way of building a parse tree; it permits the non-terminal symbol on the left-hand side to have the symbols on the right-hand side, in order, as its children in a parse tree.

Productions with the same non-terminal symbol on the left-hand side may be written in an abbreviated form: the left-hand side, the separator `::=`, and the right-hand sides separated by the special symbol `|`. This abbreviated form, using `|` to separate the right-hand sides, is for convenience only. It is equivalent to the full form, in which each production is written out separately. For example, here again is the grammar for a simple language of expressions:

```
<exp> ::= <exp> + <exp> | <exp> * <exp> | ( <exp> )
        | a | b | c
```

Here it is written in a different way, without the `|` notation:

<exp> ::= *<exp>* + *<exp>*
<exp> ::= *<exp>* * *<exp>*
<exp> ::= (*<exp>*)
<exp> ::= a
<exp> ::= b
<exp> ::= c

One final detail about grammars: the special non-terminal symbol *<empty>* is sometimes used where the grammar needs to generate an empty string—a string of no tokens. For instance, an `if-then` statement with an optional `else` part might be defined like this:

<if-stmt> ::= if *<expr>* then *<stmt>* *<else-part>*
<else-part> ::= else *<stmt>* | *<empty>*

This form for writing grammars was developed by John Backus and Peter Naur around 1960. Their reports on the development of the Algol language (Algol 60) used such grammars to describe the syntax. Their notation for grammars is now called Backus-Naur Form (BNF). The grammar examples so far have used BNF, and they will continue to do so throughout the book.

2.5 Writing Grammars

Writing a grammar is a bit like writing a program; it uses some of the same mental muscles. A program is a finite, structured, mechanical thing that specifies a potentially infinite collection of runtime behaviors. To write a program, you have to be able to imagine how the code you are crafting will unfold when it executes. Similarly, a grammar is a finite, structured, mechanical thing that specifies a potentially infinite language. To write a grammar, you have to be able to imagine how the productions you are crafting will unfold when parse trees are built. The BNF syntax is simple enough, but it takes practice to write BNF definitions for programming-language constructs. Don't worry—learning to write grammars is not as difficult as learning to program!

The most important advice for writing grammars is this: *divide and conquer*. In writing grammars, as in programming, it is very important to break problems down into simpler subproblems. Let's take an example from Java: the Java statements that define local variables. Here are three:

```
float a;
boolean a,b,c;
int a=1, b, c=1+2;
```

These statements consist of a type name, followed by a list of one or more variable names being declared. The variable names are separated by commas. The statements end with semicolons. Each of the variable names may be followed by an equal sign and an expression; this syntax is used to specify a value for initializing the variable.

Our goal is to make a BNF grammar to define the language of these Java statements. We will use *<var-dec>* as the start symbol. Our very first step is to divide the problem into smaller pieces. The major components are the type name, the list of variables, and the final semicolon. The type name and the list of variables need further elaboration, so we will use non-terminal symbols for them. This gives a production:

```
<var-dec> ::= <type-name> <declarator-list> ;
```

For type names, we can just list the primitive types of Java. (For a full Java grammar, you would have to allow class names, interface names, and array types here as well, but we will skip that part.)

```
<type-name> ::= boolean | byte | short | int
              | long | char | float | double
```

Now we are left with the problem of defining the declarator list. This is still rather complicated, so we will divide the problem again. A declarator list is a list of one or more declarators, separated by commas. We can write this as the following:

```
<declarator-list> ::= <declarator>
                    | <declarator> , <declarator-list>
```

This recursive rule says that a declarator list is either a single declarator or a declarator, followed by a comma, followed by a (smaller) declarator list. Notice how this always gives at least one declarator and gives commas between declarators.

That leaves us with the smaller problem of defining a declarator. It is a variable name followed, optionally, by an equal sign and an expression. We can write the following:

```
<declarator> ::= <variable-name> | <variable-name> = <expr>
```

For a full Java grammar, you would have to allow pairs of square brackets after the variable name, as one way of declaring arrays, and you would have to allow array initializers on the right-hand side of the equal sign. In addition, of course, we still need parts of the grammar to define legal variable names and legal expressions, but we will end this example here.

One more important piece of advice about writing a grammar: test it as you would test a program. In our Java example, we started with a list of statements in the language. We could now test the grammar to make sure these statements could be parsed and to make sure illegal examples could not be parsed. Don't forget this step when you are doing the grammar-writing exercises at the end of the chapter.

2.6 Lexical Structure and Phrase Structure

The grammars seen so far have defined a language in terms of tokens, like names, keywords, and operators. Nevertheless, a program is usually stored not as a sequence of such tokens, but as a simple text file. A text file is just one long sequence of characters—letters, numbers, spaces, tabs, end-of-line markers, and so on. How should such a sequence of characters be divided into tokens?

A grammar whose tokens are not individual characters, but meaningful chunks like names, keywords, and operators, is incomplete. It defines the *phrase structure* of the language by showing how to construct parse trees with tokens at the leaves, but it does not define the *lexical structure* of the language by showing how to divide the program text into these tokens.

It is possible to combine the two parts by writing a single grammar whose tokens are individual characters. This is almost never done, because such grammars are horribly ugly and hard to read. For example, most modern programming languages allow white space—spaces, tabs, end-of-line markers, and so on—between tokens. A definition of such a language, going all the way down to the level of individual characters, would have to mention this white space in virtually every production. Our definition for the `if-then` statement would end up looking like this:

<if-stmt> `::=` `if` *<white-space>* *<expr>* *<white-space>*
`then` *<white-space>*
<stmt> *<white-space>* *<else-part>*
<else-part> `::=` `else` *<white-space>* *<stmt>* | *<empty>*

To make matters worse, white space is required between some tokens (most languages treat `then p` differently from `thenp`), but not between others (most languages treat `a+b` the same as `a + b`). Don't forget comments too; in most modern languages, comments can occur in the middle of a line, like white space. A grammar could specify this character-by-character level of detail, but it would be very tedious to read and to write.

Most modern language definitions specify the lexical structure and the phrase structure separately. Sometimes the lexical structure is defined informally, since it is usually much simpler than the phrase structure, but more often the lexical structure and the phrase structure are specified by two separate grammars. A token-level grammar (specifying the phrase structure) defines a program as a sequence of tokens. A character-level grammar (specifying the lexical structure) defines a text file as a sequence of program elements like tokens and white space. A character-level grammar might look like this:

<program-file> ::= *<end-of-file>* | *<element>* *<program-file>*
<element> ::= *<token>* | *<one-white-space>* | *<comment>*
<one-white-space> ::= *<space>* | *<tab>* | *<end-of-line>*
<token> ::= *<name>* | *<operator>* | *<constant>* | ...

(This is an incomplete example, of course. You would go on to define all of these non-terminal symbols, down to the character level.) As you can see, there are no phrase-level language constructs, no expressions or statements; the grammar just specifies how a file is to be divided into a sequence of tokens and other elements.

These two separate parts of the syntax definition are usually reflected in the implementation of language systems. A component called the *scanner* (or *lexer*) reads an input file and converts it to a stream of tokens, discarding the white space and comments. Then another component called the *parser* reads the stream of tokens and forms the parse tree.

We can distill a piece of wisdom from the history of programming-language design and implementation: separating lexical structure from phrase structure is a good idea. It makes language definitions easier to write, it makes language systems easier to implement, and it even makes languages easier for people to read. Some early languages had features that made the separation of lexical structure from phrase structure very difficult. For example, some early languages, including dialects of Fortran and Algol, allow spaces anywhere—even in the middle of a keyword. Some languages, including dialects of Fortran and PL/I, allow variable names to be the same as keywords. These features make compiling these languages considerably trickier, since scanning and parsing cannot be cleanly separated.

Regarding older languages, one historical aspect of lexical structure should be mentioned. The end-of-line markers in a program file are usually treated as white space in modern languages. They have no more significance than a space or a tab. They could be replaced with spaces, making the file one very long line, without causing any problems other than the headache someone would get from trying to read it.

Since the end-of-line markers have no special significance, it follows that the column numbers have no special significance either. The fact that a character occurs in the sixth column rather than the seventh makes no difference in most modern languages. In some older languages, column positions are very significant. Languages that were popular when punched cards were still widely used often have a *fixed-format* lexical structure. This means that some columns in each line have special significance. In earlier dialects of Fortran, for example, there was one statement per card (we would now say "one statement per line"), and the first few columns were reserved for the statement label. Cobol also used a fixed-format lexical structure, as did Basic. The first languages that abandoned this column-oriented approach were advertised as being *free-format*. Today, since almost all modern languages are free-format (including the modern dialects of Fortran, Cobol, and Basic), few people bother to make this distinction.

2.7 Other Grammar Forms

There are many different ways of writing a grammar. They all capture the same basic ideas, but with different notational conventions. This section describes several different notations for grammars.

BNF

BNF (Backus-Naur Form) has many minor variations. Some people use = or → instead of `::=`. Some people use a distinct typeface for terminal symbols, as we have done in our examples. Some people leave out the angle brackets, relying on the typeface to show the difference between tokens and non-terminal symbols. Some people use single quotation marks around tokens. This is an especially good idea when the token is the same as one of the BNF special characters <, >, |, or `::=`. (These special characters are called *metasymbols* of the grammar; they are part of the language of the definition, not part of the language being defined.)

EBNF

A few more metasymbols can be added to BNF to help with common patterns of language definition. For example, `[`, `]`, `{`, `}`, `(`, and `)` might be added:

- `[` *something* `]` in the right-hand side of a production means that the *something* inside is optional.

- { *something* } in the right-hand side of a production means that the *something* inside can be repeated any number of times (zero or more).
- Parentheses are used to group things on the right-hand side so that |, [], and {} can be used in the same production unambiguously.

With these new metasymbols, some common patterns can be defined more simply than with plain BNF. For example, an `if-then` statement with an optional `else` part might be defined like this:

```
<if-stmt> ::= if <expr> then <stmt> [else <stmt>]
```

Remember that the square brackets are not part of the language being defined; they are metasymbols that make the `else` part optional. A list of zero or more statements, each ending with a semicolon, might have a definition like this:

```
<stmt-list> ::= {<stmt> ;}
```

Again, the curly brackets are not part of the language being defined; they are metasymbols that allow the *<stmt>* ; part to repeat zero or more times. A list of zero or more things, each of which can be either a statement or a declaration and each ending with a semicolon, might have a definition like this:

```
<thing-list> ::= { (<stmt> | <declaration>) ;}
```

The parentheses are metasymbols; they make it clear that the ; token is not part of the choice permitted by the | metasymbol.

Plain BNF can define all these patterns easily enough, but extra metasymbols like those above make the grammar easier to read. Much like the | metasymbol from plain BNF, the new metasymbols allow you to express a collection of productions succinctly.

Any grammar syntax that extends BNF in this way is called an EBNF (extended BNF). Many variations have been used. Here is an excerpt from the definition for Java. Although the notation looks completely different, you can still see the EBNF ideas. The subscript *opt*, in particular, works like our square brackets, indicating an optional part of the syntax.

While Statement:

 `while` (*Expression*) *Statement*

Do Statement:

 `do` *Statement* `while` (*Expression*) ;

For Statement:

 `for` ($ForInit_{opt}$; $Expression_{opt}$; $ForUpdate_{opt}$)
 Statement

Syntax Diagrams

Another way to express grammars is graphically, using *syntax diagrams.* A syntax diagram uses a directional graph to show the productions for each non-terminal symbol. Any path through the graph gives a legal way to add children to the parse tree.

For simple BNF-style productions, the corresponding syntax diagram is just a chain of boxes (for non-terminal symbols) and ovals (for terminal symbols). For example, a production like this:

<if-stmt> `::=` `if` *<expr>* `then` *<stmt>* `else` *<stmt>*

would be represented as a syntax diagram like this:

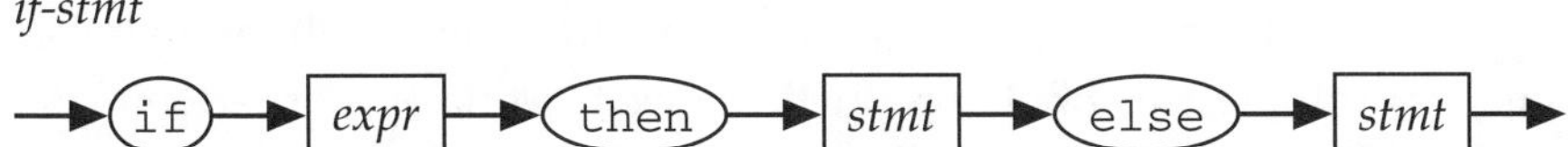

For EBNF productions that specify an optional part, the syntax diagram shows a path to bypass that part. For example, the `else` part could be made optional like this:

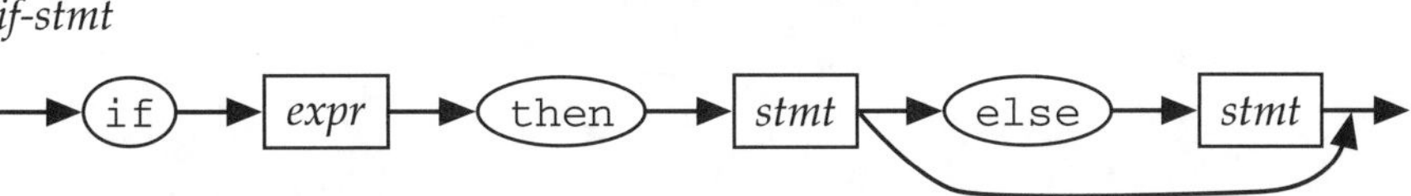

When there are multiple productions for a non-terminal symbol, the syntax diagram uses branching. For example, consider the earlier sample grammar for expressions:

<exp> `::=` *<exp>* `+` *<exp>* `|` *<exp>* `*` *<exp>* `|` `(` *<exp>* `)`
`|` `a` `|` `b` `|` `c`

These six productions could be captured in a syntax diagram like this:

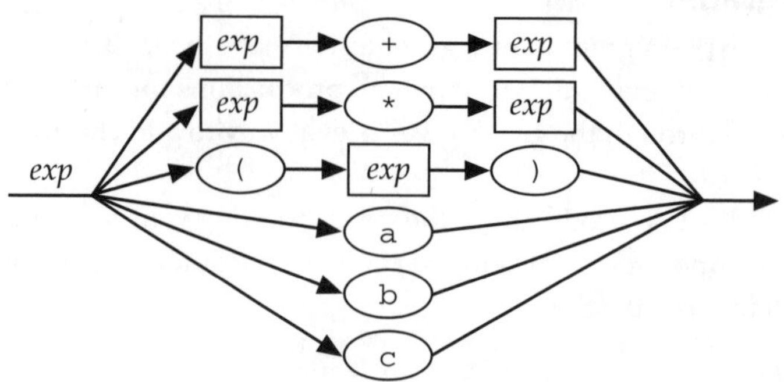

You can see why syntax diagrams are sometimes called *railroad diagrams.*

A syntax diagram can also have loops. These are a bit like the curly brackets of EBNF, since the loop can be repeated zero or more times in a path through the diagram. For example, this EBNF production specifies one or more addends separated by plus signs:

<*exp*> ::= <*addend*> {+ <*addend*>}

This syntax diagram specifies the same thing:

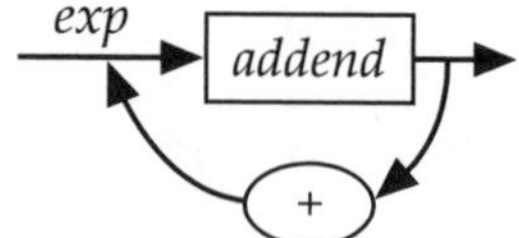

In casual use, syntax diagrams are easy to read. They are often used in elementary, tutorial descriptions of programming languages. One drawback of syntax diagrams is that they make it hard to say exactly what the resulting parse tree looks like. (We will see in Chapter 3 why it is important to know exactly what the parse tree looks like.) Another drawback of syntax diagrams is that it is difficult to make them machine readable. There are software tools that automatically generate the code for the part of a language system that parses the language. Such tools need a machine-readable grammar as input, not a syntax diagram.

Formal, Context-free Grammars

A branch of theoretical computer science called *formal languages* studies formal grammars. Books and university courses on formal languages use notation that is slightly different than what has been shown so far, like this:

```
S → aSb | X
X → cX | ∈
```

In formal languages, grammars of the kind we have been seeing are called *context-free grammars*. They are "context-free" because the children of a node in the parse tree depend only on that node's non-terminal symbol; they do not depend on the context of neighboring nodes in the tree. Other kinds of grammars include *regular grammars,* which are less expressive, and *context-sensitive grammars,* which are more expressive.[1]

2.8 Conclusion

The notations used for programming-language grammars have many variations, but they are largely cosmetic. The underlying ideas are the same. Grammars are used to define the syntax of programming languages, both at the level of the lexical structure—the division of the program text into meaningful tokens—and at the level of the phrase structure—the organization of tokens into a parse tree showing how the meaningful structures of a program (its expressions, statements, declarations, and so on) are organized.

There is a powerful connection between theory and practice here. The division between lexical structure and phrase structure is reflected in the implementation of language systems. In fact, if the grammars are in just the right form, they can be fed into parser-generators, which automatically generate those parts of the language system that scan and parse the language. When you write a grammar, you have several potential audiences: novice users, who just want to find out what legal programs look like; advanced users and language-system implementers, who need an exact, detailed definition to work from; and automatic tools, which derive other programs from your grammar automatically.

Perhaps even more important is the positive influence grammars have on language design. You can see this influence when you compare pre-BNF languages (like early Fortran) with post-BNF languages. A language with a simple, readable, short grammar has a simple, memorable phrase structure. That makes the language easier to learn and use.

1. Usually, the expressive power of regular grammars is just right for defining the lexical structure of a programming language, and the expressive power of context-free grammars is just right for defining the phrase structure.

Exercises

Exercise 1 Give a BNF grammar for each of the languages below. For example, a correct answer for "the set of all strings consisting of zero or more concatenated copies of the string ab" would be this grammar:

<*S*> ::= ab <*S*> | <*empty*>

There are often many correct answers.

a. The set of all strings consisting of zero or more as.
b. The set of all strings consisting of an uppercase letter followed by zero or more additional characters, each of which is either an uppercase letter or one of the digits 0 through 9.
c. The set of all strings consisting of one or more as.
d. The set of all strings consisting of one or more digits. (Each digit is one of the characters 0 through 9.)
e. The set of all strings consisting of zero or more as with a semicolon after each one.
f. The set of all strings consisting of the keyword begin, followed by zero or more statements with a semicolon after each one, followed by the keyword end. Use the non-terminal <*statement*> for statements, and do not give productions for it.
g. The set of all strings consisting of one or more as with a semicolon after each one.
h. The set of all strings consisting of the keyword begin, followed by one or more statements with a semicolon after each one, followed by the keyword end. Use the non-terminal <*statement*> for statements, and do not give productions for it.
i. The set of all strings consisting of one or more as, with a comma between each a and the next. (There should be no comma before the first or after the last.)
j. The set of all strings consisting of an open bracket (the symbol [) followed by a list of one or more digits separated by commas, followed by a closing bracket (the symbol]).
k. The set of all strings consisting of zero or more as, with a comma between each a and the next. (There should be no comma before the first or after the last.)
l. The set of all strings consisting of an open bracket (the symbol [) followed by a list of zero or more digits separated by commas, followed by a closing bracket (the symbol]).

Exercise 2 Give an EBNF grammar for each of the languages of Exercise 1. Use the EBNF extensions wherever possible to simplify the grammars.

Exercise 3 Give a syntax diagram for each of the languages of Exercise 1. Use branching and loops in your syntax diagrams to make them as clear as possible.

Exercise 4 Consider the earlier simple grammar for expressions:

```
<exp> ::= <exp> + <exp> | <exp> * <exp> | ( <exp> )
        | a | b | c
```

Suppose the lexical structure of the language allows any number of spaces to occur anywhere in the expression. Give a BNF grammar that defines this explicitly, at the character level, using one grammar to capture both the phrase structure and the lexical structure. For example, your grammar should generate both `(a+b)` and `( a + b)`. Use a single-quoted space, `' '`, to indicate the space character in your grammar.

Further Reading

If you are interested in algorithms for efficient parsing, try any book on compiler construction. This one is such a classic that it even has a nickname; because of the illustration on its cover, it is called the "Dragon Book."

> Aho, Alfred V., Ravi Sethi, and Jeffrey D. Ullman. *Compilers: Principles, Techniques and Tools.* Boston, MA: Addison-Wesley, 1985.

The earlier quotation from the Java language definition was taken from

> Gosling, James, Bill Joy, and Guy Steele. *The Java™ Language Specification*. Boston, MA: Addison-Wesley, 1996.

There have been occasional (unsuccessful) attempts to standardize the form of grammars for programming languages. This paper is an interesting historical example:

> Wirth, Niklaus. "What can we do about the unnecessary diversity of notation for syntactic definitions?" *Communications of the ACM,* November 1977.

A recent attempt is the ISO standard for EBNF: *ISO/IEC 14977:1996*, which may be purchased from the ISO online. (The final document for this standard is not freely available online, though you may find drafts of it at various sites.) In spite of the existence of this standard, most language definitions continue to use ad hoc EBNFs.

Chapter 3 Where Syntax Meets Semantics

3.1 Introduction

The previous chapter showed how grammars can be used to define programming-language syntax. A grammar is a set of rules for constructing parse trees; the language defined by a grammar is the set of fringes of the parse trees constructed according to those rules. There is more to a parse tree than just the fringe, however. Consider these three grammars:

G1: *<subexp>* `::= a | b | c |` *<subexp>* `-` *<subexp>*

G2: *<subexp>* `::=` *<var>* `-` *<subexp>* `|` *<var>*
<var> `::= a | b | c`

G3: *<subexp>* `::=` *<subexp>* `-` *<var>* `|` *<var>*
<var> `::= a | b | c`

G1 is the easiest to read. You can see that it generates a language of strings containing one or more `a`s, `b`s, or `c`s separated by minus signs. G2 and G3 are a bit harder to figure out. But if you think about them carefully, you will see that they generate exactly the same language. The three grammars are equivalent in that sense. But, although the three grammars generate parse trees with identical fringes, the internal structures of those parse trees are very different. This turns out to be an important difference indeed.

For example, the string `a-b-c` is in the language generated by all three grammars. But compare the parse tree generated by G2 for this string with the parse tree generated by G3:

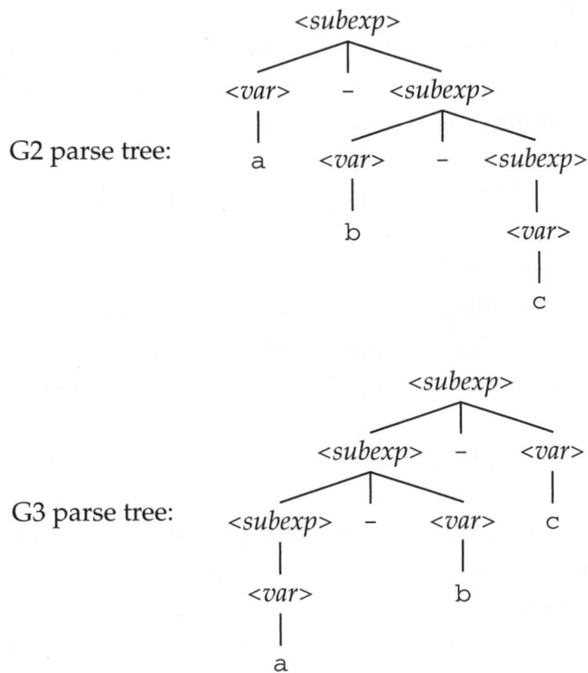

The two different parse trees seem to represent different computations. The G2 parse tree computes *b-c* in one subtree and then subtracts that from *a*, as if evaluating the expression *a-*(*b-c*). The G3 parse tree computes *a-b* in one subtree and then subtracts *c* from that, as if evaluating the expression (*a-b*)*-c*. Of course, these two different computations can produce different results: (1-2)-3 = -4, but 1-(2-3) = 2. If we use the structure of the parse tree to determine which computation to perform, the difference between these two grammars is very important. (G1 is different too. It can generate parse trees for *both* computations!)

The previous chapter ignored the internal structure of a parse tree and concentrated on the string of tokens at the fringe. From a purely syntactic point of view, that is perfectly adequate. But now we are beginning to consider program semantics. If we cannot say whether a-b-c means *a-(b-c)* or *(a-b)-c*, our language will be useless. The semantics must be unambiguous. Since we want the structure of each parse tree to correspond to the semantics of the string it generates, our grammars must do more than just define the syntax of the language. They must also generate unique parse trees that correspond to the desired semantics for the language.

3.2 Operators

Many of the examples in this chapter will make use of operators, so let's start with a little operator terminology.

Modern programming languages always include some kind of general syntax for invoking predefined, packaged operations—function calls, procedure calls, method calls, and so on. Almost all modern programming languages also include special syntax for frequently used simple operations like addition, subtraction, multiplication, and division. The word *operator* refers both to the tokens used to specify these operations (like + and *) and to the operations themselves. Not all operators are predefined; some languages allow programs to define new ones. Not all operators are associated with single tokens; some languages have multi-part operators.

The inputs to an operator are called its *operands*. For instance, in the expression 1+2, the operator is + and the operands are 1 and 2. Different operators take different numbers of operands. A *unary* operator takes a single operand; for instance, the ML language uses the token ~ as a unary negation operator, so the expression ~a has the value computed by negating the operand a. A *binary* operator takes two operands; for instance, many languages use the token + as a binary addition operator, as in the expression a+b. Occasionally you will see *ternary* operators, which take three operands; for instance, the Java expression a?b:c has the value of either b or c, depending on whether a is true or false.

In most modern programming languages, binary operators use an *infix* notation, which just means that they are written between their two operands, as in a+b. But you will sometimes see *prefix* binary operators, written before their operands as in the expression + a b, and *postfix* binary operators, written after their operands as in the expression a b +. Unary operators cannot be infix, of course; they are either prefix, as in -a, or postfix, as in the Java expression a++ (which increments a).

3.3 Precedence

The following grammar will be the starting point for a longer example. It generates a simple language of expressions using three variables, parentheses, and the binary infix operators + and *, which will be taken to mean addition and multiplication.

```
G4:    <exp> ::= <exp> + <exp>
               | <exp> * <exp>
               | ( <exp> )
               | a | b | c
```

From a purely syntactic point of view the grammar G4 is fine, but there are several problems with its parse trees. The first problem is the problem of operator *precedence*.

Consider the expression `a+(b*c)`. This clearly specifies a particular computation: a plus the product of b and c. The grammar G4 generates a single parse tree for the expression, which corresponds to that computation just as it should: it has the + operator at the root, with a left subtree for `a` and a right subtree for `b*c`. But what about the expression `a+b*c`? Does it specify $a+(b\times c)$, or $(a+b)\times c$? In most languages it specifies $a+(b\times c)$, and we say that the multiplication operator has higher *precedence* than the addition operator.

Unfortunately, the grammar G4 can generate two different parse trees for `a+b*c`, one for $a+(b\times c)$ and one for $(a+b)\times c$. Here is the one for $(a+b)\times c$:

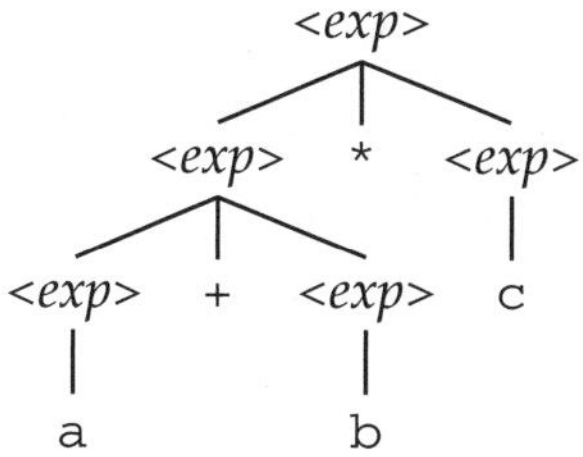

Assuming that the we want `a+b*c` to signify $a+(b\times c)$, as it does in most languages, we have to change G4 somehow to eliminate this tree. This modified grammar shows how to do it:

```
G5:    <exp> ::= <exp> + <exp> | <mulexp>
       <mulexp> ::= <mulexp> * <mulexp>
                  | ( <exp> )
                  | a | b | c
```

The new grammar generates the same language as before, but it now forces the parse tree to place * operators below + operators, like this:

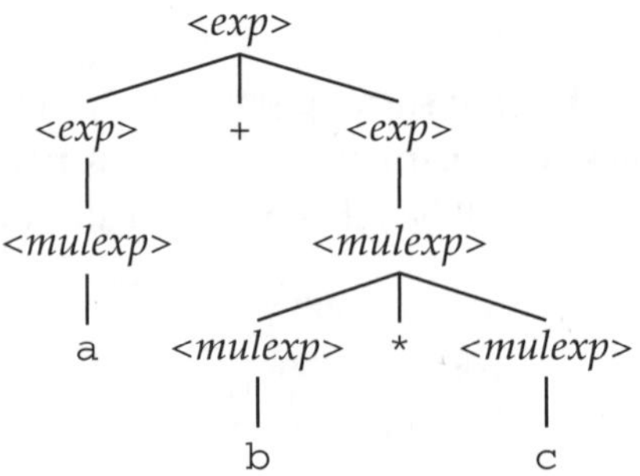

The language of G5 has just two levels of precedence: `*` at the higher level and `+` at the lower level. In general, a language may have operators at many different levels of precedence. A rough intuition about what these precedence levels mean is that higher-precedence operators are performed before lower-precedence ones, as if parenthesized. A more detailed understanding, as suggested by the example above, is tied to parse trees: the grammar does not allow lower-precedence operators to occur in the subtrees of higher-precedence ones unless explicitly parenthesized.

To solve the precedence problem with G4, we had to add a second non-terminal symbol, *<mulexp>*, to the grammar. For languages with more precedence levels, the construction is similar: we need a different non-terminal symbol for each precedence level. For example, if we wanted to add `**` to our language as an exponentiation operator with higher precedence than `*` or `+`, we could modify the grammar like this:

```
<exp> ::= <exp> + <exp> | <mulexp>
<mulexp> ::= <mulexp> * <mulexp> | <powexp>
<powexp> ::= <powexp> ** <powexp>
           | ( <exp> )
           | a | b | c
```

Notice how we end up with a chain of non-terminal symbols, from *<exp>* `::=` *<mulexp>* to *<mulexp>* `::=` *<powexp>*. The non-terminal symbols in this chain are in order of precedence, from lowest (*<exp>*) to highest (*<powexp>*). You can generalize this approach to handle any number of levels of precedence.[1]

1. Language definitions often use *<term>* and *<factor>* as non-terminal symbols in expressions. This is a custom more honored in the breach, since no part of a grammar for expressions accurately corresponds to the ordinary meaning of the words *term* and *factor*. With more levels of precedence and more operators at each level, it can be vexing to think of meaningful names for all the non-terminal symbols. It is tempting to resort to names that merely describe the precedence levels (*<level1>*, *<level2>*, and so on), an honest choice if not a particularly readable one.

Different languages have different ideas about how to organize operators into precedence levels. The C language has 15 precedence levels; Pascal has five; Smalltalk has just one for all binary operators. Saying that Smalltalk has just one precedence level is really a sneaky way of saying that there is no precedence in Smalltalk; since no binary operator has higher precedence than another, precedence is not relevant. Pascal's five precedence levels are easy to remember, but the parse trees for Pascal expressions are sometimes counterintuitive. For example, this Pascal expression shows a common beginner's mistake:

```
a <= 0 or 100 <= a
```

Since the `or` operator has higher precedence than `<=`, the subexpression `0 or 100` is evaluated first, causing an error. The example is intuitively clear to the human reader, but it is not parsed in that intuitively clear way by Pascal. It would be nice if it were possible to use a simple collection of precedence rules, like Pascal's, to make expressions that are parsed in an intuitively clear way. But the sad fact is that it often takes a complicated set of rules to make computers behave in a way that agrees with human intuition. C's complicated precedence scheme, using 15 precedence levels, enables it to parse most expressions reasonably. But C has a different problem: its precedence rules are so complicated that most C programmers cannot remember them all. For example, few C programmers could tell you exactly what computation is signified by this expression, which is completely decided by precedence:

```
a = b < c ? * p + b * c : 1 << d ()
```

Of course, almost all languages allow you to add unnecessary parentheses to make expressions more readable. Even relatively simple expressions can be more readable with explicit parentheses. Compare `a+b*c+d` with `a+(b*c)+d`, for example; the first form can be read, but the second form can be read with less effort.

3.4 Associativity

The grammar G5 still has a problem. For the expression `a+b+c`, it generates two different parse trees:

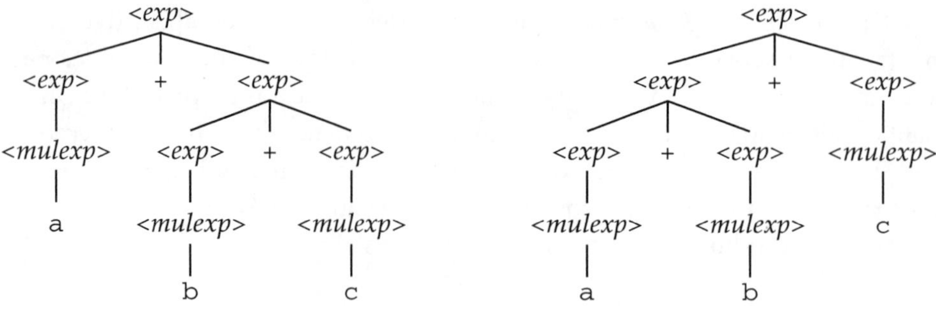

The first parse tree corresponds to *a*+(*b*+*c*), and the second corresponds to (*a*+*b*)+*c*. In this case, of course, the two different computations produce the same result. In general, however, the choice may be important; as we saw earlier, *a*-(*b*-*c*) does not produce the same result as (*a*-*b*)-*c*. The grammar for a language must generate only one parse tree for each expression. When an expression contains a sequence of operations that are not parenthesized and are all at the same level of precedence, such as `a+b+c`, which parse tree is chosen? In most languages the expression `a+b+c` specifies (*a*+*b*)+*c*, and we say that the `+` operator is *left associative*. Similarly, the `*` operator is left associative in most languages, so the expression `a*b*c` is taken to mean (*a*×*b*)×*c*.

Assuming that we want our language to work this way too, grammar G5 needs to be fixed to eliminate the right-associative parse trees for both operators. This change does the trick:

```
G6:  <exp> ::= <exp> + <mulexp> | <mulexp>
     <mulexp> ::= <mulexp> * <rootexp> | <rootexp>
     <rootexp> ::= ( <exp> )
                 | a | b | c
```

The new grammar G6 generates the same language as before, but it now forces trees to grow down to the left, like this:

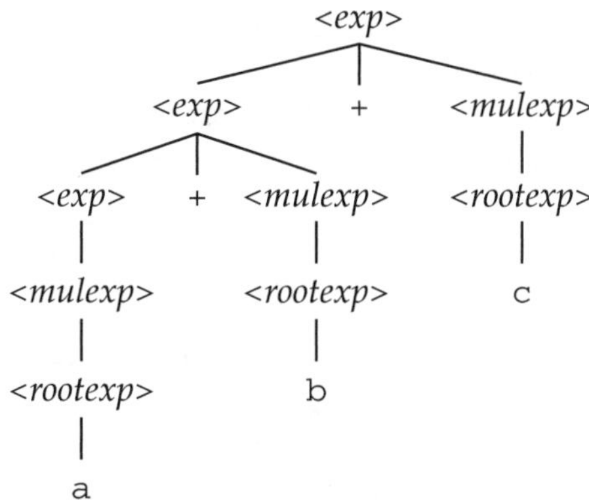

A rough intuition about what left associativity means is that a sequence of left-associative operators (at the same level of precedence and without explicit parentheses) is evaluated from left to right. A more detailed understanding, as suggested by the example above, is tied to parse trees: the grammar does not allow a left-associative operator to appear in the parse tree as the right child of another operator at the same level of precedence, without explicit parentheses.

Notice that in G6 the productions are recursive on only one side of each operator. G5 had the production *<exp>* `::=` *<exp>* `+` *<exp>*. This rule uses the nonterminal symbol *<exp>* recursively on both the left and right sides of the `+` operator. That allows the parse trees to grow down to either the left or the right. G6 uses this production instead: *<exp>* `::=` *<exp>* `+` *<mulexp>*. This is recursive only on the left side of the operator. In general, each operator in a language can be either left-associative or right-associative. Making a left-associative operator requires a left-recursive production in the grammar; making a right-associative operator requires a right-recursive production.

Most binary infix operators in most languages are left associative, but there are occasional exceptions. In Java, for example, the equal sign is treated as an operator that performs assignment. The expression `a=1` has a value (1) and a side effect (assignment of the value 1 to the variable `a`). The `=` operator is right associative. This is clearly proper, since it allows the expression `b=a=1` to neatly assign 1 to both `b` and `a`. Another example is the `::` operator in ML. This operator is used to attach a new element onto the front of a list. The ML expression `1::[2,3,4]` evaluates to the list `[1,2,3,4]`. The `::` operator is right associative. Again, this is clearly proper, since it allows the expression `1::2::[3,4]` to neatly evaluate to the list `[1,2,3,4]`. Yet another example of a right-associative operator is the exponentiation operator in Fortran, `**`. Some languages also have *non-associative* operators. In Prolog, for example, the expression `1 < 2 < 3` cannot be parsed, because < is non-associative. Explicit parentheses are required, as in the expression `1 < (2 < 3)`. (Even with parentheses, the expression is nonsense and cannot be evaluated, but without parentheses it cannot even be parsed.)

3.5 Other Ambiguities

The grammars G4 and G5 generated two different parse trees for the same string. Grammars like that are called *ambiguous* grammars.

> A grammar is *ambiguous* if it allows the construction of two different parse trees for the same string.

The structure of a parse tree should reflect the meaning of the program, so grammars certainly should be unambiguous. The last two sections showed how to eliminate ambiguities related to precedence and associativity. The resulting grammar G6 was unambiguous. So far so good. But although precedence and associativity are important concerns for expressions, other programming-language constructs can have ambiguous grammars as well.

Consider, for example, the case of the dangling `else`—a classic problem that shows up in many different languages, including Pascal, PL/I, and the C-family languages. Here is a grammar for a simple language with an `if-then-else` statement that has an optional `else` part:

```
<stmt> ::= <if-stmt> | s1 | s2
<if-stmt> ::= if <expr> then <stmt> else <stmt>
            | if <expr> then <stmt>
<expr> ::= e1 | e2
```

(For the sake of the example, this grammar treats `s1` and `s2` as statements, and it treats `e1` and `e2` as expressions.) This grammar is ambiguous, since it generates both of these parse trees for the statement `if e1 then if e2 then s1 else s2`:

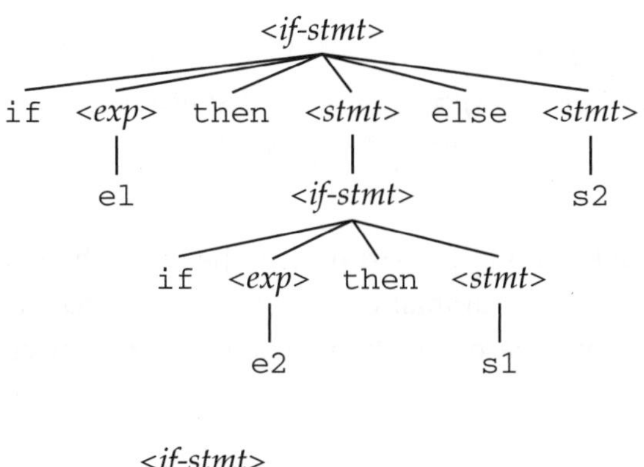

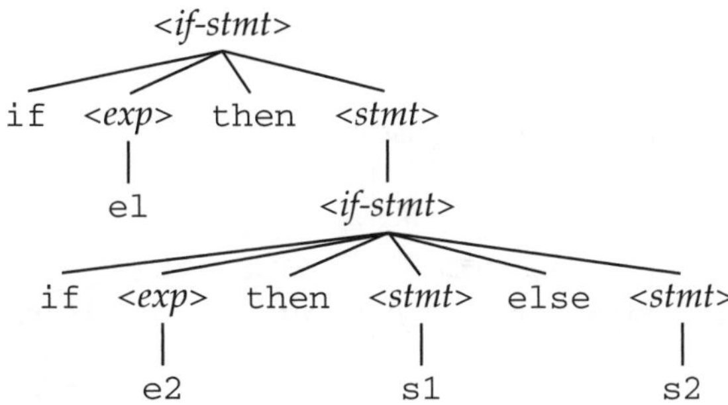

The first parse tree puts the `else` part with the first `if`. That is to say, it groups the statement this way: `if e1 then (if e2 then s1) else s2`. The second parse tree puts the `else` part with the second `if`. That is to say, it groups the statement this way: `if e1 then (if e2 then s1 else s2)`. The difference has an important impact on the behavior of the program. Which one is correct? Most languages that have the dangling-`else` problem resolve it in favor of the second parse tree above. (The usual convention is that an `else` part always goes with the nearest unmatched `if` part.)

To fix the ambiguity, we have to modify the grammar in a rather subtle way. We will first create a new non-terminal symbol, *<full-stmt>*, that generates all the same statements as our original *<stmt>*, but with the `else` part required on every `if` statement:

<full-stmt> `::=` *<full-if>* `| s1 | s2`
<full-if> `::= if` *<expr>* `then` *<full-stmt>* `else` *<full-stmt>*

Now we will substitute this new non-terminal symbol in just one place in the original grammar:

```
<stmt>    ::= <if-stmt> | s1 | s2
<if-stmt> ::= if <expr> then <full-stmt> else <stmt>
            | if <expr> then <stmt>
<expr>    ::= e1 | e2
```

We used *<full-stmt>* for the `then` part only in the case where the `else` part is present. The effect is that the grammar can match an `else` part with an `if` part only if all the nearer `if` parts are already matched. This produces a unique parse tree for the statement:

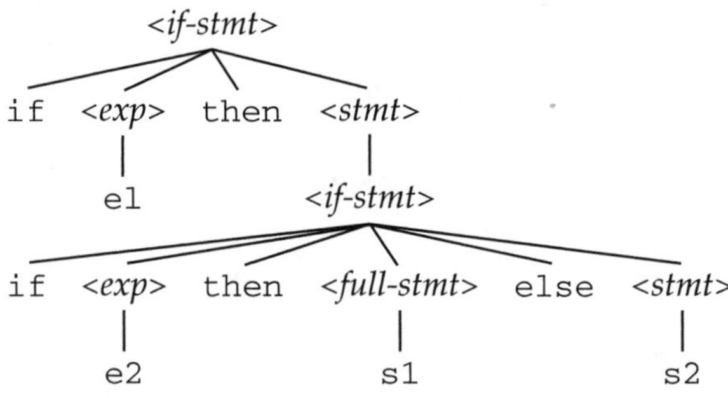

Organizing a grammar properly, as above, can eliminate the dangling-`else` ambiguity. However, the dangling `else` produces problems for people as well as grammars. A chain of `if-then-else` statements can be very hard to read, especially if some but not all of the `else` parts are present. Some languages handle conditional execution with a different syntax that does not suffer from the dangling-`else` problem and is easier for people to read. In Algol, the `then` part is not allowed to be another `if` statement. If you want to use one you must enclose it in a `begin/end` pair. In Ada, each `if` statement is terminated with an `end if`, which prevents the `else` part from dangling.

3.6 Cluttered Grammars

We have seen how to eliminate some ambiguity from grammars. This comes at a cost, however. The ambiguous G4 uses only one non-terminal symbol, *<exp>*, which naturally corresponds to expressions. The repaired, unambiguous G6 uses three non-terminal symbols. The two extra ones serve only to eliminate the technical problem of ambiguity in the grammar. They actually make G6 harder for people to read than G4. Similarly, the grammar that eliminates the dangling-`else` ambiguity is much harder to read than the original one. In each case, we got rid of ambiguity by cluttering up the grammar with extra non-terminal symbols or redundant productions. This may or may not be the right choice.

The previous chapter mentioned that there are several different audiences for a grammar: novice users, who just want to find out what legal programs look like; advanced users and language-system implementers, who need an exact, detailed definition to work from; and automatic tools, which derive other programs from your grammar automatically. A tension exists between the needs of these different audiences.

Automatic tools want a grammar that is complete and unambiguous. Such tools are not sensitive to clutter in a grammar, as long as they can generate a correct, unique parse tree for every program. We will not look at parsing algorithms here, but it turns out that more efficient algorithms require the grammar to follow certain rules. Grammars made to be used by automatic parser-generators and parsing tools may well have even more clutter than grammars we have shown, just to ensure that they follow these rules.

But automatic tools are not the only audience for a grammar. People want language definitions to be readable. It may actually make a grammar more readable to leave the ambiguity in the grammar, but explain in English how things like associativity, precedence, and the dangling `else` should be handled.

Some language definitions take one approach, and some take the other. Some language definitions do both: give a simple grammar designed for people to read, with explanations in English, and give a more cluttered grammar designed for use by parsing tools.

3.7 Parse Trees and EBNF

The EBNF extensions could be used to state the language of expressions more clearly. For example, the BNF grammar G6 contains these productions:

<exp> ::= *<exp>* + *<mulexp>* | *<mulexp>*

These two productions allow a sequence of one or more of whatever *<mulexp>* becomes, separated by plus signs. This might be easier to read in EBNF, like this:

<exp> ::= *<mulexp>* {+ *<mulexp>*}

EBNF can be easier for people to read. But since it eliminates some confusing recursions in the grammar, it tends to obscure the structure of the parse tree. What kind of parse tree would the EBNF grammar produce for the expression `a+b+c`?

There are two schools of thought about this: a strict usage and a lax usage. In strict usage, the EBNF construction above is permitted *only for left-associative operators*. For the (much rarer) right-associative operators, a recursive, BNF-style rule would have to be written. In lax usage, no parse-tree structure is implied by the EBNF curly brackets. You use them wherever you like and then add an explanation in English to clarify the associativity of the operators and resolve any other ambiguities. When you are reading EBNF language definitions, it is important to figure out what convention the authors are following.

3.8 Abstract Syntax Trees

A grammar for any realistically large language usually has many non-terminal symbols. This is especially true of grammars that are in the cluttered but unambiguous form needed by parsing tools. As we have seen, these non-terminal symbols guide the construction of a unique parse tree corresponding to a particular computation. Once this computation is determined, however, the non-terminal symbols themselves are no longer of interest.

Language systems usually store an abbreviated version of a parse tree called the *abstract syntax tree* or AST. There is no universal definition for an AST—the details differ for every language system—but usually there is a node for every operation, with a subtree for every operand. For example, this is the parse tree for the expression `a+b+c` from our unambiguous grammar G6:

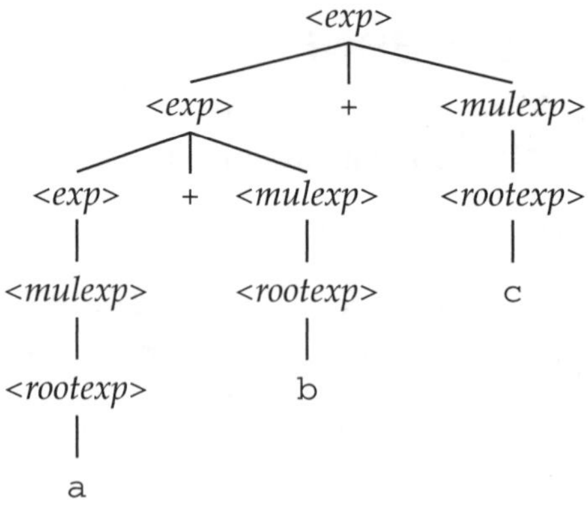

Although a parser would go through all the steps necessary to *find* this parse tree, it would not actually construct an explicit representation of it in memory. Instead, it would probably construct an AST like this:

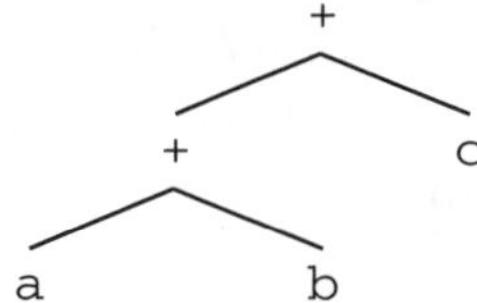

Many language systems use an AST as an internal representation of a program. Type-checking and other post-parsing steps can be carried out on the AST. Compilers can use the AST as input to the machine-code generator, and interpreters can interpret the program by traversing the AST and carrying out the operation required at each node. Chapter 23 discusses ASTs again, both as input for some little interpreters and as the starting point for some formal definitions of semantics.

3.9 Conclusion

This chapter has shown that a grammar can do more than just define the syntax of a language. By defining a unique parse tree for each program—a parse tree whose structure corresponds to the computation specified by the program—a grammar can begin to define semantics as well. Parse trees and ASTs are where syntax meets semantics.

We must now leave the question of how to define programming languages formally. Defining their syntax is the easy part. After seeing some concepts of programming-language semantics and experiencing them through some ML, Java, and Prolog programming, we will return in Chapter 23 to the question of formally defining programming-language semantics.

Exercises

Exercise 1 Start with the grammar G6, repeated here:

G6: *<exp>* ::= *<exp>* + *<mulexp>* | *<mulexp>*
<mulexp> ::= *<mulexp>* * *<rootexp>* | *<rootexp>*
<rootexp> ::= (*<exp>*)
| a | b | c

Modify it in the following ways:

a. Add subtraction and division operators (- and /) with the customary precedence and associativity.

b. Then add a left-associative operator % between + and * in precedence.
c. Then add a right-associative operator = at lower precedence than any of the other operators.

Exercise 2 Give an EBNF grammar for each of the languages of Exercise 1. Use the EBNF extensions wherever possible to simplify the grammars, but follow the strict interpretation for associativity.

Exercise 3 Show that each of the following grammars is ambiguous. (To show that a grammar is ambiguous, you must demonstrate that it can generate two parse trees for the same string.)

a. The grammar G4, repeated here:

```
G4:   <exp> ::= <exp> + <exp>
              | <exp> * <exp>
              | ( <exp> )
              | a | b | c
```

b. This grammar:

```
<person> ::= <woman> | <man>
<woman> ::= wilma | betty | <empty>
<man> ::= fred | barney | <empty>
```

c. The following grammar for strings of balanced parentheses. (A language of any number of different kinds of balanced parentheses is called a Dyck language. This type of language plays an interesting role in the theory of formal languages.)

```
<S> ::= <S> <S> | ( <S> ) | ()
```

d. This grammar:

```
<s> ::= <round> <square> | <outer>
<round> ::= ( <round> ) | ()
<square> ::= [ <square> ] | []
<outer> ::= ( <outer> ] | ( <inner> ]
<inner> ::= ) <inner> [ | )[
```

Exercise 4 For each of the grammars in Exercise 3 *except the last*, give an unambiguous grammar for the same language. (The last grammar in that exercise is a classic example of an inherently ambiguous grammar—it cannot be fixed!)

Further Reading

If you are interested in the interface between grammars and useful parse trees, there is no better reference than the Dragon Book, which was mentioned in the last chapter:

> Aho, Alfred V., Ravi Sethi, and Jeffrey D. Ullman. *Compilers: Principles, Techniques and Tools.* Boston, MA: Addison-Wesley, 1985.

If you are interested in the theoretical side of context-free grammars, there are many good books on formal languages. One excellent and classic text is

> Hopcroft, John E., and Jeffrey D. Ullman. *Introduction to Automata Theory, Languages, and Computation.* Boston, MA: Addison-Wesley, 1979.

It is only fair to warn you that in spite of the word "Introduction" in the title, the book is deeply mathematical and technical—not bedside reading for most tastes.

Chapter 4 **Language Systems**

4.1 Introduction

To make the magic of a programming language practical—to make programs work—is the job of a language system. A language system is made up of many parts, and some of the most important parts are hidden. Even though you are already familiar with at least one language system, you may not be aware of all that goes on behind the scenes to make your programming magic work. This chapter introduces some of the basic concepts of language systems.

4.2 The Classical Sequence

An *integrated development environment* is a language system that provides the programmer a single interface for editing, running, and debugging programs. It is a wonderful convenience, and many programmers today have never used anything else. But to understand language systems better, we have to start with something more old-fashioned. Let's look at an example of an un-integrated language system, a language system whose components are fully separated, so we can see the classical sequence of steps involved in running a program.

It is hard to give an example like this without going into all kinds of details about the processor, the memory architecture, and the operating system. To avoid all these details this example is artificial and generic. No language system works exactly like this, but it is representative of the kind of un-integrated language system programmers used in earlier days.

In this generic, un-integrated language system, the programmer first uses an editor to create a text file, the *source file*, containing the program. This example program in a C-like language calls the function `fred` 100 times, passing it each value of `i` from 1 through 100.

```
int i;
void main() {
  for (i=1; i<=100; i++)
    fred(i);
}
```

The program cannot be run by the hardware in this form. The source file must first be processed by a *compiler*. The job of a compiler is to translate programs into a lower-level language. The un-integrated compiler translates the program from the original high-level language into an *assembly language*, something like this:

```
i:      data word 0
main:   move 1 to i
t1:     compare i with 100
        jump to t2 if greater
        push i
        call fred
        add 1 to i
        go to t1
t2:     return
```

Each line in an assembly-language program represents either a piece of data (like `data word 0`) or an instruction for the processor (like `move 1 to i`). Before the development of the first commercial, high-level programming language (Fortran in 1957), programmers developed complete programs directly in assembly language. Today, direct assembly-language programming is reserved for those very rare occasions when there is something a compiler can't do for you; for example, when the compiler does not generate special-purpose instructions for the processor or when code the compiler generates is not fast enough or small enough.

An assembly-language program is closer to being directly executable by the hardware, but it isn't there yet. The instructions are still in a text format, still readable by people, but the hardware needs to be given instructions in its own more compact binary format. The assembly-language program also contains names—`i`, `main`, `t1`, `t2`, and `fred`. The hardware knows nothing about such names. They must all be converted into memory addresses before the program can run. An *assembler* processes the assembly-language program to convert each instruction into the machine's binary format, its *machine language*. The resulting *object file* is no longer readable by people, but it can be pictured like this:

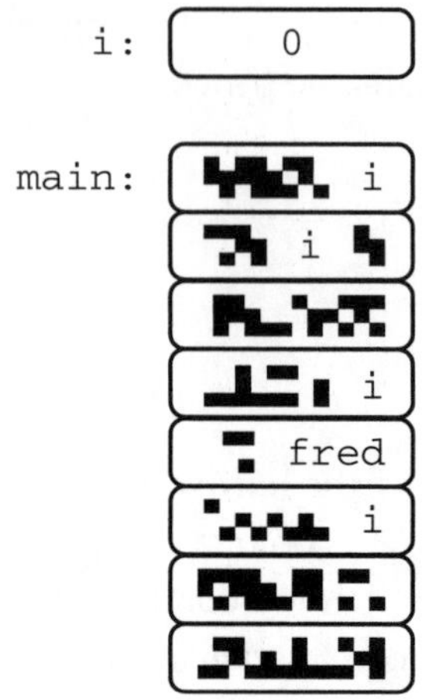

In this picture, graphics (like) show the machine-language parts of the file. As you can see, the object file is mostly machine language, but not entirely.

The assembler manages to eliminate some of the names. For example, a jump to a local label like `go to t1` becomes a relative jump: *go back 5 instructions*. But, as the illustration suggests, some of the names cannot be resolved by the assembler. The assembler does not know where in the computer's memory the variable `i` will be placed, and it does not know anything about the function called `fred`. These names cannot be resolved into actual memory addresses by the assembler, so the assembler's output is still not directly executable by the hardware.

The next step is performed by a piece of system software called a *linker* or *link editor*. The job of the linker is to collect and combine all the different parts of the program. In the example there is a reference to a function called `fred`. The linker must find the definition for `fred` and add that piece of code to the program. The function `fred` was compiled separately; it might even have been written in a different language. It might be in a system library or in one of the programmer's libraries. In some systems the linker might be able to combine `main` and `fred` into one block of code, completely resolving the call to `fred`. In other systems the linker might leave them as separate blocks that can be loaded at different addresses, like this:

The linker's output is stored in a single *executable file*. Although this file is called "executable," it may still not be entirely in machine language. There is actually one more hidden processing step before the program runs. Each time the user runs the program, the system *loader* is responsible for getting the program into memory. The loader adds any finishing touches the program needs, then starts it up.

This example is assuming a very simple kind of memory architecture, where the system's memory is organized like a single big array of words. The index of each word in this big array is the word's *address*. Before the program is loaded, the language system does not know where in this array the program will be. The loader finds a place in this memory array for each block in the executable file. Then come the loader's final touches: the references to names, `i` and `fred`, can be replaced by the actual memory addresses of those blocks. The result looks something like this in the computer's memory:

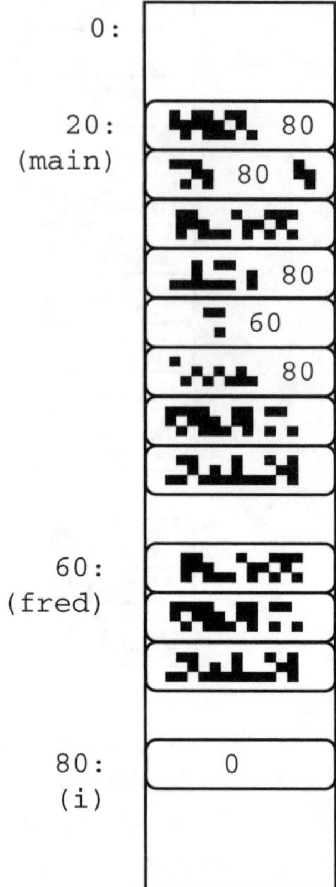

In this illustration, the `main` block is loaded at address 20, the `fred` block at address 60, and the `i` block at address 80.[1] The actual addresses are irrelevant; what is important is that each piece is loaded somewhere and all references to that piece are resolved. Now the program is directly executable by the hardware.

To summarize, this is the classical sequence of language-system steps:

1. Conventionally, memory is drawn with low addresses at the bottom of an illustration and high addresses at the top. But to remain consistent with the previous illustrations, this illustration reverses that convention.

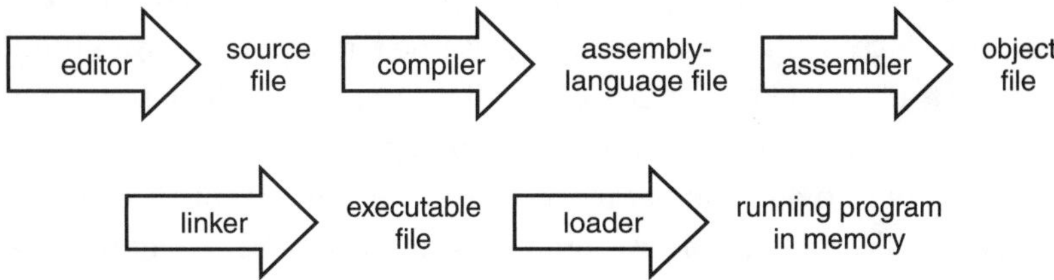

All of the steps after the compiler may be shared by several different languages. If a system is designed with this kind of compatibility in mind, compilers for different languages may generate code that can be assembled, linked, and loaded together. This allows different parts of a program to be developed in different languages.

Optimization

The code generated by a compiler is usually optimized automatically to make it run faster or take up less memory or both.[2] Optimization of generated code is not a new invention, but dates all the way back to the first Fortran compiler in 1957. Programmers who were used to writing programs in assembly language were often impressed that the Fortran compiler used many of the same tricks they were using to make their code more efficient. Compilers have become even trickier since then.

Here is an example of an optimization that most modern compilers can do. Consider this Java fragment:

```
int i = 0;
while (i < 100) {
  a[i++] = x*x*x;
}
```

This initializes the array elements `a[0]` through `a[99]` to the value `x*x*x`. The code apparently computes the value of the expression `x*x*x` over and over. This would be a waste of time. Since the value of `x` does not change inside the loop (assuming it is a local variable), it would be more efficient to do it this way:

```
int i = 0;
int temp = x*x*x;
while (i < 100) {
  a[i++] = temp;
}
```

2. The word *optimized* is a bit of a misnomer. The resulting code is *improved*, but there is no guarantee that it is optimal.

This optimization is called *loop invariant removal* and most modern compilers do it automatically. Such compilers generate the same efficient code from both of the source fragments above. (Thus, it is a waste of a programmer's time to make the optimization manually in the source code—a point addressed again in Chapter 21.)

Loop invariant removal is one of many optimizations that most modern compilers can do. Some, like loop invariant removal, add variables; others remove variables. Some reorganize the code; some add specialized copies of the code in different places; some remove unnecessary pieces of the code. The result of all this optimization is that the connection between the source code and the object code is often rather complicated. A simple question like "What assembly-language code was generated for this statement?" might have a complicated answer. The statement may have been moved, altered, or even eliminated during optimization.

In the classical sequence, optimization is done at compile time. In some of the variations discussed below, optimization may be performed at other times as well.

4.3 Variations on the Classical Sequence

Modern language systems often modify the classical sequence in important ways. This section looks at a few such variations.

Hiding the Steps

An obvious variation on the classical sequence is to hide some of the intermediate steps. Many language systems make it possible for the programmer to do the whole sequence, or at least the compile-assemble-link part, with a single command. The intermediate stages are hidden.

For example, the `gcc` command on a Unix system is used to run the Gnu C compiler. Suppose the source file were named `main.c`. Ordinarily, typing the command `gcc main.c` would compile, assemble, and link the program, producing an executable file called `a.out`. Although this simple command hides the intermediate steps, they are still there and could be executed one at a time with a little more effort. You could use the command `gcc main.c -S` to instruct the compiler to do just the first step, producing an assembly-language file called `main.s`. You could then run the assembler on that (using the command `as main.s -o main.o`), creating an object file called `main.o`. Finally, you could run the linker with an `ld` command. (The parameters for the `ld` command depend on the locations of the system libraries that you want the linker to use. See Exercise 10.)

Many modern compilers incorporate all the functionality of an assembler. Such compilers can generate object code directly, skipping the assembly-language stage completely.

Integrated Development Environments

An integrated development environment provides a single interface for editing, running, and debugging. In addition to having the advantage of presenting a single interface, an integrated environment can add power at each step. Editing, for example, can be more convenient if the editor knows the structure of the programming language. An integrated editor can automatically supply indenting, fonts, and colors to make the program text easier to read. In some integrated environments, the editor provides source-control features to track versions and coordinate collaboration. The source code may be stored in a database rather than in individual text files. Object code may also be stored in databases managed by the integrated language system; this makes linking more convenient.

When a program is built from many parts that are compiled separately, there is always the problem of how to rebuild the program when only a few parts have changed. For very large programs, it may be too expensive to recompile and link the entire program from scratch. The changed parts need to be recompiled, of course, but other parts that may depend on them also need to be recompiled. For some languages a relatively simple un-integrated tool, like the Unix `make` utility, suffices to manage the rebuilding process. In other languages the dependencies among separate compilations can be complex, even circular, and it may take a language-specific tool to do a good job of analyzing the dependencies. An integrated development environment can handle rebuilding automatically.

The part of the language system that benefits the most from integration is one we have not yet discussed: the debugger. Debuggers are discussed more below.

Interpreters

Here is a little thought experiment. Look at the following code fragment in an imaginary imperative language. What does it print?

```
x := 14;
y := 49;
while x ≠ y do
  if x < y then y := y - x else x := x - y;
print x
```

When you have figured it out, think back on the steps that you followed to find your answer. If you are like most people, you traced through the steps specified by the program, in your head or on paper. You saw that initially `x` is 14 and `y` is 49; that `x` and `y` are not equal, so the loop body executes; and that `x < y`, so the loop body changes `y` to 35. You went back to the top of the loop and saw that `x` and `y` are still not equal, and so on. You actually executed the program in your head, without going through anything like the classical sequence of a language system. In short, you *interpreted* the program. (Or perhaps you recognized Euclid's algorithm for finding the greatest common divisor and jumped immediately to the conclusion that the program prints the number 7. If so, good for you. Nevertheless, that still makes the point. You did not translate the program into a machine language and then execute it; you just chose another, deeper, way of interpreting the program.)

Carrying out the steps specified by a program, without first translating that program into another language, is something a program can do. Such a program is called an *interpreter* for the language. (We will implement some little interpreters in Prolog in Chapter 23.) Typically, language systems that interpret a program run it much more slowly than those that compile the program. Compiling takes more time up front, but it results in a machine-language program that runs at hardware speed. Interpreting starts to run right away (perhaps even before the program has been checked for syntax errors), but each step must be processed in software.

It sounds like a simple distinction, doesn't it? A compiler translates a program into machine language, and an interpreter executes the program without translating it. In fact, the distinction is not nearly that simple. There is a spectrum of language-system designs combining the two approaches. To get a perspective on this, let's consider virtual machines.

Virtual Machines

Instead of producing machine-language code that is ready to run on your computer's processor, a language system might produce code in a language for which there is no hardware. The language system might still perform the entire classical sequence of language-system steps, but the result would be "executable" code in a machine language for a *virtual machine*.

Running such a program requires a software simulator for the virtual machine. This simulator carries out the steps specified by the virtual-machine-language program. Does this sound familiar? It should—a virtual-machine simulator is really just another kind of interpreter. But now, instead of interpreting the high-level program directly, the language system compiles it into a low-level language and interprets that. The low-level language of the virtual machine is called an *intermediate code*.

Why add this extra step when you could compile directly to the physical machine language? One advantage is that an interpreter for the intermediate code can be implemented on many different machines. This way, the compiled code is platform independent—it runs the same way on different hardware platforms. Of course, you could compile to a physical-machine language and then write simulators for that machine to run on other systems. But such simulators are difficult to write. Physical-machine languages are designed to allow efficient hardware implementations; efficient software simulation is another matter entirely. An intermediate code is designed with software simulation in mind. Another advantage of intermediate-code systems is their security. Because the program being interpreted is never in control of the physical processor, it is more easily limited in how much damage it can do. The simulator for a virtual machine can intervene whenever the program being executed tries to do something it shouldn't.

Java language systems usually compile to an intermediate code. A particular intermediate code, known as the *Java virtual machine*, is supported by many different interpreters on many different physical machines. For example, almost every Web browser has an interpreter for the Java virtual machine. When you visit a Web page that contains a Java applet, that applet is a Java *bytecode* file—a file in the machine-language format of the Java virtual machine. The browser runs the applet by interpreting its bytecode. Java is by no means the first language to use this approach, but it is certainly the most successful today. Its twin advantages of cross-platform execution and heightened security are uniquely compelling for Web-browsing applications.

By varying the design of the intermediate language, we can create a whole spectrum of language-system solutions:

- If we take our intermediate language to be the same as the high-level language, we have a pure interpreter. This is not usually a good design for a language system, however, since some reasonably inexpensive pre-processing steps can produce a program that is easier to interpret.
- Most interpreted systems at least *tokenize* a program, converting it into a sequence of tokens as described in Chapter 2. A tokenized program has all the comments and white space stripped out, and it has all the keywords and punctuation identified. The tokenizing tasks need be done only once, even in loop bodies and other parts that are executed repeatedly. The tokenized form is an intermediate language, though not low-level enough to be called compiled.
- We could compile the source language into a lower-level intermediate language, like the bytecode of the Java virtual machine. Although it is

usually interpreted, Java bytecode is at a low enough level that it is possible to implement it (or large parts of it) in hardware.

- If we take our intermediate language to be the same as the physical-machine language, we have a standard, compiled language system.

A real machine is implemented in hardware, while a virtual machine is implemented in software. This sounds very definitive, but the dividing line between software and hardware is not as clear as you might think. For example, it is quite common in modern processors for some rare or particularly complicated instructions to be missing from the hardware; the missing instructions are caught by the processor and simulated in software. It is also common for the processor hardware to contain, completely hidden from the programmer, yet another translation step: the processor may implement each instruction using a sequence of internal micro-instructions. To confuse matters even more, the Java virtual machine, although it is usually implemented in software, has several hardware implementations too. At the time of this writing, several different manufacturers have developed chips to execute Java bytecode directly. The intermediate-code architecture is still called the Java *virtual* machine, even though it now exists as a real machine.

Delayed Linking

Here's a major wrinkle in the classical sequence: delaying the linking step, so that the code for library functions is *not* included in the executable file for the program that calls them. There are many different ways of doing this and, unfortunately, many different names for it.

The Microsoft Windows family of operating systems supports two different kinds of delayed linking. Many different Windows language systems give the programmer the option of using this built-in support for delayed linking. Libraries of functions for delayed linking are stored in files with special names that end with `.dll`, an abbreviation for *dynamic-link library*. One kind of delayed linking supported by the Windows system is called *load-time dynamic linking*. In this approach, the loader finds the `.dll` files and links a program to all the library functions it needs just before the program begins running. These library functions may already be in memory if they are being used by another application. The other and less widely used kind of delayed linking is called *run-time dynamic linking*. For this, a program must make explicit calls to find the `.dll` file at runtime and to load individual functions within that library.

The various Unix operating systems also support two kinds of delayed linking, similar in principle to the two Windows varieties. Many different Unix language systems give the programmer the option of using this built-in support for delayed linking. Libraries of functions for delayed linking are stored in files with special names that end with `.so` (for "shared object"), followed by a version number. In one kind of delayed linking, the `.so` files are called *shared libraries* and are linked to a program by the loader just before the program begins running. In the other kind of delayed linking, the `.so` files are called *dynamically loaded libraries,* and a program must make explicit calls to find the library at runtime and load the functions.

Java language systems, whether running on Windows, Unix, or any other platform, usually have their own scheme for delayed linking. The Java system loads and links library functions the first time a program calls them. (Well, they are not *functions* really; more accurately, they are *methods* and the classes that contain them. But we will see more about Java starting in Chapter 13.) This happens automatically, as a side effect of the program trying to call the function. The Java class loader performs a lot of work in addition to basic loading and linking. Classes are often loaded from remote sites over the Internet. Since the system cannot trust that the classes being loaded were actually created by a correct Java compiler, it has to check them thoroughly. The class loader verifies the bytecode for each loaded class, making sure that it complies with the requirements of the Java virtual machine.

There are several potential advantages of delayed linking:

- Multiple programs can share a copy of the library function. With classical linking, each program that uses a library function has a copy of that function linked in. This makes the programs' executable files take up more space on the disk, and more space in memory while running. With delayed linking there can be a single, shared copy on the disk and a single, shared copy in memory.
- The library function can be updated independently of the program. If a defect is found in the library function, it can be replaced in the library, without having any of the programs that use it altered. These programs will automatically use the repaired code the next time they are run.[3]
- Some approaches to delayed linking avoid loading functions that are never called. This can reduce the load time of a program. That is important because load time can be a significant fraction of the perceived running time of the program; for example, a simple Java applet may spend much more time arriving over your Internet connection that it does actually running. In

3. In practice, this has turned out to be a mixed blessing. It allows library updates to fix defects in many applications simultaneously, without recompiling them. It also allows library updates to *introduce* defects in many applications simultaneously. Such problems can be difficult to diagnose.

addition, some kinds of programs, like word processors, typically have huge collections of features that are rarely used. So it makes sense for the code that implements these features to be loaded only if needed.

Profiling

Compilers use many tricks to generate efficient code. Some of these tricks require the compiler to make guesses about the likely runtime behavior of a program. Which direction will a given branch go most often? Which parts of the program will be executed most often? The compiler cannot answer such questions perfectly, but it can sometimes make a reasonable guess. For example, when a program contains nested loops, the compiler may guess that the code in the innermost loop will execute most often. Then it can focus its resources on making that innermost loop efficient.

Instead of making guesses about the runtime behavior of a program, some systems use *profiling* information to improve the quality of the compiled code. The idea is to compile the program *twice*. After the first time, the program is linked, loaded, run, and profiled. Profiling collects statistics about the runtime behavior of the program; how many times each piece of the program is executed, for example. On the second pass, the profile information is used by the compiler to help it generate better code.

Dynamic Compilation

The term *dynamic compilation* covers many different techniques with one thing in common: some compiling takes place after the program starts running. A simple version of dynamic compilation is compilation of each function only when it is actually called. More sophisticated versions begin by interpreting a program and compile only those pieces that seem to be called frequently.

Still more sophisticated versions interlace running and compiling in multiple steps. Today's faster implementations of the Java virtual machine work this way. The Java source is compiled to intermediate code, as we have already seen, and the intermediate code is interpreted. But the system may decide to further compile parts of this intermediate code into the machine language of the local processor. Later on, the system may decide to perform optimization steps on the compiled code.

A catchy name for dynamic compilation is just-in-time (JIT) compilation. This is an active area of research in programming-language systems.

4.4 Binding Times

Here again is the example program for the classical sequence:

```
int i;
void main() {
  for (i=1; i<=100; i++)
    fred(i);
}
```

Many of the tokens of this program are names: `int`, `i`, `void`, `main`, `for`, and `fred`. Each name has one or more properties to be determined. What is the set of values associated with the type `int`? What is the type of `fred`? What is the memory location of the compiled code for `main`? What is the value of `i`? The act of associating properties with names is called *binding*. The binding of different properties takes place at different times, and there is a standard way of describing these times with reference to the classical sequence.

Language-Definition Time

Some properties are bound when the language is defined. In C, for example, the meaning of the keywords `void` and `for` is part of the language definition. All C language-system implementations that conform to the standard for C must treat these names the same way.

Language-Implementation Time

Some properties are left out of the language definition, either intentionally or accidentally, and are up to each implementation of the language. In C, the range of values for an `int` is implementation dependent. Each C compiler can choose the `int` that is most natural on that machine—usually, a 16-, 32-, or 64-bit twos-complement binary number. In ML, the exact meaning of `int` is also implementation dependent. (In Java, the range of an `int` is bound at language-definition time. All Java systems must implement `int` as 32 bits.)

Language implementations may also introduce limitations that are not part of the formal language specification. For example, the implementation may impose a limit on the maximum length of a name, the maximum number of array dimensions, or the maximum number of levels of nesting for nested function definitions.

Compile Time

Many properties can be determined by the compiler. In the sample program, the type of `i` is bound at compile time. (In statically typed languages like C, the types of all variables are bound at compile time. We will see more about this in Chapter 6.) Moreover, each reference to `i` is bound to the matching definition of `i` at compile time, a trivial exercise in our example, but not so in a larger program that declares many different variables named `i` in different places. (We will see more about how references are bound to definitions in Chapter 10.)

Link Time

As was shown earlier, the linker finds the definitions of library functions to match each reference in a program. In the example, the definition for `fred` is bound to the program's `fred` reference at link time.

Load Time

The loader puts finishing touches on a program just before it begins to run each time. In the example, the memory addresses for `main`, `fred`, and `i` were bound at load time.

Runtime

Of course, most of the action happens when the program actually runs. In the example, the variable `i` takes on a sequence of values. We can say that the values are bound to `i` at runtime.

One of the most important distinctions about binding times is whether a property is bound before the program starts running or after. The term *early binding* refers to all times before runtime; *late binding* is another way of saying runtime binding. Early binding generally makes things faster and more secure: there is less to do, and less that can go wrong, at runtime. Late binding generally leaves more runtime flexibility. Different languages make different decisions about this tradeoff.

Some of these binding times make sense only for language systems that follow the classical sequence. In a pure interpreter there is no compile time. With dynamic loading, the terms *link time* and *load time* are not very useful.

Each high-level language has different binding-time implications. The language definition may directly specify a binding time for some properties. For example, the Java definition specifies not only that all local variables must be assigned before being referenced, but also that this property must be checked at compile time. (It follows that no pure interpreter for Java could comply with this specification.) In other cases, the language definition may imply something about binding times without specifying it explicitly. In Lisp, for example, the type of value stored in a variable sometimes cannot be determined until runtime. While there is nothing wrong with a Lisp compiler that binds the types of some variables at compile time, it must be prepared to bind others at runtime.

4.5 Debuggers

Most language systems include *debuggers*, tools to help a programmer find program defects. Some language systems offer simple tools for postmortem analysis of a program. When the program in such a language system hits a fatal defect, it makes a *core dump*, writing a copy of its memory to a file. A language-system tool later extracts meaningful information from the dump file: the point where the problem occurred, the *traceback* of function calls leading up to that point, the values of variables at that point, and so on.

More advanced debugging tools allow a programmer to view this kind of data while the program is running. Interactive debuggers can give the programmer control over the program's execution, allowing the programmer to step through code slowly, to catch it if it ever reaches a given point, to inspect and modify the values of variables on the fly, and so on. An integrated language system can provide still more debugging features, such as editing and recompiling parts of the program while it is still running.

A debugger works with the executable program, but it must express everything in terms of the original source program. This is a thorny problem. The debugging tool can't just say, "The problem occurred in the instruction at address 4096." Instead, it should say something like, "The problem occurred at line 7 in function `fred`." It can't just say, "Memory word 8192 is 0." Instead, it should say something like, "The value of `i` is 0." How can the debugging tool get information about the names of variables and functions in the source program? In an integrated development environment this information is easily accessible. In an un-integrated system a dictionary of source-program names is commonly included in the executable file, just for the convenience of the debugger.

As observed earlier in the chapter, modern compilers use a variety of optimizations that weaken the connection between source-level code and machine-level code. This means that as compilers become more sophisticated, using more optimization tricks, debuggers must become more sophisticated as well. In effect, the debugger must conceal what the compiler has done, giving the programmer the impression of debugging the source code directly.

4.6 Runtime Support

If a program makes explicit calls to library functions, the linker is expected to include that code in the executable file. Interestingly enough, some additional code is usually included even if the program does not refer to it explicitly. This *runtime support* code is an important hidden player in any language system.

What is needed for runtime support depends on the language and language system. Here are some common components:

- Startup processing. The first thing that runs is not usually the high-level program itself. Instead, some runtime-support code runs first. It sets up the processor and memory the way the high-level code expects.
- Exception handling. What should a program do if something goes wrong—say, if it tries to divide by zero? The language may include exception handling, like the `try` statement in Java (which is discussed more in Chapter 17). Such exception handling needs to find the appropriate exception handler at runtime, and the hidden code that searches for it is part of the runtime support. If the exception is not caught within the language, the runtime system may still want to take some action before the program terminates, such as writing out a core dump. (On some systems a core dump is written by the operating system instead.)
- Memory management. Some programming languages, including ML, Java, and Prolog, implicitly require extensive memory management. Whenever a Java program creates an object, memory for that object must be allocated. Whenever an ML program adds an element to a list, memory must be allocated. Whenever a function is called, memory for its local variables must be allocated. When the program has finished using this memory, the memory should be reused somehow. Memory management is such an important part of runtime support that we will spend a whole chapter on it, Chapter 14.
- Operating-system interface. Most programs communicate with the operating system about things like keyboard and mouse input. The interface between a program and the operating system may require some special structure and special actions on the part of the program, even if the program is not interested in such input. This communication is the task of runtime support.
- Concurrent execution. Some languages, like Ada and Java, include support for writing multi-threaded programs. Others have no constructs in the language to support concurrent execution, but permit it through API calls. The study of concurrent programming techniques (and the architectural,

language-level, and API designs that support them) is a very important branch of computer science. This book does not discuss it further, but merely notes, here, that operations like interthread communication and synchronization and the creation and destruction of threads often require runtime support.

4.7 Conclusion

This chapter looked at the classical sequence of programming language systems: edit, compile, assemble, link, load, and run. It showed some of the ways in which modern language systems deviate from the classical sequence. It defined binding times for the properties of names with respect to the classical sequence. Finally, it looked at two additional parts of a programming-language system: debuggers and runtime support.

A programming language is not the same as a programming-language system, and it is important to keep the two ideas separate. Some interesting and influential programming-language designs (like the Algol languages) have been rarely, if ever, fully implemented. Conversely, a really good language system can make even a poorly designed language much more pleasant to use.

Language systems pose many interesting implementation puzzles and properly deserve their own book. Nevertheless, they have a chapter in this book. Why? Because the puzzles of language implementation interact with the puzzles of programming-language design. Programming languages have to be judged not only on how nice they are to write programs in, but also on how efficiently and cleanly they can be implemented. Language designs pose specific implementation problems; for example, Java requires garbage collection (discussed more in Chapter 14), ML requires compile-time type inference, and Fortran requires special cooperation from the linker (as you will see if you do Exercise 9). Experience with language systems also feeds back on future language designs. One of the most important annual conferences on programming languages reflects this connection. It is the annual Association for Computing Machinery (ACM) conference called PLDI—Programming Language Design and Implementation.

Exercises

Exercise 1 Choose any programming language you know well. For each of the six binding times—language-definition time, language-implementation time, compile time, link time, load time, and runtime—state one thing in the language that is bound at that time and explain how it is bound and why it is bound when it is. (If nothing in the language is bound at a given binding time, explain why not.)

Exercise 2 (for those who already know C or C++) What is the binding time for each of the following in a C or C++ program? State the binding time as precisely as possible (language-definition time, language-implementation time, compile time, link time, load time, or runtime). Explain how each of the following is bound and why it is bound when it is.

a. The location in memory of a local variable in a function.
b. The meaning of the keyword `while`.
c. The size in memory of a variable of type `int`.
d. The location in memory of a global static variable.
e. The code for the `printf` function.
f. The type of a local variable in a function.
g. The value(s) assigned to a variable.
h. The size in memory of a pointer.

Exercise 3 (for those who already know Java) What is the binding time for each of the following in a Java program? State it as precisely as possible (language-definition time, language-implementation time, compile time, link time, load time, or runtime). Explain how each of the following is bound and why it is bound when it is.

a. The location in memory of a local variable in a method.
b. The location in memory of a non-static field of a class.
c. The meaning of the keyword `while`.
d. The size in memory of a variable of type `int`.
e. The bytecode for a class.
f. The definition of the method `m` that is used when a method call of the form `a.m()` is executed, where `a` is a reference to an object.
g. The type of a local variable in a function.
h. The value(s) assigned to a variable.
i. The size in memory of a reference.

Exercise 4 Suppose the target assembly language for a compiler has these five instructions for integers:

`load` *address*`,`*reg*
`add` *reg*`,`*reg*`,`*reg*

```
sub reg,reg,reg
mul reg,reg,reg
store reg,address
```

In these instructions, an *address* is the name of a static variable (whose actual address will be filled in by the loader). A *reg* is the name of an integer register, a special extra-fast memory location inside the processor. The target assembly language has three integer registers: `r1`, `r2`, and `r3`. The `load` instruction loads the integer from the given memory address into the given register. The `add` instruction adds the second register to the first register and places the result in the third register. The `sub` instruction subtracts the second register from the first register and places the result in the third register. The `mul` instruction multiplies the first register by the second register and places the result in the third register. The `store` instruction stores the integer from the given register at the given memory address. So, for example, the compiler might translate the assignment `result := offset+(width*n)` into this:

```
load width,r1
load n,r2
mul r1,r2,r1
load offset,r2
add r2,r1,r1
store r1,result
```

Using this assembly language, give translations of the following assignment statements. Use as few instructions as possible.

a. `net := gross - costs`
b. `volume := (length * width) * height`
c. `cube := (x * x) * x`
d. `final := ((a - abase) * (b - bbase)) * (c - cbase)`

(This is an example of a *load/store architecture*. Many modern microprocessors implement an architecture like this, though usually with more registers.)

Exercise 5 Suppose the target assembly language for a compiler has these five instructions for integers:

```
push address
add
sub
mul
pop address
```

In these instructions, an *address* is the name of a static variable (whose actual address will be filled in by the loader). The machine maintains a stack of integers, which can grow to any size. The `push` instruction pushes the integer from the given memory address to the top of the stack. The `add` instruction adds the top integer on the stack to the next-from-the-top integer, pops both off, and pushes the result onto the stack. The `sub` instruction subtracts the top integer on the stack from the next-from-the-top integer, pops both off, and pushes the result onto the stack. The `mul` instruction multiplies the top integer on the stack by the next-from-the-top integer, pops both off, and pushes the result onto the stack. The `pop` instruction pops an integer off the stack and stores it at the given memory address. So, for example, the compiler might translate the assignment `result := offset+(width*n)` into this:

```
push offset
push width
push n
mul
add
pop result
```

Using this assembly language, give translations of the assignment statements in Exercise 4. Use as few instructions as possible.

(This is an example of a *stack architecture*. Such architectures have been implemented in hardware in the past, but the most well known example today is virtual—the Java virtual machine.)

Exercise 6 Give an example of an assignment statement like those in Exercise 4 that cannot be translated into the assembly language of Exercise 4 because of a shortage of registers. (Any such statement can be translated if the compiler is allowed to invent and use additional variables in memory, but do not allow this.) Give a translation of your statement into the assembly language of Exercise 5.

Exercise 7 Create a machine language to match the assembly language of Exercise 4. That is, give a binary encoding of the instruction set, so that each possible instruction has a unique encoding as a string of bits. Assume that addresses require 16 bits. Choose an encoding that is simple (so it could be implemented in hardware efficiently) but not unnecessarily wasteful of space. Different instructions need not be the same length, as long as the machine-language programs are unambiguous. Show the format you use for each instruction. Show the translation of this assembly-language program into your machine language:

```
load width,r1
load n,r2
mul r1,r2,r1
load offset,r2
add r2,r1,r1
store r1,result
```

Exercise 8 Create a machine language to match the assembly language of Exercise 5. That is, give a binary encoding of the instruction set, so that each possible instruction has a unique encoding as a string of bits. Assume that addresses require 16 bits. Choose an encoding that is simple (so it could be implemented in hardware efficiently) but not unnecessarily wasteful of space. Different instructions need not be the same length, as long as the machine-language programs are unambiguous. Show the format you use for each instruction. Show the translation of this assembly-language program into your machine language:

```
push offset
push width
push n
mul
add
pop result
```

Exercise 9 Investigate the `COMMON` keyword in Fortran. Describe how Fortran common blocks work and give an example. What happens if two named common blocks with the same name contain different variables? What is the difference between a blank common and a named common? What does the linker have to do to make this language construct work?

Exercise 10 Create this file on a Unix system, giving it the name `main.c`:

```
int main() {
  return 0;
}
```

Figure out how to compile, assemble, and link this into an executable program, not using a one-step command like `cc main.c`, but using separate steps to compile, assemble, and link. Show the exact commands that are necessary. (*Hint:* Look at the `-v` flag on the `cc` command if you get stuck.) Print out, compare, and hand in the following results:

a. The assembly-language file `main.s`.
b. The result of disassembling the file `main.o` (using the `dis` command).
c. The result of disassembling the final `a.out` file (using the `dis` command).

These three print-outs are quite different. How do you account for the differences?

Exercise 11 For a linker to do its job, it needs more than just the assembled code. For example, it needs to know where within that assembled code there are references to names that need to be resolved and where there are definitions of names that might be needed in other files.

Use the command `elfdump main.o` to examine the file `main.o` created in Exercise 10. The `elfdump` tool shows the file's *header* followed by individual *sections*. The output of `elfdump` is extensive and appears cryptic at first. You do not have to find out exactly what every part of this output means—unless you want to! Just look at it and answer some simple questions:

a. The first section is named `.text` and contains the actual code compiled from `main.c`. What are the names of the other sections?
b. Which sections actually contain data (i.e., have a non-zero section size field, `sh_size`)?
c. Which section contains the definitions of names? What names are defined there?

Chapter 5 A First Look at ML

5.1 Introduction

This chapter is an introduction to Standard ML. The ML language family has a number of dialects. The Standard ML dialect is the one used in this book; from here on it will just be referred to as ML. ML is one of the more popular functional languages, and some large commercial projects have been developed in ML. But let's be honest about this: you will probably never see an employer advertising for someone with ML skills. The point of learning ML is not to beef up your résumé, but to expand your programming language consciousness. By learning ML you will gain a new perspective—it is very different from the usual crowd of popular imperative languages. And who knows? You may find that ML is just the right language for you, and you may even choose to use it in commercial projects of your own.

This is a hands-on chapter. There are many short examples of ML. You may find it helpful to type in the examples as you go. You should do as many of the exercises as you can. By the end of the chapter, you should be able to write simple expressions and function definitions in ML and use several ML types, including tuples and lists.

5.2 Getting Started with an ML Language System

You will need an ML language system to try the examples and solve the exercises. The examples in this book were produced using SML/NJ (Standard ML of New Jersey), which is an excellent, free, open-source ML language system. If you are reading this book as part of an organized course, your teacher may give you instructions for running ML on your local systems. If not, or if you want your own copy, you can easily download and install SML/NJ on your own Unix or Windows system. The Web site for this book has up-to-date links for downloading SML/NJ.

Like most functional-language systems, SML/NJ operates in an interactive mode: it prompts you to type in an expression, you type one in, it evaluates your expression, it prints out the value, and then the whole cycle repeats. When we first run SML/NJ on our system it prints this:

```
Standard ML of New Jersey
-
```

The dash is its prompt; it is now waiting for input. Below, we have added to the session by typing an ML expression, followed by a semicolon, followed by the Enter key. (To be easier to read, the input is shown in boldface to distinguish it from ML's output. And the Enter key is not shown—that is assumed at the end of every input line.)

```
Standard ML of New Jersey
- 1 + 2 * 3;
val it = 7 : int
-
```

ML has evaluated the expression, printed the result, and prompted for another expression.

ML's response is probably more verbose than you expected. The value of `1+2*3` should be `7`, of course, but ML printed more than that. For one thing, it printed the type (`int`) as well. As we will see, ML tries to infer a type for every expression. Of course, anyone could figure out what the type of `1+2*3` must be, but ML's type system is very expressive and its type inference is unusually powerful. You might have wondered why it prints `val it = 7` instead of just `7`. Part of the explanation is that ML maintains a variable named `it` whose value is always the value of the last expression that was typed in. The rest of the explanation will have to wait until we see a few more things about ML.

The semicolon at the end of the line of input is very important. It is very easy to forget when you are first beginning to experiment with ML. In case you should forget it, here is what will happen:

```
- 1 + 2 * 3
=
```

ML assumes that you are not yet finished with the expression you want it to evaluate. (Expressions can take up more than one line.) It prompts for further input with the character =. Eventually, when the input ends with the semicolon ML is waiting for, ML will evaluate the whole thing:

```
- 1 + 2 * 3
= ;
val it = 7 : int
-
```

5.3 Constants

Let's start by looking at the simplest of expressions—constants. The example below shows ML evaluating some numeric constants. These constants illustrate the two numeric types, `int` and `real`.

```
- 1234;
val it = 1234 : int
- 123.4;
val it = 123.4 : real
```

The syntax for integer and real constants is conventional, with one important wrinkle: ML uses the tilde symbol (~) for the negation operator. So the number –1 is written as `~1` in ML.

The next example shows the ML constants `true` and `false`, which are the two values of ML's `bool` type.

```
- true;
val it = true : bool
- false;
val it = false : bool
```

There is not much else to say about them, but this is a good time to point out that ML is case sensitive. For the boolean true value, you must write `true`, not `TRUE` or `True` or anything else.

Now for some strings and characters (the ML types `string` and `char`):

```
- "fred";
val it = "fred" : string
- "H";
val it = "H" : string
- #"H";
val it = #"H" : char
```

String constants, like `"fred"`, are enclosed in double quotation marks (that is, with one double-quote character before and after—not two single-quote characters!). To enable unusual characters inside a string, ML supports the same kind of escape sequences that Java and C do; for example, `\t` for a tab, `\n` for a linefeed, or `\"` to put in a quote mark without ending the string. As you can see from the example, there is a difference between a one-character string constant and a character constant. To get a character constant, put the `#` symbol before the quoted character.

5.4 Operators

The next example shows ML's basic arithmetic operators.

```
- ~ 1 + 2 - 3 * 4 div 5 mod 6;
val it = ~1 : int
- ~ 1.0 + 2.0 - 3.0 * 4.0 / 5.0;
val it = ~1.4 : real
```

The integer binary operators for addition (`+`), subtraction (`-`), and multiplication (`*`) are standard. For integer division, ML provides two operators, written as `div` and `mod`. The `div` operator computes the integer quotient (ignoring the remainder), while `mod` returns the remainder after integer division.[1] As with constants, ML uses the tilde symbol for the negation operator. It takes a little practice to get used to this, since most languages use the minus-sign symbol both as a unary operator (for negation) and as a binary operator (for subtraction).

For real numbers, ML uses the same operators, `+`, `-`, `*`, and `~`. There is also a real-division operator (`/`). For strings, there is a concatenation operator (`^`):

```
- "bibity" ^ "bobity" ^ "boo";
val it = "bibitybobityboo" : string
```

1. The concept of integer division with a remainder appears simple enough at first glance, but it is actually subject to a variety of interpretations. What happens with negative operands? Is 5 divided by –2 equal to –2, remainder 1, or to –3, remainder -1? In Java this works one way, in ML it works the other way, and in Prolog (as in many other languages) it is machine dependent.

Then there are the ordering comparison operators: less than (<), greater than (>), less than or equal to (<=), and greater than or equal to (>=). They can be applied to pairs of strings, characters, integers, or real numbers.

```
- 2 < 3;
val it = true : bool
- 1.0 <= 1.0;
val it = true : bool
- #"d" > #"c";
val it = true : bool
- "abce" >= "abd";
val it = false : bool
```

Applied to strings, the comparisons test alphabetical order. Since `"abce"` would come before `"abd"` in the dictionary, the expression `"abce" >= "abd"` is false.

The two more fundamental comparison operators are the equality test (=) and the inequality test (<>). Some, but not all, of ML's types can be tested for equality or inequality using those operators; these are called the *equality types*. All the types we have seen so far are equality types except the real numbers. Real numbers cannot be tested for equality in ML. The reason is that most real arithmetic in computers is rounded to the limited precision of the computer hardware. Because of this rounding, two computations that should produce equal values mathematically often produce slightly different values on the computer. This means that it is usually a mistake (in any programming language) to compare two real numbers to see if they are exactly equal. This mistake is more difficult to make in ML, since ML does not allow you to compare real values for equality directly. (If you are really sure you want to, you can still accomplish it indirectly by combining a <= test with a >= test.)

For boolean values, ML has operators for logical or (`orelse`), logical and (`andalso`), and logical complement (`not`). For example:

```
- 1 < 2 orelse 3 > 4;
val it = true : bool
- 1 < 2 andalso not (3 < 4);
val it = false : bool
```

The `orelse` and `andalso` operators do not evaluate the second operand if the first one is enough to decide the result. If the first operand of an `orelse` is true, the whole result is true, so ML does not bother to evaluate the second operand. This is more than just an optimization. It is easy to write a program to test whether both operands are evaluated or not; just make the second operand something whose evaluation would cause an error and then see if the error occurs.

```
- true orelse 1 div 0 = 0;
val it = true : bool
```

Evaluating the expression `1 div 0` should cause an error, but no error occurs because the expression is not evaluated. Operators like this are called *short-circuiting* operators. (To be perfectly accurate, `orelse` and `andalso` are not really operators in ML. They are just keywords. All true ML operators evaluate all their operands. But to keep things simple, we will continue to call them operators.)

The operators seen so far are all left-associative and fall into these six precedence levels:

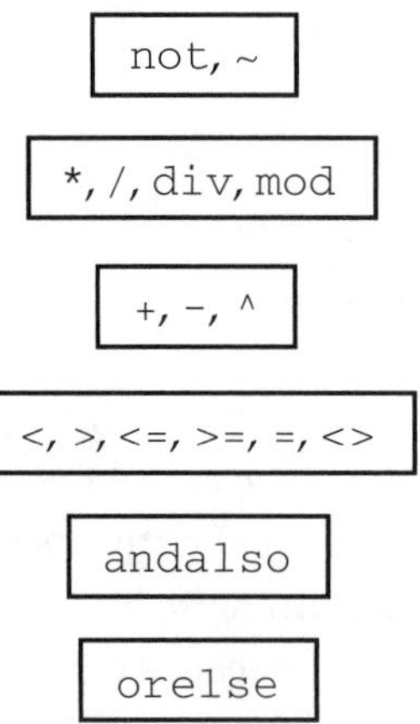

ML has additional operators and additional precedence levels, and it allows programs to define new operators and specify their precedence. However, this book will not require any further operators.

5.5 Conditional Expressions

If the language you know best is an imperative language, you are probably already familiar with if-then and if-then-else statements. However, you may not have used an if-then-else *expression* like ML's conditional:

```
- if 1 < 2 then #"x" else #"y";
val it = #"x" : char
- if 1 > 2 then 34 else 56;
val it = 56 : int
- (if 1 < 2 then 34 else 56) + 1;
val it = 35 : int
```

A conditional expression has this syntax:

<conditional-expression> `::=`
`if` *<expression>* `then` *<expression>* `else` *<expression>*

The <*expression*> in the `if` part must have the type `bool`, and the <*expression*> in the `then` part must have the same type as the <*expression*> in the `else` part. If the <*expression*> in the `if` part is true, the <*expression*> in the `then` part is evaluated and gives the value for the whole <*conditional-expression*>. Otherwise, the <*expression*> in the `else` part is evaluated and gives the value for the whole <*conditional-expression*>. Like the `orelse` and `andalso` operators described above, the conditional expression is short-circuiting. The only part evaluated is the one actually needed.

5.6 Type Conversion and Function Application

Here is an example of a type error in ML:

```
- 1 * 2;
val it = 2 : int
- 1.0 * 2.0;
val it = 2.0 : real
- 1.0 * 2;
Error: operator and operand don't agree [literal]
  operator domain: real * real
  operand:         real * int
  in expression:
    1.0 * 2
```

The first two expressions evaluated correctly. We have already seen that the `*` operator, and others like `+` and `<`, work on different types of pairs. When the same operator works differently on different types of operands, it is said to be *overloaded*. Chapter 8 will discuss overloading further. The `+` operator has one definition that applies to a pair of `int` values and another that applies to a pair of `real` values. But it does not have a definition that applies if the first operand is a `real` and the second is an `int`, so the third expression in the example above causes a type error.

In many languages, including Java, a mixed-type expression like `1.0*2` would be handled without error by converting the integer operand to a real number before multiplying. ML does not work this way. It has predefined functions that a program can use to convert values from one type to another, but it never does such conversions automatically.

Here are some of ML's predefined conversion functions:

Function	Parameter Type	Result Type	Notes
`real`	`int`	`real`	Converts integer to real.
`floor`	`real`	`int`	Rounds down.
`ceil`	`real`	`int`	Rounds up.
`round`	`real`	`int`	Rounds to the nearest integer.
`trunc`	`real`	`int`	Truncates after the decimal point, effectively rounding toward zero.
`ord`	`char`	`int`	Finds the ASCII code for the given character.
`chr`	`int`	`char`	Finds the character with the given ASCII code.
`str`	`char`	`string`	Converts a character to a one-character string.

(Note that `real` is used in ML both as the name of a predefined function and as the name of a type.) The next example shows some of these conversion functions at work.

```
- real(123);
val it = 123.0 : real
- floor(3.6);
val it = 3 : int
- floor 3.6;
val it = 3 : int
- str #"a";
val it = "a" : string
```

Did you notice that we stopped using parentheses around the function parameter in the middle of that example? To call a function in ML, you just write the function's name followed by its parameter. You can write parentheses around either the name or the parameter or both, but the preferred ML style is to avoid them. This is an important and rather unusual thing about ML syntax. The expressions `f(1)`, `(f)1`, `(f)(1)`, `(f 1)`, and `f 1` all have the same value—the value returned by function `f` when it is called with the parameter `1`.

You might have to use parentheses in a function application if ML's precedence and associativity for function application are not what you want. Function application has very high precedence, higher than anything else we have seen. For example, the expression `f a+1` is evaluated by applying `f` to `a`, then adding `1` to the result. If you want to apply `f` to the value `a+1`, you have to indicate that using parentheses: `f(a+1)`. Also, function application is left-associative (for reasons that will become clear in Chapter 9). So if you want to compute `f(g(1))`, you have to write it that way, or at least write `f(g 1)`. The expression `f g 1` won't do the same thing.

5.7 Variable Definition

The `val` keyword is used to define a new variable and bind it to a value.

```
- val x = 1 + 2 * 3;
val x = 7 : int
- x;
val it = 7 : int
- val y = if x = 7 then 1.0 else 2.0;
val y = 1.0 : real
```

Variable names defined with `val` should consist of a letter, followed by zero or more additional letters, digits, and/or underscores. As observed before, ML is case sensitive, so the variable `x` and the variable `X` are two different things.

You *can* use `val` to redefine an existing variable, giving it a new value and even a new type:

```
- val fred = 23;
val fred = 23 : int
- fred;
val it = 23 : int
- val fred = true;
val fred = true : bool
- fred;
val it = true : bool
```

It is not particularly useful to redefine variables like this, but it is mentioned here because `val` definitions do look a little like the assignment statements used in imperative languages. Do not be deceived. When you give a new definition of a variable, it does not assign a new value to the variable. It does not alter or overwrite the previous definition. It only adds a new definition on top of the previous one. When we get around to writing larger programs, this distinction becomes very important. Any part of the program that was using the old definition before you redefined it is still using the old definition afterwards. A new definition with `val` does not have side effects on other parts of the program.

We can now give the full answer to a question we skirted previously: when you type an expression into ML, why does it respond with a line beginning with `val it =`? The reason is that the ML language system actually expects keyboard input to be a series of definitions, such as `val` definitions. If you just type an expression *exp*, rather than a definition, as we have in most of the examples of this chapter, ML treats it as if you had typed `val it = ` *exp*. This makes a new instance of a variable named `it` and binds it to the value of your expression. Thus, the variable `it` always has the value of the last expression typed.

5.8 Garbage Collection

Sometimes, for no apparent reason, the SML/NJ language system prints a line that looks like this:

```
GC #0.0.0.0.1.3:    (0 ms)
```

If you have been trying the examples in this chapter, you have probably seen this at least once in the middle of ML's normal output. This message is what SML/NJ says when it is performing *garbage collection*, reclaiming pieces of memory that are no longer being used. Chapter 14 discusses garbage collection further. For now, just ignore these garbage-collection messages.

5.9 Tuples and Lists

Most languages allow functions to be called with a list of parameters, such as `f(1,2,3)`. Putting `(1,2,3)` together in parentheses groups the parameters together into an ordered parameter list that is passed to the function. An ordered collection of values of different types is sometimes called a *tuple*. ML supports tuples in a more general way than most languages. It allows tuples as expressions anywhere, not just for parameter lists.

```
- val barney = (1 + 2, 3.0 * 4.0, "brown");
val barney = (3,12.0,"brown") : int * real * string
- val point1 = ("red", (300, 200));
val point1 = ("red",(300,200)) : string * (int * int)
```

A tuple in ML is formed just by putting two or more expressions, separated by commas, inside parentheses. As the second expression above shows, tuples can even contain other tuples.

In the example above, the type of `barney` is reported by ML to be `int * real * string`. Obviously, the symbol `*` is not being used as a multiplication operator in this case. Instead, it is being used as a *type constructor*. Given any two ML types *a* and *b*, *a* `*` *b* is the ML type for tuples of two things, the first of type *a* and the second of type *b*. Parentheses are significant in tuple types;

`string * (int * int)` is not the same as `(string * int) * int`, and neither is the same as `string * int * int`.

To extract the `i`th element of a tuple `v` in ML, write the expression `#i v`. Tuple positions are numbered from left to right, starting with 1.

```
- #2 barney;
val it = 12.0 : real
- #1 (#2 point1);
val it = 300 : int
```

One final observation about tuples: they can have any length greater than one, but there is no such thing as a tuple of one. If you write a single expression inside parentheses, like `(1+2)`, the parentheses just serve to group the operations in the usual way. No tuple is constructed.

In addition to tuples, ML has lists. One important difference between a tuple and a list is that all the elements of a list must be of the same type. Lists are formed using square brackets instead of parentheses. They can contain any number of elements.

```
- [1, 2, 3];
val it = [1,2,3] : int list
- [1.0, 2.0];
val it = [1.0, 2.0] : real list
- [true];
val it = [true] : bool list
```

In the example above, the type of `[1,2,3]` is reported to be `int list`. Here, `list` is another type constructor. Given any ML type *a*, the type *a* `list` applies to lists of things of type *a*. Lists can contain any type of element, even tuples and other lists, as long as every element of the list has the same type.

```
- [(1, 2), (1, 3)];
val it = [(1,2),(1,3)] : (int * int) list
- [[1, 2, 3], [1, 2]];
val it = [[1,2,3],[1,2]] : int list list
```

Is the difference between a tuple and a list clear? Consider the next example, which shows a tuple of three integers and a list of three integers.

```
- val x = (1, 2, 3);
val x = (1,2,3) : int * int * int
- val y = [1, 2, 3];
val y = [1,2,3] : int list
```

The variable `x` is a tuple of three integers, and the variable `y` is a list of three integers. Note their different types as determined by ML. Although `x` and `y` look similar, the kinds of things you can do with them in ML are very different. In particular, a function that can take x as its parameter will apply only to tuples of three integers (values of type int * int * int). On the other hand, a function that can take y as its parameter will apply to all lists of integers—int list is the type of any list of integers, no matter what its length. The right choice depends on the problem being solved.

The empty list in ML can be written either as nil or just as []. The empty list in ML has some slight peculiarities. Unlike with all other list constants, ML cannot tell the exact type of []. Is it the empty list of integers? The empty list of strings?

```
- [];
val it = [] : 'a list
- nil;
val it = [] : 'a list
```

ML gives the type for the empty list as 'a list. Names beginning with an apostrophe, like 'a in this example, are *type variables*. A type variable stands for a type that is unknown. The type 'a list might be translated into English as "a list of elements, type unknown." A useful predefined function called null tests whether a list is empty:

```
- null [];
val it = true : bool
- null [1, 2, 3];
val it = false : bool
```

It is also possible to test whether a list is empty by comparing it for equality with the empty list, as in the expression x = []. But the function null is preferred for this, for reasons that will be described in the next section.

The @ operator in ML is used to concatenate two lists, which of course must have the same type:

```
- [1, 2, 3] @ [4, 5, 6];
val it = [1,2,3,4,5,6] : int list
```

The @ operator does for lists what the ^ operator does for strings. Both the parameters of @ must be lists. The expression 1@[2,3] is incorrect. You would either have to write [1]@[2,3] or use a different operator, the *cons* operator, which is written as :: (a double colon). Informally, you can think of the cons operator as gluing a new element onto the front of a list; for example, 1::[2,3] evaluates to the list [1,2,3].

```
- val x = #"c" :: [];
val x = [#"c"] : char list
```

```
- val y = #"b" :: x;
val y = [#"b",#"c"] : char list
- val z = #"a" :: y;
val z = [#"a",#"b",#"c"] : char list
```

At first glance, it may seem that the `@` operator would be a lot more useful than the cons operator. In fact, the cons operator is used far more often. This is for two reasons. First, it can be used naturally in recursive functions that construct lists one element at a time. Second, it is more efficient (as will be shown in Chapter 21). There are quite a few languages that provide an operator like `::` to construct lists. Such an operator was first introduced in the Lisp language, where it was called `cons` (an abbreviation for *construct*). That name has become generic, and now any operator like ML's `::` is called a cons operator.[2]

Unlike most operators in ML, the cons operator is right-associative. This turns out to be the most natural associativity for this operation. For example, you would expect `1::2::3::[]` to evaluate to the list `[1,2,3]`, and it does. If `::` were left-associative, `1::2::3::[]` would be an error, since the leftmost pair `1::2` does not even have a list as its second operand.

The two important functions for extracting parts of a list are `hd` and `tl` (which are abbreviations for *head* and *tail*).

```
- val z = 1 :: 2 :: 3 :: [];
val z = [1,2,3] : int list
- hd z;
val it = 1 : int
- tl z;
val it = [2,3] : int list
- tl(tl z);
val it = [3] : int list
- tl(tl(tl z));
val it = [] : int list
```

As you can see, the `hd` function returns the first element of the list, and the `tl` function returns the rest of the list after the first element. It is an error to try to compute the `hd` or `tl` of an empty list.

Although a string in ML is not the same as a list of characters, they obviously have a lot in common. The `explode` function converts a value of type `string` into a `char list`, and the `implode` function does the opposite conversion.

2. With continued exposure, many people find themselves using the word *cons* as a verb—to *cons* something onto a list means to attach it at the front and to *cons up* a list means to build the list by consing things onto it one at a time.

```
- explode "hello";
val it = [#"h",#"e",#"l",#"l",#"o"] : char list
- implode [#"h", #"i"];
val it = "hi" : string
```

5.10 Function Definitions

Up to this point the ML language system has looked like a calculator; you type things and it evaluates them. The next piece of ML is the first step toward making it less like a calculator and more like a programming language. To define new functions in ML you give a `fun` definition, like this:

```
- fun firstChar s = hd (explode s);
val firstChar = fn : string -> char
- firstChar "abc";
val it = #"a" : char
```

This function, `firstChar`, takes a string parameter and returns its first character. The syntax of the `fun` definition is quite simple:

<fun-def> `::=`
`fun` *<function-name>* *<parameter>* `=` *<expression>* `;`

The *<function-name>* is the name of the function being defined. It can be any legal ML name. The simplest *<parameter>* is just a variable name, as in the `firstChar` example. The *<expression>* is any ML expression. The value of the *<expression>* is the value the function returns. (This is a subset of the legal syntax for function definitions in ML. Chapter 7 discusses this further.)

Notice that ML figured out the type of `firstChar` without having to be told, just as it has done all along for expressions. That type, `string -> char`, describes functions that take a `string` parameter and return a `char` result. ML knows that the parameter `s` must be a string because the `explode` function was applied to it, and it knows that the result must be a character because that is what `hd` returns when applied to a list of characters.

The `->` symbol is another type constructor, like `*` and `list`. Given any two types *a* and *b*, *a* -> *b* is the type for functions that take a parameter of type *a* (the domain type) and return a result of type *b* (the range type).

To write a function that takes more than one input value, you can use a tuple parameter. For example, here is a function that returns the integer quotient of two integer values:

```
- fun quot(a, b) = a div b;
```

```
val quot = fn : int * int -> int
- quot (6, 2);
val it = 3 : int
```

It looks like the same kind of parameter list found in many other languages, but remember that ML handles tuple values in a much more general way. Consider this example:

```
- val pair = (6, 2);
val pair = (6,2) : int * int
- quot pair;
val it = 3 : int
```

Here we have defined the variable `pair` to be the tuple `(6,2)`, then called our function `quot` passing that tuple. This shows that there is nothing special about parameter lists on a function call. They are just tuples. Every ML function takes exactly one parameter—that parameter may be a tuple, but whether you build the tuple when you call the function, as in `quot (6,2)`, or whether you pass a tuple you have already constructed, as in `quot pair`, makes no difference to ML.

You have already seen enough ML to get a lot of work done with functions. Here, for example, is a function to compute the factorial of a non-negative integer:

```
- fun fact n =
=   if n = 0 then 1
=   else n * fact(n - 1);
val fact = fn : int -> int
- fact 5;
val it = 120 : int
```

Notice that the definition is spread out over more than one line. Like most modern languages, ML does not care where line breaks occur. They are there only to make the function definition more readable. We could have put the whole thing on one line.

The previous example was a recursive function definition. The `fact` function has a base case (`if n = 0 then 1`) that says what value to return for the smallest legal input. It has a recursive case (`else n * fact(n - 1)`) in which the function calls itself, but with a value that is closer to the base case. Recursion is used much more heavily in ML and the other functional languages than in most imperative languages. Imperative languages make heavy use of iteration: while loops, for loops, and the like. Functional languages make heavy use of recursion. It is possible to write iterative functions in ML, but it is rarely done. We will not use ML's iterative constructs at all in this book.

This next function adds up all the elements of a list:

```
- fun listsum x =
```

```
=    if null x then 0
=    else hd x + listsum(tl x);
val listsum = fn : int list -> int
- listsum [1, 2, 3, 4, 5];
val it = 15 : int
```

The `listsum` function definition illustrates a common pattern for recursive functions in ML. The base case applies when the list is `nil`, and the recursive call passes the `tl` of the list. In this way, `listsum` is called with `x`, then recursively with `tl x`, then with `tl (tl x)`, and so on all the way down to `nil`. That gives `listsum` a chance to look at each element of the list (using `hd x`). This is a pattern to consider whenever you are writing a function that has to do something for each element of a list.

A useful predefined function in ML is the `length` function, which computes the length of a list. This next example shows an implementation of it:

```
- fun length x =
=    if null x then 0
=    else 1 + length (tl x);
val length = fn : 'a list -> int
- length [true, false, true];
val it = 3 : int
- length [4.0, 3.0, 2.0, 1.0];
val it = 4 : int
```

An interesting thing about this function definition is the type ML decided for it: `'a list -> int`. As has already been shown, `'a` is a type variable. The input to `length` is a list of elements of unknown type. This is an example of a *polymorphic* function—it allows parameters of different types. We will not have to write a specialized length-computing function for every type of list, one for lists of booleans, another for lists of reals, and so on. This one `length` function will work on all types of lists. ML functions often end up being polymorphic. There is no special trick to making them that way. This example did not need to use any special syntax. ML just found the type in the usual way.

Now we can answer a question brought up in the previous section: why you should use the test `null x` instead of `x = []`. Look at what happens if `length` is defined using the test `x = []`:

```
- fun badlength x =
=    if x = [] then 0
=    else 1 + badlength (tl x);
val badlength = fn : ''a list -> int
- badlength [true, false, true];
val it = 3 : int
```

```
- badlength [4.0, 3.0, 2.0, 1.0];
Error: operator and operand don't agree
  [equality type required]
```

ML gives `badlength` the type `''a list -> int`. There is a minor difference between this and the type of `length`—a critical extra apostrophe. Type variables beginning with a double apostrophe, like `''a`, are restricted to equality-testable types. The function `badlength` works on most types of lists, but not on lists of reals, since reals cannot be tested for equality. The source of the problem is the test `x = []`. Because of this test, ML adopts the restriction that `x`'s elements must be equality testable. That is why you should use `null x` instead of `x = []`; it avoids this unnecessary type restriction.

Let's see one more example of a recursive function in ML. This one reverses a list.

```
- fun reverse L =
=   if null L then nil
=   else reverse(tl L) @ [hd L];
val reverse = fn : 'a list -> 'a list
- reverse [1, 2, 3];
val it = [3,2,1] : int list
```

In English, this function definition might be said in this way: "The reverse of an empty list is an empty list, and the reverse of any other list is the list you get by appending the first element onto the end of the reverse of the rest of the list." It's no easier to understand in English, is it?

5.11 ML Types and Type Annotations

So far we have seen the ML types `int`, `real`, `bool`, `char`, and `string`. We have also seen three type constructors: `*` for making tuple types, `list` for making list types, and `->` for making function types.

When the three type constructors are combined in a more complicated type, `list` has highest precedence and `->` has lowest precedence. For example, the type `int * int list` is the same as `int * (int list)`—the type of pairs of which the first item is an integer and the second a list of integers. The type for a list of pairs of integers would have to be written as `(int * int) list`, using parentheses to overcome the higher precedence of the `list` type constructor.

ML has discovered and written out all the types, so it might seem like a waste of time to learn how to write them yourself. Actually, it is important to know how to do it, because you do occasionally have to write ML types in an ML program.

Sometimes ML's type inference needs a little help and *type annotations* are necessary. Consider this function:

```
- fun prod(a, b) = a * b;
val prod = fn : int * int -> int
```

How did ML decide on the type `int * int -> int` for this function? Why not `real * real -> real`? Wouldn't a function to multiply two real numbers be written exactly the same way?

ML has no information about the types of `a` and `b` in `prod` other than the `*` operator that is applied to them. The `*` operator could apply to integers or to real numbers. When there are no other clues, ML uses the *default type* for `*`, which is `int * int -> int`. (The same thing would apply to the operators `+` and `-`.) If you want to define `prod` so that it applies to real numbers, you have to give ML a more definite clue: a type annotation. Here is one way to do it:

```
- fun prod(a:real, b:real) : real = a * b;
val prod = fn : real * real -> real
```

A type annotation is just a colon followed by an ML type. The example above has three type annotations that establish the types of `a`, `b`, and the returned value.

Unlike most languages, ML allows type annotations *after any variable or expression*. For instance, we could have given ML any one of these alternate clues:

```
fun prod(a, b) : real = a * b;
fun prod(a : real, b) = a * b;
fun prod(a, b : real) = a * b;
fun prod(a, b) = (a : real) * b;
fun prod(a, b) = a * b : real;
fun prod(a, b) = (a * b) : real;
fun prod((a, b) : real * real) = a * b;
```

These all work and accomplish the same thing. One hint, anywhere, is enough to help ML decide on the type. But, although ML treats these all the same, the original example is probably the best since it is the most readable. In fact, enhancing readability is probably the major reason for using type annotations in ML. ML can usually figure out types without help, but the human reader will appreciate all the help he or she can get! This book uses type annotations sparingly. That suffices only because the examples are small and are described in the text. A maturer ML programming style for larger ML projects would use type annotations more heavily. Many ML programmers give type annotations with every `fun` definition, as in the example above. Some styles of ML programming go even further, giving type annotations with variable definitions throughout the code.

5.12 Conclusion

This chapter discussed the language ML. The following parts of the language were introduced:

- The ML types `int`, `real`, `bool`, `char`, and `string` and how to write constants of each type.
- The ML operators `~`, `+`, `-`, `*`, `div`, `mod`, `/`, `^`, `::`, `@`, `<`, `>`, `<=`, `>=`, `=`, `<>`, `not`, `andalso`, and `orelse`.
- The conditional expression.
- Function application.
- The predefined functions `real`, `floor`, `ceil`, `round`, `trunc`, `chr`, `ord`, `str`, `hd`, `tl`, `explode`, `implode`, and `null`.
- Defining new variable bindings using `val`.
- Tuple construction using `(x, y, …, z)` and selection using `#n`.
- List construction using `[x, y, …, z]`.
- The type constructors `*`, `list`, and `->`.
- Function definition using `fun`, including tuples as parameters, polymorphic functions, and recursive functions.
- Type annotations.

This is enough ML to complete the exercises that follow.

Exercises

Throughout this chapter, we have used the SML/NJ language system in an interactive mode. For longer examples, it makes more sense to store your function definitions in a file. Once you have created a file containing a definition or definitions, you can load it into an ML session by using the predefined `use` function. For example, if you have created a file named `assign1.sml` in the current directory, you can run your ML language system and type `use "assign1.sml";` after the prompt. The ML language system will read the contents of the file just as if you had typed it one line at a time. After `use` finishes, you can continue typing interactive ML expressions, for example, to test the functions defined in your file.

Exercise 1 Write a function `cube` of type `int -> int` that returns the cube of its parameter.

Exercise 2 Write a function `cuber` of type `real -> real` that returns the cube of its parameter.

Exercise 3 Write a function `fourth` of type `'a list -> 'a` that returns the fourth element of a list. Your function need not behave well on lists with less than four elements.

Exercise 4 Write a function `min3` of type `int * int * int -> int` that returns the smallest of three integers.

Exercise 5 Write a function `red3` of type `'a * 'b * 'c -> 'a * 'c` that converts a tuple with three elements into one with two by eliminating the second element.

Exercise 6 Write a function `thirds` of type `string -> char` that returns the third character of a string. Your function need not behave well on strings with lengths less than 3.

Exercise 7 Write a function `cycle1` of type `'a list -> 'a list` whose output list is the same as the input list, but with the first element of the list moved to the end. For example, `cycle1 [1,2,3,4]` should return `[2,3,4,1]`.

Exercise 8 Write a function `sort3` of type `real * real * real -> real list` that returns a sorted list of three real numbers.

Exercise 9 Write a function `del3` of type `'a list -> 'a list` whose output list is the same as the input list, but with the third element deleted. Your function need not behave well on lists with lengths less than 3.

Exercise 10 Write a function `sqsum` of type `int -> int` that takes a non-negative integer *n* and returns the sum of the squares of all the integers 0 through *n*. Your function need not behave well on inputs less than zero.

Exercise 11 Write a function `cycle` of type `'a list * int -> 'a list` that takes a list and an integer n as input and returns the same list, but with the first element cycled to the end of the list n times. (Make use of your `cycle1` function from a previous exercise.) For example, `cycle ([1,2,3,4,5,6],2)` should return the list `[3,4,5,6,1,2]`.

Exercise 12 Write a function `pow` of type `real * int -> real` that raises a real number to an integer power. Your function need not behave well if the integer power is negative.

Exercise 13 Write a function `max` of type `int list -> int` that returns the largest element of a list of integers. Your function need not behave well if the list is empty. *Hint:* Write a helper function `maxhelper` that takes as a second parameter the largest element seen so far. Then you can complete the exercise by defining

```
fun max x = maxhelper (tl x, hd x);
```

Exercise 14 Write a function `isPrime` of type `int -> bool` that returns true if and only if its integer parameter is a prime number. Your function need not behave well if the parameter is negative.

Exercise 15 Write a function `select` of type `'a list * ('a -> bool) -> 'a list` that takes a list and a function *f* as parameters. Your function should apply *f* to each element of the list and should return a new list containing only those elements of the original list for which *f* returned true. (The elements of the new list may be given in any order.) For example, evaluating `select ([1,2,3,4,5,6,7,8,9,10], isPrime)` should result in a list like `[7,5,3,2]`. This is an example of a *higher-order* function, since it takes another function as a parameter. We will see much more about higher-order functions in Chapter 9.

Further Reading

This is a great book to help you learn more about ML:

Ullman, Jeffrey D. *Elements of ML Programming.* Upper Saddle River, NJ: Prentice Hall, 1998.

It covers the basics seen in this chapter, the more advanced things that will be seen in later chapters, and the even more advanced things there will not be time to discuss.

Chapter 6
Types

6.1 Introduction

You have used types in every program you have ever written. That claim can be made pretty confidently without even knowing which languages you have used, because in one way or another, types are important in almost every programming language.[1] You already know at least one type system pretty well: the type system of the programming language you use most often. You are probably very familiar with its basic type rules and with the kinds of errors caused by breaking those rules. In short, you already have a lot of concrete knowledge about types.

This chapter explores types in a more abstract way. The two main sections of this chapter deal with two basic

1. There are exceptions, but not many. If a language has operations that are meaningful on some values (like real addition for real values) and meaningless on others (like integer addition for real values), then types are a part of the picture. That description covers virtually all modern, high-level languages; it even covers most machine languages for modern processors, which have separate instructions for arithmetic on different types of operands. Only a language in which all operations are meaningful on all values could be considered free of types; BCPL, an ancestor of Java, comes to mind.

questions: what are types and what are they used for? To explore what types are, section 6.2 presents a menagerie of types, a guided tour of some of the many different types from different programming languages, organized around an interesting connection between programming-language types and mathematical sets. To explore what types are used for, section 6.3 gives an overview of some of the many ways types are used in modern programming languages.

6.2 A Menagerie of Types

There are many different programming languages (and a new one born every minute!), and there are many different types used in each language. Types are as various as the beasts of the earth, and it is dry work trying to study them all.

This section presents only a few interesting samples, using examples from only a few different languages. The organizing principle here is the interesting connection between programming-language types and mathematical sets. Almost every way of constructing sets in mathematics occurs in some programming language as a way of constructing types.

A Type Is a Set

These are the five most important words in this chapter: "A type is a set." When you declare that a variable has a certain type, you are saying that the values the variable can have are elements of a certain set. For example, consider this definition in the Java language:

```
int n;
```

Even if you do not know Java, you might well guess that the variable `n` cannot have values like the string "Hello there" or the real number 3.14. The definition says that `n` can only have values from a certain set—the `int` set, which is a bit like the mathematical set of integers (but not exactly, as is shown below).

A type is a set of values. All the elements of that set share a common representation: they are encoded in the computer's memory in the same way. For instance, all the elements of an `int` set might be represented using a 32-bit binary encoding, and all the elements of a `char` set might be represented using the 8-bit ASCII encoding.

All the elements of a type have something else in common too: the collection of operations the language supports for them. For example, in ML (as in many languages) it is legal to subtract any two `int` values, but it is not legal to subtract two `string` values. Subtraction is supported for all pairs of values of the `int` type.

As we examine some common types in the next section, we will look not only at the set of values for each type, but also at the representation and the set of supported operations.

Primitive Types and Constructed Types

Every type system starts with *primitive* types like ML's `int` and `real`. In addition, modern languages give a programmer a way to define *constructed* types in terms of primitive ones.

> Any type that a program can use but cannot define for itself is a *primitive type* in the language. Any type that a program can define for itself (using the primitive types) is a *constructed type*.

For example, here is an ML definition of a new ML type called `intpair`:

```
type intpair = int * int;
```

This defines a constructed type, the set of pairs of `int` values. Once the ML language system has processed this definition, it will recognize `intpair` as a legal type name. The type `int`, on the other hand, is a primitive type of ML. It is not possible for an ML program to make its own definition for the type `int` that works like the original.

Usually, the predefined types in a language are the primitive types, but not always. In ML, for example, there is the predefined type `bool`. ML programs use `bool` without having to give a definition for it. But it is not considered to be a primitive type of ML, because an ML program can define for itself a type exactly like the predefined `bool` (Chapter 11 shows how). The above definition of *constructed type* provides a loophole for this. A type that a program *can* define for itself is a constructed type, even if programs are allowed to assume that the definition is already given.

The definition of each programming language describes the primitive types for that language. In some cases the definition says exactly what the set for each primitive type must be. In other cases, the definition leaves some wiggle room, so that different implementations can choose different sets.

For an example of the first kind of language, consider Java. A browser displaying a Web page that contains a Java program ought to produce the same results as another browser no matter which browser it is and what kind of computer it is running on. The designers of Java wanted to define the language so that Java programs would run exactly the same on different platforms. To help make this possible, the Java language definition says exactly what the set for each primitive type must be. For example, `int` must always be the set of all integers that can be represented using a 32-bit, signed word; that is, the set of integers between -2^{31} and $2^{31}-1$, inclusive.[2]

ML and C are languages that allow different implementations to define the primitive types differently. One reason for doing this is to allow different compilers to generate efficient machine-language code for different processors. A C compiler for an Alpha processor might choose a large `int` set to match the Alpha's large word size, while a C compiler for a Pentium might choose a small `int` set to match the Pentium's small word size. Of course, this difference is visible to the program; it is all too easy to write a C program that works only on machines with a particular word size. To help programmers write portable programs, an API usually offers some way for the program to find out the exact definition of the primitive types. In C environments a standard header file called `limits.h` defines constants such as `INT_MIN` and `INT_MAX`. In ML, programs can check the values of `Int.minInt` and `Int.maxInt`. (The `int` type in ML may even be implemented with support for integers of unbounded range, limited only by available memory. In this case `Int.maxInt` has the value `NONE`, since there is no predefined maximum `int`.)

Since a language usually has relatively few primitive types, a large and expressive type system must be built with constructed types. All the types discussed below are constructed types. Most modern languages have a collection of type constructors that is expressive enough to construct infinitely many types.

Enumerations

The simplest way to construct a set in mathematics is to explicitly list all its elements. For example, if we want the set of the numbers 1 through 5, we can just write {1,2,3,4,5}. Or if we want the set of primary colors, we can just write {red, green, blue}. Similarly, many programming languages allow a programmer to define new types called *enumerations* by listing all the elements of the type. Here are some examples (using C, Ada, Pascal, and ML, in that order):

```
enum coin {penny, nickel, dime, quarter};
type GENDER is (MALE, FEMALE);
type primaryColors = (red, green, blue);
datatype day = M | Tu | W | Th | F | Sa | Su;
```

2. Java programs *ought* to appear the same on different platforms, but this ideal is notoriously difficult to achieve or even to approach. It isn't just a question of making a strict language definition. The deeper difficulty lies in making the many application programming interfaces work the same across platforms.

In each case, the fragment of code makes several definitions at once. It defines new named constants (like `nickel`) and it defines the new type as the set of those constants (like `coin`).

How are the elements of an enumeration represented? The most common way is to use a different integer for each element: `penny` = 0, `nickel` = 1, `dime` = 2, and so on. Some languages expose this representation to the programmer, and others hide it.

Pascal is a language that exposes some of the integer representation. In Pascal, an enumeration has enough integer-like properties that it can be used as the index of a `for` loop. This fragment of Pascal calls the procedure `P` three times, passing it each of the primary colors `red`, `green`, and `blue`:

```
for C := red to blue do P(C)
```

A language that carries this approach to extremes is C. In C, the elements of an enumeration are treated exactly like constants of type `int`. So it would be legal to write the expression `penny+nickel`. It would not make much sense to do so with the current definitions (`penny+nickel` would evaluate to 0+1 = 1), but C even allows the programmer to specify which integer should be used to represent each element of the enumeration:

```
enum coin {penny=1, nickel=5, dime=10, quarter=25};
```

ML goes to the opposite extreme, concealing the implementation completely. About the only thing you can do with the elements of an enumeration in ML is test them for equality. For instance, this function, using the definitions above, decides whether a given day is on a weekend:

```
fun isWeekend x = (x = Sa orelse x = Su);
```

Since no operation other than the equality test is supported, there is no way for a program to tell how the elements are being represented.

These examples of enumerations have been in C, Ada, Pascal, and ML. Why not in Java? Because Java does not support enumerations. Enumerations tend to be much less useful in object-oriented languages, as will be discussed in Chapter 16.

Tuples

The Cartesian product of two sets A and B, written $A \times B$, is the set of all pairs where the first element of the pair is from set A and the second is from set B. For example,

$$\{1,2\}\times\{r,g,b\}=\{(1,r),(2,r),(1,g),(2,g),(1,b),(2,b)\}$$

By repeated application we can produce not just pairs but triples, quadruples, and, in general, *n*-tuples.

A few languages have straightforward tuple types. Here is an example of a tuple type in ML:

```
type irpair = int * real;
```

This defines a new type `irpair` that consists of a pair of values, of which the first is an `int` and the second a `real`.

Many other languages support tuples with named components. These types are better known as *record* or *structure* types. Here is an example of a record type defined in C, followed by a similar record type defined in ML:

```
struct complex {
  double rp;
  double ip;
};

type complex = {
  rp : real,
  ip : real
};
```

This record type represents a complex number using two real numbers, one for the real part and one for the imaginary part. The only difference between these record types and pure tuples is that in the record types each element has a name. Types for values that have component values, like tuples, records, arrays, strings, and lists, are called *aggregate* types. Types for values not built from smaller component values, like primitive types and enumerations, are called *scalar* types.

A natural representation for tuple types is simply to put the representation of the tuple elements in memory, side by side. But this raises a host of further questions about representation. In what order are the elements placed? Are there any gaps between them (perhaps to align elements on word boundaries, for efficiency reasons)? Is any or all of this visible to the programmer?

As you have probably guessed by now, ML hides the representation of tuples from the programmer. The only operations permitted on tuples (other than comparing two of them for equality) are extractions of the elements. This extraction is done by number if they are pure tuples:

```
fun getFirstPart (x : irpair) = #1 x;
```

or by name if they are records:

```
fun getip (x : complex) = #ip x;
```

So all an ML program can observe is that the same values that were put in when the tuple was constructed come out again when the elements are extracted. There is no way for an ML program to tell how the tuple is represented in memory.

C programs can tell exactly how a tuple is represented. The C language standard carefully defines which parts of the representation must be the same in all C systems and which can be different in different implementations. For instance, the standard requires all C implementations to place the elements of a record in memory in the order in which they are declared (except for bit fields) and to place the first element at the beginning of the record with no gap before it. But there may be implementation-dependent gaps between elements, and the layout of bit fields is entirely implementation dependent.

Arrays, Strings, and Lists

The set A^n is the set of all vectors of length n that have elements from A in every position. The set A^* is the set of all vectors of *any* length that have elements from A in every position. These sets of vectors are just further examples of the sets of tuples already considered—A^n is just another way of writing $A \times A \times \cdots \times A$, the Cartesian product taken n times—but they are worth spending a bit more time on because the corresponding array types are particularly important. A set of vectors is a simple idea in theory, but it leads to an amazing variety of programming-language types. Almost all languages support array types of some kind, but the details differ considerably from language to language.

Consider array indices, for example. Java, like C before it, always indexes an array of n elements using the integer indices 0 through n-1. `a[0]` would refer to the first element of an array `a`. ML is another language with integer indices starting from zero (though array types are rarely used in ML programs, and not at all in the ML programs in this book).

Some other languages allow more flexibility. In Pascal and many of its descendants, arrays can be indexed using a variety of types including integers, characters, enumerations, and subranges, with low and high indexes chosen by the programmer. For example, a Pascal program that wants to keep one counter for each letter of the alphabet might use definitions like this:

```
type
  LetterCount = array['a'..'z'] of Integer;
var
  Counts: LetterCount;
```

The type `LetterCount` is the set of arrays of 26 integers indexed using the lowercase letters *a* through *z*. The variable `Counts` is an array of that type. `Counts['a']` would access the count for the letter *a*.

The indexing question is just one of many variations on the basic idea of an array. Does an array type include arrays of a particular size only (as in Pascal, and as in the set A^n) or does it include arrays of all sizes (as in Java, and as in the set A^*)? Besides indexing, what other operations are supported for arrays? In particular, do the supported operations on array values include redimensioning, making them larger or smaller? Is there a separate, perhaps primitive, type for strings that is not the same as an array of characters? Is there a separate, perhaps primitive, type for lists? Can arrays have more than one dimension, and is there any limit to the number of dimensions? Can array elements be arrays themselves, and is an array of arrays different from a two-dimensional array? In what order are the elements placed in memory, especially for higher-dimensional arrays? There are as many different implementations for array types as there are answers to the previous questions.

Unions

The union of two sets A and B, written $A \cup B$, is the set of all elements that are in either A or B (or both). The union of two types is an equally natural idea that appears in many different programming languages. Here is a union type called `element` in C, which can be either an integer or a real number:

```
union element {
  int i;
  float f;
};
```

This is a related union type in ML:

```
datatype element =
  I of int |
  F of real;
```

A union of types is more complicated than a union of sets. We still have to consider how the type will be represented and what operations will be supported for it.

Suppose, as in the examples above, we have a value that can be either an integer or a real number. How can we represent it? We can, of course, just use the integer representation if it is an integer and the real-number representation if it is a real number. That is what the C language does. The union has enough memory space for either an integer or a real number, whichever is larger. A drawback of this approach is that one cannot tell by looking at a value of type `element` whether it is supposed to be an integer or a real number; it is just a block of memory, which may have a legal interpretation as an integer and a (completely different) legal interpretation as a real number. Consider this C example using the `element` type:

```
union element e;
e.i = 100;
float x = e.f;
```

Here, the union variable `e` holds the integer value 100, and the final value of the real variable `x` will be the result of treating the memory representation of the integer 100 as if it were the memory representation of a real value. (This is machine dependent, but it is almost certainly not the real number 100.0.) This kind of type changing is usually a programming error, but C permits it. There is always the chance that it is *not* an error. Maybe the programmer has a good reason for trying to see what the integer 100 looks like if interpreted as a real number. Some people treasure C's permissiveness.

Other people prefer a language that is stricter about types, so that it can catch more errors at compile time. A stricter approach to representing unions is illustrated by ML. In this example, each value of the ML `element` type carries its inner type with it, so ML can tell at runtime whether it is an integer or a real number. Furthermore, any use of a value of type `element` in an ML program must say what to do if the value is an integer *and* what to do if it is a real number. So there is no way to get them mixed up at runtime. This function extracts a real value from an `element`:

```
fun getReal (F x) = x
  | getReal (I x) = real x;
```

Note that we have to say what real value to return in case the parameter is an integer element. Omitting this would result in a warning message from the ML language system.

Another interesting approach, and a kind of midpoint between the extremes of C and ML, is the *discriminated union* supported by several languages, including Ada and Modula-2. The idea is to support unions as part of a record that also contains an enumeration. The value of the enumeration field determines the inner type of the union part. Here is an example in Ada:

```
type DEVICE is (PRINTER, DISK);

type PERIPHERAL(Unit: DEVICE) is
  record
    HoursWorking: INTEGER;
    case Unit is
      when PRINTER =>
        Line_count: INTEGER;
      when DISK =>
        Cylinder: INTEGER;
        Track: INTEGER;
    end case;
  end record;
```

The first type definition creates an enumerated type called DEVICE, and the second creates a record type called PERIPHERAL. A PERIPHERAL contains a member called Unit of type DEVICE. The value of Unit determines which of the union elements are present in the rest of the record. This is a bit safer than the C approach, since the language system can check, on any use of one of the union fields, that the value of the enumeration is appropriate for that use.

Subtypes

Another way to construct a set is to specify some subset of an existing set. Similarly, some languages permit the definition of subtypes, whose elements are a subset of the elements of some existing type. Pascal has a specialized kind of subtype called a subrange. This Pascal fragment, for example, defines digit to be a subset of the integers:

```
type digit = 0..9;
```

Ada supports a somewhat more general kind of subtype. Recall the previous definition of the Ada record type PERIPHERAL. It was an example of a discriminated union, and it could have different fields depending on whether the peripheral in question was a PRINTER or a DISK. So the set PERIPHERAL includes some things that are printers and some things that are disks. Using subtyping, we can define a type that includes only those PERIPHERALS that are printers, like this:

```
subtype PRINTER_UNIT is PERIPHERAL(PRINTER);
```

Lisp supports a general kind of subtype, allowing any Lisp function to act as the predicate that selects members of the subtype. For example:

```
(declare (type (and integer (satisfies evenp)) x))
```

This declares the variable x to be an even integer. It says that the type of x is a subtype of integer, including only those elements of the integer set for which the function evenp returns true.

An obvious way to represent a subtype is to use the same representation that was used for the supertype. But it is also possible to optimize the representation for the subtype. For example, the Pascal type digit would fit in a single byte, and the Ada type PRINTER_UNIT would not need space for the fields that apply only to disks. (It might not even need to store the Unit field, since that must always have the value PRINTER.)

The operations allowed for a subtype usually include all the operations permitted on the supertype. In addition, further operations can be defined that make sense only on the subtype. For example, if an integer is one of the digits then it can be converted to a single character. So in Pascal we could define a new function like this:

```
function toChar(X: Digit): Char;
```

This is an important little meditation: A subtype is a subset of the values, but it can support a *superset* of the operations. This is a key idea of object-oriented languages. In object-oriented languages, a class is like a constructed type that includes both data and operations on that data, bundled together. A subclass is a subtype. It includes a subset of the objects of the superclass type, but supports a superset of the operations. We will see much more about object-oriented languages starting in Chapter 13.

Function Types

For any two sets A and B, the mathematical notation $A \rightarrow B$ refers to the set of all functions with inputs from the set A (the *domain* of the function) and outputs from the set B (the *range* of the function). Most programming languages have a similar idea of function types, types that specify the function's domain and range. The following C example declares a function whose input is a pair of characters and whose output is a single integer:

```
int f(char a, char b) {
  return a==b;
}
```

Note that the domain of the function `f` is actually a pair. C does not support such pure tuple types in general, but like many languages it does rely on them in the special case of parameter lists.

Here is a similar example in ML:

```
fun f (a : char, b : char) = (a = b);
```

The type that ML infers for this function is `char * char -> bool`. This type looks almost exactly like the mathematical function type—the set of functions whose input is a pair of characters and whose output is a boolean value.

Languages differ widely in the kinds of operations they support for functions (beyond simple function calls). Can you store a function in a variable? How about an array element? Can you pass a function value as a parameter? How about returning it from a function? Are there operators for combining functions? We take all these things for granted on simpler types of data; on integers, for example, we expect any modern language to answer yes to all these questions. But for functions the picture is quite different. Most languages support only a small number of operations on functions. The languages that support the most function operations are (surprise!) the functional languages.[3] ML is one of these. Chapter 9 will explore some of ML's advanced operations on functions.

6.3 Uses for Types

Types are used in many different ways in programming languages. This section looks at a sample.

Type Annotations

Many languages require, or at least allow, type annotations. Considering just the three key languages for this book: Java requires a definition for every variable, which includes a type annotation; ML allows type annotations to be attached, not just to variables and functions but to arbitrary expressions; and only Prolog does not allow type annotations at all.

Some languages (including Perl, many dialects of Basic, and earlier dialects of Fortran) occasionally use variables with intrinsic types—types that are determined by the name of the variable. In ANSI Basic, the name `S` automatically declares the variable to be numeric, while the name `S$` automatically declares it to be a string. A variable name that encodes a type like this is a kind of ultra-compact type annotation.

With a type annotation, the programmer supplies explicit type information to the language system. This type information may be used in many different ways, as discussed below. But even if the type information is not used by the language system at all, type annotations may still be worthwhile, simply because they make a program easier for people to read. They serve as a basic form of documentation. So perhaps it is wrong to say that Prolog does not allow type annotations; it allows anything at all in *comments*, and a well-documented Prolog program would certainly describe, at least roughly, the type of every variable.

Type Inference

Type annotations are one source of type information. Most language systems also collect type information from other sources. Constants generally have types. The integer constant `10` in Java has type `int`, but the integer constant `10L` in Java has type `long`; the real constant `1.0` has type `double` in Java, but the real constant `1.0F` has type `float`.

3. It is often said that ML and other functional languages have *first-class functions*, meaning that these languages treat function values just like values of any other type, with equally rich vocabularies of operations. Some imperative languages (like Algol 68) may also be said to have first-class functions.

In addition, expressions have types. In many languages the type of a simple expression depends only on the types of its operands (and not on the actual values), so it may be possible to infer the type of each expression before running the program. In Java, for example, if the variable `a` has type `double` then the expression `a*0` also has type `double` (the value will be `0.0`), since Java specifies that if at least one operand of a binary operator is of type `double`, the result is of type `double`. (In other languages, such as Lisp, the type of a simple expression depends on the *values* of the operands, so it cannot always be determined in advance.)

ML takes the idea of type inference to extremes. It tries to infer a type for every expression, even without any type annotations. ML allows type annotations, but these are rarely necessary and are mostly used to improve readability.

Type Checking

Consider the ML expression `not x`. This applies the logical complement operator `not` to the value of the variable `x`. Before evaluating the expression, there is an obvious consistency check to make: is the value of `x` really a boolean value? If it is not—if it is, say, an integer or a string—then applying a logical complement to it would be meaningless. This kind of consistency check is called a *type check*. There are only a few languages (Bliss and BCPL, for instance) that have no type checking and happily apply any operator to any value. Almost all modern languages perform considerable type checking, either statically or dynamically.

Static type checking determines a type for everything before running a program—every variable, every function, and every expression. The language system gets type information from annotations or from type inferences—usually from both sources—and tries to put it together into a consistent picture. If there are any problems at this stage, the language system produces an error message and does not run the program. For example, if the static type of `x` is `string`, while the static type of `not` is `bool -> bool`, the expression `not x` will cause a compile-time type error. Static type checking catches many potential errors before running a program. Most programmers appreciate this. Many modern languages, including ML and Java, are statically type checked.

A dynamic type check is the same kind of test performed at runtime. The language system runs a program without predicting whether there will be type errors. Before actually applying any operation, however, it checks the operands to make sure the types are suitable. This is still type checking—the system does not actually apply an operation to inappropriate operands, but produces a runtime error message instead. In order to perform this runtime type check, the language system must somehow be able to recognize the type of a value. This means that all data, all values that occur when a program executes, need to be tagged with a type. Maintaining this runtime type information is expensive. It makes it hard to execute dynamically type-checked programs as efficiently as statically type-checked ones. In spite of the drawbacks, some programmers like the greater freedom afforded by dynamic type checking and are attracted to languages like Lisp and Prolog that use this style of type checking.

The division between static and dynamic type checking is not as clear-cut as it has sounded so far. Many languages systems actually implement a mixture of static and dynamic type checking. The use of subtypes can cause languages that are mostly statically type checked to fall back on runtime type information. For example, the compiler might know the static type of a formal parameter to a function. But the actual runtime value of that variable—the actual parameter passed on a particular call—might belong to a subtype. When the program runs, it may be necessary to know the most precise type of the object. If this is so, each subtype value must be tagged somehow with its most precise type, just as in dynamically type-checked languages. This is especially common in object-oriented languages.

At the other end of the spectrum, languages that are mostly dynamically type checked may still support, and benefit from, type annotations and type inference. Common Lisp, for example, allows type annotations. Information from them, along with information derived by type inference, can be used by Lisp systems to decide on a static type for some parts of a program. This, in turn, helps the system to execute the program more efficiently, since it can avoid the high dynamic-type-checking overhead for those parts.

Languages that do require the presence of runtime type information may include constructs that give a programmer explicit access to that information. For instance, a Java program can explicitly test an object for membership in various types using the `instanceof` operator. The Modula-3 language supports a `typecase` statement that branches depending on the type of an object.

The purpose of type checking, whether static or dynamic, is to prevent the application of operations to incorrect types of operands. In some languages this prevention is strong enough to amount to a guarantee; the language system performs type checking so thoroughly that no type-incorrect application of an operation can go undetected. Languages with this property, like ML and Java, are called *strongly typed*. Many popular languages fall short of being strongly typed; they have "holes" in the type checking, which add flexibility to the language but weaken the guarantee. For example, we saw earlier in the chapter how the union type of C can be used to apply operations for one type to values of another type. Informally speaking, we can compare the strength of type checking in different languages by looking at how many holes of this kind they have. Java is strongly typed, Pascal just a bit weakly typed, and C considerably more weakly typed.

Type-Equivalence Issues

Many of the uses of types just discussed require the language system to decide whether two types are the same. For example, consider static type checking; a language might permit an assignment of a to b only if the static types of a and b are the same. Different languages decide this *type equivalence* question in different ways.

Consider this example in ML:

```
type irpair1 = int * real;
type irpair2 = int * real;
fun f (x : irpair1) = #1 x;
```

This fragment defines two types named irpair1 and irpair2 and then defines a function f that takes a parameter of type irpair1. What happens if you try to call f with a value of type irpair2? The answer depends on how ML decides the type-equivalence question. Obviously, the name irpair1 is different from the name irpair2, so in that sense they are two different types. *Name equivalence* is the type-equivalence rule that says that two types are equivalent if and only if they have the same name. Under name equivalence, f could not accept a value of type irpair2.

On the other hand, although irpair1 and irpair2 have different names, they were constructed in exactly the same way. Values of type irpair1 are pairs whose first element is an int and whose second element is a real. The same is true of irpair2. It was built from the same primitive using the same type constructor in exactly the same way as irpair1. *Structural equivalence* says that two types are equivalent if and only if they are constructed from the same primitive types using the same type constructors in the same order. Under structural equivalence, f could accept a value of type irpair2. That is what ML actually does for this example; it uses structural equivalence here.

For another example, consider these definitions in Pascal:

```
var
  Counts1: array['a'..'z'] of Integer;
  Counts2: array['a'..'z'] of Integer;
```

This code declares two arrays named Counts1 and Counts2. It constructs the types for the arrays on the fly, so to speak, without stopping to give names to the types. What happens if you try to assign Counts2 to Counts1? The answer depends on how Pascal answers the type-equivalence question. Under structural equivalence, the assignment would be legal, since the two types were constructed identically. Under name equivalence, however, the assignment would be illegal, since the two types do not even have names. That is what most Pascal systems actually do for this example.

Pure name equivalence and pure structural equivalence are not the only options for type equivalence—just the two easiest to explain! There are many combinations and subtle variations.

6.4 Conclusion

Types are sets, and there is a close connection between how sets are constructed in mathematics and how types are constructed in programming languages. The examples in this chapter have shown some of the ways types are used in modern programming languages.

Throughout this chapter, an important question about types has repeatedly emerged: how much of their representation is exposed to the programmer? The C language exposes much of the representation, as do related earlier languages such as B and BLISS and related later languages such as C++. Those who like such languages view this as a strength—the power to cut through type abstractions and manipulate the underlying representation directly, when it is useful or efficient or fun to do so. Other languages keep more of the representation hidden from the programmer. The term *abstract type* is sometimes used to describe types that are defined only in terms of the operations that are supported for them, without any implementation details. We have seen that the types of ML are quite abstract. Those who like such languages view this as a strength: clean, mathematical interfaces to types make it easier to write correct programs and to prove that they are correct.

As noted at the beginning of the chapter, there are far too many type systems to describe fully here. There are even far too many to categorize neatly. Categorizations like static type checking versus dynamic type checking, name equivalence versus structural equivalence, or type annotation versus type inference, and labels like abstract type and first-class function type sound very definite, but they are not definite in practice. This quick tour of types and their uses should have given you a sense of their wonderful variety.

Exercises

Exercise 1 Let X and Y be any two sets, and let $|X|$ and $|Y|$ be their sizes. What is the size of each of the following sets? If you cannot determine the answer exactly, try to give upper and lower bounds.

a. $X \cup Y$

b. $X \times Y$

c. X^n

d. X^*

Exercise 2 Give the ML type corresponding to each of the following sets:

a. $\{true, false\}$

b. $\{true, false\} \rightarrow \{true, false\}$

c. $\{(true, true), (true, false), (false, true), (false, false)\}$

Exercise 3 Investigate and report on these array varieties. Describe your findings fully, and don't forget to discuss representation issues and supported operations.

a. Arrays in the language SNOBOL4.

b. Associative arrays in Perl.

c. Arrays in APL.

Exercise 4 Suppose there are three variables `X`, `Y`, and `Z` with these types:

`X`: integer that is divisible by 3

`Y`: integer that is divisible by 12

`Z`: integer

For each of the following assignments, knowing nothing about the values of the variables except their types, answer whether a language system can tell before running the program whether the assignment is safe? Why or why not?

a. `X := Y`

b. `X := X`

c. `Y := Y + 1`

d. `Z := X`

e. `X := Z`

f. `X := X + 3`

g. `X := X + Z`

Exercise 5 Design programming-language type constructors based on set intersection and set complement. What would the representations and sets of supported operations be like? Why do you think programming languages do not usually have such types?

Chapter 7
A Second Look at ML

7.1 Introduction

This chapter continues the introduction to the ML programming language. It will discuss ML patterns, a very important part of the language. You have already used simple ML patterns without realizing it. Using patterns in a more sophisticated way, you can write functions that are both more compact and more readable. This chapter will also show how to define local variables for a function using `let` expressions.

7.2 Patterns You Already Know

ML *patterns* are a very important part of the language. You have already seen several kinds of simple patterns. For example, you have seen that ML functions take a single parameter, like the parameter `n` in this simple squaring function:

```
fun f n = n * n;
```

You have also seen how to specify a function with more than one input by using tuples, like the tuple of two items `(a,b)` in this simple multiplying function:

```
fun f (a, b) = a * b;
```

If the language you are most familiar with is C, C++, or Java, you may have an important misconception to lose. In the previous examples, `n` and `(a,b)` look like a parameter and a parameter list, but they are actually patterns in ML. ML automatically tries to match values with its patterns and takes action depending on whether or not they match. The pattern `n`, for instance, matches any parameter, while the pattern `(a,b)` matches any tuple of two items. Patterns occur in several different parts of ML syntax, not just in function parameters. It is important to start thinking about them as patterns, and not just as simple parameter lists.

Patterns do more than just match data; they also introduce new variables. The pattern `n` matches any parameter and introduces a variable `n` that is bound to the value of that parameter. The pattern `(a,b)` matches any tuple of two items and introduces two variables, `a` and `b`, that are bound to the two components of that tuple. ML supports patterns that are far more powerful than these two simple examples, but they all work by matching data and introducing new variables.

7.3 More Simple Patterns

The simplest pattern in ML is _, the underscore character. It is a pattern that matches anything and does not introduce any new variables. The following example shows a function `f` that takes one parameter and ignores its value. If the value of a parameter doesn't matter, use the _ pattern to match the parameter without introducing a variable.

```
- fun f _ = "yes";
val f = fn : 'a -> string
- f 34.5;
val it = "yes" : string
- f [];
val it = "yes" : string
```

The function `f` can now be applied to any parameter *of any type*. (The function's type, `'a -> string`, indicates that its input can be of any type and its output is always a string.) The function `f` ignores its parameter and always returns the string value `"yes"`. The function could have been defined without the underscore, as in

```
fun f x = "yes";
```

That would introduce an unused variable `x`. In ML, as in most languages, you should avoid introducing variables if you don't intend to use them.

The underscore pattern matches everything. At the other extreme, you can make a pattern that matches just one thing—a constant. The next example defines a function f that only works if its parameter is the integer constant 0:

```
- fun f 0 = "yes";
Warning: match nonexhaustive
          0 => ...
val f = fn : int -> string
- f 0;
val it = "yes" : string
```

The function f returns the string value "yes" if applied to the constant 0. No other application of the function is defined. Almost any constant can be used as a pattern. The only restriction is that it must be of an equality-testable type. You can't use real constants as patterns.

The ML language system showed f's type as int -> string, but it gave the warning message "match nonexhaustive." The language system is warning us that we defined f without using patterns that cover the whole domain type (in this case, the integers). So we have defined f in a way that can lead to runtime errors. If f is called on an integer value that isn't 0, it won't work.

```
- f 0;
val it = "yes" : string
- f 1;
uncaught exception nonexhaustive match failure
```

7.4 Complex Patterns

Any list of patterns is a legal pattern. For example, this function selects and returns the first element from a list of two elements:

```
- fun f [a, _] = a;
Warning: match nonexhaustive
          a :: _ :: nil => ...
val f = fn : 'a list -> 'a
- f [#"f", #"g"];
val it = #"f" : char
```

In the example, [a,_] is the pattern for f's parameter. Note the square brackets—this is a list, not a tuple. The pattern [a,_] matches any list of exactly two items and introduces the variable a (bound to the first element of the list). This is, again, a nonexhaustive function definition; the domain includes lists of any type, but the function will fail if a list has more or less than two elements.

The cons operator (`::`) may also appear in patterns. Any cons of patterns is a legal pattern. For example,

```
- fun f (x :: xs) = x;
Warning: match nonexhaustive
          x :: xs => ...
val f = fn : 'a list -> 'a
- f [1, 2, 3];
val it = 1 : int
```

The pattern `x :: xs` matches any non-empty list and introduces the variables `x` (bound to the head element of the list) and `xs` (bound to the tail of the list). The parentheses around `x :: xs` are not really part of the pattern, but are necessary because of precedence. Function application has higher precedence than cons, so without parentheses ML would interpret `f x :: xs` as `(f x) :: xs`, which isn't what we wanted. This example produced another nonexhaustive function definition. This one is *almost* exhaustive—it matches almost every parameter of the domain type—but it will fail on the empty list.

7.5 A Summary of ML Patterns So Far

Here is a mini-language of patterns in ML:

- A variable is a pattern that matches anything and binds to it.
- An underscore (_) is a pattern that matches anything.
- A constant (of an equality type) is a pattern that matches only that constant value.
- A tuple of patterns is a pattern that matches any tuple of the right size, whose contents match the subpatterns.
- A list of patterns is a pattern that matches any list of the right size, whose contents match the subpatterns.
- A cons of patterns is a pattern that matches any non-empty list whose head and tail match the subpatterns.

You could easily give a BNF grammar for the language of ML patterns (see Exercise 1).

7.6 Using Multiple Patterns for Functions

ML allows you to specify multiple patterns for the parameter of a function, with alternative function bodies for each one. Here's an example:

```
fun f 0 = "zero"
|   f 1 = "one";
```

This defines a function of type `int -> string` that has two different function bodies: one to use if the parameter is 0, the other if the parameter is 1. This definition is still nonexhaustive, since it has no alternative for any other integer.

Below is the general syntax for ML function definitions, allowing multiple patterns. A function definition can contain one or more function bodies separated by the `|` token.

<*fun-def*> `::=` `fun` <*fun-bodies*> `;`
<*fun-bodies*> `::=` <*fun-body*> `|` <*fun-body*> `'|'` <*fun-bodies*>

Each function body repeats the function name, but gives a different pattern for the parameter and a different expression:

<*fun-body*> `::=` <*fun-name*> <*pattern*> `=` <*expression*>

The same <*fun-name*> must be repeated in each alternative.[1]

Alternate patterns like this can have overlapping patterns. For example, this is legal:

```
fun f 0 = "zero"
|   f _ = "non-zero";
```

Here, the function `f` has one alternative that covers the constant 0 and another that covers all values. The patterns overlap, so which alternative will ML execute when the function is called? ML tries the patterns in the order they are listed and uses the first one that matches.

7.7 Pattern-Matching Style

These two function definitions are equivalent:

```
fun f 0 = "zero"
|   f _ = "non-zero";

fun f n =
  if n = 0 then "zero"
  else "non-zero";
```

1. This is redundant. From the language interpreter's point of view, it doesn't add any information to have that function name repeated over and over, and it makes extra work, since the interpreter must check that the function name is the same each time. Repeating the function name does, however, make the function definitions easier for people to read.

The first one is in the pattern-matching style; the second one accomplishes the same thing without giving alternative patterns. Many ML programmers prefer the pattern-matching style, since it usually gives shorter and more legible functions.

This example, without the pattern-matching style, was used back in Chapter 5:

```
fun fact n =
  if n = 0 then 1
  else n * fact(n - 1);
```

It can be written in the pattern-matching style like this:

```
fun fact 0 = 1
|   fact n = n * fact(n - 1);
```

This is easier to read, since it clearly separates the base case from the recursive case. Here is another earlier example that doesn't use the pattern-matching style:

```
fun reverse L =
   if null L then nil
   else reverse(tl L) @ [hd L];
```

It can be written in the pattern-matching style like this:

```
fun reverse nil = nil
|   reverse (first :: rest) = reverse rest @ [first];
```

This shows another advantage of using pattern matching. By matching the compound pattern `(first :: rest)`, we are able to extract the head and tail of the list without having to explicitly apply the `hd` and `tl` functions. That makes the code shorter and easier to read. (It doesn't make it any faster, though. In either case, the ML language system has to find the head and tail of the list.)

Functions that operate on lists often have the same structure as this `reverse` function: one alternative for the base case (`nil`) and one alternative for the recursive case (`first :: rest`), making a recursive call using the tail of the list (`rest`). Any function that needs to visit all the elements of a list will have a similar recursive structure. Suppose we want to compute the sum of all the elements of a list:

```
fun f nil = 0
|   f (first :: rest) = first + f rest;
```

See how the function definition follows the same structure? It just says that the sum of the elements in an empty list is 0, while the sum in a non-empty list is the first element plus the sum of the rest. Suppose we want to count how many `true` values are in a list of booleans:

```
fun f nil = 0
|   f (true :: rest) = 1 + f rest
|   f (false :: rest) = f rest;
```

The inductive case is broken into two parts, one to use if the first element is true and one if the first element is false. But you can still see the underlying structure. Here's one more example. Suppose we want to make a new list of integers in which each integer is one greater than it was in the original list:

```
fun f nil = nil
|   f (first :: rest) = first + 1 :: f rest;
```

This same pattern-matching structure occurs in many of the exercises at the end of this chapter.

Patterns in ML are powerful, but they have one important restriction: the same variable name cannot be used more than once in a pattern. For example, suppose you want to write a function that works on pairs and does one thing if the two elements are equal and something else if they are not. You might try to write it like this:

```
fun f (a, a) = ...for pairs of equal elements
|   f (a, b) = ...for pairs of unequal elements
```

But the pattern `(a,a)` is illegal because it uses the same variable name more than once. The only way to write this is in a non-pattern-matching style:

```
fun f (a, b) =
  if (a = b) then ...for pairs of equal elements
  else ...for pairs of unequal elements
```

Patterns occur in many places in ML programs. For instance, you can use patterns in `val` definitions like this:

```
- val (a, b) = (1, 2.3);
val a = 1 : int
val b = 2.3 : real
- val a :: b = [1, 2, 3, 4, 5];
Warning: binding not exhaustive
          a :: b = ...
val a = 1 : int
val b = [2,3,4,5] : int list
```

The "binding not exhaustive" warning is due to the fact that the pattern `a :: b` does not cover all lists—in particular, it does not cover the empty list. That does not cause any further problems in the example since the list that is matched to the pattern is not the empty list.

Later chapters will show additional ML constructs that use patterns.

7.8 Local Variable Definitions

So far, we have used only two kinds of variable definitions: `val` definitions at the top level and the variables defined by patterns for function parameters. There is a way to make additional, local variable definitions in ML, using the `let` expression. A `let` expression looks like this:

<let-exp> `::=` `let` *<definitions>* `in` *<expression>* `end`

The *<definitions>* part is a sequence of any number of definitions, such as `val` definitions, that hold only within the *<let-exp>*. The *<expression>* is evaluated in an environment in which the given definitions hold. The value of the *<expression>* is then used as the value of the entire *<let-exp>*. Here is an example:

```
- let val x = 1 val y = 2 in x + y end;
val it = 3 : int;
- x;
Error: unbound variable or constructor: x
```

The expression evaluates `x + y` in an environment in which `x` is 1 and `y` is 2. That value, 3, is the value of the entire `let` expression. The definition for `x` is not permanent. It is local to the `let` expression. Variables defined in a `let` expression between `let` and `in` are visible only from the point of definition to `end`.

For readability, you usually would not write a `let` expression all on one line. Rather, you would break it up and indent it like this:

```
let
  val x = 1
  val y = 2
in
  x + y
end
```

Some ML programmers put a semicolon after each definition. This is optional.

One reason for using a `let` expression is to break up a long expression and give meaningful names to the pieces. For example, this function converts from days to milliseconds:

```
fun days2ms days =
  let
    val hours = days * 24.0
    val minutes = hours * 60.0
    val seconds = minutes * 60.0
```

```
in
  seconds * 1000.0
end;
```

Each definition in the let part can be used in subsequent definitions, as well as in the final expression of the in part.

When you use let to define variables, you can use pattern matching at the same time to extract the individual parts of compound values. Consider this halve function. It takes a list parameter and returns a pair of lists, each containing half the elements of the original list.

```
fun halve nil = (nil, nil)
|   halve [a] = ([a], nil)
|   halve (a :: b :: cs) =
      let
        val (x, y) = halve cs
      in
        (a :: x, b :: y)
      end;
```

Notice how the val defines both x and y by pattern matching. The recursive call to halve returns a pair of lists, and the val definition binds x to the first element of the pair and y to the second. The let expression in that function could have been written like this instead:

```
let
  val halved = halve cs
  val x = #1 halved
  val y = #2 halved
in
  (a :: x, b :: y)
end;
```

The first version, using pattern matching, is more compact and easier to read. (In general, if you find yourself using the # notation to extract an element from a tuple, think twice. You can usually get a better solution using pattern matching.)

The halve function divides a list into a pair of half-lists. Here are some examples of halve in operation:

```
- halve [1];
val it = ([1],[]) : int list * int list
- halve [1, 2];
val it = ([1],[2]) : int list * int list
- halve [1, 2, 3, 4, 5, 6];
val it = ([1,3,5],[2,4,6]) : int list * int list
```

To better understand how `halve` works, let's break it down into its three alternatives:

`halve nil = (nil, nil)`	The `halve` of an empty list is, of course, just two empty half-lists.
`halve [a] = ([a], nil)`	The `halve` of a one-element list puts that one element in the first half-list and no elements in the second half-list.

`halve (a :: b :: cs) =`
`  let`
`    val (x, y) = halve cs`
`  in`
`    (a :: x, b :: y)`
`  end;`
	The `halve` of a list of two or more elements is computed recursively. It first gets the `halve` of the rest of the list, after the first two elements. Then it adds the first element to the first half-list and the second element to the second half-list.

The `halve` function is part of a simple merge-sort implementation. For more practice with ML, let's go ahead and see the rest of the merge sort. Here is a function that merges two sorted lists of integers:

```
fun merge (nil, ys) = ys
|   merge (xs, nil) = xs
|   merge (x :: xs, y :: ys) =
      if (x < y) then x :: merge(xs, y :: ys)
      else y :: merge(x :: xs, ys);
```

(The type of this `merge` function is `int list * int list -> int list`. ML infers this type because integers are the default type for the < operator.) The `merge` function takes a pair of sorted lists and combines them into a single sorted list:

```
- merge ([2], [1, 3]);
val it = ([1,2,3]) : int list
- merge ([1, 3, 4, 7, 8], [2, 3, 5, 6, 10]);
val it = [1,2,3,3,4,5,6,7,8,10] : int list
```

To better understand how `merge` works, let's break it down into its three alternatives.

`merge (nil, ys) = ys`	The `merge` of two lists, if the first one is empty, is just the second one.
`merge (xs, nil) = xs`	The `merge` of two lists, if the second one is empty, is just the first one.

`merge (x :: xs, y :: ys) =`
`  if (x < y) then x :: merge(xs, y :: ys)`
`  else y :: merge(x :: xs, ys);`
	The `merge` of two non-empty lists is computed recursively. The smallest element is attached to the front of the recursively computed `merge` of the remainder of the elements.

Now with a `halve` and a `merge` function, we can easily create a merge sort. Here, again, we take advantage of the `let` expression in ML:

```
fun mergeSort nil = nil
|   mergeSort [a] = [a]
|   mergeSort theList =
      let
        val (x, y) = halve theList
      in
        merge(mergeSort x, mergeSort y)
      end;
```

This `mergeSort` function sorts lists of integers:

```
- mergeSort [4, 3, 2, 1];
val it = [1,2,3,4] : int list
- mergeSort [4, 2, 3, 1, 5, 3, 6];
val it = [1,2,3,3,4,5,6] : int list
```

To better understand how `mergeSort` works, let's break it down into its three alternatives.

`mergeSort nil = nil`	An empty list is already sorted. `mergeSort` just returns it.
`mergeSort [a] = [a]`	A list of one element is already sorted too. `mergeSort` just returns it.

`mergeSort theList =`
`  let`
`    val (x, y) = halve theList`
`  in`
`    merge(mergeSort x, mergeSort y)`
`  end;`
	To sort a list of more than one element, `halve` it into two halves, recursively sort the halves, and `merge` the two sorted halves.

7.9 Nested Function Definitions

The previous functions halve and merge are not very useful by themselves; they are really just helpers for mergeSort. They could be locally defined inside the mergeSort definition like this:

```
(* Sort a list of integers. *)
fun mergeSort nil = nil
|   mergeSort [e] = [e]
|   mergeSort theList =
      let
        (* From the given list make a pair of lists
         * (x, y), where half the elements of the
         * original are in x and half are in y. *)
        fun halve nil = (nil, nil)
        |   halve [a] = ([a], nil)
        |   halve (a :: b :: cs) =
              let
                val (x, y) = halve cs
              in
                (a :: x, b :: y)
              end;

        (* Merge two sorted lists of integers into
         * a single sorted list. *)
        fun merge (nil, ys) = ys
        |   merge (xs, nil) = xs
        |   merge (x :: xs, y :: ys) =
              if (x < y) then x :: merge(xs, y :: ys)
              else y :: merge(x :: xs, ys);

        val (x, y) = halve theList
      in
        merge(mergeSort x, mergeSort y)
      end;
```

As this example shows, fun definitions can be made inside let, just like val definitions. The effect is to define a function that is visible only from the point of the definition to the end of the let. This organization has the advantage of making halve and merge invisible to the rest of the program, which makes it clear to the reader that they will be used in only this one place. There is another potential advantage to this nesting of functions, which was not used in the example above: the inner functions can refer to variables from the containing function. We'll see more about this in Chapter 12.

The previous example also shows the use of comments in ML. Comments in ML programs start with `(*` and end with `*)`. In ML, as in all other programming languages, programmers use comments to make programs more readable.[2]

7.10 Conclusion

This chapter introduced ML patterns and the pattern-matching style for function definitions. It introduced the ML `let` expression for local function definitions. A long merge-sort example demonstrated how to use both patterns and `let` expressions in ML. This chapter also showed how to write local function definitions in ML and how to write comments.

Exercises

Exercise 1 Give a BNF grammar for the language of ML patterns. Use the non-terminal symbol *<pattern>* as the start symbol. Use the non-terminal symbols *<name>* and *<constant>*, without defining productions for them, for the appropriate parts of the language.

In all the following exercises, wherever possible, practice using pattern-matching function definitions.

Exercise 2 Define a function `member` of type `''a * ''a list -> bool` so that `member(e,L)` is true if and only if `e` is an element of the list `L`.

Exercise 3 Define a function `less` of type `int * int list -> int list` so that `less(e,L)` is a list of all the integers in `L` that are less than `e`.

Exercise 4 Define a function `repeats` of type `''a list -> bool` so that `repeats(L)` is true if and only if the list `L` has two equal elements next to each other.

Exercise 5 Represent a polynomial using a list of its (real) coefficients, starting with the constant coefficient and going only as high as necessary. For example, $3x^2 + 5x + 1$ would be represented as the list `[1.0,5.0,3.0]` and

2. Some programmers claim that their ML programs are so clearly written as to be "self-documenting," requiring no comments. Indeed, some programmers have made this claim for their code in just about every programming language ever invented. But no program is ever as self-documenting as it seems to its author.

$x^3 - 2x$ as `[0.0,~2.0,0.0,1.0]`. Write a function `eval` of type `real list * real -> real` that takes a polynomial represented this way and a value for x and returns the value of that polynomial at the given x. For example, `eval([1.0,5.0,3.0],2.0)` should evaluate to `23.0`, because when $x = 2$, $3x^2 + 5x + 1 = 23$.

Exercise 6 Write a `quicksort` function of type `int list -> int list`. Here's a review of the quicksort algorithm. First pick an element and call it the pivot. (The head of the list is an easy choice for the pivot.) Partition the rest of the list into two sublists, one with all the elements less than the pivot and another with all the elements not less than the pivot. Recursively sort the sublists. Combine the two sublists (and the pivot) into a final sorted list.

Exercise 7 Functions can be passed as parameters just like other values in ML. For example, consider these function definitions:

```
fun square a = a * a;
fun double a = a + a;
fun compute (n, f) = f n;
```

The functions `square` and `double` take a single `int` parameter and return an `int` result. The function `compute` takes a value `n` and a function `f`, and returns the result of calling that function `f` with `n` as its parameter. So `compute(3,square)` evaluates to 9, while `compute(3,double)` evaluates to 6. Chapter 9 will explore this important aspect of ML in more detail. For this exercise, you need only the simple function-passing technique just illustrated.

Make another version of your `quicksort` function, but this time of type `'a list * ('a * 'a -> bool) -> 'a list`. The second parameter should be a function that performs the role of the < comparison in your original function. (*Hint:* This should require only minor changes to your previous `quicksort` definition.)

Why would you want to define such a function? Because it is much more useful than the original one. For example, suppose you defined `icmp` and `rcmp` like this:

```
fun icmp (a, b) = a < b;
fun rcmp (a : real, b) = a < b;
```

You could now use `quicksort(L, icmp)` to sort an integer list `L`, and you could use `quicksort(M, rcmp)` to sort a real list `M`. And if you defined

```
fun ircmp (a, b) = a > b;
```

then you could use `quicksort(L, ircmp)` to sort the integer list `L` in reverse order.

In the following exercises, implement sets as lists, where each element of a set appears exactly once in the list and the elements appear in no particular order. Do not assume you can sort the lists. Do assume that input lists have no duplicate elements, and do guarantee that output lists have no duplicate elements.

Exercise 8 Write a function to test whether an element is a `member` of a set.

Exercise 9 Write a function to construct the `union` of two sets.

Exercise 10 Write a function to construct the `intersection` of two sets.

Exercise 11 Write a function to construct the `powerset` of any set. A set's powerset is the set of all of its subsets. Consider the set $A = \{1,2,3\}$. It has various subsets: {1}, {1,2}, and so on. Of course the empty set, ∅, is a subset of every set. The powerset of A is the set of all subsets of A:

$$\{x \mid x \subseteq A\} = \{\varnothing,\{1\},\{2\},\{3\},\{1,2\},\{1,3\},\{2,3\},\{1,2,3\}\}$$

Your `powerset` function should take a list (representing the set) and return a list of lists (representing the set of all subsets of the original set). `powerset [1,2]` should return `[[1,2],[1],[2],[]]` (in any order). Your `powerset` function need not work on the untyped empty list; it may give an error message when evaluating `powerset nil`. But it should work on a typed empty list, so `powerset (nil : int list)` should give the right answer (`[[]]`).

Chapter 8
Polymorphism

8.1 Introduction

This function in the C language compares two characters to see if they are equal:

```
int f(char a, char b) {
  return a==b;
}
```

This function in ML does something similar:

```
fun f(a, b) = (a = b);
```

A major difference between the two is that the C function applies only to characters, while the ML function has type `''a * ''a -> bool`. This means that the ML function can be applied to any pair of values of the same (equality-testable) type. Functions with this kind of extra flexibility are called *polymorphic* (a word from the Greek meaning "many forms").

You may now be expecting to see a formal definition of the word "polymorphic." If so, you are in for a surprise. The word has been used to describe a wide variety of programming-language features, and finding a simple definition that exactly matches that wide variety is difficult.

This chapter will study some examples of polymorphism first. Then the end of the chapter will return to the question of trying to sum up the examples with a definition.

8.2 Overloading

Overloading is a simple kind of polymorphism.

> An *overloaded* function name or operator is one that has at least two definitions, all of different types.

Many languages have overloaded operators. In ML the + operator is overloaded. It has one definition on integer operands (with type `int * int -> int`) and a different (though related) definition on real operands (with type `real * real -> real`). In Pascal and related languages, the + operator has even more meanings: integer addition on integers, real addition on real numbers, concatenation on strings, and union on sets.

```
a := 1 + 2;
b := 1.0 + 2.0;
c := "hello " + "there";
d := ['a'..'d'] + ['f']
```

The language system uses the operands' types to determine which definition of the + operator to apply in a given situation. (This is the reverse of how ML usually works. In type inference, it uses the operator to determine the types of the operands.)

Some languages also allow the programmer to add definitions for existing operators. Here is an example from C++:

```
class complex {
  double rp, ip; // real part, imaginary part
public:
  complex(double r, double i) {rp=r; ip=i;}
  friend complex operator+(complex, complex);
  friend complex operator*(complex, complex);
};
```

This is a C++ definition for a class called `complex` that implements complex numbers. The definition specifies a new meaning for the + operator and a new meaning for the * operator. (The actual definitions for these operators would be found elsewhere in the program's source.) Having seen this class definition, the

C++ language system can now handle expressions that combine `complex` objects using the `+` and `*` operators, just as if `complex` were a predefined type.

```
void f(complex a, complex b, complex c) {
  complex d = a + b * c;
 ...
}
```

C++ allows virtually all of its operators to have additional meanings defined by the programmer. It even allows overloading of array subscripting (treating the brackets in `a[i]` as an operator) and function calls (treating the parentheses in `f(a,b,c)` as an operator). But it does not allow the syntax, and in particular the precedence, of the operators to be changed, and it does not allow the definition of new operators.

Function names can also be overloaded in some languages, including C++ and Ada. For example, in C++ we might define two meanings for the function name `square`:

```
int square(int x) {
  return x * x;
}

double square(double x) {
  return x * x;
}
```

The C++ language system uses a parameter's type to determine which `square` function to call; the first for `square(3)`, the second for `square(3.0)`.

Suppose you have a program that uses overloaded function names, and you want to convert it into one that does not. For example, suppose the previous program has this function along with the C++ definitions above:

```
void f() {
  int a = square(3);
  double b = square(3.0);
}
```

A simple way to eliminate the overloading would be to change the name for each definition of `square` to make it unique. Perhaps you could use the name `square_i` for the integer version and `square_d` for the double-precision, real-number version. Then you would go over the program, find each reference to `square`, and replace it with either `square_i` or `square_d`, depending on the type. The result would be a program with identical functionality but no overloaded function names:

```
int square_i(int x) {
```

```
    return x * x;
}

double square_d(double x) {
    return x * x;
}

void f() {
    int a = square_i(3);
    double b = square_d(3.0);
}
```

This conversion is almost exactly how most language systems implement overloading—for operators as well as functions. They create separate definitions with unique names and fix each reference to make it use the proper name, according to the types involved. In compiled language systems this happens at compile time, before the program runs.[1]

The different definitions of an overloaded function or operator are often, but not always, related. Addition on real numbers and addition on integers are obviously similar, and it seems reasonable to use the same operator for both. (In fact they are so similar that at first this scarcely seems like overloading at all—until you remember that these two operations must be implemented, usually by hardware, in very different ways.) But what about using the + operator to mean string concatenation? This operation's similarities with addition are loose. Going further in that direction, imagine overloading the symbol + with completely unrelated definitions or even with related but opposite definitions. Imagine a language in which + meant addition on integers but *subtraction* on real numbers. From the language system's point of view that would be no different from other examples of overloading, but from the programmer's point of view it would be unnatural and confusing.

In short, overloading can be obvious and reasonable, or it can be unnatural and confusing. Different languages embody different ideas about where to draw the line between the two. When a language allows a programmer to define additional meanings for operators, it involves the programmer in the decision about where to draw that line.

---

1. *Name mangling* happens when a compiler or other program creates a new, unique name that encodes extra information like parameter types along with the original name. C++ language systems are the best-known users of mangled names. Many programmers find out about mangled names for the first time when they try to link C++ functions with code written in some other language. It comes as a surprise to find that your C++ function `shazam` must be referenced from Fortran code using a mangled name such as `shazam__Fii`. (The actual mangled name is implementation dependent.)

8.3 Parameter Coercion

An implicit type conversion is called a *coercion*. ML does not perform coercion, but many languages do. For example, in Java you can write

```
double x;
x = 2;
```

Even though `x` is declared to have type `double`, it can be assigned an integer. Coercion implicitly converts the integer 2 to the `double` value 2.0 before the assignment is made. The result is exactly as if you had written an explicit type conversion:

```
double x;
x = (double) 2;
```

So far there is no polymorphism here. (In particular, the variable `x` is not polymorphic.) But if the language supports coercion of parameters on a function call or coercion of operands when an operator is applied, the result is a polymorphic function or operator. Consider a Java method that is declared to take a parameter of type `double`, like this:

```
void f(double x) {
  ...
}
```

It can be called with any type of parameter that Java is willing to coerce to type `double` in that context (namely `byte`, `short`, `char`, `int`, `long`, and `float`):

```
f((byte) 1);
f((short) 2);
f('a');
f(3);
f(4L);
f(5.6F);
```

The idea of coercion seems simple at first glance, but the documents that define programming languages often take pages and pages to define exactly when coercions are performed. To give you an idea of the complexity of the topic, here is a short sample from the Java language specification:

> Some operators apply *unary numeric promotion* to a single operand which must produce a value of a numeric type:

- If the operand is of compile-time type `byte`, `short`, or `char`, unary numeric promotion promotes it to a value of type `int` by a widening conversion.
- Otherwise, a unary numeric operand remains as is and is not converted.

Unary numeric promotion is performed on expressions in the following situations:

- The dimension expression in array creations
- The index expression in array access expressions
- Operands of the unary operators plus + and minus -

...

The specification goes on—and this addresses only one limited kind of coercion.[2] The full description of Java's coercions takes more than 20 pages. Java actually has a relatively simple collection of coercions. Many languages do more, especially some of the older languages. Algol 68 and PL/I have famously large repertoires of coercions. Coercions can simplify a programmer's task by making it unnecessary to write obvious type conversions explicitly. They can also make a programmer's task harder by performing not-so-obvious type conversions unexpectedly.

One thing that makes it tricky to design a good collection of coercions for a programming language is the potential for interaction between coercion and overloading. (This is one reason why newer languages have not been as generous with coercion as Algol 68 and PL/I were.) Consider again the earlier C++ function `square`:

```
int square(int x) {
  return x * x;
}

double square(double x) {
  return x * x;
}
```

2. You may have noticed that the Java definition does not use the word *coercion*. *Numeric promotion* is used, as is *widening conversion*. This is typical. Every language definition seems to use its own special terminology for coercion. A *numeric promotion* in Java documentation means a coercion of the numeric operands of an operator; for example, the coercion of `1` to `1.0` in the expression `1+2.0`. The same word *promotion* is used in PL/I documentation to mean coercion from a scalar to an aggregate; for example, the coercion of the integer 1 to an array containing all 1s. There is no universal definition for such terms, so *caveat lector*.

Suppose that, like C++, this language is willing to coerce a character to type `int` or to type `double`. Which definition of `square` should be used for the function call `square('a')`? Either one could work, but which will actually be called?

One solution is for the language system to give a compile-time error for `square('a')` on the grounds that it is ambiguous. Another solution is to use the integer version of `square` on the grounds that a character is somehow closer to type `int` than to type `double`. (That is what C++ does.) The problem gets even worse when you consider functions with multiple parameters. Suppose you have these two function definitions:

```
void f(int x, char y) {}
void f(char x, int y) {}
```

What should be made of the function call `f('a','b')`? By coercing the first parameter to an integer, the language system could use the first definition of `f`; by coercing the second parameter to an integer, it could use the second definition. There does not seem to be an intuitively obvious choice for the best match in this case. (By the rules C++ uses, this case is ambiguous and would result in a compile-time error.)

As was shown in Chapter 3 (in the case of operator precedence), it can sometimes take a complicated definition to make things work out in an intuitive way. So it is with overloading and coercion. The rules C++ uses to resolve overloading in the presence of coercion are quite arcane; Java's rules are only slightly less so.

8.4 Parametric Polymorphism

The chapter started with this example of a polymorphic function in ML:

```
fun f(a, b) = (a = b);
```

ML shows the type of this function as `''a * ''a -> bool`. Note the use of the type variable `''a`. The idea is that any type gotten by substituting an equality-testable ML type for that type variable `''a` will be a legal type of `f`. By substituting `int` for `''a`, you can see that `f` can have type `int * int -> bool`; by substituting `char` for `''a`, you can see that `f` can have type `char * char -> bool`. This kind of polymorphism is called *parametric polymorphism.*

> A function exhibits *parametric polymorphism* if it has a type that contains one or more type variables.

A type with type variables, like `''a * ''a -> bool`, is called a *polytype.*

Parametric polymorphism is found in quite a few languages, including C++, ML, and Ada.[3] Here is an example from C++:

```
template<class X> X max(X a, X b) {
  return a>b ? a : b;
}
void g(int a, int b, char c, char d) {
  int m1 = max(a,b);
  char m2 = max(c,d);
}
```

Using a C++ template, the example defines a polymorphic function called `max`. `X` is a type variable here. The function `max` takes two parameters of type `X` and returns a value of type `X`. The function `g` shows two uses of `max` with different types. The first uses `max` as a function of type `int * int -> int`. The second uses it as a function of type `char * char -> char`.[4] Of course, `max` cannot work on values of just any type `X`; it has to be some type for which the > comparison is defined. However, C++ allows operator overloading, so definitions of > can be added as necessary.

There are two different ways for a language system to implement parametric polymorphism. One way is to create separate copies of the polymorphic function, one for each different instantiation of the type variables, before the program runs. That is what C++ language systems do. In the case of the C++ definition above, the C++ compiler would notice that the `max` template was used with `X` = `int` and with `X` = `char`, so it would create these two (overloaded) definitions:

```
int max(int a, int b) {
  return a>b ? a : b;
}

char max(char a, char b) {
  return a>b ? a : b;
}
```

3. It is found also, perhaps, in Java. At the time of this writing, several experimental dialects of Java support parametric polymorphism, and work is under way to add parametric polymorphism to standard Java.

4. A C++ template can do more than just create polymorphic functions. A template can have function names, variable names, and constants as parameters, as well as types. Moreover, a template can create an entire C++ class definition. In Ada, the generic construct has similar powers. In ML, polymorphic functions occur without special syntax for declaring them, but the other applications of C++ templates or Ada generics would use the ML functor construct. Alas, ML functors are beyond the scope of this book.

From that point on, it would work just like overloading, as already described. All the polymorphism would be removed before the program ran. A strength of this implementation is that each definition can be optimized by the system for the particular types involved. A weakness of this implementation is that the system must make (perhaps many) similar copies of the code.

The other way to implement parametric polymorphism is for the language system to create only a single copy of the polymorphic function, which is used by all callers. This implementation avoids the problem of having to create many different copies of the polymorphic code, but it cannot be as efficient as the previous implementation since it cannot optimize the code for each instantiation of the type variables. It must generate code that is general enough to work on all types.

The statement above that there are two different ways to implement parametric polymorphism is an oversimplification. The two alternatives outlined above are two extremes; between them lie a great many variations. The development of improved implementations for parametric polymorphism is an active area of programming-language research.

8.5 Subtype Polymorphism

As shown in Chapter 6, a subtype is just a subset. If a function can work on any parameter in a given set, it certainly also can work on any parameter in a subset of that set. So it is natural for languages to permit a function that expects a parameter of some type *t* to be called with a parameter of any subtype of *t*. Here is an example from Pascal:

```
type
  Day = (Mon, Tue, Wed, Thu, Fri, Sat, Sun);
  Weekday = Mon..Fri;

function nextDay(D: Day): Day;
  begin
    if D=Sun then nextDay:=Mon else nextDay:=D+1
  end;

procedure p(var D: Day; W: Weekday);
  begin
    D := nextDay(D);
    D := nextDay(W)
  end;
```

This Pascal code defines a type `Day` and a subtype of it called `Weekday`. As you can see, the `nextDay` function can be called with a parameter of either type. This is a simple example of *subtype polymorphism*.

> A function or operator exhibits *subtype polymorphism* if one or more of its parameter types have subtypes.

Subtype polymorphism arises automatically in any language with subtypes. Pascal has only this one elementary kind of subtype. Much richer collections of subtypes occur in object-oriented languages like Java. This book has not yet covered the object-oriented languages in general or Java in particular, but here is a Java example to illustrate the idea of subtype polymorphism. Imagine a video game that involves driving cars. A car knows how to do things like respond to pressure on the brake, so the program might define a Java class called `Car` with a function called `brake`. (The functions implemented by a Java class are actually called *methods*, but that terminology can wait until Chapter 13, "A First Look at Java.")

```
public class Car {
  public void brake() { ... }
}
```

Some cars have more functions than others. Manual-transmission cars should know how to do things like respond to pressure on the clutch, so the program might define a Java class called `ManualCar` with an extra function called `clutch`.

```
public class ManualCar extends Car {
  public void clutch() { ... }
}
```

The declaration `ManualCar extends Car` says that `ManualCar` is a subtype of `Car`. It has all the abilities of `Car`, plus some special ones. (Remember this meditation from Chapter 6: a subtype is a subset of the values, but it can support a *superset* of the operations.)

Now there is a type (`Car`) and a subtype (`ManualCar`), so any function in the program that takes a parameter of type `Car` is automatically polymorphic—it will also accept a parameter of type `ManualCar`.

```
void g(Car z) {
  z.brake();
}

void f(Car x, ManualCar y) {
  g(x);
  g(y);
}
```

The function `g` brakes the car that is its parameter. That parameter can be either a `Car` or a `ManualCar`—both know how to brake—or it could be some other subtype of `Car` whose definition has not yet been seen. This is an example of subtype polymorphism.

More details of subtype polymorphism will be covered in the discussion of Java starting in Chapter 13.

8.6 Conclusion

Some languages, such as Prolog, Lisp, and Smalltalk, use dynamic type checking. For them, polymorphism is irrelevant. These languages offer a kind of total freedom—a function can be called with any type of argument, and the suitability of the argument to the function is not checked at compile time. Some programmers value this freedom, but others find that it allows too many errors to go undetected until runtime. Polymorphism is a way of gaining some of the freedom of dynamic type checking without giving up the benefits of static type checking. Polymorphic functions are statically type checked and do not risk type errors at runtime, yet they are flexible enough to handle multiple types.

This chapter discussed four kinds of programming-language phenomena that people sometimes call *polymorphism*: overloading, parameter coercion, parametric polymorphism, and subtype polymorphism. These phenomena are by no means the only ones included under the heading of polymorphism! Here are just a few other examples:

- In object-oriented languages, when a variable is an object that can be of different classes, like the parameter `z` in the function `g` in the previous example, it is sometimes called a *polymorphic variable*.
- In the previous example, `ManualCar` and `Car` both use the same definition of the `brake` function. Java allows subclasses to override such definitions, so `ManualCar` could have had a specialized implementation of `brake`. Then the call `z.brake()` in the example would actually call one of two different functions, depending on the actual class of the object `z`. Some people use the word *polymorphism* to describe this phenomenon.
- In C++ a template can be used to define a kind of parametric polymorphism that applies to an entire class definition. In Ada the same kind of thing can be done for an entire package definition. The result is sometimes called a *polymorphic class* or *polymorphic package*.
- A language that provides a rich collection of these features is sometimes called a *polymorphic language*.

On top of all that, of course, the word *polymorphic* is used to mean completely different things in geology, biology, and a host of other sciences.

In spite of all this confusion, here is an attempt at a few simple definitions. The four major examples of polymorphism were all ways to make functions work on different types of parameters. At least those four uses of the word can be covered with this definition:

> A function or operator is *polymorphic* if it has at least two possible types.

The four examples can also be divided into two major categories: *ad hoc polymorphism* and *universal polymorphism*. Something is polymorphic if it can have more than one possible type. How many different types?

> A function or operator exhibits *ad hoc polymorphism* if it has at least two but only finitely many possible types.
>
> A function or operator exhibits *universal polymorphism* if it has infinitely many possible types.

Of course, in any particular terminating run of a program, each function is called only finitely many times, so it needs only finitely many different types. The thing about universal polymorphism is that there is no limit to the number of *possible* types for the function.

Overloading is an example of ad hoc polymorphism. In overloading, each different type for a function requires a different definition, so there can be only finitely many of them in a program. The function definition (or rather, the set of function definitions for that function name) enumerates all the possible types.

Parameter coercion, too, almost certainly qualifies as ad hoc polymorphism. As long as there are only finitely many different types that could be coerced to a given parameter type, the number of different possible types for the function is also finite. (It is possible to imagine a language with some kind of universal coercion, allowing infinitely many different types to be coerced to a given parameter type. That case would qualify as universal polymorphism by the definition.)

Parametric polymorphism is a kind of universal polymorphism. In parametric polymorphism, the type variables are instantiated over some infinite universe of types.

Subtype polymorphism is almost certainly a kind of universal polymorphism. As long as there are infinitely many different possible subtypes of some type, any function that takes a parameter of that type will have infinitely many possible types itself. This certainly applies to object-oriented languages, like Java, with conventional subclasses.

Here is the resulting classification scheme:

1) Ad hoc polymorphism
   a) Overloading
   b) Parameter coercion
2) Universal polymorphism
   a) Parametric polymorphism
   b) Subtype polymorphism

It looks authoritative and organized, doesn't it? But you know now that these are only four of the many examples of polymorphism, and even they didn't fit neatly into two categories. As was shown in Chapter 6, type systems often defy simple categorizations.

Exercises

Exercise 1 Consider an unknown language with a left-associative + operator that is overloaded to have the following types: `int*real->real`, `int*int->int`, `real*int->real`, and `real*real->real`. Suppose the variable `i` has type `int` and the variable `r` has type `real`. For each + operator in each of the following expressions, say which type of + is used:

a. `i+r`

b. `i+r+i`

c. `i+(r+i)`

d. `i+i+r+(r+i)`

Exercise 2 Most languages that allow overloading of function definitions have this restriction: they do not permit two definitions for the same function to differ only in the type of value returned. Ada does not have this restriction. That means that Ada must sometimes use the context of a function call to determine which overloaded definition to use. For example, Ada must sometimes use the type of `c` to determine which definition of `f` to use in the statement `c := f(a,b)`. It must sometimes use the type of `g` to determine which definition of `f` to use in the expression `g(f(a,b))`. Even using such information, an expression with overloaded function calls may be ambiguous—there may be more than one way to resolve the overloading. Consider the statement `e := f(f(a,b),f(c,d))` in an Ada-like language. Give an example of a set of types for the overloaded function `f` that makes this statement ambiguous, even when the types of `a`, `b`, `c`, `d`, and `e` are known.

Exercise 3 Consider an unknown language with integer and real types in which `1+2`, `1.0+2`, `1+2.0`, and `1.0+2.0` are all legal expressions.

a. Explain how this could be the result of coercion, using no overloading.
b. Explain how this could be the result of overloading, using no coercion.
c. Explain how this could result from a combination of overloading and coercion.
d. Explain how this could result from subtype polymorphism, with no overloading or coercion.

Exercise 4 Consider an unknown language with integer and string types in which `1+2*3` evaluates to `7`, `"1"+"2"+"3"` evaluates to `"123"`, `"1"+2+3` evaluates to `"123"`, and `1+"2*3"` has a type error. Describe a system of precedence, associativity, overloading, and coercion that could account for this. In your system, what is the result of evaluating the expression `"1"+2*3`?

Exercise 5 Write an ML function definition for each of the following functions. Try to predict what polytype ML will infer for each function. Then check your prediction using the ML language system. What is the polytype determined by ML for each case?

a. $f(x) = 1$
b. $f(x,y) = 1$
c. $f(x) = x$
d. $f(x,y) = x$
e. $f(g) = g(1)$
f. $f(g,x) = g(x)$
g. $f(g,x,y) = g(x,y)$
h. $f(g,h,x) = g(h(x))$
i. $f(g,x) = g(g(x))$

Exercise 6 The following is a list of proposed changes to ML's type system. (All involve subtypes, which ML does not have.) For each one, give examples of ML expressions that have type errors now, but would not have type errors with the proposed change, and explain what the major benefits and drawbacks of the proposed change would be.

a. Make `char` a subtype of `string`.
b. Make `int` a subtype of `real`.
c. Make (n+1)-tuples a subtype of n-tuples. For example, make `int * int` be the type for all n-tuples with $n \geq 2$, whose first two elements are of type `int`. That way, `int * int` includes `int * int * int`.

Further Reading

If you enjoy trying to place unruly practical concepts like polymorphism in a neat mathematical framework, this paper is for you:

> Cardelli, Luca, and Peter Wegner. "On Understanding Types, Data Abstraction, and Polymorphism." *Computing Surveys* 17, no. 4 (December 1985): 472–522.

This paper introduced the categories of polymorphism used in this chapter.

The quotation from the Java language definition was taken from

> Gosling, James, Bill Joy, and Guy Steele. *The Java™ Language Specification*. Boston, MA: Addison-Wesley, 1996.

Chapter 9
A Third Look at ML

9.1 Introduction

This chapter continues the introduction to ML. It will start with some more advanced pattern-matching features. In Chapter 7 you learned about the pattern-matching style of function definitions:

```
fun f 0 = "zero"
  | f _ = "non-zero";
```

The same syntax for pattern matching can be used in several other places in ML programs, such as the `case` expression:

```
case n of
  0 => "zero" |
  _ => "non-zero"
```

After covering that, this chapter will turn to higher-order functions. A higher-order function is one that takes other functions as parameters or produces them as returned values. Such functions are used much more often in functional languages than in traditional imperative languages. By the end of this chapter you will see why.

9.2 More Pattern Matching

A *rule* is a piece of ML syntax that looks like this:

<*rule*> ::= <*pattern*> => <*expression*>

A *match* consists of one or more rules separated by the | token, like this:

<*match*> ::= <*rule*> | <*rule*> '|' <*match*>

As always, ML doesn't care how you break a match across lines, but it is easier for people to read if each rule in the match is on a line by itself. The pattern of a rule can, as always, define variables that are bound by pattern matching. The scope of those definitions runs from the point of definition to the end of the rule. A rule is a kind of block in ML. Each rule in a match must have the same type of expression on the right-hand side. A match is not an ML expression by itself, but it forms part of several different kinds of ML expressions. You have already seen something much like this for pattern-matching function definitions.

One important kind of ML expression that uses a match is the case expression. Its syntax is simple:

<*case-exp*> ::= case <*expression*> of <*match*>

For example:

```
- case 1 + 1 of
=    3 => "three" |
=    2 => "two" |
=    _ => "hmm";
val it = "two" : string
```

The value of `case` <*expression*> `of` <*match*> is the value of the expression in the first rule of the <*match*> whose pattern matches the value of the <*expression*>. In the example above, the case expression has the value 2, which matches the pattern `2`, so the value of the entire case expression is the string `"two"`.

That example does not use the full pattern-matching power of ML's case expression. Many languages have some kind of case construct that matches the value of an expression against compile-time constants, with a default entry in case there is no match. But few languages have a case expression that allows general pattern matching. For example, this expression produces the third element of `x` (an `int list`) if the list has one, the second element if the list has only two elements, the first element if the list has only one element, or the constant 0 if the list is empty:

```
case x of
  _ :: _ :: c :: _ => c |
  _ :: b :: _ => b |
  a :: _ => a |
  nil => 0
```

The case expression can easily do everything the conditional expression can do. Any expression of the form `if` exp_1 `then` exp_2 `else` exp_3 can be rewritten as a two-rule case expression like this:

```
case exp1 of
  true => exp2 |
  false => exp3
```

In fact, SML/NJ actually implements the conditional expression as a case expression. This explains some otherwise confusing error messages. For example, if you write a conditional expression in which the `then` part and the `else` part have different types, you get an error message like this:

```
- if 1 = 1 then 1 else 1.0;
  Error: types of rules don't agree [literal]
  earlier rule(s): bool -> int
  this rule: bool -> real
  in rule:
    false => 1.0
```

This error message, with its warning about a rule that looks like `false => 1.0`, does not make much sense until you understand that the conditional expression gets translated into a case expression.

9.3 Function Values and Anonymous Functions

When the ML language system starts up, many variables are already defined and bound. This includes all the predefined functions like `ord` and operators like ~:

```
- ord;
val it = fn : char -> int
- ~;
val it = fn : int -> int
```

Function names, like `ord`, and operator names, like ~, are variables just like any others in ML. They are variables that happen to be bound, initially, to functions. That is what ML is reporting in the example above; `ord` is a variable whose value is a function of type `char -> int`, and ~ is a variable whose value is a function of type `int -> int`.

The definition `val x = 7` binds `x` to the integer 7. In the same way, this next example binds `x` to the function denoted by the `~` operator.

```
- val x = ~;
val x = fn : int -> int
- x 3;
val it = ~3 : int
```

As you can see, `x` now denotes the same function that `~` does. It was applied to the operand 3 to negate it.

This can be a hard concept to follow at first, especially if you are accustomed to a conventional imperative language. In most imperative languages, a function definition gives a unique, permanent name to the function. In ML, a function is not tied to a particular function name. We may speak informally of "the function `f`" in some ML program, but it would be more accurate to speak of "the function currently bound to the name `f`." Functions themselves do not *have* names, though one or more names may be bound to a particular function.

Then how can a function be created without a name? The `fun` syntax creates a new function and binds a name to the function automatically. But there is another way to define a function, a way that does not involve giving it a name. To define such an anonymous function, simply give the keyword `fn` followed by a match. Here is a named function `f`, defined using the original `fun` syntax, that adds 2 to its integer parameter:

```
- fun f x = x + 2;
val f = fn : int -> int
- f 1;
val it = 3 : int
```

Here is the same computation using an anonymous function defined with an `fn` expression:

```
- fn x => x + 2;
val it = fn : int -> int
- (fn x => x + 2) 1;
val it = 3 : int
```

The anonymous function `fn x => x + 2` is exactly the same as the named function `f` and can be applied to parameters in exactly the same way. In fact, what `fun` does can now be defined in terms of `val` and `fn`, since `fun f x = x + 2` has the same effect as `val f = fn x => x + 2`.[1]

---

1. There is actually a slight but important difference between a definition with `fun` and one with `val` and `fn`. The scope of the definition of `f` produced by `fun f` includes the function body being defined, while the scope of the definition of `f` produced by `val f = fn` does not. So only the `fun` version can be recursive.

Anonymous functions are useful when you need a small function in just one place and don't want to clutter up the program by giving that function a name. For example, suppose a sorting function called `quicksort` takes two inputs—the list to be sorted and a comparison function that decides whether one element should come before another. (You implemented such a function if you did Exercise 7 in Chapter 7.) The comparison function is trivial. It seems ugly to clutter up the program with a named function like this:

```
- fun intBefore (a,b) = a < b;
val intBefore = fn : int * int -> bool
- quicksort ([1,4,3,2,5], intBefore);
val it = [1,2,3,4,5] : int list
```

It would be simpler just to make an anonymous comparison function at the point where it is needed, as in these two examples:

```
- quicksort ([1,4,3,2,5], fn (a,b) => a < b);
val it = [1,2,3,4,5] : int list
- quicksort ([1,4,3,2,5], fn (a,b) => a > b);
val it = [5,4,3,2,1] : int list
```

There is an even shorter way to write the two previous examples. The anonymous comparison functions in those examples do exactly what the < and > operators do. Why not just use the < and > operators directly as the comparison functions? Unfortunately, we cannot just write `quicksort(x, <)`, since ML expects < to be used as a binary operator. But there is a way to extract the function denoted by an operator: the `op` keyword. The value of the expression `op <` is the function used by the operator <. Using this trick, we can simply write:

```
- quicksort ([1,4,3,2,5], op <);
val it = [1,2,3,4,5] : int list
- quicksort ([1,4,3,2,5], op >);
val it = [5,4,3,2,1] : int list
```

Most functional languages have an expression like ML's `fn` expression, whose value is an anonymous function.[2]

---

2. The idea of an expression whose value is an anonymous function goes back to the first versions of Lisp, which used the name `lambda` for something that works like `fn` in ML. In a theoretical form, the idea goes back to the branch of mathematics called the "lambda calculus," which manipulates anonymous functions with a notation that uses the Greek letter lambda (λ) to introduce a function. The name has become generic, so that any expression like ML's `fn` expression is called a "lambda expression."

9.4 Higher-Order Functions and Currying

Every function has an *order*, defined as follows:

> A function that does not take any functions as parameters and does not return a function value has *order 1*.
>
> A function that takes a function as a parameter or returns a function value has *order n+1*, where *n* is the order of its highest-order parameter or returned value.

A function of order *n* is called an *nth order function*, and a function of any order greater than 1 is called a *higher-order function*. Higher-order functions are used much more often in functional languages like ML than in imperative languages.

As you know, functions in ML take exactly one parameter. You have already seen one way to squeeze multiple parameters into a function, which is to pass a tuple as the parameter. There is another way to do it using higher-order functions. You can write a function that takes the first parameter and returns another function. The new function takes the second parameter and returns the ultimate result. This trick is called *currying*.[3] The next example shows a function `f` with a tuple parameter, and a curried function `g` that does the same thing:

```
- fun f (a,b) = a + b;
val f = fn : int * int -> int
- fun g a = fn b => a + b;
val g = fn : int -> int -> int
- f (2,3);
val it = 5 : int
- g 2 3;
val it = 5 : int
```

The function `g` takes the first parameter and returns an anonymous function that takes the second parameter and returns the sum. Notice that `f` and `g` are called differently. `f` expects a tuple, but `g` expects just the first integer parameter. Because function application in ML is left associative, the expression `g 2 3` means `(g 2) 3`; that is, first apply `g` to the parameter `2` and then apply the resulting function (the anonymous function `g` returns) to the parameter `3`.

We do not have to create a tuple when calling `g`, but that is not the main advantage of currying. The real advantage is that we can call curried functions, passing

3. "Currying" is named not for the spicy food, but for the mathematician Haskell Brooks Curry (1900–1982), who made significant contributions to the mathematical theory of functional programming. There is also a major functional programming language named for him: Haskell.

only some of their parameters and leaving the rest for later. For example, we can call g with its first parameter only:

```
- val add2 = g 2;
val add2 = fn : int -> int
- add2 3;
val it = 5 : int
- add2 10;
val it = 12 : int
```

Here g was used to create a function called add2 that knows how to add 2 to any parameter. In effect, add2 is a specialized version of g, with the first parameter fixed at 2 but the second parameter still open.

For a more practical example, imagine defining the quicksort function as a curried function that takes the comparison function first and the list to sort second. So it would have this type:

```
('a * 'a -> bool) -> 'a list -> 'a list
```

We could use this curried quicksort in the usual way, giving all of its parameters at once:

```
- quicksort (op <) [1,4,3,2,5];
val it = [1,2,3,4,5] : int list
```

Or we could use it to create specialized sorting functions by giving just the first parameter, like this:

```
- val sortBackward = quicksort (op >);
val sortBackward = fn : int list -> int list
- sortBackward [1,4,3,2,5];
val it = [5,4,3,2,1] : int list
```

As you can see, the curried quicksort is useful in more ways than a quicksort that takes its parameters as a tuple.

Of course, currying could be generalized for any number of parameters. Here is an example that adds three numbers together, first using a tuple and then in curried form:

```
- fun f (a,b,c) = a + b + c;
val f = fn : int * int * int -> int
- fun g a = fn b => fn c => a + b + c;
val g = fn : int -> int -> int -> int
- f (1,2,3);
val it = 6 : int
- g 1 2 3;
val it = 6 : int
```

Once you are sure that you understand how these currying examples work, you can be let in on a little secret: there is a much easier way to write curried functions. For example, these two definitions do exactly the same thing:

```
fun g a = fn b => fn c => a + b + c;
fun g a b c = a + b + c;
```

The second way is much shorter to write but identical in meaning. ML treats it as an abbreviation for the first way. This section started out showing you how to write curried functions the long way because the long way makes all the intermediate anonymous functions explicit. But once you really understand how this works, you should use the short way, since it is much easier to write and read.

9.5 Predefined Higher-Order Functions

This section will use three important predefined higher-order functions: `map`, `foldr`, and `foldl`. (As you might guess from the names, `foldr` and `foldl` are very similar, with one subtle but important difference.) Once you get comfortable using these functions you will find them very helpful. The exercises at the end of this chapter will give you some idea of the versatility of these functions.

The map Function

The `map` function is used to apply some function to every element of a list, collecting a list of the results. For example:

```
- map ~ [1,2,3,4];
val it = [~1,~2,~3,~4] : int list
```

This example applies the negation function, ~, to every element of the list `[1,2,3,4]`. The result is the original list, with every element negated. Here are some other examples:

```
- map (fn x => x + 1) [1,2,3,4];
val it = [2,3,4,5] : int list
- map (fn x => x mod 2 = 0) [1,2,3,4];
val it = [false,true,false,true] : bool list
- map (op +) [(1,2),(3,4),(5,6)];
val it = [3,7,11] : int list
```

The last example applies the function of the + operator to a list of pairs. The result is a list of the sums formed from each pair.

You can tell from the way `map` is called that it is a curried function. It takes two parameters, but they are not grouped together as a tuple. Its type is

```
('a -> 'b) -> 'a list -> 'b list
```

If you call it with just the first parameter, you get a function that transforms lists using a fixed function. For example:

```
- val f = map (op +);
val f = fn : (int * int) list -> int list
- f [(1,2),(3,4)];
val it = [3,7] : int list
```

The most important thing to remember about using `map` is that the result will always be a list that is the same length as the input list. When you have a problem to solve that involves converting one list into another list of the same length, and when each element of the output list depends only on the corresponding element of the input list, you may be able to use `map` to solve the problem. If these requirements are not met, you may be able to use `foldr` or `foldl` instead.

The `foldr` Function

The `foldr` function is used to combine all the elements of a list into one value. This example adds up all the elements of a list:

```
foldr (op +) 0 [1,2,3,4];
```

The `foldr` function takes three parameters: a function f, a starting value c, and a list of values $[x_1, \ldots, x_n]$. It starts with the rightmost element x_n and computes $f(x_n,c)$. Then it folds in the next element x_{n-1}, computing $f(x_{n-1},f(x_n,c))$. It continues in this way until all the elements have been combined. The result is

$$f(x_1,f(x_2,\ldots f(x_{n-1},f(x_n,c))\ldots))$$

For example, `foldr (op +) 0 [1,2,3,4]` adds up the list by computing 1+(2+(3+(4+0))). Here is `foldr` in action:

```
- foldr (op +) 0 [1,2,3,4];
val it = 10 : int
- foldr (op * ) 1 [1,2,3,4];
val it = 24 : int
- foldr (op ^) "" ["abc","def","ghi"];
val it = "abcdefghi" : string
- foldr (op ::) [5] [1,2,3,4];
val it = [1,2,3,4,5] : int list
```

Did you notice the space after the `*` in the expression `(op * )`? Writing the expression without that extra space would confuse ML, since `*)` is used to close ML comments.

You can tell from the way `foldr` is called that it is a curried function. It takes three parameters, but not grouped together as a tuple. This is its type:

```
('a * 'b -> 'b) -> 'b -> 'a list -> 'b
```

One common way to use `foldr` is to give it the first two parameters, but not the third. The result is a function that takes a list and folds it with a fixed function and an initial value:

```
- val addup = foldr (op +) 0;
val addup = fn : int list -> int
- addup [1,2,3,4,5];
val it = 15 : int
```

The examples above show `foldr` being used with operators: `op +`, `op ::`, and so forth. In the exercises at the end of the chapter, you will rarely find that there is an operator that performs exactly the function you need. Usually, you have to write a little anonymous function for `foldr`, so the call will look more like this:

```
foldr (fn (a,b) => function body) c x
```

Here, *c* is the starting value for the fold—usually a constant—and *x* is the input list. Some important tips for using `foldr`:

- On the first call of the anonymous function, `a` will be the rightmost element from the list *x* and `b` will be the starting value *c*.
- On each subsequent call of the anonymous function, `a` will be the next element from the list *x* and `b` will be the result accumulated so far—that is, the previous value returned by the anonymous function.
- These values all have the same type: `b`, *c*, the value returned by the anonymous function, and the value returned by the `foldr`.
- The type of the elements of the list *x* is the same as the type of `a`.
- The starting value *c* is what `foldr` will return if the list *x* is empty.

These tips can help you figure out how to use `foldr` to solve programming problems. For example, suppose you want to write a function `thin` that takes an `int list` and returns the same list, but with all the negative numbers eliminated. You can rule out using `map` for this, since the result list does not necessarily have the same length as the input list. So you start with the pattern described above:

```
fun thin L = foldr (fn (a,b) => function body) c L;
```

The result is supposed to be an `int list`, so it follows that `b`, *c*, and the value returned by the anonymous function must also be of type `int list`. Furthermore, if the input list `L` is the empty list, the output should also be the empty list; so it follows that the starting value *c* should be `[]`. All that remains is to write the body of the anonymous function. It takes an `int a` and an `int list b`, and returns either `a::b` (if `a` is to be accumulated in the result) or just `b` (if `a` is to be omitted). This is simply

```
fun thin L =
  foldr (fn (a,b) => if a < 0 then b else a::b) [] L;
```

The `foldl` Function

Like `foldr`, the `foldl` function is used to combine all the elements of a list into one value. In fact, `foldr` and `foldl` sometimes produce the same results:

```
- foldl (op +) 0 [1,2,3,4];
val it = 10 : int
- foldl (op * ) 1 [1,2,3,4];
val it = 24 : int
```

All the tips about how to use `foldr` also apply to `foldl`, with one subtle difference: `foldl` starts with the leftmost element in the list and proceeds from left to right.

The `foldl` function takes the same three parameters as `foldr`: a function *f*, a starting value *c*, and a list of values $[x_1, \ldots, x_n]$. It starts with the *leftmost* element x_1 and computes $f(x_1,c)$. Then it folds in the next element x_2, computing $f(x_2,f(x_1,c))$. It continues in this way until all the elements have been combined. The result is

$$f(x_n,f(x_{n-1},\ldots f(x_2,f(x_1,c))\ldots))$$

For example, `foldl (op +) 0 [1,2,3,4]` adds up the list by computing 4+(3+(2+(1+0))). Compare this with the function computed by `foldr`. The `foldr` function starts with the rightmost element of the list; the `foldl` function starts with the leftmost element of the list. For operations that are associative and commutative, like addition and multiplication, this difference is invisible. For other operations, like concatenation, it matters a lot. Compare these `foldr` and `foldl` results:

```
- foldr (op ^) "" ["abc","def","ghi"];
val it = "abcdefghi" : string
- foldl (op ^) "" ["abc","def","ghi"];
val it = "ghidefabc" : string
- foldr (op -) 0 [1,2,3,4];
val it = ~2 : int
- foldl (op -) 0 [1,2,3,4];
val it = 2 : int
```

9.6 Conclusion

This chapter introduced the following parts of ML:

- The general syntax for a match.
- The `case` expression (using matches).
- The idea of function values and anonymous functions.
- The `fn` expression for creating anonymous functions (using matches).
- The idea of higher-order functions.
- The idea of currying.
- The long and short forms for writing curried functions.
- The predefined, curried, higher-order functions `map`, `foldr`, and `foldl`.

Exercises

The first 25 exercises should all have one-line solutions using `map`, `foldr`, or `foldl`. You can also use other predefined functions, of course, but *do not write any additional named functions and do not use explicit recursion.* If you need helper functions, use anonymous ones. For example, if the problem says "write a function `add2` that takes an `int list` and returns the same list with 2 added to every element," your answer should be

```
fun add2 x = map (fn a => a + 2) x;
```

You have seen some of these problems before. The trick now is to solve them in this new, concise form.

Exercise 1 Write a function `il2rl` of type `int list -> real list` that takes a list of integers and returns a list of the same numbers converted to type `real`. For example, if you evaluate `il2rl [1,2,3]` you should get `[1.0,2.0,3.0]`.

Exercise 2 Write a function `ordlist` of type `char list -> int list` that takes a list of characters and returns the list of the integer codes of those characters. For example, if you evaluate `ordlist [#"A",#"b",#"C"]` you should get `[65,98,67]`.

Exercise 3 Write a function `squarelist` of type `int list -> int list` that takes a list of integers and returns the list of the squares of those integers. For example, if you evaluate `squarelist [1,2,3,4]` you should get `[1,4,9,16]`.

Exercise 4 Write a function `multpairs` of type `(int * int) list -> int list` that takes a list of pairs of integers and returns a list of the products of each pair. For example, if the input is `[(1,2),(3,4)]`, your function should return `[2,12]`.

Exercise 5 Write a function `inclist` of type `int list -> int -> int list` that takes a list of integers and an integer increment, and returns the same list of integers but with the integer increment added to each one. For example, if you evaluate `inclist [1,2,3,4] 10` you should get `[11,12,13,14]`. Note that the function is curried.

Exercise 6 Write a function `sqsum` of type `int list -> int` that takes a list of integers and returns the sum of the squares of those integers. For example, if you evaluate `sqsum [1,2,3,4]` you should get `30`.

Exercise 7 Write a function `bor` of type `bool list -> bool` that takes a list of boolean values and returns the logical OR of all of them. If the list is empty, your function should return `false`.

Exercise 8 Write a function `band` of type `bool list -> bool` that takes a list of boolean values and returns the logical AND of all of them. If the list is empty, your function should return `true`.

Exercise 9 Write a function `bxor` of type `bool list -> bool` that takes a list of boolean values and returns the logical exclusive OR of all of them. (It should return `true` if the number of `true` values in the list is odd and `false` if the number of `true` values is even.) If the list is empty, your function should return `false`.

Exercise 10 Write a function `dupList` of type `'a list -> 'a list` whose output list is the same as the input list, but with each element of the input list repeated twice in a row. For example, if the input list is `[1,3,2]`, the output list should be `[1,1,3,3,2,2]`. If the input list is `[]`, the output list should be `[]`.

Exercise 11 Write a function `mylength` of type `'a list -> int` that returns the length of a list. (Of course, you may not use the predefined `length` function to do it.)

Exercise 12 Write a function `il2absrl` of type `int list -> real list` that takes a list of integers and returns a list containing the absolute values of those integers, converted to real numbers.

Exercise 13 Write a function `truecount` of type `bool list -> int` that takes a list of boolean values and returns the number of trues in the list.

Exercise 14 Write a function `maxpairs` of type `(int * int) list -> int list` that takes a list of pairs of integers and returns the list of the max elements from each pair. For example, if you evaluate `maxpairs [(1,3),(4,2),(~3,~4)]` you should get `[3,4,~3]`.

Exercise 15 Write a function `myimplode` that works just like the predefined `implode`. In other words, it should be a function of type `char list -> string` that takes a list of characters and returns the string containing those same characters in that same order.

Exercise 16 Write a function `lconcat` of type `'a list list -> 'a list` that takes a list of lists as input and returns the list formed by appending the input lists together in order. For example, if the input is `[[1,2],[3,4,5,6],[7]]`, your function should return `[1,2,3,4,5,6,7]`. (There is a predefined function like this called `concat`, which of course you should not use.)

Exercise 17 Write a function `max` of type `int list -> int` that returns the largest element of a list of integers. Your function need not behave well if the list is empty.

Exercise 18 Write a function `min` of type `int list -> int` that returns the smallest element of a list of integers. Your function need not behave well if the list is empty.

Exercise 19 Write a function `member` of type `''a * ''a list -> bool` so that `member(e,L)` is true if and only if `e` is an element of list `L`.

Exercise 20 Write a function `append` of type `'a list -> 'a list -> 'a list` that takes two lists and returns the result of appending the second one onto the end of the first. For example, `append [1,2,3] [4,5,6]` should evaluate to

[1,2,3,4,5,6]. Do not use predefined appending utilities, like the @ operator or the concat function. Note that the function is curried.

Exercise 21 Define a function less of type int * int list -> int list so that less(e,L) is a list of all the integers in L that are less than e (in any order).

Exercise 22 Write a function evens of type int list -> int list that takes a list of integers and returns the list of all the even elements from the original list (in the original order). For example, if you evaluate evens [1,2,3,4] you should get [2,4].

Exercise 23 Write a function convert of type ('a * 'b) list -> 'a list * 'b list, that converts a list of pairs into a pair of lists, preserving the order of the elements. For example, convert [(1,2),(3,4),(5,6)] should evaluate to ([1,3,5],[2,4,6]).

Exercise 24 Define a function mymap with the same type and behavior as map, but without using map. (Note this should still be a one-liner: use foldl or foldr.)

Exercise 25 Represent a polynomial using a list of its (real) coefficients, starting with the constant coefficient and going only as high as necessary. For example, $3x^2 + 5x + 1$ would be represented as the list [1.0,5.0,3.0] and $x^3 - 2x$ as [0.0,~2.0,0.0,1.0]. Write a function eval of type real list -> real -> real that takes a polynomial represented this way and a value for x and returns the value of that polynomial at the given x. For example, eval [1.0,5.0,3.0] 2.0 should evaluate to 23.0, because when $x = 2$, $3x^2 + 5x + 1 = 23$. (This is the same as Exercise 5 in Chapter 7, except that it is now a curried function and must be written as a one-liner.)

These remaining exercises are not one-liners. They should be written without using map, foldl, or foldr.

Exercise 26 Define a function mymap with the same type and behavior as map.

Exercise 27 Define a function myfoldr with the same type and behavior as foldr.

Exercise 28 Define a function myfoldl with the same type and behavior as foldl.

Chapter 10
Scope

10.1 Introduction

Imagine a world in which every person had to have a unique name. It would be a simpler world in some respects. You could say, "I ran into Bob yesterday," and no one would have to ask, "Bob who?" But in other respects, it would be a much more complicated world. The task of naming a new baby would be formidable. All the nice short names would quickly be used up. Even if you invented a strange-looking long name, someone else could still be inventing the same name for their child at the same time.

Of course, we get along fine without insisting on unique names. Although there are many people named Bob, this fact does not render all "Bob"-laden communication ambiguous. In many cases, the context makes it clear which person is meant; in other cases, the speaker can add more information (such as Bob's family name). Although this is slightly troublesome, it is much easier than trying to make sure everyone has a unique name.

For much the same reasons, modern programming languages do not insist on unique names for variables. Consider this fragment of an ML program:

```
fun square n = n * n;
fun double n = n + n;
```

The code contains two different variables, both of which happen to be named n. To modern programmers this is obvious and natural. It would not be practical to require that a program use the name n only once, especially since programs often consist of many parts developed independently. In fact, with the exception of some early dialects of older languages like Fortran and Basic, it is hard to think of any language that forces the programmer to come up with unique names for all variables.

When a language allows different variables to have the same name, it must have some way to ensure that each use of the name is unambiguous. This means that there must be some way to control the scope of definitions. Even without name conflicts, programmers often want a way to control the scope of definitions, making some definitions widely visible in the program and others restricted. This chapter looks at the scoping problem and some common solutions.

This chapter faces the same kind of difficulty with scope as Chapter 6 had with types. There are many different solutions to the scoping problem—usually several solutions at once in each programming language—and it would be dry work to catalog them all. This chapter is not an encyclopedia of scoping, but just a quick tour of some common solutions to the scoping problem.

10.2 Definitions and Scope

Before examining the problem of controlling the scopes of definitions, let's step back and define these terms. The problem of deciding which definition should apply to a given instance of a name is just another binding question, like those introduced in Chapter 4. When there are different variables with the same name, there are different possible bindings for that name. Each occurrence of the name must be bound to exactly one of the variables. The language must specify how to decide which of the bindings to use in each case. This binding question arises not only for variables, but also (depending on the language) for other things that might be bound to names—functions, types, constants, classes, and so on.

Programming languages offer many different ways to set up possible bindings for names. The terminology for such definitions varies from language to language; sometimes the word *definition* is used, sometimes *declaration*, and sometimes both terms to mean slightly different things. This book will stick to *definition*.

A *definition* is anything that establishes a possible binding for a name.[1]

In ML, you have seen function definitions:

```
fun square n = n * n;
```

This establishes a *possible* binding for the name `square`. The same name may be used for different things elsewhere in the program. It also establishes a possible binding for the name `n`—the `square` function's formal parameter. So that one example contains two different definitions. The function could be legally written like this:

```
fun square square = square * square;
```

This establishes two possible bindings for the name `square`; it can be bound to the function or to the function's parameter. ML has no trouble with this. According to ML's rules, occurrences of `square` inside the function body should be bound to the parameter, while occurrences of `square` outside the function body should be bound to the function. (You will see more about ML's rules below.)

This next example shows definitions of some constant, type, and variable names in Pascal:

```
const
  Low = 1;
  High = 10;
type
  Ints = array [Low..High] of Integer;
var
  X: Ints;
```

Again, these definitions establish *possible* bindings for names. `Low` and `High` may be bound to integer constants, `Ints` to an array type, and `X` to a variable. But these same names may also be reused for completely different purposes elsewhere in the program.

Not all definitions are explicit. Some languages, including dialects of Fortran, PL/I, and Basic, have implicit variable definitions. When a Fortran program uses a name that was not explicitly defined, Fortran treats it as a variable—an integer variable if the name begins with one of the letters 'I' through 'N' and a real variable otherwise. You could say that the first use of an undefined name is treated as an

1. If you feel slightly queasy, it could be because you just read a definition for the word *definition*. We bound the name *definition* to "anything that gives a possible binding for a name," and that might well make your head spin. But rest assured, the effect lasts only as long as the book is open. This book is the scope of this definition of the scope of a definition.

implicit definition of that variable. Or you could just as well say that all names have pre-established possible bindings as variables.

The question remains, which definition applies to each occurrence of a name?

> An occurrence of a name is *in the scope of* a given definition of that name whenever the definition governs the binding for the occurrence.

To revisit the previous example:

```
- fun square square = square * square;
val square = fn : int -> int
- square 3;
val it = 9 : int
```

There are two definitions for `square`. The two occurrences of `square` in the function body are in the scope of the second definition (`square` = the function's parameter). The occurrence of `square` following the function definition is in the scope of the first definition (`square` = the function). How ML decides this will be seen shortly.

What is wanted, then, is a way to control the scopes of definitions. The sections that follow look at several different approaches.

10.3 Scoping with Blocks

Most modern programming languages use *blocks* to solve at least part of the scoping problem.

> A *block* is any language construct that contains definitions and also contains the region of the program where those definitions apply.

The `let` construct in ML is an example of a block.

```
let
  val x = 1;
  val y = 2;
in
  x + y
end
```

As you can see, the `let` construct contains definitions (`x` and `y` in our example) and also entirely contains the region of the program where those definitions apply—from the point of each definition to the final `end`.

An ML `let` expression is a nice example of a block, because it serves no other purpose. All it does is contain definitions, plus an expression in which those definitions apply. Many other kinds of language constructs have other purposes and serve as blocks too. In ML, the obvious purpose of a `fun` definition is to define a function. But `fun` definitions also serve as blocks:

```
fun cube x =
  x * x * x;
```

This contains a definition of `x`. It also entirely contains the region of the program where that `x` is visible—the expression that is the function body. With a pattern-matching function, we actually get multiple blocks:

```
fun f (a :: b :: _) = a + b
|   f [a] = a
|   f [] = 0;
```

The first pattern introduces definitions for `a` and `b`, which apply only in the first expression (`a + b`). The second pattern introduces another definition for `a`, which applies only in the second expression. In general, each pattern can introduce definitions, and those definitions apply only in the corresponding expression.

In the C language, you can collect statements together into a single *compound statement* using braces. For example, you might use a compound statement as the body of a loop:

```
while (i < 0) {
  p += i * i * i;
  q += i * i * i;
  i -= step;
}
```

Any compound statement in C can also serve as a block. It can start with variable definitions, which normally apply from the point of definition to the closing brace. For example, the above loop could be rewritten as

```
while (i < 0) {
  int c = i * i * i;
  p += c;
  q += c;
  i -= step;
}
```

Many different constructs serve as blocks in different languages. People used to use the term *block-structured* to refer to languages that use some kind of block to delimit scopes. Today, since almost all modern languages are block-structured, few people bother to make this distinction.

A block associates definitions with a particular region of the program text. This makes it easy to figure out which definition of a name governs the binding for a given occurrence of that name. There is only one hitch: what happens if a block contains another block and both the outer and inner blocks have definitions of the same name? For example, what should the value of this ML expression be?

```
let
  val n = 1
in
  let
    val n = 2
  in
    n
  end
end
```

In ML, the value of that expression is 2. In the inner block, the inner definition of `n` overrides the outer definition.

As already noted, most modern languages have blocks of some kind. Indeed, most modern languages have blocks that can be nested, and most allow names to be defined in an outer block and then redefined in an inner block. So most modern languages have exactly the same problem as the previous ML example and solve it using the same rule, or some minor variation of it. This might be called the classic block scope rule:

> The scope of a definition is the block containing that definition, from the point of definition to the end of the block, minus the scopes of any redefinitions of the same name in interior blocks.

There are, as always, many minor variations. For example, Scheme (a modern dialect of Lisp) has three slightly different block constructs like ML's `let`, called `let`, `let*`, and `letrec`, that differ only in the exact starting point of the scope of the definitions. C++ has a C-like block structure, but allows variable definitions and statements to be interleaved. In C all the definitions must come at the beginning of a block. Java has a C++-like block structure, but prohibits redefinitions in inner blocks on the grounds that they are confusing for people to read. Ada has an interesting way for inner blocks to access definitions from outer blocks, even when the names have been redefined.

10.4 Scoping with Labeled Namespaces

Most modern languages offer, in addition to blocks, some kind of *labeled namespace*:

> A *labeled namespace* is any language construct that contains definitions and a region of the program where those definitions apply, and also has a name that can be used to access those definitions from outside the construct.

ML has a kind of labeled namespace called a `structure`. Here is an example:

```
structure Fred = struct
  val a = 1;
  fun f x = x + a;
end;
```

Within the structure is a list of definitions. In the above example, the definition for the variable `a` is visible in the function body for `f`. The scope of a definition within the structure extends from the point of definition to the end of the structure, just like in a block. Structures can even be nested, just like blocks. Outside of the structure, the names `a` and `f` are undefined, again like in a block. But unlike the definitions in a block, the definitions in an ML structure can be accessed from outside the structure by using the structure's name. We can access the variable `a` from outside the structure as `Fred.a`, and the function `f` as `Fred.f`.

An ML structure is a nice example of a labeled namespace, because it serves no other purpose. C++ has a simple labeled namespace as well, which uses (appropriately enough) the keyword `namespace`. Modula-3 has `module`; Ada calls it a `package`. Java also uses `package` for a kind of labeled namespace that is very different from Ada's. A construct that serves as a labeled namespace may also serve other purposes. In object-oriented languages, the definition of a class often serves as a labeled namespace. This is true in C++ and in Java. For example, this Java class defines integer variables named `min` and `max`:

```
public class Month {
  public static int min = 1;
  public static int max = 12;
}
```

These variables would be visible within any other definitions in the class, while from outside the class they could be referred to as `Month.min` and `Month.max`. Of course, classes also serve another purpose altogether in Java, which will be shown in Chapter 13.

Why do so many languages have labeled namespaces? What is the advantage? One advantage is that labeled namespaces reduce "namespace pollution." If you introduce a definition with broad, perhaps global, scope, you face the unique-naming problem mentioned in the introduction to this chapter. Programmers naturally want to choose memorable, meaningful names like `min` and `max`, but a large program may have many different variables that could reasonably use those names. There may be a `max` month, a `max` weight, and a `max` bid. They can't all be called `max` in the same namespace, but they could be in different namespaces as `Month.max`, `Weight.max`, and `Bid.max`. Of course, the same thing could be accomplished with a naming convention. Variables named `maxMonth`, `maxWeight`, and `maxBid` could be in the same namespace. But there are other advantages to using labeled namespaces.

Like blocks, namespaces contain a region of a program where their definitions apply directly. If the definitions in a namespace are logically related (and they are, if the program is well designed), this is useful. Within the context of a `Month`, it makes sense to use the short names `max` and `min`. That could not be done with a mere naming convention.

But there is more. Once you gather related definitions together into a namespace, you sometimes find that they are not all of interest outside that namespace. For example, suppose you are implementing some kind of dictionary that supports the operations `create`, `insert`, `search`, and `delete`. You start with a namespace labeled `dictionary`, like this outline (this is prototypical and not meant to be in any particular language):

```
namespace dictionary contains
   a function definition for create
   a function definition for insert
   a function definition for search
   a function definition for delete
end namespace
```

You decide to implement it using hash tables, so you add a `hashTable` type, a `hash` function, an `initialSize` constant, and a `reallocate` function to reallocate a table if it grows too large. Now you have

```
namespace dictionary contains
   a constant definition for initialSize
   a type definition for hashTable
   a function definition for hash
   a function definition for reallocate
   a function definition for create
   a function definition for insert
```

```
    a function definition for search
    a function definition for delete
end namespace
```

Then you realize that although `initialSize`, `hashTable`, `hash`, and `reallocate` are important parts of the solution, you don't want other parts of the program to use them. You want the rest of the program to use only the original interface and not depend on this particular implementation. This is a good impulse, too; making `dictionary` an *abstract datatype*, a datatype whose implementation is concealed, helps make that part of the program more reusable and maintainable. But the point here is not about abstract datatypes in particular, it is about *information hiding* in general. Many programmers have learned from bitter experience that it is best to keep scopes small. For one reason or another you may find that some of the definitions in a namespace do not need to be visible outside of it. In this example, other parts of the program should not have access to implementation details like `dictionary.initialSize`.

To accommodate the programmer's desire to hide information, most namespace constructs have some way to allow part of the namespace to be kept private. There seem to be two general approaches to this. One is to have the namespace define the visibility of each definition, like this:

```
namespace dictionary contains
    private:
    a constant definition for initialSize
    a type definition for hashTable
    a function definition for hash
    a function definition for reallocate
    public:
    a function definition for create
    a function definition for insert
    a function definition for search
    a function definition for delete
end namespace
```

This is the approach taken for C++ classes. An alternative is to have a separate definition of the namespace's intended interface. This is, as the example shows, wordier, but it is also more flexible. (Notice that the definitions in the interface give the name and its type, but no more of the definition—not, for instance, the function body for functions. You will see more about this in the discussion of separate compilation below.)

```
interface dictionary contains
    a function type definition for create
    a function type definition for insert
```

```
   a function type definition for search
   a function type definition for delete
end interface

namespace myDictionary implements dictionary contains
   a constant definition for initialSize
   a type definition for hashTable
   a function definition for hash
   a function definition for reallocate
   a function definition for create
   a function definition for insert
   a function definition for search
   a function definition for delete
end namespace
```

This is the approach taken for ML structures. (The interface definition is called a `signature` in ML.) It is also the approach taken in Modula-3. Some other languages, including Ada and Java, cook up a combination of the two approaches.[2]

10.5 Scoping with Primitive Namespaces

Here is something not to do in ML:

```
- val int = 3;
val int = 3 : int
```

It is, as this example shows, perfectly legal to have a variable named `int`. ML does not get confused by this, nor does it somehow lose its definition of the name `int` as a primitive type. We could even write

```
- fun f int = int * int;
val f = fn : int -> int
- f 3;
val it = 9 : int
```

Ordinarily, the phrase `int * int` in ML would be a type (the type of pairs of `int` values). But ML's syntax keeps types and expressions firmly separated. The grammar for ML specifies types in special places (such as after the colon in a type

2. Labeled namespaces are often one of the most difficult parts of a modern programming language to understand and use properly. Many languages have several kinds of labeled namespaces that interact with each other. For example, Java classes are one kind of labeled namespace. They can implement interfaces, another kind of labeled namespace; they are contained in Java packages, another kind of labeled namespace; they can be nested; and they can be subclasses. All this makes for many more possible levels of visibility than just "public" and "private" and bewilders many programmers at all levels of experience.

annotation), so the ML language system always knows whether it is looking for a type or for something else. We could even rewrite the previous example this way:

```
fun f(int : int) = (int : int) * (int : int);
```

The ML language system knows that the first `int` in `(int : int)` is a variable and the second is a type. Because of this segregation, ML is free to keep the bindings for type names separate from other bindings. It has two separate namespaces—two separate collections of names and definitions. Whenever it encounters something like `fun f(x : y)`, it looks for a definition of `x` in the ordinary namespace, but looks for a definition of `y` in the namespace for types.

These namespaces have a significant effect on scoping. Recall that an occurrence of a name is in the scope of a given definition of that name whenever the definition governs the binding for the occurrence. It follows that, in something like `fun f(int:int)`, the first `int` is in the scope of one definition, while the second `int` is in the scope of another. As you can see, the scopes associated with namespaces are fragmented, unlike the scopes associated with blocks (which are continuous, except for redefinitions in inner blocks).

These are called *primitive namespaces* because, like primitive types, they are not explicitly created using the language. They are part of the language definition. As this simple example already shows, scoping with blocks and scoping with namespaces can work together—in fact, they usually do. In the example, scoping with blocks limits the scope of the parameter named `int` to the body of the function `f`. Scoping with namespaces then further limits the scope of the parameter named `int` to those points in the body where a type is not expected.

If you had not just read about it here, you might have programmed in ML for years without realizing the existence of these primitive namespaces. No reasonable person would *want* to make a variable named `int`! But some languages have a more extensive collection of primitive namespaces than ML, and some programmers find them useful.

Java, for example, has separate primitive namespaces for packages, types, methods, fields, and statement labels. Some respectable styles of Java programming allow limited use of the same name in different primitive namespaces. For example, a public Java method to access the value of a private field might have the same name as the field itself. Since a reference to a field (like `fred`) is visibly different from a method call (like `fred()`), there is little danger of confusion. On the other hand, by using the same name in too many different primitive namespaces, it is easy to write code that is mystifying to the human reader, but clear to the Java language system. This example, from *The Java Programming Language* by Ken

Arnold and James Gosling, shows how bad it can get. The name `Reuse` is the only name that occurs, but it occurs in different namespaces as a class name, a method name, the name of a formal parameter, and a statement label.

```
class Reuse {
    Reuse Reuse(Reuse Reuse) {
      Reuse:
        for (;;) {
            if (Reuse.Reuse(Reuse) == Reuse)
                break Reuse;
        }
        return Reuse;
    }
}
```

10.6 Dynamic Scoping

All the tools for scoping seen so far are static; they answer the question of whether a given instance of a name is in the scope of a given definition at compile time.[3] Another approach, though rarely used in modern languages, makes an interesting contrast. It is known as *dynamic scoping* because it has the unique property that it does not answer the scoping question until runtime. Scoping rules that are decided before runtime, by contrast, are called *static* or *lexical scoping*.

In dynamic scoping, an environment of definitions is associated with each function. If a name that occurs in a function is not found in that function's environment, the environment of that function's caller is searched. If a definition is not found there, the caller's caller is search, and so on back through the chain of callers until a definition is found. The way this lookup works makes it tricky to describe the scope of a particular definition. A definition may reach not only within the defining function, but also to other functions when they are called (even indirectly) by the defining function. This might be called the classic dynamic scope rule:

> The scope of a definition is the function containing that definition, from the point of definition to the end of the function, along with any functions when they are called (even indirectly) from within that scope—minus the scopes of any redefinitions of the same name in those called functions.

3. Traditionally, the terms *static scoping* and *lexical scoping* have been used to refer specifically to scoping with blocks using some variation of the classic block scope rule. This book is using these terms more generally, since scoping with namespaces can also reasonably be described as static and lexical.

If you compare this with the classic block scope rule, you will see some similarities. Both definitions say, "minus the scopes of any redefinitions of the same name." (When a scope is limited by a redefinition in this way, the gap is known as a *scope hole*.) The difference is that block scoping refers only to regions of the program text, so it can be applied at compile time. Dynamic scoping refers to events at runtime ("functions when they are called"), and so cannot be decided until runtime.

Here is an ML example that shows the difference.

```
fun g x =
  let
    val inc = 1;
    fun f y = y + inc;
    fun h z =
      let
        val inc = 2;
      in
        f z
      end;
  in
    h x
  end;
```

Before you read on, try to answer this question: what is the value of `g 5` using this function definition (remembering that ML uses classic block scoping)? The evaluation of `g 5` results in an evaluation of `h 5`, which in turns evaluates `f 5`, and that returns the value `5+inc`. So the only question is this: what is the value of `inc` in function `f` when the expression `5+inc` is evaluated? There are obviously only two possibilities: there is a definition of `inc` as 1 and another definition of `inc` as 2. So clearly `g 5` must evaluate to either 6 or 7. But which one is it?

The correct answer is that when `5+inc` is evaluated, `inc` has the value 1. That's block scoping. There is no definition of `inc` in the block for `f`, but there is a definition for `inc` in the block that contains `f`—the `let` block of function `g`. The occurrence of the name `inc` in function `f` is bound (at compile time) to the variable `inc` = 1. The value of `g 5` is 6.

If ML used dynamic scoping, the other answer would be correct. Since there is no definition of `inc` in the function `f`, the name `inc` would be bound (at runtime) to the variable `inc = 2` that was defined by `f`'s caller. The value of `g 5` would be 7.

Dynamic scoping is used in only a few languages—some dialects of Lisp, for instance, and APL. Modern dialects of Lisp rarely use it, though it is available as an option in Common Lisp. Dynamic scoping has several drawbacks. For one thing, it is difficult to implement efficiently, since language systems must look up bindings at runtime. Another problem is that dynamic scoping tends to result in large and complicated scopes, since the scopes of definitions extend into called functions. This violates the principle, already mentioned, that scopes should be as small as possible. With dynamic scoping, the choice of variable names in the calling function may affect the behavior of called functions. This can be useful, but it can also be a source of debugging headaches.

10.7 A Word about Separate Compilation

Many programming languages are designed to support *separate compilation* of the kind seen in the classical sequence of language-system steps. A program is written in many small pieces, each perhaps stored in a different file. Each piece is compiled separately, and then the linker combines the results. To do its job, the linker needs at least some of the names from the original source files; for example, it needs to connect a call of a function `f` from one file with the definition of the function `f` from another file.

The C language helps make this possible by having two different kinds of definitions. One kind is a full definition. The other (called a *declaration* in C documentation) is a definition that gives only the name and its type—not the function body, if it is a function, and not the initialization value, if it is a variable. For example, if several C source files want to use the same integer variable `x` initialized to 3, they might all contain the declaration `extern int x`, but only one would give the full definition (outside of any function body) as `int x = 3`. In terms of scoping, these two kinds of definitions are equivalent; they both define a possible binding for `x` as an integer variable. The difference comes when the linker runs. The linker treats a declaration as a reference to a name defined in some other file, and then expects to see exactly one file with the full definition for that name. Note that the C definition `extern int x` does not say where the definition of `x` is to be found. The effect is only to require that the linker find a definition of `x` somewhere.

An older Fortran solution is the `COMMON` block. Suppose two separate Fortran compilations want to share the variables `A`, `B`, and `C`. They can both define the variables in the normal way, and then both include the statement `COMMON A, B, C`. The `COMMON` statement tells the linker to put the variables in the same memory location. (It actually has nothing to do with the names of the variables, only their positions in the list. If one Fortran compilation contains `COMMON A, B, C` and the other contains `COMMON X, Y, Z`, the effect will be to identify `A` with `X`, `B` with `Y`, and `C` with `Z`.) Modern dialects of Fortran have additional mechanisms: a way to define data in a separate compilation (a `MODULE`) and a way to import those definitions into a separate compilation (with the `USE` statement). Unlike in the C approach, the `USE` statement says what module the definitions are to be found in, but does not say what those definitions are. The Fortran compiler must examine the compiled module.

It seems to be a trend in recent languages (and recent dialects of older languages) to have "separate compilation" be less and less separate. To handle modules, the Fortran compiler must at least examine the results of separate compilations. Java classes can depend on each other, even circularly, and a Java compiler may have to handle this by compiling many classes simultaneously. ML is not really suitable for separate compilation at all, although a separate tool for the SML language system (called CM, the Compilation Manager) makes separate compilation possible for most ML programs.

10.8 Conclusion

This chapter presented several common mechanisms for controlling the scopes of definitions: scoping with blocks, scoping with labeled namespaces, scoping with primitive namespaces, and dynamic scoping. It touched only on some highlights of scoping techniques. The techniques have many variations, and most languages use several different scoping mechanisms at once.

You may have noticed that the chapter never really gave a definition of *scope*. There is a reason for this. It defined what it means for an occurrence of a variable to be *in the scope of* a definition, and from that you can infer how the scope of a definition might be defined. But to give a direct definition of the scope of a definition is an interesting exercise—Exercise 1, to be precise.

The single most important thing to take away from this chapter is the ability to use the word *scope* correctly in a sentence. Be careful: names do not have scopes, definitions do. Too many people say things like, "What is the scope of `x`?" That is sloppy usage and often reflects a poor understanding of scope. The name `x` is only a name, and occurrences of that name may be bound in many different ways in a program. The correct way to ask the question is, "What is the scope of *this definition* of `x`?"

Exercises

Exercise 1 Give a definition of *the scope of a definition*. Try to make it as concise as possible, but be careful not to define scope in a way that rules out dynamic scoping or any of the other scoping mechanisms in this chapter.

Exercise 2 Investigate and report on the block constructs named `let`, `let*`, and `letrec` in the language Scheme. Explain the scoping differences fully.

Exercise 3 Here again is the example used to show the difference between scoping with blocks and dynamic scoping:

```
fun g x =
  let
    val inc = 1;
    fun f y = y + inc;
    fun h z =
      let
        val inc = 2;
      in
        f z
      end;
  in
    h x
  end;
```

Copy it and then annotate it as follows:

a. Draw a circle around every block, and number the blocks.
b. Identify each definition of a name.
c. For each definition, describe its scope in terms of your block numbers.
d. For each occurrence of a name (other than a definition of that name), show which definition is used to bind it. Check that this agrees with your scopes.

Exercise 4 (for those who already know Java) Here again is the example used to show primitive namespaces in Java:

```
class Reuse {
    Reuse Reuse(Reuse Reuse) {
      Reuse:
        for (;;) {
            if (Reuse.Reuse(Reuse) == Reuse)
                break Reuse;
        }
        return Reuse;
    }
}
```

Copy it and then annotate it as follows:

a. For each occurrence of the name `Reuse` that is a definition, describe what binding for `Reuse` is established.

b. For each occurrence of `Reuse` that is not a definition, show which definition is used to bind it.

Exercise 5 Suppose there are the following operations on a stack of dictionaries:

- `pushEmptyDictionary()`: push a new empty dictionary on top of the stack
- `popDictionary()`: pop the top dictionary off the stack and discard it
- `addDefinition(name,thing)`: add a definition, a possible binding of the given name to the given thing, to the dictionary that is on top of the stack
- `lookup(name)`: look up the binding for the given name by searching the stack of dictionaries, starting from the top one, until the name is found

A compiler can use these operations to implement block scoping. The idea is that as it reads the program, the compiler uses `pushEmptyDictionary` whenever it encounters a new block and `popDictionary` whenever it reaches the end of a block. It uses `addDefinition` whenever it encounters a definition and `lookup` whenever it needs to look up the binding to use for a name.

Suppose a compiler reads the example from Exercise 5 as a sequence of tokens and starts with a single empty dictionary on top of the stack. Annotate the code to show where in this sequence of tokens the compiler uses each operation on the stack of dictionaries. Each time the stack of dictionaries changes in any way (that is, after any operation except `lookup`), show the new state of it. For each `lookup`, make sure the binding it finds is correct.

Exercise 6 The operations from Exercise 5 can also be used at runtime to implement dynamic scoping. When should each operation be used to make this work?

Further Reading

The `Reuse` example, demonstrating labeled namespaces in Java, is from

Arnold, Ken, and James Gosling. *The Java™ Programming Language*. Boston, MA: Addison-Wesley, 1996.

Chapter 11
A Fourth Look at ML

11.1 Introduction

You may recall from Chapter 6 that the type `bool` is not primitive in ML. Although it is a predefined type, it is actually constructed with an ML definition—*this* ML definition:

```
datatype bool = true | false;
```

Similarly, the `list` type constructor is not primitive—it is predefined, but its ML definition is simply this:

```
datatype 'element list = nil |
   :: of 'element * 'element list
```

You can write your own `datatype` definitions in ML, defining types as simple as `bool` (which is really just an enumeration) or as complicated as polymorphic tree structures. Defining new ML types is the subject of this chapter. This is also the last chapter on ML, so its conclusion gives an overview of the parts of ML that weren't covered.

11.2 Enumerations

One of the simplest uses of the datatype definition in ML is to create an enumerated type. Here is an example:

```
- datatype day = Mon | Tue | Wed | Thu | Fri | Sat | Sun;
datatype day = Fri | Mon | Sat | Sun | Thu | Tue | Wed
- fun isWeekDay x = not (x = Sat orelse x = Sun);
val isWeekDay = fn : day -> bool
- isWeekDay Mon;
val it = true : bool
- isWeekDay Sat;
val it = false : bool
```

This example defined an enumerated type called day and its members, Mon through Sun. The type was then used in a function isWeekDay. Notice that ML's usual type inference applies to new types as well; ML decided that the domain type for isWeekDay must be day, since the function compares its input for equality with the day values Sat and Sun.

The name day in this example is called a *type constructor* and the member names are called *data constructors.* (This terminology will make more sense in later examples, when you see how type constructors and data constructors can both have parameters.) A common ML style convention is to capitalize the names of data constructors, as was done in the example.

Here is another example of an enumeration:

```
- datatype flip = Heads | Tails;
datatype flip = Heads | Tails
- fun isHeads x = (x = Heads);
val isHeads = fn : flip -> bool
- isHeads Tails;
val it = false : bool
- isHeads Mon;
Error: operator and operand don't agree [tycon mismatch]
  operator domain: flip
  operand:         day
```

As you can see, ML is strict about these new types—it is not allowing us to pass a value of type day to a function that expects a value of type flip. In some languages, the underlying representation the language system uses for enumerations is visible to the programmer. In C, for example, an enum definition creates named constants with integer values, so any value of an enumeration can be used just like an integer. ML does not expose the underlying representation. It may be using small integers to represent the different day values, and it may be using the same small integers to represent the different flip values, but there is no way to tell. ML does not permit any operations that would allow the program to detect the representation. The only operations permitted are comparisons for equality (either explicitly or implicitly through the use of patterns).

You can use the data constructors in patterns. For example, we could, and probably should, rewrite the isWeekday function using a pattern-matching style:

```
fun isWeekDay Sat = false
|   isWeekDay Sun = false
|   isWeekDay _ = true;
```

In this simple case the data constructors work just like constants in a pattern.

11.3 Data Constructors with Parameters

You can add a parameter to a data constructor by adding the keyword of followed by the type of the parameter. Here, for example, is a datatype definition for a type exint with three data constructors, one of which has a parameter:

```
datatype exint = Value of int | PlusInf | MinusInf;
```

The exint type includes three different kinds of things: Value, PlusInf, and MinusInf. By declaring the Value data constructor as Value of int, we are saying that each Value will contain an int, which is to be given as a parameter to the data constructor: Value 3, Value 65, and so on. For each different int there is a different possible Value. A Value is like a wrapper that contains an int, while a PlusInf or a MinusInf is like an empty wrapper. This illustration shows some possible things of type exint.

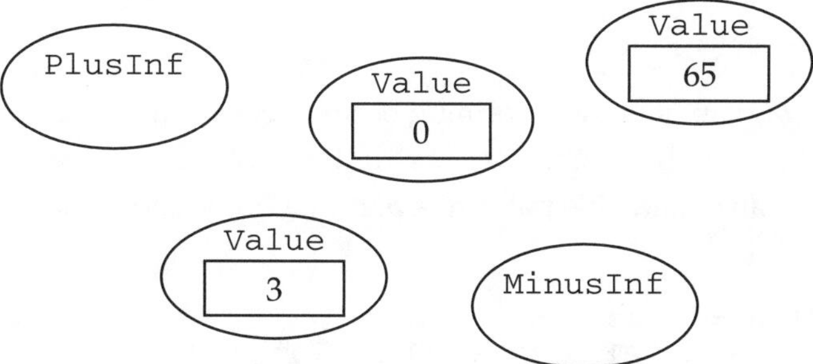

You might use the exint type as an extended kind of integer that includes representations for all the int values, plus special representations for positive and negative infinities.

If you look at how ML reports the types of the data constructors, you will see that while `PlusInf` and `MinusInf` look like constants of type `exint`, `Value` is a function that takes an `int` and returns an `exint`.

```
- PlusInf;
val it = PlusInf : exint
- MinusInf;
val it = MinusInf : exint
- Value;
val it = fn : int -> exint
- Value 3;
val it = Value 3 : exint
```

Although each `Value` contains an `int`, it cannot be treated as an `int`. For example, if we try to add one `Value` to another, we get an error:

```
- val x = Value 5;
val x = Value 5 : exint
- x + x;
Error: overloaded variable not defined at type
  symbol: +
  type: exint
```

So how can we get the wrapped-up `int` out of a `Value`? It's simple—by pattern matching. We can treat `(Value x)` as a pattern that not only matches a `Value`, but also binds the variable `x` to the integer inside it. Remember that pattern matching is used in many different places in ML: in `val` definitions, in `case` expressions, and most commonly in pattern-matching function definitions. Here we use a pattern in the `val` definition to extract the integer from the previous variable `x`:

```
- val (Value y) = x;
Warning: binding not exhaustive
          Value y = ...
val y = 5 : int
```

The "binding not exhaustive" warning occurs because the pattern `Value y` matches some but not all possible `exints`. It does not match `PlusInf` or `MinusInf`. Here an exhaustive pattern is part of a `case` expression to convert each `exint` into a string:

```
- val s = case x of
=           PlusInf => "infinity" |
=           MinusInf => "-infinity" |
=           Value y => Int.toString y;
val s = "5" : string
```

Int.toString is a predefined function that takes an int parameter and returns the corresponding string.

This pattern-matching function definition defines a function square that returns an exint representing the square of an exint input.

```
- fun square PlusInf = PlusInf
= |   square MinusInf = PlusInf
= |   square (Value x) = Value (x * x);
val square = fn : exint -> exint
- square MinusInf;
val it = PlusInf : exint
- square (Value 3);
val it = Value 9 : exint
```

Pattern-matching function definitions are especially important when you are working with your own datatype definitions, since pattern matching is the only way to extract the values that were passed to the data constructors.

Incidentally, one more use of pattern matching in ML is for exception handling. This book will not cover ML's exception handling (although it will look at Java's exception handling later on), but here is one example of it just to whet your appetite. This example extends the previous function so that it handles integer overflow on the multiplication by returning a PlusInf.

```
- fun square PlusInf = PlusInf
= |   square MinusInf = PlusInf
= |   square (Value x) = Value (x * x)
=       handle Overflow => PlusInf;
val square = fn : exint -> exint
- square (Value 10000);
val it = Value 100000000 : exint
- square (Value 100000);
val it = PlusInf : exint
```

11.4 Type Constructors with Parameters

The type constructor for a datatype definition can have parameters too. The parameters for a type constructor are type parameters, and the result is a polymorphic type constructor. For example, here is the option type constructor, which is predefined in ML:

```
datatype 'a option = NONE | SOME of 'a;
```

The type constructor is named `option`. It takes a type `'a` as a parameter. The data constructors are `NONE` and `SOME`. The `SOME` constructor takes a parameter of type `'a`.

It seems odd at first that the parameter `'a` is placed before the type constructor name, but that is how it will be used. Just as the `list` type constructor makes types like `int list` and `real list`, the `option` type constructor will make types like `int option` and `real option`.

```
- SOME 4;
val it = SOME 4 : int option
- SOME 1.2;
val it = SOME 1.2 : real option
- SOME "pig";
val it = SOME "pig" : string option
```

The `option` type constructor is useful for functions whose result is not always defined. For example, the result of an integer division is not defined when the divisor is zero, so we might write:

```
- fun optdiv a b =
=   if b = 0 then NONE else SOME (a div b);
val optdiv = fn : int -> int -> int option
- optdiv 7 2;
val it = SOME 3 : int option
- optdiv 7 0;
val it = NONE : int option
```

Many predefined ML functions use `option`. You can use it in your own functions too.

Here is a longer example of a polymorphic `datatype` definition. It defines a type constructor called `bunch` so that a value of type `'x bunch` is either a single element of type `'x` or a list of elements of type `'x`.

```
datatype 'x bunch =
   One of 'x |
   Group of 'x list;
```

As usual, ML figures out the actual type of any `bunch` value.

```
- One 1.0;
val it = One 1.0 : real bunch
- Group [true,false];
val it = Group [true,false] : bool bunch
```

Although ML can figure out the type of a bunch value, it does not have to resolve the type of a bunch in all cases. Polymorphic functions like size, below, can work on values of any bunch type.

```
- fun size (One _) = 1
= |   size (Group x) = length x;
val size = fn : 'a bunch -> int
- size (One 1.0);
val it = 1 : int
- size (Group [true,false]);
val it = 2 : int
```

Here is an example of a use of bunch that does force ML to resolve the type:

```
- fun sum (One x) = x
= |   sum (Group xlist) = foldr op + 0 xlist;
val sum = fn : int bunch -> int
- sum (One 5);
val it = 5 : int
- sum (Group [1,2,3]);
val it = 6 : int
```

Because the + operator (through foldr) is applied to the list elements, ML knows that the type of the parameter to sum must be int bunch.

11.5 Recursively Defined Type Constructors

In the data constructors of a datatype definition, you can use the type constructor being defined. This kind of recursive definition is a source of expressive power in ML programs. Here, for example, is a definition of a type constructor called intlist, which is almost like the ML type int list.

```
datatype intlist =
  INTNIL |
  INTCONS of int * intlist;
```

Notice the recursion. The second element of the pair required by the INTCONS data constructor is of the type being defined—intlist. This new type works just like a plain int list, but with INTNIL in place of nil and with the INTCONS constructor in place of the :: operator. This illustration shows some possible values of type intlist.

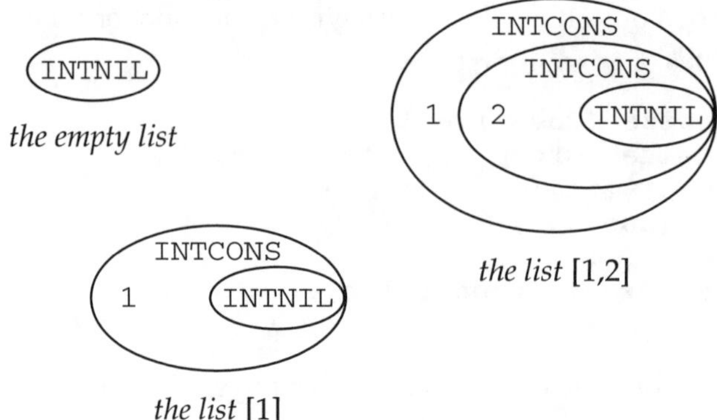

the empty list

the list [1,2]

the list [1]

This ML session constructs the values pictured above:

```
- INTNIL;
val it = INTNIL : intlist
- INTCONS (1,INTNIL);
val it = INTCONS (1,INTNIL) : intlist
- INTCONS (1,INTCONS(2,INTNIL));
val it = INTCONS (1,INTCONS (2,INTNIL)) : intlist
```

Of course, ML does not display those values in the standard list notation; you would have to write your own function to do that. The function `intlistLength`, below, computes the length of an `intlist`. Compare this with the function `listLength` that follows it, which computes the length of an ordinary `int list` using the same method. See how similar the two types are?

```
fun intlistLength INTNIL = 0
  | intlistLength (INTCONS(_,tail)) =
      1 + (intListLength tail);

fun listLength nil = 0
  | listLength (_::tail) =
      1 + (listLength tail);
```

Of course, there is one major difference between the predefined `list` type constructor and `intlist`: the predefined `list` is parametric, while `intlist` works only for lists of integers. This is easily remedied. The following datatype, `mylist`, is just like `intlist`, but parametric. Compare the two definitions and you will see that the only change was to replace the `int` type with a type variable, added as a parameter for the type constructor.

```
datatype 'element mylist =
  NIL |
  CONS of 'element * 'element mylist;
```

This is now a parametric list type constructor, just like the predefined `list`. We can make a `real mylist` or an `int mylist`, and ML's type inference handles it in the usual way.

```
- CONS(1.0, NIL);
val it = CONS (1.0,NIL) : real mylist
- CONS(1, CONS(2, NIL));
val it = CONS (1,CONS (2,NIL)) : int mylist
```

Almost no change is necessary to the length-computing function to make it handle this new polymorphic list. We just have to use the new data constructors `CONS` and `NIL`.

```
fun myListLength NIL = 0
  | myListLength (CONS(_,tail)) =
      1 + myListLength(tail);
```

Almost anything you can do with the predefined `list` types you can now do with a `mylist` type. Here is a function to add up the elements of an `int mylist`. This is not polymorphic, since the use of the `+` operator forces ML to nail down the element type.

```
fun addup NIL = 0
  | addup (CONS(head,tail)) =
      head + addup tail;
```

With predefined `list` types, we would not bother to write a function like `addup`. As was shown in Chapter 9, it is easier to use `foldr` to add up an `int list x` just by writing `foldr op + 0 x`. Here is an implementation of `foldr` for the `mylist` type:

```
fun myfoldr f c NIL = c
  | myfoldr f c (CONS(a,b)) =
      f(a, myfoldr f c b);
```

We can now add up an `int mylist x` just by writing `myfoldr op + 0 x`.

In short, the type constructor `mylist` works just like the predefined type constructor `list`. Take any function that works on `list` types, replace `nil` with `NIL` and `::` with `CONS`, and you have a function that works on `mylist` types. Of course, you would not really want to replace the predefined list types with your own list types. The point of these examples is to demonstrate the use of `datatype` to make polymorphic type constructors and to emphasize that there is no primitive magic to the predefined list types. They can be defined using ordinary ML constructs.

Actually, there is still one minor difference between the `mylist` type constructor and the predefined `list` type constructor: the predefined `::` function is an operator, while `CONS` is not. This is trivial to fix. How new ML operators are defined won't be shown in any detail, but here is an example to whet your appetite:

```
- infixr 5 CONS;
infixr 5 CONS
- 1 CONS 2 CONS NIL;
val it = 1 CONS 2 CONS NIL : int mylist
```

Now you can write `1 CONS 2 CONS NIL` just as you can write `1::2::nil` using the predefined list types. (The `infixr` statement declares that the function in question should now be treated as a right-associative binary operator. The 5 in the example is the precedence level—in ML, this is the same precedence level as the `::` operator.)

The `mylist` type constructor shows how a recursively defined `datatype` can be used for polymorphic lists. The same trick can be used for polymorphic binary trees. Here is the `datatype` definition:

```
datatype 'data tree =
   Empty |
   Node of 'data tree * 'data * 'data tree;
```

In this definition, a tree can be empty or can consist of a left child, a data element, and a right child. The type variable `'data` is the type of the element stored in the node. This illustration shows some possible values of type `int tree`:

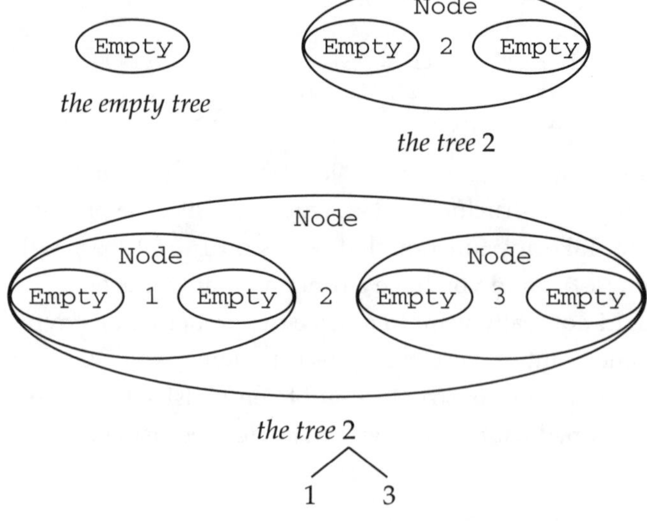

This ML session constructs the values pictured above:

```
- val treeEmpty = Empty;
val treeEmpty = Empty : 'a tree
- val tree2 = Node(Empty,2,Empty);
val tree2 = Node (Empty,2,Empty) : int tree
- val tree123 = Node(Node(Empty,1,Empty),
=                    2,
=                    Node(Empty,3,Empty));
```

Here are some examples of functions that operate on these trees. This one takes an `int tree` parameter and returns a similar tree, but with 1 added to each integer:

```
fun incall Empty = Empty
  | incall (Node(x,y,z)) =
      Node(incall x, y+1, incall z);
```

For example, applying it to the previous value `tree123` produces this result:

```
- incall tree123;
val it = Node (Node (Empty,2,Empty),
               3,
               Node (Empty,4,Empty)) : int tree
```

This next function adds up all the numbers in an `int tree`:

```
fun sumall Empty = 0
  | sumall (Node(x,y,z)) =
      sumall x + y + sumall z;
```

Applying it to the value `tree123` produces this result:

```
- sumall tree123;
val it = 6 : int
```

The previous functions `incall` and `sumall` are not polymorphic, since they work only on `int tree` values. This polymorphic function takes any type of tree and produces a list of its values:

```
fun listall Empty = nil
  | listall (Node(x,y,z)) =
      listall x @ y :: listall z;
```

For example, applying it to the value `tree123` produces this result:

```
- listall tree123;
val it = [1,2,3] : int list
```

One more polymorphic example: this is an exhaustive search of any type of tree for a given value:

```
fun isintree x Empty = false
  | isintree x (Node(left,y,right)) =
       x = y
       orelse isintree x left
       orelse isintree x right;
```

Using it to search the value `tree123` produces these results:

```
- isintree 4 tree123;
val it = false : bool
- isintree 3 tree123;
val it = true : bool
```

Note that the `isintree` function makes no assumptions about the order in which elements appear in the tree; it searches the whole tree until the element is found. For ordered trees (such as binary search trees) you can do better—can and will, if you do Exercise 12.

11.6 Conclusion—Farewell to ML

This chapter discussed the `datatype` definition in ML. It explored some examples showing simple enumerations, data constructors with parameters, type constructors with parameters, and recursively defined types for lists and trees. This is the end of the introduction to ML.

At this point, which of these describes you best?

A. I just couldn't get comfortable with ML. I hope I never have to write another piece of code in a functional language.

B. I really liked ML and I want to do more.

Did you answer A? Don't worry; you are not alone. Learning a little bit of a language like ML is an interesting and mind-expanding exercise, but not everyone feels comfortable with ML programming. The next language is Java. Perhaps that will suit you better.

Did you answer B? Then you may be interested in some of the parts of ML that were skipped. Here is a list of some of them:

- Records—ML supports records, which are handled a bit like tuples except that the elements are named instead of numbered.

- Arrays—ML supports arrays, with elements that can be altered. This is not in the purely functional part of ML, but for some applications arrays are just too useful to leave out.
- References—Again, this is an imperative part of ML. References can be used to get the effect of assignable variables.
- Exception handling—ML uses pattern matching in its exception handling mechanism.
- Encapsulation—For larger programs, you want a way to build separate modules whose parts can be hidden from each other. This is a big part of ML (and of any modern language), though these small examples and exercises did not require it. ML supports *structures*, which are collections of datatypes, functions, and so on; *signatures*, which give a way of describing the interface of a structure, separate from its implementation; and *functors*, which are like functions that operate on whole structures.
- API—As always, the language libraries dwarf the language itself. The *standard basis* defines the functions (not to mention type constructors, structures, signatures, functors, and so on) that are predefined in standard ML environments. Some of these are present in the *top-level* environment and are referred to by their simple names, like `concat` and `explode`. Most, however, are in structures and are referred to by their full names, like `Int.maxInt`, `Real.Math.sqrt`, and `List.nth`. Many other popular libraries are not part of the standard basis. For example, a library called eXene is for developing ML applications that work in X Window System.
- Compilation Manager—A system for managing the many files that make up large ML applications. This serves some of the same purposes as the Unix `make` facility.

This book has used Standard ML, but there several other dialects of ML. For example, OCaml is a dialect that adds class-based, object-oriented features.

ML supports a function-oriented style of programming. It favors a problem-solving approach that composes solutions to algorithmic problems using many small (usually side-effect-free) functions. That same general style is supported by other functional languages as well. If you find that this style suits you, you might want to look at other functional languages, like Lisp and Haskell. The "Further Reading" section at the end of this chapter includes a reference for each of them.

Exercises

Exercise 1 Write a datatype definition for a type suit whose values are the four suits of a deck of playing cards.

Exercise 2 Using your definition from Exercise 1, write a function suitname of type suit -> string that returns a string giving the name of a suit.

Exercise 3 Write a datatype definition for a type number whose values are either integers or real numbers.

Exercise 4 Using your definition from Exercise 3, write a function plus of type number -> number -> number that adds two numbers, coercing int to real only if necessary.

Exercise 5 Write a function addup of type intnest -> int that adds up all the integers in an intnest. Use this definition for intnest. (Be careful as you type. INT is not the same as int!)

```
datatype intnest =
  INT of int |
  LIST of intnest list;
```

Exercise 6 Write a function prod of type int mylist -> int that takes an int mylist x and returns the product of all the elements of x. If the list is NIL your function should return 1. Here again is the definition of mylist, as seen earlier in this chapter:

```
datatype 'element mylist =
  NIL |
  CONS of 'element * 'element mylist;
```

Exercise 7 Write a function reverse of type 'a mylist -> 'a mylist that takes a mylist a and returns a mylist of all the elements of a, in reverse order. (Use the mylist definition from Exercise 6.)

Exercise 8 Write a function append of type 'a mylist -> 'a mylist -> 'a mylist that takes two mylist values, a and b, and returns the mylist containing all the elements of a followed by all the elements of b. (Use the mylist definition from Exercise 6.)

Exercise 9 Write a function `appendall` of type `'a list tree -> 'a list` that takes a tree of lists and returns the result of appending all the lists together. Put the list for a node together in this order: first the contents of the left subtree, then the list at this node, and then the contents of the right subtree. Here again is the definition of `tree`, as seen earlier in this chapter:

```
datatype 'data tree =
   Empty |
   Node of 'data tree * 'data * 'data tree;
```

Exercise 10 A complete binary `tree` is one in which every `Node` has either two `Empty` children or two `Node` children, but not one of each. Write a function `isComplete` of type `'a tree -> bool` that tests whether a `tree` is complete. (Use the `tree` definition from Exercise 9.)

Exercise 11 A binary search tree is a binary tree with special properties. It may be `Empty`. It may be a `Node` containing a left subtree, a data item `x`, and a right subtree. In this case all the data items in the tree are different, all the items in the left subtree are smaller than `x`, all the items in the right subtree are greater than `x`, and the left and right subtrees are also binary search trees. Write a function `makeBST` of type `'a list -> ('a * 'a -> bool) -> 'a tree` that organizes the items in the list into a binary search tree. The tree need not be balanced. You may assume that no item in the list is repeated.

Exercise 12 Write a function `searchBST` of type `''a tree -> (''a * ''a -> bool) -> ''a -> bool` that searches a binary search tree for a given data element. (Refer to Exercise 11 for the definition of a binary search tree.) You should not search every node in the tree, but only those nodes that, according to the definition, might contain the element you are looking for.

Further Reading

This excellent introductory book on ML has already been mentioned:

Ullman, Jeffrey D. *Elements of ML Programming*. Upper Saddle River, NJ: Prentice Hall, 1998.

This ML book is somewhat more advanced:

Paulson, Larry C. *ML for the Working Programmer.* New York: Cambridge University Press, 1996.

If you liked ML, you may also be interested in other functional languages. Two important ones are Lisp and Haskell. Lisp is the oldest of the functional languages and is still widely used for artificial-intelligence research. This book does not focus on AI, but gives a variety of examples of Lisp code:

> Graham, Paul. *ANSI Common Lisp*. Upper Saddle River, NJ: Prentice Hall, 1995.

Haskell is a modern functional language that differs from ML in several important ways. One major difference is that Haskell is a *lazy* language; it evaluates only as much of the program as necessary to get the answer.

> Thompson, Simon. *Haskell: The Craft of Functional Programming*. Boston, MA: Addison-Wesley, 1999.

Chapter 12
Memory Locations for Variables

12.1 Introduction

In an imperative language, there is an obvious connection between variables and memory locations. When a value is assigned to a variable, it must be stored somewhere. That *somewhere* is the memory location associated with the variable. Some programming languages make the idea of "the memory location of a variable" explicit. For example, in C and C++, the expression `&x` yields the memory location of the variable `x`. But even without such a construct, the connection between variables and memory locations in an imperative language is obvious.

In a language without assignment—a purely functional language, like the subset of ML seen so far—the fact that variables are associated with memory locations is more hidden. Without assignment, you do not have to be aware of the steps the language system must take to record the values of variables, and of course no expression, like `&x`, gives access to the memory location of a variable. The fact that variables must somehow be stored at memory locations is treated as an implementation detail.

Whether it is exposed or hidden, all programming languages face this implementation problem: each variable needs at least one memory location. How are these memory locations determined? This is really just another binding question: how are a program's variables bound to memory locations? This chapter will explore some of the many interesting answers to this deceptively simple question.

12.2 Activation-Specific Variables

Most languages have a way to declare a variable that is bound to a memory location only for a particular execution of a function. The variables in this ML example from Chapter 7 have short lifetimes of this kind.

```
fun days2ms days =
  let
    val hours = days * 24.0
    val minutes = hours * 60.0
    val seconds = minutes * 60.0
  in
    seconds * 1000.0
  end;
```

When the `days2ms` function is called, memory locations are needed to hold the values of `days`, `hours`, `minutes`, and `seconds`. Later calls of the same function will have different values for these variables, values that have no connection with the values from previous calls. Note that the variables may or may not be bound to the same memory locations on later calls—for ML programs there is no way to tell.

It is important here to think carefully about what function lifetimes are like. When a function is called, it performs its computation, perhaps calls other functions, and finally returns to its caller. The lifetime of this one execution of the function, from call to corresponding return, is called an *activation* of the function. Variables like those in the previous example are called *activation specific*.[1] In most modern languages, local variables are activation specific by default.

A variable might be specific to an activation of a particular block within a function. In the example above, the variable `days` is a formal parameter of the function, but `hours`, `minutes`, and `seconds` are local variables inside the block of the `let` expression. In that example it makes little difference, but the distinction can be important if the block in question is not always executed when the function is called, as in this expression of the factorial function:

---

1. Some authors use the term *dynamic* for activation-specific variables; others use the term *automatic*.

```
fun fact n =
  if (n = 0) then 1
  else let val b = fact (n - 1) in n * b end;
```

Here, the block defining `b` is not always executed. A language system might bind `b` to a memory location only if its block is entered. The variable `b` is still activation specific, but it is specific to an activation of the `let` block, not the whole `fact` function.

Other Kinds of Variables

There are other kinds of lifetimes for variables. Most imperative languages have a way to declare a variable that is bound to one memory location for the entire runtime of the program. In the C language, any variable declared outside of a function has this kind of long lifetime:

```
int count = 0;
int nextcount() {
  count = count + 1;
  return count;
}
```

Each time the `nextcount` function is called, it increments the previous value of `count` and returns the new value. Although `count` may have many different values, it only ever has one memory location where those values are stored. Static allocation is the obvious way to handle these long-lifetime variables, so they are called *static* variables.

Note that the question of whether a variable has local scope is independent of whether it has an activation-specific lifetime. The C language, for example, allows the definition of static variables with several different kinds of scope. In the previous example, the variable `count` was declared in such a way that it would be visible throughout the program. Other functions defined in the same file and other functions in different files could all refer to that same variable. The variable could also be defined in this way:

```
int nextcount() {
  static int count = 0;
  count = count + 1;
  return count;
}
```

This limits the scope of the variable to the single function `nextcount`. But even though `count` now has local scope, it still has a static lifetime.

In addition to activation-specific variables and static variables, there are other possibilities. For object-oriented languages like Java, it is common to have variables whose lifetimes are associated with object lifetimes—the fields of an object. Other languages support *persistent* variables, variables with super-long lifetimes that extend across multiple executions of the program. But in modern languages, most variables are activation specific. They are the most common case and the most interesting case for binding to memory locations. The rest of the chapter focuses on them.

12.3 Activation Records

A function may have many different activations during the execution of a program, since it may be called many times. Even in ordinary, single-threaded programs, often more than one activation is alive at a time. This happens when one function calls another. In that case, the called function's activation begins before the caller's activation has ended, so both activations are alive at the same time. They aren't *executing* at the same time, of course, since the calling activation is suspended until the called activation returns. But when the called activation returns, the calling activation resumes, and it expects its activation-specific variables to have been preserved across the call.

Additional activation-specific data must be stored in memory. This usually includes a function's *return address,* which is the location within the calling function's code where execution should resume when the called function returns. (Each activation may have a different return address, since a function may be called from many different places within the program.) Language implementations usually gather all the activation-specific variables and other activation-specific data together into one block of memory called an *activation record*.

When a block within a function body is entered, memory locations for the variables of that block must be found. Most language systems optimize this case and do not create a complete new activation record every time a block is entered. Space for the variables in each block can often be preallocated within the activation record for the whole function. That is how the examples that follow will be illustrated; one activation record will be shown for each activation of a function, including space for all the variables that are local to blocks within the function. This assumes that the amount of memory required for each variable is known when the function is entered. (If the amount of memory required is not known until the block is entered—for instance, if the language allows a local variable in a block to be an array whose size was computed just before the block was entered—blocks must be handled in some other way. One approach is to extend the activation record for the function when the block is entered and then shrink it back down when the block is exited.)

12.4 Static Allocation of Activation Records

Here is a simple way to handle activation records: allocate one for every function, *statically*. That means allocate one for each function before the program begins running. This has efficiency advantages, since no allocation has to be done at runtime.

Older dialects of Fortran and Cobol used this system. Consider this old-style Fortran function, which computes the mean of an array of real numbers:

```
      FUNCTION AVG (ARR, N)
      DIMENSION ARR(N)
      SUM = 0.0
      DO 100 I = 1, N
        SUM = SUM + ARR(I)
100   CONTINUE
      AVG = SUM / FLOAT(N)
      RETURN
      END
```

Whenever this function is called, it needs memory space for its three local variables—the integer `I`, the real number `SUM`, and the function's returned value `AVG`. It also needs memory space for the parameters `ARR` and `N`. In Fortran, the parameters are not the numbers themselves, but the addresses of the numbers. (Chapter 18 discusses this further.) The function also needs space to record its return address.

All this activation-specific data needs an activation record. The first thing we need to know is how much space each of the items takes up. Let's say that the Fortran implementation uses two words for each real number (`SUM` and `AVG`), one word for each integer (`I`), and one word for each address (`ARR`, `N`, and the return address). So we need a block of $2 \times 2 + 1 + 3 = 8$ words. We might lay it out like this:

N address
ARR address
return address
I
SUM
AVG

The order of the components of the activation record depends on the implementation. We can now allocate this block of eight words statically.

Recall the question posed at the beginning of this chapter: how are the memory locations for variables determined? This system—static allocation of activation records, along with static allocation of any explicitly static variables—is the simplest and most efficient answer. Unfortunately, the chapter can't end here, because this system suffers from a severe limitation. Since every activation of a given function uses the same block of memory for its activation-specific data, this system will fail if there is ever more than one activation of a function alive at the same time.

How would a program get more than one activation of the same function going at once? One way is for a function to be called recursively. When a function calls itself, the calling activation and the called activation are both alive at the same time. The two (or more) activations of the same function will overwrite each other's variables if they share a single, static activation record. The early dialects of Fortran and Cobol got around this problem by making recursion illegal. This seemed like a sensible trade-off 40 years ago. Static allocation for activation records made programs slightly faster, and recursion didn't seem that important. But today, almost all languages support recursion, including the modern dialects of Fortran and Cobol. Recursion necessitates a more sophisticated way of allocating activation records.

12.5 Dynamic Stacks of Activation Records

Languages that support recursion need to be able to allocate a new activation record for each activation. This means that activation records have to be allocated dynamically. When a function is called, the language system prepares to execute it by allocating a new activation record for it. In many languages, like C, that activation record can be deallocated when the function returns. The activation records form a stack at runtime. Activation records are pushed on call and popped on return. This is such a popular system that activation records are sometimes known simply as *stack frames*.

Each function must know how to find the address of its current activation record. Since activation records are now dynamically allocated, their addresses can't be known at compile time. Instead, a machine register is usually dedicated to this purpose at runtime. When a function returns, two addresses are important now: the address of the machine code to return to in the calling function and the address of the activation record that function was using.

Here's an example of a recursive C function. This function, called `fact`, takes a non-negative integer and returns the factorial of that integer.

```
int fact(int n) {
  int result;
  if (n<2) result = 1;
  else result = n * fact(n-1);
  return result;
}
```

Let's trace the operation of this function when the expression `fact(3)` is evaluated. This illustration shows the first activation record, just before the recursive call to evaluate `fact(2)` is made. The variable `result` has not yet been assigned a value. The "return address" field tells where to resume in the caller's code when the `fact(3)` call returns. The "previous activation record" field holds the address of the caller's activation record (which isn't shown).

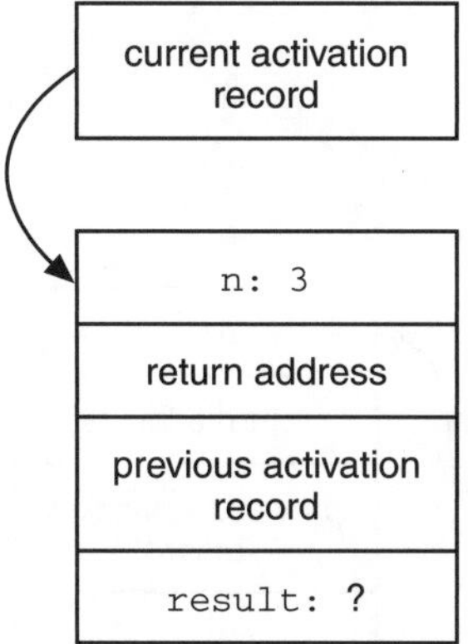

The next illustration shows the contents of memory during the second activation of `fact`. The first activation record is still present, although the first activation is suspended until the second one returns. The illustration shows the state of memory just before the recursive call to evaluate `fact(1)` is made.

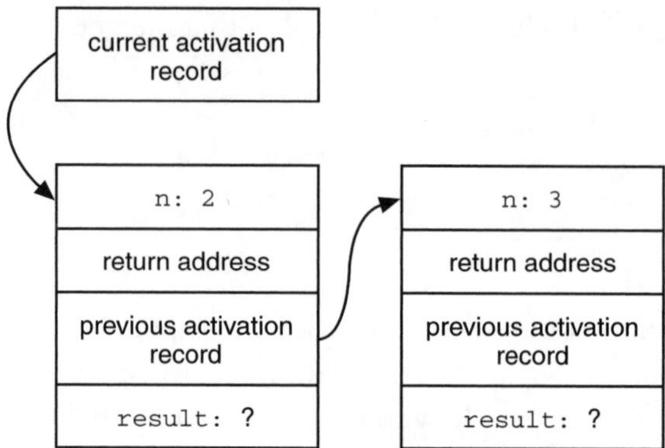

The next illustration shows the situation during the third activation of `fact`. Since now `n`<2, the function assigns 1 to the variable `result` without making a recursive call and is about to return that to its caller.

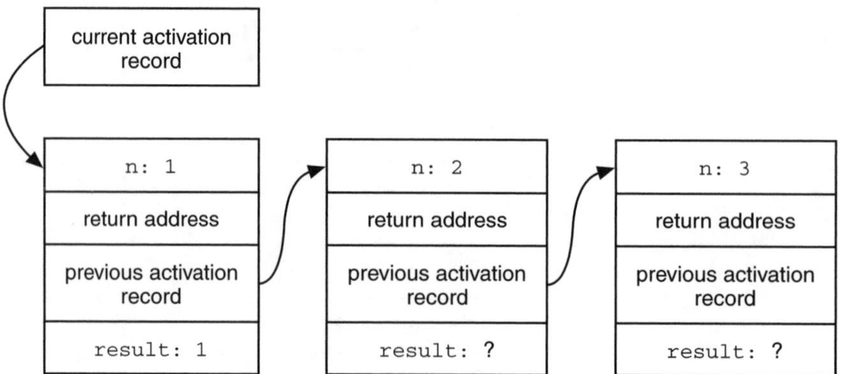

When the third activation returns to the second, the second activation gets the value 1 for `fact(1)` and sets `result` $= 2 \times 1 = 2$. The following picture shows the situation just before the second activation returns. The activation record for the third activation has been popped off the stack.

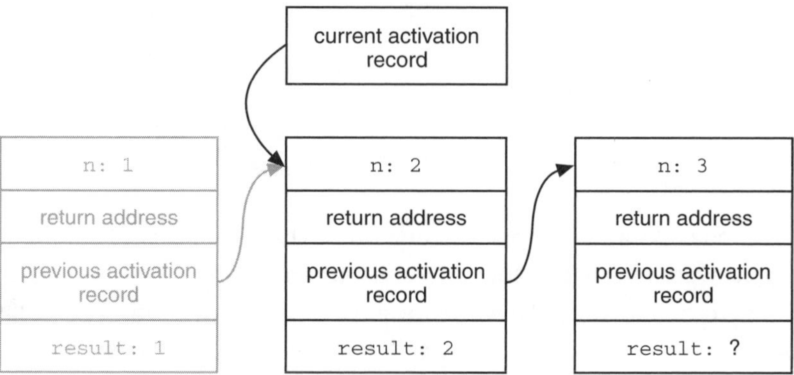

Finally, the second activation returns to the first. The first activation gets the value 2 for `fact(2)` and sets `result` = 3 × 2 = 6. The following picture shows the situation just before the first activation returns. The activation record for the second activation has been popped off the stack.

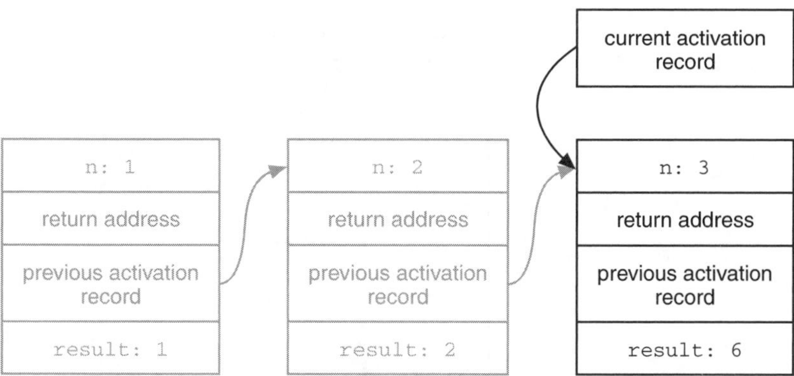

What becomes of the activation records that are popped off the stack? That depends on the language and the implementation. In many languages, including C, a popped activation record can be deallocated and its memory space can be reused. (As will be shown in Chapter 14, it is possible to implement stack-structured allocation and deallocation very efficiently.)

To drive this idea home let's see one more example. For a little more ML practice, this one will be in ML. Recall the `halve` function from Chapter 7. It takes a list parameter and returns a pair of lists, each containing half of the elements of the original list.

```
fun halve nil = (nil, nil)
|   halve [a] = ([a], nil)
|   halve (a::b::cs) =
      let
        val (x, y) = halve cs
      in
        (a::x, b::y)
      end;
```

Let's trace the operation of this function on the list `[1,2,3,4]`. In the initial activation, the third alternative for `halve` is chosen. The variables `a`, `b`, and `cs` are defined by pattern matching. This picture shows the first activation record, just before the function makes its recursive call to `halve [3,4]`. The variables `x` and `y` do not yet have their values, and the value that the function will return is not yet known.

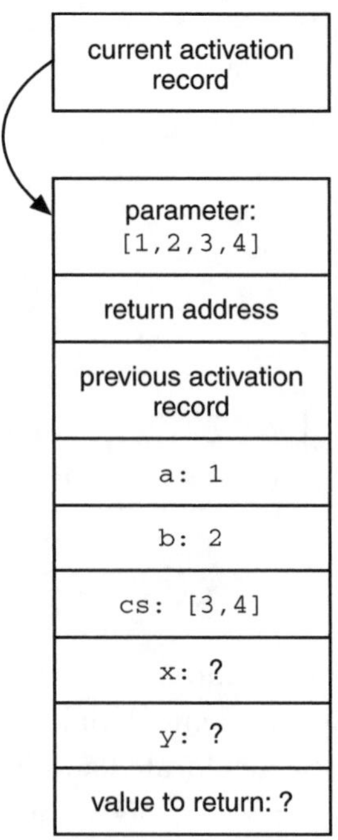

The next illustration shows the contents of memory during the execution of the second activation of `halve`. Again, the third alternative for `halve` has been chosen and the variables `a`, `b`, and `cs` have been defined by pattern matching. This shows the second activation record, just before the recursive call to `halve []`.

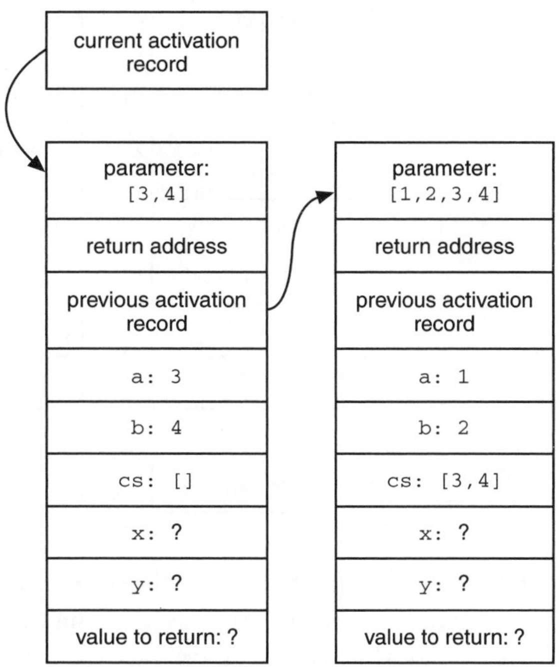

The next illustration shows the contents of memory during the execution of the third activation of `halve`. This time, the first alternative for `halve` is chosen, since the parameter is the empty list. Instead of making a recursive call, it immediately returns a pair of empty lists to its caller. This illustration shows the situation just before the third activation returns.

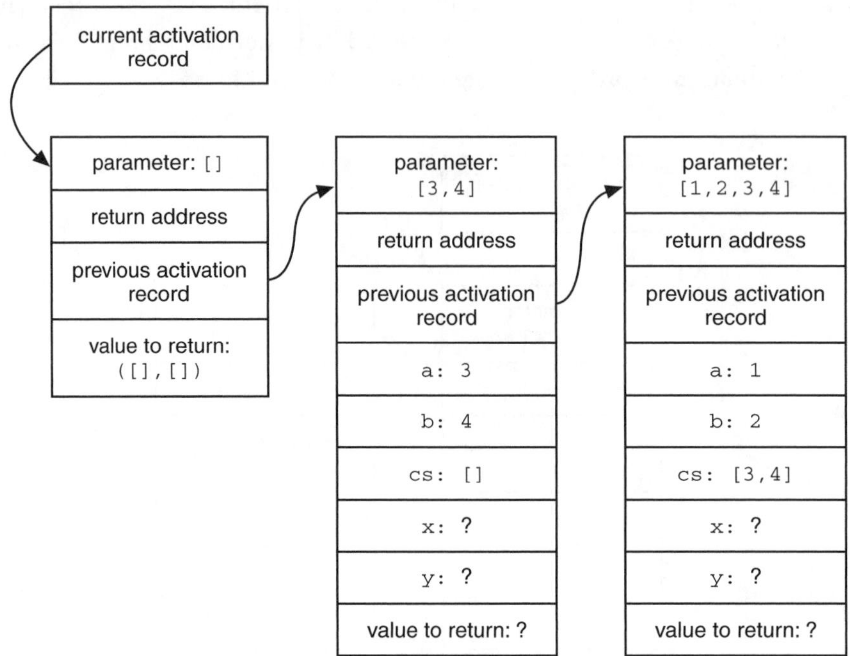

When the third activation returns to the second, the second activation gets definitions for `x` and `y` by pattern matching `(x, y)` with the value `([], [])`. It then constructs its return value. This picture shows the situation just before the second activation returns. The activation record for the third activation has been popped off the stack.

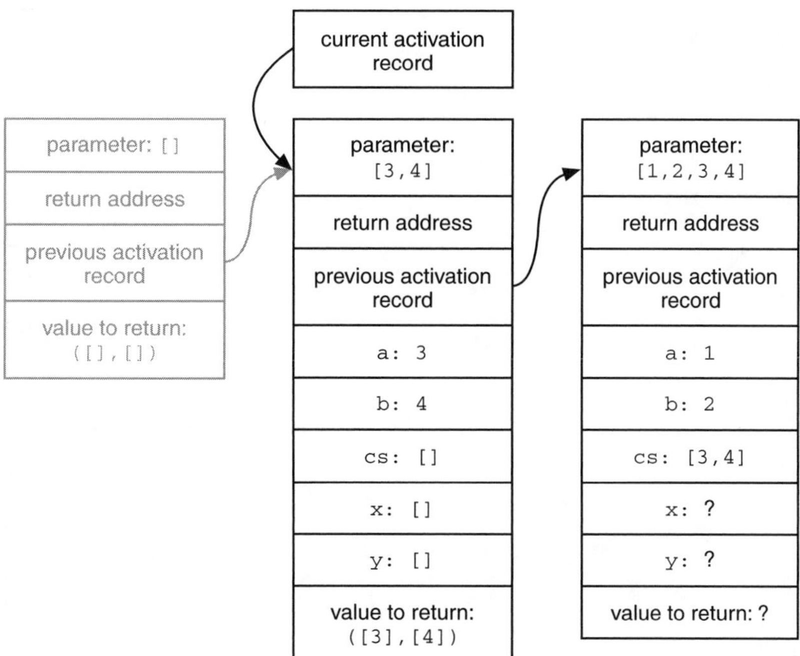

When the second activation returns to the first, the first activation gets definitions for `x` and `y` by pattern matching `(x, y)` with the value `([3], [4])`. It then constructs its return value. This picture shows the situation just before the first activation returns to its caller. This concludes the example. The value returned by ML for the expression `halve [1,2,3,4]` is `([1,3],[2,4])`.

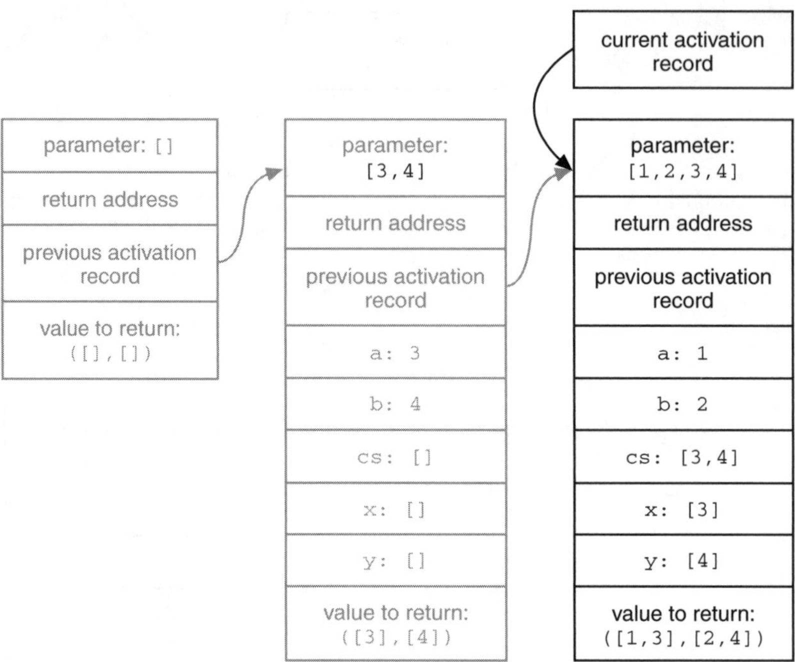

The system of stack-structured dynamic allocation of activation records is used in almost all modern language implementations. Unfortunately, the chapter cannot end here. As you will see, several extra tricks are required to handle advanced language features.

12.6 Handling Nested Function Definitions

The prior system for allocating activation records is just right for the C language, but not quite enough for languages like Pascal, Ada, and ML, which allow nested function definitions with non-local references. In C, any reference that is not local must refer to a static variable, and you already know how to handle those. But many other languages have an intermediate kind of reference: a reference to a variable that is not local but is also not static—a reference to a variable that is in some other function's activation record.

Here's an example—an implementation of the quicksort algorithm in ML. Before you study this to see how it works, scan it quickly for the variable named `pivot`. It has one definition and two references to it. One of those references is the source of the problem that needs to be addressed.

```
fun quicksort nil = nil
|   quicksort (pivot :: rest) =
      let
        fun split(nil) = (nil,nil)
        |   split(x :: xs) =
              let
                val (below, above) = split(xs)
              in
                if x < pivot then (x :: below, above)
                else (below, x :: above)
              end;
        val (below, above) = split(rest)
      in
        quicksort below @ [pivot] @ quicksort above
      end;
```

In this example, the function `quicksort` contains a nested function called `split`. The `split` function splits a list into two parts—those less than a special element called the pivot and those greater than or equal to the pivot. (This simple implementation always chooses the first element of the list to be the pivot.) An example of this kind of nested function was in Chapter 7 in a merge sort. The `split` function is nested for the same reason: to restrict the visibility of its definition to the only likely caller.

Inside `split` there is an underlined reference to the variable `pivot`. This is a non-local reference, the kind that causes trouble for activation records. The variable `pivot` is not a local variable of `split`; it is a local variable of `quicksort`. `pivot` could be passed from `quicksort` to `split` as a parameter, but then `pivot` would also have to be passed when `split` calls itself recursively. These extra parameters would be misleading, since the value of `pivot` is the same in each recursive `split` call.

So when `split` is executing, how does it find the variable `pivot`? It can't look in its own activation record. It can't assume that `pivot` is in its caller's activation record either. Since `split` is recursive, it may be its own caller. It needs to find the activation record for `quicksort`. It could link back from caller to caller's caller and so on, until it finds an activation record for `quicksort`, but that is too much work to do at runtime. This picture shows the problem:

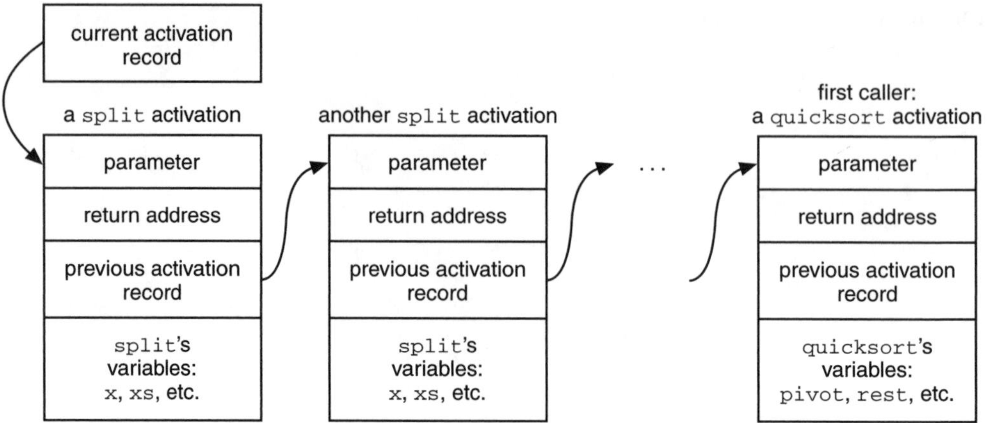

The illustration shows what happens when a `quicksort` activation calls `split` and `split` then makes recursive calls to an arbitrary depth. The current activation is a `split` activation, and it needs to find the `pivot`. Unfortunately, `pivot` is not in the current activation record, nor in any record nearby. (The illustration does not show the value of the function name `split`. There's more about function values below.)

The activation record already contains the address of the previous activation record—the immediate caller of this activation. But to solve the `pivot` problem we need to find a different address—the address of the most recent activation record for the function within which the function's definition is nested. This address is called the *nesting link*.[2] The following example adds the nesting links to the previous illustration. The nesting links for all the recursive activations of `split` are the same, since they all have the same nearest caller. The nesting link for the `quicksort` activation is null, since `quicksort` is not nested within another function definition.

2. Some authors use the term *access link* for the nesting link; others use the term *static link*. The first seems too vague (every link accesses something), the second just misleading (the link itself is decidedly not static, though it points to the most recent activation record for the function within which our function is statically nested).

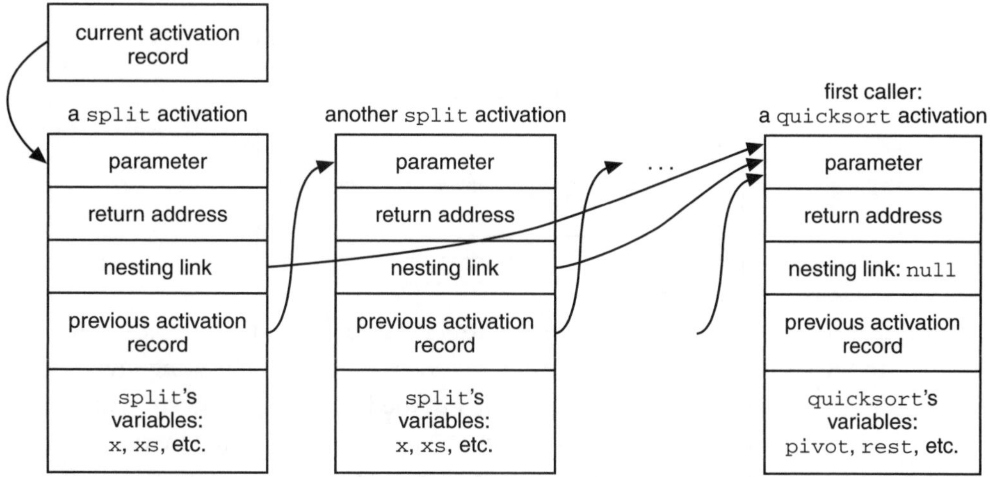

It is not hard to see how the nesting link should be maintained when there is only one simple level of nesting:

- When calling a top-level function like `quicksort`, set the nesting link for the called activation to `null`. (It will not be used.)
- When calling from a top-level function to a nested function, like `quicksort`'s call to `split`, set the nesting link to the address of the caller's activation record.
- When calling from a nested function to a nested function, like `split`'s recursive call, set the nesting link for the called activation the same as the caller's nesting link.

Then, whenever a nested function needs to make a non-local reference, it can use its nesting link to find the right activation record.

Languages that allow nested function definitions at all generally allow them to be nested arbitrarily deep. But such programs can still be handled using nesting links. For example, suppose a program text has function and variable definitions nested as in this diagram:

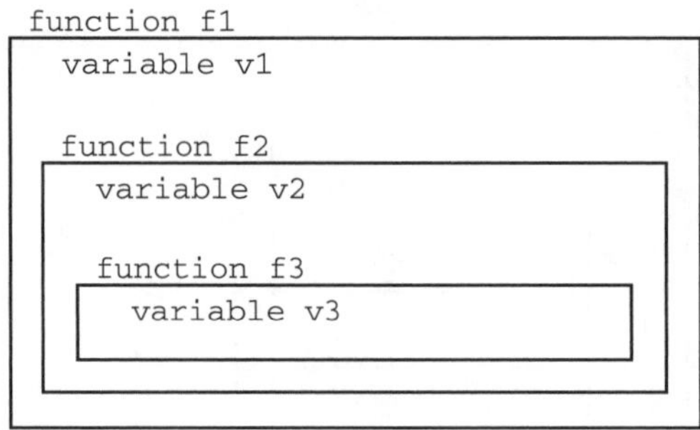

Ordinary local references—`f1` referring to `v1`, `f2` to `v2`, and `f3` to `v3`—are handled in the current activation record. References that are one nesting level away—`f2` referring to `v1` and `f3` to `v2`—are handled by using the nesting link. References that are *two* nesting levels away—`f3` to `v1`—are handled by using the nesting links *twice*. When the current activation record is for `f3`, its nesting link is the address of an activation record for `f2`, and the nesting link from there is the address of an activation record for `f1`, which contains the variable `v1`. In general, references that are *n* nesting levels away can be handled by working back along *n* nesting links.

When functions are nested more than one level deep, a more complete set of rules is needed to say how the nesting link should be set when a call is made. Suppose a function nested *n* levels deep calls one nested *m* levels deep. How should the new activation record's nesting link be initialized? It is an interesting exercise (Exercise 2, at the end of this chapter) to work out all the possibilities.

Consider what is known about the program at compile time. The compiler knows how each activation record will be laid out, so it knows the offset of each variable into its activation record. The compiler also knows the nesting depth of each function definition, so it knows how many nesting levels away each reference is from the variable. Thus we know statically how many nesting links back to travel, and we know statically where within the activation record the variable will be. But we do not know the actual addresses, the values of those nesting links, until runtime.

Although a language may officially allow nesting to be arbitrarily deep, it is not uncommon to find that language implementations impose their own restrictions on nesting depth. One almost never sees programs with function definitions nested more than three levels deep. If a compiler just gives up on programs that are nested more than, say, 10 levels deep, no customer may ever observe this defect.[3]

The solution shown, using nesting links in the activation records, is not the only solution to this problem. Another variation on this solution is to keep all the nesting links in a single static array called a *display*. A third, very different approach, called *lambda lifting*, solves the problem by passing each function all the variables it needs for non-local references as extra, hidden parameters.

By implementing nesting links, we can handle languages that allow non-local references from nested function definitions. But the chapter cannot end here. We need still another trick for languages that allow functions to be passed as parameters.

12.7 Functions as Parameters

Many languages allow functions to be passed as parameters to other functions. Chapter 9 showed the usefulness of this in ML. When a function `f` is passed as a parameter to a function `g`, the implementation of `f` must be passed so that `g` can call it. This part of the problem is straightforward: pass the source code for `f`, the compiled code for `f`, or whatever the implementation requires when calling a function. But it turns out that just passing the implementation of `f` is not enough—at least not for ML and languages like it. Here is a simple ML example that illustrates the problem:

```
fun addXToAll (x,theList) =
  let
    fun addX y =
      y + x;
  in
    map addX theList
  end;
```

This function takes a number `x` and a list `theList` as parameters and returns a new list that is like `theList` but with `x` added to every element. For example, evaluating `addXToAll (1,[1,2,3])` gets the list `[2,3,4]`. The function works

3. There are, however, many anecdotes about language-system disasters caused by the assumption that programs are written by sensible people. Of course, not all programmers are sensible, and not all are people. One must always consider the possibility that the program was written by an automatic tool, like a language translator, that has no particular preference for good style. Ten levels of nesting depth may be enough for any sensible person, but that doesn't mean the language system can safely rest there.

by creating a function `addX` that knows how to add the given `x` to a number. Then it applies that function to every element of the list using `map`.

You can see that the `addX` function has a non-local reference. It uses the variable `x`, which is in the activation record of `addXToAll`. So `addX` really will need a correct nesting link when it runs. But how can it get that link? `addXToAll` calls `map` passing `addX` as a parameter. It is `map` that will eventually call `addX`. Since `map` is a top-level function and `addX` is a nested function, the previous rule for initializing the nesting link was this:

- When calling from a top-level function to a nested function, set the nesting link to the address of the caller's activation record.

But that isn't the right thing to do here. The address of the caller's activation record is the right nesting link only if the nested function is actually nested inside the caller. When you have function parameters, this simple rule no longer works. A function can call any function it received as a parameter. That callee might be nested in some function other than the caller, as `addX` is.

To pass a function as a parameter in ML, or in any other language that allows nested functions with non-local references, you need to pass both the implementation and the nesting link to use when calling it. In fact, the language system must always keep the implementation and the corresponding nesting link together. In languages like ML, function values appear in many places, not just as parameters, but as the values of expressions, the values of local variables, and the values returned from functions. Wherever a function value appears, you may need both the implementation and the nesting link to use with it.

This illustration shows what is in memory for the `addXToAll` example, just before the `map` function is called:

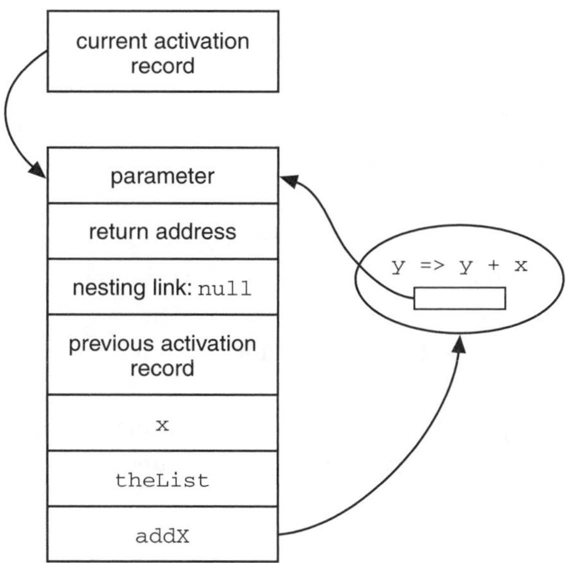

Recall from Chapter 9 that the function definition `fun addX y = y + x` simply defines a variable `addX` whose value is the function—exactly the same as if we had written the definition using a match, as `val addX = y => y + x`. The illustration shows the value of `addX` as the match `y => y + x`, but also shows the nesting link that goes with it. Now when we want to pass `addX` as a parameter, we can treat it just like any other variable. Its value includes the nesting link to use when calling it.

For a contrast, it is instructive to see how this is done in a lower-level language. In C, for example, a `quicksort` function that takes a comparison function as a parameter is declared this way:

```
void quicksort(void *list[], int (*lt)(void *, void *));
```

This declares a function called `quicksort` whose first parameter `list` is an array of addresses of the items to be sorted and whose second parameter `lt` is the *address of* a suitable comparison function. The C language does not allow you to pass a function as a parameter, but it allows you to pass the address of a function. In C this important distinction is very visible to the programmer. If `lt` were a function, you would write `lt(i1,i2)` in the usual way to call it with the parameters `i1` and `i2`. But since `lt` is the address of a function, you must write `(*lt)(i1,i2)`. (The expression `(*lt)` performs an operation called *dereferencing*. It says, in effect, "take the thing to which `lt` points.") No nesting link is required since functions cannot be nested in C.

12.8 Long-Lived Functions

There is one final complication to consider: some languages allow function values to persist after the function that created them has returned. That has not happened in any of the examples so far. `quicksort` creates a `split` function and uses it internally, but there is no way for that `split` to be used outside of `quicksort`—no way for it to be used after `quicksort` returns. The `addXToAll` function creates an `addX` function and passes it to another function, but again there is no way for that `addX` function to be used after `addXToAll` returns.

The following example, by contrast, shows how function values in ML may persist after the function that created them has returned.

```
fun funToAddX x =
  let
    fun addX y =
      y + x;
  in
    addX
  end;
```

This example creates a function `addX`, just as `addXToAll` did, but then returns that function to the caller. The value of `funToAddX 3`, for example, would be a function that adds 3 to any parameter. That means that this `test` function should always return the value 8:

```
fun test =
  let
    val f = funToAddX 3;
  in
    f 5
  end;
```

When `test` is run, it calls `funToAddX`, passing it the value 3. This illustration shows the contents of memory just before `funToAddX` returns. The local variable `f` in `test` does not yet have a value.

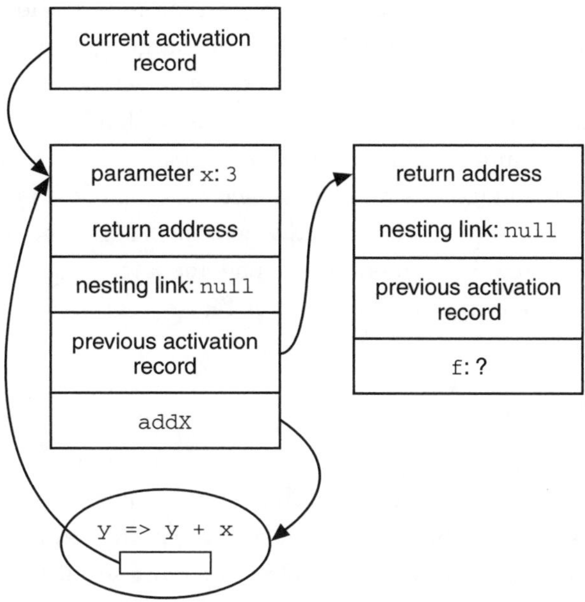

Now funToAddX returns its addX value, which becomes the value of f in test. That leaves this picture:

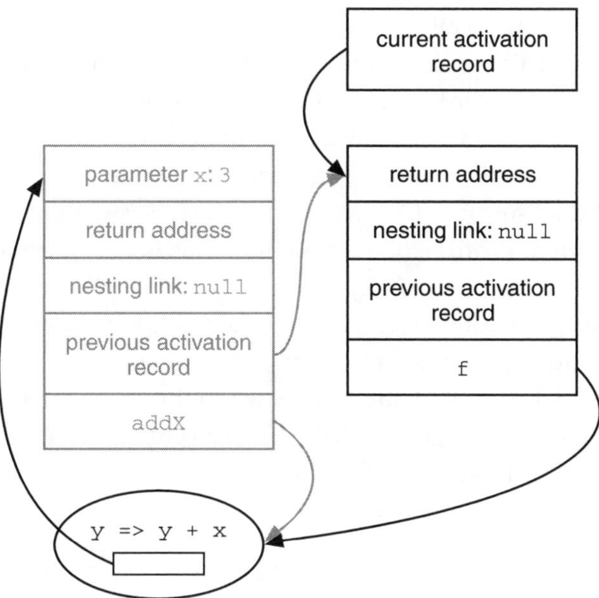

Now you can see the problem. When `test` calls `f`, `f` uses its nesting link to find the value of `x`. But that `x` is in an activation record for an activation of `funToAddX` that has already returned. To handle this situation, language implementations for languages like ML cannot just deallocate and reuse an activation record as soon as the activation returns. An activation record may be needed long after the function has returned. In this example, it can be reused as soon as `test` returns to its caller. But in general, activation records may be needed indefinitely. The memory space for an activation record can only be reused when the program no longer has any active links to it. This requires a memory-management technique called *garbage collection*, which will be introduced in Chapter 14.

12.9 Conclusion

This chapter looked at the problem of binding variables to memory locations. You saw how this depends on the lifetimes of the variables. For static variables, static allocation is an easy answer. But it is not always so easy to handle the activation records that hold activation-specific variables. The more sophisticated the language, the more difficult this binding problem.

- For languages that do not allow more than one activation of a function to be alive at once, you can allocate activation records statically. This works for older Fortran and Cobol implementations, which did not support recursion.
- For languages that do allow more than one activation of a function to be alive at once, you can allocate activation records dynamically. The natural behavior of function calls and returns produces a stack of activation records. A new activation record is pushed when a function is called and popped when it returns. This works for the C language.
- Languages that allow non-local references from nested function definitions need additional support. One way to handle this is with an additional field in the activation record—the nesting link. This is necessary for Pascal, Ada, and ML.
- For languages that allow references into activation records for activations that have returned, you need to be aware that activation records cannot necessarily be deallocated and reused when they are popped off the stack. This happens in languages like ML, when a function value persists after the function that created it has returned.

Exercises

Exercise 1 Continuing the example of the `test` function on page 202, draw the activation records and links that show the situation when function `f` has been called and is about to return to its caller (`test`).

Exercise 2 Consider a block-structured language implemented using nesting links. Suppose a function nested n levels deep makes a legitimate reference to a local variable of a function nested m levels deep. Describe exactly how to find the variable at runtime. *Hint:* You do not have to worry about the cases where $m > n$; be sure you explain why not.

Exercise 3 Consider a block-structured language implemented using nesting links. Suppose a function nested n levels deep makes a legal call to one nested m levels deep. How should the new activation record's nesting link be initialized? Describe exactly how to find the correct nesting link for all cases—$m < n$, $m = n$, and $m > n$. *Hint:* You do not have to worry about the cases where $m > n + 1$, but be sure you explain why not.

Exercise 4 Write the shortest ML function you can that would not work correctly if implemented using statically allocated activation records. Explain why it would fail.

Exercise 5 Write the shortest ML function you can that would not work correctly if implemented using simple, stack-allocated activation records (without nesting links). Explain why it would fail.

Exercise 6 Write the shortest ML function you can that would not work correctly if implemented using a dynamically allocated stack of activation records plus nesting links. Explain why it would fail.

Exercise 7 For each of the following ML functions, could the activation record for the function be deallocated as soon as the function returns? Explain why or why not.

a. `fun f x = x + 1;`
b. `fun f x = fn y => x + y;`
c. `fun f x = fn y => y + 1;`
d. `fun f x = map ~ x;`

Exercise 8 Each of the following ML functions contains a function call that passes a function parameter `f`. In each case, will the function `f` use its nesting link when it is called? Explain.

a.
```
fun addone theList =
  let fun f x = x + 1;
  in map f theList
  end;
```

b.
```
fun addall n theList =
  let fun f x = x + n;
  in map f theList
  end;
```

c.
```
fun do123 f =
  map f [1,2,3];
```

Chapter 13
A First Look at Java

13.1 Introduction

This chapter is an introduction to the Java programming language. By the end of the chapter, you should be able to write simple expressions, statements, methods, and class definitions in Java. This chapter also gives an elementary introduction to the object-oriented style of programming.

In this chapter and throughout the book, Java is used to illustrate some of the concepts of object-oriented programming languages and of imperative programming languages in general. Java is a language of considerable and rising popularity, especially for the development of Web-based applications. With all this popularity, a brief reminder may be in order: this book's interest in Java is purely linguistic. It will not cover the large and rapidly growing Java API, which supports (among other things) the creation of active Web pages. It will rarely even create complete Java programs. Nevertheless, if you find that Java appeals to you, this should provide a good starting point for your own further study and experimentation with the language.

This chapter was designed for readers who have not seen an imperative or object-oriented language before.

Perhaps you are not one of them. Perhaps you have already programmed in Java; in C++, which is a similar object-oriented language; or in C, which, although not object oriented, has expressions, statements, and declarations that are quite similar to Java's. Perhaps you have programmed in some other imperative language, like Fortran, Ada, Pascal, or Cobol. In that case, you will probably still recognize more in Java than in ML or Prolog. Of the three core languages of this book, Java is the one most likely to be familiar to you already. Even if you are familiar with it, you are encouraged to read this chapter anyway. Try looking at imperative programming and object-oriented programming with the eyes of a beginner. It is a good way to deepen your insight.

13.2 Thinking about Objects

Java is an object-oriented language. Chapter 16 will investigate more methodically what it means for a language to be *object oriented*. For now, here is an example to illustrate the style of programming that object-oriented languages are designed to support.

Suppose we want the computer to do something with colored points on the screen. We might start by asking two questions: What data goes into making a colored point on the screen? What should a colored point be able to do? For this example, let's answer the first question by saying that a colored point on the screen has a position (that is, x and y coordinates) and a color. And let's answer the second question by saying that a colored point on the screen should be able to move itself and should be able to report its position.

Now imagine that we have a bunch of these points. Each one has its own x and y coordinates and color, and each one knows how to move itself and how to report its position.

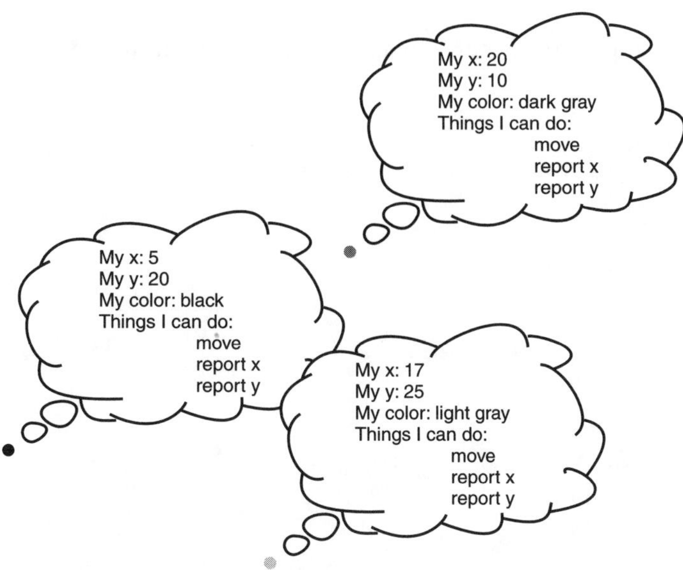

There is Java terminology for many of the things in this example:

- *Object*—Each of the colored points in the picture is an object. Each object has its own data—its own position and color—not shared with the other points.
- *Field*—Each object includes three fields: an x coordinate, a y coordinate, and a color.
- *Method*—The things that the objects know how to do are called the methods of the objects. The points all know how to move themselves and how to report their positions.
- *Instance* of a *class*—The points may be different, but they have a lot in common. They are all points, after all. They all contain three fields (not the same data, but the same kinds of data), and they have the same methods. In Java, they are all instances of the same class.

This example illustrates an object-oriented way of thinking about programming problems. You may have noticed the almost anthropomorphic descriptions of the actions a point might take: "a colored point on the screen should be able to move itself." That is the object-oriented point of view. In object-oriented programming, programs are designed using objects—little bundles of data that know how to do things to themselves. We don't say, "the computer knows how to move the point." Instead we say, "the point knows how to move itself." That makes all the difference.

Object-oriented languages, like Java, are designed to make this way of thinking easier.

Here is a quick preview, a bare-bones Java definition of the `Point` class:

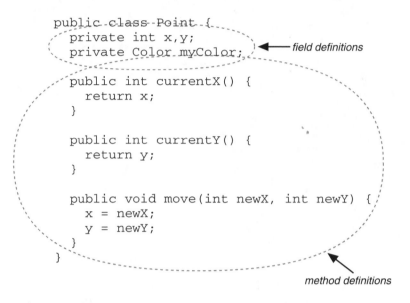

```
public class Point {
  private int x,y;
  private Color myColor;

  public int currentX() {
    return x;
  }

  public int currentY() {
    return y;
  }

  public void move(int newX, int newY) {
    x = newX;
    y = newY;
  }
}
```


13.3 Simple Expressions and Statements

We will return to Java class definitions later. We will start with the simplest constructs: expressions and statements.

Constants and Types

The primitive types of Java that you will be using are `int`, `char`, `double`, `boolean`, `void`, and `null`. (The other primitive types—`byte`, `short`, `long`, and `float`—are just specialized sizes of numbers and would not add anything to the discussion.) As was shown in Chapter 6, the Java specification says exactly what the primitive types are. Unlike many other languages, it does not leave anything about the meaning of these types up to the implementation.

The `int` type is the set of 32-bit, twos-complement binary numbers—that is, the set of integers in the range from -2^{31} to $2^{31}-1$. Constants of type `int` are written in the usual way (using `-`, not `~`, for negation).

Constants of type `char` are written as characters with single quotes around them, like `'a'`. For unusual `char` values, Java supports the same kind of escape sequences that ML and C do; for example, `'\t'` for a tab, `'\n'` for a linefeed, or

`'\''` for the single quote character. In Java, as in all the C-family languages, `char` is an integral type. You can assign an integer value to a `char` variable or use a `char` constant as an integer in an expression, such as `'a'+1`. Not that you would, necessarily. Most Java programs ignore the integral nature of `char` and treat it as a distinct type, as it is in ML. The `char` type is the set of 16-bit, unsigned binary numbers—that is, the set of integers in the range from 0 to 2^{16}-1. To interpret those integral `char` values as written characters, Java uses the Unicode character set. This is unusual. Most languages leave the character set unspecified or specify the ASCII character set. Unicode is a much larger character set than ASCII. It tries to provide all the characters used in written texts in all the world's languages.

The `double` type is used to represent real numbers. It is the set of double-precision, 64-bit, floating-point numbers as defined by IEEE standard 754. For `double` constants, Java uses either standard decimal notation or scientific notation using `e` or `E` before the exponent. As in ML, when you use scientific notation, you do not get an integer, even if the value has no fractional part. `1e2` evaluates to the `double` number 100.0, not the `int` 100.

The `boolean` type includes only the constants `true` and `false`. Like ML, Java is case sensitive, so you cannot write `True` or `TRUE` to mean `true`. The `void` type is the empty set—there are no values of type `void`. It is used as the return type for methods that do not actually return a value. The `null` type contains only one value—the special constant `null`. You cannot declare a variable to have type `null`, so Java programmers are often unaware of this type. But the special constant `null` has to have some type, and it doesn't fit anywhere else. The `null` constant is a special value that can be assigned to any variable of any *reference type*. (In this, Java differs from C and C++, which make the integer 0, assigned to a pointer, serve a similar purpose.)

In Java, any value that is not of a primitive type is a reference to an object. The types of such values are constructed and are called *reference types*. There are three kinds of reference types:

- Any class name, like the `Point` class, is a reference type. Obviously, this type includes all references to `Point` objects. Less obviously, it includes references to all objects of subclasses of the `Point` class, which Chapter 15 will discuss further.
- Any *interface* name is a reference type. There will be more about interfaces in Chapter 15.
- Any array type is a reference type. For example, the type for an array of `int` values would be `int[]`; the type for a two-dimensional array of references

to `Point` objects would be `Point[][]`. Chapter 14 will discuss arrays further.

Unlike ML, Java has no primitive type for strings. Instead, it has an important predefined class called `String`. An object of the `String` class contains a string of `char` values. A string of characters enclosed in double quotes is a string constant, much as in ML. But in Java it would be more accurate to say that a string of characters enclosed in double quotes is as an instance of the `String` class, containing the given string of characters. For example, `"Hello there"` is really an object like this:

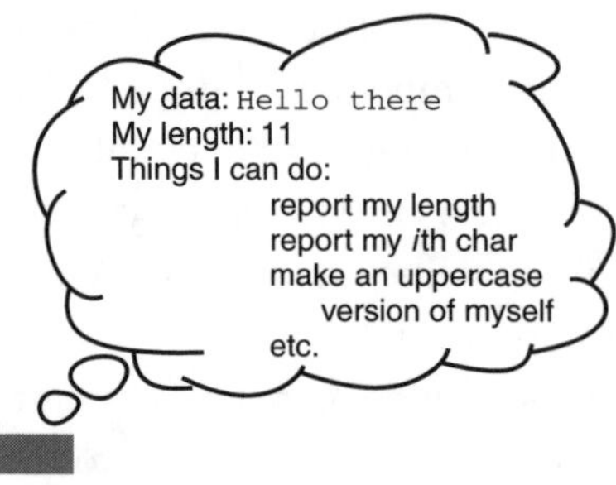

Operators for Integer Arithmetic

Java has the usual binary arithmetic operators `+`, `-`, `*`, and `/`. On integers, the `/` operator does integer division (like the ML `div` operator), discarding any remainder. The operator `%` gets the integer remainder, like the ML `mod` operator. The `-` operator can also be used as a unary operator, for negation. (The `+` operator can also be used as a unary operator, but it is not particularly useful in that capacity.)

Java Expression	Value
`1+2*3`	`7`
`15/7`	`2`
`15%7`	`1`
`-(5*5)`	`-25`

Operators for Real Arithmetic

The binary arithmetic operators `+`, `-`, `*`, and `/` are overloaded for real arithmetic on operands of type `double`. The `-` operator is overloaded for unary negation of a `double` operand.

Java Expression	Value
`13.0*2.0`	`26.0`
`15.0/7.0`	`2.142857142857143`

Concatenation of Strings

Other classes are treated uniformly by Java, but the `String` class has a special relationship with the language. One example of this, which you have already seen, is the syntax for `String` constants. No other objects can be created so easily. Creating an object normally requires a special expression using the keyword `new`, which you will see below. Another aspect of the special treatment for the `String` class is that the binary operator `+` has special overloading and coercion behavior for the class `String`.

The `+` operator concatenates two `String` values. More generally, the `+` operator means concatenation when *either* of the operands is a `String`. If one operand is a `String` and the other is not, the non-string operand is coerced to a `String` before concatenation. The Java language system knows how to coerce any primitive-type value to a `String`; the `int` value `123` becomes `"123"`, `null` becomes `"null"`, and so on. The language system can also coerce any reference-type value to a `String`. It just asks the object in question to produce a `String` version of itself by calling the `toString` method of that object. (Every object inherits a `toString` method from the `Object` class, though many objects implement their own `toString` method instead. Chapter 15 discusses inheritance further.) In short, whenever either operand is a `String`, the `+` operator produces a concatenated `String` value.

Java Expression	Value
`"123"+"456"`	`"123456"`
`"The answer is " + 4`	`"The answer is 4"`
`"" + (1.0/3.0)`	`"0.3333333333333333"`
`1+"2"`	`"12"`
`"1"+2+3`	`"123"`
`1+2+"3"`	`"33"`

In the last example, the left-associativity of the `+` operator causes the subexpression `1+2` to be evaluated first. Since neither of the operands is a `String`, the result is the `int` value `3` rather than the `String` value `"12"`. Concatenating the string `"3"` onto that produces the final result, `"33"`.

Comparison Operators

Java has the usual ordering comparison operators: `<`, `<=`, `>=`, and `>`. These can be used on values of any numeric type. The equality comparisons, `==` and `!=`, can be used on values of any type. (Unlike ML, the `double` type is not excluded.)

Java Expression	Value
`1<=2`	`true`
`1==2`	`false`
`true!=false`	`true`

For the `==` and `!=` comparisons, two references are considered to be equal if and only if they refer to the same object. Even if two different objects contain exactly the same data, they are still not equal in the sense of `==` since they are not the same object. For example, if `a` and `b` are references to two different `String` objects, then `a==b` is automatically false—even if both objects contain the string `"Hello there"`. To compare the *contents* of `String` objects for equality, you would use the `equals` method, which is described below.

Boolean Operators

The binary operators `&&` and `||` behave like ML's `andalso` and `orelse`. They are short-circuiting operators that work only on operands of type `boolean`. The unary operator `!` complements a `boolean` operand, like ML's `not` operator. Conditional expressions have a terse syntax; the Java expression `a ? b : c` is equivalent to ML's `if a then b else c`.

<table>
<tr><th>Java Expression</th><th>Value</th></tr>
<tr><td><code>1<=2 && 2<=3</code></td><td><code>true</code></td></tr>
<tr><td><code>1<2 || 1>2</code></td><td><code>true</code></td></tr>
<tr><td><code>1<2 ? 3 : 4</code></td><td><code>3</code></td></tr>
</table>

Operators with Side Effects

When an operator changes something in the environment, like the value of a variable or the contents of an array, that change is called a *side effect*. An operator that has no side effects is called *pure*. All our ML operators were pure, of course, since we looked at only the functional part of ML. But Java is not a functional language; it is an imperative (and object-oriented) language. Some of Java's most important operators have side effects. The most important one is the assignment operator.

Java Expression	Side Effect
`a=b`	Changes the value of `a`, making it equal to `b`

The equal sign takes on many different meanings in different languages. In mathematical notation, `a=b` is an assertion; in English it might read, "`a` *is equal to* `b`." In ML it is used as an equality test; in English it might read, *"Is it true that* `a` *is equal to* `b`*, or is it false?"* In Java it is used as a command; in English it might read, "*Change* `a` *to make it equal to* `b`." (There will be yet another meaning in Prolog!)

Some things can be assigned to, and others cannot. This may seem obvious; clearly, `a=1` makes sense while `1=a` does not. But consider this more deeply for a moment. What kinds of things can appear on the right-hand side of an assignment expression, and what kinds of things can appear on the left?

Almost all Java expressions have a value and can appear on the right-hand side of an assignment expression. The only exception is a call of a method that returns `void`. A variable like `a` has a value; a constant like `1` has a value; an expression like `a+1` has a value. Anything with a value can appear on the right-hand side of an assignment expression.

The left-hand side is more restricted. To appear on the left-hand side, an expression must have a *memory location*—a place in memory where a value can be stored. A variable like `a` has a memory location; a constant like `1` does not; an expression like `a+1` does not. Anything with a memory location can appear on the left-hand side of an assignment expression. In Java, this includes local variables, parameters, array components, and fields.

Notice that these assignable things can actually appear on either side of an assignment operator, since they have both a value and a memory location. When you write `a` on the left-hand side of an assignment operator, you mean `a`'s memory location. When you write `a` on the right-hand side, you mean `a`'s value. In Java, as in most imperative languages, the context makes it clear which of these two attributes is signified. These two attributes are sometimes called the *lvalue* and the *rvalue*—lvalues are assignable memory locations, as on the *left* side of an assignment statement, and rvalues are values, as on the *right* side.

Like Java, most languages rely on context to distinguish between lvalues and rvalues, but there are a few exceptions. One is Bliss, in which an assignment statement would look like `x := .y`. The variable `y` by itself always means `y`'s location in memory. The `.` operator must be used to explicitly *dereference* that location, fetching the value currently stored there. ML is another such language. We saw only ML's functional part, but ML also supports some imperative constructs. In ML, the type `int ref` is the type for alterable memory locations containing integers, and the `!` operator is used for dereferencing. If `x` and `y` are both of type `int ref`, you could write `x := !y`.

Anyway, back to Java. The assignment operator must have an lvalue as its first operand, and it has the side effect of changing the value stored in that location. After you store a value in a variable, it holds that value until you store something else there. If you assign to a variable more than once, which is how programs generally use variables, the variable always holds the value you assigned most recently.

Java supports shortened ways of writing expressions with side effects: compound assignment operators and the increment and decrement operators. First, here are *compound assignment* operators:

Long Java Expression	Short Java Expression
`a=a+b`	`a+=b`
`a=a-b`	`a-=b`
`a=a*b`	`a*=b`

Java has compound assignment operators for many of the pure binary operators, including `+=`, `-=`, `*=`, `/=`, and `%=`. There are even shorter ways of handling the common case of adding one to a variable (*incrementing* it) or subtracting one from a variable (*decrementing* it). These are the *increment* and *decrement* operators shown below.

Long Java Expression	Short Java Expression
`a=a+1`	`++a`
`a=a-1`	`--a`

An expression with side effects is not just a command; it has a value, just like expressions using pure operators. That value may be used as part of a larger expression. Consider the expression `a+(b=c)`. It makes no sense at all mathematically, but in Java it is legal and even useful. The subexpression `(b=c)` has the side effect of changing the value of `b`, making it equal to `c`. The subexpression `(b=c)` also has a value—the value that gets assigned to `b`—and that value is used as the second operand for the addition.

For simple assignments and compound assignments, the value of an expression is the value that is assigned, as these examples demonstrate:

Java Expression	Value	Side Effect
`a+(x=b)+c`	The sum of `a`, `b`, and `c`	Changes the value of `x`, making it equal to `b`
`(a=d)+(b=d)+(c=d)`	Three times the value of `d`	Changes the values of `a`, `b`, and `c`, making them all equal to `d`
`a=b=c`	The value of `c`	Changes the values of `a` and `b`, making them equal to `c`

In the third example above, you can see that the assignment operator is right associative; `a=b=c` is equivalent to `a=(b=c)`. (If it were left-associative, `a=b=c` would be illegal, since `a=b` does not have an lvalue.)

Although expressions with side effects do have values like pure expressions, good programmers usually resist the urge to take advantage of this. Of the three examples above, only the last, `a=b=c`, is the sort of thing you might actually want to write as part of a Java program. The others are perfectly legal and their behaviors are well-defined, but they are hard for people to read.

For the increment and decrement operators, the value of an expression depends on whether the operator is before or after the variable:

Java Expression	Value	Side Effect
`a++`	The old value of `a`	Adds one to `a`
`++a`	The new value of `a`	Adds one to `a`
`a--`	The old value of `a`	Subtracts one from `a`
`--a`	The new value of `a`	Subtracts one from `a`

When the increment or decrement operator is placed before a variable, as in `++a` or `--a`, it is called a *pre-increment* or *pre-decrement*. It changes the variable first, then takes the value of the result. When the increment or decrement operator is placed after a variable, as in `a++` or `a--`, it is called a *post-increment* or *post-decrement*. It takes the value of the variable first, then makes the change.

When you speak a foreign language it is very hard to sound like a native speaker. Even if you start with a reasonable idea, express it grammatically, and pronounce it perfectly, you may not have chosen the way of expressing that idea that a native speaker would have chosen. Native speakers speak *idiomatically*, following conventions that are not captured in dictionary definitions and rules of grammar. This is true of programming languages too. In Java there are usually several different ways to say the same thing. For example, you have seen several different ways to change a variable by adding one to it. If you are interested only in the side effect, any one of these can be used:

Java Expression	Side Effect
`a=a+1`	Changes the value of `a`, making it greater by 1
`a+=1`	Changes the value of `a`, making it greater by 1
`a++`	Changes the value of `a`, making it greater by 1
`++a`	Changes the value of `a`, making it greater by 1

All are correct, but if you use the first expression you will give yourself away as a non-native Java speaker. Fluent Java programmers prefer the shorter forms. You will need to understand them if you want to be able to read other people's Java code.

Method Calls

A Java method call is much like a function call in other languages. It takes a list of zero or more parameters and can return a single value. Here are some examples using instance methods of the `String` class, assuming that `s` and `r` are references to `String` objects.

Java Expression	Value
`s.length()`	The length of the `String s`
`s.equals(r)`	`true` if `s` and `r` are equal, `false` otherwise
`r.equals(s)`	`true` if `s` and `r` are equal, `false` otherwise
`r.toUpperCase()`	A `String` object that is an uppercase version of the `String r`
`r.charAt(3)`	The `char` value in position 3 in the `String r` (that is, the fourth character, since the first character is at position 0)
`r.toUpperCase().charAt(3)`	The `char` value in position 3 in the uppercase version of the `String r`

These are all examples of calls to *instance methods*. Instance methods require an object to operate on. As you can see, the reference to the object on which an instance method operates is not passed as an explicit parameter. In a call of an instance method, the reference to the object comes first, followed by a period, followed by the method name, and finally followed by the list of zero or more parameters enclosed in parentheses:

<method-call> `::=` *<reference-expression>*`.`*<method-name>*`(`*<parameter-list>*`)`

Of course, the method has to know what object it is acting on, so the reference is somehow passed to the method. Java takes care of that behind the scenes. In a non-object-oriented language, you might have a freestanding `length` function, and you would get the length of a string `s` using the function call `length(s)`. In Java, the `String` class has a `length` method, and if `s` is a reference to a `String`, you get its length using the method call `s.length()`.

Some Java methods do not require a particular object to operate on. These are called *class methods*. For example, the `String` class has a number of methods called `valueOf`, which construct strings from other types:

Java Expression	**Value**
`String.valueOf(1==2)`	`"false"`
`String.valueOf(5*5)`	`"25"`
`String.valueOf(1.0/3.0)`	`"0.3333333333333333"`

A call of a class method looks like a call of an instance method, except with the class name in place of a reference to an object of that class:

<method-call> `::=` *<class-name>*`.`*<method-name>*`(`*<parameter-list>*`)`

Actually, you *can* use a reference to call a class method, if you happen to have an object of that class around. For example, if `s` is a reference to a `String`, you can write `s.valueOf(1==2)`. But that is not usually a good way to express it, since `s` is not really involved in the computation. Class methods do not operate on an existing object of the class. In fact, there really isn't anything object oriented about class methods; the class just functions as a labeled namespace, as was shown in Chapter 10. By writing `String.valueOf`, you specify which `valueOf` method you are talking about—not `Date.valueOf`, nor `Time.valueOf`, nor `BigInteger.valueOf`, nor any of the other predefined methods named `valueOf`.

The previous example shows that Java allows methods to be overloaded; `String.valueOf` has more than one type. There can be many methods in a class with the same name, provided that they take different types of parameters.

You have seen how to call instance methods and how to call class methods. There is also a way to abbreviate these method calls, if the caller and the called method are in the same class:

<method-call> `::=` *<method-name>* `(`*<parameter-list>*`)`

For example, if another instance method of the `String` class wants the fourth character of the string, it can express the method call as `charAt(3)`, rather than *x*`.charAt(3)`. When the abbreviated form is used, it is understood that the called method will operate on the same instance as the caller. (It follows that the caller must be an instance method, not a class method, since class methods do not have an instance to operate on.) Similarly, if any method of the `String` class wants to call `String.valueOf(1==2)`, it can abbreviate it as `valueOf(1==2)`. Here again, the class functions merely as a labeled namespace.

Object Creation Expressions

<creation-expression> `::=` `new` *<class-name>* `(`*<parameter-list>*`)`

The keyword `new` is used to create a new object—a new instance of a class. When a new object is created, a special kind of instance method called a *constructor* is called to initialize it. Just like an instance method, a constructor expects a list of zero or more parameters. A class definition ordinarily includes definitions of one or more of these constructors. Here are some object creation expressions that use the constructors of the `String` class:

Java Expression	Value
`new String()`	A new `String` of length zero
`new String(s)`	A new `String` that contains a copy of `String s`
`new String(chars)`	A new `String` that contains the `char` values from the `chars` array

In some languages, allocated memory stays allocated until the program explicitly deallocates it. In C++, for every use of `new`, there must eventually be a corresponding use of `delete` to free up the allocated memory. But Java (like ML) uses garbage collection to reclaim allocated memory. A program does not have to take explicit steps to announce to the language system that it is finished with an object. When the language system sees that the program no longer has any references to the object, it cleans up the object automatically. Chapter 14 will discuss garbage collection further.

Associativity, Precedence, Coercion, and All That

All Java operators are left associative, except for the assignment operators, as was already noted. The operators of Java are grouped into 15 precedence levels, but the details are not important here. Some of the precedence orderings are obvious (`*` has higher precedence than `+`) and others less obvious (`<` has higher precedence than `!=`). In general, unless the orderings are obvious, it is a good plan to use parentheses rather than rely on precedence. It makes your code more readable.

Unlike ML, Java performs coercions. It takes many pages of the Java language specification to define exactly how coercion works. Java coerces `null` to any reference type; if `x` is a reference variable, you can always use the expression `x=null`. It coerces any value to type `String` for concatenation, as was already discussed. It coerces one reference type to another under certain circumstances—Chapter 15 will have more about that kind of coercion.

Java also coerces in numeric expressions. It coerces `char` values to `int` before applying any operator. In binary expressions containing a mixture of `int` and `double` values, Java coerces the `int` to `double` before applying the binary operator.

Java Expression	Value
`'a'+'b'`	`195`
`1/3`	`0`
`1/3.0`	`0.3333333333333333`
`1/2+0.0`	`0.0`
`1/(2+0.0)`	`0.5`

Chapter 8 showed that there can be tricky interactions between coercion and overloading. Java supports both, and that is part of what makes it so difficult to give an exact definition of Java coercion. But for the simple examples you will be working with, you should not encounter any problems of that kind.

Expression Statements

<expression-statement> `::=` *<expression>* `;`

A statement in Java is a phrase that gives a command. Unlike an expression, it has no value; it is executed only for its side effects. Statements are the heart of any imperative language. In Java, every method consists of a sequence of statements (actually, a *compound statement,* which you will see more about in a moment).

The simplest kind of Java statement is an expression statement. Just write a semicolon after an expression and you have a statement. The value of the expression is discarded, so only its side effect is important. Unlike C and C++, Java requires that the *<expression>* be something that could actually have a side effect. It must be an expression using one of the operators with side effects, a method call, or an object creation expression. Java does not, for example, allow `x==y;` as a statement, although C does.

Java Statement	Equivalent Command in English
`speed = 0;`	Store a 0 in `speed`.
`a++;`	Increase the value of `a` by 1.
`inTheRed = cost > balance;`	If `cost` is greater than `balance`, set `inTheRed` to `true`. Otherwise set it to `false`.

Compound Statements

```
<compound-statement> ::= { <statement-list> }
<statement-list> ::= <statement> <statement-list> | <empty>
```

A compound statement consists of an opening brace, followed by any number of statements, followed by a closing brace. In the most common case, the statements inside the compound statement are expression statements. As you saw in the last section, expression statements all end with a semicolon. So you would get something that looks like this:

```
{
  expression;
  expression;
  ...
  expression;
}
```

But that is only one possibility. Each statement inside a compound statement may be any Java statement, and not all Java statements end with a semicolon.

A compound statement is a command to do the component statements in the order given. Here is the idea behind the compound statement: there are many places in the syntax of Java where only one statement is allowed. You will often find that you want to squeeze several statements into the place of one. No problem: that one statement can be a compound statement, which always lets you fit in as many statements as necessary. It is like being granted one wish and using that one to wish for more wishes.

Java Statement	Equivalent Command in English
`{ a = 0; b = 1; }`	Store a 0 in `a`, then store a 1 in `b`.
`{ a++; b++; c++; }`	Increment `a`, then increment `b`, and then increment `c`.
`{ }`	Do nothing.

A compound statement in Java also serves as a block for scoping. Definitions of new local variables within a compound statement are made by *declaration statements*.

Declaration Statements

<declaration-statement> ::= *<declaration>* ;
<declaration> ::= *<type>* *<variable-name>*
| *<type>* *<variable-name>* = *<expression>*

A declaration statement introduces a local variable. The new variable may be assigned an initial value as part of the declaration. Java uses the classic block scope rule for the new definition; its scope extends from the point of definition to the end of the block (usually, the compound statement) in which it is declared.

Java Statement	Equivalent Command in English
`boolean done = false;`	Define a new variable named `done` of type `boolean`, and initialize it to `false`.
`Point p;`	Define a new variable named `p` of type `Point`. (Do not initialize it.)
`{ int temp = a; a = b; b = temp; }`	Swap the values of the integer variables `a` and `b`.

The same *<declaration>* syntax is also used in class definitions for declaring the fields of a class.

The `if` Statement

<if-statement> `::=` `if (`*<expression>*`)` *<statement>*
  `|` `if (`*<expression>*`)` *<statement>* `else` *<statement>*

The *<expression>* may be any boolean-valued expression. The `else` part is optional. The parentheses are *not* optional. Note that the fragment of grammar shown above has the dangling-else ambiguity. This is resolved in the usual way, as was discussed in Chapter 3.

The `if` statement is a command to evaluate the expression and, if that value is true, carry out the first statement. The second form also gives an alternative statement, to be carried out if the value is false.

Java Statement	Equivalent Command in English
`if (i > 0) i--;`	Decrement `i`, but only if it is greater than zero.
`if (a < b) b -= a;` `else a -= b;`	Subtract the smaller of `a` or `b` from the larger.

`if (reset) {`
`  a = b = 0;`
`  reset = false;`
`}`
	If `reset` is `true`, zero out `a` and `b` and then set `reset` to `false`.

The `while` Statement

<while-statement> `::=` `while (`*<expression>*`)` *<statement>*

The *<expression>* may be any boolean-valued expression. The `while` statement evaluates the *<expression>*. If that value is false, nothing else happens; the *<statement>* is not executed. If that value is true, the *<statement>* is executed. Then the whole thing repeats. The value of the *<expression>* is retested, and the while loop continues until the *<expression>* finally becomes false.

Java Statement	Equivalent Command in English
`while (a < 100) a += 5;`	As long as `a` is less than 100, keep adding 5 to `a`.

`while (a != b)`
  `if (a < b) b -= a;`
  `else a -= b;`
	Subtract the smaller of `a` or `b` from the larger. Continue to do this until `a` and `b` are equal. (This is Euclid's algorithm for finding the greatest common denominator, GCD, of two positive integers. The resulting value of `a` and `b` is the GCD of the original values.)

`while (time > 0) {`
  `simulate();`
  `time--;`
`}`
	As long as `time` is greater than zero, call the `simulate` method of the current class and then decrement `time`.

`while (true) work();`	Call the `work` method of the current class over and over, forever.

Java has three different kinds of loops, using the keywords `while`, `for`, and `do`. This book will not use `for` and `do` loops. `while` loops are the simplest and are all you need for the exercises in this book.

The `return` Statement

<return-statement> `::=` `return` *<expression>*`;`
`|` `return;`

Methods that can return a value must eventually execute the statement `return` *<expression>*`;`. This statement causes the execution of the body of the method to stop. The method immediately returns the value of the *<expression>* to its caller. The *<expression>* must have the right type—the type that the method declaration says the method returns.

Methods that do not return a value—those with the return type `void`, as you will see below—do not have to execute an explicit `return` statement at all. When the compound statement that forms the method body is finished, such a method returns to its caller automatically. Nevertheless, the statement `return;` (with no *<expression>*) can be used to return immediately to the caller, even if the end of the method body has not yet been reached.

13.4 Class Definitions

Now that you have seen some Java expressions and statements, you can (at last!) get around to writing complete class definitions. Let's start with an example you are already familiar with—a linked list of integers, implemented much like ML's `int list` type.

```
/**
 * A ConsCell is an element in a linked list of
 * ints.
 */
public class ConsCell {
  private int head; // the first item in the list
  private ConsCell tail; // rest of the list or null

  /**
   * Construct a new ConsCell given its head and tail.
   * @param h the int contents of this cell
   * @param t the next ConsCell in the list or null
   */
  public ConsCell(int h, ConsCell t) {
    head = h;
    tail = t;
  }

  /**
   * Accessor for the head of this ConsCell.
   * @return the int contents of this cell
   */
  public int getHead() {
    return head;
  }

  /**
   * Accessor for the tail of this ConsCell.
   * @return the next ConsCell in the list or null
   */
  public ConsCell getTail() {
    return tail;
  }
}
```

This example contains comments. In Java, everything on a line after `//` and everything between `/*` and the following `*/` is taken to be a comment. Comments are largely ignored by the language system.[1]

Everything in the class is defined using one of the access specifiers `public` or `private`, and so is the class itself. A `public` definition is one that can be used from anywhere in the program. A `private` definition can be used only from within the class. For now, follow a simple policy: declare all fields `private` and everything else `public`. In a real Java program you would make more subtle choices, but this simple policy is a pretty good place to start. Objects should behave like little bundles of data that know how to do things to themselves. Other parts of the program should not be able to alter the fields of an object, so they are all `private`. Other parts of the program should be able to ask an object to do things, so its methods are `public`. (Java has two other intermediate levels of accessibility: `protected` and the default *package* access. These interact with more advanced things in Java—packages and inheritance—so they will not be used in this chapter.)

The definition of the `ConsCell` class contains two fields, `head` and `tail`. Notice that the syntax for declaring fields in a class is the same as the syntax you already saw for declaration statements, with the addition of the access specifier (this declaration used `private`).

After the fields in the `ConsCell` definition comes the definition of a constructor for the class. The constructor expects an `int` and a `ConsCell` as parameters. It uses them to initialize the `head` and `tail` fields of the new object. As you can see, a constructor is defined by giving an access specifier (`public` in this case), followed by a repetition of the name of the class (`ConsCell`), followed by the parameter list, followed by a compound statement for the body of the constructor. As already shown, the parameters passed by an object creation expression must match those expected by a constructor. For `ConsCell`, an object creation expression must specify the head and tail for the cell; for example, `new ConsCell(1,null)`.

Notice that the constructor can access the fields of the object under construction by using their simple names, just as if they were local variables. The same is true in the instance methods that follow the constructor, `getHead` and `getTail`. An instance method is defined by giving an access specifier (`public` in this case), followed by the type returned by the method, followed by the method name,

1. There is a simple standard for formatting block comments. A language-system tool called `javadoc` can be used on programs that follow this standard. The `javadoc` tool extracts the block comments from a Java program and generates Web documents from them. This book will not discuss this standard commenting style any further, but it does follow it in block comments. This style has merits even when `javadoc` is not used.

followed by the parameter list, followed by a compound statement for the body of the method. The `getHead` and `getTail` methods are accessors. They do nothing but return the values of fields.

A constructor definition looks like a method definition, *except that a constructor definition has no return type* and its name is the name of the class. Adding a return type to a constructor definition is a sure way to get a confusing error message from the compiler, so be careful!

The `ConsCell` class can almost be used as it stands to implement lists the way ML does (at least lists of integers). Consider this sequence of ML definitions:

```
val a = nil;
val b = 2 :: a;
val c = 1 :: b;
val x = (length a) + (length b) + (length c);
```

To write something like this in Java requires operations equivalent to ML's `::` operator and `length` function. Remember that we cannot write a freestanding function as in ML; whatever functions we write must be methods of some class.

We will look at two different solutions. The first is to implement `length` and `cons` as class methods of the `ConsCell` class. We can add these methods to our class definition for `ConsCell`:

```
/**
 * Get the length of a list of ConsCells.
 * @param a the first ConsCell in the list or null
 * @return the int length
 */
public static int length(ConsCell a) {
  int len = 0;
  while (a != null) {
    len++;
    a = a.getTail();
  }
  return len;
}

/**
 * Return the result of consing an int onto a
 * list of ConsCells.
 * @param a the int to cons onto the list
 * @param b the first ConsCell in the list or null
 * @return the first ConsCell in the new list
 */
public static ConsCell cons(int a, ConsCell b) {
  return new ConsCell(a,b);
}
```

Notice the keyword `static`. This differentiates class-method definitions from instance-method definitions. As class methods, these are like plain ML functions; they operate only on their explicit parameters and have no fields (no `head` or `tail`) to work with. Using these methods, we can imitate the ML sequence of operations pretty closely:

```
ConsCell a = null;
ConsCell b = ConsCell.cons(2,a);
ConsCell c = ConsCell.cons(1,b);
int x = ConsCell.length(a) + ConsCell.length(b)
              + ConsCell.length(c);
```

Unfortunately, this solution is not a good example of an object-oriented style. (Writing a lot of class methods in Java can be a symptom of non-object-oriented thinking.) The `length` and `cons` methods do things to lists passed as parameters. To achieve a more object-oriented style, we should implement these operations as things lists know how to do to themselves. The class method call `ConsCell.length(b)` says, in effect, "compute the length of `b`." We want an instance method call `b.length()` that says, in effect, "ask `b` for its length."

There is just one problem with implementing it that way: we are using `null` to represent the empty list. In this example, we are not going to be able to compute `a`'s length with an expression like `a.length()` because `a` is `null`—there is no object there with methods we can call. That will not do. All the list operations you might want to implement—`length`, `append`, `reverse`, and so on—ought to work on the empty list as well as on non-empty lists.

The solution is to create a separate `IntList` class that uses the `ConsCell` class. Here is an example that includes a `cons` method and a `length` method:

```
/**
 * An IntList is a list of ints.
 */
public class IntList {
  private ConsCell start; // first in the list or null

  /**
   * Construct a new IntList given its first ConsCell.
   * @param s the first ConsCell in the list or null
   */
  public IntList(ConsCell s) {
    start = s;
  }
```

```
    /**
     * Cons the given element h onto us and return the
     * resulting IntList.
     * @param h the head int for the new list
     * @return the IntList with head h and us for a tail
     */
    public IntList cons (int h) {
      return new IntList(new ConsCell(h,start));
    }

    /**
     * Get our length.
     * @return our int length
     */
    public int length() {
      int len = 0;
      ConsCell cell = start;
      while (cell != null) { // while not at end of list
        len++;
        cell = cell.getTail();
      }
      return len;
    }
}
```

Using this class definition, we can match the ML sequence of operations in a more object-oriented style:

```
IntList a = new IntList(null);
IntList b = a.cons(2);
IntList c = b.cons(1);
int x = a.length() + b.length() + c.length();
```

You have now seen two solutions to the problem of implementing ML-style integer lists in Java. The first used class methods heavily and ended up with an implementation much like you would see in an ordinary imperative language. The second solution made heavier use of instance methods. Thinking in terms of objects—little bundles of data that know how to do things to themselves—leads to that kind of implementation. Both implementations were imperative; both cases used assignments and `while` loops, rather than recursion. But the second implementation was more object oriented than the first.

This is a question of style. As you can see, Java does not force you to write in an object-oriented style. It encourages it, certainly. For example, Java does not allow freestanding functions, but forces you to write functions as methods of a class. But you can get around that by implementing a single big class with many class methods. The result would be much like a C program and not object oriented at all. Java also encourages an imperative style. It has many side-effecting expressions and several looping constructs. But you can get around that by avoiding side effects and always using recursion instead of loops. The result would be something like an ML program and not imperative at all. For example, the `length` method for the `IntList` class could have been written in a functional style like this:

```
public int length() {
  if (start == null) return 0;
  else return start.length();
}
```

It uses a `length` method for the `ConsCell` class, which might also have been written in a functional style:

```
public int length() {
  if (tail == null) return 1;
  else return 1 + tail.length();
}
```

The resulting implementation is still object oriented, but is now functional rather than imperative. It would be a good way to compute the length of a list in ML, but in Java it is unnatural. That is not to say that recursion is always unnatural in imperative languages. There are times when a recursive solution works out better, even in Java, and you will see examples in later chapters. But to use recursive functions in place of a simple counting loop in Java is just plain contrary.

13.5 About References and Pointers

The `IntList` class has a field called `start`, which is a reference to a `ConsCell` object. But what exactly *is* a reference? If you have previously used a language with pointers, like C or C++, you know a simple explanation for references: a reference is a pointer. A reference is the address of the piece of memory used for the object. Here again is the constructor for the `IntList` class:

```
public IntList(ConsCell s) {
  start = s;
}
```

What gets passed in parameter `s` is not the object itself—it is the address of the object. What gets stored in the local variable `start` is not a copy of the object—it is the address of the object. No copy of the object is made.

On the other hand, you will sometimes hear it said that Java is like C++, but without pointers. This is true, from a certain point of view. C and C++ have pointer operations that reveal the underlying representation of pointers as memory addresses. For example, in C and C++, if `p` is a pointer to an array element, then `p+1` is a pointer to the next element in the array. That kind of operation exposes quite a bit of the machine-level, memory-address nature of C and C++ pointers. By contrast, there is very little you can do with a Java reference. You can use it to access the object's methods and variables, you can compare it with another reference for equality, you can pass it as a parameter or store it in a variable, but you certainly cannot do any arithmetic with it. A Java reference may be implemented as a pointer, but from the Java program's point of view it just functions as a unique identifier for an object. There is no way for a Java program to tell whether a reference is actually a pointer to the object. It might be a pointer to a pointer to the object, for example, or it might be an index into an array of objects.

This sometimes confuses people who already know C++ and are trying to learn Java. In C++, a local variable can be an object or it can be a pointer to an object. In Java, a local variable cannot be an object; it can only be a reference to an object. Java objects are never allocated in activation records.[2] Here's a side-by-side comparison:

C++	Equivalent Java

`IntList* p;`
`p = new IntList(0);`
`p->length();`
`p = q;`
	`IntList p;`
	`p = new IntList(null);`
	`p.length();`
	`p = q;`

`IntList p(0);`
`p.length();`
`p = q;`
	No equivalent.

The first row shows both languages using the local variable `p` as a pointer to an object. The second row shows C++ using the local variable `p` as an actual object, which is not possible in Java. Notice that C++ has two selection operators: `p->x` selects method `x` when `p` is a pointer to an object and `p.x` selects method `x` when `p` is an actual object. Java has only one selection operator: `p.x` selects method `x` when `p` is a reference to an object.

2. More accurately, Java objects have lifetimes that do not end automatically when the activation that allocated them is finished. If the language system can prove that a certain object will not be used again after the activation that allocated it is finished, it is free to allocate that object in the activation record if it wants to. Some implementations of the Java virtual machine do this as an optimization, but it is not visible to the programmer. There have been proposals to add C++-style, activation-specific objects to Java, but these have not (yet) made it into the language standard.

13.6 Getting Started with a Java Language System

The interactive approach of ML language systems made it easy to experiment with small pieces of ML code in previous chapters. With most Java language systems it is not quite so easy. You must write a small program to test your code and print some results. This section describes how to write and run a Java program that produces some output.

You will need a Java language system to experiment with Java code and to solve the exercises. The Java 2 Software Development Kit, Standard Edition version 1.3, was used to test the examples and exercises. It is an excellent, free, Java language system provided by Sun Microsystems, Inc. If you are reading this book as part of an organized course, your teacher may give you instructions for running Java on your local system. If not or if you want your own copy, you can easily download and install the Java SDK on your own Unix or Windows system. The Web site for this book (**http://www.webber-labs.com/mpl.html**) has up-to-date links for downloading the Java SDK.

The SDK includes a variety of tools: a debugger, a disassembler, an applet viewer, and so on. But you will need only two tools for the exercises: the Java compiler, `javac`, and the Java launcher, `java`. You will see how to use these two tools in a moment, but first let's make a small program to try them out on.

To get output we will use a predefined Java object called `System.out`. It has two instance methods, `print` and `println`, which can be used for simple output. The first, `System.out.print(x)`, simply prints out its parameter `x`. `System.out.println(x)` does the same thing, but starts a new line right after it. Here, for example, is a definition of a `print` method for the `IntList` class, so that an `IntList` knows how to print itself out:

```
/**
 * Print ourself to System.out.
 */
public void print() {
  System.out.print("[");
  ConsCell a = start;
  while (a != null) {
    System.out.print(a.getHead());
    a = a.getTail();
    if (a != null) System.out.print(",");
  }
  System.out.println("]");
}
```

With that method added to the IntList class, all we need to test our code is a *main method*. A main method is a static, public method named main that takes an array of String values as a parameter. (The String values in that parameter are from the command line that runs the program. Ignore them for now.) The Java language system calls the main method to start the program when it is run. Here is a class named Driver that contains a main method for testing the IntList class:

```
class Driver {
  public static void main(String[] args) {
    IntList a = new IntList(null);
    IntList b = a.cons(2);
    IntList c = b.cons(1);
    int x = a.length() + b.length() + c.length();
    a.print();
    b.print();
    c.print();
    System.out.println(x);
  }
}
```

Any class can have a main method. We could have added it to IntList or to ConsCell. But to keep separate things separate, we put it in a class of its own.

Now we only need to compile the three classes (ConsCell, IntList, and Driver) and then run the main method of the Driver class. If you are using the Java SDK tools, the first step is to save the three class definitions in three files in the same directory: ConsCell.java, IntList.java, and Driver.java. Be careful with the capitalization. The file names must match the class names exactly. Now type the command javac Driver.java. This runs the Java compiler on Driver.java and, indirectly, on the other classes it needs (ConsCell.java and IntList.java). If everything was typed in correctly, there should be no errors and no output from this. If you now check the directory, you will find three new files, ConsCell.class, IntList.class, and Driver.class. These are the compiled Java files, which contain Java bytecode for the Java virtual machine (as was discussed back in Chapter 4).

Now you can run the program by typing the command java Driver. This launches the Java program by running the main method of the Driver class. The main method prints its output:

```
[]
[2]
[1,2]
3
```

That's all there is to it.

There are, by the way, two conventional ways for a Java program to run: as an *application* or as an *applet*. This example is an *application*. A Java language system runs it by executing the main method of a class. A Java application is like an ordinary program in any other language. It can read and write files, open and close windows, and do anything else the operating system and hardware permit. By contrast, an *applet* is a Java program that runs under a Web browser. An applet's powers are strictly limited to ensure security, to make sure, for example, that visiting a Web page with a Java applet in it cannot give your computer a virus. Applets have no main method, but instead have methods for responding to particular events. For example, an applet has a `paint` method that the system calls whenever the applet needs to redraw its part of the Web page. The Java API includes a predefined `Applet` class that provides an appropriate interface for applets. As usual, this book will not be looking at the extensive Java API, so the Java examples will present applications rather than applets.

13.7 Conclusion

This chapter introduced Java. It introduced the following parts of the language:

- The Java types `int`, `char`, `double`, `boolean`, `null`, and `String`, and how to write constants of each type.
- The pure Java operators `+`, `-`, `*`, `/`, `%`, `<`, `>`, `<=`, `>=`, `==`, `!=`, `&&`, `||`, and `!`.
- The conditional (`x ? y : z`) expression.
- Operators with side effects (`+=`, `-=`, `*=`, `/=`, `%=`, `++`, and `--`).
- Calling instance methods, and the `String` instance methods `length`, `equals`, `charAt`, and `toUpperCase`.
- Calling class methods, and the `String` class methods named `valueOf`.
- Object creation expressions with the `new` keyword.
- Simple statements: expression statements, compound statements, declaration statements, and the `if`, `while`, and `return` statements.
- Class definitions, using the `public` and `private` access specifiers.

This is enough Java to complete the exercises that follow.

Exercises

Unless the exercise says otherwise, you should implement your solutions to these exercises in an imperative, object-oriented style. Test your solutions with a `Driver` class, as we did in this chapter.

Exercise 1 Follow the instructions in section 13.6 to test the classes from this chapter—`ConsCell` (without those extra static methods), `IntList`, and `Driver`. Compile and run them with your Java language system.

Exercise 2 Add a `contains` instance method to the `IntList` class, so that `x.contains(n)` returns `true` if the `int` value `n` occurs in the `IntList x` and returns `false` otherwise.

Exercise 3 Add an `equals` instance method to the `IntList` class, so that `x.equals(y)` returns `true` if the `IntList x` and the `IntList y` have exactly the same integers in the same order and returns `false` otherwise. It should be true that `x.equals(y)` is always equivalent to `y.equals(x)`. It should also be true that if `x==y` then `x.equals(y)`, although the reverse should not necessarily be true.

Exercise 4 Add an `append` instance method to the `IntList` class, so that `x.append(y)` returns an `IntList` that is equal to the `IntList x` followed by the `IntList y`. There should be no side effect on `x` or `y`. (*Hint:* You will need to make a copy of `x`.)

Exercise 5 Add a `reverse` instance method to the `IntList` class, so that `x.reverse()` returns an `IntList` that is the reverse of the `IntList x`. There should be no side effect on `x`.

Exercise 6 Add a `reverseMe` instance method to the `IntList` class, so that `x.reverseMe()` returns no value but has the side effect of reversing the contents of `x`. (This is easier if you start by making a backwards copy of `x`. It is harder, and more interesting, to do the reversal in place, without creating any new `ConsCell` objects.)

Exercise 7 Add a `sort` instance method to the `IntList` class, so that `x.sort()` returns an `IntList` that is a version of the `IntList x`, sorted in non-decreasing order. You may use any sorting algorithm you like. There should be no side effect on `x`.

Exercise 8 Add a `sortMe` instance method to the `IntList` class, so that `x.sortMe()` returns no value but has the side effect of sorting the contents of the

IntList x into non-decreasing order. Use a merge sort algorithm, and do not create any new ConsCell objects.

Exercise 9 Implement append (from Exercise 4) in a recursive, functional style (but still object oriented), as was done for length in this chapter.

Exercise 10 Create a class Int with the following components:

a. A field to store an int value.
b. A constructor so that new Int(x) creates an Int object that stores the int value x.
c. An instance method toString so that x.toString() returns the value of the Int object x in String form.
d. An instance method plus so that x.plus(y) returns a new Int object whose value is the value of the Int x plus the value of the Int y. There should be no side effects.
e. Instance methods minus, times, and div, similar to the plus method described above. (The div method should perform integer division, like the / operator on int values.)
f. An instance method isPrime so that x.isPrime() returns true if the value of the Int x is a prime number.

In some object-oriented languages, like Smalltalk, absolutely everything is an object—integers, booleans, characters, strings, everything. In such languages, arithmetic really works a bit like this exercise, though the language may provide a more natural syntax for operators.

Exercise 11 The primitive type long in Java has the same operators as int, but uses twice as many bits—a 64-bit, twos-complement binary representation. Modify the Int class from Exercise 10 to make it work entirely with long values instead of int values. Compare the two implementations of the Int class, and make a list of all the changes you had to make.

Exercise 12 Create an IntVar class with the following components:

a. A field to store an Int reference (using the Int class from Exercise 10).
b. A constructor so that new IntVar(x) creates an Int object in an uninitialized state.
c. An instance method write so that x.write(y) stores the Int y in the IntVar x.

d. An instance method `read` so that `x.read()` returns the `Int` reference stored in the `IntVar x`. The behavior of `x.read()` is undefined if the `IntVar x` is in an uninitialized state.
e. An instance method `isInitialized()` so that `x.isInitialized()` returns `true` if the `IntVar x` is in an initialized state—that is, if `x.write` has ever been called—or returns `false` otherwise.

Consider the two classes `Int` and `IntVar`. Which one corresponds to an lvalue, and which one corresponds to an rvalue? Explain.

Exercise 13 In this exercise you will create a class `IntSet` that represents a set of integers. There are many different ways to implement this, but for this exercise you should use a binary search tree (see Exercise 11 in Chapter 11) as the internal data structure for storing the set. The tree need not be balanced. In addition to the actual `IntSet` class, you will need to create an additional class or classes to represent nodes of the binary search tree. The `IntSet` class should have the following components:

a. A constructor so that `new IntSet()` creates an `IntSet` object that represents the empty set.
b. A `find` instance method so that `x.find(n)` returns `true` if `n` is an element of the `IntSet x` and returns `false` otherwise. (The `find` method should not search every node in the tree, but only those nodes that, according to the definition of a binary search tree, might contain `n`.)
c. An `add` instance method so that `x.add(n)` returns no value, but adds the integer `n` to the set `x`. If `n` is already present in `x`, `x` should not be changed.
d. A `toString()` instance method so that `x.toString()` returns a `String` representing the sorted contents of the set. For example, if `x` represents the set {1,7,2,5}, `x.toString()` should return `"{1,2,5,7}"`.

Further Reading

There are many good books and online resources to help you get started with Java. This is an excellent one:

> Campione, Mary, Kathy Walrath, and Alison Huml. *The Java ™ Tutorial*. 3rd ed. Boston, MA: Addison-Wesley, 2000.

It covers the basics and (unlike this language-oriented introduction) pays plenty of attention to the Java API. The book is based on the online tutorial at **www.java.sun.com**.

Chapter 14
Memory Management

14.1 Introduction

When a program runs, many different kinds of data must be stored in the computer's memory. The program itself must be stored in memory somewhere. Room must be found for the constant data used by the program: numeric constants, string constants, and so on. The values taken on by the program's variables must be stored in memory. Often, auxiliary data structures like the buffers for files must be allocated in memory. And, of course, memory space must be allocated to satisfy explicit program requests; for example, a `malloc` in C or a `new` in Java.

You may have noticed that every sentence in the last paragraph is in the passive voice—room "must be found," values "must be stored," memory space "must be allocated." Who does all this finding, storing, and allocating? Static code and data are allocated in memory by the loader, before the program begins running, as was shown in Chapter 4. But an interesting hidden player is at work here: runtime memory management. Most modern languages require a complex and largely hidden library of runtime support code to perform the chores of dynamic memory allocation and deallocation. This chapter looks at some of the techniques of memory management.

14.2 A Memory Model Using Java Arrays

The techniques of memory management are slightly different for every different combination of language, operating system, and memory architecture. This chapter will assume that the operating system grants each running program one or more fixed-size regions of memory to use for its dynamic allocation. Today's general-purpose computers have operating systems and memory architectures that are more flexible and more complicated than this. The end of the chapter will return to some of these complications. For now, this simple model will suffice to illustrate some key ideas of memory management.

To make this more concrete (and to get more practice with Java), let's look at implementations of some memory-management techniques in Java. This requires a piece of Java not addressed in Chapter 13—arrays. Here is an example of an array declaration and initialization in Java:

```
int[] a = null;
```

This declares `a` to be a reference to an array of `int` values and initializes it to `null`. An array is really an object, so all the things you read in Chapter 13 about references and reference-type variables apply to arrays too. The type `int[]` means an array of `int` values. In general, to specify an array type in Java, give the element type followed by a pair of square brackets. For example, `char[]` is the type for arrays of `char` values and `String[]` is the type for arrays of strings. (`String[][]` is the type for arrays of arrays of strings—in effect, two-dimensional arrays of strings—but this book will not be using arrays of more than one dimension.) The declaration above initializes `a` to `null`, so although `a` *can* hold a reference to an array of `int` values, it does not initially hold a reference to anything.

To make `a` be a reference to an array, allocate an array and assign the reference to `a` like this:

```
a = new int[100];
```

This creates a new array of 100 `int` values and stores a reference to that new array in `a`. To create an array you use the keyword `new`, much as when creating an object; but instead of constructor parameters, you give the size of the array in square brackets. `a` could have been declared and had an array allocated for it in one line like this:

```
int[] a = new int[100];
```

This loop stores the value 5 in each of the 100 elements of the array.

```
int i = 0;
while (i < a.length) {
  a[i] = 5;
  i++;
}
```

The elements of the array are referred to using the indexing notation *array*`[`*index*`]`, where *array* is an expression whose value is an array reference and *index* is an expression of type `int`. The indexes of arrays in Java always start at zero, so the expression `a[0]` refers to the first element of array `a`. Since `a` has 100 elements, the indexes of those elements range from 0 to 99. An expression *array*`[`*index*`]` can be used anywhere a variable is permitted in Java. You can assign to it, use its value in an expression, or pass it as a parameter. (If the array element happens to be an object, you can even call one of its methods.) You can get the number of elements in an array `a` using the expression `a.length`. Notice that the example above used `(i<a.length)` instead of `(i<=a.length)`. This is because the loop shouldn't run when `i` is equal to 100; the last legal index is 99.

Arrays are a particular strength of imperative languages. Many important computational problems are best solved using arrays whose contents change as the program runs. For example, programs that simulate the formation of physical systems, from galaxies to planetary climates to molecular structures, often model the systems using large arrays. Such problems are difficult to solve efficiently using a programming language that lacks arrays, like a purely functional language. (ML has arrays—one of the non-functional parts of the language that was skipped.)

Getting back to memory management, it is assumed that the operating system grants each running program one or more fixed-size regions of memory to use for its dynamic allocation. These regions of memory will be treated as `int[]` arrays. The memory-management techniques that are implemented in the following pages will be Java classes of this form:

```
public class MemoryManager {
  private int[] memory;

  /**
   * MemoryManager constructor.
   * @param initialMemory the int[] of memory to manage
   */
```

```
  public MemoryManager(int[] initialMemory) {
    memory = initialMemory;
  }
  ...
}
```

The initial `memory` array is an argument to the constructor. Imagine that this is one of those fixed-size regions of memory for dynamic allocation granted by the operating system to the running program. The memory manager provides methods that can be called by the running program to allocate and deallocate blocks of addresses within the `memory` array.

Needless to say, you would probably not actually implement memory management for a real language system in this way. The goal in presenting memory managers as Java objects is to illustrate some of the algorithms and to give you more practice reading and writing Java.

14.3 Stacks

Chapter 12 looked at the question of finding memory locations for variables. In particular, it looked at the organization of activation records—blocks of memory that contain variables and other data specific to an activation of a function. You saw that the simplest way to implement activation records is to allocate them statically. This implementation does not require any runtime memory management, since the loader finds space for all statically allocated blocks of data before the program begins running.

You also saw in Chapter 12 that static allocation of activation records is sufficient only if the function cannot have two records active at the same time. In particular, it works only if the function is not recursive. Since most modern languages, including modern dialects of older languages, do allow recursion, we need to consider how to allocate activation records at runtime. For many languages, activation records form a stack at runtime. They are pushed on call and popped on return. How can allocation and deallocation for such a stack of activation records be implemented? This is one of the simplest memory-management problems. The memory manager can take advantage of the stack order—the fact that the first activation record allocated will be the last one deallocated.

For implementation of a stack manager, place the activation records in the memory array, starting at the highest addresses and growing downward.[1] This illustration shows an initial, empty memory array of eight words. The stack manager records the address of the top of the stack. Initially top is 8, since the stack is growing downwards from the highest addresses and is initially empty.

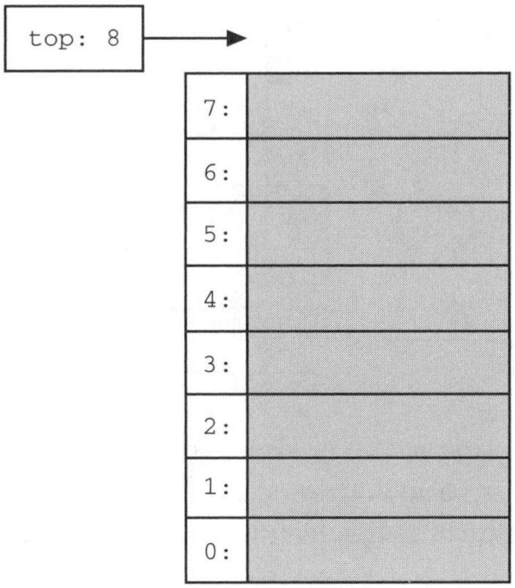

top: 8 →	
7:	
6:	
5:	
4:	
3:	
2:	
1:	
0:	

Throughout this chapter, free areas of the memory array will be shown in gray. These are addresses that are not currently allocated to the running program.

Suppose the running program now needs an activation record of three words. It requests the allocation from the stack manager. In this model, the stack manager is a reference m to an object that manages the memory array. The running program calls the method m.push(3), telling the stack manager how many words are needed. That method returns the address 5—the first address in a block of three words now allocated to the running program. The memory array now looks like this:

1. It would be more intuitive to have stacks start at the lowest addresses and grow upward. But downward-growing stacks are quite common in memory-management systems and in hardware implementations of stacks, as well. One advantage of the downward-growing arrangement is that the address of the start of the most recent activation record is the same as the address of the limit of the stack. Exercise 3 illustrates another reason for downward-growing stacks.

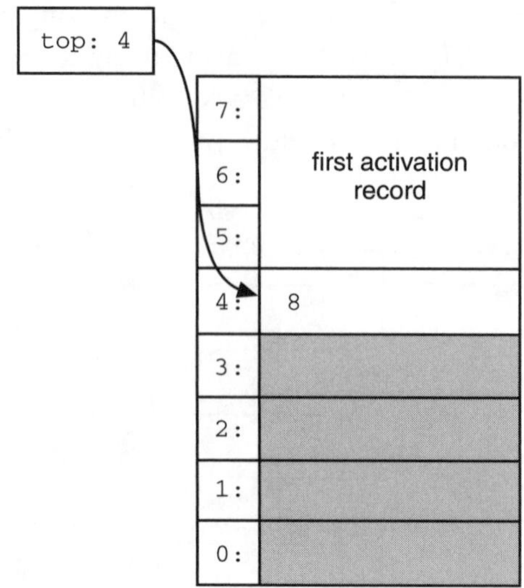

Although the first activation record occupies addresses 5, 6, and 7, the block allocated for it actually starts at address 4. The stack manager uses the extra word to store the previous value of `top`, which will be needed when the record is popped.[2]

Suppose the running program now needs an activation record of two words. It calls the stack manager method, `m.push(2)`, telling it how many words are needed. That method returns the address 2—the first address in a block of two words now allocated to the running program. The `memory` array now looks like this:

2. This is not strictly necessary. When a function is called, it allocates an activation record. When it returns, it deallocates the record. Since that function knows how much space it allocated, it could compute the address of the previous activation record by adding that amount to its current activation record's address. But this seems to be rare in practice. Other parts of the language system, like debuggers and exception-handling mechanisms, need to be able to link back through the activation records on the stack. For their sake, it works better to have each activation record start with an explicit link to the previous one (or, equivalently, start with its own size).

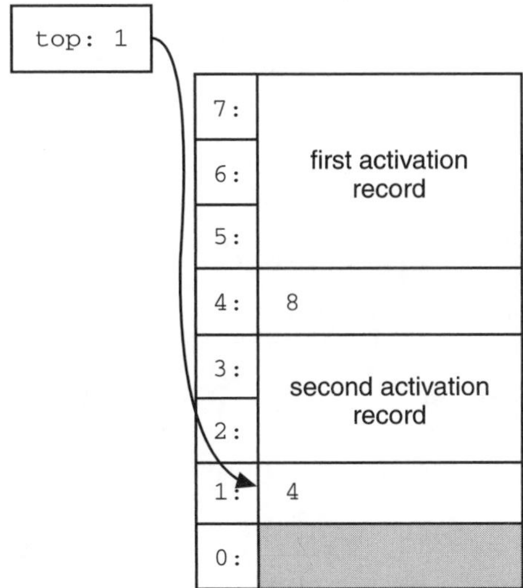

Although the second activation record occupies addresses 2 and 3, the block allocated for it actually starts at address 1. As before, the stack manager uses the extra word to store the previous value of `top`. The `memory` array now has one word free. This is not enough for any more activation records (even a one-word record actually requires two words, because of the extra word for `top`). Any subsequent call to `push` will therefore result in a stack overflow.

When the function using the second activation record is finished it will call another stack manager method, `m.pop()`, to deallocate the record. All `m.pop()` will have to do is reload `top` from the previous value stored in the memory array—`top = memory[top]`. The stack management will return to the state shown in the previous illustration. A second call to `m.pop()` will pop the first activation record, returning the array to the initial, empty-stack state.

Now that you have seen an example of this stack-management algorithm in action, here is an implementation of it in Java. (This implementation uses one Java statement not seen before—the `throw` statement. The `push` method uses it to signal a stack overflow. The `throw` statement will be examined in detail in Chapter 17.)

```
public class StackManager {
  private int[] memory; // the memory we manage
  private int top; // index of top (lowest) stack block

  /**
   * StackManager constructor.
   * @param initialMemory the int[] of memory to manage
   */
```

```
  public StackManager(int[] initialMemory) {
    memory = initialMemory;
    top = memory.length;
  }

  /**
   * Allocate a block and return its address.
   * @param requestSize int size of block, > 0
   * @return block address
   * @throws StackOverflowError if out of stack space
   */
  public int push(int requestSize) {
    int oldtop = top;
    top -= (requestSize + 1); // extra word for oldtop
    if (top < 0) throw new StackOverflowError();
    memory[top] = oldtop;
    return top + 1;
  }

  /**
   * Pop the top stack frame. This works only if the
   * stack is not empty.
   */
  public void pop() {
    top = memory[top];
  }
}
```

Although there are many minor variations on this, the general "bump-the-pointer" technique used by `StackManager` is very common. Allocation and deallocation are nothing more than simple adjustments to the `top` address. They are extremely efficient; a good thing, since they are needed by the running program on every function call and return. But remember that this efficiency depends on the fact that allocation and deallocation are restricted to stack order. Without that restriction, memory management is a more difficult problem.

14.4 Heaps

Many languages have constructs that require unordered runtime memory allocation and deallocation. Some are explicit:

- C programs explicitly allocate and deallocate memory by calling the library routines `malloc` and `free`.
- C++ programs use the `new` and `delete` operators to create new objects and dispose of those no longer needed.

- PL/I programs use the `allocate` and `free` statements to allocate and free up memory dynamically.

Other language constructs implicitly require similar allocation and deallocation. A language might, for example, support buffered file I/O, with file buffers that need to be allocated when the file is opened and deallocated when it is closed. A language might support dynamically resizable arrays, so that when an array is redimensioned, new space needs to be allocated for it and its prior space needs to be deallocated. In addition, as was shown in Chapter 12, in some languages (like ML) activation records are not always allocated and deallocated in stack order.

The previous section considered memory management in stack order. Now consider *unordered* runtime memory allocation and deallocation. The program is free to allocate and deallocate blocks in any order.

> A *heap* is a pool of blocks of memory, with an interface for unordered runtime memory allocation and deallocation.[3]

We will implement a heap manager that provides allocation and deallocation services through two functions, `allocate` and `deallocate`. The `allocate` function takes an integer parameter—the number of words of memory to be allocated—and returns the address of a newly allocated block of at least that many words. The `deallocate` function takes the address of an allocated block—one of those addresses returned by prior calls to `allocate` and not yet deallocated—and frees up the block beginning at that address, so that it is eligible to be reused. This is like C's functions `malloc` and `free` and is representative of the kind of interface a heap manager presents to the running program. (Of course, the programmer may see a more abstract model. In Pascal, for example, the `new` procedure allocates space for a value of a particular type, without revealing how much memory that might be. But the language system must implement such abstractions with low-level calls like `allocate` and `deallocate`.)

Assume, for now, that the heap manager has no other interaction with the language system. A later section will look at heap managers that have a way to examine, and perhaps modify, the addresses being used by the running program.

---

3. The word *heap* has another, unrelated meaning in computing: a binary tree whose nodes appear in a certain partial order. This data structure is used in the classical heap-sort algorithm and as a way of implementing priority queues. According to Donald Knuth, the word *heap* began to appear in print in its memory-management sense around 1975 (see *The Art of Computer Programming,* Vol. 1, 3rd ed., Boston, MA: Addison-Wesley, 2000, p. 435). The data-structure sense is at least 10 years older. This book will always use the word *heap* in its memory-management sense.

A First-Fit Mechanism

First consider the following simple mechanism:

- The heap manager maintains a linked list of free blocks, initially containing one big free block.
- To allocate a block, the heap manager searches the free list for the first sufficiently large free block. If there is extra space at the end of the block, the block is split and the unused portion at the upper end is returned to the free list. The requested portion at the lower end is allocated to the caller.
- To free a block, the heap manager returns it to the front of the free list.

This is one of the simplest mechanisms for heap management: *first fit*, with a free list in last-in-first-out order. Consider a `HeapManager m` with a `memory` array of 10 words, and look at the following sequence of calls:

```
p1=m.allocate(4);
p2=m.allocate(2);
m.deallocate(p1);
p3=m.allocate(1);
```

The following illustration shows an initial, empty `memory` array of 10 words. The heap manager maintains a variable called `freeStart`, which is a link to the head of the linked list of free blocks. Initially, the entire `memory` array is one big free block:

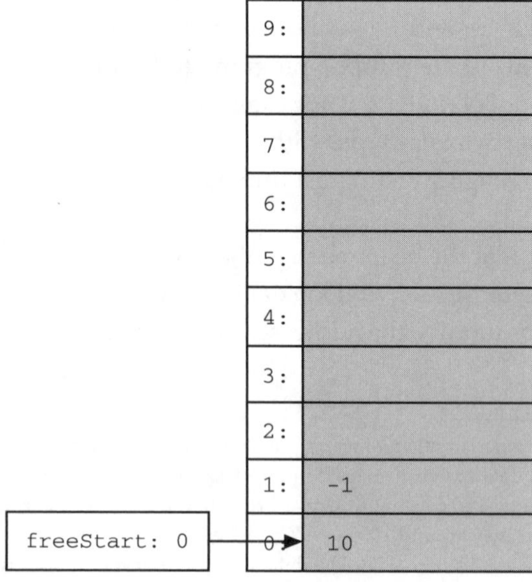

Every block in the heap, whether allocated or free, has its length in its first word. For free blocks, the second word is also used. It is the address of the next free block in the free list. The value –1 is used to represent the null link, the link from the last block in the list.

The running program now makes its first allocation, `p1=m.allocate(4)`. The heap manager finds that the first (and only) block in the free list is large enough. In fact, it is too large. The heap manager allocates five words (the requested four plus one for the length word) and returns the remainder to the free list. The address returned to the running program is 1, the first of the four requested words.

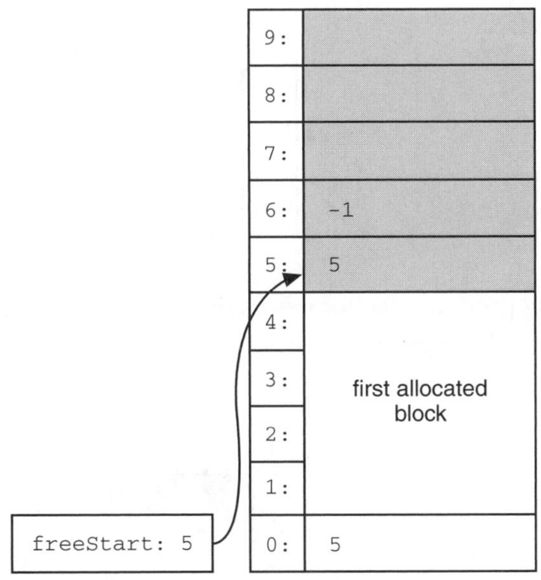

Next, the running program makes its second allocation, `p2=m.allocate(2)`. The heap manager finds that the first (and only) block in the free list is large enough. As before, it is too large. The heap manager allocates three words (the requested two plus one for the length word) and returns the remainder to the free list. The address returned to the running program is 6, the first of the two requested words.

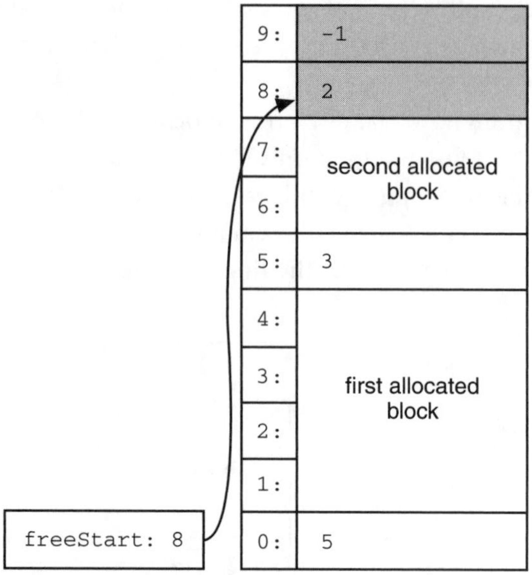

Next, the running program deallocates its first allocated block, `m.deallocate(p1)`. The heap manager returns it to the front of the free list.

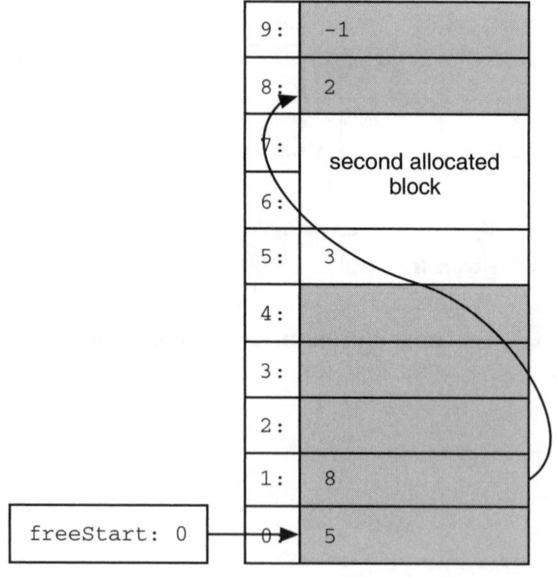

The free list now contains two blocks, one of five words and one of two words. When the running program makes its final memory allocation, `p3=m.allocate(1)`, the memory manager finds the five-word block at the head of the free list. It allocates two words of this (the requested one plus one for the length) and returns the remaining three words to the free list.

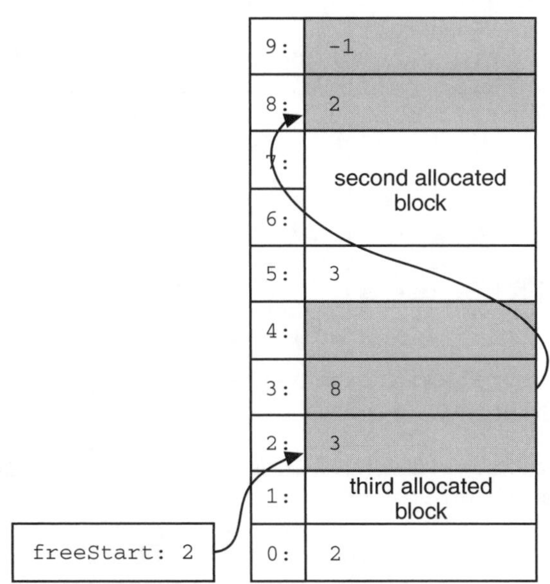

The heap manager had two alternatives for the last allocation. Either of the two free blocks would have worked, and the other one had the advantage of being exactly the right size. But the first-fit mechanism chooses the first block in the free list that is large enough.

Now that you have seen an example of a simple heap-management mechanism in action, here is an implementation of it in Java. This implementation uses a kind of Java declaration you have not seen before. The variable `NULL` is declared to be `static`, `private`, and `final`. Declaring it `static` means there is only one for the whole class, not one field in each object of the class. Declaring it `final` means that it cannot be reassigned after it is initialized—`NULL` will always be –1. This is the way to declare named constants in Java. The value –1 should be used as the link from the last block in the free list, and this declaration lets the name `NULL` be used for that purpose.

```
public class HeapManager {
  static private final int NULL = -1; // our null link
```

```
public int[] memory; // the memory we manage
private int freeStart; // start of the free list

/**
 * HeapManager constructor.
 * @param initialMemory the int[] of memory to manage
 */
public HeapManager(int[] initialMemory) {
  memory = initialMemory;
  memory[0] = memory.length; // one big free block
  memory[1] = NULL; // free list ends with it
  freeStart = 0; // free list starts with it
}

/**
 * Allocate a block and return its address.
 * @param requestSize int size of block, > 0
 * @return block address
 * @throws OutOfMemoryError if no block big enough
 */
public int allocate(int requestSize) {
  int size = requestSize + 1; // size including header

  // Do first-fit search: linear search of the free
  // list for the first block of sufficient size.

  int p = freeStart; // head of free list
  int lag = NULL;
  while (p != NULL && memory[p] < size) {
    lag = p; // lag is previous p
    p = memory[p + 1]; // link to next block
  }
  if (p == NULL) // no block large enough
    throw new OutOfMemoryError();
  int nextFree = memory[p + 1]; // block after p

  // Now p is the index of a block of sufficient size,
  // lag is the index of p's predecessor in the
  // free list, or NULL, and nextFree is the index of
  // p's successor in the free list, or NULL.

  // If the block has more space than we need, carve
  // out what we need from the front and return the
  // unused end part to the free list.

  int unused = memory[p]-size; // extra space in block
  if (unused > 1) { // if more than a header's worth
    nextFree = p + size; // index of the unused piece
```

```
      memory[nextFree] = unused; // fill in size
      memory[nextFree+1] = memory[p+1]; // fill in link
      memory[p] = size; // reduce p's size accordingly
    }

    // Link out the block we are allocating and done.

    if (lag == NULL) freeStart = nextFree;
    else memory[lag + 1] = nextFree;
    return p+1; // index of useable word (after header)
  }

  /**
   * Deallocate an allocated block. This works only if
   * the block address is one that was returned by
   * allocate and has not yet been deallocated.
   * @param address int address of the block
   */
  public void deallocate(int address) {
    int addr = address - 1;
    memory[addr + 1] = freeStart;
    freeStart = addr;
  }
}
```

As you can see, a heap is a lot more complicated than a stack. And this mechanism is not yet complicated enough. It has a defect that would render it impractical, even for relatively undemanding applications.

Coalescing Free Blocks

The previous mechanism breaks big blocks into little blocks, but never reverses the process. Consider this sequence of operations on a `HeapManager m` with a `memory` array of 10 words:

```
p1=m.allocate(4);
p2=m.allocate(4);
m.deallocate(p1);
m.deallocate(p2);
p3=m.allocate(7);
```

The mechanism allocates the two blocks `p1` and `p2`, then returns them to the free list. After the deallocations, all memory is free—the running program is not holding any allocated blocks. However, the free list consists of two smaller blocks, so the final allocation, `m.allocate(7)`, fails, even though there is plenty of free memory.

To alleviate this problem, we will modify the `deallocate` method to make it *coalesce* adjacent free blocks. The new `deallocate` method does not just put the free block on the head of the free list. Instead, it maintains the free list *sorted* in increasing order of addresses. It finds the right insertion point in this list for the newly deallocated block, inserts it into the list, and merges it with the previous free block and with the following free block if they are adjacent. Here is an implementation of this new `deallocate` method:

```
/**
 * Deallocate an allocated block. This works only if
 * the block address is one that was returned by
 * allocate and has not yet been deallocated.
 * @param address int address of the block
 */
public void deallocate(int address) {
  int addr = address - 1; // real start of the block

  // Find the insertion point in the sorted free list
  // for this block.

  int p = freeStart;
  int lag = NULL;
  while (p != NULL && p < addr) {
    lag = p;
    p = memory[p + 1];
  }

  // Now p is the index of the block to come after
  // ours in the free list, or NULL, and lag is the
  // index of the block to come before ours in the
  // free list, or NULL.

  // If the one to come after ours is adjacent to it,
  // merge it into ours and restore the property
  // described above.

  if (addr + memory[addr] == p) {
    memory[addr] += memory[p]; // add its size to ours
    p = memory[p + 1]; //
  }

  if (lag == NULL) { // ours will be first free
    freeStart = addr;
    memory[addr + 1] = p;
  }
  else if (lag+memory[lag]==addr) { // block before is
                                    // adjacent to ours
    memory[lag] += memory[addr]; // merge ours into it
    memory[lag + 1] = p;
  }
```

```
    else { // neither, just a simple insertion
      memory[lag + 1] = addr;
      memory[addr + 1] = p;
    }
  }
```

With this more complicated method for deallocation, the heap manager now coalesces adjacent free blocks. It cannot, of course, coalesce free blocks that are *not* adjacent—a fragmentation problem that will be taken up later in the chapter.

Quick Lists and Delayed Coalescing

The sequence of `allocate` and `deallocate` calls that a heap manager sees depends, of course, on the running program. Different programs make different demands on memory. There is, however, an observation that applies across many programs, languages, and language systems: small blocks tend to be allocated and deallocated much more frequently than large blocks. A common way to improve the performance of a heap manager is to have it maintain separate free lists for the popular (small) block sizes. On these *quick lists*, all the blocks are the same size. For example, here is how we could add quick lists for block sizes 2 through 9 to the previous `HeapManager`. First, add a private array `quickGet` to hold the addresses of the individual quick lists. The array is indexed by block sizes 2 through 9. Elements 0 and 1 are unused, since there are no blocks of those sizes. Initialize the array with `NULL` addresses, showing that all the quick lists are initially empty:

```
public class QuickHeapManager {
  static private final int NULL = -1; // our null link
  static private final int QLSIZE = 10; // quickGet size
  public int[] memory; // the memory we manage
  private int freeStart; // head of general free list
  private int[] quickGet; // heads of quick lists

  /**
   * QuickHeapManager constructor.
   * @param initialMemory the int[] of memory to manage
   */
  public QuickHeapManager(int[] initialMemory) {
    memory = initialMemory;
    memory[0] = memory.length; // one big free block
    memory[1] = NULL; // free list ends with it
    freeStart = 0; // free list starts with it
    quickGet = new int[QLSIZE]; // quick list heads
    int i = 0; // all quick lists are initially empty
    while (i < QLSIZE) quickGet[i++] = NULL;
  }
  ...
```

`deallocate` needs to be modified to make it free blocks directly to the appropriate quick list if they are the right size for the list.

```
public void deallocate(int address) {
  int addr = address - 1; // real start of the block
  int size = memory[addr]; // size of the block

  // If possible, add to quick list.

  if (size < QLSIZE) {
    memory[addr + 1] = quickGet[size];
    quickGet[size] = addr;
    return;
  }

  // Not quick, continue normal deallocation...
  ...
```

A check of the quick lists needs to be added as a new first step for `allocate`.

```
public int allocate(int requestSize) {
  int size = requestSize + 1; // size including header

  // If possible, take from quick list.

  if (size < QLSIZE) { // if quick list exists
    int p = quickGet[size];
    if (p != NULL) { // if there is one, use it
      quickGet[size] = memory[p + 1];
      return p + 1;
    }
  }

  // No quick list, continue normal allocation...
  ...
```

As you can see, `allocate` now checks the quick lists first. If there is a list for the requested size and if there is a free block on that list, it returns it. If this really is a common case—if small blocks really are frequently allocated and deallocated—there will be a significant performance improvement, since the new code speeds up that common case considerably and slows down the less common case only slightly.

Notice that quick-list blocks are not being coalesced when they are freed. (Since they are not in the main free list, they will not be coalesced when adjacent blocks are freed either.) This brings back the old problem again. The heap may not be able to satisfy an allocation, not because there is insufficient free memory, but because the free memory has been cut up into small blocks that are sitting unused on the quick lists. One way to alleviate this problem is to have `allocate` take an extra step if an allocation fails: remove blocks from the quick lists, free them to the general free list and coalesce as usual, and then try the allocation again. The rest of this code will not be shown here, but this makes an interesting exercise—Exercise 2, at the end of the chapter.

Fragmentation

As was already observed, the heap manager cannot combine non-adjacent free blocks. Consider this sequence of operations on a `MemoryManager m` with a `memory` array of 10 words:

```
p1=m.allocate(4);
p2=m.allocate(1);
m.deallocate(p1);
p3=m.allocate(5);
```

The final call to `m.allocate(5)` fails, because after the first three operations the heap looks like this:

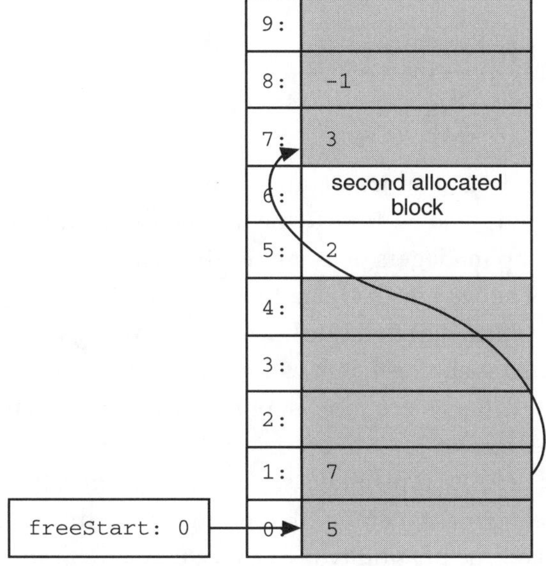

Although there is plenty of free memory, it is fragmented. The two free blocks are not adjacent, so they cannot be merged into a single free block. The illustration shows the block `p1` having been freed to the general free list, not to a quick list. But that makes no difference here. Either way, the final allocation request fails even though the heap has enough free space.

Ideally, the running program should be able to allocate a block of a given size whenever there is at least that much space not currently allocated. This is not the case if the heap is fragmented. Fragmentation is a classic problem for heap managers and for many other kinds of storage managers. Allocation of memory space on a disk, or of floor space in a warehouse, is subject to the same kind of problem.[4]

Other Heap Mechanisms

The mechanisms discussed so far are among the simplest of an amazing variety of mechanisms for heap management that have been implemented for language systems. But even these simple mechanisms illustrate three major issues in heap management: placement, splitting, and coalescing.

A heap manager must decide on a *placement* for every block allocated. When it sees a request to allocate a block, the allocator usually has many positions in memory to choose from. The simple mechanism of first-fit allocation from a first-in-first-out free list is only one of many ways to make that choice. Consider again the sequence of operations on a `MemoryManager m` with a `memory` array of 10 words, which led to fragmentation in the previous example:

```
p1=m.allocate(4);
p2=m.allocate(1);
m.deallocate(p1);
p3=m.allocate(5);
```

The mechanism placed `p1` at address 0 and `p2` at address 5. If only `p1` had been placed at address 2 and `p2` at address 0, the fragmentation would not have occurred. Of course, heap managers do not have the luxury of knowing in advance what the sequence of allocations and deallocations will be. A heap manager must choose a position for each allocated block without knowing what other operations are coming. Some placement mechanisms use a list of free blocks, as the first-fit `HeapManager` does. Others use a more sophisticated data structure such as a balanced binary tree.

A heap manager usually implements some block *splitting*. If it decides to allocate a block within a free region of memory that is larger than the requested size, it has more choices to make. One possibility is to allocate exactly the requested amount,

---

4. Some authors use the term *fragmentation* to mean exactly the situation illustrated above: free regions separated from each other by allocated blocks, so that the remaining free memory cannot be allocated as a single block. Other authors (especially Paul Wilson—see the Further Reading section at the end of the chapter) use it more generally to describe any state in which a heap manager is unable to allocate memory even though it is free. This more general meaning includes cases where the heap manager does not coalesce adjacent free blocks and cases where the heap manager has wasted some free memory by allocating larger blocks than requested.

leaving the rest as a free block. (This is what `HeapManager` does.) This looks reasonable, but a heap manager can often get better performance by doing a little less splitting. If the requested amount is nearly the same size as the free block, it might make more sense to just go ahead and use the whole thing. More generally, the heap manager has a range of possibilities between these two extremes. It can choose to include some but not all of the extra free space in the allocated block.[5]

A heap manager also usually implements some block *coalescing*. When adjacent blocks are free, the heap manager may decide to combine them into a single free block. On the other hand, a heap manager can often get better performance by doing a little less coalescing. You saw this with the delayed coalescing of quick-list blocks. When a small block is deallocated, it may be of a popular size that will soon be needed again. In that case it would be a waste of time to coalesce it into neighboring free blocks.

In addition to the basic decisions about placement, splitting, and coalescing, there are many other possible refinements for heap-management mechanisms. Among all these possible mechanisms, some work better than others, but there is no obvious winner. No mechanism can be perfect. Every run of every program generates its own sequence of allocations and deallocations. For any heap mechanism there is always some sequence that will lead to poor performance and severe fragmentation.[6] The trick is to find mechanisms that work well in practice—mechanisms that perform well on the sequences of allocations and deallocations generated by real programs. This is an active area of language-systems research.

14.5 Current Heap Links

To the heap managers of the previous section, the running program was nothing more than a source of `allocate` and `deallocate` requests. This section will show some tricks available to heap managers that have a bit more awareness of what the

---

5. Real heap managers usually round all allocation sizes up to some multiple, such as the nearest multiple of 16 bytes. This avoids the creation of odd-size blocks and results in more successes with quick lists. Another reason for doing it this way is that memory hardware often handles memory references more efficiently if they are aligned on multiples of some underlying memory-block size.

6. Programmers sometimes decide to avoid using a language system's heap manager for a particular application (at least for explicit allocations and deallocations) because they find that it is giving poor performance or because they anticipate that it will do so. This can mean enduring the limitations of static allocation, or it can mean implementing an *ad hoc* dynamic allocation scheme. In some cases this may be a rational and practical decision. In other cases, it is biased by the programmer's natural preference for low-level solutions (which this author shares) and is done mainly for fun.

running program does with the heap addresses allocated to it. In particular, it will look at heap managers that make use of the running program's *current heap links*:

> A *current heap link* is a memory location where a value is stored that the running program will use as a heap address.

Information about current heap links can be extremely valuable to heap managers, allowing tricks like heap compaction and garbage collection. You will see more about such tricks presently. First, consider the basic problem of tracing current heap links.

Tracing Current Heap Links

To illustrate what a heap manager has to do to trace current heap links, consider a Java `main` method starting with this code:

```
IntList a = new IntList(null);
int b = 2;
int c = 1;
a = a.cons(b);
a = a.cons(c);
```

Recall from Chapter 13 that an `IntList` object represents a list of integers. It contains a reference to the head of a linked list of `ConsCell` objects, one for each integer in the list. A Java language system can put activation records in a stack, but must put objects in a heap. So after the five statements have executed, memory looks like this:

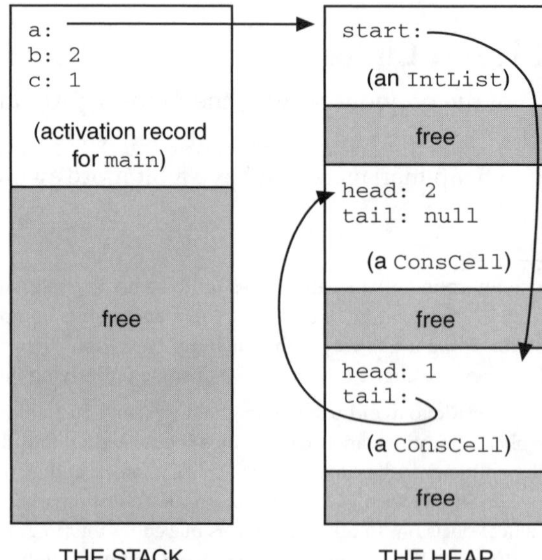

(As you can see, the illustration does not show absolute addresses for allocated blocks. This section will not be showing implementations in Java, so it will illustrate things a bit more abstractly than the previous section.)

Suppose that after these five statements, the heap manager decides that it needs to trace the current heap links. Its first step is to look at all the variables that might be used by the program. These are `a`, `b`, and `c`—all the variables in the activation record for `main`. This gives it {`a,b,c`} as a potential set of current heap links. (Of course, {`a,b,c`} really means the set of memory locations for those variables in the activation record for `main`.)

The heap manager's next step might be to eliminate `b` and `c` on the grounds that they have type `int`. Java's type system is rigid enough to guarantee that no variable with the static type `int` will ever be used as a heap address, even if its value happens to *be* a legal heap address. This leaves the set {`a`}, which is called the *root set*.

The heap manager cannot stop with the root set. There are other memory locations whose contents the running program might use as heap addresses. For example, the running program might call the method `a.length()`, which would traverse the linked list of `ConsCell` objects to count its length. That computation would use not just `a`, but every `ConsCell` link reachable from `a`. In general, the heap manager needs to find not just the root set, but every memory location reachable from the root set. Its next step is to add to the root set every field of the object referred to by `a`. This produces the set {`a`, `a.start`}. Then it adds every field of the object referred to by `a.start` to the root set, giving the set {`a`, `a.start`, `a.start.head`, `a.start.tail`}. As before, it might eliminate `a.start.head` on the grounds that it has type `int`. It then considers every field of the object referred to by `a.start.tail`. Neither of these fields needs to be added to the set. `a.start.tail.head` has type `int`, and `a.start.tail.tail` has the value `null`, so neither one can be used as a heap address. The heap manager's final set of memory locations is {`a`, `a.start`, `a.start.tail`}.

Is that result correct? Is it the exact set of current heap links after the first five statements of the program? It might be, but there is no way to tell. Remember, the current heap links are those that the program actually *will use* as heap addresses. We did not even show the rest of the code for the main method; who knows whether it ever uses `a`, `a.start`, or `a.start.tail`? In general, the heap manager cannot know what actions the running program will take in the future. The example found all the reachable heap links. The running program can use only those memory locations it can reach; so this set certainly contains all the current heap links. That is the best that can be hoped for.

The example illustrated the general procedure heap managers follow to trace current heap links:

1. Start with the *root set*, the set of memory locations of all the running program's variables, including all those statically allocated and all those in activation records for activations that have not yet returned. Omit all those whose values obviously cannot be used as heap addresses.
2. For each memory location in the set, look at the allocated block it points to and add all the memory locations within that block, but omit those whose values obviously cannot be used as heap addresses, as before. Repeat this until no new memory locations are found.

The details of this process vary with each language system. Some of the details are related to the language itself.

It is especially interesting to consider how the language affects the decision about which values "obviously" cannot be used as heap addresses. In some languages, like Java, a variable can be omitted if it has the wrong static type. Whether this is actually done is another matter. The implementation may be unable to recover the static type at runtime, or the implementers may judge that the improvement gained by excluding such variables is not worth the cost of all that runtime type checking. In other languages, like C, the static type of a variable may not be useful in the same way. A C program can use an integer variable as a memory address (by performing some type conversions), so a variable `i` might be a current heap link in spite of having type `int`.

Usually, a variable can be omitted if its value is not the address of an allocated heap block. (Depending on the language, it may or may not be necessary to consider variables whose values are addresses in the *middle* of an allocated heap block.) The value of a variable may have dynamic type information—some computer architectures tag values with type information even at the hardware level—and this might help exclude some variables from the set.

As you can see, tracing current heap links is not an exact operation. It is prone to several kinds of errors. These errors can be divided into three categories:

- *Exclusion errors*: a memory location that actually is a current heap link is accidentally excluded from the set.
- *Unused inclusion errors*: a memory location is included in the set, but the program never actually uses the value stored there.
- *Used inclusion errors*: a memory location is included in the set, but the program uses the value stored there as something other than a heap address; as an integer, for example.

For the kinds of things a heap manager uses current heap links for, which you will see below, it is critical to avoid exclusion errors. Somehow, every memory location that could possibly be a current heap link must be included. This makes unused inclusion errors inevitable, as you saw in the previous Java example. When we find something that *might* be used as a heap link we must include it, even though the program might not actually get around to using it at all.[7]

That leaves used inclusion errors, memory locations that might be used as heap links that actually end up being used as something else. Such errors may be avoidable, but it depends on the language and language system. Consider a C union like this:

```
union {
  char *p;
  char tag[4];
} x;
```

This `x` contains either the address of a character or an array of four characters. The static type of `x` is obviously of no help in determining whether it could be a current heap link. The value stored in `x` may also be of no help. It might have both a legal interpretation as the address of an allocated block and a legal interpretation as a character string. `x` must be included as a possible current heap link to avoid exclusion errors. But this may be a used inclusion error, since the program might actually use `x` as an array of characters.

Heap Compaction

Without current heap links, a heap manager is powerless to move blocks once they are allocated. That is part of what makes the placement problem for heap allocators so important. Once placement is determined for an allocated block, it is fixed until the running program deallocates it. Using current heap links, however, the heap manager can move allocated blocks around without disturbing the running program. It simply copies the block to a new location, then updates all the current heap links to the old block, making them point to the new location.

Some heap managers use this capability to perform *heap compaction*. They move all the allocated blocks together at one end of the heap, leaving all the free space in a single free block at the other end. This eliminates all fragmentation in the heap. Heap compaction is expensive, so it is usually done only as an operation of last

---

7. Compilers often face variations of this problem. For many optimizations a compiler needs to know whether a variable will be used after a given point in the program. This property is undecidable, so compilers must settle for an approximation called *liveness*—whether there is some path from that point to a use of the variable, regardless of whether that path will ever be taken.

resort. For example, a heap manager might attempt a compaction if some allocation is about to fail and then try that allocation again.

Moving allocated blocks is safe only if the set of current heap links has no exclusion errors and no used inclusion errors. Any exclusion error can result in the running program using a link to the old location of an allocated block after it has been moved; the heap manager did not find that link, so it was not updated. Any used inclusion error can result in damage to some value used by the running program. The heap manager updated the value, thinking that it was an address within a moved block, but it was actually used by the running program for some other purpose.

Simple heap compaction is not an option for languages like C, for which used inclusion errors are unavoidable. For other languages, language systems sometimes implement a form of garbage collection that accomplishes the same thing.

Garbage Collection

Here is a fragment of Pascal code that illustrates a common kind of heap-related defect:

```
type
  p: ^Integer;
begin
  new(p);
  p^ := 21;
  dispose(p);
  p^ := p^ + 1
end
```

In this fragment, a heap block is allocated (with the statement `new(p)`) and the variable `p` is used as its address. The integer 21 is stored in that block. The block is then deallocated (with the statement `dispose(p)`). Then the variable `p` (now a *dangling pointer*, a pointer to a block that is no longer allocated) is again used as an address, and the integer at that address is incremented. This is the defect. Since the block was deallocated, the heap manager may now be using that address for something else. This kind of bug is often fatal but hard to find. The program may run for quite a long time before the fact that some unknown value in the heap was incremented causes any visible problems.

This Pascal procedure illustrates another common kind of heap-related defect:

```
procedure Leak;
  type
    p: ^Integer;
  begin
    new(p)
  end;
```

This has a *memory leak*. It allocates a heap block and then loses track of it and forgets to deallocate it. This is an extremely common problem in larger programs. If a program occasionally allocates a heap block that it neglects to deallocate, the heap will gradually fill up with these unused but allocated blocks. The program will use more and more memory and may eventually run out of heap space unexpectedly. It is quite common for developers to ship commercial software with memory leaks, since this defect may not show up in routine testing.

Both these defects are related to improper heap deallocation. The first deallocates a block too soon, before the program is finished using it. The second forgets to deallocate the block at all. Some language systems eliminate this kind of defect by doing away with deallocation altogether. The running program allocates heap space but never deallocates it. The heap manager finds the allocated blocks that the running program is no longer using and reclaims them automatically—an operation called *garbage collection*.

For most garbage collection techniques, the heap manager uses current heap links. If an allocated block is the target of some current heap link, it is not garbage; the program is still going to use it. If an allocated block is not the target of any current heap link, it is garbage and can be collected. Three basic techniques for garbage collection are *mark-and-sweep*, *copying*, and *reference counting*.

A *mark-and-sweep* garbage collector carries out a two-phase process. In the *mark* phase, the garbage collector traces current heap links and marks all the allocated blocks that are the targets of those links. In the *sweep* phase, the garbage collector makes a pass over the heap, finding all the blocks that did not get marked and adding them to the free list (or to whatever data structure holds free blocks for later allocation). Mark-and-sweep collectors do not move allocated blocks; the heap remains fragmented after garbage collection. For this reason they can tolerate both kinds of inclusion errors. Extra inclusions in the current heap link set merely cause some garbage blocks to be retained. This is not serious as long as it is reasonably rare.

Another kind of garbage collector that uses current heap links is called a *copying collector*. A heap manager with a copying collector uses only one half of its available memory at a time. When that half becomes full, it finds the current heap links and copies all the non-garbage blocks into the other half. It compacts as it goes, so in the new half all the allocated blocks are together and all the free space is in a single free block. Then it resumes normal allocation in the new half. When that half becomes full, it repeats the process, copying and compacting back into the other half. Copying collectors do move allocated blocks, so (as with heap compaction) they are sensitive to used inclusion errors.

A very different kind of garbage collector, one that does not need to trace current heap links, is the *reference-counting collector*. In a reference-counting system, every allocated heap block includes a counter that keeps track of how many copies of its address there are. The language system maintains these reference counters, incrementing them when a reference is copied, and decrementing them when a reference is discarded. When a reference counter becomes zero, that block is known to be garbage and can be freed. Reference-counting systems suffer from poor performance generally, since maintaining the reference counters adds a substantial overhead to simple pointer operations.

Reference-counting collectors have another weakness. They cannot collect cycles of garbage. Suppose the running program gets into the situation pictured below. A local variable named `circle` is a reference to one of three objects linked to each other circularly:

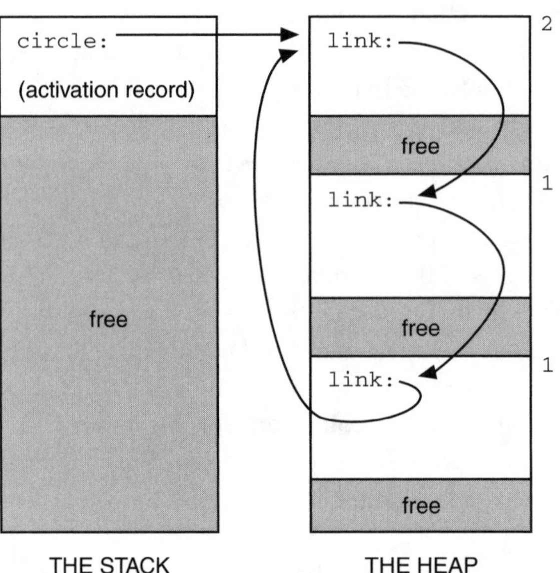

The reference counter for each allocated heap block is shown to its right—the number of references that point to it. If the running program now assigns `null` to `circle`, that decrements one reference counter, leaving this situation:

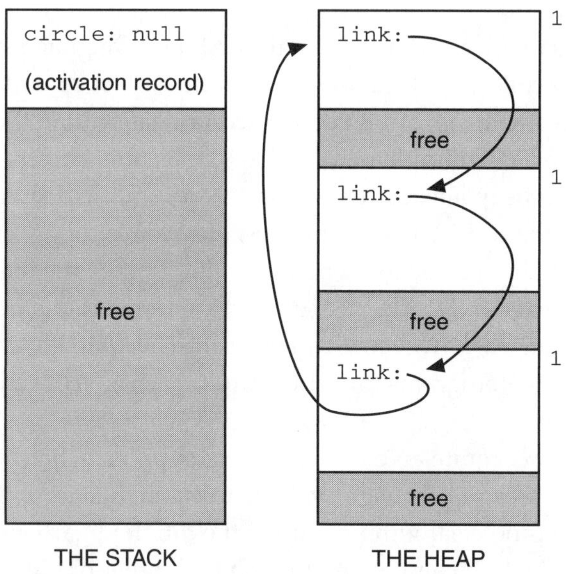

None of the heap blocks has a reference counter of zero, so they all remain allocated. But they cannot be reached by current heap links from the root set. They are actually garbage, and the other methods would reuse them.

Because of the high overhead and the difficulty with cycles of garbage, reference-counting garbage collectors are relatively rare. There are techniques for dealing with both problems. In some applications the advantages may outweigh the difficulties.

You have seen three basic techniques for garbage collection, but there are many possible refinements. Some garbage collectors take advantage of a common pattern of heap usage: blocks that have been in use for a long time tend to remain in use, while recently allocated blocks are more likely to become garbage. A *generational* collector divides its collection of allocated blocks into generations according to age, and garbage-collects (using one of the previously mentioned methods) most often within the youngest generations.

One drawback of the basic mark-and-sweep and copying approaches to garbage collection is that they can give very uneven performance—very good most of the time, but with occasional long pauses while the heap manager collects garbage. For some systems (like real-time control systems) such delays are unacceptable, even though they happen rarely. *Incremental collectors* recover a little garbage at a time, while the program is running, instead of doing it all at once in response to some memory allocation.

Some languages require garbage collection. All Java language systems must implement garbage collection, because Java has an explicit construct (`new`) for allocating objects on the heap, but no construct for deallocating them. Similarly, all ML language systems must implement garbage collection, because ML programs can perform implicit heap allocations whose corresponding deallocations cannot be placed statically in the code. Other languages, like Ada, strongly encourage the use of garbage collection but can be implemented without it. Some languages, like C and C++, make garbage collection difficult and are rarely implemented with it. Even for these languages, however, it can be used. There are libraries that can be linked with C and C++ programs that substitute a garbage-collecting heap manager for the standard one.

Garbage collection is quite an old idea, but its popularity has increased in recent years. It is an active area of language-systems research. Just as with basic heap management, there is no clear winner among the different garbage collection techniques. It is difficult to compare them with each other or with heap managers that use explicit deallocation. Their performance depends on the language, the language system, the operating system, the architecture, and the behavior of the running program. Roughly speaking, an application written for and running on a garbage-collecting language system usually runs at about the same speed as, or perhaps a little slower than, a similar application written for and running on a language system using explicit deallocation. Programmers who like garbage collection feel that the programmer time it saves (by avoiding pointer errors and making deallocation unnecessary) is worth the processor time it spends.

14.6 Conclusion

This chapter has shown some of the techniques of runtime memory management. Efficient and reliable memory management is an important hidden player in any language system.

This chapter assumed that memory management worked with fixed-size blocks of memory and treated those blocks of memory like simple arrays. The real story is far subtler than this. Real memory managers can usually ask the operating system for many independent blocks of memory for heaps and stacks and can ask it to increase the sizes of these segments as needed. Virtual-memory architectures make it possible for these to increase well beyond the size of the machine's main memory, so real memory managers rarely have to worry about running out of memory.

Instead, they have to worry about running slower and slower as the system begins to swap parts of the heap and the stack out to the disk and back in again. A memory-management system can and should cooperate with the many tricks of the memory architecture it runs on: multi-level cache effects, paging effects, virtual address translation effects, and all the rest.

Even without these details, you can see that memory management is an extremely subtle problem. It seems so simple at first—just `allocate` and `deallocate`; what could be so hard about that? But it is a problem that has challenged language-systems programmers for many years. It is a side of programming languages that eludes abstract analysis and is more often characterized by experimentation and (truth to tell) by seat-of-the-pants engineering.

Exercises

Exercise 1 The `HeapManager` in this chapter implements a first-fit mechanism. It uses the first block on the free list that is at least as large as the requested size. Another fairly simple mechanism is called *best-fit*. As you might guess, the idea is to search the free list for a sufficiently large block that is as close to the requested size as possible. If there is an exact fit on the free list, the best-fit mechanism can stop the search early. Otherwise, it has to search all the way to the end of the free list. This has the advantage that it does not break up large blocks unnecessarily. For example, if there is an exact fit somewhere on the list, the best-fit mechanism will find one, so it will not have to split a block at all.

Implement a version of `HeapManager` with a best-fit mechanism. Start with a renamed copy of the `HeapManager` class, and then modify the `allocate` method to implement a best-fit search. (The code for `HeapManager` is available on the Web site for this book. It includes the coalescing version of `deallocate`, which is the one you should use.)

After this has been tested and works, find a simple sequence of operations for which your best-fit manager succeeds while the first-fit one fails. *Hint:* There is a sequence that begins like this:

```
mm = new HeapManager(new int[7]);
int a = mm.allocate(2);
int b = mm.allocate(1);
int c = mm.allocate(1);
mm.deallocate(a);
mm.deallocate(c);
```

By extending this sequence with just two more calls to `mm.allocate`, you can get something that will succeed for best-fit and fail for first-fit.

Although best-fit is often a better placement strategy than first-fit, there are examples for which it is worse. Find a simple sequence of operations for which the first-fit manager succeeds while your best-fit one fails. *Hint:* There is a sequence that begins like this:

```
mm = new HeapManager(new int[11]);
a = mm.allocate(4);
b = mm.allocate(1);
c = mm.allocate(3);
mm.deallocate(a);
mm.deallocate(c);
```

By extending this sequence with just three more calls to `mm.allocate`, you can get something that will succeed for first-fit and fail for best-fit.

Exercise 2 Complete `QuickHeapManager`, the class implementing heap allocation with quick lists introduced in this chapter. Start with a renamed copy of the `HeapManager` class, and then modify the declarations and the `allocate` and `deallocate` methods as suggested. (The code for `HeapManager` is available on the Web site for this book. It includes the coalescing version of `deallocate`, which is the one you should use.) Make sure that your `allocate` implements delayed coalescing of quick-list blocks. If it cannot find a sufficiently large free block, it should remove everything from the quick lists, freeing to the general free list and coalescing as usual, and should then attempt the allocation again. The allocation should fail only if this second attempt fails. Your class should work on this test sequence:

```
QuickHeapManager m = new QuickHeapManager(new int[20]);
int p1 = m.allocate(4);
int p2 = m.allocate(4);
int p3 = m.allocate(4);
int p4 = m.allocate(4);
m.deallocate(p1);
m.deallocate(p2);
m.deallocate(p3);
m.deallocate(p4);
int p5 = m.allocate(5);
```

This test allocates and then frees all memory to the quick lists. When the final allocation is made, all the memory is on the quick lists (of the wrong size), but it should succeed anyway because of the (delayed) coalescing.

Exercise 3 Older language systems often managed one heap and one stack together in the same big block of memory. Embedded systems are sometimes still implemented this way. The heap lives at the low end of the block and the stack at the high end. The memory manager prevents them from running into each other, but does not use a fixed partition. A program can use a lot of stack space and a little heap, or a lot of heap space and a little stack, as it chooses.

Implement a `MemoryManager` class that combines the features of the `StackManager` and the `HeapManager` classes from this chapter. (The code for `StackManager` and `HeapManager` is available on this book's Web site.) Like them, it should have a constructor that takes as a parameter the memory array to be managed:

```
public MemoryManager(int[] initialMemory)...
```

Like `StackManager` it should have methods to `push` and `pop` stack blocks:

```
public int push(int requestSize)...
public void pop()...
```

Like `HeapManager` it should have methods to `allocate` and `deallocate` heap blocks:

```
public int allocate(int requestSize)...
public void deallocate(int address)...
```

Your implementation should start with an empty stack and an empty heap. The heap should grow upwards only as necessary to satisfy allocation requests. Make sure to handle both ways of running out of memory cleanly. Don't let the stack run into the heap or the heap run into the stack. (When the `push` method finds that it is going to run into the heap, it could check whether the last block in the heap is free and, if so, remove it from the heap and use that space for the stack. But you do not have to implement this refinement. Your heap needs to be able to grow up toward the stack, but need never shrink.)

Further Reading

This is a critical survey of basic heap-allocation techniques, not including compaction and garbage collection. It is interesting as a survey of the many different techniques and as a critique of research methods in the area of memory management.

Wilson, Paul R., Mark S. Johnstone, Michael Neely, and David Boles. "Dynamic storage allocation: a survey and critical review." *Proc. 1995 Int'l Workshop on Memory Management.* New York: Springer-Verlag, 1995.

Paul Wilson is also the author of an excellent survey paper on garbage collection:

Wilson, Paul R. "Uniprocessor garbage collection techniques." *ACM Computing Surveys,* to appear.

Chapter 15
A Second Look at Java

15.1 Introduction

You have seen that in Java you can use a name, like the name of a class, as the type of a variable with a declaration like this:

```
Person x;
```

Does this declare `x` to be a reference to an object of the `Person` class? Well, not exactly. It is possible for `x` to refer to an object of some other class, as long as that class is related to `Person` in a certain way. Java has polymorphism—a kind of subset polymorphism, which was touched on in Chapter 8. This chapter introduces the parts of Java that get you such polymorphism: interfaces and subclasses.

15.2 Implementing Interfaces

An *interface* in Java is a collection of method prototypes, method declarations that omit the method body. Here is an example of an interface called `Drawable`:

```
public interface Drawable {
  void show(int xPos, int yPos);
  void hide();
}
```

As you can see, the `Drawable` interface contains two method prototypes: `show` and `hide`. The prototypes include the return type, the method name, and the parameter lists, but no method bodies. Since there are no method bodies, the names of the parameters are irrelevant. But as always, you should choose meaningful names if possible. You can include the access specifier `public` for the methods if you want to, but Java treats them as public whether you declare them that way or not.

There is a way to declare that a class implements a given interface. To implement the `Drawable` interface, a class must first announce that it does so by using an `implements` clause and then must actually provide public methods named `show` and `hide` that match the prototypes in the interface. Here is an example:

```
public class Icon implements Drawable {
  public void show(int x, int y) {
    ... method body ...
  }
  public void hide() {
    ... method body ...
  }
  ... more methods and fields ...
}
```

When a class uses an `implements` clause, like `implements Drawable` above, it is promising to provide a public implementation of all the methods in that interface. The names of the parameters do not have to match those used in the interface declaration, but the method names and the types must match. A class may implement more than one interface. The interface names are separated by commas, like this:

```
public class Square implements Drawable, Scalable {
  ...
}
```

In that case the class must give definitions of all the methods required by all the interfaces it implements.

An interface can be, and in large applications usually is, implemented by many different classes. The `Drawable` interface might be supported by any class for things that are drawn on the screen, perhaps things like these:

```
public class Window implements Drawable ...
public class MousePointer implements Drawable ...
public class Oval implements Drawable ...
```

The pay-off for using interfaces is that you can use the name of an interface as the type in a type declaration. For example:

```
Drawable d;
d = new Icon("i1.gif");
d.show(0,0);
d = new Oval(20,30);
d.show(0,0);
```

Here the variable `d` is used polymorphically. It holds first a reference to an object of class `Icon`, then a reference to an object of class `Oval`. Java allows this since both classes implement the `Drawable` interface. Here is another example:

```
static void flashoff(Drawable d, int k) {
  int i = 0;
  while (i < k) {
    d.show(0,0);
    d.hide();
    i++;
  }
}
```

Here, Java has no way of knowing at compile time what class of object `d` refers to. It only knows that it is some class that implements the `Drawable` interface. This is an important source of polymorphism in Java. `flashoff` is a polymorphic method, since it can accept parameters of many different types. The formal parameter `d` may be a reference to an object of any class that implements the `Drawable` interface, an `Icon`, a `Window`, a `MousePointer`, and so on. Java can receive it as a parameter and call its `show` method without knowing exactly what class of object it is. An important point here is that the object must be of a class that actually promises to implement the `Drawable` interface using an `implements` clause. It is not enough for the class merely to have appropriate `show` and `hide` methods.

Let's look at a more complete example. `Worklist` will be defined as a collection of `String` objects that can be added to, removed from, and tested for emptiness. Here is a suitable interface definition:

```
/**
 * An interface for collections of Strings.
 */
public interface Worklist {
```

```
    /**
     * Add one String to the worklist.
     * @param item the String to add
     */
    void add(String item);

    /**
     * Test whether there are more elements in the
     * worklist; that is, test whether more elements
     * have been added than have been removed.
     * @return true if there are more elements
     */
    boolean hasMore();

    /**
     * Remove one String from the worklist and return
     * it. There must be at least one element in the
     * worklist.
     * @return the String item removed
     */
    String remove();
  }
```

Comments are especially important in an interface, since no code is there to help the reader figure out what each method does. You should think of the comments as part of the contract; along with the method prototypes, the comments specify what each class that implements the interface should do. Notice that the comments on the `Worklist` interface do not say anything about the order in which elements are added and removed. So when you implement a `Worklist`, you could do it as a stack, a queue, a priority queue, or some other data structure. And, of course, the comments do not say anything about implementation details, so when you implement a `Worklist` you could use arrays, linked lists, or some other technique.

The `Worklist` interface will be implemented as a stack, using linked lists. A class will be needed for the nodes in the list:

```
/**
 * A Node is an object that holds a String and
 * a link to the next Node. It can be used to
 * build linked lists of Strings.
 */
public class Node {
  private String data; // Each node has a String...
  private Node link;   // ...and a link to the next Node
```

```
  /**
   * Node constructor.
   * @param theData the String to store in this Node
   * @param theLink a link to the next Node
   */
  public Node(String theData, Node theLink) {
    data = theData;
    link = theLink;
  }

  /**
   * Accessor for the String data stored in this Node.
   * @return our String item
   */
  public String getData() {
    return data;
  }

  /**
   * Accessor for the link to the next Node.
   * @return the next Node
   */
  public Node getLink() {
    return link;
  }
}
```

Using objects of this class for the nodes in a linked list, this `Stack` class implements the `Worklist` interface:

```
/**
 * A Stack is an object that holds a collection of Strings.
 */
public class Stack implements Worklist {
  private Node top = null; // The top Node in the stack
  /**
   * Push a String on top of this stack.
   * @param data the String to add
   */
  public void add(String data) {
    top = new Node(data,top);
  }
  /**
   * Test whether this stack has more elements.
   * @return true if this stack is not empty
   */
  public boolean hasMore() {
    return (top != null);
  }
```

```
  /**
   * Pop the top String from this stack and return it.
   * This should be called only if the stack is not empty.
   * @return the popped String
   */
  public String remove() {
    Node n = top;
    top = n.getLink();
    return n.getData();
  }
}
```

Now an object of the class `Stack` can be used wherever an object of the type `Worklist` is needed. For example:

```
Worklist w;
w = new Stack();
w.add("the plow.");
w.add("forgives ");
w.add("The cut worm ");
System.out.print(w.remove());
System.out.print(w.remove());
System.out.println(w.remove());
```

The `Worklist` interface makes no guarantees about the order in which items that were added are removed. But since this `Worklist` was implemented as a stack, this code would print "`The cut worm forgives the plow.`" Other implementations of the `Worklist` interface are also possible, as you will see if you do Exercise 1.

15.3 Extending Classes

There is another, more complex, source of polymorphism in Java. Suppose that you want to implement a fancy version of `Stack` that lets you peek at the top element on the stack without popping it off. Since this is a clean addition to the functionality already provided by `Stack` objects, it would be a shame to have to rewrite the whole class. Luckily, you do not have to. Here is an implementation of `PeekableStack`:

```
/**
 * A PeekableStack is an object that does everything a
 * Stack can do and can also peek at the top element
 * of the stack without popping it off.
 */
public class PeekableStack extends Stack {
```

```
    /**
     * Examine the top element on the stack, without
     * popping it off. This should be called only if the
     * stack is not empty.
     * @return the top String from the stack
     */
    public String peek() {
      String s = remove();
      add(s);
      return s;
    }
}
```

The phrase `extends Stack` in the class definition establishes a special relationship between the new class `PeekableStack` and the old class `Stack`. The new class `PeekableStack` will *inherit* all the fields and methods of `Stack`, so they do not have to be redefined. As you can see, we only defined the method we added, which was the `peek` method. The `PeekableStack` class inherits the definitions of the methods `add`, `hasMore`, and `remove`, and also inherits the `top` field. Nothing like this happened with interfaces. Interfaces do not contain method bodies. When a class says that it `implements` an interface, all it gets is the obligation to provide definitions for all the required methods. When a class says that it `extends` another class, however, it inherits all the field and method definitions of that class. Consider this example:

```
PeekableStack s = new PeekableStack();
s.add("drive");
s.add("cart");
s.remove();
System.out.println(s.peek());
```

As you can see, even though we did not write explicit definitions of `add`, `hasMore`, and `remove`, these methods are present in the object of the class `PeekableStack`. It got them by inheritance.

Inheritance is an important part of virtually all class-based, object-oriented languages. Java, C++, Smalltalk, Eiffel, and so on all have a similar construct. The terminology is often different, however. Some people refer to `Stack` as a *superclass* and `PeekableStack` as a *subclass* of it. For Java programs, most people refer to `Stack` as a *base class* and `PeekableStack` as a *derived class*. Those are the terms used in this chapter.

In addition to inheritance, you also get polymorphism, as with interfaces. A reference of type `Stack` can actually refer to an object of the class

PeekableStack. Why not, since by construction a PeekableStack can do anything a Stack can do? We can write the following:

```
Stack s1 = new PeekableStack();
PeekableStack s2 = new PeekableStack();
s1.add("drive");
s2.add("cart");
System.out.println(s2.peek());
```

s1 and s2 both refer to objects of the class PeekableStack, even though s1 has type Stack. Incidentally, because s1's type does not include a peek method, Java will not allow the method call s1.peek(), even though the object s1 refers to at runtime actually does provide such a method. It is the declared type of a variable, not the actual class at runtime, that determines the operations Java will permit.

The implementation of the peek method is inefficient. It works by popping the top item from the stack and then pushing it right back on. There is a reason for doing it this way. In the original Stack definition, the reference to the top Node on the stack is held in a private field named top. Since this field is private, no other class can access it—not even PeekableStack. So there is no way to peek directly at that top element. If this inefficiency is a serious problem in the application, we could expose the top field by changing its visibility declaration from private to protected. A protected definition is visible within the class and within any class that extends that class (and in other classes in the same *package*—but we will not be looking at Java packages). We can change the definition of top in the class Stack to this:

```
protected Node top = null;
```

Then we could change the definition of peek in the class PeekableStack to this:

```
public String peek() {
  return top.getData();
}
```

This illustrates an important and common kind of challenge for program designers using object-oriented languages. Inheritance is a very useful mechanism, but you have to plan ahead for it. You have to anticipate the ways in which a class like Stack might need to be extended, and you have to design for them (with things like protected access where appropriate). Inheritance is a good way to reuse existing code, but the benefit is lost if you have to make a lot of changes to the base class before it can be extended the way you want.

A class that is formed by extending another class can itself be extended. For example, `PeekableStack` could be extended with yet another method, this time for peeking at the element just below the top one.

```
public class DoublePeekableStack extends PeekableStack {

  /**
   * Examine the next-to-top element on the stack,
   * without changing the stack. This should be called
   * only if the stack contains at least two elements.
   * @return the next-to-top String from the stack
   */
  public String doublepeek() {
    String s = remove();
    String r = remove();
    add(r);
    add(s);
    return r;
  }
}
```

We now have a chain of inheritance; `DoublePeekableStack` inherits from `PeekableStack`, which in turn inherits from `Stack`. In fact, every class but one inherits from some other class, since if you do not include an `extends` clause, Java provides one implicitly—`extends Object`. The class `Object` is the predefined ultimate base class in Java. All other classes extend `Object` through a chain of one or more steps. From the class `Object`, all classes inherit a number of useful methods. For example, all classes inherit a method `toString()` that returns a representation of the object in `String` form. (Recall that Java coerces any `x` to type `String` before concatenating, in an expression such as `"It is " + x`. If `x` is a reference, Java uses the `toString` method of that object to accomplish this coercion. All objects have such a method since all classes inherit one from `Object`.)

Sometimes you want to inherit some of the methods of a base class, but change others. In Java this can be accomplished by *overriding* the inherited definitions. There is no special mechanism for this. A definition of a method in a class will override any inherited definition for a method with the same name and type. (Remember that Java does allow method overloading, so you can have several methods with the same name but different types. A new method overrides an inherited method only if both the name and type are identical.)

Each time you use an `extends` clause, you are adding one link to the chain of inheritance. The word "chain" is not necessarily accurate here, since inheritance more generally forms a tree. Suppose, for example, that you are writing a program with a graphical user interface, and you have these classes named `Icon` and `Label`:

```
public class Icon {
  private int x,y;
  private int width,height;
  private Gif image;
  public void move(int newX, int newY) {
    x = newX;
    y = newY;
  }
  public Gif getImage() {
    return image;
  }
}

public class Label {
  private int x,y;
  private int width,height;
  private String text;
  public void move(int newX, int newY) {
    x = newX;
    y = newY;
  }
  public String getText() {
    return text;
  }
}
```

As you can see, `Icon` and `Label` have a lot in common. They have identical instance variables `x`, `y`, `width`, and `height`, and they have identical `move` methods. Yet neither one is an extension of the other. An `Icon` has an image, while a `Label` has a text string. So you cannot just have `public class Icon extends Label` or `public class Label extends Icon`. What you need is a common base class, from which both `Label` and `Icon` can inherit their shared implementation.

```
public class Graphic {
  protected int x,y;
  protected int width,height;
  public void move(int newX, int newY) {
    x = newX;
    y = newY;
  }
}
```

```
public class Icon extends Graphic {
  private Gif image;
  public Gif getImage() {
    return image;
  }
}

public class Label extends Graphic {
  private String text;
  public String getText() {
    return text;
  }
}
```

The resulting inheritance structure is a tree:

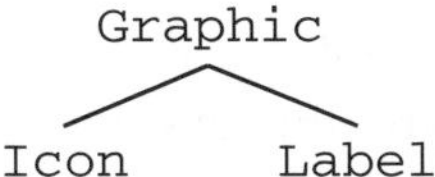

This use of inheritance should already seem familiar to you, no matter what language you are most comfortable with. That is because all modern languages give the programmer some way to avoid writing the same piece of code over and over again. When, for example, you find yourself writing the same block of code repeatedly, you should think, "I should collect that code into a method that I can call." Reusing code this way instead of replicating it is almost always a good thing. It saves your time, it reduces errors, it trims down the program size, and (most importantly) it makes the code easier to maintain. Tree-structured inheritance has the same effect at a higher level. When you find yourself writing the same method repeatedly, you should think, "I should collect that method into a class that I can extend." Of course, it is far better if you can perceive the need for a shared base class early in the design stage, before you actually create a lot of redundant code that needs to be reorganized.

Part of the challenge of object-oriented design is to construct a hierarchy of classes that helps you solve whatever problem you are facing. It is natural, and often very useful, to choose a hierarchy that corresponds to the intuitive real-world categories of things the program will manipulate. For example, a program operating an automatic teller machine might have a base class for cards, which has derived classes for credit cards, debit cards, ATM cards, and so on. Connecting your design to intuitive categories like this is often a good idea, but it can be overdone. One mistake that beginners often make is to ignore the question of how derived classes will extend the functionality of their base classes. For example, suppose you are writing a program that works with geometrical figures. You might leap in with a class hierarchy like this one:

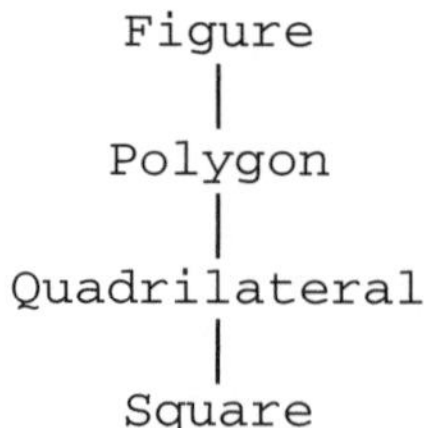

That makes sense, right? Every square is a quadrilateral, every quadrilateral is a polygon, and every polygon is a figure, so this is a nice intuitive categorization. However, there is no way to tell whether this makes sense as a design for a class hierarchy until you know what operations you want each object to support. Perhaps you want any `Figure x` to be able to skew itself—stretch itself out of shape. But it does not make sense for `Square` to inherit a `skew` method from `Figure`, since a skewed square is no longer square. This example shows that nice intuitive categorizations do not always translate into classes of objects that cleanly inherit functionality from each other. In Java, a derived class supports all the functionality of its base class and adds more. Remember this meditation from Chapter 6: "A subtype is a subset of the values, but it can support a superset of the operations." A derived class (treated as a type) is a subset of the base class, but it offers a superset of the functionality of the base class.[1]

15.4 Extending and Implementing

Classes often use `extends` and `implements` together. To see how this works, let's look at their operation in more detail.

For every Java class, the Java language system keeps track of several properties. These include:

A. The interfaces that it implements.
B. The methods that it is obliged to define.
C. The methods that are defined for it.
D. The fields that are defined for it.

1. The designers of Java made a good choice when they chose the keyword `extends`. It helps the programmer to remember the superset-of-functionality part, and not focus exclusively on the subset-of-values part.

A method definition in a class affects only C; it adds one method to the set of methods defined by the class. Similarly, a field definition in a class affects only D. An `implements` clause in a class affects A and B; it adds the interfaces that are listed in the `implements` clause to the set of interfaces implemented by the class, and it adds all the methods of those interfaces to the set of methods the class is obliged to define. This is still fairly simple. An `implements` clause does not affect parts C and D.

An `extends` clause is more complicated. It affects all four properties. It adds all the methods of the base class to C and all the fields of the base class to D—that is what is usually meant by *inheritance,* that the implementation of the base class is inherited by the derived class. It also adds all the interfaces implemented by the base class to A and adds all the methods that the base class is obliged to define to B. This is also a form of inheritance; the derived class inherits the interfaces and method obligations of the base class.

Consider the previous class `PeekableStack`. It extends the class `Stack`, and the class `Stack` implements the `Worklist` interface. Accordingly, `PeekableStack` also has `Worklist` as one of the interfaces it implements, though it does not say so explicitly. It inherits the `Worklist` interface from `Stack`. Because of this inherited interface, any variable of type `Worklist` is permitted to refer to an object of the class `PeekableStack`.

A class thus inherits all four properties back along its whole chain of ancestors in the inheritance tree. Normally, it ends up with all of its obligations satisfied; that is, the final set C is a superset of the final set B. Normally, it is an error if a class ends up with any obligations that it does not satisfy. A class can be declared `abstract`, in which case it need not meet all its obligations. A class whose only function is to serve as a base class that other classes will extend, like the `Graphic` example above, is often declared this way. A class can also declare an `abstract` method, which is a way of adding to the method obligations for the class without using an interface. But space doesn't permit exploring abstract methods and classes further.

15.5 Multiple Inheritance and How to Live without It

A Java class extends only a single base class. This is not true of all object-oriented languages. C++ allows a class to extend multiple base classes. This seems simple enough at first. A class would just inherit all the fields and methods from all the base classes, right? But there are, as always, complications.

Imagine that you are creating a `MultiFunction` class as part of the software controlling a multi-function printer—one that serves as a printer, copier, scanner, and fax machine. Since it should have the abilities of the different machines it replaces, you might want to use multiple inheritance for it, like this:

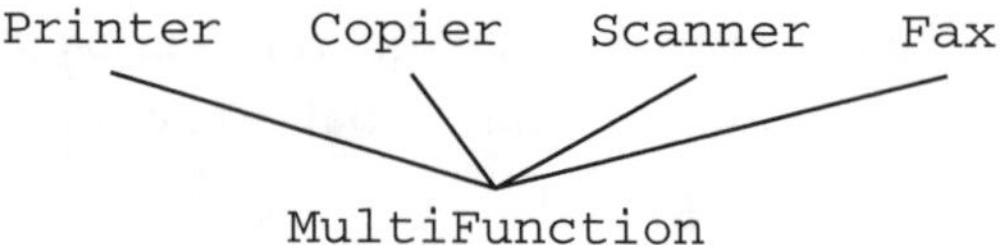

This can result in useful code-sharing, in a way that is not possible with single inheritance. It can also make the code more difficult to understand and maintain, since the different base classes may not have been designed to be combined. `Scanner` and `Fax` might, for example, both have a method named `transmit`. When you use the `transmit` method of a `Multifunction` object, does it transmit a scanned document to the computer or does it send a fax? Another kind of complexity is incurred by the possibility of *diamond inheritance:*

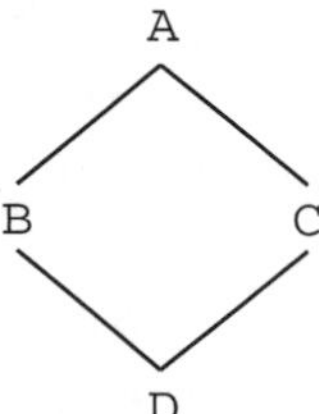

Here, class `D` has `A` as an ancestor through two different paths in the inheritance graph. If `A` has a field named `x`, then `B` inherits an `x` and C inherits an `x`. Does `D` then inherit two fields named `x`, or just one?

A language that supports multiple inheritance needs to define how such cases will be handled. This is not so very difficult—the question is whether the additional power you gain with multiple inheritance is worth the additional language complexity. This question has been debated thoroughly, without convincing many partisans on either side. Java, at any rate, is of the school that allows only single inheritance.

One reason multiple inheritance is attractive is that it allows a class to have several types that are not related to each other. In the example, an object of the class `MultiFunction` can be used anywhere a `Printer`, a `Copier`, a `Scanner`, or a `Fax` is expected. In Java you can get the same effect by using multiple interfaces. Remember that a class can implement as many interfaces as it wants. Another reason multiple inheritance is attractive is that it allows a class to inherit from several base classes. This cannot be so easily accomplished in a single-inheritance language like Java. Suppose that you want the effect of a multiple inheritance, like this:

```
public class MultiFunction
    extends Printer, Copier, Scanner, Fax {
  ...
}
```

Since Java does not allow multiple inheritance, you could instead have each `MultiFunction` object contain a reference to four other objects, a `Printer`, a `Copier`, a `Scanner`, and a `Fax`. Since there would be no inheritance, you would have to write methods for `MultiFunction` that pass along method calls to whichever of the member objects knows how to handle them. For example:

```
public class MultiFunction {
  private Printer myPrinter;
  private Copier myCopier;
  private Scanner myScanner;
  private Fax myFax;

  public void copy() {
    myCopier.copy();
  }
  public void transmitScanned() {
    myScanner.transmit();
  }
  public void sendFax() {
    myFax.transmit();
  }
  ...
}
```

This technique is called *forwarding*. The forwarding methods do not actually implement the functionality, they just forward the call and parameters to another object.

15.6 Generics and How to Live without Them

This is a good place to mention something else that is missing from Java: type variables. The `Node` class used in the `Stack` example earlier in this chapter had a lot in common with the `ConsCell` class from Chapter 13. In fact, they are nearly identical classes for linked-list elements. They both store an item and a link to the next element. There is just one critical difference: the type of the item. `ConsCell` stored an `int` item, while `Node` stored a `String`. Do you feel that there should be a way for the same class to handle both purposes? Many people do, and there has been a lot of discussion about extending Java with *generics* (that is, parameterized polymorphic classes and interfaces) to handle this more naturally.

ML uses type variables for this kind of thing. You could write

```
datatype 'a node =
  NULL |
  CELL of 'a * 'a node;
```

This would create a type constructor called `node` that could be used to create an `int node` or a `string node`. Something similar could be done with C++ and Ada. In Java, it would be nice to be able to give some type variables when defining an interface or class. Perhaps it would look something like this, using a type variable `T` for the type of element stored in `Node`:

```
public class Node<T> {
  private T data;
  private Node<T> link;
  public Node(T theData, Node<T> theLink) {
    data = theData;
    link = theLink;
  }
  public T getData() {
    return data;
  }
  public Node<T> getLink() {
    return link;
  }
}
```

This would give a generic `Node`, one that could be specialized to `Node<T>` for any type `T` and used to build linked lists containing items of any type. A generic `Stack` could then be written:

```
public class Stack<T> implements Worklist<T> {
  private Node<T> top = null;
  public void add(T data) {
    top = new Node<T>(data,top);
  }
  public boolean hasMore() {
    return (top != null);
  }
  public T remove() {
    Node<T> n = top;
    top = n.getLink();
```

```
    return n.getData();
  }
}
```

That generic `Stack` class might even implement a generic `Worklist` interface:

```
interface Worklist<T> {
  void add(T item);
  boolean hasMore();
  T remove();
}
```

You would use the generic `Stack` class like this:

```
Stack<String> s1 = new Stack<String>();
Stack<int> s2 = new Stack<int>();
s1.add("hello");
String s = s1.remove();
s2.add(1);
int i = s2.remove();
```

All this is not really part of Java. At least not as of the time of this writing. By the time you read this book, Java may have been extended in something like this way.

It is possible to implement a generic stack without using type variables, but it will not be as easy to use or as efficient. To implement a generic stack, you first need a class for a generic node. Instead of `Node` with its `String` variable, define `GenericNode` with a variable of type `Object`. Since `Object` is the ultimate base class for all classes in Java, a reference variable of type `Object` can refer to any class of object at runtime.

```
public class GenericNode {
  private Object data;
  private GenericNode link;
  public GenericNode(Object theData,
       GenericNode theLink) {
    data = theData;
    link = theLink;
  }
  public Object getData() {
    return data;
  }
  public GenericNode getLink() {
    return link;
  }
}
```

Similarly, you could define a `GenericStack` (and `GenericWorklist`) using the type `Object` instead of the type `String`.

One thing that makes `GenericStack` less easy to use than a truly generic `Stack<T>` is that a `GenericStack` object loses the type of the item. The following code would cause a compile-time error. Do you see what the error is?

```
GenericStack s1 = new GenericStack();
s1.add("hello");
String s = s1.remove();
```

The error is that the return type of the `remove` method is `Object`, but it is being assigned to a reference of type `String`. Since not all `Object` values are `String` values, Java will not permit this assignment. Of course you know that this particular `Object` actually *is* a `String`, since it is the value `"hello"` that you just pushed onto the stack. In Java you can use a *type cast* to convert the type of the value returned by `remove` to `String`. It looks like this:

```
GenericStack s1 = new GenericStack();
s1.add("hello");
String s = (String) s1.remove();
```

It is a pain to have to write this every time you call `remove`. It is an inefficiency as well—Java actually checks at runtime to make sure the object whose reference is being cast to the type `String` actually is a `String`.

Another thing that makes `GenericStack` less easy to use than a truly generic `Stack<T>` is that primitive types must be first stored in an object before being placed on the stack. The type `Object` in Java, which is the type `GenericStack` wants, includes all references but does not include primitive types like `int` and `boolean`. So to put integer values on the stack, you would have to do something like this:

```
GenericStack s2 = new GenericStack();
s2.add(new Integer(1));
int i = ((Integer) s2.remove()).intValue();
```

The expression `new Integer(1)` creates an object of the class `Integer` that holds the integer value 1. The `Integer` class is predefined in Java and is meant for just such occasions as this. All it does is hold an `int` value. (Such classes are sometimes called *wrapper* classes.) The example then pushes that object onto the stack. To get the top integer off the stack, as the example shows, you must unwrap the `int` value. First use the `remove` method, then cast the reference it returns to type `Integer`, and finally ask that `Integer` object for the `int` it holds by calling its `intValue` method. This is, again, both a pain to type and an inefficiency at runtime.

Notice that GenericStack allows items of different types to be placed on the same stack. A truly generic Stack<T> does not allow this; it only allows items of type T, whatever that is. This is usually a good thing, since it gives you stronger compile-time error checking. For example, if you intend to use a stack to hold only integers, you want the compiler to warn you if you try to push a string. But for those applications that really do want to push different kinds of things on the same stack, you could always use the generic type Stack<Object>, which would work just like GenericStack.

15.7 Conclusion

This chapter looked at two related techniques in Java: how to use interfaces and how to extend classes. Using interfaces is simpler, since it involves only polymorphism. Extending classes is more complicated, since it involves both polymorphism and inheritance. Most object-oriented languages include similar kinds of polymorphism and inheritance.

This chapter also showed two related features that Java does not (at the time of this writing) support: generic classes and multiple inheritance. These are more advanced forms of polymorphism and inheritance. The chapter looked at some simple examples of how to make do without them.

The exercises that follow are longer than most of the others in this book. They are not more difficult, but they do involve larger pieces of code. The reason for this is simple: interfaces and derived classes are useful primarily for organizing large programs. There is no way to practice using these techniques in short exercises! Even the longer exercises that follow are still too short to demonstrate the full benefits of interfaces and derived classes in Java. But at least they should help you get the idea.

Exercises

All the Java code you need for these exercises is available both in print in this chapter and on this book's Web site, **http://www.webber-labs.com/mpl.html**.

Exercise 1 For this exercise you will need the definition of the Worklist interface from page 275 and the definition of the Node and Stack classes starting on page 276. Write two additional classes, as follows:

a. Write a class Queue that implements the Worklist interface, using a first-in-first-out order. Implement your Queue using a linked list.

b. Write a class `PriorityQueue` that implements the `Worklist` interface. No matter in what order strings are added with the `add` method, the `remove` method should always return the alphabetically first string still in the worklist. (To compare two strings alphabetically, use the `compareTo` method of the `String` class. `s.compareTo(r)` is less than zero if `s` comes before `r`, equal to zero if `s` and `r` are equal, and greater than zero if `s` comes after `r`.) You need not implement a high-efficiency data structure; an implementation using linked lists will do.

You may modify the `Node` class if necessary, but do not change it in a way that breaks the original `Stack` class.

You will need to write some code to test your classes. You can implement `Driver`-type classes to test your code, as in Chapter 13. An alternative is to add a `main` method directly to each class you want to test. For example, if you add the following method to the `Stack` class, you can then run `Stack` as an application and check that the strings come out in stack order:

```
public static void main(String[] args) {
  Worklist w = new Stack();
  w.add("able");
  w.add("charlie");
  w.add("baker");
  while (w.hasMore()) {
    System.out.println(w.remove());
  }
}
```

A similar method to test `Queue` and `PriorityQueue` is a good place to start. (Test your code more thoroughly than this!)

You also might be interested in testing your code using an interactive tester with a graphical user interface. The class `WorklistDemo`, available on this book's Web site, can be run as an application or as an applet. When you place `WorklistDemo.java` in a directory with the other class definitions it needs (`Worklist.java`, `Node.java`, `Stack.java`, `Queue.java`, and `PriorityQueue.java`), you can compile and run it, testing your `Worklist` implementations interactively. Though the Java API is not covered in this book, you might be interested in looking at the source code for `WorklistDemo`. It shows how to use the API to create a simple applet with a graphical user interface.

Exercise 2 This exercise deals with dictionaries of strings. A dictionary object has a collection of key strings and associates each one with a value string. You might think of the key as a word in the dictionary and the associated value as the definition of that word. A dictionary object has three basic methods: `find`, `size`, and `associate`. The `find` method takes a key (a parameter of type `String`) and returns the corresponding value, or `null` if that key is not found in the dictionary. The `size` method returns the integer number of distinct keys in the dictionary. A dictionary is initially empty, but the `associate` method adds a new entry (or replaces an existing entry). It takes two `String` parameters, the key and the value, and adds that pair to the dictionary. It returns the previous value associated with that key, or `null` if that key was not previously in the dictionary.

You will see three different ways of implementing this functionality. The first two use a simple linked list of key/value pairs. An object of the class `ANode` is an element of such a list:

```
public class ANode {
  private String key;
  private String value;
  private ANode link;
  public ANode(String k, String v, ANode li) {
    key = k;
    value = v;
    link = li;
  }
  public String getKey() {
    return key;
  }
  public ANode getLink() {
    return link;
  }
  public String getValue() {
    return value;
  }
  public void setValue(String v) {
    value = v;
  }
}
```

The `AList` class that follows uses a linked list of `ANode` objects to implement a dictionary of strings. Notice that the only mutator for `ANode` objects is `setValue`. The value associated with a given key may be changed, but otherwise the dictionary changes only by growing. Existing entries are not removed or reordered, and keys are not changed.

```
public class AList {
  private ANode head = null;
  public String associate(String key, String value) {
```

```
    ANode n = nodeLookup(key);
    String oldValue;
    if (n != null) {
      oldValue = n.getValue();
      n.setValue(value);
    }
    else {
      n = new ANode(key, value, head);
      head = n;
      oldValue = null;
    }
    return oldValue;
  }
  public String find(String key) {
    ANode n = nodeLookup(key);
    return (n == null) ? null : n.getValue();
  }
  private ANode nodeLookup(String key) {
    ANode n = head;
    while (n!=null && !n.getKey().equals(key)) {
      n = n.getLink();
    }
    return n;
  }
  public int size() {
    ANode n = head;
    int length = 0;
    while (n!=null) {
      n = n.getLink();
      length++;
    }
    return length;
  }
}
```

Here is another way of implementing a dictionary of strings. This is similar to the first, but it keeps track of its length in an integer field. That way, when the `size` method is called, it is able to respond in constant time, instead of having to traverse the linked list to compute the size.

```
public class SizedAList {
  private ANode head = null;
  private int size = 0;
  public String associate(String key, String value) {
    ANode n = nodeLookup(key);
    String oldValue;
    if (n != null) {
      oldValue = n.getValue();
```

```
        n.setValue(value);
      }
      else {
        n = new ANode(key, value, head);
        head = n;
        oldValue = null;
        size++;
      }
      return oldValue;
    }
    public String find(String key) {
      ANode n = nodeLookup(key);
      return (n == null) ? null : n.getValue();
    }
    private ANode nodeLookup(String key) {
      ANode n = head;
      while (n!=null && !n.getKey().equals(key)) {
        n = n.getLink();
      }
      return n;
    }
    public int size() {
      return size;
    }
  }
```

A good way to implement a dictionary of strings is already available as part of the Java API. The predefined class `java.util.Hashtable` is a general-purpose, hash-table-based dictionary that is not limited to strings. The three methods can be implemented as simple "forwarding" calls to a `Hashtable` object like this:

```
  public class AHash {
    private java.util.Hashtable table =
      new java.util.Hashtable();
    public String associate(String key, String value) {
      return (String) table.put(key,value);
    }
    public String find(String key) {
      return (String) table.get(key);
    }
    public int size() {
      return table.size();
    }
  }
```

For this exercise, rewrite all three of the classes above and add any classes or interfaces you need to achieve the following goals:

- The three basic dictionary-of-strings methods should be part of an interface named `DictionaryOfStrings`, which should be implemented by all three classes. With this in place, you would be able to pass an `AList`, a `SizedAList`, or an `AHash` object to a method that expects a parameter of type `DictionaryOfStrings`, and that method would be able to use `find`, `size`, and `associate` without knowing the exact class of the object.
- You should use inheritance where appropriate to minimize the amount of duplicated code among the three implementations. Notice, in particular, that the current implementations of `AList` and `SizedAList` have much code in common.
- You should comment the class appropriately; that is, comment every interface, every class, every field, and every method, as well as anything in the code that you think needs explanation.

Do not make any material changes to the method bodies. Check that your code compiles. Other than that, there is no need to test your code, since the method bodies given already work.

Exercise 3 Write `GenericAList`, a generic version of the `AList` class from the previous exercise, that works with keys and values that are objects of any class. (You will need a generic version of `ANode` as well.)

When comparing keys for equality, continue to use the `equals` method; that is, test `x.equals(y)` instead of switching to `x==y`. You might ask, what if `x` is now of some class that does not have an `equals` method? Don't worry, there is no such class. One of the methods that all classes inherit from the root class `Object` is the `equals` method. If `x` is a reference to any object and `y` is any reference-type variable, you can always evaluate `x.equals(y)`—in effect, asking `x` to report whether or not it is equal to `y`. The inherited implementation is the simplest. `x.equals(y)` is more or less the same as `x==y`. But classes are free to override this inherited method with a more sophisticated test. (For example, if `x` and `y` are `String` objects, `x.equals(y)` will be true if they contain the same sequence of characters, even if they are not the same object.)

Now write a class `IntAList` that implements a dictionary with `int` keys and values and uses a `GenericAList` to store them. Your `IntAList` class should have these three methods:

```
public void associate(int key, int value);
public int find(int key);
public int size();
```

Notice that the `associate` method in `IntAList` does not need to return a value.

Exercise 4 Consider again the `AList` class from Exercise 2. Suppose you wanted to write Java code to implement this pseudocode:

> *for each key in the* `AList x {`
> *look up the value for that key in* `x`
> *print out the key and value*
> `}`

Of course, it would be easy to do if you had access to the private variables of the `AList` class. But the more interesting design problem is this: how can a container class (like `AList`) provide a way for its users to iterate over its contents (as needed in the pseudocode), without revealing its own implementation details?

One popular object-oriented solution to this problem is to use an *iterator*, an object whose only function is to iterate over the contents of some container. Using an iterator, you might implement the pseudocode this way:

```
StringIterator i = x.getIterator();
while (i.hasNext()) {
  String key = i.next();
  String value = x.find(key);
  System.out.println(key + " - " + value);
}
```

As you can see, the `AList` object `x` would have a method called `getIterator`, which would return an object of type `StringIterator`. (Typically, `StringIterator` would actually be an interface implemented by the iterator object, so that each different kind of string dictionary could have a different kind of iterator, but all the iterators would implement a common interface.) The `StringIterator` has a method called `hasNext` that reports whether there are any more items to go and a method called `next` that returns the next key in the `AList`.

Implement this idea for the `AList` class as follows:

a. Write a `StringIterator` interface with the two iterator methods used.
b. Write an `AListIterator` class that implements the `StringIterator` interface for iterating over the contents of an `AList`.
c. Add a `getIterator` method to the `AList` class. (You should not need to make any other changes to `AList`.)

If you did Exercise 2, it would be natural to add the `getIterator` method to the `DictionaryOfStrings` interface. The `SizedAList` class would be able to use the same iterator as `AList`. The `AHash` class would, of course, need a completely different implementation, but you would not have to do that for this exercise.

There is, by the way, a general-purpose interface in the Java API called `Iterator`. The `Hashtable` class can supply an `Iterator` for iterating over its contents, as can many other predefined container classes in the API. The `Iterator` class includes similar `hasNext` and `next` methods, although `next` is generic. It returns a value of type `Object`. (There we go again—another place where we might want to use generics if Java supported them.) The `Iterator` interface also has an optional `remove` method, so you can remove items as you iterate over the container. It is a bit more complicated than the interface, since it makes use of exceptions in Java. You will see all about exceptions in Chapter 17.

Chapter 16 **Object Orientation**

16.1 Introduction

This was said about object-oriented programming and object-oriented languages back in Chapter 13:

> In object-oriented programming, programs are designed using objects—little bundles of data that know how to do things to themselves. We don't say, "the computer knows how to move the point." Instead we say, "the point knows how to move itself." That makes all the difference. Object-oriented languages, like Java, are designed to make this way of thinking easier.

That was a casual description, but not a definition. What exactly is object-oriented programming? What exactly is an object-oriented language?

If you have read the previous chapters, you know those questions are not going to be answered! In the first place, there is a lot of disagreement about exactly what those terms mean.[1] Moreover, definitions for those terms are not very useful. Object orientation is not a black-and-white issue. Some programming styles, and some languages, are more object oriented than others. You must use your own judgment and decide for yourself how object oriented a programming style or a language is—and whether you like it that way or not. A casual intuitive understanding is, in this instance, more serviceable than a rigorous definition, and less boring.

Without definitions, however, some important generalizations about object orientation can still be made. This chapter offers two:

1. Object-oriented programming is not the same thing as programming in an object-oriented language.
2. Object-oriented languages are not all like Java.

Section 16.2 makes the first point using two examples. It shows how one can develop an object-oriented programming style in virtually any language, and how one can write completely un-object-oriented programs in an object-oriented language. Section 16.3 makes the second point by giving a guided tour of object-oriented language features. There are many object-oriented languages out there that illustrate many different ideas about how a language can support an object-oriented programming style.

16.2 Object-Oriented Programming

You can program in an object-oriented style in virtually any language—in assembly language, if need be. On the other hand, you can use virtually any object-oriented language in a non-object-oriented way. To illustrate this point, consider two longer examples in this section: an object-oriented stack implementation in ML and a non-object-oriented stack implementation in Java.

Object-Oriented ML

To illustrate object-oriented programming in a non-object-oriented language, let us revisit the stack example from the previous chapter. This time, we will implement it in ML.

Recall that we used a `Node` class in the Java implementation for objects representing elements in a linked list. Here it is again (with the comments suppressed this time):

---

1. Part of this argument is driven by marketing forces. *Object oriented* is, at the moment, a trendy and positive appellation—a buzzword. Software marketers (and language advocates in general) want definitions that are broad enough to include their products or, alternatively, narrow enough to exclude competitors' products.

```
public class Node {
  private String data;
  private Node link;
  public Node(String theData, Node theLink) {
    data = theData;
    link = theLink;
  }
  public String getData() {
    return data;
  }
  public Node getLink() {
    return link;
  }
}
```

In ML, we will implement objects as functions. What else? Objects will be functions that take a message and return a response. We will define a type `message` for messages and a type `response` for responses, and the type for objects will be `message -> response`.

Here is a simple implementation of a `node` object in ML. The messages for `node` objects correspond to the Java methods `getData` and `getLink`.

```
datatype message =
    GetData
  | GetLink;

datatype response =
    Data of string
  | Object of message -> response;

fun node data link GetData = Data data
  | node data link GetLink = Object link;
```

Notice that the `node` function is curried. Supplying the first two parameters results in a function that takes a message (`GetData` or `GetLink`) and returns the appropriate response. In other words, if we supply the first two parameters, *the result is an object*. For example, let `f` be any object, and let `g` be the value of `node "fred" y`. Clearly, `g` is a function. It was constructed by giving `node` its first two parameters only, so it is still waiting for a `message`, which will be `GetData` or `GetLink`. Depending on that message, it will return one of two things. `g GetData` will evaluate to `Data "fred"`, while `g GetLink` will evaluate to `Object x`. In short, `g` is an object; you give it a `message`, it produces a `response`.

So the function `node` not only corresponds to the Java class definition `Node`, but also takes the place of the Java constructor. To experiment with this, we will need one more definition—an object that corresponds to the Java value `null`. In order to use `node`, we need a value for the `link` parameter. That value must have the object type `message -> response`. This definition will serve for now (in a moment, we will come up with something more general):

```
fun null _ = Data "null";
```

To see how this `node` function works, use it to create some `node` objects and see how they respond to a `GetData` message:

```
- val n1 = node "Hello" null;
val n1 = fn : message -> response
- val n2 = node "world" n1;
val n2 = fn : message -> response
- n1 GetData;
val it = Data "Hello" : response
- n2 GetData;
val it = Data "world" : response
```

The full stack implementation that follows uses this same object-oriented style. The `message` and `response` types have been enlarged to accommodate the `add`, `hasMore`, and `remove` methods for stacks. In the Java implementation, the `add` and `remove` methods have side effects on the object: they make the object change its state. That can be done in ML too, but not using the purely functional part. Instead, the ML versions of these methods return a new object. The original object continues to exist in its original state, and the new object reflects the results of the `Add` or `Remove` message. Notice that the `null` class has been implemented more uniformly. A `null` object handles the `IsNull` message by returning `Pred true`.

```
datatype message =
    IsNull
  | Add of string
  | HasMore
  | Remove
  | GetData
  | GetLink;

datatype response =
    Pred of bool
  | Data of string
  | Removed of (message -> response) * string
  | Object of message -> response;

fun root _ = Pred false;
```

```
fun null IsNull = Pred true
  | null message = root message;

fun node data link GetData = Data data
  | node data link GetLink = Object link
  | node _ _ message = root message;

fun stack top HasMore =
      let val Pred(p) = top IsNull in Pred(not p) end
  | stack top (Add data) = Object(stack (node data top))
  | stack top Remove =
      let
        val Object(next) = top GetLink
        val Data(data) = top GetData
      in
        Removed(stack next, data)
      end
  | stack _ message = root message;
```

All the objects, whether they are `node` objects or `stack` objects or something else, have the type `message -> response`. This makes weak use of ML's typing. In particular, there is no compile-time warning if an inappropriate message is passed to an object. The Java type system warns you at compile time if you try to call a method that an object does not implement. But in this ML implementation, we have to define the behavior of objects in response to inappropriate messages. For example, what should a `node` object do with a `HasMore` message? The example above includes a root class called `root`. The `null`, `node`, and `stack` objects pass unexpected messages to `root`. In effect, they inherit the behavior of `root` on these messages—which is to return `Pred false`.

This shows the ML objects at work, on an example from Chapter 15:

```
- val a = stack null;
val a = fn : message -> response
- val Object(b) = a (Add "the plow.");
val b = fn : message -> response
- val Object(c) = b (Add "forgives ");
val c = fn : message -> response
- val Object(d) = c (Add "The cut worm ");
val d = fn : message -> response
- val Removed(e,s1) = d Remove;
val e = fn : message -> response
val s1 = "The cut worm " : string
- val Removed(f,s2) = e Remove;
val f = fn : message -> response
val s2 = "forgives " : string
```

```
- val Removed(_,s3) = f Remove;
val s3 = "the plow." : string
- s1^s2^s3;
val it = "The cut worm forgives the plow." : string
```

To make the last example more readable, many compiler warnings were edited out. This is what the ML language system actually says in response to that first `val` definition using `Remove`:

```
- val Removed(e,s1) = d Remove;
   Warning: binding not exhaustive
          Removed (e,s1) = ...
val e = fn : message -> response
val s1 = "The cut worm " : string
```

For all the compiler knows, `d Remove` might produce any value of type `response`. The type of `d`, after all, is just `message -> response`, like any other object. The `val` definition assumes that the response will match the pattern `Removed(e,s1)`. Although that is true in this case, it is not guaranteed by the types involved. The many "binding not exhaustive" warnings are a result of the weak typing of objects in this style of object-oriented programming in ML.[2]

Chapter 15 went on to implement a derived Java class named `PeekableStack`. This class inherits from `Stack` and adds a `peek` method for peeking at the top of the stack without popping the element off. If `Peek` is added to the message type, the same thing can be implemented in ML this way:

```
fun peekableStack top Peek = top GetData
  | peekableStack top message = stack top message;
```

`peekableStack` "inherits" the behavior of `stack` for everything except the new `Peek` message.

The example above uses messages for communicating with objects, passes unhandled messages back to a "superclass" to get the effect of inheritance, and does not use much typing. All the messages have the same type, all the objects have the same type, and all the responses have the same type. Consequently, an incorrect message to an object or an incorrect response would not be caught at compile time. The approach is a bit like a classical implementation of the Smalltalk language (which is not statically type checked at all). It is not the only way, or even the best way, to do object-oriented programming in ML. It merely illustrates that it is possible to develop an object-oriented programming style in ML. Not natural, perhaps, but possible.

---

2. The ML dialect OCaml adds class-based objects to ML in a way that makes stronger use of the type system. Like Java, at compile time it rules out the error of sending an incorrect message to an object.

Non-Object-Oriented Java

Java forces a programmer to create classes (or at least one class) and to write methods for it (or at least one method). But that does not guarantee that the resulting program is object oriented—not at all. To illustrate the point, here is a non-object-oriented implementation of the stack of strings in Java. It still uses the classes named `Node` and `Stack`, as follows:

```
public class Node {
  public String data; // Each node has a String...
  public Node link;   // ...and a link to the next Node
}

public class Stack{
  public Node top;  // The top node in the stack
}
```

These classes no longer have any methods or constructors. All their fields are public. They are, in effect, just like records in many older languages. In this implementation, all the code is organized into static methods of a class named `Main`:

```
public class Main {
  private static void add(Stack s, String data) {
    Node n = new Node();
    n.data = data;
    n.link = s.top;
    s.top = n;
  }
  private static boolean hasMore(Stack s) {
    return (s.top != null);
  }
  private static String remove(Stack s) {
    Node n = s.top;
    s.top = n.link;
    return n.data;
  }
  public static void main(String[] args) {
    Stack s = new Stack();
    add(s,"able");
    add(s,"charlie");
    add(s,"baker");
    while (hasMore(s)) {
      System.out.println(remove(s));
    }
  }
}
```

As you can see, Java allows you to read and write the fields of a class directly. For instance, the expression `s.top = n.link` copies the value in the `link` field of the object referred to by `n` into the `top` field of the object referred to by `s`. The static methods of `Main` use this technique to operate on the data stored in `Node` and `Stack` objects. Since the data for a stack is completely separate from the code that operates on it, this would not be called an object-oriented solution.

Chapter 15 developed an interface called `Worklist` that could be implemented by different classes for managing collections of strings—stacks, queues, or priority queues, for example. Interfaces (in a truly object-oriented Java program) are a very useful source of polymorphism. A client can call the `add` method of an object without knowing the exact class of the object. Non-object-oriented programs sometimes try to achieve this kind of behavior manually.

Here is a non-object-oriented class definition for a `Worklist`. A `Worklist` can hold the data for a stack, a queue, or a priority queue. It includes a "type" code that tells what kind of `Worklist` it is.

```
public class Worklist {
  public static final int STACK = 0;
  public static final int QUEUE = 1;
  public static final int PRIORITYQUEUE = 2;
  public int type; // one of the above Worklist types
  public Node front; // front Node in the list
  public Node rear; // unused when type==STACK
  public int length; // unused when type==STACK
}
```

The example above declares the variables `STACK`, `QUEUE`, and `PRIORITYQUEUE` to be `public`, `static`, and `final`. A `static final` variable is simply a named constant in Java. The three constants together make up a kind of artificial enumeration, a list of the three possible kinds of `Worklist` structures the program is going to support. Each `Worklist` object contains a `type` field that will be assigned one of the three constant values. The other fields have meanings that depend on what kind of `Worklist` it is. Two of them are unused if the `Worklist` is a stack.

To implement this, all the methods that operate on a `Worklist` have to branch on the value of the `type` field. The `Main` class needs an `add` method like this:

```
private static void add(Worklist w, String data) {
  if (w.type == Worklist.STACK) {
    Node n = new Node();
    n.data = data;
    n.link = w.front;
    w.front = n;
  }
```

```
    else if (w.type == Worklist.QUEUE) {
      the implementation of add for queues
    }
    else if (w.type == Worklist.PRIORITYQUEUE) {
      the implementation of add for priority queues
    }
  }
```

Every method that operates on a `Worklist` has to contain a similar branching:

```
  private static String remove(Worklist w) {
    String item = null;
    if (w.type == Worklist.STACK) {
      Node n = w.front;
      w.front = n.link;
      item = n.data;
    }
    else if (w.type == Worklist.QUEUE) {
      the implementation of remove for queues
    }
    else if (w.type == Worklist.PRIORITYQUEUE) {
      the implementation of remove for priority queues
    }
    return item;
  }
```

This is a common design pattern in non-object-oriented, imperative programs. To implement the same set of operations on a variety of different kinds of records, an enumeration defines a code for each different kind of record, each record starts with the code identifying what kind of record it is, and each relevant method branches on this identifying code.

This non-object-oriented technique has drawbacks. Programming the same branching structure over and over, in every relevant method, is tedious and error-prone. Depending on the language, there may be no way to avoid wasting space in the records, when the different kinds of records require different fields. Worst of all, common maintenance tasks require modifying many widely scattered pieces of the program. For example, adding a new kind of record to such a system would be difficult, since the whole program would have to be examined and more code added to each place where the identifying codes were used.[3]

---

3. This is not too difficult if the program makes disciplined use of the identifying codes, as in the neatly patterned branching examples. Unfortunately, it is very tempting to use those small-integer identifying codes in tricky ways, as branch offsets, for example, or as indexes into an array. These uses can be much harder to find and update when the codes are expanded or altered. The author has encountered code like this in legacy systems in assembly language, PL/I, and C. Encountered it, and created it. *Mea culpa.*

Object-oriented programming avoids these drawbacks. When a method of an interface is called, the language system automatically dispatches the call to the correct implementation for the actual class of the object. (In effect, the language system does the branch-on-the-identifying-code step for you automatically.) Different implementations of the same interface need have nothing in common beyond the methods the interface requires; in particular, they need not include unused fields. Finally, by grouping all the code that applies to a given kind of object together, object-oriented program organization makes many common maintenance tasks easier. For example, to add a new class that implements an interface, you do not have to modify existing code at all.[4]

Summary

Object-oriented programming is not the same thing as programming in an object-oriented language. An object-oriented style can be used in any language, and object-oriented languages can be used in non-object-oriented ways. There are occasionally good reasons for doing one or the other. But for the most part, object-oriented languages and an object-oriented style of programming do and should go together. You can do object-oriented programming in ML, but it is not quite natural and not usually a good idea. You can write Java programs that make heavy use of enumerations, but this also is not quite natural, and you usually get a better Java design by using a more object-oriented style. (Java encourages this by not including a separate type constructor for enumerations.)

16.3 A Menagerie of Object-Oriented Language Features

The last section looked at some issues in object-oriented program design. This is an important topic, but any further discussion of it would be outside the scope of this book. It is a large subject and deserves a book of its own. This book's interest is in programming languages. Object-oriented languages have features designed to support an object-oriented style of programming. This section looks at some of these features.

This is just a guided tour of some of the highlights. There are many object-oriented programming languages. Some are very different from Java.

---

4. Object-oriented program organization can also make some maintenance tasks harder. In particular, it makes the task of adding a new operation to an interface more difficult, since all the separate classes that implement the interface have to be modified. Andrew Appel gives a good example of this in his book, *Modern Compiler Implementation in Java*. He encounters a particular design problem in Java for which, he argues, avoiding the object-oriented style produces a better solution.

Classes

Most object-oriented languages, including Java, have some kind of class construct. A class can serve a variety of purposes:

- A class groups together the fields and methods that a set of objects have. This is central to the earlier casual description of an object—a bundle of data (the fields) that knows how to do things to itself (the methods).
- A class is *instantiable.* That is, a running program can create as many objects of the class as it needs. A class contains the constructors that the program can use to allocate and initialize new objects of that class. A class is like a mold for objects. The constructors stamp out new objects using that mold.
- A class is the unit of inheritance. A derived class inherits, as a group, the fields and methods of its base class.
- In statically type checked languages, a class can serve as a type. Objects (or references to objects) can have a class or superclass as their static type.
- In some languages, including Java, a class can include static fields and methods. Static fields have only one instance, not one per object. Static methods are called without an object of the class to operate on, so they can access static fields only.
- A class can serve as a labeled namespace (as was shown in Chapter 10). In some languages, a class can control the degree to which its contents are visible outside of the class.

Prototypes

Imagine an object-oriented language without classes. How would it work? With classes, the constructor for a class can create a new object, like this:

```
x = new Stack();
```

Without classes, an object could be created from scratch by listing all its methods and fields on the spot:

```
x = {
  private Node top = null;
  public boolean hasMore() {
    return (top != null);
  }
  public String remove() {
    Node n = top;
    top = n.getLink();
    return n.getData();
  }
  ...
}
```

Alternatively, if an object `y` is similar to the one that needs to be created (a stack of some kind), `y` could be used as a prototype for the new object. `y` could be copied and then have some of its fields modified:

```
x = y.clone();
x.top = null;
```

Object-oriented languages that work this way are called *prototype-based* languages. Self is an example of such a language. A prototype is just an object that is copied to make other, similar objects. Prototype-based languages have constructs for creating objects from scratch (by defining methods and fields) and for making modified copies of existing objects. When making modified copies, a program not only can change the contents of fields, but also can add or remove fields or methods.

This is only one part of getting along without classes; that is, creating new objects without the class-and-constructor mechanism. But if you look back at the list of things classes do in class-based languages, you will see several other things a classless language must do without. Without classes, it is difficult to devise useful static types for objects. Most prototype-based languages are not statically type checked at all, so they do not need static types for objects. Without classes, there is no framework on which to build a static inheritance hierarchy. Many prototype-based languages use a related dynamic mechanism called *delegation,* which is discussed below.

There is also a philosophical difference between class-based and prototype-based languages. For example, consider the question, "What is a cat?" The class-based language answers with a list of properties (that is, fields and methods): "A cat is an animal with four legs, a tail, fur, and whiskers that can run, jump, eat, catch mice… ." By contrast, the prototype-based language answers with an example: "A cat is like Tabby here." The meaning of "like Tabby" is flexible. The more things something has in common with the prototypical Tabby, the more catlike it is. Even if it cannot catch mice it can still be a cat, according to this definition, since it can still have a lot in common with Tabby. People who like the prototype approach argue that the class approach is too crisp to accurately model the natural fuzziness of many concepts.

Inheritance

The general idea of inheritance is simple enough. Two classes, a base class and a derived class, have a relationship such that the derived class gets things from the base class. But exactly what a derived class gets from its base class (or classes) varies considerably from language to language. Here are some of the points on which languages differ:

- Can a derived class have more than one base class? That is, does the language support multiple inheritance? Languages that allow only single inheritance include Smalltalk and Java. Languages that support multiple inheritance include C++, CLOS, and Eiffel. Some of the complexities of multiple inheritance were discussed in Chapter 15.
- Must a derived class inherit all the methods and fields of the base class, or can it pick and choose? Derived classes in Java inherit all methods and fields. In Sather, a derived class can *rename* inherited methods (which can be used to work around some of the complexities of multiple inheritance), or it can simply undefine them.
- Is there a common root to the inheritance hierarchy—a class from which all other classes inherit? Java has one (the class `Object`). C++ does not.
- What happens when a derived class has a method or field definition with the same name and type as an inherited one? In Java, method definitions in the derived class can sometimes override matching inherited method definitions. But not always; a method definition in the base class can be declared `final`, indicating that no overriding is permitted. And overriding is not permitted to restrict the visibility of methods, for example, by overriding a `public` definition with a `private` one. Field definitions in the derived class hide matching definitions in the base class, but the base-class definitions are still present and can be accessed using namespace constructs. Such details differ considerably from language to language.
- Does a derived class inherit specification from the base class? In Java, a derived class inherits a collection of method obligations from the base class. These are method prototypes for which matching method definitions must be supplied. This is a rudimentary kind of specification. Some languages, like Eiffel, take the idea of inherited specification much further. For example, an Eiffel class inherits *invariants* specified for its base class. Invariants are assertions about the class that are always true; for example, the assertion that an integer field is always positive. A derived class is not allowed to break its inherited invariants.
- Does a derived class inherit membership in types from the base class? In Java, a derived class inherits membership in all the types of the base class—all its interfaces, all its inherited types, and the base-class type itself.

Prototype-based languages cannot have inheritance in the usual sense, since they have no classes. The corresponding mechanism for prototype-based languages is called *delegation*. When an object gets a method call that it cannot handle, it can arrange to delegate it to another object. If an object delegates to the object from which it was originally cloned, delegation can end up working quite a bit like inheritance. But delegation can be more elaborate. Some languages permit an object to choose an arbitrary object to delegate to and to change its delegation as the program runs.

Encapsulation

Encapsulation is an important part of virtually all modern programming languages, not just the object-oriented ones. Without encapsulation, every part of a program is visible to every other part. This sounds nice and friendly, but it makes large programs extremely difficult to develop and maintain. Decades of practical experience have taught programmers the importance of building large programs from small parts whose correctness can be judged in isolation. Programming languages help by offering constructs that enforce, or at least encourage, the isolation of small parts. Encapsulated parts present a controlled interface to the rest of the program. Beyond that defined interface, their internal workings are invisible and independent. In object-oriented languages, these encapsulated parts are the objects.

One important tool for encapsulation in Java is the controlled visibility of the fields and methods of an object. If a field is declared to be `private`, only the methods of the class can access it. The rest of the program does not need to be checked to make sure no one else writes to that field, because the language system enforces the declared visibility. Similarly, if a method is declared to be `private`, there can be no calls to that method from other parts of the program. It is part of the invisible, independent, *encapsulated* workings of objects of that class.

Java `interface` types provide another kind of aid for encapsulation. When you work with a reference variable whose declared type is an interface name, you are permitted to use only the methods that are part of that interface. A compile-time error will alert you if you try to use any of the other methods and fields that may be offered by the object in question. This is not as strict as controlling the visibility of the fields—you could always use a typecast to access the other visible parts of the object. But it does encourage, if not enforce, encapsulation.

Other object-oriented languages vary in the amount of encapsulation they provide. Some, like Smalltalk, Loops, and Self, provide little; all fields and all methods are, in effect, public. Eiffel, by contrast, provides very precise control over visibility; methods and fields ("features," in Eiffel parlance) can be made visible to a specified set of client classes. Other languages, like Dylan, allow access to fields only through accessor and mutator functions, which are included at the programmer's discretion. (That is the style followed in this book's Java examples, but Java also allows direct access to fields, while Dylan does not).

Polymorphism

Polymorphism plays a role in many modern languages, but object-oriented languages have a peculiar need for it. When objects of different classes have a method of the same name and type, it often makes sense to be able to call that method in contexts where the exact class of the object is not known at compile time. For example, both stack objects and queue objects may have an `add` method, and that method might have to be used in contexts where it is not known at compile time whether the container being added to is a stack or a queue. To make this work in a statically type checked language, some kind of polymorphism is necessary.

As was shown for Java in Chapter 15, the declared type of a reference variable and the exact class of an object to which that variable refers at runtime are not necessarily the same. In Java, the declared type may be a base class extended by the object's exact class, or it may be an interface implemented by the object's exact class. This gives a kind of subtype polymorphism. The exact class is a subtype of the declared type. Most statically type checked, class-based, object-oriented languages provide polymorphism in a similar way.

Such polymorphism has a hidden cost. At compile time, when the language system sees a method call, it knows the declared type of the object but not (necessarily) the exact class of the object. Not knowing the exact class at compile time, the language system cannot decide which implementation of the target method to call. It must defer the decision until runtime, when the actual class of the object is known. This facility is called *dynamic dispatch*. C++ offers dynamic dispatch as an option; in Java and most other object-oriented languages, dynamic dispatch is always used. Remember the non-object-oriented implementation of a worklist in Java, where each method had to branch on the worklist type. Dynamic dispatch has to do exactly the same kind of branching. Because of this hidden branching, polymorphic method calls are slowed down a little. (Dynamic dispatch also requires the language system to represent the exact class of objects at runtime. This may make objects take a little more space in memory—though most object-oriented languages have other features that already require each object to carry information about its exact class.)

To support this kind of polymorphism, a language must include some way for classes to have supertypes. Java has two ways to do this: by implementing an interface and by extending a base class. When a class implements an interface, it gets a supertype only. It must implement the methods necessary to qualify for the specified interface type. When a class extends a base class, it gets a supertype and inherits implementation. It gets the base class as a supertype, and inherits all the method and field definitions of the base class.

With these two overlapping mechanisms, Java makes a partial distinction between getting a supertype and inheriting implementation. Other object-oriented languages vary in the degree to which they separate these two aspects of inheritance. C++ provides less separation than Java. It has only one mechanism for general inheritance, and a derived class gets both supertype and implementation from its base classes. (If the base class does not specify any implementation, the derived class gets type only. Using private inheritance, the derived class can conceal the inherited type, in effect getting implementation only.) By contrast, Sather provides more separation of the two aspects of inheritance than Java—really, complete separation. A Sather class can *include* other classes, in which case it gets only implementation but not type. A class can also declare that it is a subclass of an abstract class (the Sather equivalent of an interface), in which case it gets only supertype but not implementation.

Some object-oriented languages are not statically type checked. Smalltalk and Self are two examples. Smalltalk implements method calls rather like the object-oriented ML example in the previous section. To call a method of an object, you send the object a message containing the name of the method along with any parameters. An object may or may not be capable of responding to that particular message, but no check is made at compile time. (At runtime, if the language system finds that the object's class cannot handle the message, it tries the superclass and so on back to the root class.) This is total freedom. Any method of any object can be called in any context. Polymorphism is a way of gaining some of this freedom, without giving up the benefits of static type checking. It is not relevant for languages like Smalltalk that are not statically type checked at all.

16.4 Conclusion

There are many programmers whose only exposure to object orientation is the Java language. This provincialism sometimes leads to a pair of misconceptions: that object-oriented programming is the same as using an object-oriented language, and that using an object-oriented language is the same as using Java. This chapter tried to banish both of these misconceptions.

Removing this kind of misconception is really what the study of programming languages is all about, and what this book is all about. Knowing more than one language—especially, knowing several very different languages—provides the perspective to tell general principles from linguistic idiosyncracies.

This cosmopolitan perspective is especially important for object-oriented programming and languages, because they are trendy and are evolving quickly. The chapter avoided giving definitions for object orientation not only because there are no widely accepted definitions (and to avoid boring the reader), but also because object orientation is a moving target. There is no one object-oriented style of programming. New styles are evolving. There is no one set of features that make a language object oriented. Opinions on this are evolving, and there are, no doubt, new object-oriented language features yet to be invented.

Exercises

Exercise 1 Implement an object-oriented `queue` in ML, using the same message-passing style as the `stack` example beginning on page 302. Your queue should handle the same messages `stack` handles (`Add`, `HasMore`, and `Remove`).

Exercise 2 The following Java class, `FormattedInteger`, stores a single integer value. It has the methods `getInt` and `setInt` to get and set the stored value. It also has the methods `getString` and `setString`, which allow a client to get and set the stored value using a string representation. The class handles three different string representations: ordinary signed decimal integers, such as `"-2"`; hex integers starting with `"0x"`, such as `"0xfffffffe"`; and octal integers starting with `"0"`, such as `"037777777776"`. (All three of these examples are string representations for the same number.) The class uses an enumeration to encode which of the three formats it will understand. The `setString` method is the only slightly complicated one. It checks the string to make sure it has the appropriate format and returns an error message if there is any problem. Here is the code for this class, which is also available on this book's Web site (**http://www.webber-labs.com/mpl.html**):

```
public class FormattedInteger {
  public static final int HEX = 0;
  public static final int PLAIN = 1;
  public static final int OCTAL = 2;
  private int value;
  private int format;
  public FormattedInteger(int f) {
    format = f;
  }
```

```
public int getInt() {
  return value;
}
public String getString() {
  String result = null;
  if (format == HEX)
    result = "0x" + Integer.toHexString(value);
  else if (format == PLAIN)
    result = Integer.toString(value);
  else if (format == OCTAL)
    result = "0" + Integer.toOctalString(value);
  return result;
}
public void setInt(int v) {
  value = v;
}
public String setString(String s) {
  if (format == HEX) {
    if (!s.startsWith("0x"))
      return "Hex strings must start with \"0x\".";
    int i = 2;
    while (i < s.length()) {
      char c = s.charAt(i);
      if (!(('0' <= c && c <= '9') ||
            ('a' <= c && c <= 'f') ||
            ('A' <= c && c <= 'F')))
        return "Hex digits are 0..9 and A..F" +
               " (or a..f).";
      i++;
    }
    value = (int) Long.parseLong(s.substring(2),16);
  }
  else if (format == PLAIN) {
    boolean negative = false;
    if (s.charAt(0) == '-') {
      negative = true;
      s = s.substring(1);
    }
    else if (s.charAt(0) < '0' || s.charAt(0) > '9')
      return "First char must be a decimal digit" +
             " or a minus sign.";
    int i = 0;
    while (i < s.length()) {
      char c = s.charAt(i);
      if (!('0' <= c && c <= '9'))
        return "Decimal digits must be 0..9";
      i++;
    }
```

```
      value = Integer.parseInt(s);
      if (negative) value = -value;
    }
    else {
      if (s.charAt(0) != '0')
        return "Octal requires a leading zero.";
      int i = 0;
      while (i < s.length()) {
        char c = s.charAt(i);
        if (!('0' <= c && c <= '7'))
          return "Octal digits must be 0..7";
        i++;
      }
      value = (int) Long.parseLong(s,8);
    }
    return "";
  }
}
```

Although `FormattedInteger` works, it is ugly. It is not written in a fully object-oriented style. It has no comments. Your job is to replace it with a more beautiful implementation of the same thing, using three separate classes for the three different behaviors of `FormattedInteger`. Your implementation must use a fully object-oriented style (eliminating the enumerations); "factor out" redundant code and variables into superclasses, as necessary; provide polymorphism, using a new `FormattedInteger` as a common superclass or interface for the three classes; be generally beautiful, neat, and well commented; and still work.

Extensive testing is not necessary, but you might be interested in seeing the code run with a graphical user interface. The class `FormattedIntegerDemo`, available on this book's Web site, can be run as an application or as an applet. In its current form it runs using the original `FormattedInteger` class. You should be able to make it run with your classes by changing only the initializers on these three declarations:

```
private FormattedInteger decimal =
  new FormattedInteger(FormattedInteger.PLAIN);
private FormattedInteger hex =
  new FormattedInteger(FormattedInteger.HEX);
private FormattedInteger octal =
  new FormattedInteger(FormattedInteger.OCTAL);
```

To make this work you must still use the name `FormattedInteger`, as a superclass or an interface, so that it can still serve as a common type for the three objects.

Exercise 3 Suppose two reference variables `x` and `y` have the declared types `R` and `S` like this:

```
R x;
S y;
```

When the types guarantee that this is safe (i.e., when `S` is a subtype of `R`), Java will allow the assignment `x = y`, coercing the value of `y` to type `R`. When the types guarantee that this cannot work (i.e., when no object of type `S` can also have type `R`), Java will forbid the assignment `x = y`. When neither of these conditions holds, the assignment might or might not be possible at runtime, and Java will permit it only with an explicit type cast, `x = (R) y`. (This kind of type cast is called a *downcast*.) With this explicit type cast, the Java language system performs a runtime check to make sure that the exact class of `y` at runtime is in the type `R`.

Suppose the following Java declarations:

```
class C1 implements I1 {
}
class C2 extends C1 implements I2 {
}
class C3 implements I1 {
}
```

and suppose a variable of each type:

```
C1 c1;
C2 c2;
C3 c3;
I1 i1;
I2 i2;
```

For each possible assignment of one of these five variables to another, say whether Java allows it, disallows it, or allows it only with a downcast, and explain why. (*Hint:* An assignment of `c1` to `i2` is allowed with a downcast, even though the class `C1` clearly does not implement interface `I2`. Think carefully about why.)

Exercise 4 Suppose a derived class `C2` defines a method `m` of type `A2->B2` that overrides a method `m` of type `A1->B1`, inherited from the base class `C1`. Different languages have very different rules about how the types `A1` and `A2`, and `B1` and `B2`, must be related. Investigate and report on this aspect of inheritance, citing the sources you used. Answer the following questions:

a. Explain how this works in Java.
b. What is the rule called *covariance*? Give an example of a language that uses the covariant rule. Explain the advantage of this rule.

c. What is the rule called *contravariance*? Give an example of a language that uses the contravariant rule. Explain the advantage of this rule.

Further Reading

If you are interested in learning more about object-oriented language concepts, the following book is a good place to start. It describes and gives references on a range of languages, including some that you would otherwise find only in research conference proceedings.

Craig, Iain. *The Interpretation of Object-Oriented Programming Languages*. New York: Springer-Verlag, 1999.

If you like object-oriented programming, you may be interested in learning object-oriented languages other than Java. There is no shortage. In addition to all the recent designs, object-oriented features have been added to dialects of many older languages like Fortran and Cobol.

Chapter 17
A Third Look at Java

17.1 Introduction

This Java program demonstrates integer division:

```
public class Test {
  public static void main(String[] args) {
    int i = Integer.parseInt(args[0]);
    int j = Integer.parseInt(args[1]);
    System.out.println(i / j);
  }
}
```

Stored in a file named `Test.java`, it can be compiled and run like this:

```
> javac Test.java
> java Test 6 3
2
>
```

As you can see, the program reads two integers from the command line and prints out their integer quotient. At least, that is what it does if nothing goes wrong. But quite a few things could go wrong. For example, the program might be run without enough input on the command line:

```
> java Test
Exception in thread "main"
java.lang.ArrayIndexOutOfBoundsException: 0
        at Test.main(Test.java:3)
```

Or it might be run with zero as the divisor:

```
> java Test 6 0
Exception in thread "main"
        java.lang.ArithmeticException: / by zero
        at Test.main(Test.java:4)
```

These are examples of *exceptions* in Java. An exception is an error condition that stops the ordinary flow of a computation.

In early languages, exceptions were fatal. The program that encountered an exception crashed. Perhaps, as in the Java examples above, it printed an error message that identified the kind of exception and the part of the program that caused it. Perhaps the program wrote a core dump—a copy of its memory at the time of the exception—before crashing, so that a post mortem examination could figure out what went wrong. But these things were, in early languages, extralingual; the language system or the operating system implemented these behaviors, but the language itself said nothing about them.

Most modern languages, including Java, have constructs for handling exceptions. A Java program can catch its own exceptions and even recover from them. This chapter will look at exception handling in Java.

When a language supports exception handling, it gives rise to a different programming style. Programmers find more uses for exceptions—things that would never have been treated as fatal conditions in the old days. Where exceptions used to be thought of as error conditions that stop the ordinary flow of a computation, they are now thought of as special cases in the ordinary flow of a computation. Some longer examples will demonstrate the style of programming that exception handling supports.

This is also the last chapter on Java, so it will conclude with an overview of the parts of Java that were skipped.

17.2 Throwable Classes

Many different kinds of exceptions are predefined for Java programs. Here are some common ones, with examples of Java code that would cause them:

Java Exception	Code to Cause It
`NullPointerException`	`String s = null;` `s.length();`

`ArithmeticException`	`int a = 3;`
	`int b = 0;`
	`int q = a / b;`

`ArrayIndexOutOfBoundsException`	`int[] a = new int[10];` `a[10];`

`ClassCastException`	`Object x =`
	`  new Integer(1);`
	`String s = (String) x;`

`StringIndexOutOfBoundsException`	`String s = "Hello";` `s.charAt(5);`

You can also create your own kinds of exceptions. But before getting into that, what exactly is an exception?

As you might guess, since Java is an object-oriented language, an exception is an object. The names of exceptions, like `NullPointerException`, are the names of classes. The exceptions themselves are objects of those classes. When something happens that causes an exception, like the code samples in the previous table, Java automatically creates an object of the appropriate class and *throws* that object. If the program has not taken any steps to *catch* the exception, the program terminates and the language system gives an error message like those in the introduction to this chapter.

There is a special part of the class hierarchy for objects that can be thrown as exceptions. To be throwable, an object must be of a class that inherits from the predefined class `Throwable`. `Throwable` has a couple of special subclasses as well. Here are the roots of that part of the class hierarchy:

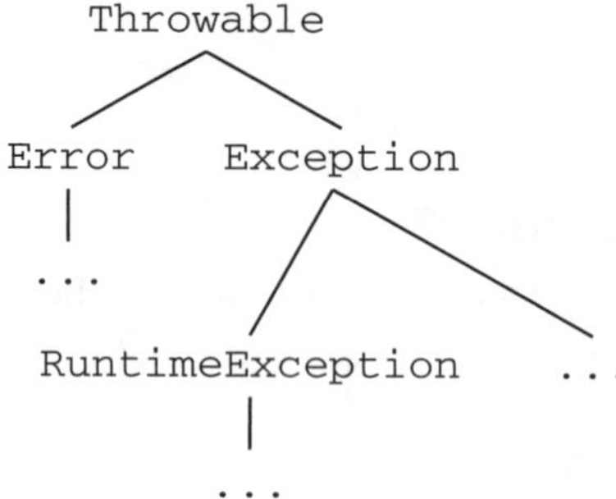

`Throwable` is the root of this part of the hierarchy. It is derived directly from `Object`. Java will not throw an object unless it is of a class descended from `Throwable`. The `Error` class is the superclass for system-generated exceptions that are serious and usually cannot be recovered from. Classes derived from `Error` include `ClassFormatError` (one of the `.class` files for the program is corrupt), `StackOverflowError` (the language system has run out of space for activation records), and `OutOfMemoryError`.

The class `Exception` is the superclass for the more ordinary exceptions, those that a program might want to catch and recover from. The class `RuntimeException`, derived from `Exception`, is the superclass for "normal" system-generated exceptions, including all those in the previous table. You can also add your own exceptions to this hierarchy. Usually, exception classes you create will be derived from `Exception`. More will be said about creating and throwing your own exceptions below. First let's look at the basic mechanism for catching exceptions.

17.3 Catching Exceptions

The `try` statement is used to handle exceptions in Java. In its simplest form, it contains two compound statements: the first to execute and the second to execute only if an exception is thrown from the first. The syntax looks like this:

<try-statement> `::=` *<try-part>* *<catch-part>*
<try-part> `::=` `try` *<compound-statement>*
<catch-part> `::=` `catch (`*<type>* *<variable-name>*`)` *<compound-statement>*

(This is a little simplified. The full syntax will be shown later in this chapter.) The *<type>* must be a class name that is `Throwable` or one of its descendants. Java executes the *<compound-statement>* in the *<try-part>*. If no exception occurs, it ignores everything in the *<catch-part>*. However, if an exception object is thrown during the execution of the *<try-part>* and if that object has the given *<type>*, Java executes the *<compound-statement>* in the *<catch-part>*. (You will see what the *<variable-name>* part is for later.)

For example, here is a modification of the program in the introduction to this chapter. It uses an exception handler to print a special message in case of division by zero.

```
public class Test {
  public static void main(String[] args) {
    try {
      int i = Integer.parseInt(args[0]);
      int j = Integer.parseInt(args[1]);
      System.out.println(i / j);
    }
    catch (ArithmeticException a) {
      System.out.println("You're dividing by zero!");
    }
  }
}
```

When this program is run, it handles any `ArithmeticException` itself. Other exceptions still get the language system's default behavior:

```
> java Test 6 3
2
> java Test 6 0
You're dividing by zero!
> java Test
Exception in thread "main"
java.lang.ArrayIndexOutOfBoundsException: 0
        at Test.main(Test.java:3)
```

By specifying the type of exception in the `catch` part, you can choose to catch a broader or narrower category of exceptions. By specifying `RuntimeException`, for example, this example program would have caught the `ArrayIndexOutOfBoundsException` as well as the `ArithmeticException`, because they are both subclasses of `RuntimeException`. By specifying `Throwable`, the program would have caught all possible exceptions. (This is rarely a good idea, since serious errors like an `OutOfMemoryError` can leave the language system unable to continue executing the program properly, in spite of attempts at exception handling.)

A `try` statement can be just another in a sequence of Java statements. If no exception occurs, or if an exception occurs and is handled by the `catch` part, Java then continues with the next statement following the `try` statement. Consider this fragment:

```
System.out.print("1, ");
try {
  String s = null;
  s.length();
}
catch (NullPointerException e) {
  System.out.print("2, ");
```

```
    }
    System.out.println("3");
```

When run, it prints the line "`1, 2, 3`."

The `try` statement guards not just the textual body of the `try` block, but the whole period of its execution, including the execution of any methods that it might call. Suppose a method `f` calls a method `g` from within a `try` block:

```
void f() {
  try {
    g();
  }
  catch (ArithmeticException a) {
    ...
  }
}
```

If `g` throws an `ArithmeticException` that it does not handle, `f`'s `catch` block is executed. In fact, the point of the throw can be separated from the point of the catch by any number of method invocations. Suppose `g` calls another method `h`, and `h` calls `i`, and so on, so that at runtime there is a stack of activation records like this:

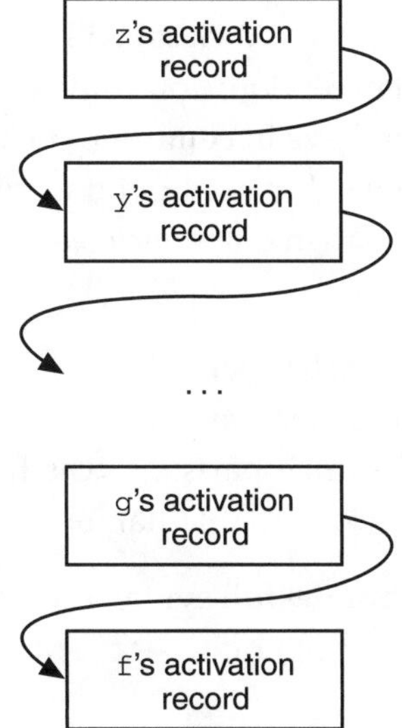

Suppose `z` throws an `ArithmeticException`. If the throw occurs within a suitable `try` block in `z`—one with a `catch` for `ArithmeticException` or some superclass of it—the exception is handled by that `catch` block and the execution of `z` continues. If the throw does not occur within a suitable `try` block, the exception is not caught in `z`. `z` is halted and its activation record is popped off the stack. That is not the end of the story. `z`'s caller `y` then gets a chance to catch the exception. If `y`'s call to `z` is made from inside a suitable `try` block, the exception is handled by the corresponding `catch` block and the execution of `y` continues. If the exception is not caught in `y`, `y` is halted and its activation record is popped off. Then `y`'s caller gets a chance at catching the exception, and so on all the way back to `f`. `f` definitely did make its call to `g` from within a suitable `try` block. So if none of the other methods catch the `ArithmeticException` that was thrown from `z`, `f` will catch it.

This kind of long-distance throw is one of the big advantages of exception handling. Without it, how would you get all the method invocations from `g` through `z` to give up after an error condition observed by `z`? You would have to have every method, `g` through `z`, explicitly check whether an error condition requires them to return immediately. For example, you might have the method `z` set a global flag signaling the error condition and have all the other methods check that flag after every method call. Exception handling can simplify programs that need this kind of behavior, as you will see if you do Exercise 2.

Notice that a `catch` block specifies the class of exception it catches. An exception that is not of that class (or a derived class) will not be caught there. If you want to catch more than one kind of exception, you could specify a superclass that all the exceptions you are interested in have in common, such as `RuntimeException`. But to handle different exceptions differently, you would normally include multiple `catch` blocks. You just list more than one *<catch-part>* after the same *<try-part>*. The syntax looks like this:

<try-statement> ::= <try-part> <catch-parts>
<try-part> ::= `try` <compound-statement>
<catch-parts> ::= <catch-part> <catch-parts> | <catch-part>
<catch-part> ::= `catch (`<type> <variable-name>`)` <compound-statement>

(This is still a little simplified, but the full syntax is coming.) For example, separate handling for the `ArrayIndexOutOfBoundsException` could be added to the previous example, like this:

```
public static void main(String[] args) {
  try {
    int i = Integer.parseInt(args[0]);
    int j = Integer.parseInt(args[1]);
    System.out.println(i / j);
  }
```

```
    catch (ArithmeticException a) {
      System.out.println("You're dividing by zero!");
    }
    catch (ArrayIndexOutOfBoundsException a) {
      System.out.println("Requires two parameters.");
    }
  }
```

What if an exception is thrown whose class matches the type for two or more different `catch` blocks? Consider this code:

```
  public static void main(String[] args) {
    try {
      int i = Integer.parseInt(args[0]);
      int j = Integer.parseInt(args[1]);
      System.out.println(i / j);
    }
    catch (ArithmeticException a) {
      System.out.println("You're dividing by zero!");
    }
    catch (ArrayIndexOutOfBoundsException a) {
      System.out.println("Requires two parameters.");
    }
    catch (RuntimeException a) {
      System.out.println("Runtime exception.");
    }
  }
```

If this code is run with the command `java Test 6 0`, it throws an `ArithmeticException`. Since `ArithmeticException` is derived from `RuntimeException`, both the first and the third catch blocks have matching types. Which one executes—or do they both execute?

```
> java Test 6 0
You're dividing by zero!
```

Only the first one executes. Java executes at most one `catch` block—the first one that matches the exception. The example above shows a common pattern, with special handling for specific `RuntimeException` subclasses followed by a general `catch` block that covers the rest.

Incidentally, a Java compiler will not allow unreachable `catch` blocks. For example, if the `catch` blocks in the example were reordered to put the one for `RuntimeException` first, the other two `catch` blocks would be unreachable. Since any `ArithmeticException` or `ArrayIndexOutOfBoundsException` is a `RuntimeException`, the first `catch` block would always match the exception and the other two would never have a chance. A Java compiler will give an error message for such code. (This is a general property of Java compilers. They do not allow unreachable code. This is not up to the language implementation, but is part of the language specification.)

17.4 Throwing Exceptions

Exceptions are automatically created and thrown by the Java language system when it encounters an error condition while executing a Java program. It is also possible, and sometimes very useful, for a program to create and explicitly throw its own exceptions.

Here is the syntax for the `throw` statement:

<*throw-statement*> `::=` `throw` <*expression*> `;`

The value of the <*expression*> must be a reference to an object whose class is `Throwable` or derived from `Throwable`. In most applications, the program creates an exception object right before throwing it, so the <*expression*> is usually an object creation expression. For example, a program can throw a `NullPointerException` with this statement:

```
throw new NullPointerException();
```

This is not a very useful example, though, since the `NullPointerException` already has a specific meaning in Java. An exception of that class is automatically created and thrown whenever the program tries to use a reference variable whose value is `null` as if it were a reference to an object (by trying to call one of its methods, for instance). Occasionally there is a good reason to imitate one of these predefined exceptions using an explicit throw, but in most applications it makes more sense to use a custom exception class.

`OutOfGas` is an example of a custom exception class:

```
public class OutOfGas extends Exception {
}
```

As you can see, it extends the predefined class `Exception`. (It is also possible for a custom exception class to be derived from `Error` or `RuntimeException` or to extend `Throwable` directly. The next section will explain why a derivation from `Exception` is usually the right choice.) The custom exception class does not need to define any additional fields or methods, since it inherits everything it needs for objects to be thrown and caught just like a predefined exception.

```
System.out.print("1, ");
try {
  throw new OutOfGas();
}
catch (OutOfGas e) {
  System.out.print("2, ");
}
System.out.println("3");
```

The `catch` part has what looks like a parameter, `(OutOfGas e)`. The type `OutOfGas` defines the exceptions the `catch` block can catch. But what about that variable `e`? It actually does work a bit like a parameter. Within the `catch` block it is a reference to the exception object that was caught.

The exception object can be used to communicate information from the point of the throw to the catcher. For example, all throwable objects contain information about the contents of the stack of activation records at the point of the throw: a *stack trace.* A stack trace can be used to print an error message showing which method threw the exception, which method called it, and so on back through the stack. Classes derived from `Throwable` inherit a method `printStackTrace()` that can be used to print out this information.

Another thing all throwable objects have is a string field for storing a detailed error message. This field can be accessed using the `getMessage()` method (again, inherited from `Throwable`). There is no way to set this message except from the constructor, so a constructor for the `OutOfGas` class must be defined:

```
public class OutOfGas extends Exception {
  public OutOfGas(String details) {
    super(details);
  }
}
```

This uses a bit of Java not seen before: the keyword `super`. This particular use of `super` is a call of the constructor for the superclass (`Exception`) that takes a `String` parameter. This initializes all the inherited parts of the `OutOfGas` object, just like for `new Exception(details)`. In particular, it uses the string `details` as the value that will be returned by the `getMessage()` method.

A number of things about Java constructors have been ignored so far. All constructors (except in the root class `Object`) begin with a call to another constructor, either another constructor of the same class or one of the constructors of the base class. If a constructor does not start with such a call, Java supplies a call to the zero-parameter constructor for the base class, `super()`, automatically. This insures that all inherited fields are initialized by the constructors for the superclasses that defined those fields. Another thing about constructors that has been ignored is that all classes have at least one constructor. If one is not defined, Java includes a zero-parameter constructor automatically. So the original, skimpy definition of `OutOfGas` is actually equivalent to this one:

```
public class OutOfGas extends Exception {
  public OutOfGas() {
    super();
  }
}
```

That is, it contained an implicit zero-parameter constructor, which implicitly called the zero-parameter constructor of the superclass.[1]

Getting back to exceptions, with the necessary constructor, a program can place a detailed error message in the exception object when it is created. This error message is carried along inside the exception from the thrower to the catcher:

```
try {
  throw new OutOfGas("You have run out of gas.");
}
catch (OutOfGas e) {
  System.out.println(e.getMessage());
}
```

Placing a detailed error-message string in an exception is easy, since almost everything is inherited from `Throwable`. It is only slightly harder to include other information as well. All that is needed is an additional field in the exception class, an additional parameter for the constructor, and an additional accessor method. Here, an integer field is added to the `OutOfGas` exception:

```
public class OutOfGas extends Exception {
  private int miles;
  public OutOfGas(String details, int m) {
    super(details);
    miles = m;
  }
  public int getMiles() {
    return miles;
  }
}
```

1. Some Java programmers write all constructors and all superconstructor calls explicitly, even those that Java would have supplied automatically. This convention has the benefit of reminding the reader about the existence of these otherwise hidden parts of the program. If you do follow this convention, you should follow it rigorously, since the reader may be lulled into forgetting that these parts are present even when not explicit.

This exception class can now carry both a detailed message string and an integer from the thrower to the catcher.

```
try {
  throw new OutOfGas("You have run out of gas.", 19);
}
catch (OutOfGas e) {
  System.out.println(e.getMessage());
  System.out.println("Odometer: " + e.getMiles());
}
```

The previous example illustrates the mechanics of creating, throwing, and catching custom exceptions. It does not, however, illustrate the usefulness of custom exceptions. There is no point to a `try` statement that does nothing but throw an exception and then catch it. The benefits are more clear when the throw is not in the same method as the catch.

17.5 Checked Exceptions

Here is a method that throws the `OutOfGas` exception and does not catch it:

```
void z() {
  throw new OutOfGas("You have run out of gas.", 19");
}
```

As it stands, this method will not be accepted by a Java compiler. The error message from the compiler will be something like this: "The exception `OutOfGas` is not handled."

Why is the Java language system complaining now about something it did not complain about before? Several example methods have thrown exceptions they do not catch. The `main` method from the example in the introduction to this chapter can throw a variety of exceptions—`ArithmeticException` and `ArrayIndexOutOfBoundsException`, among others—and although these are not caught, the language system still allows this program to compile and run. Why is it now insisting that `z` must handle the exception it throws?

It turns out that Java distinguishes between two kinds of exceptions: checked exceptions and unchecked exceptions. Checked exceptions are the class `Exception` and its subclasses, except for classes derived through `RuntimeException`. This illustration shows where the checked exceptions occur in the hierarchy of exception classes:

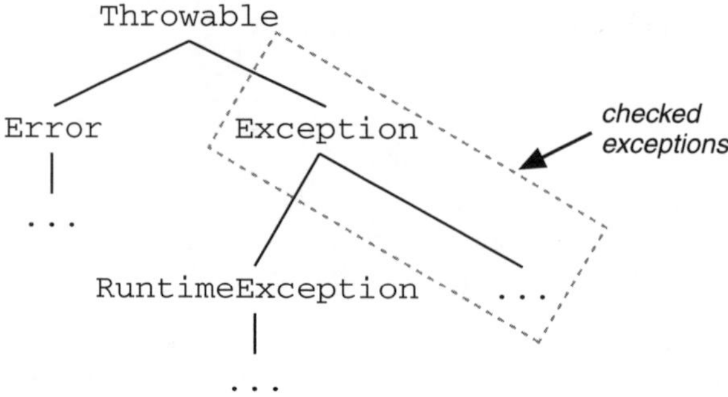

All other exceptions are unchecked.

A method that can get a checked exception is not permitted to ignore it. It must either catch the checked exception or declare that it does not catch it. You have already seen how to catch an exception: put the code that can throw it inside a `try` statement with a `catch` part for that exception type. Alternatively, a method may declare that it does not catch the exception. This is done using a `throws` clause.

```
void z() throws OutOfGas {
  throw new OutOfGas("You have run out of gas.", 19);
}
```

A `throws` clause lists one or more exception types, separated by commas. The method `z` always throws an `OutOfGas` exception. In general, however, the `throws` clause should not be taken to mean that the method actually does throw the given exceptions. A method is *permitted*, not *required*, to throw the checked exceptions declared in its `throws` clause.

Every checked exception that a method might throw must be listed in the `throws` clause, even if the exception is thrown indirectly, by calling another method that throws and does not catch it. Consider this method `f`:

```
void f() {
  try {
    g();
  }
  catch (OutOfGas e) {
    System.out.println(e.getMessage());
    System.out.println("Odometer: " + e.getMiles());
  }
}
```

This `f` calls a method `g`. Suppose that `g` calls `h`, and `h` calls `i`, and so on, so that at runtime there is a stack of activation records like this:

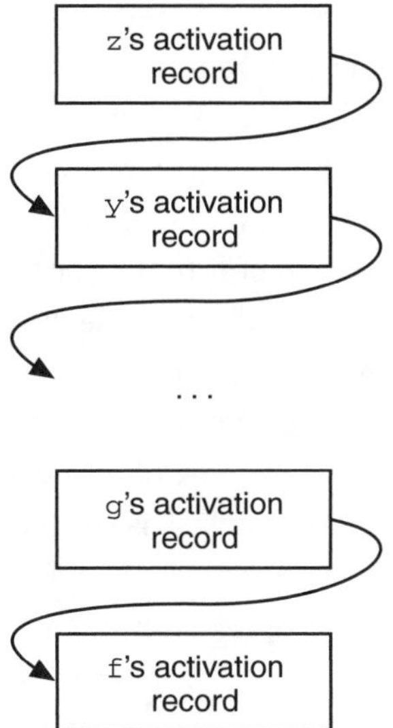

That final method z is the one already defined. It throws an OutOfGas exception. It says so in its throws clause. If y does not catch the exception, it too must say that it throws OutOfGas. The same applies to y's caller, and its caller, and so on. If the exception thrown by z is not caught before the try statement in f, then every method z through g must declare that it throws OutOfGas.

The Java compiler tests to make sure that all checked exceptions that can be thrown in a method are caught there or are declared in that method's throws clause. If a method fails this test, there will be an error message from the compiler: "The exception OutOfGas is not handled" or something like that. These error messages can be very useful. They are reminders about exceptions that might occur that the programmer may have forgotten about. The programmer must decide whether the right way to handle the exception is to catch it or to add it to the throws clause. (The compiler cannot tell which solution to recommend, which is why this error message is usually vague.) Once all the throws clauses are correct, they serve to make the program more readable. They are like documentation explaining what exceptions may result from a call of the given method. Except, unlike ordinary comments, they are guaranteed to be correct by the compiler.

Since checked exceptions offer the benefit of this extra compile-time checking, why are there unchecked exceptions at all? The reason is that although exception checking has benefits, it also places an additional burden on the programmer. Sometimes this burden clearly outweighs the benefits. As an example of an exception that clearly should be unchecked, consider OutOfMemoryError. Few programs attempt to catch this, yet almost all methods can (in principle) throw it, since almost all methods do something that requires some memory allocation. If OutOfMemoryError were a checked exception, it would be nothing but a nuisance. The compiler would force the programmer to put it in the throws clause of almost every method. That would not make the program any more comprehensible, or any more likely to be correct, than before. In general, if an exception is thrown from most methods and caught in few, the whole exception-checking mechanism is unhelpful. In Java, all the automatically generated exceptions are unchecked. These are usually the kinds of exceptions that many different methods can generate and few will catch, like OutOfMemoryError. Custom exceptions can also be unchecked. This happens if the exception class is derived from Error or directly from Throwable instead of from Exception.

In short, checked exceptions are optional in Java. You are never forced to use checked exceptions or to write throws clauses for methods. (Well, almost never. Parts of the API, including the standard classes supporting file I/O, throw checked exceptions.) But there are benefits to exception checking, and you should consider using it for your custom exceptions. Used properly, it can make programs easier to read and more likely to be correct. To use checked exceptions, all you have to do is to write your custom exception classes so they extend Exception.

17.6 Error Handling

Using exceptions is only one way of handling error conditions in a program. This section presents a longer example and considers several different approaches for handling class-specific errors. Let's start with the following class for a simple stack of integers. This is basically the same as the stack of strings in Chapter 15.

```
/**
 * An IntStack is an object that holds a stack of ints.
 */
public class IntStack {
  private Node top = null; // The top Node in the stack

  /**
   * Test whether this stack has more elements.
   * @return true if this stack is not empty
   */
  public boolean hasMore() {
    return (top != null);
  }
```

```
  /**
   * Pop the top int from this stack and return it. This
   * should be called only if the stack is not empty.
   * @return the popped int
   */
  public int pop() {
    Node n = top;
    top = n.getLink();
    return n.getData();
  }

  /**
   * Push an int on top of this stack.
   * @param data the String to add
   */
  public void push(int data) {
    top = new Node(data,top);
  }
}
```

As always, many things could go wrong while using an `IntStack`. The system could run out of space for activation records while calling `hasMore`. It could run out of memory space for objects while trying to allocate a new `Node` in the `push` method. It could simply fail to find a definition for the `Node` class when trying to load it dynamically. Errors of this kind can occur throughout every program and are handled by the language system in a uniform way; it automatically throws an exception derived from `Error`, such as a `StackOverflowError`, an `OutOfMemoryError`, or a `NoClassDefFoundError`. As already noted, few programs try to catch and recover from such errors.

Something specific to `IntStack` could also go wrong: the client could try to pop the stack when it is empty. There are many approaches to handling such class-specific error conditions. Several of these are outlined below, with the approach using exceptions presented last.

Preconditions Only

`IntStack` illustrates one perfectly reasonable approach. It does not handle errors at all, but documents the *preconditions* for each method—the things that must be true when the method is called in order to avoid errors. The documentation for the `pop` method says, "This should be called only if the stack is not empty." A program that wants to pop but is not sure whether the stack is empty must check before popping.

```
if (s.hasMore()) x = s.pop();
else ...
```

In effect, the preconditions-only technique leaves it up to the caller to ensure that error conditions do not occur.[2]

If the caller makes a mistake and calls pop when the stack is empty, the IntStack class has an unhelpful behavior. Consider this fragment:

```
IntStack s = new IntStack();
s.push(1);
s.pop();
s.pop();
```

The final pop call, made when the stack is empty, causes a NullPointerException. (Look at the code for pop. Do you see why it throws this exception?) If the program does not catch a NullPointerException, the result is an inscrutable error message for the user—one that talks only about null pointers and not about empty stacks. If the program *does* catch a NullPointerException, it is relying on an undocumented part of the behavior of IntStack. An implementation of IntStack using arrays instead of linked lists would almost certainly generate a different exception when popping an empty stack.

Total Definition

Another approach to error handling is to define a "normal" behavior for every condition. IntStack does not say what its behavior is if it pops an empty stack. What if the pop method were changed to make it safely return some fixed value in this case? The problem could be defined away by declaring that the result of popping an empty stack is the integer zero:

```
/**
 * Pop the top int from this stack and return it.
 * If the stack is empty we return 0 and leave the
 * stack empty.
 * @return the popped int or 0 if the stack is empty
 */
public int pop() {
  Node n = top;
  if (n == null) return 0;
  top = n.getLink();
  return n.getData();
}
```

2. In some languages, notably Eiffel, preconditions are more than just comments. They are part of the program. For such languages, the compiler can generate code to check the precondition automatically when the method is entered.

This approach is sometimes used for character-by-character file I/O in various languages and APIs. What should be the result of trying to read a character from a file if you are already at the end of the file? In the standard API for C, the `fgetc` function returns the special character `EOF` in case the end of the file is encountered or any other file error occurs. This is a practical approach since most character-by-character readers immediately branch on the value of the character returned. Using the special `EOF` character, they can handle the end-of-file condition at the same time.

Another common example of this total-definition approach is the IEEE standard for floating-point arithmetic. What should be the result of trying to divide 0.0 by 0.0? The IEEE standard defines a special value as the result—Not-a-Number, usually abbreviated as NaN. Many microprocessors implement this standard. The Java language specification requires it. Integer division by zero in Java results in an `ArithmeticException`. But `0.0/0.0` does not result in an exception, it results in a special floating-point value that prints out as `NaN`.

Total definition can be a useful technique in some circumstances, but it is probably not a good approach for `IntStack`. If the client pops more than it pushes, there might well be a serious problem that should be caught right away. The proposed total definition would mask the problem, making the program harder to debug.

Fatal Errors

At the opposite extreme from the total-definition approach, any method that detects an error condition can print an error message and terminate the program:

```
/**
 * Pop the top int from this stack and return it.
 * This should be called only if the stack is
 * not empty. If called when the stack is empty,
 * we print an error message and exit the program.
 * @return the popped int
 */
public int pop() {
  Node n = top;
  if (n == null) {
    System.out.println("Popping an empty stack!");
    System.exit(-1);
  }
  top = n.getLink();
  return n.getData();
}
```

As you can see, this includes commented preconditions. But unlike the preconditions-only method, it takes decisive action if the preconditions are not met. This certainly calls attention to the error as soon as it is detected. But this approach is not usually good, especially in object-oriented languages. An object-oriented style expects objects to have local effects. Calling a method should make the object do something to itself. Terminating the entire program is about as non-local an effect as you can get. (In fact, if a program is running as an applet, the Java language system may not allow it to shut down this way at all. The `System.exit` call does not guarantee to shut down the Java virtual machine. It tries to do so, but it throws a `SecurityException` if that form of exit is denied.)

The fatal-error approach is an inflexible kind of error handling. Each client may want to handle errors in its own way, some by simply terminating, others by cleaning up and then terminating, others by ignoring the error and continuing, and others by repairing the error and continuing. If a class takes the fatal-error approach, it allows only one of these options.

Error Flagging

A common way of handling errors is to have the method that identifies the error flag it in some way. The method might return a special value that indicates an error, as memory allocation does in the standard API for C. This example allocates a block of memory and then tests whether the allocation failed:

```
char *p = (char *) malloc(n);
if (p == NULL) ...
```

Of course, this technique is possible only if there is some value in the returned type that can be reserved to signal an error, like the `NULL` pointer. That could not be done for `pop`, since any integer could be the result of a correct `pop` call. Alternatively, the method might set a global flag, like the global value `errno` in the standard API for C. This example raises `x` to the `y` power, then checks whether there was an error in doing so:

```
errno = 0;
z = pow(x,y);
if (errno) ...
```

Another variation is for the method to record the error in a way that can be checked by another method call. File errors in the standard C API often work this way. This example writes a string `s` to a file `f`, one character at a time, and then checks to see whether there was an error:

```
while (c=*s++) putc(c,f);
if (ferror(f)) ...
```

These examples are superficially different, but they have one important thing in common: the caller must perform an explicit check after a call (or after a series of calls) to see whether an error occurred. Something similar can be implemented for a stack of integers by adding a private `error` field to the `IntStack` class. A new version of `pop` sets the flag if an attempt is made to pop an empty stack. It also needs a method to test the flag and (to support error recovery) a method to reset it.

```
/**
 * Pop the top int from this stack and return it. This
 * should be called only if the stack is not empty. If
 * called when the stack is empty, we set the error flag
 * and return an undefined value.
 * @return the popped int if stack not empty
 */
public int pop() {
  Node n = top;
  if (n == null) {
    error = true;
    return 0;
  }
  top = n.getLink();
  return n.getData();
}

/**
 * Return the error flag for this stack. The error
 * flag is set true if an empty stack is ever popped.
 * It can be reset to false by calling resetError().
 * @return the error flag
 */
public boolean getError() {
  return error;
}

/**
 * Reset the error flag. We set it to false.
 */
public void resetError() {
  error = false;
}
```

The main drawback of this style of error handling is that the caller must explicitly check for an error. To see how this looks, let's look at an example of a client.

A *stack machine* is a computational engine that gets its operands from a stack and returns its results to the stack. Using a stack machine `s`, the computation `c = a+b` looks like this:

```
s.push(a);
s.push(b);
s.add();
c = s.pop();
```

(Incidentally, the Java virtual machine is a stack machine, as was mentioned in Chapter 4.) Here is a class called `StackMachine` that extends `IntStack`. This stack machine knows how to add, subtract, multiply, and divide.

```
/**
 * A stack machine for simple integer arithmetic.
 */
public class StackMachine extends IntStack {
  /**
   * Pop the two top integers from the stack, add
   * them, and push their integer sum. There
   * should be at least two integers on the stack
   * when we are called. If not, we leave the stack
   * empty and set the error flag.
   */
  public void add() {
    int i = pop();
    int j = pop();
    if (getError()) return;
    push(i + j);
  }

  /**
   * Pop the two top integers from the stack, divide
   * them, and push their integer quotient. There
   * should be at least two integers on the stack
   * when we are called. If not, we leave the stack
   * empty and set the error flag.
   */
  public void divide() {
    int i = pop();
    int j = pop();
    if (getError()) return;
    push(i / j);
  }
```

```
    /**
     * Pop the two top integers from the stack, multiply
     * them, and push their integer product. There
     * should be at least two integers on the stack
     * when we are called. If not, we leave the stack
     * empty and set the error flag.
     */
    public void multiply() {
      int i = pop();
      int j = pop();
      if (getError()) return;
      push(i * j);
    }

    /**
     * Pop the two top integers from the stack, subtract
     * the second from the first, and push their integer
     * difference. There should be at least two
     * integers on the stack when we are called. If not,
     * we leave the stack empty and set the error flag.
     */
    public void subtract() {
      int i = pop();
      int j = pop();
      if (getError()) return;
      push(i - j);
    }
}
```

The methods in this stack machine make use of the error flagging implemented by `IntStack`. They check for the empty-stack error after popping their two operands off the stack. (Notice that it is not necessary to check after the first pop, since there is no harm in continuing to the second, which leaves the error flag set.) If there is an error, these methods skip the final step of making the computation and pushing the result to the stack. This is important for two reasons. It avoids spurious errors that would result from continuing the computation with bogus operands. For example, it avoids the division by zero that would result from completing a division operation when the stack is empty. It also avoids pushing a bogus integer result onto the stack.

There is, of course, a runtime cost to checking the error flag. Often, the really costly part is that the error flag may have to be checked repeatedly. The caller of the `add` method may also be in the middle of a computation that should be aborted if there is an error, so it may also have to check the flag. And *its* caller may have to check the flag, and so on. This can clutter up a program, as you will see if you do Exercise 2.

Throwing Exceptions

Last but not least, a class can handle errors by throwing custom exceptions. Here is an implementation of the `pop` method that throws its own checked exception, called `EmptyStack`:

```
/**
 * Pop the top int from this stack and return it.
 * @return the popped int
 * @throws EmptyStack if stack is empty
 */
public int pop() throws EmptyStack {
  Node n = top;
  if (n == null) throw new EmptyStack();
  top = n.getLink();
  return n.getData();
}
```

This allows us to simplify the client code in `StackMachine`, since there is no need for an explicit error check.

```
public class StackMachine extends IntStack {
  /**
   * Pop the two top integers from the stack, add
   * them, and push their integer sum.
   * @throws EmptyStack if stack runs out
   */
  public void add() throws EmptyStack {
    int i = pop();
    int j = pop();
    push(i + j);
  }

  /**
   * Pop the two top integers from the stack, divide
   * them, and push their integer quotient.
   * @throws EmptyStack if stack runs out
   */
  public void divide() throws EmptyStack {
    int i = pop();
    int j = pop();
    push(i / j);
  }
```

```
    /**
     * Pop the two top integers from the stack, multiply
     * them, and push their integer product.
     * @throws EmptyStack if stack runs out
     */
    public void multiply() throws EmptyStack {
      int i = pop();
      int j = pop();
      push(i * j);
    }

    /**
     * Pop the two top integers from the stack, subtract
     * the second from the first, and push their integer
     * difference.
     * @throws EmptyStack if stack runs out
     */
    public void subtract() throws EmptyStack {
      int i = pop();
      int j = pop();
      push(i - j);
    }
  }
```

The exception-throwing method solves some of the problems of other error-handling methods. Unlike the preconditions-only method, it provides a sensible error message if the program does not handle the error. The `EmptyStack` class could even be defined with a detailed error message like this:

```
  public class EmptyStack extends Exception {
    public EmptyStack() {
      super("Trying to pop an empty stack.");
    }
  }
```

That way, if the error is not caught, at least the user sees something more meaningful than `NullPointerException`.

Unlike the preconditions-only method, the exception-throwing method does not expose unwanted implementation details. An array-based implementation of `IntStack` could still throw the same exception. Unlike the total-definition approach, throwing an exception catches errors right away. Unlike the error-flagging approach, it does not require the caller to explicitly check for an error. Unlike the fatal-error approach, it still leaves things flexible for the caller. The caller can decide whether to handle the exception. For client methods like `add`, `subtract`, `multiply`, and `divide` that want to immediately terminate their computations in the event of an error, exceptions work out very well. The default behavior for exceptions—terminating the method and passing the exception back to the caller—is exactly what these methods want. But a client method that wants to take a different action can do so by catching the exception.

All this is not to say that exceptions are the best solution for every error-handling problem. It is, as always, up to the programmer to choose the best technique for each situation. But exceptions are an important technique to have in your repertoire. Exceptions are available in many modern, high-level languages. PL/I was the first widely used language to include exception handling. Other languages with exception handling include C++, Ada, and ML.

17.7 Finally

There is one last part to the syntax of the `try` statement: the optional `finally` block. Here, as promised, is the full syntax for the `try` statement:

<try-statement> ::= *<try-part>* *<catch-parts>*
| *<try-part>* *<catch-parts>* *<finally-part>*
| *<try-part>* *<finally-part>*
<try-part> ::= `try` *<compound-statement>*
<catch-parts> ::= *<catch-part>* *<catch-parts>* | *<catch-part>*
<catch-part> ::= `catch (`*<type>* *<variable-name>*`)` *<compound-statement>*
<finally-part> ::= `finally` *<compound-statement>*

If the *<try-part>* finishes without getting an exception, the *<finally-part>* is executed. If the *<try-part>* throws an exception that is caught by one of the *<catch-parts>*, the *<finally-part>* is executed (after the *<catch-part>*). If the *<try-part>* throws an exception that is not caught by any of the *<catch-parts>*, the *<finally-part>* is executed (before the statement terminates with an uncaught exception). In short, the *<finally-part>* is *always* executed when the *<try-statement>* is finished, no matter what else happens.

A `finally` block is used for cleanup operations: code that absolutely must be executed at the end of the `try` statement. Suppose you want to open a file, work with it, and then close it. You might write a sequence of method calls like this:

```
file.open();
workWith(file);
file.close();
```

(These are not real Java API calls.) Suppose something goes wrong inside the `workWith` method, so that it throws an exception (and does not catch it). Then the final statement, `file.close()`, is never executed. This can be a serious problem.

To absolutely guarantee that the file is closed, you would use a `try` block with a `finally` clause, like this:

```
file.open();
try {
  workWith(file);
}
finally {
  file.close();
}
```

Often, a `finally` block is used in combination with `catch` blocks, like this:

```
System.out.print("1");
try {
  System.out.print("2");
  if (true) throw new Exception();
  System.out.print("3");
}
catch (Exception e) {
  System.out.print("4");
}
finally {
  System.out.print("5");
}
System.out.println("6");
```

The code fragment above prints the line "`12456`." The statement that would have printed `3` is not executed because of the exception. (The `if (true)` is necessary to make Java compile this fragment without complaining about unreachable code.) What would happen if the statement `throw new Exception()` were changed to `throw new Throwable()`? (See if you can figure it out before reading on.) If the thrown exception is of the class `Throwable`, it will still not print `3` because of the exception. It will not print `4` because the exception is not caught. It will print `5` because the `finally` block always executes. It will not print `6`. Since the exception was uncaught, the statement after the `try` statement is not executed. The effect of the entire fragment is to print "`125`", then terminate with an exception.

17.8 Conclusion—Farewell to Java

This chapter showed the `try` and `throw` statements in Java. It explored some examples showing the use of checked and unchecked exceptions for error handling. This is the end of the introduction to Java.

Java is a popular language at present. There is no shortage of books, courses, and online tutorials to help you learn more about it. Here is a list of some of the parts of Java that were skipped:

- Fundamentals—Some of Java's primitive types—`byte`, `short`, `long`, and `float`—were skipped. Also some kinds of Java statements were skipped. Only the `while` loop was shown, but Java has a full collection of C-like looping constructs: `do` loops and `for` loops, with `break` and `continue` statements. Java does not have a `goto` statement, but does have labels that can be the target of a `break` or `continue`. For conditional execution, only the `if` statement was discussed, but Java also has a C-like `switch` statement for multiple-way branching.
- Packages—Cooperating classes in Java are ordinarily grouped into labeled namespaces called *packages*. The default visibility for fields and methods is called *package access*. If `public`, `private`, or `protected` is not specified, the field or method is visible from all other classes in the same package. An entire Java application can be written in a single package, as has been done here, but most significant Java programs use multiple packages. The Java API comes in many separate packages.
- Threads—Java supports *concurrent programs*, programs that contain multiple threads running simultaneously. The API includes ways to create and manage multiple threads. The language itself includes constructs that threads can use to synchronize their operations.
- API—Java is a fairly small language with a very large API. The API includes container classes (stacks, queues, hash tables, and so on) and classes for implementing graphical user interfaces, for 2D and 3D graphics, for advanced mathematics, for network and file I/O, for encryption and security, for remote method invocation, and for interfacing to databases and other tools.

Exercises

Exercise 1 Write a class that implements the following interface:

```
/**
 * An interface for iterators over the chars in a
 * string. It is expected that implementers will
 * have a constructor that takes a string
 * parameter--the string over which to iterate.
 */
public interface CharIter {
```

```
    /**
     * Test whether there are more characters to go.
     * @return true if more chars (next can be called)
     */
    boolean hasNext();

    /**
     * Get the next char in the string. This should be
     * called only if there is a next char--see hasNext.
     * @return the next char
     */
    char next();
}
```

Write a method that demonstrates the class by using it to print out the characters in a test string, one per line.

Next, write a class that implements this alternate interface for iterating over the characters in a string:

```
/**
 * An interface for iterators over the chars in a
 * string. It is expected that implementers will have a
 * constructor that takes a string parameter--the string
 * over which to iterate.
 */
public interface CharIterX {
    /**
     * Get the next char in the string.
     * @return the next char
     * @throws IteratorExhausted if there is no next char
     */
    public char next() throws IteratorExhausted;
}
```

As you can see, this interface works in a different way. There is no way to test whether the end of the string has been reached, so the caller is expected to continue calling `next` until there is an `IteratorExhausted` exception. (You will have to write the `IteratorExhausted` class as a checked exception.) Write a method that demonstrates the class by using it to print out the characters in a test string, one character at a time. Your test method should catch and handle the `IteratorExhausted` exception.

Decide which technique for iteration you like best and write a paragraph arguing for it.

Exercise 2 The following two Java classes implement a simple calculator that understands a language of numeric expressions. The language allows numeric constants; the operators `+`,`-`,`*`, and `/`; and parentheses. The calculator observes proper precedence and associativity. The first class, `CalcLexer`, divides a string containing an expression into a sequence of tokens. The class `CalcParser` parses that sequence of tokens according to a grammar. `CalcParser` uses a style of parsing called *recursive descent*, which uses a different method for each non-terminal symbol in the grammar. If you look at the methods `parseExpression`, `parseMulexp`, and `parseRootexp` you will recognize the productions of EBNF grammars like those in Chapter 3. `CalcParser` does not construct a parse tree, but instead computes the value of the resulting expression as it parses.

Here is the code for these two classes. (This code is available on the book's Web site, **http://www.webber-labs.com/mpl.html**.)

```
/**
 * A CalcLexer provides a simple scanner for a CalcParser.
 * We hold the string being parsed, and the CalcParser
 * uses us to read the string as a sequence of tokens.
 */
public class CalcLexer {
  /**
   * The string being parsed, held in a StringTokenizer.
   */
  private java.util.StringTokenizer tokens;

  /**
   * The error message. This will be null if there
   * has been no error.
   */
  private String errorMessage = null;

  /**
   * The current token.
   */
  private int tokenChar;

  /**
   * If the current token is NUMBER_TOKEN, this is
   * the number in question.
   */
  private double tokenNum;
```

```
/**
 * Non-character values for tokenChar. By choosing
 * negative values we are certain not to collide
 * with any char values stored in the int tokenChar.
 */
public static final int NUMBER_TOKEN = -1;
public static final int EOLN_TOKEN = -2;

/**
 * Constructor for a CalcLexer. Our parameter is the
 * string to be tokenized.
 * @param s the String to be tokenized
 */
public CalcLexer(String s) {

  // We use a StringTokenizer to tokenize the string.
  // Our delimiters are the operators, parens, and
  // white space. By making the third parameter true
  // we instruct the StringTokenizer to return those
  // delimiters as tokens.

  tokens = new java.util.StringTokenizer(
                      s," \t\n\r+-*/()",true);

  // Start by advancing to the first token. Note that
  // this may get an error, which would set our
  // errorMessage instead of setting tokenChar.

  advance();
}

/**
 * Advance to the next token. We don't return anything; the
 * caller must use nextToken() to see what that token is.
 */
public void advance() {

  // White space is returned as a token by our
  // StringTokenizer, but we will loop until something
  // other than white space has been found.

  while (true) {

    // If we're at the end, make it an EOLN_TOKEN.

    if (!tokens.hasMoreTokens()) {
      tokenChar = EOLN_TOKEN;
      return;
    }
```

```
      // Get a token--if it looks like a number,
      // make it a NUMBER_TOKEN.

      String s = tokens.nextToken();
      char c1 = s.charAt(0);
      if (s.length()>1 || Character.isDigit(c1)) {
        try {
          tokenNum = Double.valueOf(s).doubleValue();
          tokenChar = NUMBER_TOKEN;
        }
        catch (NumberFormatException x) {
          errorMessage = "Illegal format for a number.";
        }
        return;
      }

      // Any other single character that is not
      // white space is a token.

      else if (!Character.isWhitespace(c1)) {
        tokenChar = c1;
        return;
      }
    }
  }

  /**
   * Return our error message. This will be null if no
   * error has occurred.
   *
   * @return error String or null if no error
   */
  public String getErrorMessage() {
    return errorMessage;
  }

  /**
   * Return the value of a numeric token. This should only
   * be called when nextToken() reports a NUMBER_TOKEN.
   *
   * @return the double value of the number
   */
  public double getNum() {
    return tokenNum;
  }
```

```
  /**
   * Return the next token. Repeated calls will
   * return the same token again; the caller should
   * use advance() to advance to another token.
   * @return the next token as an int
   */
  public int nextToken() {
    return tokenChar;
  }
}

/**
 * A CalcParser is a calculator that evaluates a String
 * containing a numeric expression. We handle numbers,
 * the operators +,-,*, and / with the usual precedence
 * and associativity, and parentheses.
 */
public class CalcParser {

  /**
   * We use a CalcLexer object to tokenize the input string.
   */
  private CalcLexer lexer;

  /**
   * Our error message or null if there has been no error.
   */
  private String errorMessage = null;

  /**
   * The result of evaluating the expression (if no error).
   */
  private double value;

  /**
   * Constructor for CalcParser. This actually does all the
   * work. We parse and evaluate the string from here. Our
   * caller should then use the getErrorMessage() method to
   * see if there has been an error and, if not, the
   * getValue() method to get the value we calculated.
   *
   * @param s the string to be parsed
   */
  public CalcParser(String s) {

    // First make a CalcLexer to hold the string. This
    // will get an error immediately if the first token
    // is bad, so check for that.
```

```
    lexer = new CalcLexer(s);
    errorMessage = lexer.getErrorMessage();
    if (errorMessage != null) return;

    // Now parse the expression and get the result.

    value = parseExpression();
    if (errorMessage != null) return;

    // After the expression we should be at the end of
    // the input.

    match(CalcLexer.EOLN_TOKEN);
    if (errorMessage != null) return;

  }

  /**
   * Get the error message or null if none.
   *
   * @return the error message or null
   */
  public String getErrorMessage() {
    return errorMessage;
  }

  /**
   * Get the value of the expression as a string. This should
   * only be called if getErrorMessage() returned null.
   *
   * @return the value of the expression as a String
   */
  public String getValue() {
    return Double.toString(value);
  }

  /**
   * Match a given token and advance to the next. This
   * utility is used by our parsing routines. If the given
   * token does not match lexer.nextToken(), we generate an
   * appropriate error message. Advancing to the next token
   * may also cause an error.
   *
   * @param token the token that must match
   */
  private void match(int token) {

    // First check that the current token matches the
    // one we were passed; if not, make an error.
```

```
    if (lexer.nextToken() != token) {
      if (token == CalcLexer.EOLN_TOKEN)
        errorMessage =
          "Unexpected text after the expression.";
      else if (token == CalcLexer.NUMBER_TOKEN)
        errorMessage = "Expected a number.";
      else errorMessage =
             "Expected a " + ((char) token) + ".";
      return;
    }

    // Now advance to the next token.

    lexer.advance();
    errorMessage = lexer.getErrorMessage();
  }

  /**
   * Parse an expression. If any error occurs we
   * return immediately.
   *
   * @return the double value of the expression
   * or garbage in case of errors.
   */
  private double parseExpression() {

    // <expression> ::=
    //     <mulexp> { ('+' <mulexp>) | ('-' <mulexp>) }

    double result = parseMulexp();
    if (errorMessage != null) return result;

    while (true) {
      if (lexer.nextToken() == '+') {
        match('+');
        if (errorMessage != null) return result;
        result += parseMulexp();
        if (errorMessage != null) return result;
      }
      else if (lexer.nextToken() == '-') {
        match('-');
        if (errorMessage != null) return result;
        result -= parseMulexp();
        if (errorMessage != null) return result;
      }
      else return result;
    }
  }
```

```
/**
 * Parse a mulexp, a subexpression at the precedence level
 * of * and /. If any error occurs we return immediately.
 *
 * @return the double value of the mulexp or
 * garbage in case of errors.
 */
private double parseMulexp() {

  // <mulexp> ::=
  //   <rootexp> { ('*' <rootexp>) | ('/' <rootexp>) }

  double result = parseRootexp();
  if (errorMessage != null) return result;

  while (true) {
    if (lexer.nextToken() == '*') {
      match('*');
      if (errorMessage != null) return result;
      result *= parseRootexp();
      if (errorMessage != null) return result;
    }
    else if (lexer.nextToken() == '/') {
      match('/');
      if (errorMessage != null) return result;
      result /= parseRootexp();
      if (errorMessage != null) return result;
    }
    else return result;
  }
}

/**
 * Parse a rootexp, which is a constant or
 * parenthesized subexpression. If any error occurs
 * we return immediately.
 *
 * @return the double value of the rootexp or garbage
 * in case of errors
 */
private double parseRootexp() {
  double result = 0.0;

  // <rootexp> ::= '(' <expression> ')'

  if (lexer.nextToken() == '(') {
    match('(');
```

```
      if (errorMessage != null) return result;
      result = parseExpression();
      if (errorMessage != null) return result;
      match(')');
      if (errorMessage != null) return result;
    }

    // <rootexp> ::= number

    else if (lexer.nextToken()==CalcLexer.NUMBER_TOKEN){
      result = lexer.getNum();
      if (errorMessage != null) return result;
      match(CalcLexer.NUMBER_TOKEN);
      if (errorMessage != null) return result;
    }

    else {
      errorMessage =
        "Expected a number or a parenthesis.";
    }

    return result;
  }

}
```

Although this calculator works, it would benefit from the use of exception handling. As you see when you read the code, it uses the error-flagging technique. In many places a method is invoked and then a check is made afterward to see whether an error occurred.

Modify both `CalcParser` and `CalcLexer` so that they handle errors internally by throwing checked exceptions. To get started, create a new class `CalcError` that extends `Exception`. Whenever an error is first detected, modify the code to make it `throw new CalcError(message)`, where `message` is the error message you want to use. Do not change the interface `CalcParser` presents to its clients; the client of `CalcParser` should not receive `CalcError` exceptions and should still use the `getErrorMessage` method of the `CalcParser` to check for errors. But internally, you should be able to eliminate almost all other references to the `errorMessage` instance variable in `CalcParser`, and you should be able to entirely eliminate the `errorMessage` instance variable in `CalcLexer`. *Hint:* The program should become noticeably shorter and simpler as a result. If not—if it seems to be getting longer and more complicated—you are doing something wrong.

You can test your CalcParser and CalcLexer by adding a simple main method to CalcParser, such as this one:

```
public static void main(String[] args) {
  CalcParser p = new CalcParser(args[0]);
  if (p.getErrorMessage() == null)
    System.out.println(p.getValue());
  else System.out.println(p.getErrorMessage());
}
```

This tests it on input from the command line. For example, you can type the command `java CalcParser 1+2` and get the output `3.0`. (Unix systems usually preprocess input from the command line and give special treatment to symbols like `(`, `)`, and `*`. On these systems, you should enclose the argument to CalcParser in quotes, as in `java CalcParser "(1+2*3)"`.)

You might also be interested in seeing the code run with a graphical user interface. The class CalcDemo, available on this book's Web site, can be run as an application or as an applet. It lets you type in an expression and displays its value (or an error message). This should continue to work, without any changes, using your new versions of CalcParser and CalcLexer.

Exercise 3 Modify the CalcParser class from the previous exercise. Instead of evaluating the expression, make it produce a string containing commands to evaluate the expression on a stack machine. You should be able to test it with the same main method as before. For example, if you give the command `java CalcParser 1+2*3`, the output should be a sequence of stack commands such as this:

```
push 1.0
push 2.0
push 3.0
multiply
add
```

For the command `java CalcParser (1+2)*3`, on the other hand, it should print a sequence like this:

```
push 1.0
push 2.0
add
push 3.0
multiply
```

You may start from either the original CalcParser and CalcLexer or your modified version from the previous exercise, whichever you prefer.

Exercise 4 The behavior of the `try` statement in Java can be rather complicated, since the `try` block, the `catch` block, and the `finally` block can all finish their execution in different ways. For each of the following scenarios, what happens? Which parts of the `try` statement are executed, in what order, and what happens immediately after? Write simple test programs in Java to demonstrate the answers to the following questions about the behavior of `finally`. Include your program, its output, and your conclusions for each part.

a. The `try` block completes normally, and the `finally` block completes normally.
b. The `try` block completes normally, and the `finally` block stops by throwing an exception.
c. The `try` block completes normally, and the `finally` block stops by executing an explicit `return` statement.
d. The `try` block stops by throwing an exception that is not caught, and the `finally` block completes normally.
e. The `try` block stops by throwing an exception that is not caught, and the `finally` block stops by throwing a *different* exception.
f. The `try` block stops by throwing an exception that is not caught, and the `finally` block stops by executing an explicit `return` statement.
g. The `try` block stops by throwing an exception that is caught, the relevant `catch` block completes normally, and the `finally` block completes normally.
h. The `try` block stops by throwing an exception that is caught, the relevant `catch` block completes normally, and the `finally` block stops by throwing an exception.
i. The `try` block stops by throwing an exception that is caught, the relevant `catch` block completes normally, and the `finally` block stops by executing an explicit `return` statement.
j. The `try` block stops by throwing an exception that is caught, the relevant `catch` block stops by throwing a *different* exception, and the `finally` block completes normally.
k. The `try` block stops by throwing an exception that is caught, the relevant `catch` block stops by throwing a *different* exception, and the `finally` block stops by throwing *another different* exception.
l. The `try` block stops by throwing an exception that is caught, the relevant `catch` block stops by throwing a *different* exception, and the `finally` block stops by executing an explicit `return` statement.

m. The `try` block stops by throwing an exception that is caught, the relevant `catch` block stops by executing an explicit `return` statement, and the `finally` block completes normally.
n. The `try` block stops by throwing an exception that is caught, the relevant `catch` block stops by executing an explicit `return` statement, and the `finally` block stops by throwing a *different* exception.
o. The `try` block stops by throwing an exception that is caught, the relevant `catch` block stops by executing an explicit `return` statement, and the `finally` block stops by executing an explicit `return` statement, returning a *different* value.
p. The `try` block stops by executing an explicit `return` statement, and the `finally` block completes normally.
q. The `try` block stops by executing an explicit `return` statement, and the `finally` block stops by throwing a exception.
r. The `try` block stops by executing an explicit `return` statement, and the `finally` block stops by executing an explicit `return` statement, returning a *different* value.

Further Reading

The `throws` clause in Java is part of a gray area of programming languages, somewhere between source code and documentation. It does not really *do* anything, nor does it tell the language system anything it could not have figured out anyway. It is like documentation, except that the language system verifies it and enforces its requirements on the method's callers.

This chapter mentioned the idea of preconditions for a method. Preconditions can be considered in this same light. Imagine a language with a `preconditions` clause, like a `throws` clause. To what extent could a language system verify that the given preconditions are adequate to ensure that the method works correctly? To what extent could a language system enforce the requirement that all callers guarantee the preconditions? Questions like these are part of an active area of research on program *annotations*. There is a thought-provoking language of program annotations for Java called JML, which you can read about here:

Leavens, Gary T., Albert L. Baker, and Clyde Ruby. "Preliminary design of JML." *Technical Report* 98-060, Iowa State University (May 2001).

The bibliography of this document cites many related works on program annotations.

Chapter 18
Parameters

18.1 Introduction

Ever since Chapter 5, the first ML chapter, you have been reading examples and doing exercises that involve calling functions or methods and passing parameters to them. It is now time for a closer look at this familiar operation. Exactly how are parameters passed from caller to callee? This chapter will look at seven different methods and compare their costs and dangers.

First, some basic terminology. Here is a method definition and call in a Java-like language, with the key parts labeled:

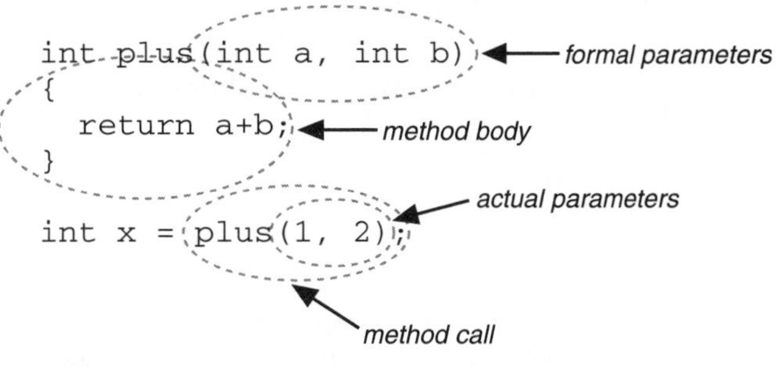

It is important to distinguish between the *actual parameters*, the parameters passed at the point of call, and the *formal parameters*, the variables in the called method that correspond to the actual parameters.[1]

This chapter will use the word *method* instead of *function* and will use a Java-like syntax for most of the examples. Real Java cannot illustrate the many different parameter-passing mechanisms used in different languages. In fact, it implements only one of them. So be aware that most of the examples in this chapter are fictitious.

18.2 Correspondence

Before looking at the parameter-passing mechanisms, a preliminary question must be dealt with: how does a language decide which formal parameters go with which actual parameters? In the simplest case, as in ML, Java, and Prolog, the correspondence between actual parameters and formal ones is determined by their positions in the parameter list. Most programming languages use such *positional parameters*, but some offer additional parameter-passing features. Ada, for example, permits *keyword parameters* like this:

```
DIVIDE(DIVIDEND => X, DIVISOR => Y);
```

This call to an Ada procedure named `DIVIDE` passes two actual parameters, `X` and `Y`. It matches the actual parameter `X` to the formal parameter named `DIVIDEND` and the actual parameter `Y` to the formal parameter named `DIVISOR`, regardless of the order in which those formal parameters appear in the definition of `DIVIDE`. To call a procedure, the programmer does not have to remember the order in which it expects its parameters; instead, the programmer can use the names of the formal parameters to make the correspondence clear. (Of course, an Ada compiler would resolve the correspondence at compile time, so there is no extra runtime cost for using keyword parameters.) Other languages that support keyword parameters include Common Lisp, Dylan, Python, and recent dialects of Fortran. These languages also support positional parameters and allow the two styles to be mixed; the first parameters in a list can be positional, and the remainder can be keyword parameters.

---

1. Some authors use the word *parameter* to mean a formal parameter and use the word *argument* to mean an actual parameter. Many people also use the word *parameter* informally, referring to either a formal parameter or an actual parameter. This author will always say either *formal parameter* or *actual parameter*, thus avoiding any argument.

Another parameter-passing feature offered by some languages is a way to declare optional parameters with default values. The formal parameter list of a function can include default values to be used if the corresponding actual parameters are not given. This gives a very short way of writing certain kinds of overloaded function definitions. For example, consider a C++ definition like this one:

```
int f(int a=1, int b=2, int c=3) {
  function body
}
```

With this definition, the caller can provide zero, one, two, or three actual parameters. The actual parameters that are provided are matched with the formal parameters in order. Any formal parameters that are not matched with an actual parameter are initialized with their default values instead. In effect, C++ treats the definition above like the following overloaded collection of four definitions:

```
int f() {f(1,2,3);}
int f(int a) {f(a,2,3);}
int f(int a, int b) {f(a,b,3);}
int f(int a, int b, int c) {
  function body
}
```

A few languages, including C, C++, and most of the scripting languages like JavaScript, Python, and Perl, allow actual parameter lists of any length. In C, for example, an ellipsis can appear as the last item in a formal parameter list. The `printf` library function for C, which takes a format string followed by any number of additional parameters, would be declared like this:

```
int printf(char *format, ...) {
  function body
}
```

The function body must use C library routines to access the additional actual parameters. This is a weak spot in C's static type checking, of course, since the types of the additional parameters cannot be checked statically.

18.3 By Value

The first parameter-passing mechanism this chapter will look at is the most common—passing parameters by value.

> For by-value parameter passing, the formal parameter is just like a local variable in the activation record of the called method,

with one important difference: it is initialized using the value of the corresponding actual parameter, before the called method begins executing.

The by-value mechanism is the simplest. It is the only one used in real Java. The actual parameter is used only to initialize the corresponding formal parameter. After that, the called method can do anything it wants to with the formal parameter, and the actual parameter is not affected. For example:

```
int plus(int a, int b) {
  a += b;
  return a;
}
void f() {
  int x = 3;
  int y = 4;
  int z = plus(x, y);
}
```

In this Java code, when the method `f` calls the method `plus`, the values of `f`'s variables `x` and `y` are used to initialize `plus`'s variables `a` and `b`. When the `plus` method begins executing, the activation records look like this:

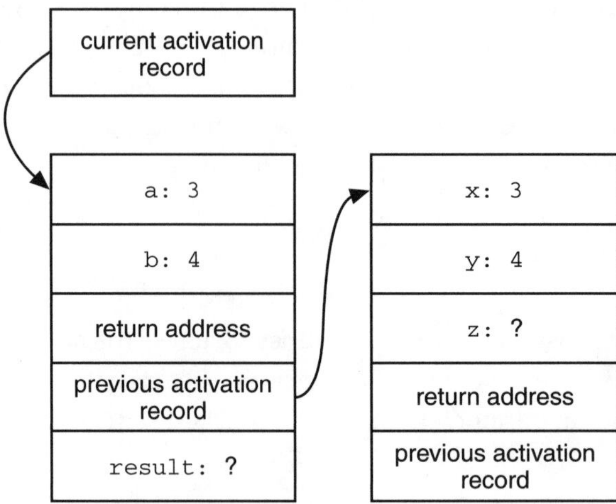

`plus`'s assignment `a += b` changes only its own formal parameter `a`, not the variable `x` in `f` that was the corresponding actual parameter on the call.

When parameters are passed by value, changes to the formal parameter do not affect the corresponding actual parameter. That does not mean that the called method is unable to make any changes that are visible to the caller. Consider the `ConsCell` class from the previous chapter with this method added:

```
/**
 * Mutator for the head field of this ConsCell.
 * @param h the new int for our head
 */
public void setHead(int h) {
  head = h;
}
```

The method `setHead` is a *mutator*—a method that changes the value of a field. Now consider this method `f`:

```
void f() {
  ConsCell x = new ConsCell(0,null);
  alter(3,x);
}

void alter(int newHead, ConsCell c) {
  c.setHead(newHead);
  c = null;
}
```

As you can see, the method `f` creates a `ConsCell` object and passes its reference to the method `alter`. When `alter` begins to execute, the activation records look like this:

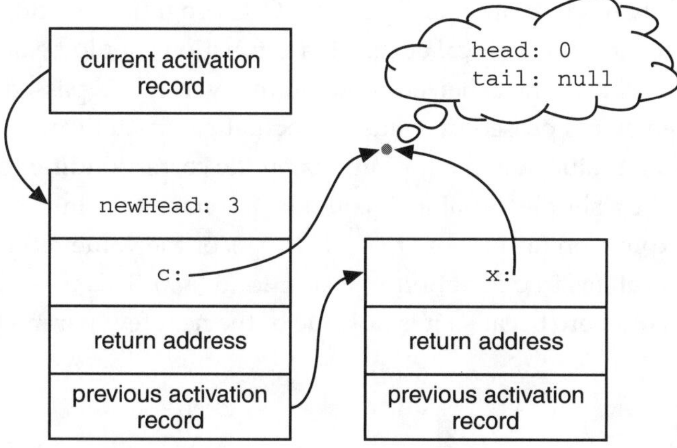

As the illustration shows, the formal parameter `c` is a copy of the actual parameter `x`. This does not mean that there is a copy of the `ConsCell` object—only that the reference `c` is a copy of the reference `x`, so both refer to the same object. Now when the first statement of `alter` executes, it calls the `setHead` method of that object. The object's `head` becomes 3. That change is visible to the caller. When `alter` returns, the object to which `f`'s variable `x` refers will have a new `head` value. On the other hand, when the second statement of `alter` executes, it changes `c` to `null`. This has no effect on the object or on the actual parameter `x`. When `alter` is ready to return, this is the situation:

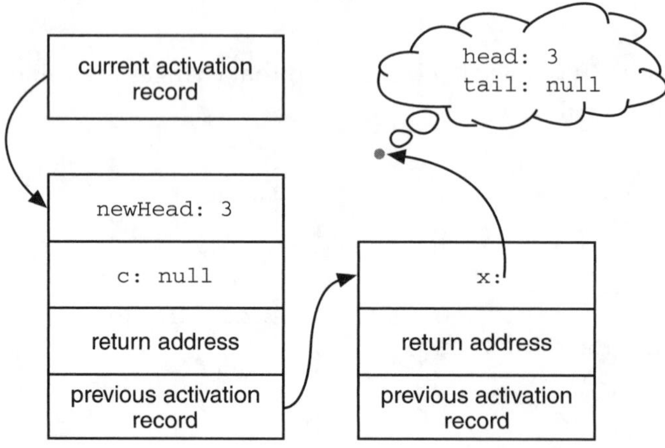

In general, when a Java method receives a parameter of a reference type, any change it makes to the *object* (like `c.setHead(3)`) is visible to the method's caller, while any change it makes to the *reference* (like `c = null`) is purely local. Another language that only has by-value parameters is C. C programmers often use the same kind of trick to get non-local effects. If a C function should be able to change a variable that is visible to the caller, a pointer to that variable is passed.

When a parameter is passed by value, the actual parameter can be any expression that yields an rvalue suitable for initializing the corresponding formal parameter. It need not be a simple variable. It could be a constant (as in `c.setHead(3)`), an arithmetic expression (as in `c.setHead(1+2)`), or the value returned by another method call (as in `c.setHead(x.getHead())`). This may seem obvious, but it is pointed out here because it is not true of the next few parameter-passing methods.

18.4 By Result

A parameter that is passed *by result* is, in a way, the exact opposite of a parameter that is passed by value.

> For by-result parameter passing, the formal parameter is just like a local variable in the activation record of the called method—it is uninitialized. After the called method finishes executing, the final value of the formal parameter is assigned to the corresponding actual parameter.

Notice that the actual parameter is not evaluated, only assigned to. No information is communicated from the caller to the called method. A by-result parameter works only in the opposite direction, to communicate information from the called method back to the caller. Here is an example, in a Java-like language but with a fictitious `by-result` keyword. (Parameters not otherwise declared are assumed to be passed by value, as in normal Java.)

```
void plus(int a, int b, by-result int c) {
  c = a + b;
}
void f() {
  int x = 3;
  int y = 4;
  int z;
  plus(x, y, z);
}
```

In this example, the method `f` calls the method `plus`. The third parameter is passed by result. This means that the actual parameter `z` does not need to be initialized before the call, since its value is never called for. When `plus` starts, its formal parameter `c` is uninitialized:

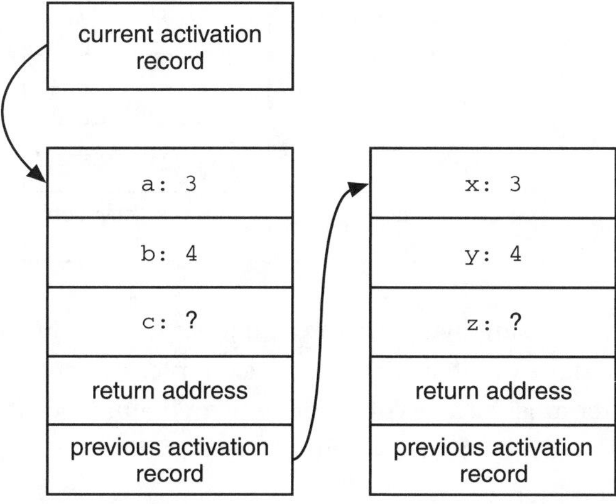

When `plus` is ready to return, its formal parameter `c` has had a value assigned to it. This has had no immediate effect on the corresponding actual parameter `z`:

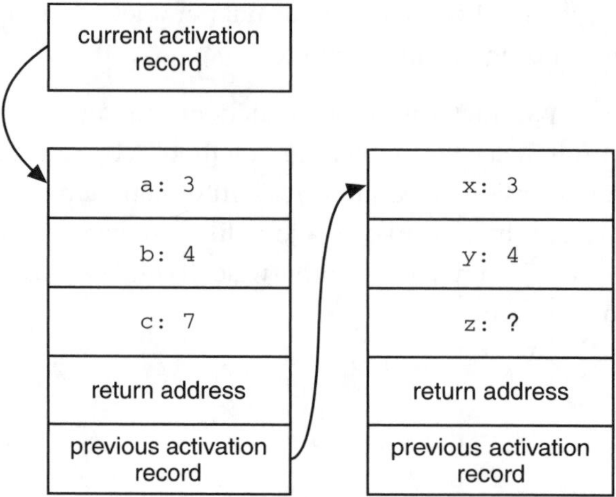

Only when `plus` actually returns is the final value of `c` automatically copied to `z`:

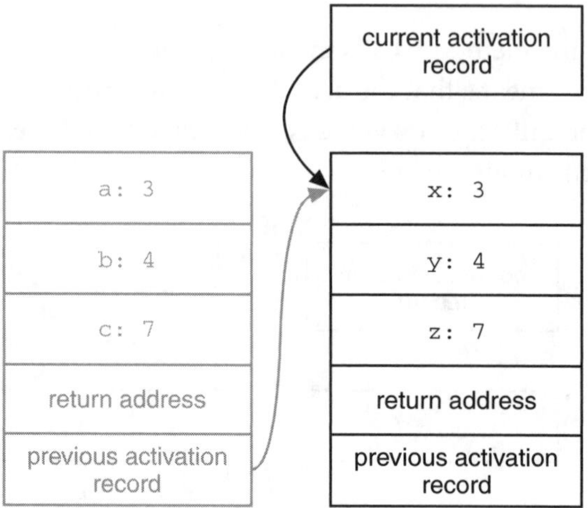

To use parameter passing by result, the actual parameter must be something that can have a value assigned to it; a variable, for example, and not a constant. In fact, the actual parameter must be an expression with an lvalue—something that could appear on the left-hand side of an assignment, as was discussed in Chapter 13.

By-result parameter passing is also sometimes called *copy-out*, for obvious reasons. Relatively few languages support pure by-result parameter passing. Algol W is one. Ada language systems also sometimes use the by-result mechanism.

18.5 By Value-Result

You have seen by-value parameters for communicating information from the caller to the called method, and you have seen by-result parameters for communicating information in the opposite direction. What about bidirectional communication? What if you want to pass a value into a method through a parameter, and get a different value out through that same parameter? One way to do this is to pass the parameter by *value-result*, which is a simple combination of by-value and by-result. If you look at the descriptions of by-value and by-result, you will see that the first describes things that happen before the called method begins executing, while the second describes things that happen after it has finished. If you combine the two, you get value-result:

> For passing parameters by value-result, the formal parameter is just like a local variable in the activation record of the called method. It is initialized using the value of the corresponding actual parameter, before the called method begins executing. Then, after the called method finishes executing, the final value of the formal parameter is assigned to the actual parameter.

This method behaves like by-value when the method is called and like by-result when the method returns. Because (like by-result) it assigns a value to the actual parameter, it needs the actual parameter to be an lvalue. For example:

```
void plus(int a, by-value-result int b) {
  b += a;
}
void f() {
  int x = 3;
  plus(4, x);
}
```

When `plus` is called, but before it begins executing, the activation records look like this:

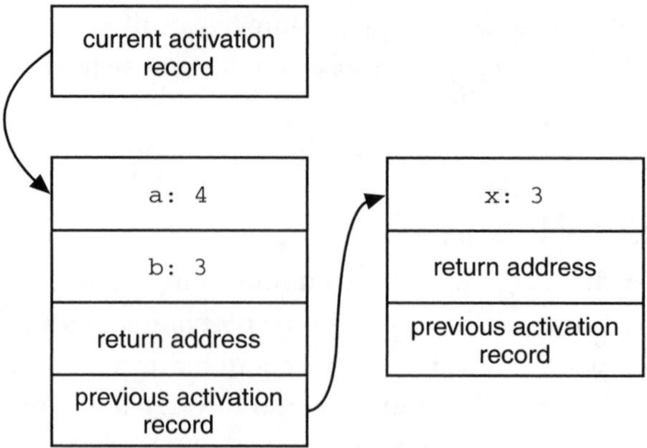

As the illustration shows, the formal parameter `b` has been initialized using the value of the actual parameter `x`. When `plus` has finished, but not yet returned, its value for `b` has changed. But the value of the caller's `x` has not yet been changed:

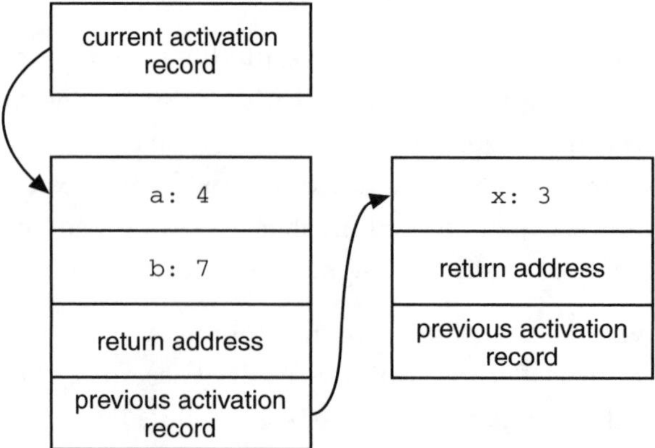

Only when the method actually returns is the final value of the formal parameter copied back to the actual parameter, like this:

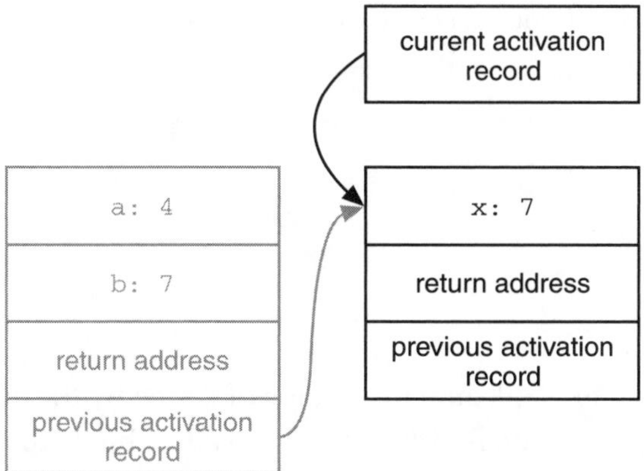

Value-result parameter passing is sometimes called *copy-in/copy-out*, for obvious reasons. Ada language systems sometimes use the value-result mechanism.

18.6 By Reference

The three methods of parameter passing seen so far require copying values into and out of the called method's activation record. This can be a problem for languages in which values that take up a lot of space in memory can be passed as parameters. Copying a whole array, string, record, object, or some other large value to pass it as a parameter can can be seriously inefficient, both because it slows down the method call and because it fattens up the activation record. This is not a problem in Java, because no primitive-type or reference-type value takes up more than 64 bits of memory. Objects, including arrays, can be large, but they are not passed as parameters—only references are. But languages other than Java sometimes need another method of parameter passing to handle large parameters more efficiently.

One solution is to pass the parameter *by reference*:

> For passing parameters by reference, the lvalue of the actual parameter is computed before the called method executes. Inside the called method, that lvalue is used as the lvalue for the corresponding formal parameter. In effect, the formal parameter is an alias for the actual parameter—another name for the same memory location.

Here is an example. It is the same as the example used for value-result parameter passing, except for the (fictional) keyword `by-reference` to indicate the parameter-passing technique.

```
void plus(int a, by-reference int b) {
  b += a;
}
void f() {
  int x = 3;
  plus(4, x);
}
```

As in the value-result example, the final value of `x` seen by the method `f` is 7. But the mechanism is quite different. When `plus` is called, but before it begins executing, the activation records look like this:

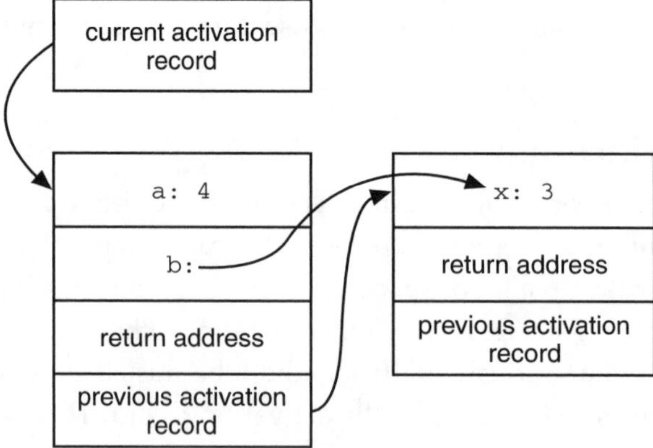

There is no separate memory location for the value of `b`. The lvalue for `b` (that is, the address where `b`'s value is stored) is the same as the lvalue for `x`, which is indicated with an arrow in the illustration. The effect is that `b` is an alias—just another name for `x`. So when the `plus` method executes the expression `b += a`, the effect is to add 4 to `x`. Unlike value-result, the caller's actual parameter is affected even before the called method returns.

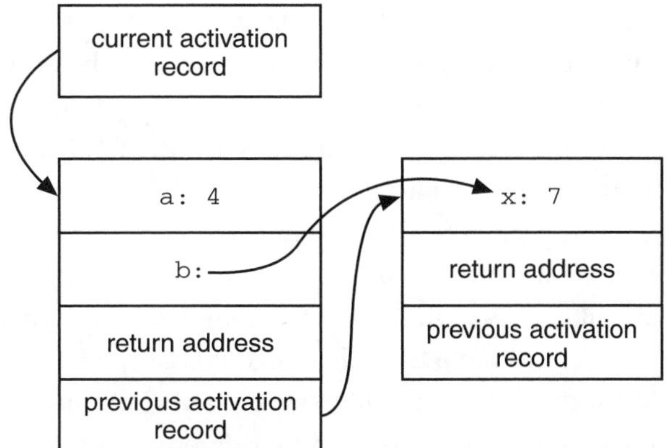

No extra action needs to be taken when the method returns, since the change to x has already been made. Notice that no copying of the values of the parameters ever took place. This makes little, if any, difference in efficiency in this example, since copying the value of x is probably no more expensive than setting up b to be an alias for x. But if x were some large value, like an array, passing it by reference would be less expensive than the previous parameter-passing methods.

The discussion of by-value parameter passing mentioned a trick that C programmers often use: passing a pointer to a variable rather than the variable itself. By-reference parameter passing *is* that same trick, really, except that the language system hides most of the details. Although C only has by-value parameter passing, a C program can exhibit the same behavior as the previous example, like this:

```
void plus(int a, int *b) {
  *b += a;
}

void f() {
  int x = 3;
  plus(4, &x);
}
```

The declaration `int *b` means that `b` is a pointer to an integer. The expression `*b` refers to the integer to which `b` points. The expression `&x` gives a pointer to the integer `x`. An implementation of by-reference parameter passing might well work exactly like this C example. Passing by reference can be implemented simply by passing the actual parameter's address by value.

By-reference parameter passing is the oldest parameter-passing technique in commercial high-level languages, since it was the only one implemented in early dialects of Fortran. When Fortran was developed, the whole idea of writing programs in a high-level language instead of assembly language was new and strange. People doubted that a high-level program could approach the efficiency of an assembly-language program. So efficiency was one of the top design goals for Fortran, and by-reference parameter passing was a suitably efficient mechanism. Early implementations of Fortran had a famous defect related to this. When a constant was passed as a parameter, the one-and-only, in-memory copy of that constant was passed by reference. So if the called method changed the corresponding formal parameter, it changed all uses of the constant throughout the program. The function call `F(2)` could have the side effect of changing all the program's uses of the constant 2! Modern Fortran still allows constants (and other expressions that do not ordinarily have lvalues) to be passed by reference, but it implements this safely, by storing the value before the call in a temporary local variable allocated for the purpose. If the called method changes the corresponding formal parameter, only the temporary local variable is changed. That has no effect on the rest of the program.

Although by-reference parameters can be more efficient, they can also be perilous to use. The heart of the problem is aliasing.

> Two different expressions that have the same lvalue are *aliases* of each other.

Aliases make programs difficult to understand. When you see an expression like `x=y+z`, you might naturally assume that it can change `x` but not `y` or `z`. This natural assumption is wrong if `x` and `y` are aliased; any change to `x` will also be a change to `y`. Aliasing arises in many different ways. Languages with explicit pointers (or references, as in Java) get aliasing in an obvious way:

```
ConsCell x = new ConsCell(0,null);
ConsCell y = x;
```

Now `x` and `y` are references to the same object, so `x.head` and `y.head` have the same lvalue. The method call `x.setHead(3)` would change the head of `y` as well. Languages with arrays also get some obvious kinds of aliasing, as in this expression:

```
A[i]=A[j]+A[k]
```

If the integer variables `i` and `j` are equal, then `A[i]` and `A[j]` have the same lvalue. The expression changes the value of `A[j]` as well as `A[i]`.

The aliasing that can occur when parameters are passed by reference can be much more deceptive. Consider this example:

```
void sigsum(by-reference int n, by-reference int ans) {
  ans = 0;
  int i = 1;
  while (i <= n) ans += i++;
}
```

This `sigsum` method takes two integer parameters, `n` and `ans`, by reference. When it is called properly, it stores the sum of the numbers 1 through `n` in `ans`. For example, this function uses it to compute the sum of the numbers 1 through 10:

```
int f() {
  int x,y;
  x = 10;
  sigsum(x,y);
  return y;
}
```

The simple aliasing that occurs in this example is not a problem. `sigsum`'s variable `n` aliases `f`'s variable `x`, and `sigsum`'s variable `ans` aliases `f`'s variable `y`. Since the aliases have scopes that do not overlap, there is no danger from this. But consider what happens when `sigsum` is called this way:

```
int g() {
  int x;
  x = 10;
  sigsum(x,x);
  return x;
}
```

You might expect this function `g` to return the same value as `f`, but it does not. Because the function `g` passes `x` for both parameters, `sigsum`'s variables `n` and `ans` are actually aliases for each other. (That's what makes this kind of aliasing so deceptive. The variables *look* innocent enough. It might not occur to you that, depending on how the function is called, they can actually have the same lvalue.) This is how the activation records look when `sigsum` is called, before it begins executing:

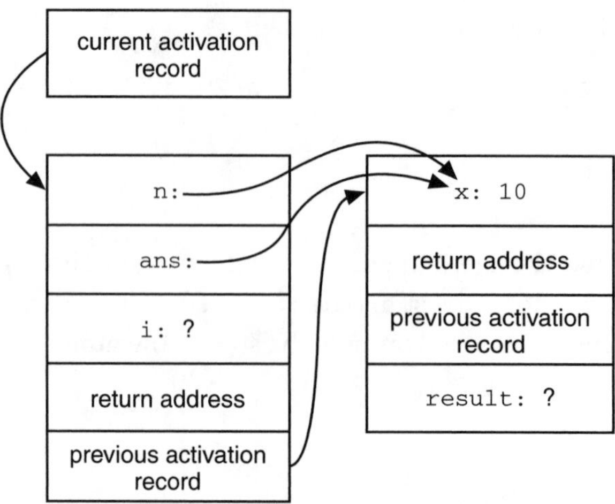

The first thing `sigsum` does is initialize `ans` to zero. Since `ans` and `n` are aliased, this also sets `n` to zero. That makes the loop guard for `sigsum`'s while loop, `(i<=n)`, immediately false, so `sigsum` returns to its caller. This is how the activation records look:

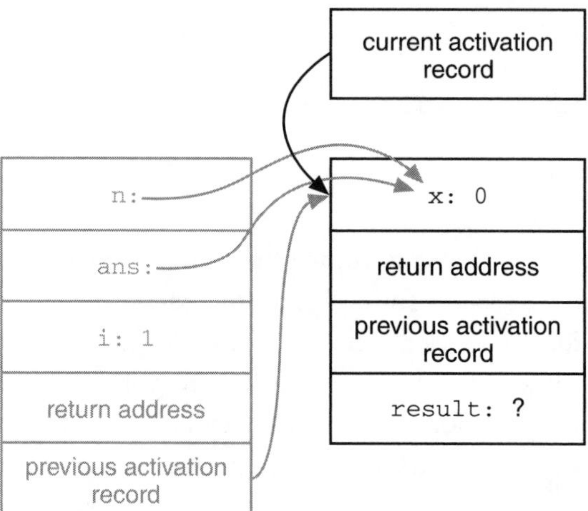

The function `g` returns the value 0, instead of the sum of the numbers 1 through 10.

18.7 By Macro Expansion

And now for something completely different—macro expansion. Here is an example of a definition of a macro for the C language:

```
#define MIN(X,Y) ((X)<(Y)?(X):(Y))
```

Here is a corresponding use of the macro:

```
a = MIN(b,c);
```

Although macros look like methods, and sometimes seem to work like methods, they are not methods. Before a program is run—before it is even compiled—a preprocessing step replaces each use of the macro with a complete copy of the macro body, with the actual parameters substituted for the formal parameters. In the example, the statement that uses the macro will be turned into this one:

```
a = ((b)<(c)?(b):(c))
```

The C compiler will see only the transformed version of the statement. It will never see the macro definition itself or any use of the macro. For C, and other languages with this kind of preprocessing step, another binding time should perhaps be added to the list from Chapter 4: *macro-expansion time,* coming right before compile time.

Macro expansion is an even older technique than by-reference parameter passing, since it was implemented in assembly-language systems long before high-level languages were built. It has some odd properties. Each actual parameter is reevaluated every time it is used. `MIN(f(),g())` becomes `((f())<(g())?(f()):(g()))`, which calls either `f` or `g` twice. (If by any chance a formal parameter is not used, the corresponding actual parameter is never evaluated.) The consequences can be especially odd if the actual parameters are expressions that have side effects; for example, `MIN(a++,b++)` increments either `a` or `b` twice.

One of the oddest properties of macro expansion is demonstrated by the following macro, which swaps two integers.

```
#define intswap(X,Y) {int temp=X; X=Y; Y=temp;}
```

The `intswap` macro defines a block containing a local variable named `temp` and uses that variable in the usual three-step swap. Most of the time, this macro works as expected. But consider this application:

```
int main() {
  int temp=1, b=2;
  intswap(temp,b);
  printf("%d, %d\n", temp, b);
}
```

This program prints the string "`1, 2`", showing that it does not swap the two variables. (See if you can figure out why, before reading on!)

The macro expansion shows why. Before the compiler sees the program, the preprocessing step expands the macro this way:

```
int main() {
  int temp=1, b=2;
  {int temp= temp ;  temp = b ;  b =temp;} ;
  printf("%d, %d\n", temp, b);
}
```

The actual parameter `temp` is evaluated in an environment that has a new, local definition of a variable called `temp`. This is a kind of behavior that programmers usually find surprising. They have the habit of thinking that the names of local variables in the called method are irrelevant to the caller. But macros are not methods, and the names of local variables in a macro body may be critically important to the caller.

This phenomenon has a name—*capture*. In any program fragment, an occurrence of a variable that is not statically bound within the fragment is *free*. For example, in this fragment, the occurrences of `temp` are bound while the occurrences of `a` and `b` are free:

```
{int temp= a ;  a = b ;  b =temp;}
```

In the problematic use of the `intswap` macro, `intswap(temp,b)`, the two actual parameters are program fragments with free variables, `temp` and `b`. When these program fragments are substituted into the body of the macro, the free variable `temp` is "captured" by the local definition of `temp` in the macro body. Capture can also occur when the macro body is substituted into the body of the caller. If the macro contains occurrences of a global variable and if the caller has a local definition of the same name, the macro's occurrences will be captured by the caller's definition.

The other parameter-passing methods you have seen can be mixed, and are mixed in some languages. In Pascal, for example, a procedure can take some of its parameters by reference and others by value. But macro expansion is really an all-or-nothing affair. Just substituting the text of an actual parameter for the formal parameter would be nearly useless, since the actual parameter could not then refer to variables in the caller's context. To pass parameters by macro expansion, you must also substitute the text of the macro body back into the caller's code. When it is implemented by textual substitution like this, a macro does not have an activation record of its own, and generally cannot be recursive.

Macro expansion has been explained in terms of textual substitutions that happen before compilation and execution. This is the easiest way to think about it. But the trick of making textual substitution is just an implementation technique—one that is useful for compiled language systems like C, but not the only one that can be imagined. The important thing about macro expansion is not its implementation, it is its effect. The body of a macro must be evaluated in the caller's context, so that free variables in the macro body can be captured by the caller's definitions. Each actual parameter must be evaluated on every use of the corresponding formal parameter, in the context of that occurrence of the formal parameter, so that free variables in the actual parameter can be captured by the macro body's definitions. Any implementation that achieves this can be said to pass parameters by macro expansion, even if it does not do textual substitution before compilation.

> For passing parameters by macro expansion, the body of the macro is evaluated in the caller's context. Each actual parameter is evaluated on every use of the corresponding formal parameter, in the context of that occurrence of that formal parameter (which is itself in the caller's context).

18.8 By Name

The phenomenon of capture is a drawback for macro expansion. One way to eliminate it is to pass parameters *by name*. In this technique, each actual parameter is evaluated in the caller's context, on every use of the corresponding formal parameter. Macro expansion puts each actual parameter in the context of a use of the formal parameter, and then puts the whole macro body in the caller's context. In this way the actual parameters can get access to the caller's local definitions. But it happens in an indirect way that risks capture. Passing parameters by name skips the middle man; the actual parameter is evaluated directly in the caller's context.

> For passing parameters by name, each actual parameter is evaluated in the caller's context, on every use of the corresponding formal parameter.

As with macro expansion, if a formal parameter passed by name is not used in the called method, the corresponding actual parameter is never evaluated.

Passing parameters by name is simple to describe in the abstract, but it is rather difficult to implement. It can be done by macro-style substitution, if the names used in the method body are changed to avoid capture. But this is not efficient enough for practical implementations. In practical implementations, the actual parameter is treated like a little anonymous function. Whenever the called method needs the value of the formal parameter (either its lvalue or its rvalue), it uses that little anonymous function to get it. Here is an example:

```
void f(by-name int a, by-name int b) {
  b=5;
  b=a;
}
int g() {
  int i = 3;
  f(i+1,i);
  return i;
}
```

This is what the activation records look like when `g` calls `f`, before `f` starts executing:

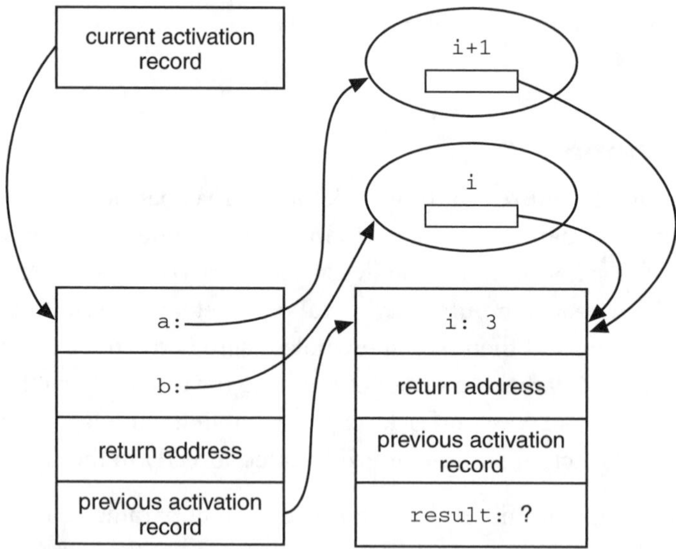

This illustration shows how the formal parameters `a` and `b` are bound to two anonymous functions. The function for `a` knows how to compute the value for `i+1`, and the function for `b` knows how to compute `i`. These little anonymous functions need the caller's context to get the variable `i` from the caller. As was shown in Chapter 12 when passing functions as parameters, the thing that is passed from caller to callee has two parts: the code for the actual parameter and the nesting link to use with it.[2]

When `f` executes the expression `b=5`, it calls for the lvalue of `b`. The anonymous function for `b` supplies `i`'s lvalue. The result is that the value 5 is stored in the caller's variable `i`. So far this seems to be working like a by-reference parameter—the change to the formal parameter immediately changed the corresponding actual parameter. But there is more to the story. When `f` executes the expression `b=a`, it calls again for the lvalue of `b` (which is recomputed) and for the rvalue of `a`. The anonymous function for `a` computes the value `i+1` in the caller's context—using the current value for `i`—which produces the value 6. This 6 is the value stored back in `i` and is the value that the function `g` returns.

Notice the similarities between by-name parameter passing and the anonymous functions experimented with in ML. A method call like `f(i+1,i)`, if it passes parameters by name, is like a shorthand notation for passing two little anonymous functions without parameters. In ML, this might be written as

```
f(fn () => i+1, fn () => i);
```

As in ML, the functions are passed with nesting links that allow them to access variables in the caller's context.

By-name parameter passing was introduced in Algol 60 (which also introduced by-value parameter passing). It can be used to do some impressively tricky things, but on the whole it was not a successful invention. It is difficult to implement and can be inefficient. Moreover, most programmers prefer a parameter-passing technique that is easier to understand, even if it is not as flexible. By-name parameter passing is one of the few things introduced in Algol 60 that has not been widely copied in later languages. However, the variation shown next, by-need parameter passing, is used in many functional languages.

18.9 By Need

An actual parameter that is passed by name (or by macro expansion) must be reevaluated every time the corresponding formal parameter is used in the called method. This can be useful, but more often it is merely wasteful. Reevaluations of

2. There is a customary name for the little-anonymous-function-and-nesting-link used to implement by-name parameter passing. It is called a *thunk*.

an actual parameter usually produce the same value as the first evaluation (except for unusual examples like the one above, in which the evaluation of the actual parameter is affected by some intervening side effect). Passing parameters *by need* eliminates this unnecessary recomputation.

> For passing parameters by need, each actual parameter is evaluated in the caller's context, on the first use of the corresponding formal parameter. The value of the actual parameter is then cached, so that subsequent uses of the corresponding formal parameter do not cause reevaluation.

The previous example—the one that demonstrates parameters passed by name—would produce the same result if the parameters were passed by need. Each actual parameter would be evaluated only once. But the parameter `i+1` would be evaluated after the value 5 was assigned to `i`, so the outcome would be the same. On the other hand, here is an example that shows the difference between by-name and by-need parameters:

```
void f(by-need int a, by-need int b) {
  b=a;
  b=a;
}
void g() {
  int i = 3;
  f(i+1,i);
  return i;
}
```

When `f` is called, its first assignment expression `b=a` has the same effect as evaluating `i=i+1` in the caller's context; it changes `g`'s variable `i` to 4. But the second assignment does not reevaluate the actual parameters. It just sets `i` to 4 again. By-name parameters would be reevaluated for the second assignment, so `i` would end up as 5. As you can see, the difference depends on the side effects. Without side effects, the only way to detect the difference between by-name and by-need parameter passing is by the difference in cost. If a formal parameter is used frequently in the called method and if the corresponding actual parameter is an expensive expression to evaluate, by-name parameters can be much slower than by-need parameters.

All three of the last parameter-passing methods—macro expansion, passing by name, and passing by need—have the property that if the called method does not use a formal parameter, the corresponding actual parameter is never evaluated. Consider this function, which implements the `&&` operator of Java:

```
boolean andand(by-need boolean a, by-need boolean b) {
  if (!a) return false;
  else return b;
}
```

This example short-circuits, just like Java's `&&` and ML's `andalso`. If the first parameter is false, Java decides the result is false without ever evaluating the second parameter. This can make a big difference, in more than just efficiency. For example:

```
boolean g() {
  while (true) {
  }
  return true;
}

void f() {
  andand(false,g());
}
```

When `f` calls `andand`, it passes the expressions `false` and `g()` by need. Since the first parameter is `false`, `andand` never evaluates the second parameter; that is, it never calls `g`. This is easily observable when the program runs, since the function `g` has an infinite loop. If `f` did call it, the program would hang. As it is, `f` completes normally.

By-need parameter passing is used in so-called lazy functional languages, such as Haskell. Such languages evaluate only as much of the program as necessary to get an answer. Consistent with that philosophy, they only evaluate an actual parameter if the corresponding formal parameter is really used. As in the example above, lazy languages can produce an answer where an eager language hangs or gets an exception.

18.10 Specification Issues

You have now seen seven different methods of passing parameters. Are these techniques part of the language specification? Does a programmer know and rely on the peculiarities of the parameter-passing technique used by the language system, or are they just hidden system-implementation details? The answer depends on the language.

In languages without side effects, the exact parameter-passing technique is often invisible to the programmer. For functional languages, the big question is whether actual parameters are always evaluated (*eager evaluation*) or whether they are evaluated only if the corresponding formal parameter is actually used (*lazy evaluation*). ML uses eager evaluation. It guarantees to evaluate all actual parameters, whether they are used in the called method or not. It follows that an ML language system does not pass parameters by name, by need, or by macro expansion. But it is difficult to distinguish among the other possibilities without side effects, and there are no side effects in the subset of ML seen.

In imperative languages, it is possible to write a program whose behavior differs with each of our seven parameter-passing techniques. In that sense the technique is perfectly visible to the programmer. Nevertheless, some imperative language specifications define parameter passing abstractly, so that the language system is free to use one of several techniques. Ada, for example, has three parameter-passing "modes": `in`, `out`, and `in out`. An `in` parameter is used to pass values into the called method. The language treats `in`-mode formal parameters rather like constants in the called method and does not permit assignments to them. An `out` parameter is used to pass values out of the called method. The language requires assignment to `out`-mode formal parameters in the called method, and does not permit their values to be read. An `in out` parameter is used for two-way communication. It may be both read and assigned within the called method. None of this specifies whether the formal parameters are copies of the actual parameters or references to the actual parameters. For scalar values, the Ada standard specifies copying. But for aggregates like arrays and records it permits implementations to go either way. For example, an implementation might pass `in out` parameters by reference or by value-result. A program that can tell the difference (like some of the examples in this chapter) is simply not considered to be a valid Ada program.

This exemplifies the abstract definition of parameter passing. In this approach, the parameter-passing techniques in this chapter are all considered to be implementation details—they belong in the language system, not in the definition of the language itself. The language definition specifies parameter passing abstractly, not saying how parameters should be implemented, but only how they should be used. Any program that tries to make use of implementation-specific, parameter-passing properties not guaranteed by the language deserves what it gets.

18.11 Conclusion

The parameter-passing techniques described in this chapter are among the most commonly used, but they are certainly not the only techniques that have been tried. In particular, Prolog handles parameters in a completely different way, as you will see starting in the next chapter. Further, there are many minor variations on the different techniques, as you will see if you do some of the exercises that follow. There certainly is a lot of unexpected complexity to parameter passing. It all seems so simple at first glance! But a corollary of Murphy's Law is particularly well-suited to computing: *inside every little problem there is a big problem waiting to get out.*

Exercises

Exercise 1 One important question about by-result parameter passing that was not mentioned is this: when does the language system compute the lvalue of the actual parameter? (The lvalue of the actual parameter is the memory location to which the final value of the formal parameter is written.) You might have assumed that this would be computed, like a by-reference parameter, before the called method executes. But since it is not needed until the called method returns, its computation could be delayed until it is needed, like a by-name parameter. Ada does it the early way, while Algol W does it at the last minute.

Here is an example that illustrates the difference:

```
void f(int[] A) {
  int i = 0;
  g(i,A[i]);
}

void g(by-reference int i, by-result int j) {
  j = 2;
  i = 1;
  j = 3;
}
```

For each of these two different interpretations of by-result parameter passing, explain what happens when `f` calls `g`. In particular, say exactly what happens when any change is made to `i` or `A`.

Exercise 2 An important detail of by-result and value-result parameter passing is the *order* in which the final values of the formal parameters are written back to the actual parameters. A method `f(a,b)` might write back first `a` then `b`, or first `b` then `a`. Or the language specification might leave the order unspecified, leaving it up to the language system. The order can make a significant difference.

Write two Java-like methods `f` and `g` that illustrate this distinction. Your method `f` should call only `g`, passing parameters by value-result. Your `g` method should make no calls. Your methods should produce different results (that is, different final values in the variables of `f`) depending on the order in which the value-result parameters of g are written back. Explain the results that two different write-back orders would produce for your example.

Exercise 3 Make an experiment with the ML language system that demonstrates that ML does not pass parameters by name. Show the results of your experiment, and explain what results by-name parameter passing would have given.

Exercise 4 Make an experiment with the ML language system that demonstrates that ML does not recopy lists when they are passed as parameters. (*Hint:* The only way to tell the difference, without side effects, is by timing.) Show the results of your experiment, and explain what results you would expect if ML recopied list parameters.

Exercise 5 Write two ML functions f and g that demonstrate that ML does not implement function calls using macro expansion. Your f should call only g, and your g should make no calls. Explain the results macro expansion would give for your function, and show the results ML actually gives.

Exercise 6 This code fragment uses arrays in Java. The first line declares and allocates an array of two integers. The next two lines initialize it. (Java arrays are indexed starting from 0.)

```
int[] A = new int[2];
A[0] = 0;
A[1] = 2;
f(A[0],A[A[0]]);
```

Function f is defined as

```
void f(int x, int y) {
      x = 1;
      y = 3;
}
```

For each of the following parameter-passing methods, say what the final values in the array A would be, after the call to f. (There may be more than one correct answer.)

a. By value.
b. By reference.
c. By value-result.
d. By macro expansion.
e. By name.

Exercise 7 One of the tricks associated with by-name parameter passing is called *Jensen's device.* Research Jensen's device, give an example using a Java-like syntax (augmented with `by-name`), and write a paragraph explaining the idea and how it works.

Chapter 19 A First Look at Prolog

19.1 Introduction

This chapter begins the introduction to Prolog. By the end of the chapter, you should be able to write simple Prolog code and use Prolog to manipulate lists.

Prolog is a logic programming language. All programming uses logic, of course, but in Prolog the use of logic is much more explicit than in other languages. A Prolog program *is* logic, you might say—a collection of facts and rules for proving things. You do not "run" a Prolog program; you pose questions, and the language system uses the program's collection of facts and rules to try to answer them. Interestingly, this turns out to be much more flexible than it sounds. You can do anything in Prolog that you can do in ML or Java or any other general-purpose programming language. But Prolog is especially useful in domains that involve searching for solutions to problems that are specified logically. It is, for example, one of the two most popular languages for artificial intelligence programming (along with Lisp).

ML is one of many functional languages. Java is one of many object-oriented languages. Logic programming languages are less common. Prolog is really the only widely used one—though it does have dialects, like virtually all languages. There are a few experimental logic languages, such as λ–Prolog and Gödel, and a few languages that combine functional and logic programming, such as Escher and Curry. On the whole, though, when people speak of logic programming, they usually mean Prolog.

This is a hands-on chapter. There are many short examples of Prolog. You may find it helpful to type in the examples as you go. You should do as many of the exercises as you can.

19.2 The Building Blocks—Prolog Terms

Before you jump in and start using the Prolog language system, there are a few important things you should know. Prolog programs look very different from programs in most other languages. Java and ML have, in appearance anyway, much more in common with each other than with Prolog. The good news is that Prolog is syntactically a very simple language. Everything in a Prolog program—both the program itself and the data it manipulates—is built from Prolog *terms*. There are three kinds of terms: constants, variables, and compound terms.

The simplest kind of term is a constant—an integer, a real number, or an *atom*. Integers and real numbers are straightforward. Hexadecimal, octal, binary, and character codes have some special syntax, but the basic integers and real numbers have the familiar forms:

```
123
-123
1.23
-1.23e-2
```

Any name that starts with a lowercase letter (followed by zero or more additional letters, digits, or underscores) is an *atom*. Although atoms may look like the variables of other languages, they are treated as constants in Prolog. The atom `n` is never equal to anything but the atom `n`. In ML or Java terms, an atom is much like a string constant. Sequences of most non-alphanumeric characters (like `*`, `+`, `-`, `.`, and so on) are also atoms. There are also several special atoms, including `[]` (the empty list), `!`, and `;`. All the following are atoms:

```
fred
m1
*
.
=
@#$
[]
```

The second kind of Prolog term is a *variable*. A variable is any name beginning with an uppercase letter or an underscore, followed by zero or more additional letters, digits, or underscores. For example, these are all variables:

```
X
Child
Fred_123
_123
_
```

Variables beginning with an underscore, including the variable _, get special treatment in Prolog. Most of the variables you write will begin with an uppercase letter.

The last kind of Prolog term is a *compound term*. Compound terms have an atom followed by a parenthesized, comma-separated list of terms. These are some examples of compound terms:

```
x(y,z)
parent(adam,seth)
parent(adam,Child)
x(Y,x(Y,Z))
+(1,2)
.(1,[])
```

Warning: Compound terms may look like function calls in other languages, but they almost never work anything like function calls. It will help if you just think of them as structured data.

You have now seen just about every kind of Prolog term. A term is either a constant, a variable, or a compound term. From such terms all Prolog programs and data are built. Later you will see some other ways of writing terms; for example, the term `+(1,2)` can be (and usually is) written as `1+2`. But such forms are just abbreviations, not new kinds of terms. Here is a simplified, partial grammar for terms:

```
<term> ::= <constant> | <variable> | <compound-term>
<constant> ::= <integer> | <real number> | <atom>
<compound-term> ::= <atom> ( <termlist> )
<termlist> ::= <term> | <term> , <termlist>
```

Pattern-matching using Prolog terms is called *unification*. Prolog makes heavy use of pattern-matching—even more so than ML. Two terms are said to *unify* if there is some way of binding their variables that makes them identical. Consider these two terms:

```
parent(adam,Child)
parent(adam,seth)
```

These unify by binding the variable `Child` to the atom `seth`. Finding a way to unify two terms can be tricky. Chapter 20 discusses it further. For now we will stay away from examples and exercises that involve tricky unification, and stick to cases where the unification is obvious.

A Prolog language system maintains a collection of facts and rules of inference, a kind of internal database that changes as the system runs. A Prolog program is just a set of data for this database. The simplest kind of thing in such a database is a *fact*, which is just a term followed by a period. This Prolog program consists of six facts, one on each line:

```
parent(kim,holly).
parent(margaret,kim).
parent(margaret,kent).
parent(esther,margaret).
parent(herbert,margaret).
parent(herbert,jean).
```

An atom that starts a compound term with *n* parameters is called a *predicate of arity n*. The program above gives some facts about a `parent` predicate of arity 2. They would naturally be interpreted as facts about families; Kim is a parent of Holly, Margaret is a parent of Kim, and so on.

19.3 Getting Started with a Prolog Language System

You will need a Prolog language system to try the examples and solve the exercises in this chapter. The examples were produced using SWI-Prolog, which is a good, free Prolog language system. If you are reading this book as part of an organized course, your teacher may give you instructions for running Prolog on your local system. If not, or if you want your own copy, you can easily download and install SWI-Prolog on your own Unix or Windows system. This book's Web site has up-to-date links for downloading SWI-Prolog.

You can, of course, use another implementation of Prolog. But be warned: Prolog is less standardized than many languages. There is an ISO standard for Prolog, and SWI-Prolog conforms to it in most respects. If you use a different Prolog system that implements the ISO standard, or one that implements the so-called Edinburgh syntax (from which the ISO standard was derived), it should run the examples in this book. But even Prolog implementations that are based on the ISO standard are often rather casual about conforming to it. Some dialects of Prolog are quite different.

SWI-Prolog operates in an interactive mode, as the ML language system did. It prompts you to type in a query. You type one in. It tries to prove your query, it prints out the result, and then the whole cycle repeats. When SWI-Prolog first runs it prints this:

```
Welcome to SWI-Prolog (Version 3.4.2)
Copyright (c) 1990-2000 University of Amsterdam.
Copy policy: GPL-2 (see www.gnu.org)

For help, use ?- help(Topic). or ?- apropos(Word).

?-
```

The `?-` is its prompt. It is now waiting for input. Suppose that the set of `parent` facts from the previous section is stored in a file called `relations`. The predefined predicate `consult` can then be used to read it in. (The input is shown in boldface, to distinguish it from the language system's output. The Enter key is not shown—that is assumed at the end of every input line.)

```
?- consult(relations).
% relations compiled 0.00 sec, 0 bytes

Yes
?-
```

The `consult` predicate has the side effect of adding the contents of the file to the system's internal database of facts. It can now respond to queries about the `parent` predicate.

```
?- parent(margaret,kent).

Yes
?- parent(fred,pebbles).

No
?-
```

A query asks whether the language system is able to prove something. The first query asked, "Can you prove `parent(margaret,kent)`?" The system answered `Yes`. It was able to prove that easily, since the query term unifies trivially with one of the fact terms from the program. The second query asked, "Can you prove `parent(fred,pebbles)`?" The system answered `No`. That term is not a fact in the database, nor is it implied by anything in the database. All interaction with the

Prolog language system takes place through such queries. Even the initial loading of the program was phrased as a query. The language system attempted to "prove" `consult(facts)` and succeeded, with the side effect of adding the contents of the file to the system's internal database.

The period at the end of a query is very important and very easy to forget when you are first beginning to experiment with Prolog. In case you should forget it, here is what will happen:

```
?- parent(margaret,kent)
|
```

SWI-Prolog assumes that you are not yet finished with the query. (Queries can take up more than one line.) It prompts for further input with the character `|`. Eventually, when the input ends with the period SWI-Prolog is waiting for, it will respond to the whole thing:

```
?- parent(margaret,kent)
|    .

Yes
?-
```

Any term can appear as a query, including a term with variables. For example, the query `parent(P,jean)` asks whether there is a parent of Jean—and finds one if there is.

```
?- parent(P,jean).

P = herbert

Yes
?- parent(P,esther).

No
```

The Prolog system shows the binding for `P` that was necessary to prove `parent(P,jean)`; in this case, the binding that made the query term unify with a fact term from the program. (After it shows the binding, it waits for more input. Pressing Enter at that point makes it proceed.)

In most other languages, a function to look up parent facts would be less flexible. In Java, for instance, you might have a `parentOf` method to look up a parent for a given child (taking the child as a parameter), and a `childOf` method to look up a child of a given parent (taking the parent as a parameter). In Prolog a predicate need not be treated so strictly. The previous examples used `parent` queries with a variable in the first position to look up a parent for a given child. Simply by having the variable in the second position, the query looks up a child for a given parent:

```
?- parent(esther,Child).

Child = margaret

Yes
```

Putting variables in both positions checks for the existence of any parent-child pair—or for a person who is his or her own parent:

```
?- parent(Parent,Child).

Parent = kim
Child = holly

Yes
?- parent(Person,Person).

No
```

A query can be a list of terms separated by commas. The system treats such a query as the logical conjunction of the terms in the list. For example:

```
?- parent(margaret,X),parent(X,holly).

X = kim

Yes
```

The query asks whether there is some `X` such that both `parent(margaret,X)` and `parent(X,holly)` can be proved, and the system finds one.

Often, there is more than one binding for the variables of a query that allows it to be proved. For example, this program has two facts that unify with `parent(margaret,Child)`. The Prolog system will report the bindings it used for its first successful proof. Ordinarily, you then hit Enter—one success is enough. It is also possible to ask the Prolog system to continue searching for other ways to prove your query. When it prompts after showing a binding, type a semicolon (and, if necessary, then hit Enter). You can repeat this over and over until the system has reported all solutions:

```
?- parent(margaret,Child).

Child = kim ;

Child = kent ;

No
```

Notice the final `No`. The system was asked for a third way to prove the query. It reports that it cannot find any more, even though it did have two initial successes.

This next query asks whether Kim has grandparents. This again asks for all solutions:

```
?- parent(Parent,kim),parent(Grandparent,Parent).

Parent = margaret
Grandparent = esther ;

Parent = margaret
Grandparent = herbert ;

No
```

This last example asks whether Esther has great-grandchildren:

```
?- parent(esther,Child),
|     parent(Child,Grandchild),
|     parent(Grandchild,GreatGrandchild).

Child = margaret
Grandchild = kim
GreatGrandchild = holly

Yes
```

19.4 Rules

The last example made a lengthy query to ask for great-grandchildren of Esther. It would be nicer if `greatgrandparent(esther,GreatGrandChild)` could be queried directly. One way to do this would be to add a bunch of `greatgrandparent` facts to the program. That would be laborious and error-prone. The `greatgrandparent` facts should follow logically from the `parent` facts. What is needed is a *rule* that says how to prove a great-grandparent relation. In Prolog it looks like this:

```
greatgrandparent(GGP,GGC) :-
  parent(GGP,GP), parent(GP,P), parent(P,GGC).
```

The syntax for Prolog rules is simple: a term called the *head* of the rule (`greatgrandparent(GGP,GGC)`), followed by the token `:-`, followed by a comma-separated list of terms called the *conditions* of the rule, with a period at the end.

A rule says how to prove something—to prove the head, prove the conditions. Notice that in the rule above, the conditions include variables that do not appear in the head (`GP` and `P`). Translated into English, the rule might be expressed this way:

> To prove `greatgrandparent(GGP,GGC)`, find some `GP` and `P` for which you can prove `parent(GGP,GP)`, then `parent(GP,P)` and then `parent(P,GGC)`.

This rule can be added to the `relations` program:

```
parent(kim,holly).
parent(margaret,kim).
parent(margaret,kent).
parent(esther,margaret).
parent(herbert,margaret).
parent(herbert,jean).
greatgrandparent(GGP,GGC) :-
  parent(GGP,GP), parent(GP,P), parent(P,GGC).
```

This program now contains two kinds of *clauses*: facts and rules. It permits direct greatgrandparent queries:

```
?- greatgrandparent(esther,GreatGrandchild).

GreatGrandchild = holly

Yes
```

Let's look at the sequence of steps a Prolog system might follow in response to that initial query. Let's start with one *goal* (a term to be proved), which is the query term:

```
greatgrandparent(esther,GreatGrandchild)
```

To prove this goal, try to unify it with some fact, or with the head of some rule, in the database. The goal unifies with the head of the `greatgrandparent` rule. "To prove the head, prove the conditions." The conditions of the rule are now adopted as the new list of goals:

```
parent(esther,GP), parent(GP,P), parent(P,GreatGrandchild).
```

The same bindings of variables that made the head of the rule unify with the original query have been applied to the conditions of the rule to make the new list of goals. Now there are three things to prove. To prove the first remaining goal, `parent(esther,GP)`, again try to find some matching fact or rule in the database. The goal unifies with the fact `parent(esther,margaret)`. This proves the first goal in the list, leaving this new list of goals:

```
parent(margaret,P),  parent(P,GreatGrandchild).
```

Again, the variable bindings that were used in the previous unification step have been applied to the remaining goals in the list. To prove the next remaining goal, `parent(margaret,P)`, again try to find some matching fact or rule in the database. The goal unifies with the fact `parent(margaret,kim)`. This proves that goal, leaving only one goal to go:

```
parent(kim,GreatGrandchild).
```

This remaining goal can be proved by unifying with the fact `parent(kim,holly)` from the database. This completes the proof. A Prolog system will report success with the binding `GreatGrandchild = holly`. Notice that the system reports bindings only for the variables that actually occurred in the query. To solve the query, it needed to find bindings for `GGP`, `GP`, `P`, and `GGC` as well, but it keeps them to itself.

Instead of `greatgrandparent` being directly defined, it could be defined indirectly by way of a separate `grandparent` predicate:

```
grandparent(GP,GC) :-
  parent(GP,P), parent(P,GC).

greatgrandparent(GGP,GGC) :-
  grandparent(GGP,P), parent(P,GGC).
```

Notice that both rules contain a variable named `P`. That brings up the whole question of scope, which is quite simple for Prolog:

> The scope of the definition of a variable is the clause that contains it.

The first occurrence within a clause of a name beginning with a capital letter serves as a definition of a variable with that name. All other occurrences of the same name in that clause are in the scope of that definition and are bound to the same variable. For example, the name `P` occurs twice in the `grandparent` rule. Those two occurrences are bound to the same variable. Whenever that variable is bound to some term, both occurrences are affected. The name `P` also occurs twice in the `greatgrandparent` rule. Those occurrences get bound to a completely different variable named `P`, with no connection with the variable of the same name in the `grandparent` rule.

The `greatgrandparent` rule uses a `grandparent` term as one of its conditions. A rule can be recursive, with a condition that unifies with its own head. That, as in ML, is how all the really interesting work gets done in Prolog. Here is an example—an `ancestor` predicate defined in terms of `parent` facts:

```
ancestor(X,Y) :- parent(X,Y).
ancestor(X,Y) :-
  parent(Z,Y),
  ancestor(X,Z).
```

This predicate is defined using two rules. The first says that `X` is an ancestor of `Y` if `X` is a parent of `Y`. The second says that `X` is an ancestor of `Y` if `X` is an ancestor of a parent of `Y`. As many different rules as necessary can be given for the same predicate. In this example, the first rule is the base case of a recursive definition, and the second rule is the inductive case. Prolog language systems search for proofs by trying rules in the order they are given, so base-case rules and facts should almost always be put first. Here are some example queries on the new `ancestor` predicate:

```
?- ancestor(jean,jean).

No
?- ancestor(kim,holly).

Yes
?- ancestor(A,holly).

A = kim ;

A = margaret ;

A = esther ;

A = herbert ;

No
```

You have now seen the complete core syntax of Prolog. A Prolog program is a sequence of clauses, each of which is either a fact or a rule.

<clause> ::= *<fact>* | *<rule>*
<fact> ::= *<term>* .
<rule> ::= *<term>* :- *<termlist>* .
<termlist> ::= *<term>* | *<term>* , *<termlist>*

Full Prolog has a bit more syntax than this, but not very much. It is syntactically a very simple language.

19.5 The Two Faces of Prolog

You have seen that Prolog rules say how to prove something; to prove the head, prove the conditions. Chapter 20 will discuss further Prolog's model of execution. When you understand Prolog's model of execution and you know what rules and facts are in a program (and in what order), you can predict exactly what will happen for any query.

That is one way of thinking of Prolog—a procedural way of thinking of it. But one of the charms of Prolog is that there is another, purely logical side to the story. Instead of thinking of rules as instructions on how to prove something, you can just focus on their logical content. For instance, consider the `greatgrandparent` rule again:

```
greatgrandparent(GGP,GGC) :-
  parent(GGP,GP), parent(GP,P), parent(P,GGC).
```

Procedurally, this is described as a recipe for proving `greatgrandparent` queries:

> To prove `greatgrandparent(GGP,GGC)`, find some `GP` and `P` for which you can prove `parent(GGP,GP)`, then `parent(GP,P)`, and then `parent(P,GGC)`.

Focusing on its logical content, it can be described instead as an assertion that relates `parent` facts to `greatgrandparent` facts by implication:

> For all bindings of `GGP`, `GP`, `P`, and `GGC`, if `parent(GGP,GP)` and `parent(GP,P)` and `parent(P,GGC)` are true, then `greatgrandparent(GGP,GGC)` is true.

In the mathematical language of first-order logic, this can be written as

$$\forall GGP,GP,P,GGC\ .\ \text{parent}(GGP,GP) \wedge \text{parent}(GP,P) \wedge \text{parent}(P,GGC) \\ \Rightarrow \text{greatgrandparent}(GGP,GGC)$$

Viewed this way, a Prolog program is just a formula in first-order mathematical logic. It does not say how to *do* anything in particular; it just makes some logical assertions. What a language system may or may not do with that information in response to some query is an implementation detail. This is a *declarative* way of thinking about Prolog.

Prolog is called a declarative language. Each piece of the program (each Prolog fact or rule) is like a declaration that corresponds to a simple mathematical abstraction (a formula in first-order logic). A formula does not talk about computers at all—no steps to be followed, no processor states, no contents of memory, no untidy details of mechanical execution. Functional programming languages are also called declarative, again because each piece of the program (each function definition) is like a declaration that corresponds to a simple mathematical abstraction (a function). Many people use *declarative* as the opposite of *imperative*. The declarative languages include both the logic programming languages and the functional languages.[1]

Some people feel strongly that the more declarative a language is, the better. Imperative languages are doomed to subtle side effects and interdependencies, or so the argument goes. The more declarative a language is, the simpler its semantics, and the easier it is to develop and maintain correct programs. Adding to the appeal of declarative languages is the attractive idea of *automatic programming*, the idea of having computers automatically write their own programs, given a description of the problem to be solved.[2] The detailed description of a programming problem seems like a job for a declarative language rather than an imperative one, since programmers want to declare what the problem is, not give orders on how to solve it. In some ways Prolog programming is like that. A Prolog program can be a logical specification of a problem domain, and the query can be a request for a solution to a problem in that domain. One example of this is at the end of the chapter, and there are more in Chapter 22.

---

1. One variety of programming-language semantics, *denotational semantics*, does manage to treat each piece of an imperative program as a declaration that corresponds to a mathematical abstraction. But the mathematical abstractions for imperative languages are quite complicated, since they must represent machine states.

2. Automatic programming is a well-established thread of research in artificial intelligence. The phrase *automatic programming* was once used to describe early Fortran systems. They automatically produced the assembly language that programmers used to write by hand, thus (some said) making programmers obsolete. In its early days, the whole high-level language thing seemed wonderfully AI-ish. However, the novelty wore off, programmers turned out not to be obsolete after all, and *automatic programming* came to have its present, much more ambitious meaning. This is an example of an effect that has long been an annoyance to AI researchers; once a problem is solved, people no longer think of it as an AI problem.

But Prolog programming is not magic, and Prolog is not purely declarative. It has a declarative aspect, so each fact and rule can be thought of as a formal, logical assertion. It also has a procedural aspect, each rule can be thought of as an instruction that says how to prove a given kind of goal, within the framework of Prolog's overall algorithm for proving things. It is important to be aware of both aspects when working with Prolog.

19.6 A Word about Term Interpretation

Beginning Prolog programmers sometimes mistakenly assume that the language system understands atoms. Consider the following Prolog program:

```
pays(miller,apprentice).
pays(cook,miller).
pays(cook,farmer).
pays(diner,cook).
pays(housekeeper,cook).
pays(housekeeper,butler).
```

Does it look familiar? It should. It is exactly the same as the first `relations` program, except that the eight atoms have been renamed.

To the human reader, the programs look very different, but to Prolog the difference is trivial. The names of the atoms suggest obvious interpretations to the human reader. While such interpretations are indispensible for understanding a program, it is important to remember that they are not part of Prolog. For example, you know many common-sense things about parenthood, such as the fact that two people cannot be each other's parents. But a Prolog language system does not know such things, and they will not apply to a predicate named `parent` unless they are explicitly included as facts and rules in the database. The names of atoms in Prolog are no more significant than the names of variables in ML and Java. Meaningful names are chosen not because they matter to the language, but only because they make the program more readable.

19.7 Operators

Prolog has a number of predefined operators. An operator is a special predicate for which the Prolog language system will accept operator notation. For example, the predefined predicate named `=` takes two parameters and is provable if and only if those two parameters can be unified.

```
?- =(parent(adam,seth),parent(adam,X)).

X = seth

Yes
```

The = predicate is an operator, so it can be (and usually is) written this way:

```
?- parent(adam,seth)=parent(adam,X).

X = seth

Yes
```

Writing it as an operator is a convenient shorthand. No matter which way you write it, however, you get the same thing—a compound term with the predicate =.[3]

Prolog has a number of predefined operators, including the arithmetic operators +, -, *, and /, with the usual precedence and associativity. For example, `1+2*3` can be used as a shorthand for the term `+(1,*(2,3))`, like this:

```
?- X = +(1,*(2,3)).

X = 1+2*3

Yes
?- X = 1+2*3.

X = 1+2*3

Yes
```

Although the Prolog system prints out that term using the operator notation and allows it to be entered that way, the term really is `+(1,*(2,3))`. Notice that the term is not evaluated. It unifies with the term `+(X,Y)`, but not with the term `7`:

```
?- +(X,Y) = 1+2*3.

X = 1
Y = 2*3

Yes
?- 7 = 1+2*3.

No
```

3. At least, that is what an operator is in Prolog implementations that comply with the ISO standard. This is an area where different implementations of Prolog sometimes work very differently.

There is a way to get Prolog to evaluate terms (at least, those that use *evaluable predicates* like + and *), but that will wait until Chapter 22. Notice, by the way, that Prolog observes parentheses, operator precedence, and associativity when it constructs terms from expressions with operators. For example, to get the term `*(+(1,2),3)`, you would have to write `(1+2)*3`, like this:

```
?- *(X,Y) = (1+2)*3.

X = 1+2
Y = 3

Yes
```

Incidentally, you have already seen two other Prolog operators. One is the `:-` operator used to define rules. For example, the rule `p(X):-q(X)` is just a shorthand notation for the term `:-(p(X),q(X))`. Another is the comma operator, used to separate the conditions of a rule or the terms in a conjunctive query. When the syntax for rules and the syntax for facts were described separately, that was not the whole story. All clauses, both rules and facts, have the same syntax. They consist of a single term followed by a period. For rules, that term is a compound with `:-` as its predicate.

19.8 Lists

Lists in Prolog work a bit like lists in ML. The atom `[]` represents the empty list. The `.` predicate in Prolog corresponds to the `::` operator in ML. This chart shows some ML list expressions and corresponding Prolog terms side by side:

ML Expression	Prolog Term
`[]`	`[]`
`1::[]`	`.(1,[])`
`1::2::3::[]`	`.(1,.(2,.(3,[])))`
No equivalent	`.(1,.(parent(X,Y),[]))`

As that last example shows, any term can be an element of any Prolog list. A Prolog list can contain a mixture of different types of elements, unlike an ML list.

In spite of the similarities, there is an important difference between the ML `::` operator and the Prolog `.` predicate. In ML, expressions that contain `::` are evaluated. The expression `1::[]` evaluates to a list containing the integer 1. ML does not reveal how that list is represented. The representation may have nothing to do with the :: operator that produced the list. By contrast, a Prolog term using the . predicate is not something that evaluates to a list—it *is* a list. Prolog exposes its representation of lists. It represents them as terms using the . predicate.

Special Notation for Lists

Prolog also allows a simple ML-style list notation for lists:

List Notation	Term Denoted
`[]`	`[]`
`[1]`	`.(1,[])`
`[1,2,3]`	`.(1,.(2,.(3,[])))`
`[1,parent(X,Y)]`	`.(1,.(parent(X,Y),[]))`

The list notation with square brackets is just a shorthand way of writing the list term using the . predicate. Lists expressed in either notation can be used as terms in Prolog. SWI-Prolog usually prints lists using the square-bracket notation, which makes them easier to read:

```
?- X = .(1,.(2,.(3,[]))).

X = [1, 2, 3]

Yes
?- .(X,Y) = [1,2,3].

X = 1
Y = [2, 3]

Yes
```

The Prolog notation for lists has an extra feature that ML does not have. After the list of elements, but before the closing square bracket, there can appear the symbol | followed by a final term for the tail of the list. For example:

List Notation	Term Denoted
`[1|X]`	`.(1,X)`
`[1,2|X]`	`.(1,.(2,X))`
`[1,2|[3,4]]`	`[1,2,3,4]`

The notation using | can be useful for making terms that serve as patterns. For example, the term `[1,2|X]` unifies with any list that starts with the elements 1 and 2, binding the variable `X` to the rest of the list:

```
?- [1,2|X] = [1,2,3,4,5].

X = [3, 4, 5]

Yes
```

append and Other Flexible Predicates

Prolog systems include a number of predefined predicates for lists. Consider the append predicate. append(X,Y,Z) is provable if and only if Z is the result of appending the list Y onto the end of the list X.

```
?- append([1,2],[3,4],Z).

Z = [1, 2, 3, 4]

Yes
```

This example used the append predicate to compute the result of appending two lists, much as the @ operator would have been used in ML. But the append predicate is more flexible. For example, what can [3,4] be appended to that will result in the list [1,2,3,4]? The append predicate can be used to find the answer.

```
?- append(X,[3,4],[1,2,3,4]).

X = [1, 2]

Yes
```

What two lists can be appended to get the list [1,2,3]? The append predicate can be used to find them all.

```
?- append(X,Y,[1,2,3]).

X = []
Y = [1, 2, 3] ;

X = [1]
Y = [2, 3] ;

X = [1, 2]
Y = [3] ;

X = [1, 2, 3]
Y = [] ;

No
```

Here is an implementation of an append predicate that works like the predefined append:

```
append([], B, B).
append([Head|TailA], B, [Head|TailC]) :-
  append(TailA, B, TailC).
```

The first clause, the fact append([],B,B), simply says that the result of appending any list B to the empty list is the same list B again. The recursive rule is more complex. Notice that it applies only to cases where the first parameter and the third parameter are lists with the same first element, Head. In such cases, the rule says that you can prove the append relation by proving another append relation, using the tail of the first list, the same second list, and the tail of the third list. Since the condition of this rule is an append relation with a shorter first list, repeated applications of the rule eventually result in an append goal in which the first parameter is the empty list. Then the base case applies.

It is interesting to compare this with an append function written in ML. This one returns true when the Prolog predicate would be provable and false otherwise:

```
fun append(nil,b,c) = (b=c)
|   append(heada::taila,b,headc::tailc) =
      heada=headc andalso append(taila,b,tailc)
|   append(_,_,_) = false;
```

The two implementations have a few similarities. ML and Prolog both use pattern-matching to bind values to variables. In the ML append function, the pattern head::taila matches any list that contains at least one element, binds the variable head to the first element, and binds the variable taila to the rest of the list. In the Prolog append predicate, the term .(Head,TailA) (which in the example was written as [Head|TailA]) does pretty much the same thing. It unifies with any list of at least one element, binding Head to the first element and TailA to the rest of the list.

One difference between the two implementations is that the ML version explicitly tests whether b=c (in the first alternative) and whether heada=headc (in the second alternative). The Prolog version performs the same tests more compactly by using the same variable more than once in a term. ML does not allow the same variable to appear more than once in a pattern. The Prolog version could be rewritten to avoid using this trick.

```
append([], B, C) :- B = C.
append([HeadA|TailA], B, [HeadC|TailC]) :-
  HeadA = HeadC,
  append(TailA, B, TailC).
```

This looks more like the ML version, but it is not a natural style for Prolog.

Another difference is that the ML version has to explicitly return either true or false. That is why the third alternative in the ML definition is required—so that the function will return false if the parameters do not match either of the patterns for the first two alternatives. In Prolog you only say what to do to make a proof succeed; you do not have to show all the ways in which it can fail. If you try to prove something that does not match either the `append` fact or the head of the `append` rule, the Prolog system fails to prove it and simply says `No`.

There is a more profound difference between the two implementations. The Prolog version is much more flexible. It can, for example, be used to find any one of the parameters given the other two. The ML version works only on fully instantiated parameters. It can decide whether `append([1],[2],[1,2])` is true, but it cannot be used to find the `X` for which `append([1],[2],X)` is true. Naturally, it would be possible to write a function to compute the result of that particular kind of goal:

```
fun append (nil, b) = b
|   append (head::taila, b) = head :: append(taila, b);
```

But the new function is still useful for one kind of goal only.

Prolog has a number of other predefined predicates for lists. Here are a few important ones:

Predicate	Description
`member(X,Y)`	Provable if the list `Y` contains the element `X`.
`select(X,Y,Z)`	Provable if the list `Y` contains the element `X`, and `Z` is the same as `Y` but with one instance of `X` removed.
`nth0(X,Y,Z)`	Provable if `X` is an integer, `Y` is a list, and `Z` is the `X`th element of `Y`, counting from 0.
`length(X,Y)`	Provable if `X` is a list of length `Y`.

These are all flexible about their parameters, like `append`. Queries using them can contain variables anywhere, and always produce logically correct results. The flexibility of these list predicates can be very useful, once you get the hang of it. For example, `select` can be used not only to remove an element from a list, but also to insert one:

```
?- select(2,[1,2,3],Z).

Z = [1, 3] ;

No
?- select(2,Y,[1,3]).

Y = [2, 1, 3] ;

Y = [1, 2, 3] ;

Y = [1, 3, 2] ;

No
```

`reverse` and Other Inflexible Predicates

There is a predefined predicate for reversing a list, called `reverse`.

```
?- reverse([1,2,3,4],Y).

Y = [4, 3, 2, 1] ;

No
```

Here is an implementation of a `reverse` predicate that works like the predefined one:

```
reverse([],[]).
reverse([Head|Tail],X) :-
  reverse(Tail,Y),
  append(Y,[Head],X).
```

The Prolog `reverse` predicate is very similar to this ML `reverse` function:

```
fun reverse nil = nil
|   reverse (head::tail) = reverse tail @ [head];
```

This turns out to be quite an inefficient way of reversing a list, in ML and in Prolog. You will see why, and look at a more efficient version, in Chapter 21.

The `reverse` predicate cannot be used as flexibly as `append`. For example, it does not work well if given an unbound variable as its first parameter. It can find one solution, but asking for more sends the system into an infinite loop. Here is what happens:

```
?- reverse(X,[1,2,3,4]).

X = [4, 3, 2, 1] ;

Action (h for help) ? a
% Execution Aborted
?-
```

It is quite easy to make non-terminating queries by accident, so it is important to know what to do with your Prolog language system when this happens. In the example above using SWI-Prolog, when the semicolon was typed to ask for another solution, the system printed nothing further. After a little while, it was clear that the system was not going to terminate. It could not find a proof, but was stuck endlessly searching for one. Typing Control-C, which did not produce any visible character, halted the language system's search for a proof. The system then printed the message `Action (h for help) ?` Typing `a` for abort made the system give up the search and prompt for a new query. (SWI-Prolog accepts some simple debugging commands in addition to `a`. They will not be used in this book, but you can read more about them by typing `h` for help at that point.)

Chapter 20 will look at Prolog's proof technique in more detail and show what goes wrong with that query to cause an infinite loop. For now, the details are unimportant. The important thing is that it can happen. Some predicates are not flexible about how their parameters can be used. The `reverse` predicate is one. It is intended to be used to reverse its first parameter, unifying the result with a variable as its second parameter. This is another example of the two faces of Prolog. In a purely declarative, logical sense, `reverse(X,[1,2,3,4])` and `reverse([1,2,3,4],X)` should be equivalent. Procedurally, however, one works and the other gets into an infinite loop.

Another example of an inflexible predicate is the predefined `sort`.

```
?- sort([2,3,1,4],X).

X = [1, 2, 3, 4] ;

No
```

The `sort` predicate succeeds when the first parameter is a list of things in any order and the second is a list of the same elements sorted. Logically, you should be able to use the query `sort(X,[1,2,3,4])` to unsort the list—to see all permutations of the list. But the `sort` predicate is not that flexible. The first parameter is not permitted to be a variable.

```
?- sort(X,[1,2,3,4]).
ERROR: Arguments are not sufficiently instantiated
```

Other things being equal, it is better for predicates to be fully flexible like `append`, not restricted like `reverse` and `sort`. Fully flexible predicates are more useful and easier to understand. They are more declarative, with fewer procedural quirks to consider. But restricted implementations are sometimes chosen on the grounds of efficiency or simplicity. A `sort` predicate could be written that is flexible enough to unsort too, but it would not sort as efficiently as the predefined, restricted `sort`.

The Anonymous Variable

Prolog terms and ML patterns both use the symbol _ as a kind of wild card. In Prolog, the term _ is an anonymous variable. Every occurrence of _ is bound independently of every other. For example, to bind a variable to the first element of a list while ignoring the rest of the list, you would use the ML pattern `head::_` or the Prolog term `[Head|_]`. The following fact defines a Prolog predicate `tailof`, with the property that `tailof(X,Y)` succeeds when `X` is a non-empty list and `Y` is the tail of that list:

```
tailof([_|A],A).
```

It could be written using an ordinary variable instead of _ like this:

```
tailof([Head|A],A).
```

But it is bad style to introduce a variable that is never used. SWI-Prolog gives a warning message complaining that `Head` is a "singleton variable," meaning that it is a variable that occurs only once in the clause. In general, when you need to match a term but do not need to use the resulting binding, you should use _.

By the way, those "singleton variable" warnings are the only hint the Prolog language system gives that you have misspelled a variable name. For example, this definition of `append` has such an error:

```
append([], B, B).
append([Head|TailA], B, [Head|TailC]) :-
  append(TailA, B, Tailc).
```

Do you see the error? There are two variables, one named `TailC` and one named `Tailc`, that are supposed to be the same. The predicate will run incorrectly because it will find solutions that do not bind those two variables to the same value. The only warning about this is a "singleton variable" warning. If you are in the habit of ignoring those warnings—especially if it is, say, two in the morning—this kind of error can be very frustrating. So it is important to get into the habit of eliminating those warnings, either by using _ if you don't care about the binding or by fixing the spelling if you do.

19.9 Negation and Failure

Don't worry, this section is not as depressing as its heading makes it sound. So far, only the question of how Prolog proves things has been addressed. What about *disproving* things—proving that some assertion is false?

Mathematicians use the symbol ¬ for logical negation. For any assertion P, the assertion ¬P is true if and only if P is false. Prolog has a related predicate called `not`.

```
?- member(1,[1,2,3]).

Yes
?- not(member(4,[1,2,3])).

Yes
```

For simple applications, `not` often works quite a bit like logical negation. In the example above, it is not true that the atom `4` is a member of the list `[1,2,3]`, so the query `not(member(4,[1,2,3]))` succeeds. But be aware of the procedural side of the `not` predicate.

The way Prolog tries to prove the goal `not(member(4,[1,2,3]))` is by trying to prove the goal `member(4,[1,2,3])`. If it *fails* to find a proof of that, the `not` goal succeeds. This is another example of the two faces of Prolog. The logical, declarative meaning of `not(X)` is simple—`X` is false. But the procedural meaning of `not(X)` is more complicated. If the Prolog system can complete an exhaustive search for a proof of `X` without finding one, the goal `not(X)` will succeed. If the Prolog system finds a proof of `X`, the goal `not(X)` will fail. If the Prolog system gets into an infinite loop looking for a proof of `X`, it will also get into an infinite loop on the goal `not(X)`.[4]

This non-declarative behavior can produce quirky results. Consider this `sibling` predicate:

```
sibling(X,Y) :- parent(P,X), parent(P,Y).
```

4. The name `not` is traditional, but a bit misleading. ISO Prolog calls this predicate `fail_if`, which reflects its procedural behavior more accurately.

At first glance this looks right. Two people are siblings if they have a parent in common. But it has one shortcoming: it will allow the system to prove `sibling(X,Y)` in cases where `X` and `Y` are the same person. One way to correct that is to add a condition using `not`, like this:

```
sibling(X,Y) :- not(X=Y), parent(P,X), parent(P,Y).
```

With the addition of this first condition, the rule no longer allows a person to be his or her own sibling. Thus (using the earlier `relations` facts) it handles some queries properly:

```
?- sibling(kim,kent).

Yes
?- sibling(kim,kim).

No
```

On other queries, though, it behaves badly:

```
?- sibling(X,Y).

No
```

How could it fail on `sibling(X,Y)`, when it already succeeded on `sibling(kim,kent)`?

To answer that, you have to remember the procedural behavior of the `not` predicate. Starting with the goal `sibling(X,Y)`, the Prolog system unifies it with the head of the `sibling` rule. That generates this new list of goals:

```
not(X=Y), parent(P,X), parent(P,Y).
```

Then it starts on the first goal in the list, `not(X=Y)`. To prove this, it sees whether the goal `X=Y` will fail. It will *not* fail, of course, since `X` and `Y` are unbound variables. It is perfectly possible to find bindings for `X` and `Y` for which `X=Y`. Since `X=Y` succeeds, `not(X=Y)` fails. Since that goal fails, the entire query fails.

The problem here occurs because the variables `X` and `Y` are unbound when the `not` goal is attempted. This can be fixed simply by reordering the conditions of the rule. Rewrite the `sibling` rule like this:

```
sibling(X,Y) :- parent(P,X), parent(P,Y), not(X=Y).
```

Declaratively, listing the conditions in a different order changes nothing. Procedurally, it makes a great deal of difference.

```
?- sibling(X,Y).

X = kim
Y = kent ;

X = kent
Y = kim ;

X = margaret
Y = jean ;

X = jean
Y = margaret ;

No
```

Using the new rule, Prolog already has bindings for X and Y by the time it gets to the not goal. For example, for the first solution above, Prolog has already bound X to kim and Y to kent by the time it gets to the not goal, so it has only to prove not(kim=kent).

19.10 What Prolog Is Good For

So far the examples in this chapter have been quite pedestrian, and you may be wondering what Prolog is really good for. This section gives an example of the kind of problem that is easier to solve with Prolog than with ML or Java.

The problem is based on an old riddle. A man is traveling with a wolf, a goat, and a cabbage. He comes to the west bank of a river and wants to cross. A tiny rowboat is available, but it is so small that the man can take at most one of his possessions with him in the boat. If he leaves the goat and the cabbage alone together, the goat will eat the cabbage. If he leaves the wolf and the goat alone together, the wolf will eat the goat. How can the man get to the east bank without losing any of his possessions?

To solve this problem, represent a configuration using a list that tells which side of the river each thing is on in a fixed order—man, wolf, goat, cabbage. (Ignore the boat, which will always be on the same side of the river as the man.) The two sides of the river will be the atoms e and w. So the initial configuration is [w,w,w,w]; everything is on the west side of the river. If the man first takes the wolf across, the resulting configuration is [e,e,w,w]. Of course, in that configuration, the goat eats the cabbage, so that would not be a wise move. The desired final configuration is [e,e,e,e]. None of the intermediate configurations can have the wolf and the goat, or the goat and the cabbage, alone together on either side of the river.

In each move, the man crosses the river taking at most one possession with him. So there are four basic moves, which will be represented with four atoms—wolf, goat, cabbage, or nothing—indicating what the man takes with him as he crosses. Each move transforms one configuration to another. This can be written in Prolog as a predicate move(Config,Move,NextConfig), where Config is a configuration, Move is one of the four basic moves, and NextConfig is the configuration that results from applying that move to the first configuration. For example, the goal move([w,w,w,w],wolf,[e,e,w,w]) would succeed. That could be encoded with a fact:

```
move([w,w,w,w],wolf,[e,e,w,w]).
```

But it would take too many such facts to encode all the possible moves. One way to get more power from the same basic fact is to note that, for this move, the goat and cabbage do not change positions. So if it were written like this, it could cover more cases:

```
move([w,w,Goat,Cabbage],wolf,[e,e,Goat,Cabbage]).
```

There's a similar fact for moving the wolf from east to west. Both directions could be covered with one rule, like this:

```
move([X,X,Goat,Cabbage],wolf,[Y,Y,Goat,Cabbage]) :-
  change(X,Y).
```

That assumes a change predicate with two solutions: change(e,w) and change(w,e). In this way the whole collection of legal moves can be defined:

```
change(e,w).
change(w,e).

move([X,X,Goat,Cabbage],wolf,[Y,Y,Goat,Cabbage]) :-
  change(X,Y).
move([X,Wolf,X,Cabbage],goat,[Y,Wolf,Y,Cabbage]) :-
  change(X,Y).
move([X,Wolf,Goat,X],cabbage,[Y,Wolf,Goat,Y]) :-
  change(X,Y).
move([X,Wolf,Goat,C],nothing,[Y,Wolf,Goat,C]) :-
  change(X,Y).
```

Next, configurations need to be tested for safety (nothing gets eaten). Here the predicate oneEq(X,Y,Z) tests whether at least one of Y or Z is equal to X. If at least one of the goat or the wolf is on the same side as the man, and if at least one of the goat or the cabbage is on the same side as the man, then the configuration is safe:

```
oneEq(X,X,_).
oneEq(X,_,X).

safe([Man,Wolf,Goat,Cabbage]) :-
  oneEq(Man,Goat,Wolf),
  oneEq(Man,Goat,Cabbage).
```

With `move` and `safe`, the puzzle can be solved. A solution is a starting configuration and a list of moves that takes you to the goal configuration. A solution from `[e,e,e,e]` would be the empty list. No moves are required from there. Otherwise, a solution is a list of moves with the property that the first move takes you to a safe configuration, and the rest of the list is a solution from there.

```
solution([e,e,e,e],[]).
solution(Config,[Move|Rest]) :-
  move(Config,Move,NextConfig),
  safe(NextConfig),
  solution(NextConfig,Rest).
```

Care is required with using this predicate to solve the puzzle, because it does not specify the length of the solution. (Unfortunately there is no built-in limit to the length of a possible solution—the man could just row back and forth with the goat forever.) But if Prolog is asked for a solution of a specific length, say seven moves, it will oblige:

```
?- length(X,7), solution([w,w,w,w],X).

X = [goat, nothing, wolf, goat, cabbage, nothing, goat]

Yes
```

This is the solution Prolog found: first cross with the goat, then cross back empty, then cross with the wolf, then cross back with the goat (leaving the wolf on the east side), then cross with the cabbage (leaving the goat on the west side again), then cross back empty, and finally cross with the goat.

Planning a sequence of moves like this is a classic AI problem. Prolog found the answer easily. An important thing to notice here is that the Prolog program says nothing about how to search for the solution. The problem just had to be specified logically; Prolog's method of searching for proofs finds the solution from there. This is the kind of problem Prolog is especially good for. Chapter 22 has more examples. But before you can reliably apply Prolog to solve such problems, you have to understand Prolog's method of searching for proofs. You will see more about that in Chapter 20.

19.11 Conclusion

This chapter introduced some Prolog fundamentals:

- Terms: integers, real numbers, atoms, and compound terms.
- Facts, rules, and queries.
- Operators, as a special notation for compound terms.
- Lists: the `[]` atom, the . predicate, and special notation for list terms like `[1,2,3]` and `[1,2,3|X]`.
- Some useful predefined predicates for lists: `append`, `member`, `select`, `nth0`, `length`, `reverse`, and `sort`.
- The anonymous variable _.
- The `not` predicate.

In addition, this chapter introduced the two important aspects of Prolog—declarative and procedural—and introduced the use of the SWI-Prolog language system. That is enough for you to be able to complete the exercises that follow.

In fact, you now know most of the syntax of Prolog. Subsequent chapters will show more Prolog programming techniques and more about how the Prolog language system proves things.

Exercises

Define your answers to Exercises 1 through 6 in terms of the base relations `parent(X,Y)`, `female(X)`, and `male(X)`. To test your code, define some `parent` facts like those in this chapter, along with appropriate `female` and `male` facts. But your solutions should be general enough to work with any set of such facts.

Exercise 1 Define a `mother` predicate so that `mother(X,Y)` says that `X` is the mother of `Y`.

Exercise 2 Define a `father` predicate so that `father(X,Y)` says that `X` is the father of `Y`.

Exercise 3 Define a `sister` predicate so that `sister(X,Y)` says that `X` is a sister of `Y`. Be careful, a person cannot be her own sister.

Exercise 4 Define a `grandson` predicate so that `grandson(X,Y)` says that `X` is a grandson of `Y`.

Exercise 5 Define the `firstCousin` predicate so that `firstCousin(X,Y)` says that `X` is a first cousin of `Y`. Be careful, a person cannot be his or her own cousin, nor can a brother or sister also be a cousin.

Exercise 6 Define the `descendant` predicate so that `descendant(X,Y)` says that `X` is a descendant of `Y`.

Exercise 7 Define a `third` predicate so that `third(X,Y)` says that `Y` is the third element of the list `X`. (The predicate should fail if `X` has fewer than three elements.) *Hint:* This can be expressed as a fact.

Exercise 8 Define a `firstPair` predicate so that `firstPair(X)` succeeds if and only if `X` is a list of at least two elements, with the first element the same as the second element. *Hint:* This can be expressed as a fact.

Exercise 9 Define a `del3` predicate so that `del3(X,Y)` says that the list `Y` is the same as the list `X` but with the third element deleted. (The predicate should fail if `X` has fewer than three elements.) *Hint:* This can be expressed as a fact.

Exercise 10 Define a `dupList` predicate so that `dupList(X,Y)` says that `X` is a list and `Y` is the same list, but with each element of `X` repeated twice in a row. For example, if `X` is `[1,3,2]`, `Y` should be `[1,1,3,3,2,2]`. If `X` is `[]`, `Y` should be `[]`. Check that your predicate works in both directions—that is, check that it works on queries like `dupList(X,[1,1,3,3,2,2])` as well as on queries like `dupList([1,3,2],Y)`.

Exercise 11 Define a predicate `isDuped` so that `isDuped(Y)` succeeds if and only if `Y` is a list of the form of the lists `Y` in Exercise 10. That is, the predicate should succeed if and only if the first and second elements are equal, and the third and fourth elements are equal, and so on to the end of the list. It should fail for all odd-length lists.

Exercise 12 Define the `oddSize` predicate so that `oddSize(X)` says that `X` is a list whose length is an odd number. *Hint:* You do not need to compute the actual length, or do any integer arithmetic.

Exercise 13 Define the `evenSize` predicate so that `evenSize(X)` says that `X` is a list whose length is an even number. *Hint:* You do not need to compute the actual length, or do any integer arithmetic.

Exercise 14 Define the `prefix` predicate so that `prefix(X,Y)` says that `X` is a list that is a prefix of `Y`. That is, each element of `X` is equal to (unifies with) the corresponding element of `Y`, but `Y` may contain additional elements after that. Check that your predicate works when `X` is uninstantiated: given a query like `prefix(X,[1,2,3])`, it should find all the prefixes of the list `[1,2,3]`.

In Exercises 15 through 20, you should implement sets as lists, where each element of a set appears exactly once in its list, but in no particular order. Do not assume you can sort the lists. Do assume that input lists have no duplicate elements, and do guarantee that output lists have no duplicate elements.

Exercise 15 Define the `isMember` predicate so that `isMember(X,Y)` says that element `X` is a member of set `Y`. Do not use the predefined list predicates.

Exercise 16 Define the `isUnion` predicate so that `isUnion(X,Y,Z)` says that the union of `X` and `Y` is `Z`. Do not use the predefined list predicates. Your predicate may choose a fixed order for `Z`. If you query `isUnion([1,2],[3],Z)` it should find a binding for `Z`, but it need not succeed on both `isUnion([1],[2],[1,2])` and `isUnion([1],[2],[2,1])`. Your predicate need not work well when `X` or `Y` are unbound variables.

Exercise 17 Define the `isIntersection` predicate so that `isIntersection(X,Y,Z)` says that the intersection of `X` and `Y` is `Z`. Do not use the predefined list predicates. Your predicate may choose a fixed order for `Z`. Your predicate need not work well when `X` or `Y` are unbound variables.

Exercise 18 Define the `isEqual` predicate so that `isEqual(X,Y)` says that the sets `X` and `Y` are equal. Two sets are equal if they have exactly the same elements, regardless of the order in which those elements are represented in the set. Your predicate need not work well when `X` or `Y` are unbound variables.

Exercise 19 Define the `powerset` predicate so that `powerset(X,Y)` says that the powerset of `X` is `Y`. The powerset of a set is the set of all subsets of that set. For example, consider the set $A = \{1,2,3\}$. It has various subsets: $\{1\}$, $\{1,2\}$, and so on.

And of course the empty set ∅ is a subset of every set. The powerset of A is the set of all subsets of A:

$$\{x \mid x \subseteq A\}=\{\varnothing,\{1\},\{2\},\{3\},\{1,2\},\{1,3\},\{2,3\},\{1,2,3\}\}$$

For your `powerset` predicate, if `X` is a list (representing the set), `Y` will be a list of lists (representing the set of all subsets of the original set). So `powerset([1,2],Y)` should produce the binding `Y = [[1,2],[1],[2],[]]` (in any order). Your predicate may choose a fixed order for `Y`. Your predicate need not work well when `X` is an unbound variable.

Exercise 20 Define the `isDifference` predicate so that `isDifference(X,Y,Z)` says that the set `Z` contains the elements of `X` that do not also appear in `Y`. But unlike Exercises 16, 17, and 19, make a relation that works no matter what order `Z` is in. Your predicate need not work well when `X` or `Y` are unbound variables.

Exercise 21 Try the man-wolf-goat-cabbage solution starting on page 412. (The code for this is also available on this book's Web site, **http://www.webber-labs.com/mpl.html**.) Use this query:

```
length(X,7), solution([w,w,w,w],X).
```

Use the semicolon after each solution to make it print them all; that is, keep hitting the semicolon until it finally says No. As you will see, it finds the same solution more than once. How many solutions does it print, and how many of them are distinct? Modify the code to make it find only distinct solutions. (*Hint:* The problem is in the `oneEq` predicate. As written, a goal like `oneEq(left,left,left)` can be proved in two different ways.)

Further Reading

The following book is a good resource for learning Prolog. The first half of the book introduces the language and covers quite a bit more of it than this book does. The second half focuses on artificial intelligence applications of Prolog—expert systems, planning, learning, game playing, and so on.

Bratko, Ivan. *Prolog Programming for Artificial Intelligence*. 2nd ed., Boston, MA: Addison-Wesley, 1990.

Chapter 20 A Second Look at Prolog

20.1 Introduction

The previous chapter, the first look at Prolog, showed that it has both a declarative aspect and a procedural aspect. It is possible to write Prolog code even if you don't really understand the procedural side, but it is chancy. You can easily end up with solutions that are non-terminating or grossly inefficient, and fixing them without understanding how Prolog really works can be a frustrating process of trial and error. This chapter focuses on the procedural side of Prolog.

This book has interleaved the practical chapters and the abstract chapters. This chapter deviates from that plan, but only a little. It starts with three different but complementary views of Prolog's model of execution: how a Prolog language system uses a program to solve queries. This part of the chapter, although it is very Prolog-specific, requires some abstract thinking. The end of the chapter, for a change of pace, will look at the lighter side of Prolog programming. It will show some very non-declarative dirty tricks that are unique to Prolog and apply them in a longer example.

20.2 Unification

At the heart of Prolog's model of execution is the pattern-matching technique called *unification*. To begin with, a *substitution* is a set of bindings for variables. When a Prolog system succeeds with a query, it reports the substitution for the variables in the query term that it used to find a proof:

```
?- append([1,2],[3,4],Z).

Z = [1, 2, 3, 4]

Yes
```

In this example, Prolog reports that it can prove the query using the substitution of the term `[1,2,3,4]` for the variable `Z`. Prolog uses substitutions frequently while trying to prove queries; the ones it reports after the query is proved are only a tiny sample.

Substitutions will be written as functions that map variables to terms, like this:

```
σ = {X→a, Y→f(a,b)}
```

Greek letters are used for substitutions to stress the fact that they are *not* Prolog terms. Substitutions are used internally by the Prolog language system, but are not directly manipulated by Prolog programs. The example above is a substitution that maps the variable `X` to the term `a` and maps the variable `Y` to the term `f(a,b)`.

The result of applying a substitution to a term is an *instance* of that term. For example, the term `append([1,2],[3,4],[1,2,3,4])` is an instance of the term `append([1,2],[3,4],Z)` using the substitution {`Z→[1,2,3,4]`}. When Prolog proves a query, it reports the substitution it needed to make a provable instance of the query term.

Two Prolog terms t_1 and t_2 are said to *unify* if there is some substitution σ (their *unifier*) that makes them identical, $\sigma(t_1) = \sigma(t_2)$.[1] For example:

- `a` and `b` do not unify
- `f(X,b)` and `f(a,Y)` unify: a unifier is {`X→a`, `Y→b`}
- `f(X,b)` and `g(X,b)` do not unify
- `a(X,X,b)` and `a(b,X,X)` unify: a unifier is {`X→b`}
- `a(X,X,b)` and `a(c,X,X)` do not unify
- `a(X,f)` and `a(X,f)` do unify: a unifier is {}

---

1. Many authors use a postfix notation for substitutions, writing $t\sigma$ instead of $\sigma(t)$. It means the same thing: the result of applying the substitution to the term.

Two terms that unify might have more than one unifier. For example, the terms `parent(X,Y)` and `parent(fred,Y)` unify. One unifier is σ_1 = {X→fred}, and another is σ_2 = {X→fred, Y→mary}. The unifier σ_1 does just enough substitution to make the terms unify, converting them both to the term `parent(fred,Y)`, which is a common instance of both original terms. The unifier σ_2 does more substitution than necessary, converting them both to the common instance `parent(fred,mary)`.

Which one is preferred? The Prolog language system wants to bind variables only when necessary to prove the query, so it chooses unifiers like σ_1 that do just enough substitution to make the terms unify. Such unifiers are called MGUs—most general unifiers. To define an MGU more formally, let us say that a term x_1 is *more general than* a term x_2 if x_2 is an instance of x_1 but x_1 is not an instance of x_2. So, for example, `parent(fred,Y)` is more general than `parent(fred,mary)`. Then a unifier σ_1 of two terms t_1 and t_2 is an MGU if there is no other unifier σ_2 such that $\sigma_2(t_1)$ is more general than $\sigma_1(t_1)$.

Can there be more than one MGU for a given pair of terms? Well, yes, though the differences are slight. Continuing with the previous example, the terms `parent(X,Y)` and `parent(fred,Y)` also have the unifier σ_3 = {X→fred, Y→Z}. This unifier converts both terms to the common instance `parent(fred,Z)`. This is no less general than the result of the unifier σ_1 = {X→fred}, which was `parent(fred,Y)`. In fact, the two results are identical except for the names of variables. This always turns out to be the case for MGUs: all MGUs for a pair of terms are identical except for the way they rename variables.[2]

Unification is a critical utility for Prolog programs.

- Where other languages have parameter-passing mechanisms, Prolog has unification. In the goal `reverse([1,2,3],X)`, unification is how the list `[1,2,3]` is passed to the `reverse` predicate and how the result list `[3,2,1]` is bound to the variable `X`.
- Where other languages have assignment, Prolog has unification. The goal `X=0` uses unification to bind `X` to `0`.
- Where other languages have data constructors, Prolog has unification. The goal `X=.(1,[2,3])` uses unification to bind `X` to the newly constructed list `[1,2,3]`.
- Where other languages have data selectors, Prolog has unification. The goal `[1,2,3]=.(X,Y)` uses unification to bind `X` to `1` and `Y` to the list `[2,3]`.

2. People sometimes refer to *the* MGU of two terms, as if it were unique, but with the understanding that there is actually a whole family of MGUs that differ only in the names of variables.

The Occurs Check

When you are trying to unify two terms and one of them is a variable, it is usually easy to find an MGU. For example:

- `X` and `b` unify: an MGU is {`X`→`b`}
- `X` and `f(a,g(b,c))` unify: an MGU is {`X`→`f(a,g(b,c))`}
- `X` and `f(a,Y)` unify: an MGU is {`X`→`f(a,Y)`}

You might be tempted to conclude that for a variable `X` and any term *t*, an MGU for `X` and *t* is {`X`→*t*}. There is an important exception to this: if *t* is a compound term in which the same variable `X` occurs, then it cannot be unified with `X` at all. For example, consider the terms `X` and `f(X)`. It should be clear that no matter what term you substitute for `X`, the terms `X` and `f(X)` will not be identical. In particular, the substitution {`X`→`f(X)`} gets you nowhere. Applied to `X` it gives `f(X)`, and applied to `f(X)` it gives `f(f(X))`. Before concluding that you can unify a variable `X` and a term *t* using {`X`→*t*}, therefore, you must check for this special case. It is called the *occurs check*—checking whether a particular variable `X` occurs in a term *t*.

The occurs check is part of any algorithm for finding the MGU of any two terms. Such algorithms do need to perform the occurs check rather frequently. Because the speed of unification is a critical factor in the overall speed of a Prolog system and because the occurs check rarely fails in real Prolog programs, *most Prolog systems implement unification without the occurs check*. This is a weakness that Prolog programmers tolerate for the sake of speed.

The visible symptom of this weakness in a Prolog system's unification is that it will misbehave on unifications that should fail the occurs check; for example, it might get into an infinite loop, or it might claim that the terms do unify and produce a (faulty) unifier for them. You will probably never see this behavior unless you go looking for it. But just as an example, consider the predefined `append` predicate:

```
append([], B, B).
append([Head|TailA], B, [Head|TailC]) :-
  append(TailA, B, TailC).
```

Here is a strange query for `append`: it asks for a list `X` whose head is the atom `a` and whose tail is the list `X` again. There is no such list, but the query succeeds anyway.

```
?- append([], X, [a | X]).

X = [a, a, a, a, a, a, a, a, a|...]

Yes
```

The first clause for `append` is the only one involved in the proof. The Prolog system tries to unify the query term with the fact term `append([], B, B)`. In the process, it tries to unify `X` with `[a | X]`. If it were performing the occurs check, it would fail at that point. But it isn't, and it doesn't. The answer even makes sense, in a certain way. If `X` were an infinite list of `a`s, that might be thought to satisfy the query. But it is not a correct answer for Prolog, which does not handle infinite terms generally. It is just an anomaly that reveals that this Prolog system, like most, is not doing the occurs check. The ISO standard for Prolog says that the result of a unification of two terms that should fail the occurs check is undefined. This means that Prolog language systems are allowed to skip the occurs check, and Prolog programmers are not allowed to depend on the results.

20.3 A Procedural View

Thinking of each rule as giving a procedure for proving a particular kind of goal can help you understand how Prolog works. Consider this simple rule:

```
p :- q, r.
```

This rule can be thought of as a procedure for proving goals: to prove a goal, unify it with `p`, then prove `q`, and then prove `r`. If all three of these steps succeed, the goal is proved. If any one of these three steps fails, the goal cannot be proved with this procedure. Facts can also be thought of as procedures. Consider this fact:

```
s.
```

Taking the procedural view, it can be thought of as a procedure for proving goals: to prove a goal, unify it with `s`. If this step succeeds, the goal is proved. If not, the goal cannot be proved with this procedure.

This program gives a complete way to prove a goal term `p`:

```
p :- q, r.
q :- s.
r :- s.
s.
```

The sequence of steps taken by a Prolog system when the goal `p` is attempted with this program is easy to imagine procedurally. It is a bit like the sequence of steps taken by a Java system when the method `p` is called in this program:

```
boolean p() {return q() && r();}
boolean q() {return s();}
boolean r() {return s();}
boolean s() {return true;}
```

Similarly, consider the sequence of steps taken by a Prolog system when the goal p is attempted with this program:

```
p :- p.
```

It is an infinite loop, a bit like the sequence of steps taken by a Java system when the method p is called in this program:

```
boolean p() {return p();}
```

Unfortunately, the procedural view of Prolog rarely parallels a conventional procedural execution this simply. There are two major complications: backtracking and substitution.

Backtracking

Let's look at backtracking first. Consider this program (where the clauses are numbered for future reference):

```
1.  p :- q, r.
2.  q :- s.
3.  q.
4.  r.
5.  s :- 0=1.
```

This program gives two different procedures for proving the goal q. Which one will Prolog use? The answer is that Prolog uses backtracking to explore all possible targets of a procedure call in the order given, until it finds as many successes as the caller requires or until it exhausts all the possibilities. In the example above, with the goal term p, Prolog follows the procedure of clause 1 and first tries to prove q. To do that, it follows the procedure of clause 2 and tries to prove s. To do that, it follows the procedure of clause 5 and tries to prove 0=1. That fails, so it looks for any other procedure for proving s. There isn't one, so it backtracks to an earlier point and looks for any other procedure for proving q. Now it finds the procedure for proving q in clause 3, and from there the rest of the proof runs smoothly.

Substitution

The other major complication in the Prolog execution model is substitution. The previous examples were free of variables, but no realistic Prolog program is that simple. A procedure computes substitutions for variables as it goes. The initial substitution is the MGU of the goal term and the head of the clause. An additional substitution is supplied by the proof of each condition in a rule. Before the proof of a condition in a rule is attempted, all the substitutions for the rule up to that point are applied to it.

For example, consider this rule, annotated with substitutions:

```
            σ1          σ2           σ3
p(f(Y))  :-  q(Y)   ,  r(Y)       .
```

This procedure for `p` computes the three substitutions shown. The first, σ_1, is the initial substitution: the MGU of the goal being proved and the head term of the rule, `p(f(Y))`. This substitution is applied to the first condition, so what the system tries to prove as the first condition is not `q(Y)`, but σ_1(`q(Y)`). The proof of this first condition produces the next substitution σ_2. Now *both* substitutions are applied to the second condition, so what the system tries to prove as the second condition is not `r(Y)`, but σ_2(σ_1(`r(Y)`)). The proof of that second condition produces the next substitution σ_3. Finally, all three substitutions are composed, making a new substitution σ such that for any term x, $\sigma(x) = \sigma_3(\sigma_2(\sigma_1(x)))$. This is the substitution the procedure for `p` will return to its caller—the substitution used to make a provable instance of the original goal term.

Substitution and backtracking work together. Backtracking tries different ways of proving a goal. Each way makes its own series of substitutions. Consider this program (numbered for future reference), which includes the same rule for `p` that was just examined:

```
1.  p(f(Y)) :- q(Y),r(Y).
2.  q(g(Z)).
3.  q(h(Z)).
4.  r(h(a)).
```

Let's start with the goal term `p(X)`. Prolog uses the procedure of clause 1 to prove it. Prolog starts with the substitution σ_1 = {`X`→`f(Y)`}, which is an MGU of the goal term and the head of clause 1. Now it advances to the first condition of the rule. It tries to prove σ_1(`q(Y)`), which is just `q(Y)`, using the procedure of clause 2. The MGU of this goal and the fact is σ_2 = {`Y`→`g(Z)`}. This substitution is returned to the procedure for `p`. The next step is to try to prove σ_2(σ_1(`r(Y)`)), which is the term `r(g(Z))`. The only clause for `r` is a fact that does not unify with this goal, so that fails. Backtracking, Prolog looks for any other way to prove `q(Y)` and finds one using the procedure of clause 3. The MGU of this goal and the fact is σ_2 = {`Y`→`h(Z)`}—this is a *different* σ_2, as the system has backtracked to a point before the first σ_2 was found. This substitution is returned to the procedure for `p`. The next step is to try to prove σ_2(σ_1(`r(Y)`)), which now is the term `r(h(Z))`. Prolog finds the fact in clause 4; the MGU of the goal and this fact is σ_3 = {`Z`→`a`}. This substitution is returned to the procedure for `p`. The result of applying all three substitutions to the original goal term gives the instance of the goal that was actually proved: $\sigma_3(\sigma_2(\sigma_1($`p(X)`$)))$ = `p(f(h(a)))`.

As the previous example shows, you have to think not only of the flow of control, but also of the flow of substitutions. Thinking of Prolog clauses as procedures, substitutions are like hidden parameters to those procedures. They carry information from the goal term into the procedure, and from each condition in a rule to the next, and finally back out again. Once you get the hang of the procedural view, it is reasonably intuitive and easy to work with. But it does not really explain backtracking properly. It just leaves it up to the Prolog system to somehow explore all possible targets of a procedure call in the order given. Now let's turn to a different way of thinking about how Prolog works, one that is more specific about backtracking.

20.4 An Implementational View

For a complementary view of Prolog's model of execution, let's turn to a simple implementation of a Prolog interpreter.

The Resolution Step

The basic step this interpreter uses is an operation called *resolution*. Resolution applies one clause from a program to make one step of progress on a list of goal terms to be proved. Here it is implemented as a function that takes a clause from the program and a list of goal terms to be proved and returns a new list of goal terms:

```
function resolution(clause, goals):
  let sub = the MGU of head(clause) and head(goals)
  return sub(tail(clause) concatenated with tail(goals))
```

This pseudo-code implementation treats a clause `c` as a list of terms. For a rule, the list contains the head term followed by the conditions. For a fact, the list contains only the one fact term. The pseudo-code uses the terms *head* and *tail* in their usual list-processing sense: the head is the first element of the list, and the tail is all the rest of the elements after the first.

As you can see, `resolution` removes one term (the first) from the list of goals and adds zero or more terms in its place (the conditions of the rule). And, very importantly, it applies the MGU that unified the rule head and the goal term to all of the new goal list. Of course, this only works if the head of the clause and the head of the list of goals actually do unify—the caller of `resolution` is expected to verify this before making the call.[3]

Suppose there is a list of goals `[p(X),s(X)]` and a rule `p(f(Y)) :- q(Y),r(Y).` Resolution should be used to get a new list of goals. This call,

```
resolution([p(f(Y)),q(Y),r(Y)], [p(X),s(X)])
```

unifies the head of the clause, `p(f(Y))`, with the first goal in the list, `p(X)`. The unifier is the substitution {`X`→`f(Y)`}. It then forms a new goal list by concatenating the conditions of the rule with the tail of the goal list, and it applies the substitution to each term in the list. The resulting term list is `[q(Y),r(Y),s(f(Y))]`.

The Prolog Interpreter

The resolution step is used by the Prolog interpreter, which is implemented as a function named `solve`. This `solve` function takes one parameter named `goals`, which is a list of goal terms to be proved. Each time `solve` finds a way to prove the list of goal terms, by reducing it to an empty list, it calls a function named `succeed` to report its success. When it has done this as often as it can, it finishes (returning no value to its caller).

```
function solve(goals)
  if goals is empty then succeed()
  else for each clause c in the program, in order
    if head(c) does not unify with head(goals) then do nothing
    else solve(resolution(c, goals))
```

As you can see from this implementation, each call to `solve` with a non-empty list of goals looks at every clause in the program, in order, and does one of two things with it. If the head of the clause does not unify with the first goal term, nothing happens for that clause. Otherwise, a new list of goals is formed by resolution, and `solve` calls itself recursively to solve the new list of goals.

Let's examine the behavior of this procedure on the previous program:

```
1.  p(f(Y)) :- q(Y),r(Y).
2.  q(g(Z)).
3.  q(h(Z)).
4.  r(h(a)).
```

3. Prolog language systems are not the only programs that use resolution. Many resolution-based theorem-proving systems have been implemented. Prolog applies resolution in a way that always chooses the first of the list of goal terms to operate on, and treats that list as a stack. This is only one of many possible orderings for resolution. Different resolution orders lead to inference techniques of different efficiency and power.

To solve the initial query p(X), make an initial call to solve:

```
solve([p(X)])
```

The call looks at each of the four clauses in turn. The first clause has a head that unifies with p(X), so resolution is called to apply the resolution step and make a new goal list. The new list, [q(Y),r(Y)], is not empty, so solve calls itself recursively on that new list. Let's postpone looking at what happens in that recursive call—no matter what it does there, solve then goes on to examine the other three clauses in the program. They do not unify with p(X), so for those clauses nothing happens. So far the behavior of solve([p(X)]) can be summarized like this:

```
solve([p(X)])
 1. solve([q(Y),r(Y)])
        ...
 2. nothing
 3. nothing
 4. nothing
```

This shows the four iterations of solve's loop, one for each clause in the program. The first produces a recursive call, and the other three do nothing.

What happens for that recursive call, solve([q(Y),r(Y)])? Again, it tries each of the four clauses in the program, trying to unify with the first goal term, q(Y). This time, both the second and third clauses can be used, so there are two recursive calls. Again, let's postpone looking into the behavior of those two recursive calls and summarize what is known so far about the entire execution:

```
solve([p(X)])
 1. solve([q(Y),r(Y)])
     1. nothing
     2. solve([r(g(Z))])
          ...
     3. solve([r(h(Z))])
          ...
     4. nothing
 2. nothing
 3. nothing
 4. nothing
```

The first of those new recursive calls tries all four clauses in vain; no clause has a head that unifies with r(g(Z)). The final recursive call also tries all four clauses, looking for a match for r(h(Z)). The first three clauses do not unify, but the fourth one does. Furthermore, the result of the resolution step with this rule is an empty goal list, so `solve` calls the function `succeed` to report a successful proof. Here is the complete trace of `solve([p(X)])`:

```
solve([p(X)])
 1. solve([q(Y),r(Y)])
     1. nothing
     2. solve([r(g(Z))])
         1. nothing
         2. nothing
         3. nothing
         4. nothing
     3. solve([r(h(Z))])
         1. nothing
         2. nothing
         3. nothing
         4. solve([]) —success!
     4. nothing
 2. nothing
 3. nothing
 4. nothing
```

Collecting the Substitutions

The `solve` procedure is unlike what Prolog language systems really do in one important way: it reports each success it finds by calling `success`, but it has no way to report the substitutions it used to find that success, as real Prolog language systems must. It does not even collect all the substitutions; it just applies them immediately to the goal list. One way to fix this, and make the procedure behave more like a real Prolog language system, is to pass the original query along as a parameter to `solve` and `resolution`. Every time `resolution` applies a substitution to the goal list, it also applies that same substitution to the original query. That way the effect of all the substitutions is collected and `success` is passed the instance of the query that was actually proved:

```
function resolution(clause, goals, query):
  let sub = the MGU of head(clause) and head(goals)
  return (sub(tail(clause) concatenated with tail(goals)), sub(query))

function solve(goals, query)
  if goals is empty then succeed(query)
  else for each clause c in the program, in order
    if head(c) does not unify with head(goals) then do nothing
    else solve(resolution(c, goals, query))
```

This now generates the same trace as before, but with the substituted query term carried along in a new parameter, and eventually passed to `succeed`:

```
solve([p(X)],p(X))
 1. solve([q(Y),r(Y)],p(f(Y)))
     1. nothing
     2. solve([r(g(Z))],p(f(g(Z))))
         1. nothing
         2. nothing
         3. nothing
         4. nothing
     3. solve([r(h(Z))],p(f(h(Z))))
         1. nothing
         2. nothing
         3. nothing
         4. solve([],p(f(h(Z))))
     4. nothing
 2. nothing
 3. nothing
 4. nothing
```

Imagine that the `succeed` function prints the substitutions used in the proved query, then gives the user a chance to press Enter (to quit) or type a semicolon (for more solutions). If the user types a semicolon, `succeed` just returns and the `solve` function continues finding solutions. If the user presses Enter, `succeed` aborts the search, for example by throwing an exception. With that, you have something that behaves very much like any Prolog language system.

This view of Prolog's model of execution is exact enough to be implementable (though it is still missing one important step, which will be shown in the next section). Indeed, early Prolog implementations often worked something like `solve`. This implementability is either a strength or a weakness of this view of Prolog, depending on your perspective. It is nice to have a view of Prolog that is unambiguous. However, modern Prolog compilers do *not* work anything like this; they produce the same behavior by a very different technique. Next, you will see a view that is a bit more general and applies to all correct implementations of Prolog.

20.5 An Abstract View—Proof Trees

The traces of `solve` that you saw in the previous section are the key to finding a less implementation-specific view of Prolog execution. It does not matter how a Prolog system is implemented; it must somehow explore the same possible proofs in the same order. If you can define that order clearly, then you have the essence of Prolog.

Proof-Tree Definition

A *proof tree* for a given program and list of query terms is defined as follows:

- A proof tree contains two kinds of nodes, called *nothing nodes* and *solve nodes*.
- Each *nothing* node is a leaf (that is, it has no children in the tree).
- Each *solve* node contains a list of terms. If this list is empty, the *solve* node is a leaf. Otherwise, the *solve* node has one child for each clause in the program, in order. If a given clause does not unify with the head of the list at that *solve* node, the corresponding child is a *nothing* node. Otherwise, the corresponding child is a *solve* node containing the list of terms formed from the current list of terms and the clause by applying the resolution step.
- The root of the tree is a *solve* node containing the list of query terms.

This corresponds to the behavior of the previous `solve` function quite closely. Each *solve* node in the tree records the `goals` parameter from a call of the `solve` function. The children of that node record what that call of the `solve` function did for each clause in the program. Arranging the traces in the previous section as trees results in the proof trees just defined. For example, let's look again at the query `[p(X)]` and this program:

```
1.  p(f(Y)) :- q(Y),r(Y).
2.  q(g(Z)).
3.  q(h(Z)).
4.  r(h(a)).
```

Here is the proof tree for that query:

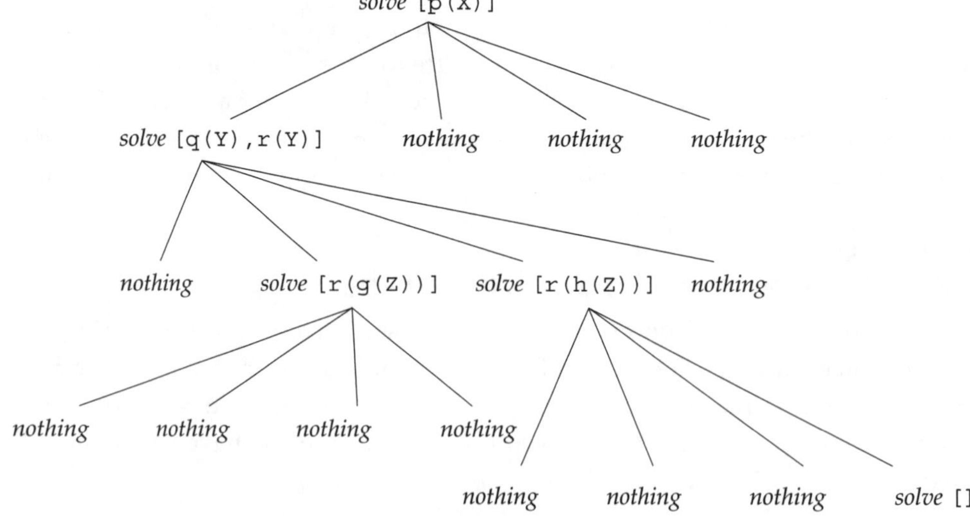

Notice that every non-leaf node has four children—one for each clause in the program, in order. The proof tree exactly matches the trace of the `solve` function in the previous section. Once you understand the connection, you might prefer to work with proof trees where the *nothing* nodes are suppressed. Some people draw them this way:

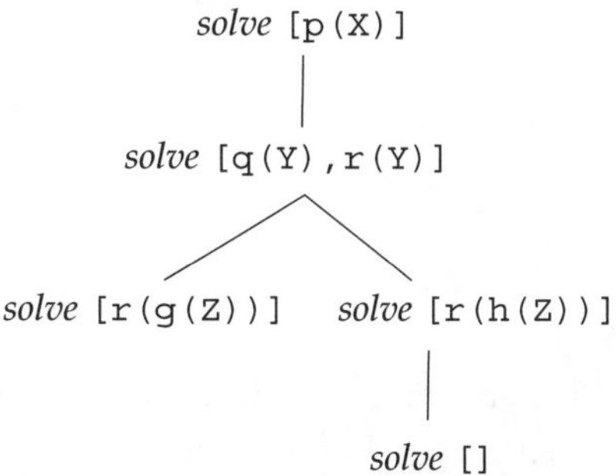

This compressed form shows one child for every clause whose head unifies with the first goal term, instead of one child for every clause in the program.

Proof trees can be used to give a more abstract account of Prolog's execution model:

> Given a program and a query, a Prolog language system must act in the order given by a depth-first, left-to-right traversal of the proof tree.

It need not use the method of the previous section to explore the proof tree. It need not actually construct the proof tree. But it must find successes in the proof-tree order. More than that: it must use clauses in the proof-tree order, even in branches of the tree that do not lead to successes. As you will see below, Prolog clauses can have side effects, such as printing on the screen or altering the database. These side effects must occur in the proof-tree order.

Infinite Proof Trees

By the above definition, a proof tree can easily be infinite. For example, consider this program:

```
p :- p.
p.
```

Here is part of the infinite proof tree for the query `p`:

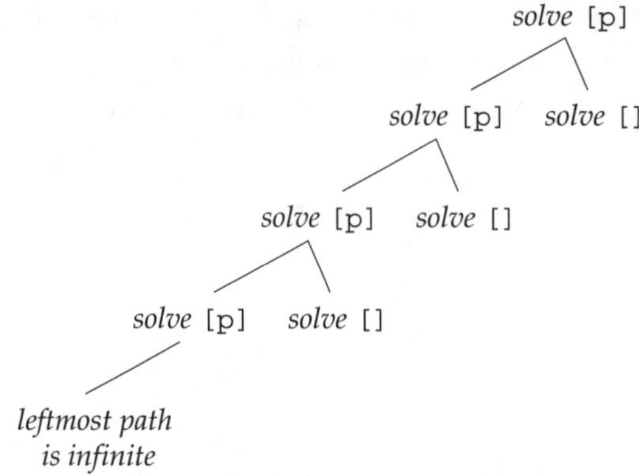

Each *solve* node has two children, corresponding to the two clauses of the program. The first clause leaves the goal list unchanged; the second solves it. It is clear that there are successful proofs of `p`—in fact, infinitely many of them. But it is also clear that in a depth-first, left-to-right visit of the proof tree, the Prolog language system will never find even one of them. Instead, it will proceed down that infinite leftmost path.

Changing the order of clauses in the program changes the order of children in the proof tree. This does not change whether it is an infinite proof tree or not, but it can change Prolog's behavior drastically. For example, suppose the previous program is reordered like this:

```
p.
p :- p.
```

Now the proof tree, though it still contains all the same elements and is still infinite, has a different shape:

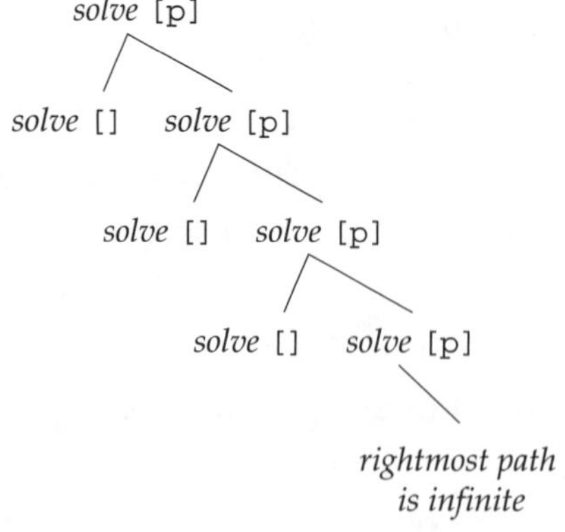

In this proof tree, a Prolog language system will immediately find a proof of p. Although the proof tree is still infinite, the depth-first, left-to-right traversal finds a proof without trying to visit that infinite path. (The next chapter, when examining cost models, will show some of the ways in which reordering the clauses of a program, or the conditions within a rule, can be used to make programs more efficient.)

Variable Renaming

All three of the prior views of Prolog's model of execution are missing a small but critical ingredient: variable renaming. The models worked on the examples chosen, but on other examples they would fail. Here is one example that shows the problem, using this reverse predicate from Chapter 19:

```
reverse([],[]).
reverse([Head|Tail],X) :-
  reverse(Tail,Y),
  append(Y,[Head],X).
```

This is the proof tree specified for reverse([1,2],X). In this tree each *solve* node with a reverse as the first goal term has two children, one for each of the two clauses above. Since the predicates for append are not being shown, each *solve* node that has an append as its first goal term will be drawn with a single child. That child will be either a *nothing* node, if the append cannot be solved, or a *solve* node, with the append solved and the rest of the goals in the list substituted accordingly.

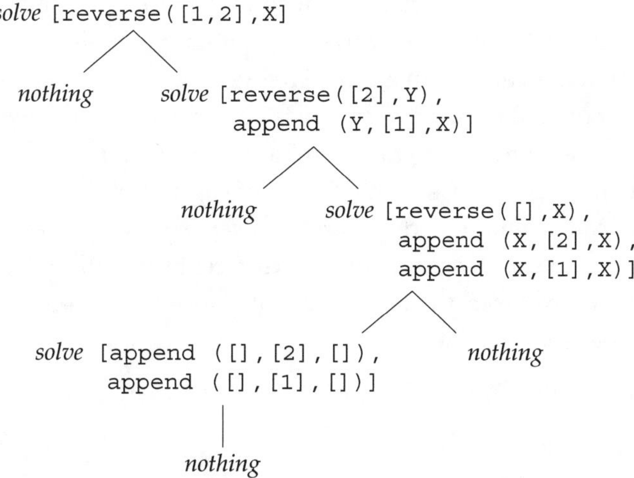

Obviously, something is wrong with the model. This proof tree says that there is no solution for `reverse([1,2],X)`, but there should be a solution where {`X`→`[2,1]`}. What went wrong?

The first *solve* goal list just has the original query term. There is nothing wrong there. The second *solve* goal list also looks fine. There should be a solution to these goals using the substitution {`Y`→`[2]`, `X`→`[2,1]`}. But something has definitely gone wrong by the third goal list. No single substitution for the variable `X` can satisfy all the goals in that list.

That incorrect goal list was formed by the resolution step, using the previous (correct) goal list and a (correct) rule for `reverse`. The previous goal list was

```
[reverse([2],Y),append(Y,[1],X)]
```

The rule used was

```
reverse([Head|Tail],X) :-
  reverse(Tail,Y),
  append(Y,[Head],X).
```

Notice that the goal list and the rule both contain variables named `X` and `Y`. Therein lies the problem: the resolution step combined these two without realizing that the `X` and `Y` in the rule are not the same as the `X` and `Y` in the goals. It unified the head of the rule with the first goal term using the substitution {`Head`→2, `Tail`→`[]`, `Y`→`X` }, then applied that same substitution to all the rest of the new goal term. That was a mistake: the `Y`s in the goal list are not the same as the `Y`s in the rule and should not have been mapped to `X`.

In short, the model is not paying attention to Prolog's scope rules: the scope of the definition of a variable is the clause that contains it. The variables in a clause should be independent of any other variables that happen to have the same names. The problem is that if a variable in a clause happens to have the same name as a variable in the list of goal terms, the variables are treated as if they were the same. Remember the phenomenon of *capture* that affects macro expansion, as shown in Chapter 18? The problem here is another kind of capture problem.

This problem can be eliminated by *variable renaming*. Every time a clause is used, it will be given a fresh set of variable names, different from all the other names that have been used. For example, the first time that clause for `reverse` is used, the variables might be renamed like this:

```
reverse([Head1|Tail1],X1) :-
  reverse(Tail1,Y1),
  append(Y1,[Head1],X1).
```

The second time it is used, it might be renamed like this:

```
reverse([Head2|Tail2],X2)  :-
  reverse(Tail2,Y2),
  append(Y2,[Head2],X2).
```

Generating a new set of names for every use of the clause avoids accidentally using any of the variable names that already appear in the list of goal terms. Following this strategy, here is a new and correct proof tree:

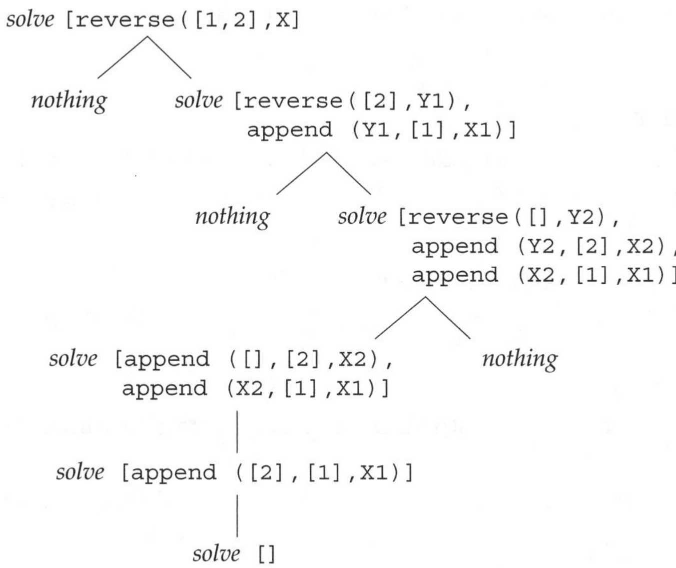

To be correct, all three of the views of Prolog execution need to be modified to incorporate this same step. Before using a clause from the program, always generate a fresh set of variables for it.

20.6 The Lighter Side of Prolog

This chapter has spent a lot of time trying to come to grips with Prolog's model of execution. This is an important exercise, but a strenuous one. You may be starting to think that Prolog is too much trouble altogether—all unification and proof trees, and not enough fun. This section will look at some fun Prolog programming tricks. Dirty tricks, in fact: all the techniques introduced here involve side effects.

Quoted Atoms as Strings

Any string of characters enclosed in single quotes is a term in Prolog. In fact, it is a kind of term you have already seen, since it is treated as a big atom. The atom 'abc' is the same as the atom abc; they are just two different ways of writing the same thing. But by using single quotes you can write atoms that contain spaces, such as 'hello world'. You can also write atoms that start with capital letters, such as 'Hello world'. Even though it starts with a capital letter, it is treated as an atom and not as a variable since it is a quoted string. Using these quoted atoms is the easiest way to manipulate simple strings in Prolog.

Quoted atoms can contain the same kinds of backslash sequences used in ML and Java: \n for a new line, \t for a tab, \' for a single quote, and \\ for a backslash.

write and read

The predicate write(X) is a predefined predicate with a side effect. Logically speaking, write(X) is true for any X. But whenever it is called, it prints out its parameter X:

```
?- write('Hello world').
Hello world

Yes
```

The predefined predicate nl (with no parameters) starts a new line. It has the same effect as write('\n').

There is a corresponding predicate read(X) for reading typed input:

```
?- read(X).
|    hello.

X = hello

Yes
```

In this example, the Prolog system prompted for input with the | character, then read in a term. That term was unified with the read parameter X. The read predicate requires the user to enter a Prolog term, complete with a period at the end. Prolog also has predicates for doing general character-by-character input and output, but read and write are easier to use.

One use for write is in debugging. For example, here is a predicate that clearly cannot be proved:

```
p :-
  append(X,Y,[1,2]),
  X=Y.
```

There are three solutions for `append(X,Y,[1,2])`, but none of them have `X=Y`, so the query `p` is bound to fail. To see exactly what happens when it fails, insert some writes into the conditions for `p`, like this:

```
p :-
  append(X,Y,[1,2]),
  write(X), write(' '), write(Y), write('\n'),
  X=Y.
```

Now let's see what happens in response to the query `p`:

```
?- p.
[] [1, 2]
[1] [2]
[1, 2] []

No
```

The first solution Prolog gets for `append(X,Y,[1,2])` is `X=[],Y=[1,2]` The `write` goals print those out. But that is not all that gets printed, because the final condition `X=Y` fails. The Prolog system backtracks and tries another solution for the `append` goal and another. Each one gets printed out by the calls to `write`.

`assert` and `retract`

The predicate `assert(X)` adds the term `X` as a fact in the database. For example:

```
?- green(light).
ERROR: Undefined procedure: green/1
?- assert(green(light)).

Yes
?- green(light).

Yes
```

The corresponding predicate `retract(X)` removes the term `X` from the database:

```
?- green(light).

Yes
?- retract(green(light)).

Yes
?- green(light).

No
```

Retracting a term does not necessarily make it fail as a subsequent query. It did in the example above, but only because the only way of proving `green(light)` that was in the database at the time was retracted. If there had been another way to prove it—for example, if `green(_)` had also been a fact in the database—the query `green(light)` would still have succeeded. Retracting a term does not necessarily make it unprovable; it just removes one clause from the database. If you retract a term that is not fully instantiated, with a query like `retract(green(_))`, the first thing in the database that unifies with the retracted term will be removed, and any others will remain. To retract all the things in the database that unify with a given term, you can use the `retractall` predicate. For example, the goal `retractall(green(_))` removes all `green` facts of arity 1 from the database.

When you have loaded a predicate using `consult`, SWI-Prolog will not permit its definition to be changed by `assert` or `retract`. For example, if you use `consult` to bring in a database of `parent` facts, and then try to use `assert` to add the fact `parent(fred,pebbles)`, you will get an error message. Not all Prolog systems are as fussy about this as SWI-Prolog, and even in SWI-Prolog it is possible to circumvent this restriction. But these examples will not need to do so. They will stick to simple applications of `assert` and `retract`, using them only on facts, only with predicates that are not otherwise defined in the program, and only in situations where the clause order has no importance.

Using `assert` and `retract` as queries can be confusing, since they make on-the-fly modifications to the current program. It can be even more confusing when a program uses `assert` and `retract` in the conditions of its own rules. Such programs are self-modifying, and their behavior can be very difficult to reason about. It isn't safe, it isn't at all declarative, and most implementations do not make it particularly efficient; but simple cases of this self-modifying behavior can be quite tempting in Prolog, as the following longer example shows.

An Adventure Game

Developing a little text-based adventure game will demonstrate the lighter side of Prolog. To play the game, you give typed commands to move around in an imaginary world.[4] The program begins with descriptions of all the places in this world:

---

4. Text-based, solo adventure games are a peculiar genus. A game called Adventure (also known as Colossal Cave or Advent) introduced the idea in 1972. It was originally a realistic cave crawl. It was ported to numerous mainframe systems, to the dismay of some systems administrators. It evolved through many versions and inspired many similar games, such as Zork. Later species introduced the fantasy elements and had commercial success as personal computer games. The genus is now largely extinct.

```
/*
  This is a little adventure game. There are three
  entities: you, a treasure, and an ogre. There are
  six places: a valley, a path, a cliff, a fork, a maze,
  and a mountaintop. Your goal is to get the treasure
  without being killed first.
*/

/*
  First, text descriptions of all the places in
  the game.
*/
description(valley,
  'You are in a pleasant valley, with a trail ahead.').
description(path,
  'You are on a path, with ravines on both sides.').
description(cliff,
  'You are teetering on the edge of a cliff.').
description(fork,
  'You are at a fork in the path.').
description(maze(_),
  'You are in a maze of twisty trails, all alike.').
description(mountaintop,
  'You are on the mountaintop.').
```

This example contains comments. In Prolog, everything on a line after `%` and everything between `/*` and the following `*/` is taken to be a comment. The example defines a predicate `description(X,Y)`, where `X` is a location and `Y` is a string describing that location. The locations are `valley`, `path`, `cliff`, `fork`, and `mountaintop`, along with some locations of the form `maze(X)`. (This example will use `maze(0)`, `maze(1)`, `maze(2)`, and `maze(3)`, but all the maze locations have the same description—that's what makes it a maze.) The descriptions will be used when reporting a player's current location:

```
/*
  report prints the description of your current
  location.
*/
report :-
  at(you,X),
  description(X,Y),
  write(Y), nl.
```

This `report` predicate uses the condition `at(you,X)` to look up the player's current location `X`. An `at` predicate has not been written yet, but one of the nice things about Prolog programming is that it is easy to test fragments of the program before the whole thing is written. Here, assert and retract are used to establish some at facts and test the resulting behavior of report:

```
?- assert(at(you,cliff)).

Yes
?- report.
You are teetering on the edge of a cliff.

Yes
?- retract(at(you,cliff)).

Yes
?- assert(at(you,valley)).

Yes
?- report.
You are in a pleasant valley, with a trail ahead.

Yes
```

A map of this world needs to specify how the locations are related to each other. For example, if a player is in the valley and moves forward, where is the player then? A collection of connect facts is used to establish this map:

```
/*
  These connect predicates establish the map.
  The meaning of connect(X,Dir,Y) is that if you
  are at X and you move in direction Dir, you
  get to Y. Recognized directions are
  forward, right, and left.
*/
connect(valley,forward,path).
connect(path,right,cliff).
connect(path,left,cliff).
connect(path,forward,fork).
connect(fork,left,maze(0)).
connect(fork,right,mountaintop).
connect(maze(0),left,maze(1)).
connect(maze(1),right,maze(2)).
connect(maze(2),left,fork).
connect(maze(0),right,maze(3)).
connect(maze(_),_,maze(0)).
```

The connect facts say what happens when the player moves; for example, the first fact says that going forward from valley gets the player to path. Going left from `fork` gets the player to `maze(0)`. From there, the player must go `left`, `right`, and `left` again to get back to `fork`. Other sequences of moves simply wander around in the maze. The final `connect` fact ensures that all maze moves other than those previously defined take the player back to `maze(0)`.

The `connect` facts establish the moves that are permitted. To accomplish those moves, a `move` predicate is defined:

```
/*
  move(Dir) moves you in direction Dir, then
  prints the description of your new location.
*/
move(Dir) :-
  at(you,Loc),
  connect(Loc,Dir,Next),
  retract(at(you,Loc)),
  assert(at(you,Next)),
  report.
/*
  But if the argument was not a legal direction,
  print an error message and don't move.
*/
move(_) :-
  write('That is not a legal move.\n'),
  report.

/*
  Shorthand for moves.
*/
forward :- move(forward).
left :- move(left).
right :- move(right).
```

The first clause for `move` handles the legal moves. If the player starts at a given location (`Loc`), and if the `connect` predicate says that a move from there in the requested direction leads to the new location `Next`, it is a legal move. The player is moved by retracting the old fact `at(you,Loc)` and asserting the new fact `at(you,Next)`, then reporting what is visible at the new location. The second clause for `move` handles the illegal moves (when the first clause fails). It prints an error message and does not move the player. The predicates `forward`, `left`, and `right` are also defined, just to save the player a little typing. Here is a demonstration of the code so far:

```
?- assert(at(you,valley)).

Yes
?- forward.
You are on a path, with ravines on both sides.

Yes
?- forward.
You are at a fork in the path.

Yes
?- forward.
That is not a legal move.
You are at a fork in the path.

Yes
```

Next, the game includes an ogre, who kills the player in a fanciful and grisly manner if they meet:

```
/*
  If you and the ogre are at the same place, it
  kills you.
*/
ogre :-
  at(ogre,Loc),
  at(you,Loc),
  write('An ogre sucks your brain out through\n'),
  write('your eye sockets, and you die.\n'),
  retract(at(you,Loc)),
  assert(at(you,done)).
/*
  But if you and the ogre are not in the same place,
  nothing happens.
*/
ogre.
```

The goal `ogre` always succeeds: it succeeds by killing the player if the player and ogre are at the same location, or by doing nothing otherwise. This predicate will have to be called each time the player (or the ogre) moves. A similar approach can be used to implement the special behaviors of the treasure (the player wins if he or she finds it) and the cliff (the player falls off and dies if he or she goes there):

```
/*
  If you and the treasure are at the same place, you
  win.
*/
```

```
treasure :-
  at(treasure,Loc),
  at(you,Loc),
  write('There is a treasure here.\n'),
  write('Congratulations, you win!\n'),
  retract(at(you,Loc)),
  assert(at(you,done)).
/*
  But if you and the treasure are not in the same
  place, nothing happens.
*/
treasure.

/*
  If you are at the cliff, you fall off and die.
*/
cliff :-
  at(you,cliff),
  write('You fall off and die.\n'),
  retract(at(you,cliff)),
  assert(at(you,done)).
/*
  But if you are not at the cliff nothing happens.
*/
cliff.
```

Winning and losing are handled by establishing a special `at` fact: `at(you,done)`. The main loop for the game lets the user move around until `at(you,done)` is achieved:

```
/*
  Main loop. Stop if player won or lost.
*/
main :-
  at(you,done),
  write('Thanks for playing.\n').
/*
  Main loop. Not done, so get a move from the user
  and make it. Then run all our special behaviors.
  Then repeat.
*/
main :-
  write('\nNext move — '),
  read(Move),
  call(Move),
  ogre,
  treasure,
  cliff,
  main.
```

This uses a predefined predicate not seen before: `call(X)` treats the term `X`, whatever it is, as a goal. That allows the program to take the move the user typed in and run it. Now the game is almost ready to go. All that is needed is a predicate to start up the game with some initial `at` facts:

```
/*
  This is the starting point for the game. We
  assert the initial conditions, print an initial
  report, then start the main loop.
*/
go :-
  retractall(at(_,_)), % clean up from previous runs
  assert(at(you,valley)),
  assert(at(ogre,maze(3))),
  assert(at(treasure,mountaintop)),
  write('This is an adventure game. \n'),
  write('Legal moves are left, right, or forward.\n'),
  write('End each move with a period.\n\n'),
  report,
  main.
```

Notice the initial `retractall`—an important step if the program is going to be run more than once, since a game should not start with old `at` facts still in the database. Here is a sample run of the complete game:

```
?- go.
This is an adventure game.
Legal moves are left, right, or forward.
End each move with a period.

You are in a pleasant valley, with a trail ahead.

Next move - forward.
You are on a path, with ravines on both sides.

Next move - forward.
You are at a fork in the path.

Next move - right.
You are on the mountaintop.
There is a treasure here.
Congratulations, you win!
Thanks for playing.

Yes
```

It is a simple game, but easily extended, as you will see if you do Exercise 6.

For this kind of program, the procedural view of Prolog is perfect. The program's use of unification is trivial. Moreover, it never backtracks very far, because while unifications with the basic fact terms `connect` and `at` sometimes fail, the other predicates in the program always succeed.

The game program makes use of something about Prolog that was stressed back in Chapter 19: everything is a term. A Prolog program is a collection of terms. The data on which a Prolog program operates is also represented as terms. A program may choose to keep a strict division between code and data, but the language does not enforce one. This game program takes advantage of this flexibility. For example, it treats the atom `ogre` as data in the fact `at(ogre,maze(3)))`, but as code in the predicate `ogre`. It reads commands typed by the player, treating them as data in `read(Move)`, then immediately treats the same term as code in `call(Move)`. It changes the database using `assert`, thus modifying its own code.

20.7 Conclusion

This chapter presented three different views of Prolog's model of execution. This is just another way of saying that this chapter presented three different definitions of Prolog's semantics. Semantics is that part of the programming-language definition that describes how programs work: their behavior and meaning. And that is what this chapter tried to illuminate.

Defining the semantics of any programming language is difficult. What you saw in this chapter is a good introduction to some of the typical difficulties. If you try to make a clear and intuitive description (as with the procedural view of Prolog), you often end up with something that is not really a rigorous, detailed definition of how the language works. One way to make a rigorous, detailed definition is to describe how to implement an interpreter for the language (as with the implementational view). The drawback here is that you end up with a description of a particular implementation, rather than a definition of the language being implemented. To solve *that*, you can try to make a definition that is abstract enough to say exactly what it means for an implementation of the language to be correct, without talking about the implementation mechanism. The problem there (as with the proof-tree view) is that you end up with something so abstract that it is hard to think about. You will see more about the general problem of defining programming language semantics in Chapter 23; it is a problem that has, today, no entirely satisfactory solution.

This chapter also showed the lighter side of Prolog: some of the dirty programming tricks that are unique to the language. Prolog makes it uniquely easy to write self-modifying code and to break down the line between code and data. Prolog does not require the programmer to use such tricks. For serious Prolog programming it is probably best to avoid them and to write programs that are as declarative as possible. But, thank goodness, programming does not always have to be serious.

Exercises

Exercise 1 What is the MGU used in each of the following resolution steps, and what is the new list of goal terms that results?

a. `resolution([p,q,r],[p,x,y])`

b. `resolution([p(a)],[p(X)])`

c. `resolution([p(X,b),q(X)],[p(a,Y),r(Y)])`

d. `resolution([append(X,Y,[1,2])],[append([],B,B)])`

e.
```
resolution([append(X,Y,[1,2])],
           [append([Head|TailA], B, [Head|TailC]),
            append(TailA,B,TailC)])
```

Exercise 2 Consider the following `append` predicate:

```
append([], B, B).
append([Head|TailA], B, [Head|TailC]) :-
  append(TailA, B, TailC).
```

Using the implementation view from this chapter, show the trace of `solve([append(X,Y,[1,2])])`. Do not stop after the first `succeed`—show the full trace, finding all possible solutions. Use the version of `solve` on page 426, which does not collect the substituted query term. Be careful to rename the variables before each use of an `append` clause.

Exercise 3 Repeat Exercise 2, using the version of `solve` on page 428, which collects the substituted query term. Again, be careful to rename the variables before each use of an `append` clause.

Exercise 4 Can a Prolog program with a finite proof tree run forever? Explain why or why not. If the answer is yes, give an example of such a program. Can a Prolog program that does not run forever have an infinite proof tree? Explain why or why not. If the answer is yes, give an example of such a program.

Exercise 5 Consider the following `reverse` predicate:

```
reverse([],[]).
reverse([Head|Tail],X) :-
  reverse(Tail,Y),
  append(Y,[Head],X).
```

Draw the proof tree for this query: `reverse(X,[1,2])`. As in the example on page 435, each *solve* node with a `reverse` as the first goal term should have two children, one for each of the two `reverse` clauses. Each *solve* node that has an `append` as its first goal term should have a single child: either a *nothing* node, if the `append` cannot be solved, or a *solve* node, with the `append` solved and the rest of the goals in the list substituted accordingly. (*Hint:* If you are not sure how Prolog handles a particular `append` goal term, you can always try it and see.) Be careful to rename the variables before using each clause from the program. The tree for `reverse(X,[1,2])` is an infinite tree. So when you see where it has an infinite branch, cut off the drawing there and explain where and how the infinite branch grows.

With reference to your proof tree, explain this example from Chapter 19:

```
?- reverse(X,[1,2,3,4]).

X = [4, 3, 2, 1] ;

Action (h for help) ? a
% Execution Aborted
?-
```

That is, explain why `reverse` runs forever trying to find a second solution for this query.

Exercise 6 Add the following features to the adventure game from this chapter:

- There is a gate between the fork in the path and the mountaintop. The gate is a separate location; that is, the player must move from `at(you,fork)` to `at(you,gate)` and then to `at(you,mountaintop)`.
- To move forward through the gate the player must first unlock it with a key.
- The key is somewhere in the maze. The player must find it and explicitly pick it up.
- If the player tries to pass through the gate while still holding the key, he or she is killed by lightning. (To get the treasure, the player must first open the gate, then put down the key, and then pass through.)

Start from the code in this chapter (which is also available on this book's Web site, **http://www.webber-labs.com/mpl.html**). Part of your implementation should be a general way for the player to pick things up, carry them, and put them down. Design your solution so that it would be easy to add additional objects for the player to pick up and put down.

Chapter 21 Cost Models

21.1 Introduction

Suppose `X` is a Prolog list of a hundred integers. Which is faster: adding a new element to the front of the list or adding it to the rear? That is, which goal will be computed faster: `Y=[1|X]` or `append(X,[1],Y)`?

Experienced Prolog programmers know that adding a new element to the front of a list is much faster than adding it to the rear. This kind of information is rarely explicit in the language definition, but it is an important part of every competent programmer's expertise. Every experienced programmer has a *cost model* of the language—a mental model of the relative costs of various operations. Cost models are the subject of this chapter.

This chapter is concerned only with relative costs, not absolute costs. No programmer has a mental model so accurate that he or she can predict how many nanoseconds it will take to execute a given piece of code. For one thing, such models are extremely complex. To model absolute costs accurately, you would have to take into account the behavior of the language system, the operating system, the processor, the memory system—really, the whole computer, hardware and software. It could not be a general cost model for the language; it would have to be a specific cost model for a specific computer system. Relative costs, on the other hand, can sometimes be modeled in a very general way. There are even some things about relative costs that a programmer can reasonably assume will be true for all implementations of the language on all machines.

21.2 A Cost Model for Lists

As shown in Chapter 19, Prolog has two different notations for lists: the more convenient notation using square brackets and the more detailed notation using the . predicate. For example, these are two different ways of writing the same Prolog term:

```
[1,2,3,4]
.(1,.(2,.(3,.(4,[]))))
```

The more detailed notation suggests the underlying representation, which is illustrated below. The illustration shows a Prolog goal that binds the variables A, B, and C to the lists [], [1], and [1,2], respectively. Next to the Prolog session is a picture of how the lists are represented in memory.

```
?-   A = []
|    B = .(1, []),
|    C = .(1, .(2, [])).

A = []
B = [1]
C = [1, 2]

Yes
```

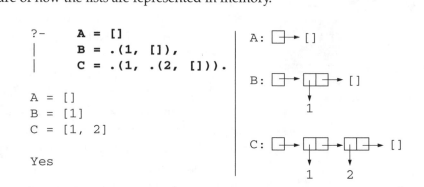

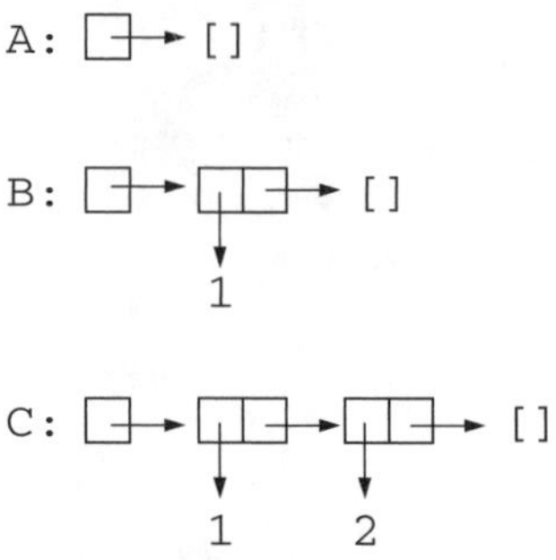

As the illustration shows, a list is represented using a chain of pairs of pointers. The first pointer in a pair points to an element of the list, and the second points to the rest of the list. Pairs of pointers used this way to implement a list are commonly called *cons cells.* With this implementation, a compound term using the . predicate is a cons cell.

An important consequence of this representation is that lists can share structure with each other, as the next illustration shows.

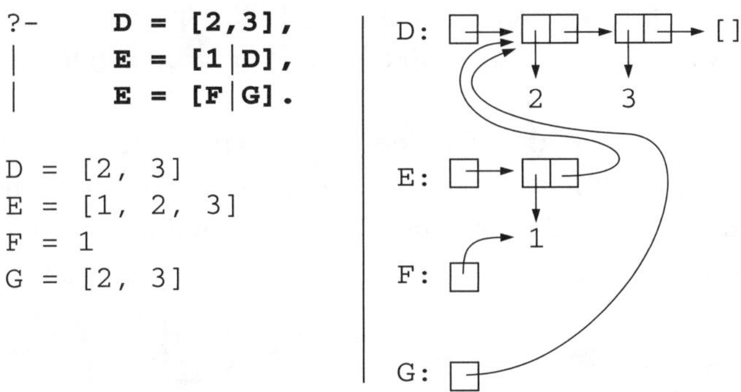

The variable D is bound to the list [2,3], which is represented in memory by a list of cons cells, which is also the tail of the list E. The lists D and G are completely shared—not just equal, but represented by the same list of cons cells.

How do we know that Prolog represents lists this way? How do we know that it does not make a complete copy of the list D when satisfying the goal E = [1|D], so that E and D do not share any structure at all? This is a very important question. The answer (for Prolog) is that we know only because of the costs of the operations. There is nothing in the language specification that says it uses the cons-cell representation. A Prolog program can test only whether two lists are equal; it has no direct way to tell the difference between lists that are copied and lists that share representations. Nevertheless, we can observe that a goal like E = [1|D] is satisfied in a constant amount of time, using a constant amount of memory. *It does not depend on the length of the list*—so we know that the representation is not being recopied when a new element is consed onto the front of an old list. Similarly, extracting the head and tail of a list, as we did with the goal E = [F|G], is observably a constant-time operation.

The length predicate, on the other hand, takes an amount of time that does depend on the length of the list. In fact, when length is used like a function (that is, when the first parameter is instantiated to a list and the second is not instantiated), it takes an amount of time proportional to the length of the list. As you can see from the representation, the length of a list is not recorded anywhere. There is no way to find the length of a list except to follow the trail of cons cells, counting how many steps it takes to reach the [] at the end. In effect, the Prolog system has to implement the length predicate in pretty much the same way ML would:

```
fun length nil = 0
|   length (head :: tail) = 1 + length tail;
```

(You will see an implementation of this in Prolog in Chapter 22.) There are various things a Prolog language system can do to improve the speed of this computation, but even with improvements it must still take time proportional to the length of the list.

Appending two lists is another operation that can be expensive when the cons-cell representation is used. To append a list `I` onto the end of a list `H`, the language system must make a copy of the list `H` and then have the final tail pointer of the copy point to list `I`, like this:

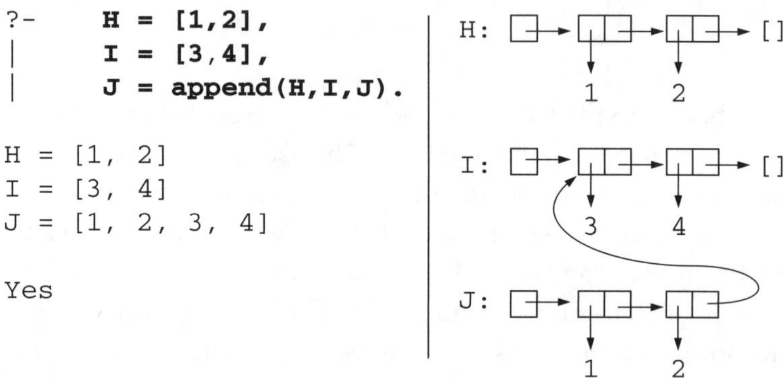
?- H = [1,2],
| I = [3,4],
| J = append(H,I,J).
H = [1, 2]
I = [3, 4]
J = [1, 2, 3, 4]
Yes
H:
[]
1
2
I:
[]
3
4
J:
1
2

In effect, the Prolog language system has to implement the `append` predicate pretty much the same way you would:

```
append([],X,X).
append([Head|Tail],X,[Head|Suffix]) :-
  append(Tail,X,Suffix).
```

When `append` is used like a function (that is, when the first two parameters are instantiated to lists and the third is not instantiated), it conses up a copy of the first list, then connects it to the end of the second list. The time it takes to do this is proportional to the length of that first list. Again, there are various things a Prolog language system can do to improve the speed of the computation, but even with improvements it must still take time proportional to the length of the first list.

Unifying lists is another potentially expensive operation. Although two equal lists may share structure, they do not have to. This next example shows three lists that are all equal to each other, though only the first two share structure:

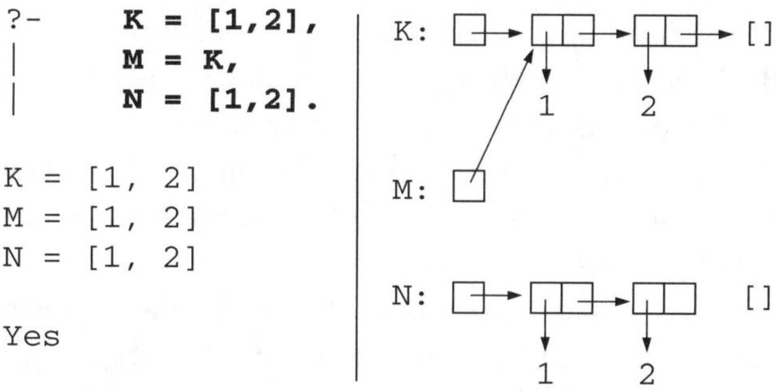
?- K = [1,2],
M = K,
N = [1,2].
K = [1, 2]
M = [1, 2]
N = [1, 2]
Yes
K:
[]
1
2
M:
N:
[]
1
2

If the program now tried to unify the lists `M` and `K` (for example, by trying the goal `M=K` again), the Prolog language system might notice that they are bound to the same thing and immediately conclude that `M=K` is satisfied. But `K=N` is also true, even though `K` and `N` do not share structure. So it is not enough for the unifier to check for shared structure. In the absence of shared structure, it must unify the two lists element by element. In effect, the Prolog language system has to implement unification for lists pretty much the same way you would:

```
xequal([],[]).
xequal([Head|Tail1],[Head|Tail2]) :-
  xequal(Tail1,Tail2).
```

Again, the Prolog language system may be able to improve the speed of this; for example, by taking a shortcut if it finds shared structure. But in the worst case it must still unify each element of the first list with the corresponding element of the second list, until one or both of the lists are exhausted.

This is even worse than the computations that `length` and `append` must make. The `length` and `append` predicates have to visit the cons cells in the list, but they do not have to visit the list elements themselves. Computing the length of the list `[1,2,3]` takes exactly the same amount of time as computing the length of any other list of three elements, such as `[[1,2,3],[4,5,6],[7,8,9]]`. But that is not the case for the equality comparison. The second rule for the `xequal` predicate has to unify the two list `Head` elements—and if those elements are lists, that means unifying all *their* elements, and so on. The whole structure of the two lists must be visited, not just the top level. That means that the worst-case time required for the unification is proportional to the total size (not just the length) of the shorter of the two lists.[1]

1. The actual time required depends on the unification algorithm. Some unification algorithms have linear worst-case complexity.

To summarize, here is the basic cost model for lists:

- Consing onto the front of a list always takes constant time.
- Extracting the head of a list always takes constant time.
- Extracting the tail of a list always takes constant time.
- When length is used like a function (that is, when the first parameter is instantiated to a list and the second is not instantiated), it always takes time proportional to the length of the list.
- When append is used like a function (that is, when the first two parameters are instantiated to lists and the third is not instantiated), it always takes time proportional to the length of its first parameter.
- Unifying lists, in the worst case, takes time proportional to the size (not just the length) of the shorter list.

This cost model for lists can reasonably be supposed to apply to all implementations of Prolog and to all implementations of ML, Lisp, and other languages that use the cons-cell implementation.

How does this cost model influence implementation decisions? For example, here is a simple predicate that defines the reverse of a list:

```
reverse([],[]).
reverse([Head|Tail],Rev) :-
  reverse(Tail,TailRev),
  append(TailRev,[Head],Rev).
```

Although this function is easy to understand, the fact that it repeatedly appends an element to the end of a list makes it highly inefficient. The cons-cell cost model guides programmers toward implementations that add to the front of a list instead of to the rear. After some thought, you can find an implementation of `reverse` that works by adding to the front of the list, such as this one:

```
reverse(X,Y) :- rev(X,[],Y).
rev([],Sofar,Sofar).
rev([Head|Tail],Sofar,Rev) :-
  rev(Tail,[Head|Sofar],Rev).
```

The second implementation of `reverse` is a bit harder to understand, but it is much more efficient than the first one. It uses a helper predicate with an *accumulating parameter*, `Sofar`, that collects the partially reversed list. (Accumulating parameters will be covered more in the next section's discussion of tail calls.) The biggest advantage of the faster `reverse` is that it is able to build the resulting list from the front instead of the back. Used as functions, the faster `reverse` always takes time proportional to the length of the list, and the slower `reverse` takes time proportional to the *square* of the length of the list. For most applications, the faster `reverse` is well worth the additional effort it takes to write and understand it. If you have doubts about the benefits of this improvement, try both implementations on a reasonably long list. For instance, try this goal with both definitions of `reverse`:

```
length(X,5000),  reverse(X,Y).
```

You will be convinced!

Languages that use the cons-cell representation for lists differ in how much of that representation they expose to the programmer. Lisp has several different equality tests, including `equal` and `eq`. `equal` works like ML's `=`, but `eq` only tests for shared structure. (So the `eq` test is a constant-time operation.) Lisp also has functions for directly altering the two parts of a cons cell: `setcar` and `setcdr`. In general, Lisp makes the cons-cell implementation of lists entirely visible to the programmer.

Prolog and ML make the representation somewhat less visible. There is no way for a Prolog or ML program to make the equivalent of the Lisp `eq` test, and the difference between shared structure and recopied structure is almost invisible in these languages. In general, they treat the implementation of lists (and tuples) as an internal matter and none of the programmer's business. *Except, of course, for the cost model.* Even though Prolog and ML try to conceal the implementation details, they cannot quite succeed, because experienced programmers know and use the cons-cell cost model.

21.3 A Cost Model for Function Calls

The stack implementation of activation records was shown back in Chapter 12. The next example of a cost model has to do with the implementation of function calls, so let's start with a quick review of stacks of activation records. ML will be used for the initial example. Then later the same cost model will be applied to other languages, including Prolog.

Here is an ML implementation of the faster reverse algorithm. Compare this with the previous Prolog `reverse` predicate.

```
fun reverse x =
  let
    fun rev(nil,sofar) = sofar
    |   rev(head::tail,sofar) = rev(tail,head::sofar);
  in
    rev(x,nil)
  end;
```

Suppose the expression `rev([1,2],nil)` is evaluated. Since the first parameter is not `nil`, the second alternative is used. So the first activation record for `rev` looks like this:

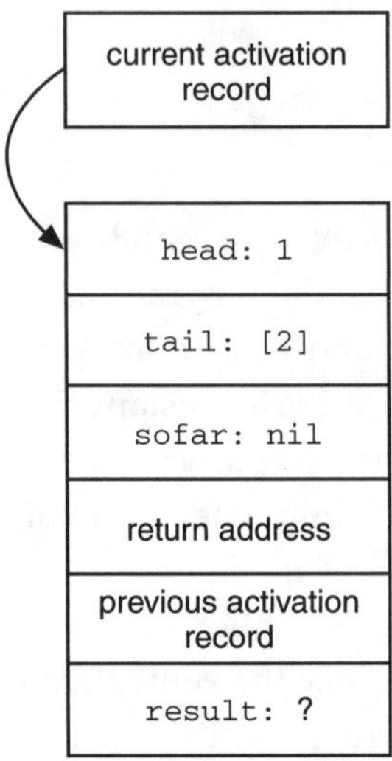

The function now makes the recursive call `rev(tail,(head::sofar))`. Again, the first parameter is not `nil`, so the second alternative is used. When the second activation of `rev` begins, the stack looks like this:

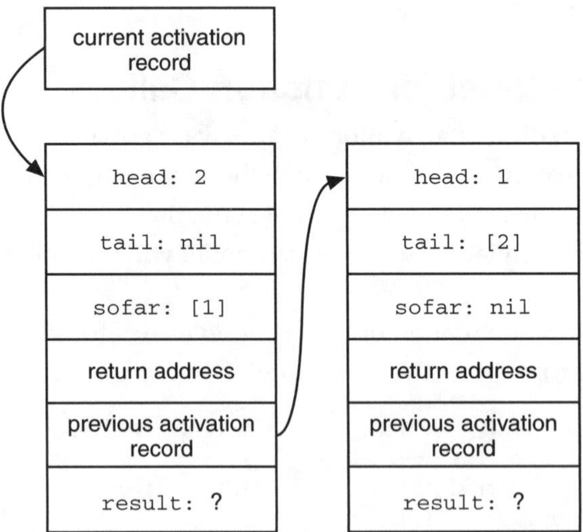

The function makes another recursive call to `rev(tail,(head::sofar))`. This time, the first parameter is `nil`, so the first alternative is used. The new activation immediately prepares to return the result value `nil`. This picture shows the stack just before the third activation of `rev` returns:

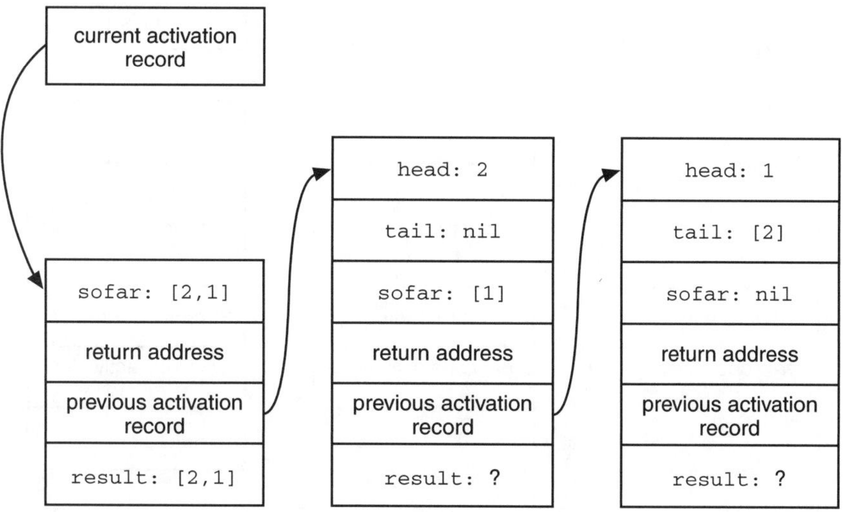

Now the top activation of `reverse` returns the result `[2,1]`, and its activation record is popped off the stack. The second activation prepares to return the same value `[2,1]` to its caller:

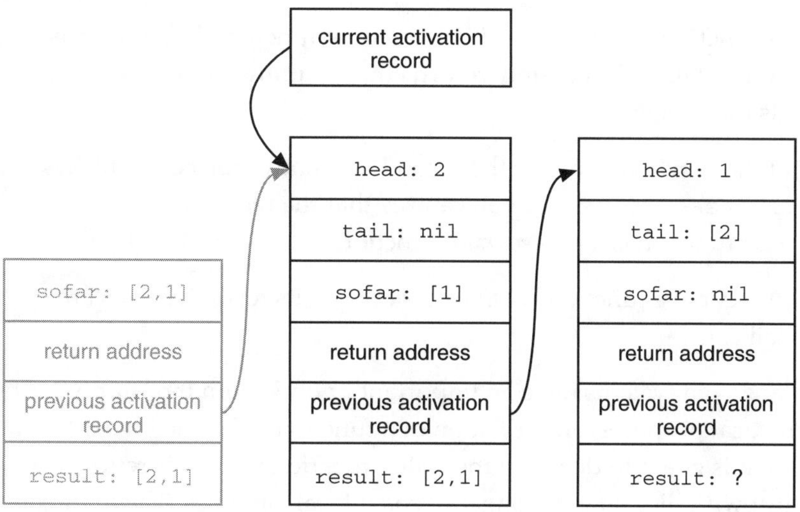

Next, the second activation of `reverse` returns the same result `[2,1]`, and its activation record is popped off the stack. The first activation prepares to return the same value `[2,1]` to its caller:

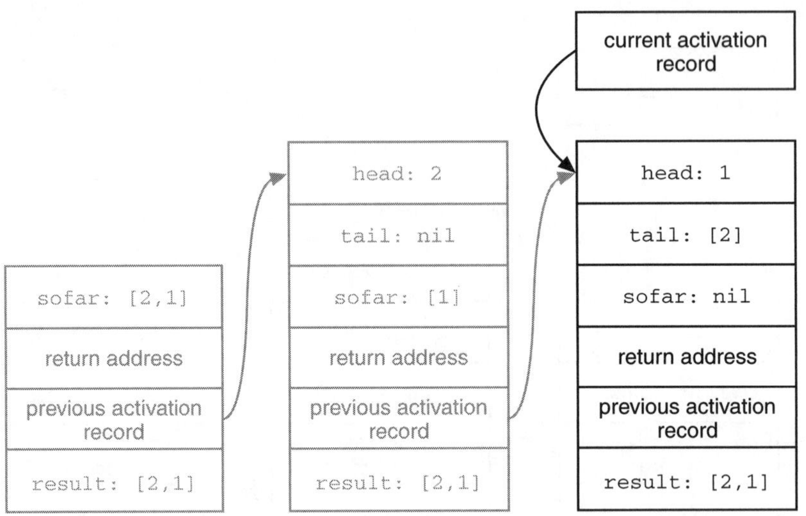

Thus the value of the expression `rev([1,2],nil)` is `[2,1]`, as was expected: the reversed list.

Notice that after each activation's (recursive) call, it did no further computation. All it did was return the value to its own caller. There is a special name for this kind of function call:

> A function call is a *tail call* if the calling function does no further computation, but merely returns the resulting value (if any) to its own caller.

Looking at the function body for the second alternative for `rev`, which is simply `rev(tail,(head::sofar))`, you can see that the recursive function call is a tail call. The `rev` function is a *tail-recursive* function:

> A recursive function is *tail recursive* if all its recursive calls are tail calls.

Most language systems have an important optimization they apply for tail calls. For all practical purposes, an activation of a function is finished when it makes a tail call. All it is going to do when the called function returns is return the same value to its own caller, so it no longer needs it local variables. The optimization for tail calls is to have the called function reuse the calling function's activation record. This way, a new activation record doesn't have to be allocated for the called function, there's no cleaning up when the called function returns, and the called function can return directly to the calling function's caller.

Let's look at the example again, this time applying the optimization for tail calls. The expression `rev([1,2],nil)` is evaluated. Since the first parameter is not `nil`, the second alternative is used. So the first (and only!) activation record for `rev` looks like this:

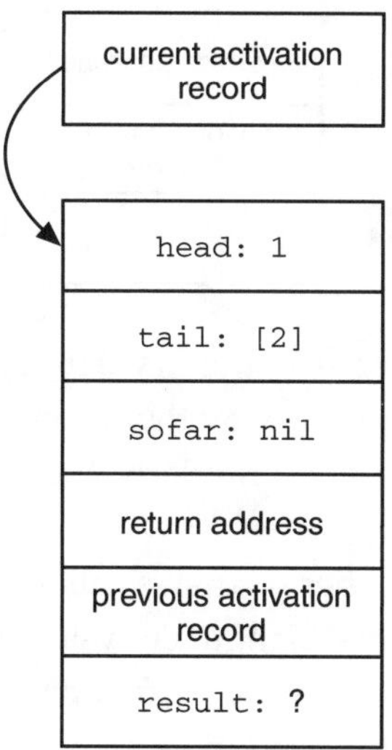

The function now makes the recursive call `rev(tail,(head::sofar))`. Since this is a tail call, this smart language system does not push a new activation record onto the stack. Instead, it overwrites the parameters using the values for the new activation:

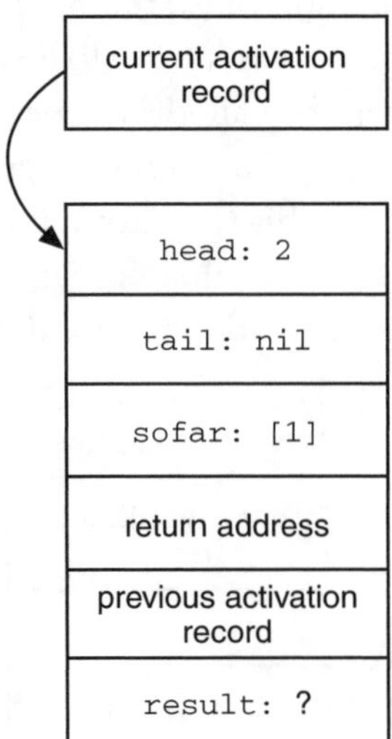

The return address is unchanged—all the first activation was going to do was return the value to its caller, and this way the second activation will just return directly to the first activation's caller. Similarly, the address of the previous activation record is unchanged.

The function now makes another recursive call to `rev(tail,(head::sofar))`. This is another tail call, so the smart language system reuses the same activation record for the third activation. This time, the first parameter is `nil`, so the first alternative is used. Notice that the activation record needed for the first alternative is smaller—that's no problem, just leave some of it unused:

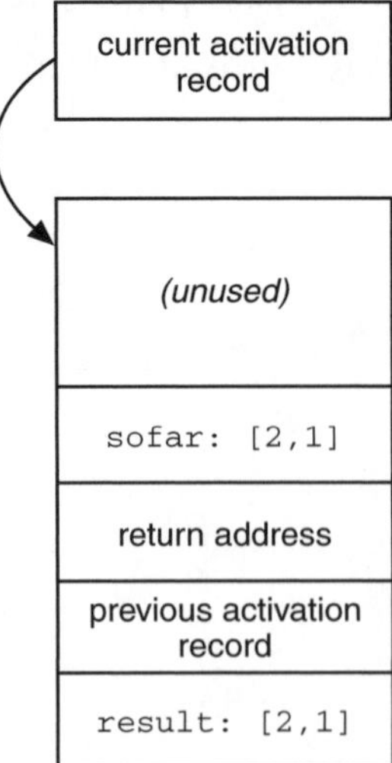

As before, the return address and the link to the previous activation record are left unchanged. So when the third activation returns the value `[2,1]`, it returns directly to the caller of the first activation.

Knowing that a language system optimizes tail calls gives programmers a tail-call cost model. Under this model, tail calls are considerably faster than non-tail calls, and they take less memory space. In fact, the reduction in the memory space needed can ultimately be more important than the speed-up. A recursive solution that does not use tail calls may run out of memory, where an optimized tail-recursive solution does not. The tail-call cost model guides programmers toward solutions that use tail calls, even if that means making the code somewhat longer and harder to understand.

The tail-recursive `rev` function, as you have already seen, is much more efficient than the simple `reverse`. But in that example, the benefit from optimizing the tail call is minor compared with the benefit from using the `::` operator instead of `@`. For another example, consider again this `length` function in ML:

```
fun length nil = 0
|   length (head :: tail) = 1 + length tail;
```

This function is deceptive, since the recursive call looks like a tail call. But don't be fooled: even though the recursive call, `length tail`, is the last piece of the function body, it is not the last thing the function does before returning. It takes the value returned by the recursive call, *adds one to it*, and returns that. So the recursive call in that function is *not* a tail call. With some effort it can be rewritten using tail calls, like this:

```
fun length thelist =
  let
    fun len (nil,sofar) = sofar
    |   len (head::tail,sofar) = len (tail,sofar+1);
  in
    len (thelist,0)
  end;
```

This is similar to the fast `reverse` function. Both use a helper function that takes an extra parameter. This extra parameter is called an *accumulating parameter*, because on each recursive call it accumulates a little more of the solution. For the `reverse` function, the accumulating parameter is the reverse of that part of the list seen so far, and progress is made by consing one more element onto it. For the `length` function, the accumulating parameter is the length of that part of the list seen so far, and progress is made by adding one to it.

Converting functions to a form that uses tail calls often involves adding parameters like this. It is an exercise that gets easier with practice. It is always possible to restructure a program to make it use tail calls, but it is not always worth doing. It can make the program much more difficult to understand and maintain. The tail-call cost model spells out the advantages, but as always it is up to the programmer's discretion to decide whether these advantages outweigh the disadvantages.

A language system may be able to perform the optimization for any tail call, not just recursive ones. Tail-call optimization is especially important for functional languages, since these languages encourage a style of programming that makes heavy use of function calls and recursion. But tail-call optimization is not just for functional languages. Many modern imperative language systems perform some kind of tail-call optimization, including most C and C++ systems.[2]

Many Prolog systems implement a kind of tail-call optimization. For example, the faster Prolog implementation of `reverse` on page 454 can be compiled to a form that makes tail calls, both where `reverse` calls `rev` and where `rev` calls itself. Although it is easy to see the similarity between ML and Prolog tail-call optimization in the last example, the Prolog tail call can be harder to identify. The general idea is the same: a call is a tail call if it is the very last thing the predicate does. In Prolog, therefore, only the last condition in a rule can be a tail call. But because of Prolog's backtracking, the last condition in a rule is not always a tail call. In this example, the condition `r(X)` is not (necessarily) a tail call:

```
p :- q(X), r(X).
```

Why might `r(X)` not be a tail call here? Because it might not be the very last thing this rule for predicate `p` does. If `r(X)` fails for one binding, Prolog may need to backtrack into the condition `q(X)` to find another binding for `X`. In general, when execution reaches the last condition in a rule for some predicate, *and if there is no possibility of backtracking within that rule*, then a Prolog compiler can apply a kind of tail-call optimization.

2. At least one popular language is rarely, if ever, implemented with tail-call optimization: Java. At the time of this writing, tail-call optimization is not part of the popular implementations of the Java virtual machine.

21.4 A Cost Model for Prolog Search

Chapter 20 showed how a Prolog program is executed. To summarize, a Prolog system

- works on goal terms from left to right;
- tries rules from the database in order, trying to unify the head of each rule with the current goal term; and
- backtracks on failure—there may be more than one rule whose head unifies with a given goal term, and the system tries as many as necessary.

Declaratively, a Prolog program is a logical specification of a solution. It describes what should be computed, but not how. Yet in practice, there are many different and *logically* equivalent ways of specifying a solution, which are not at all equivalent in efficiency. Some are solved faster by the Prolog system, some slower, and some are never solved. The Prolog programmer needs a cost model to guide him or her toward an efficient solution. Knowledge of how a Prolog system searches for solutions provides that model.

This cost model was studied thoroughly in Chapter 20, so not much more will be said about it here. It is difficult in any case to reduce it to simple efficiency guidelines. In most cases, the best order for the conditions in a rule, or for the clauses in a program, depends on the underlying database of facts and on the expected form of the query (see Exercise 9).

Here is one rough efficiency guideline that can be taken from Prolog's search strategy: *restrict early*. Stop searching useless alternatives as soon as possible. For example, consider this rule:

```
grandfather(X,Y) :-
  parent(X,Z),
  parent(Z,Y),
  male(X).
```

A Prolog system works on the terms from left to right, so this rule can be thought of as three steps, one for each term.

1. Find a binding for `X` and for `Z` such that parent`(X,Z)`; then
2. using those bindings, find a binding for `Y` such that parent`(Z,Y)`; and finally
3. using those bindings, check that `male(X)`.

Clearly, if the `X` from step 1 is not male, the work of step 2 will be wasted. It is a useless alternative, and exploration of it should stop as soon as possible. Assuming that step 1 instantiates X and Z, which seems likely, step 3 is just a restriction—it just fails on some of the bindings generated by the previous steps. The Prolog cost model guides the programmer toward solutions that restrict early. In this case, a more efficient order would be to exchange steps 2 and 3, like this:

```
grandfather(X,Y) :-
  parent(X,Z),
  male(X),
  parent(Z,Y).
```

Similarly, the order of rules in the database can influence the efficiency of a Prolog program.

Prolog programmers also make critical use of the cost model in deciding where to use the *cut* operation. The cut operation won't be covered here, but it is an important practical tool for improving program efficiency by eliminating unnecessary backtracking.

21.5 A Cost Model for Arrays

Many languages support multidimensional arrays. This, for example, is a declaration of a two-dimensional array in C:

```
int a[1000][1000];
```

For each pair of indexes i and j with $0 \le$ i < 1000 and $0 \le$ j < 1000, there is one array element a[i][j], making a million elements in all. (This section will assume for simplicity that array indexes are consecutive integers starting from zero, as in C, Java, and ML.)

Two C functions do the same thing: they sum up all the elements in an array of that type.

```
int addup1(int a[1000][1000]) {
  int total = 0;
  int i = 0;
  while (i < 1000) {
    int j = 0;
    while (j < 1000) {
      total += a[i][j];
      j++;
    }
    i++;
  }
  return total;
}
```

```
int addup2(int a[1000][1000]) {
  int total = 0;
  int j = 0;
  while (j < 1000) {
    int i = 0;
    while (i < 1000) {
      total += a[i][j];
      i++;
    }
    j++;
  }
  return total;
}
```

These two functions do the same thing. The only difference is the order in which the array elements are accessed. The `addup1` function counts `i` up from zero in the outer loop and counts `j` up from zero in the inner loop. So it adds up all the elements `a[0][0]` through `a[0][999]`, then moves on to all the elements `a[1][0]` through `a[1][999]`, and so on. The `addup2` function varies `j` in the outer loop and `i` in the inner loop. So it adds up all the elements `a[0][0]` through `a[999][0]`, then moves on to all the elements `a[0][1]` through `a[999][1]`, and so on. Although these pieces of code look almost identical, perform the same number of steps, and compute the same results, there is a significant difference in their speed (with most C language systems). To understand why, you have to understand how arrays are represented in memory.

Chapter 14 treated computer memory as a sequence of memory words with consecutive integer addresses. This is a reasonable approximation to the way memory hardware works. The array-like organization of memory hardware makes it easy to handle one-dimensional arrays in high-level languages. The only complication is that the size of the array elements may not be the same as the hardware's natural size for addressable units of memory. For example, consider a one-dimensional array *A* of *n* elements, where each element requires *size* words. The simplest approach, and by far the most common, is simply to allocate all *n* elements, one after the other, in a single block of $n \times size$ words. The address to use for an array reference *A*[*i*] is computed as $base + i \times size$, where *base* is the starting address of the block allocated for array *A*.

There is one important additional observation to make about memory hardware: it is usually optimized for sequential accesses. That is, when software accesses the memory word at address *i*, the hardware anticipates in various ways that the word at address *i*+1 will soon be called for too. Because consecutive array elements are placed at consecutive addresses, and because memory hardware is optimized for sequential access, there is a simple cost model for arrays: *accessing array elements sequentially is faster than accessing them non-sequentially*. This cost model guides programmers toward solutions that visit array elements in order. For one-dimensional arrays, such solutions are natural. Indeed, they are hard to avoid. When accessing all the elements of an array, you would have to go out of your way to visit array elements in a non-sequential order. But for higher-dimensional arrays the matter is not quite so simple.

Let's consider the case of two-dimensional arrays. It is common to visualize a two-dimensional array as a grid, with an element $A[i][j]$ stored at row i, column j. For example, a two-dimensional array of elements $A[i][j]$ with $0 \le i < 3$ and $0 \le j < 4$ can be visualized as a 3-by-4 grid like this:

	column 0	*column 1*	*column 2*	*column 3*
row 0	0,0	0,1	0,2	0,3
row 1	1,0	1,1	1,2	1,3
row 2	2,0	2,1	2,2	2,3

Although this arrangement is fairly standard, it is by no means universal. In computer graphics, for example, an image is often treated as a two-dimensional array of pixels $A[x][y]$, where the first index is the x-coordinate (the column) and the second index is the y-coordinate (the row). This confusion is unfortunate, since the words *row* and *column* lend such a nice visual intuition to two-dimensional arrays. They are used here in the sense of the standard arrangement illustrated above. An m-by-n array A is a collection of elements $A[i][j]$ with $0 \le i < m$ and $0 \le j < n$. A *row* of A is the collection of all elements $A[i][j]$ for some fixed i, and a *column* is the collection of all elements $A[i][j]$ for some fixed j.

The problem here is to represent an m-by-n array of elements, where each element requires *size* words. One approach is to store the whole first row in order, followed by the whole second row, and so on. This is called *row-major order*. Consider the 3-by-4 array from the illustration above. In row-major order, the elements would be placed in memory like this:

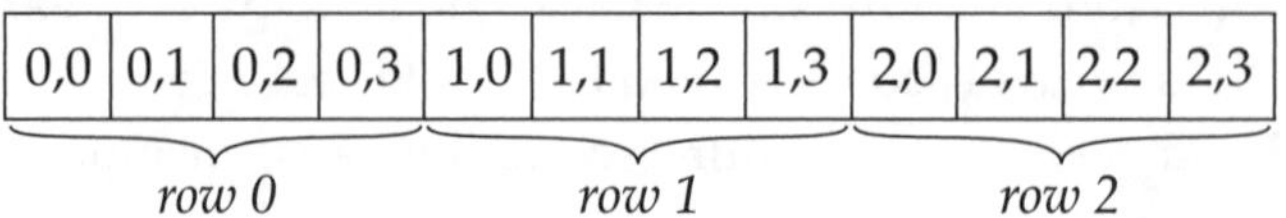

In general, if array A is an m-by-n array of elements, each of which requires *size* words, this representation uses a single block of $m \times n \times size$ words. The address to use for an array reference $A[i][j]$ is $base+(i\times n\times size)+(j\times size)$, where *base* is the starting address of the array's block of memory.

Another array organization is *column-major order*, which places the whole first column in memory, followed by the whole second column, and so on. Continuing the previous example, using column-major order, the elements in the array would be placed in memory like this:

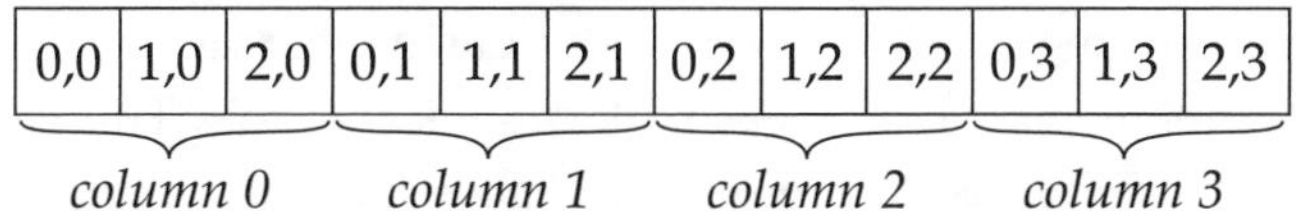

In general, if array A is an m-by-n array of elements, each of which requires *size* words, this representation uses, as before, a single block of $m \times n \times size$ words. However, the address to use for an array reference $A[i][j]$ is computed differently. It is $base+(i\times size)+(j\times m\times size)$, where *base* is the starting address of the array's block of memory.

Now let's return to the question that started this section: which is faster, `addup1` or `addup2`? The `addup1` function adds up the whole first row, then the whole second row, and so forth. The `addup2` function proceeds by columns instead. In C, arrays are allocated in row-major order. So `addup1` is faster, since it accesses the elements in the same order in which they are allocated in memory. Memory hardware is optimized for sequential access, and `addup1` takes advantage of that. The cost model for two-dimensional arrays is the same as before: *accessing array elements sequentially is faster than accessing them non-sequentially*. This cost model guides programmers toward solutions that visit array elements in the same order in which they are allocated in memory. To do this, a programmer must know whether the language system allocates arrays in row-major or column-major order.

Languages vary in how much of the representation of arrays they expose to the programmer. The C language exposes the representation through pointer arithmetic. A pointer variable `p` can hold the address of an array element `a[i][j]`, in which case `p+1` is the address of the element `a[i][j+1]` (or `a[i+1][0]` if `j` is the last index in the row). The C language specifies row-major order. It is not up to the implementation. Fortran exposes the representation less dramatically, but it is still possible to write Fortran code that depends for correctness on the array representation. The Fortran language specifies column-major order. (It is one of the few languages to do so.) Ada, by contrast, hides the array representation thoroughly. A programmer can see only that an array *A* behaves like a collection of separate variables, one *A*[*i*][*j*] for each pair of values *i* and *j*. A program cannot depend for correctness on how these values are stored in memory. An implementation of such a language could conceivably use some completely different representation for arrays. But even with a language that hides the implementation details and presents arrays as an abstract data type, programmers still know and use the appropriate cost model, favoring sequential access whenever possible. Ada language systems generally use row-major order, although they are not required to do so.

You have seen only two ways of allocating two-dimensional arrays. There are others. A common strategy is to treat a two-dimensional array as an array of pointers to one-dimensional arrays, each allocated separately. This can still be done either by rows or by columns. This illustration shows it done by rows:

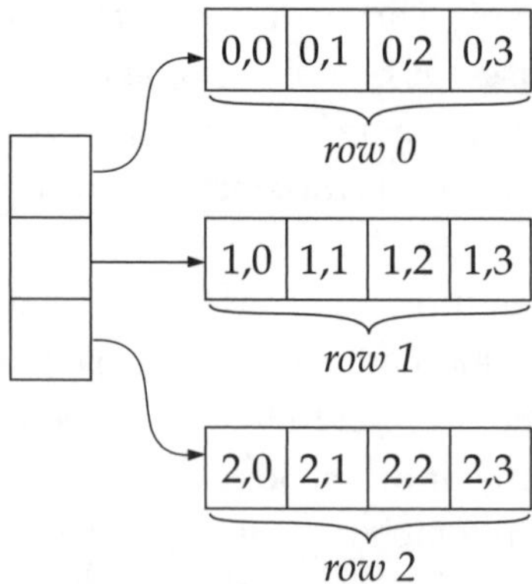

In general, if array *A* is an *m*-by-*n* array of elements, each of which requires *size* words, this representation uses a single block of *m* pointers plus *m* separate blocks of *n*×*size* words. The address to use for an array reference *A*[*i*][*j*] is computed by first finding *B* = *A*[*i*], the base of the *i*th row, using conventional one-dimensional array indexing and then finding *B*[*j*], again using conventional one-dimensional array indexing. This is the way multidimensional arrays are handled in Java. Allocating arrays this way imposes some inefficiencies, but gains greater flexibility. For example, the rows can be different sizes, and unused rows can be left unallocated. The cost model for this organization still guides the programmer toward solutions that operate sequentially across rows.

All the approaches for array allocation can be generalized for arrays of higher dimensions as well. There are two natural ways to visit all the elements of an *n*-dimensional array. You can vary the rightmost subscripts fastest, like this:

for each i_0
  for each i_1
    . . .
      for each i_{n-2}
        for each i_{n-1}
          access $A[i_0][i_1] \ldots [i_{n-2}][i_{n-1}]$

Or you can vary the leftmost subscripts fastest, like this:

for each i_{n-2}
  for each i_{n-1}
    . . .
      for each i_1
        for each i_0
          access $A[i_0][i_1] \ldots [i_{n-2}][i_{n-1}]$

When the array elements are stored in a single block, in the first order given above, that is row-major order. (Row-major order is also called *odometer order*, which makes more sense for higher-dimensional arrays.) When the array elements are stored in a single block, in the second order given above, that is column-major order. An n-dimensional array can also be implemented as a one-dimensional array of pointers to n-1 dimensional arrays. In any event, the same basic cost model still applies: experienced programmers try to access array elements in the order in which they are stored in memory.

21.6 Spurious Cost Models

Here is a C program that calls a function `max` 100,000,000 times:

```
int max(int i, int j) {
  return i>j?i:j;
}

int main() {
  int i,j;
  double sum = 0.0;
  for (i=0; i<10000; i++) {
    for (j=0; j<10000; j++) {
      sum += max(i,j);
    }
  }
  printf("%d\n", sum);
}
```

If the line that makes the function call, `sum += max(i,j)`, is replaced with a direct computation, `sum += (i>j?i:j)`, how much faster will the program be?

The proposed change replaces a function call with the body of the called function (an optimization called *inlining*). Sometimes this is a good idea, because of the overhead involved in making a function call. The language system must jump to the called function and set up an activation record for it. When the function returns, it must clean up the activation record and return to the caller. For functions of any significant length this overhead is much smaller than the cost of executing the function body, and so not worth worrying about. But a call of a really simple function like `max` might spend more time on overhead than it does actually executing the function body. Since this program does almost nothing but call `max` over and over, it might well be something like twice as fast with the proposed change.

This is a little cost model for function calls that many programmers carry around. It guides them toward solutions that use inline code instead of function calls for short functions. (In C it also guides programmers toward solutions that use macros instead of function calls.) It is just another piece of the cost-model knowledge that experienced programmers use.

Unfortunately, this particular cost model is often wrong, because *any respectable C compiler can perform inlining automatically.* A C compiler might have various optimization options; on Unix systems, the current version of the Gnu C compiler does inlining only with the `-O3` optimization flag set. But most modern C compilers are capable of making this optimization automatically. With this compiler optimization turned on, this program runs at exactly the same speed whether the `max` function is inlined manually or by the compiler.

This is an issue that arises in many languages, not just C. In general, it is a mistake to clutter up a program with manually inlined copies of function bodies. It makes the program harder to read and maintain, without making it any faster after automatic optimization. It is certainly true that the overhead for calls of a simple function is significant. But since such calls may not actually be performed in the code produced by an optimizing compiler, it rarely makes sense to worry about this overhead. To put it another way, it is not usually a good idea to let this cost model guide your implementation choices.

This shows how some cost models change over time. For perhaps the first 10 years of C programming, compilers smart enough to do a good job of automatic inlining were not generally available. In those days it made sense for C programmers to manually inline simple functions (in performance-critical code). Today it is usually a mistake, not because the language has changed, but because improved language systems are widely available.

Another example of how cost models can change over time is the C (and C++) keyword `register`. This can appear in declarations for activation-specific variables, like this:

```
register int i;
```

The `register` keyword hints to the C compiler that the variable in question will be heavily used. Registers are special extra-fast pieces of computer memory. Different architectures have different numbers of registers, but the number is always very limited, so it makes sense to keep only the most heavily used variables in registers. The `register` keyword is a suggestion that the variable being declared should be one of them.

The cost model programmers use with the `register` keyword is usually rather vague. They know that variables in registers can be read and written much faster and that only a small number of variables can be in registers. Guided by this model, programmers try to identify a few variables that would benefit the most from being stored in registers and mark them with the `register` declaration. This was once a valuable way of improving the performance of C programs. But in modern language systems, it is just a waste of effort. Any respectable C compiler is capable of doing just as good a job of using the machine's registers without such hints.

The cost model for arrays discussed in the previous section may be heading in the same direction. It is a bit beyond the reach of ordinary C compilers today, but advanced compilers can automatically reorganize both the code and the array layout to take best advantage of the underlying memory architecture.

21.7 Conclusion

Cost models lie in the gray area between programming-language definition and language-system implementation. All the cost models in this chapter help programmers to write more efficient programs by using inside knowledge of how a language is implemented. These implementation details—cons cells, tail-call optimization, search strategy in Prolog, array layout, and others—are an important part of a competent programmer's expertise, whether or not they are an official part of a programming-language definition. Even for the more declarative languages, programmers use cost models to help choose implementations that will have good performance.

Some cost models are language-system specific. Those that depend on whether the language system performs (or does not perform) a particular optimization are good examples. These cost models are not very robust. That is not to say you should never use such cost models—just that you should be aware of their limitations. It is a shame to spend a lot of effort improving the performance of a piece of code, and uglifying it in the process, only to find that a better compiler could have made the work unnecessary.

Other cost models are not language-system specific, though they are still language specific. For example, the cons-cell cost model can be relied on for all Lisp systems. Lisp would not be Lisp without cons cells. It can be safely relied on for ML and Prolog as well. The Scheme language requires language systems to implement the tail-call optimization, so the tail-call cost model is reliable for Scheme. It is fairly safe to rely on it for all functional languages, since it is too important an optimization for any respectable functional-language compiler to omit. All these cost models are quite robust.

To carry this to its logical conclusion, the strongest possible cost models would be completely language independent. Such cost models could be relied on for all language systems and all languages. No such cost models have been mentioned. Do they exist? Yes, but such super-robust cost models do not belong to the study of programming languages; they belong to the study of algorithms. The design and analysis of algorithms is where computer science rises above both language and system. Language-based cost models are an important part of a programmer's expertise, but remember, nothing is as important as choosing an appropriate algorithm in the first place.

Exercises

Exercise 1 Figure out what the following mystery predicate does, then reimplement it as efficiently as possible.

```
riddle(X,_) :-
  length(X,XL),
  XL = 0.

riddle(_,Y) :-
  length(Y,YL),
  YL = 0.
```

Exercise 2 Figure out what the following mystery predicate does, then reimplement it without using `append`.

```
mystery(Item,List) :-
  append(_,[Item],List).
```

Exercise 3 Figure out what the following mystery predicate does, then reimplement it without using append.

```
enigma(List1,N,List2) :-
  length(Dummy,N),
  append(List2,Dummy,List1).
```

Exercise 4 Here is a factorial predicate in Prolog:

```
xfactorial(1,1).
xfactorial(N,FN) :-
  NextN is N-1,
  xfactorial(NextN,FNextN),
  FN is FNextN * N.
```

Rewrite it to make it tail recursive.

Exercise 5 Rewrite the halve function from Chapter 7 in tail-recursive form.

Exercise 6 The following ML function prefixCopy x n returns a list equal to x, in which the first n cons cells of the list are copies, while all the others are shared. (When n >= length(x), it returns a full copy of x.)

```
fun prefixCopy x 0 = x
|   prefixCopy nil _ = nil
|   prefixCopy (head::tail) n =
      head::(prefixCopy tail (n-1));
```

Rewrite this to make it tail recursive. Which implementation do you think is more efficient, and why?

Exercise 7 The problem described in Chapter 12, section 12.8, can restrict the use of tail-call optimization. Explain how, and give an example.

Exercise 8 For each of the following, give a formula for computing the address to use for the array reference. Assume that the array A is allocated as a single block at address *base*, and let *size* be the size of an individual array element.

a. The element $A[i]$, where $0 \le i < n$.
b. The element $A[i]$, where $1 \le i \le n$.
c. The element $A[i][j]$, where $1 \le i \le m$ and $1 \le j \le n$, and where the array is allocated in row-major order.
d. The element $A[i][j][k]$, where $0 \le i < m$, $0 \le j < n$, and $0 \le k < p$, and where the array is allocated in column-major order.

Exercise 9 In many cases, the most efficient order for the conditions in a Prolog rule cannot be determined just by looking at the rule. It depends on other parts of the program. Consider these two grandfather predicates:

```
grandfather1(X,Y) :-
  parent(X,Z),
  male(X),
  parent(Z,Y).

grandfather2(X,Y) :-
  male(X),
  parent(X,Z),
  parent(Z,Y).
```

a. Suppose the database has many `parent` facts but only a few `male` facts. Which grandfather predicate would you prefer, and why?
b. Suppose the database has many `male` facts but only a few `parent` facts. Which grandfather predicate would you prefer, and why?
c. Consider the following facts: `male(joe)`, `male(bob)`, `parent(joe,bob)`, and `parent(bob,alice)`. Give an order of these facts for which the query `grandfather1(X,Y)` finds the solution without backtracking, while `grandfather2(X,Y)` must backtrack. Give a different order for which the query `grandfather1(X,Y)` must backtrack, while `grandfather2(X,Y)` finds the solution without backtracking. In each case, explain the steps taken by the Prolog system to find the solution, showing where backtracking occurs.

Chapter 22 A Third Look at Prolog

22.1 Introduction

You have made it this far in Prolog without any numerical computation. That is as it should be, since it is the manipulation of terms, not numbers, that is central to Prolog. However, Prolog programs can perform numerical computation when they need to. This chapter will show how.

Then it will turn to the kind of problem Prolog is best for: problem space search. A Prolog program can be a logical specification of a problem domain, and the query can be a request for a solution to a problem in that domain. Taking advantage of Prolog's proof-tree search lets you write simple solutions for complicated problems.

This is also the last chapter on Prolog, so the conclusion gives an overview of the parts of Prolog that were skipped.

22.2 Numeric Computation

Terms in Prolog are not evaluated—at least not without special effort. These terms, for example, are all different ways of writing the term `.(1,.(2,.(3,[])))`:

```
.(1,[2,3])
[1 | [2,3]]
[1,2,3]
```

The term is unevaluated in Prolog. It is, without any processing, the representation for the list of the integers 1 through 3. Similarly, these terms are all different ways of writing the term `+(1,*(2,3))`:

```
1+ *(2,3)
+(1,2*3)
(1+(2*3))
1+2*3
```

Again, the term is unevaluated in Prolog. It is not the same as the constant term `7`. Predefined predicates can be used to evaluate terms like that one, to perform numerical computation when necessary.

Numeric Evaluation

The predefined predicate `is` can be used to evaluate terms.

```
?- X is 1+2*3.

X = 7

Yes
```

As you can see from that example, the `is` predicate is an operator. The term `is(X,1+2*3)` is usually written using the operator notation, as `X is 1+2*3`. When the Prolog system tries to solve an `is` goal, it evaluates the second parameter and unifies the result with the first parameter.

For most uses, the first parameter of `is` is a variable, which gets bound to the result of the evaluation of the second parameter. The second parameter must be fully instantiated (it can't have any unbound variables in it). Consider these three queries:

```
?- Y=X+2, X=1.

Y = 1+2
X = 1

Yes
?- Y is X+2, X=1.
ERROR: Arguments are not sufficiently instantiated
?- X=1, Y is X+2.
```

```
X = 1
Y = 3

Yes
```

The first query is solved without trouble. But it does not evaluate the expression `1+2`, because it uses `=` instead of `is`. In the second query the `=` is changed to `is`, but now there is another problem: the value of `X` is not known when the goal `Y is X+2` is attempted. All variables in the term must be bound before the term is evaluated. In the third query the order of the two goals is changed. Now it first binds `X` to 1, and then attempts the goal `Y is X+2`. That works as expected, binding `Y` to `3`.

The predicates used in the expression being evaluated must be *evaluable predicates*. The evaluable predicates include the binary numeric operators `+`, `-`, `*`, and `/` and the unary numeric operator `-`, with the usual precedence and associativity. A collection of arithmetic functions is also available as evaluable predicates, like `abs(X)` (the absolute value of X) and `sqrt(X)` (the square root of X). You will not be using anything beyond the basic arithmetic operators.

Recall that Prolog constant terms include both integers and real numbers. Many operators and other evaluable predicates are defined for both types. This can make it seem as if there is only one numeric type, where an integer is merely a real number that happens to have a zero fractional part:

```
?- X is 1/2.

X = 0.5

Yes
?- X is 1.0/2.0.

X = 0.5

Yes
?- X is 2/1.

X = 2

Yes
?- X is 2.0/1.0.

X = 2

Yes
```

In these examples, it almost looks like there is only one numeric type—like `2` and `2.0` are actually two different ways of writing the same constant. But it is not so. The constants `2` and `2.0` do not unify (so the goal `2=2.0` would fail), which shows that they are not the same in Prolog's eyes. Prolog is not statically type checked, but is dynamically type checked: a Prolog language system is aware of the type of each value at runtime. The operators just mentioned, and many of the other evaluable predicates, are overloaded for various combinations of real and integer operands. The overloading is resolved at runtime, according to the dynamic types of the operands.[1]

Numeric Comparisons

There are six special operators for comparing numeric values: `<`, `>`, `=<`, `>=`, `=:=` (equality), and `=\=` (inequality). When the Prolog system tries to solve one of these goals, it evaluates both parameters and compares the results numerically. Both parameters, therefore, must be fully instantiated.

```
?- 1+2 < 1*2.

No
?- 1<2.

Yes
?- 1+2>=1+3.

No
?- X is 1-3, Y is 0-2, X =:= Y.

X = -2
Y = -2

Yes
```

Equality comparisons in Prolog can be a little confusing, since there are several different but related operators. The three you have seen are

- `is`: The goal `X is Y` evaluates `Y` and unifies the result with `X`. This is the correct operator to use when you want to evaluate an expression and bind a (formerly unbound) variable to its value. The second operand must be fully

---

1. This is another area where different implementations of Prolog sometimes work very differently. Many implementations, including the current version of SWI-Prolog, automatically convert real results to integers when the fractional part is zero, though this is not part of the ISO standard. For example, the goal `X is 1.0` binds `X` to the integer 1 in these implementations, not to the real number 1.0. This can produce odd results. For example, the goal `1.0 is 1.0` fails in SWI-Prolog.

instantiated; the goal `X is 1+Y` generates a runtime error when `Y` is unbound. The goal `3 is 1+2` succeeds, but the goal `1+2 is 3` fails.

- `=`: The goal `X=Y` unifies `X` and `Y`. Unification does not evaluate numeric expressions at all, but only pays attention to term structure. The goal `1+X=1+2` succeeds with the substitution {X?2}. The goal `3=1+2` fails, as does `1+2=3`, since `1+2` and `3` are distinct terms that do not unify.
- `=:=`: The goal `X=:=Y` evaluates both `X` and `Y` and succeeds if and only if they have the same value. Both the goals `3=:=1+2` and `1+2=:=3` succeed. Both operands must be fully instantiated.

As if that were not enough, there are at least two more variations—the == operator and a predicate called `unify_with_occurs_check`. But you will not be needing them. Be careful also of the odd form of =<: it is easy to make the mistake of typing <= instead, which is not defined in Prolog.

Examples

With numeric evaluation and numeric comparisons, you can write some numeric predicates in Prolog. Here, for example, is an implementation of the predefined `length` predicate:

```
mylength([],0).
mylength([_|Tail], Len) :-
  mylength(Tail, TailLen),
  Len is TailLen + 1.
```

(This actually does not work exactly like the predefined `length` predicate in cases where the first parameter is not fully instantiated. But it is close.) Here it is at work:

```
?- mylength([1,2,3,4,5],X).

X = 5

Yes
?- mylength([a,b,c],X).

X = 3

Yes
?- mylength(X,3).

X = [_G266, _G269, _G272]

Yes
```

What would happen if = were used in place of is in the mylength predicate? It would not evaluate the length of the list, but instead would build an expression for the length of the list.

```
?- mylength([1,2,3,4,5],X).

X = 0+1+1+1+1+1

Yes
```

That is clearly not what a length predicate should do!

The next example computes the sum of a list of numbers. This is similar to the mylength predicate:

```
sum([],0).
sum([Head|Tail],X) :-
  sum(Tail,TailSum),
  X is Head + TailSum.
```

Here is the sum predicate in action:

```
?- sum([1,2,3],X).

X = 6

Yes
?- sum([1,2.5,3],X).

X = 6.5

Yes
```

Notice that the list being summed can contain a mixture of integer and real values. It must, however, be fully instantiated. The goal sum([1,2,X],6) would cause a runtime error.

This next example computes the greatest common divisor of two integers using Euclid's algorithm.

```
gcd(X,Y,Z) :-
  X =:= Y,
  Z is X.
gcd(X,Y,Denom) :-
  X < Y,
  NewY is Y - X,
  gcd(X,NewY,Denom).
gcd(X,Y,Denom) :-
  X > Y,
```

```
    NewX is X - Y,
    gcd(NewX,Y,Denom).
```

These three clauses handle the computation in three cases: `X =:= Y`, `X < Y`, and `X > Y`. The first clause says that any number is its own GCD. You might be tempted to write the first clause as the much simpler fact `gcd(X,X,X)`, but that would compare the first and second parameters by unification rather than numerically, resulting in some strange behavior. For example, `gcd(fred,fred,fred)` would succeed, but `gcd(1+2,2+1,X)` would fail. Here is the `gcd` predicate at work:

```
?- gcd(5,5,X).

X = 5

Yes
?- gcd(12,21,X).

X = 3

Yes
?- gcd(91,105,X).

X = 7

Yes
?- gcd(91,X,7).
ERROR: Arguments are not sufficiently instantiated
```

As the last test shows, the predicate requires the first two parameters to be fully instantiated. It cannot be used to solve for some `X` such that the greatest common denominator of 91 and `X` is 7.

A final numeric example: here is a predicate for computing the factorial function.

```
fact(X,1) :-
  X =:= 1.
fact(X,Fact) :-
  X > 1,
  NewX is X - 1,
  fact(NewX,NF),
  Fact is X * NF.
```

This predicate requires the first parameter to be fully instantiated. The first clause says that the factorial of 1 is 1. The second says how to compute the factorial of any number greater than 1. Here is the `fact` predicate at work:

```
?- fact(5,X).

X = 120

Yes
?- fact(20,X).

X = 2.4329e+018

Yes
?- fact(-2,X).

No
```

The factorial for negative numbers or for zero was not defined, so the goal `fact(-2,X)` fails.

22.3 Problem Space Search

Although Prolog can handle numeric computation, it does not really shine on such problems. As seen in Chapter 19, Prolog is particularly well suited to problems that involve searching in a logically defined space of possible solutions. This section will look at some more problems of that kind.

The Knapsack Problem

Imagine that you are packing for a camping trip. You go to your pantry and find that it contains the following items:

Item	Weight in Kilograms	Calories
bread	4	9,200
pasta	2	4,600
peanut butter	1	6,700
baby food	3	6,900

Your knapsack for food can hold 4 kilograms. The items cannot be divided; each is packaged so that you must bring it all or bring none of it. Which items should you bring to maximize the number of calories you are carrying?

This is an instance of the *knapsack problem*, a famous and famously difficult allocation problem. Greedy methods do not work on the knapsack problem. For example, if you try fill the knapsack by taking the highest-calorie items first, you get bread only: not the best solution at 9,200 calories. If you try to fill the knapsack by taking the lowest-weight items first, that fails too: you get peanut butter and pasta at 11,300 calories, also not the best solution. (The best solution, though perhaps not the most appetizing, is peanut butter and baby food at 13,600 calories.) No algorithm is known that runs significantly faster than a search through all possible combinations of the items.[2]

That is good news for us, since searching is what Prolog does best. To solve the problem, represent each food item as a term `food(N,W,C)`, where `N` is the food name, `W` is its weight, and `C` is the number of calories. The contents of the pantry can then be represented by a list of food terms:

```
[food(bread,4,9200),
 food(pasta,2,4600),
 food(peanutButter,1,6700),
 food(babyFood,3,6900)]
```

The same representation, a list of `food` terms, can be used for the contents of the knapsack. We will need predicates that compute the total weight and total number of calories in a given knapsack:

```
/*
   weight(L,N) takes a list L of food terms, each
   of the form food(Name,Weight,Calories). We
   unify N with the sum of all the Weights.
*/
weight([],0).
weight([food(_,W,_) | Rest], X) :-
  weight(Rest,RestW),
  X is W + RestW.

/*
   calories(L,N) takes a list L of food terms, each
   of the form food(Name,Weight,Calories). We
   unify N with the sum of all the Calories.
*/
calories([],0).
calories([food(_,_,C) | Rest], X) :-
  calories(Rest,RestC),
  X is C + RestC.
```

2. For those who have studied algorithmic complexity, the knapsack problem is NP-complete. An interesting solution using dynamic programming takes time that is polynomial in the maximum weight. This is a pseudo-polynomial time solution, not truly polynomial. Like all known solutions for NP-hard problems, it takes time that is exponential in the number of bits used to represent the problem instance.

A knapsack will hold a subset of the contents of the pantry. In the list representation, a knapsack will be a subsequence of the pantry list—a copy of the list with zero or more elements omitted. Here is a predicate that defines this subsequence property for lists:

```
/*
  subseq(X,Y) succeeds when list X is the same as
  list Y, but with zero or more elements omitted.
  This can be used with any pattern of instantiations.
*/
subseq([],[]).
subseq([Item | RestX], [Item | RestY]) :-
  subseq(RestX,RestY).
subseq(X, [_ | RestY]) :-
  subseq(X,RestY).
```

The first clause is the base case: the empty list is a subsequence of itself. The second and third clauses are the recursive cases. Each element of the original list either is (second clause) or is not (third clause) included in the subsequence. Here is a demonstration of `subseq` in action:

```
?- subseq([1,3],[1,2,3,4]).

Yes
?- subseq(X,[1,2,3]).

X = [1, 2, 3] ;

X = [1, 2] ;

X = [1, 3] ;

X = [1] ;

X = [2, 3] ;

X = [2] ;

X = [3] ;

X = [] ;

No
```

As you can see, `subseq` can do more than just test whether one list is a subsequence of another; it can *generate* subsequences of a list, which is how it will be used in solving the knapsack problem. All possible knapsacks (subsequences of the pantry list) will be generated and then examined.

This predicate tests for the existence of a solution that achieves at least a specified number of calories:

```
/*
  knapsackDecision(Pantry,Capacity,Goal,Knapsack)
  takes a list Pantry of food terms, a positive number
  Capacity, and a positive number Goal. We unify
  Knapsack with a subsequence of Pantry representing
  a knapsack with total calories >= Goal, subject to
  the constraint that the total weight is =< Capacity.
*/
knapsackDecision(Pantry,Capacity,Goal,Knapsack) :-
  subseq(Knapsack,Pantry),
  weight(Knapsack,Weight),
  Weight =< Capacity,
  calories(Knapsack,Calories),
  Calories >= Goal.
```

This predicate does not necessarily find the optimal solution—more on that in a moment—but it does say whether or not there is a solution that meets or exceeds the goal, and it does find such a solution. This test asks it whether there is a solution with at least 10,000 calories:

```
?- knapsackDecision(
|    [food(bread,4,9200),
|     food(pasta,2,4600),
|     food(peanutButter,1,6700),
|     food(babyFood,3,6900)],
|    4,
|    10000,
|    X).

X = [food(pasta, 2, 4600), food(peanutButter, 1, 6700)]

Yes
```

It found a solution with that property. To actually find the knapsack that maximizes the number of calories is a bit more difficult. Let's make use of another predefined Prolog predicate: `findall`.

The `findall` predicate takes three parameters: `findall(X,Goal,L)`. `Goal` is a goal term, and `findall` finds all the ways of proving that goal. The predicate unifies `L` with a list of terms, one for each way of proving `Goal`. The terms in the list `L` are instances of the parameter `X`; for each substitution that makes a provable instance of Goal, the same substitution is applied to X, and the resulting instance of X is added to the list L. For example, if X is a constant, findall just collects a list of Xs whose length is the number of solutions to Goal:

```
?- findall(1,subseq(_,[1,2]),L).

L = [1, 1, 1, 1]

Yes
```

This shows that there are four solutions to subseq(_,[1,2]), but it does not say what they are. To collect all the provable instances of the goal, have the first and second parameters to findall be the same:

```
?- findall(subseq(X,[1,2]),subseq(X,[1,2]),L).

X = _G396
L = [subseq([1, 2], [1, 2]), subseq([1], [1, 2]),
     subseq([2], [1, 2]), subseq([], [1, 2])]

Yes
```

To collect all the Xs such that subseq(X,[1,2]) can be proved—that is, to collect all the subsequences of [1,2]—have the first parameter to findall be just the one variable from the goal term:

```
?- findall(X,subseq(X,[1,2]),L).

X = _G312
L = [[1, 2], [1], [2], []]

Yes
```

That is perhaps the most common way of using findall: the first parameter is a variable, the second parameter is a goal containing that variable, and the final parameter collects a list of all the instantiations of that variable encountered in successful proofs of the goal.

Now back to the knapsack problem. The strategy will be to collect all the legal knapsack arrangements (those within the capacity of the knapsack) in a list by using findall, then to select the one with the greatest number of calories. First, a predicate must be defined that says what a legal knapsack is: a subsequence of the pantry, within the knapsack capacity.

```
/*
  legalKnapsack(Pantry,Capacity,Knapsack) takes a list
  Pantry of food terms and a positive number Capacity.
  We unify Knapsack with a subsequence of Pantry whose
  total weight is =< Capacity.
*/
legalKnapsack(Pantry,Capacity,Knapsack):-
  subseq(Knapsack,Pantry),
  weight(Knapsack,W),
  W =< Capacity.
```

Next there has to be a way to find the entry in a list of knapsacks that has the maximum total number of calories. Here is a predicate `maxCalories` that uses a helper predicate `maxC` to find the element using tail calls:

```
/*
  maxCalories(List,Result) takes a List of lists of
  food terms. We unify Result with an element from the
  list that maximizes the total calories. We use a
  helper predicate maxC that takes four parameters:
  the remaining list of lists of food terms, the best
  list of food terms seen so far, its total calories,
  and the final result.
*/
maxC([],Sofar,_,Sofar).
maxC([First | Rest],_,MC,Result) :-
  calories(First,FirstC),
  MC =< FirstC,
  maxC(Rest,First,FirstC,Result).
maxC([First | Rest],Sofar,MC,Result) :-
  calories(First,FirstC),
  MC > FirstC,
  maxC(Rest,Sofar,MC,Result).
maxCalories([First | Rest],Result) :-
  calories(First,FirstC),
  maxC(Rest,First,FirstC,Result).
```

Now the solution for the knapsack optimization problem is to find all legal knapsacks, then choose one with maximum total calories.

```
/*
  knapsackOptimization(Pantry,Capacity,Knapsack) takes
  a list Pantry of food items and a positive integer
  Capacity. We unify Knapsack with a subsequence of
  Pantry representing a knapsack of maximum total
  calories, subject to the constraint that the total
  weight is =< Capacity.
*/
```

```
knapsackOptimization(Pantry,Capacity,Knapsack) :-
  findall(K,legalKnapsack(Pantry,Capacity,K),L),
  maxCalories(L,Knapsack).
```

Here is a demonstration of `knapsackOptimization`:

```
?- knapsackOptimization(
|     [food(bread,4,9200),
|      food(pasta,2,4600),
|      food(peanutButter,1,6700),
|      food(babyFood,3,6900)],
|     4,
|     Knapsack).

Knapsack = [food(peanutButter, 1, 6700),
             food(babyFood, 3, 6900)]

Yes
```

The Eight-Queens Problem

The eight-queens problem is related to the game of chess. But don't worry, you do not need to be a chess player to understand it. You only need to know a few simple facts about the game.

The game of chess is played on a chess board, an 8-by-8 grid. The different game pieces can move from square to square on this board in different ways, but this problem uses only one kind of piece, the queen. A queen can move any number of spaces vertically, horizontally, or diagonally. Two queens have each other *in check* when they are in the same row, the same column, or the same diagonal of the board, so that they could move to each other's squares.

That's all the background information you need. The eight-queens problem is this: how can eight queens be placed on an empty chess board, so that no queen has any other queen in check?

To solve this problem with Prolog, you first need a way to use terms to represent configurations of queens on the chess board. If the rows and columns of the chess board are numbered from one to eight, then each queen on the chess board can be represented by its two coordinates. A new compound term could be used for this, something like `queen(2,5)` to represent a queen in column 2, row 5. This would be more readable (and less trouble to type) if something more compact were used. There will be nothing but queens on the board—no `king(2,5)` or `pawn(2,5)`—so all that is really needed is the coordinates themselves. A queen in column 2, row 5, can be represented with just the term `2/5`. Of course, these terms will never be evaluated numerically; / is not being used as an evaluable predicate, but just as a handy constructor for a term. Each queen will be represented by a term of that `X/Y` form, and a configuration of queens on the chess board will be represented by a list of them. For example, the list `[2/5,3/7,6/1]` represents this configuration:

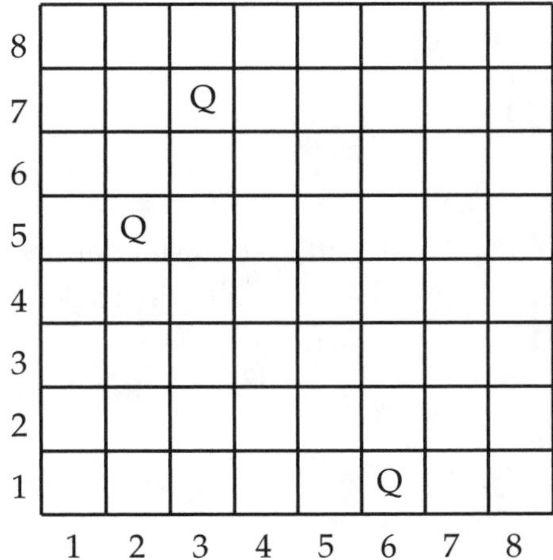

In this configuration, the `2/5` and `6/1` have each other in check.

With this representation it is easy to decide whether a queen `X/Y` holds another queen `X1/Y1` in check. Clearly the answer is yes if they are in the same column (`X=:=X1`) or in the same row (`Y=:=Y1`). If they are in the same diagonal, like `2/5` and `6/1` in the example above, then their horizontal distance from each other must be the same as their vertical distance. This can be expressed in Prolog as `abs(Y1-Y) =:= abs(X1-X)`. The following predicate, `nocheck(X/Y,List)`, will be used. It succeeds if and only if the given queen `X/Y` does not hold in check any of the queens in the `List`.

```
/*
  nocheck(X/Y,L) takes a queen X/Y and a list
  of queens. We succeed if and only if the X/Y
  queen holds none of the others in check.
*/
nocheck(_, []).
nocheck(X/Y, [X1/Y1 | Rest]) :-
  X =\= X1,
  Y =\= Y1,
  abs(Y1-Y) =\= abs(X1-X),
  nocheck(X/Y, Rest).
```

Now a legal placement of queens on the board is one where all the queens are in range (with coordinates between 1 and 8) and no queen holds any other in check.

```
/*
  legal(L) succeeds if L is a legal placement of
  queens: all coordinates in range and no queen
  in check.
*/
legal([]).
legal([X/Y | Rest]) :-
  legal(Rest),
  member(X,[1,2,3,4,5,6,7,8]),
  member(Y,[1,2,3,4,5,6,7,8]),
  nocheck(X/Y, Rest).
```

This predicate can be used with any pattern of instantiation—which means that enough is already written to solve the eight-queens problem. A goal term of the form `legal(X)` finds all legal placements of queens:

```
?- legal(X).

X = [] ;

X = [1/1] ;

X = [1/2] ;

X = [1/3] ;
```

That takes too long, of course. As it is asked for more solutions, it first enumerates all 64 legal placements for one queen, then starts on the legal placements for two queens, and so on. A query like this makes it concentrate right away on solutions for eight queens:

```
?- X = [_,_,_,_,_,_,_,_], legal(X).

X = [8/4, 7/2, 6/7, 5/3, 4/6, 3/8, 2/5, 1/1]

Yes
```

The Prolog system has found the eight-queens configuration shown below:

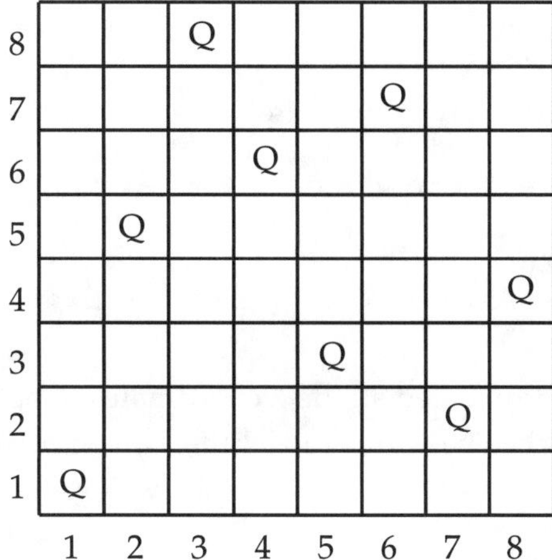

Although the program finds a solution, let's look at some ways to improve it. It is rather slow—on the author's machine it takes about 20 seconds to find a solution. Also, if you ask for more solutions, subsequent answers will be trivial permutations of the first:

```
?- X = [_,_,_,_,_,_,_,_], legal(X).

X = [8/4, 7/2, 6/7, 5/3, 4/6, 3/8, 2/5, 1/1] ;

X = [7/2, 8/4, 6/7, 5/3, 4/6, 3/8, 2/5, 1/1] ;

X = [8/4, 6/7, 7/2, 5/3, 4/6, 3/8, 2/5, 1/1] ;

X = [6/7, 8/4, 7/2, 5/3, 4/6, 3/8, 2/5, 1/1]
```

These first four are all really the same solution. They just list the first few queens in different orders.

An improvement that can be made, to help with the speed and the redundant answers, is to make a more specific query. There are eight queens and eight columns, so there must be one queen in each column. Thus every solution can be written in a fixed order, like this:

```
X = [1/_,2/_,3/_,4/_,5/_,6/_,7/_,8/_]
```

Starting with a query term of that form will be more efficient since it will significantly reduce the number of different configurations explored. By the same token, it will force the system to find answers that really are distinct. So let's use this predicate to start the search:

```
/*
  eightqueens(X) succeeds if X is a legal
  placement of eight queens, listed in order
  of their X coordinates.
*/
eightqueens(X) :-
  X = [1/_,2/_,3/_,4/_,5/_,6/_,7/_,8/_],
  legal(X).
```

Since the query has already forced all the `X` coordinates to be in range and distinct, the other two predicates can be optimized a little, by commenting out unnecessary conditions:

```
nocheck(_, []).
nocheck(X/Y, [X1/Y1 | Rest]) :-
  % X =\= X1, assume the Xs are distinct
  Y =\= Y1,
  abs(Y1-Y) =\= abs(X1-X),
  nocheck(X/Y, Rest).

legal([]).
legal([X/Y | Rest]) :-
  legal(Rest),
  % member(X,[1,2,3,4,5,6,7,8]), assume X in range
  member(Y,[1,2,3,4,5,6,7,8]),
  nocheck(X/Y, Rest).
```

This new program finds a solution much faster (without perceptible delay on the author's machine) and also quickly finds additional distinct solutions:

```
?- eightqueens(X).

X = [1/4, 2/2, 3/7, 4/3, 5/6, 6/8, 7/5, 8/1] ;

X = [1/5, 2/2, 3/4, 4/7, 5/3, 6/8, 7/6, 8/1] ;
```

To understand this solution a little better, let's try a few experiments. You might have wondered, for example, about that apparently inefficient test the `legal` predicate makes for legal `Y` coordinates: `member(Y,[1,2,3,4,5,6,7,8])`. Would it not be more efficient to make the test numerically, like this:

```
legal([]).
legal([X/Y | Rest]) :-
  legal(Rest),
```

```
    % member(X,[1,2,3,4,5,6,7,8]), assume X in range
    1=<Y, Y=<8, % was member(Y,[1,2,3,4,5,6,7,8]),
    nocheck(X/Y, Rest).
```

It would certainly be more efficient, but it would be less flexible. Using numeric comparisons would add the requirement that `Y` be already instantiated as a number. In fact, `Y` is not instantiated when `legal` is called. The modified version would just do this:

```
?- eightqueens(X).
ERROR: Arguments are not sufficiently instantiated
```

The original version used the condition `member(Y,[1,2,3,4,5,6,7,8])` not just to *test* whether `Y` is a legal coordinate, but to *instantiate* `Y` as a legal coordinate. That is how the program generates `Y` coordinates for the proof-tree search.

Here is a related experiment: what happens if the conditions of `legal` are reordered like this?

```
legal([]).
legal([X/Y | Rest]) :-
  % member(X,[1,2,3,4,5,6,7,8]), assume X in range
  member(Y,[1,2,3,4,5,6,7,8]),
  nocheck(X/Y, Rest),
  legal(Rest). % formerly the first condition
```

It looks like a plausible thing to try. `legal(Rest)` will be an expensive call, and it makes sense to postpone it until after the two less expensive conditions have been passed. However, this is what happens with the modified version:

```
?- eightqueens(X).
ERROR: Arguments are not sufficiently instantiated
```

It is the same error again—and for much the same reason as before. The condition `legal(Rest)` serves not just to *test* whether `Rest` is a legal arrangement with one less queen, but to *instantiate* `Rest` as a legal arrangement with one less queen. The `nocheck` predicate will not work until after `Rest` is fully instantiated, so that the condition `legal(Rest)` cannot be moved to the end of the clause.

22.4 Conclusion—Farewell to Prolog

This chapter showed some predefined predicates for numeric computation in Prolog. It explored the techniques of problem space search with the knapsack problem and the eight-queens problem. This is the end of the introduction to Prolog.

Here is a list of some of the parts of Prolog that were skipped:

- Cut—The cut is a special goal term, written as !, which always succeeds, but only once. Since it always succeeds, it has no declarative meaning. But since it succeeds only once it has a large procedural effect. It cuts off backtracking and can be used to make Prolog programs more efficient.
- Exception handling—Prolog has predefined predicates **catch** and **throw** that implement exception handling, both for system-generated exceptions and for those explicitly thrown by the program. Like the cut, these are part of the procedural side of Prolog.
- API—The set of predefined predicates for ISO Prolog is fairly small. Most implementations of Prolog provide significant supersets. In addition, there are many public Prolog libraries: basic data structures, network and file I/O, graphical user interfaces, interfaces to other languages, object-oriented extensions, and so on.

The list of the parts skipped is not as long as it was for ML or Java, because Prolog is a small language with a simple syntax. As you have probably observed, that does not mean that it is a weak language—or an easy one to master. The most important thing about Prolog that was skipped is not really a part of the language at all. It is the collection of programming techniques that experienced Prolog programmers use. This syntactically simple language can express elegant solutions to some rather subtle programming problems, as the examples in this chapter were meant to suggest.

Exercises

Exercise 1 Define a predicate `max(X,Y,Z)` that takes numbers `X` and `Y` and unifies `Z` with the maximum of the two.

Exercise 2 Define a predicate `maxlist(L,M)` that takes a list `L` of numbers and unifies `M` with the maximum number in the list. The predicate should fail if the list `L` is empty.

Exercise 3 Define a predicate `ordered(L)` that succeeds if and only if the list of numbers `L` is in non-decreasing order—each element is less than or equal to the next.

Exercise 4 Define a predicate `mergesort(In,Out)` that makes a sorted version of a list `In` of numbers and unifies that result with `Out`. Your predicate should use a merge-sort algorithm. SWI-Prolog has a predefined predicate called `merge`. Don't use it, but choose another name for yours. (*Hint:* An ML merge sort was presented in Chapter 7.)

Exercise 5 Define a predicate `nqueens(N,X)` that takes an integer `N` and finds a solution `X` to the `N`-queens problem. The `N`-queens problem is like the eight-queens problem, but requires placing `N` queens on an `N`-by-`N` chess board. (*Hint:* Start with the eight-queens code from this chapter, which is also available on this book's Web site. Most of it can still be used on this more general problem.)

Exercise 6 Define the predicate `subsetsum(L,Sum,SubL)` that takes a list `L` of numbers and a number `Sum` and unifies `SubL` with a subsequence of `L` such that the sum of the numbers in `SubL` is `Sum`. For example:

```
?- subsetsum([1,2,5,3,2],5,SubSet).

SubSet = [1,2,2];
SubSet = [2,3];
SubSet = [5];
SubSet = [3,2];

No
```

Your predicate should assume that `L` and `Sum` are instantiated, and should succeed once for each distinct subsequence of `L` that adds up to `Sum`.

Exercise 7 Define a predicate `multiknap(Pantry,Capacity,Knapsack)` that works like the `knapsackOptimization` predicate from this chapter, but solves the *multiple-choice* knapsack problem. In this version of the problem you are allowed to take any number of each kind of item in the refrigerator. So if `Pantry` is

```
[food(bread,4,9200),
 food(pasta,2,4600),
 food(peanutButter,1,6700),
 food(babyFood,3,6900)],
```

your knapsack can contain zero or more copies of `food(bread,4,9200)`, zero or more copies of `food(pasta,2,4600)`, and so on.

Exercise 8 Another famously hard problem is the set cover problem. You are given two lists, `Set` and `Subsets`. `Subsets` is a list of lists, each of which is a subsequence of `Set`. The problem is to find a minimum-size `Cover`: a minimum-length subsequence of `Subsets` with the property that every element of `Set` is an element of some list in the `Cover`. Suppose `Set` is `[1,2,3,4,5]` and `Subsets` is `[[1,2],[2,4],[3,5],[1,3],[3,4,5]]`. Then a minimum-size `Cover` (in this case, the unique minimum-size `Cover`) is `[[1,2],[3,4,5]]`.

a. Write a predicate `coverDecision(Set,Subsets,Goal,Cover)` that takes a list `Set`, a list `Subsets` containing subsequences of `Set`, and a positive number `Goal`. It unifies `Cover` with a subsequence of `Subsets` that covers `Set` and has length `=< Goal`. It fails if there is no such `Cover`. Your solution should be able to generate all covers satisfying the goal.
b. Write a predicate `coverOptimization(Set,Subsets,Cover)` that takes a list `Set` and a list `Subsets` containing subsequences of `Set`. It unifies `Cover` with a subsequence of `Subsets` that covers `Set` and has minimum length. It fails if there is no covering subsequence. Your solution should be able to generate all minimum-length covers.

Further Reading

This excellent introductory book on Prolog has already been recommended:

Bratko, Ivan. *Prolog Programming for Artificial Intelligence.* 2nd ed., Boston, MA: Addison-Wesley, 1990.

This is the classic reference on Prolog, now in its fourth edition:

Clocksin, W. F., and C. S. Mellish. *Programming in Prolog.* 4th ed., New York: Springer-Verlag, 1994.

This book is an interesting collection of advanced Prolog techniques, with thoughts on how to write Prolog code that is elegant and effective. After the first chapter, you can read it in any order:

O'Keefe, Richard A. *The Craft of Prolog (Logic Programming).* Cambridge, MA: MIT Press, 1990.

Chapter 23 Formal Semantics

23.1 Introduction

Chapters 2 and 3 started a story: the story of how programming languages can be defined rigorously. Grammars were used to define the syntax of a language, its lexical and phrase-level structure. The story got as far as parse trees and abstract syntax trees—where syntax meets semantics. Now you are ready to continue the story and see how the semantics of a programming language can be defined rigorously.

There are many different techniques for formally defining the semantics of a programming language. Most are highly abstract and mathematical, and for that reason are out of bounds for this book. But there are a few techniques that can be understood without much mathematics. One in particular, the so-called *natural semantics*, is a technique that should be very accessible to the reader, since its notation is closely related to Prolog.

This chapter will develop a natural semantics for several tiny functional languages, side by side with Prolog interpreters for those languages. The last section will survey some of the other techniques of formal semantics.

23.2 Language One

Let's review the results of Chapters 2 and 3 by defining the syntax of a tiny language of integer expressions. Let's call this Language One. As was shown back in Chapter 3, the syntax of a language includes both its lexical structure and its phrase structure. For lexical structure, this language will allow only the tokens `+`, `*`, `(`, and `)`, along with integer constants composed of sequences of one or more decimal digits. The phrase structure of the language is defined in terms of these tokens by the following grammar:

<exp> ::= *<exp>* + *<mulexp>* | *<mulexp>*
<mulexp> ::= *<mulexp>* * *<rootexp>* | *<rootexp>*
<rootexp> ::= (*<exp>*) | *<constant>*

Notice that Language One is a subset of ML expressions, of Java expressions, and of Prolog terms.

The grammar is unambiguous: it defines a unique parse tree for each expression in the language. Here is a parse tree for the expression `1+2*3`:

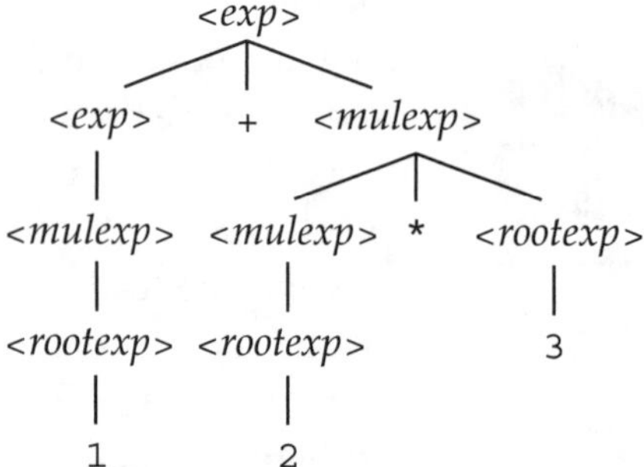

Chapter 3 showed that once a grammar has been used to construct a parse tree, most language systems retain only a simplified tree structure, the abstract syntax tree or AST. The AST records the operation and the operands, but no longer records the non-terminal symbols from the grammar. For the expression `1+2*3`, the AST would be

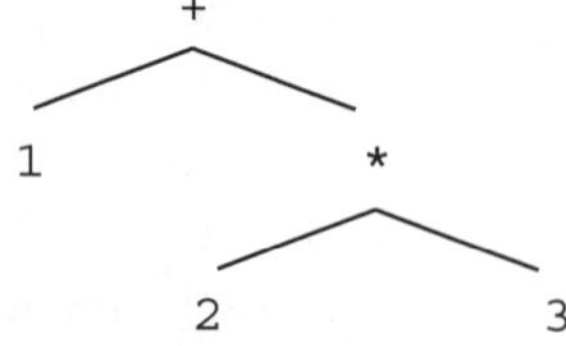

How can the AST be represented? In ML, a `datatype` might be used to define this language of parse trees:

```
datatype AST =
    Const of int |
    Plus of AST * AST |
    Times of AST * AST;
```

In Java, classes for `Const`, `Plus`, and `Times` might be defined that all extend a common `AST` base class (or implement a common `AST` interface). In Prolog, compound terms for `plus`, `const`, and `times` could be used. For example, the AST illustrated above could be represented by this Prolog term:

```
plus(const(1),times(const(2),const(3)))
```

This chapter will implement interpreters using Prolog, so the Prolog representation for an AST will be used.

The language of legal ASTs is sometimes called the *abstract syntax* of the language, and it can be defined by a grammar. Here is a grammar for the abstract syntax of Language One, given as Prolog terms:

```
<exp> ::= plus(<exp>,<exp>)
        | times(<exp>,<exp>)
        | const(<constant>)
```

At any rate, construction of an AST is where syntax ends—where syntax meets semantics. Now you are ready to think about how to continue the story. How can a definition be given of what such tree structure means—what happens when an AST from Language One is evaluated?

An Interpreter

One way to define it is to give an interpreter for the ASTs of the language. Then the interpreter can be treated as definitive. It can say to the world, "Language One programs behave the way *this interpreter* says they behave." This purpose requires a simple interpreter. It should not do anything tricky for the sake of efficiency, for example. The simpler it is, the more likely it is to be correct, and the more understandable it will be.

Here, for example, is a simple interpreter for Language One written in Prolog:

```
val1(plus(X,Y),Value) :-
  val1(X,XValue),
  val1(Y,YValue),
  Value is XValue + YValue.
```

```
val1(times(X,Y),Value) :-
  val1(X,XValue),
  val1(Y,YValue),
  Value is XValue * YValue.

val1(const(X),X).
```

The `val1` predicate, defined above, says how to evaluate a Language One expression, thus defining its semantics.

```
?- val1(const(1),X).

X = 1

Yes
?- val1(plus(const(1),const(2)),X).

X = 3

Yes
?- val1(plus(const(1),times(const(2),const(3))),X).

X = 7

Yes
```

This may seem to be a solid definition of the semantics of Language One, but the closer you look the more holes you find. For example, how is a string of digits interpreted as an integer value in Language One? The `val1` predicate says only that the value of `const(X)` is `X`. So on the question of how a string of decimal digits is to be interpreted as an integer value, the semantics says only that Language One does it the same way Prolog does it. Unfortunately, different implementations of Prolog do this differently. The SWI-Prolog system uses 32-bit signed integers with a range from -2^{31} to $2^{31}-1$. If the value of a string of decimal digits lies outside that range, the system treats it as a floating-point constant.

```
?- val1(const(2147483647),X).

X = 2147483647

Yes
?- val1(const(2147483648),X).

X = 2.14748e+009


Yes
```

Oops! Language One was never intended to manipulate floating-point numbers. But it does, according to this semantics.

Similarly, the `val1` predicate says that the `plus` operator in the AST has the same function as the + predicate in Prolog, as evaluated by the `is` operator. Unfortunately, the evaluation of the + predicate in Prolog is not at all standardized, so `val1` will give different results on different implementations of Prolog. When integer operations overflow in SWI-Prolog, the result becomes a floating-point number:

```
?-  val1(plus(const(2147483646),const(1)),X).

X = 2147483647

Yes
?-  val(plus(const(2147483647),const(1)),X).

X = 2.14748e+009

Yes
```

Because of such problems, the `val1` predicate is not satisfactory as a definition of Language One semantics. It is too implementation specific. To say to the world, "Language One programs behave the way this interpreter says they behave, *running under this implementation of Prolog on this computer system,*" would be unambiguous but not very useful. People who need to know how Language One works will not be able to tell by reading the `val1` predicate. They will have to get the same implementation of Prolog running on the same computer system and experiment with it. Like all large programs, this implementation of Prolog has defects. If any of these impact the way the `val1` predicate works, then those defects have just been made an official part of the definition of Language One.

The problems mentioned above could be avoided by writing a really portable Prolog definition of `val1`. It would have to include definitions of predicates to evaluate integer constants and to perform addition and multiplication, without using the corresponding non-portable parts of Prolog. It would be much more complicated, but it is possible. But a deeper problem is lurking here. Defining the semantics of Language One programs by giving a Prolog program to evaluate them, even a perfectly portable Prolog program, begs the question: what is the semantics of Prolog? Using Prolog in Language One's definition assumes that Prolog's semantics is given and that the reader understands it. This is probably not a wise move. The semantics of Prolog is challenging to define, even informally. In general, all attempts at defining formal semantics have this meta-definition problem: the skeptical reader can always ask, "What is the semantics of the notation you are using to define your programming-language semantics?" Although always present, this problem is made more difficult than necessary by using Prolog (or any other real programming language) as the notation for defining the semantics. Something simpler is needed.

A Natural Semantics

There is a formal notation that can capture the same basic proof rules used in the `val1` predicate, without resorting to Prolog. The semantics for Language One should define a relation between ASTs and their results when evaluated. Let's use the symbol $\rightarrow$ to represent this relation, writing $E \rightarrow v$ to mean that the evaluation of the AST E produces the final value v. So, for example, the semantics should conclude that `times(const(2),const(3))`$\rightarrow$6.

This $\rightarrow$ relation can be defined by giving a collection of rules. The rules are a bit like Prolog rules, but written using a different notation. For example, here is the rule for `times` nodes in the AST:

$$\frac{E_1 \rightarrow v_1 \quad E_2 \rightarrow v_2}{\texttt{times}(E_1,v_1) \rightarrow v_1 \times v_2}$$

Above the line are the conditions; below the line is the conclusion. This rule can be read as saying that if the evaluation of E_1 produces the final value v_1, and if the evaluation of E_2 produces the final value v_2, then the evaluation of `times`(E_1,E_2) produces the final value $v_1 \times v_2$. Here are all the rules defining the $\rightarrow$ relation for Language One, side by side with the corresponding clauses for the `val1` predicate:

$$\frac{E_1 \rightarrow v_1 \quad E_2 \rightarrow v_2}{\texttt{plus}(E_1,v_1) \rightarrow v_1 \times v_2}$$

```
val1(plus(X,Y),Value) :-
  val1(X,XValue),
  val1(Y,YValue),
  Value is XValue + YValue.
```

$$\frac{E_1 \rightarrow v_1 \quad E_2 \rightarrow v_2}{\texttt{times}(E_1,v_1) \rightarrow v_1 \times v_2}$$

```
val1(times(X,Y),Value) :-
  val1(X,XValue),
  val1(Y,YValue),
  Value is XValue * YValue.
```

$$\texttt{const}(n) \rightarrow eval(n)$$

```
val1(const(X),X).
```

These three rules form a *natural semantics* for Language One. Notice that the natural semantics still needs low-level definitions for operations. Those functions +, ×, and *eval* still have to be specified in detail, although those specifications are not given here. Notice also that the natural semantics still has a meta-definition problem. It is not hard to see, informally, how a set of rules like the one above defines a → relation, but defining that connection formally requires a bit more mathematics than will be ventured here. Take the author's word for it, however: it is vastly simpler than giving a formal semantics for Prolog!

A natural semantics may have more than one rule for an AST node—something you will need to know if you try Exercise 2. For a language with an ML-style if-then-else expression, the natural semantics might have rules like this:

$$\frac{E_1 \to true \quad E_2 \to v_2}{\texttt{if}(E_1,E_2,E_3) \to v_2}$$

$$\frac{E_1 \to false \quad E_3 \to v_3}{\texttt{if}(E_1,E_2,E_3) \to v_3}$$

In this case, of course, at most one of these rules can apply to a given AST node. In general, it may be necessary to prove that the language defined is deterministic—that there is no program for which the → relation defines more than one possible final value. In Prolog terms, this would be like proving that for every AST `P` there is no more than one `X` for which `val1(P,X)`.

23.3 Language Two—Adding Variables

Now Language One will be extended by the addition of variables, along with an ML-style `let` expression for defining them. Some new tokens will be added: variable names and the tokens `let`, `val`, `=`, `in`, and `end`. Here is the syntax for Language Two:

```
<exp> ::= <exp> + <mulexp> | <mulexp>
<mulexp> ::= <mulexp> * <rootexp> | <rootexp>
<rootexp> ::= let val <variable> = <exp> in <exp> end
            | (<exp>) | <variable> | <constant>
```

For example, this program in Language Two makes use of the new constructs:

```
let val y = 3 in y*y end
```

Two new types of AST nodes need to be defined for programs in Language Two: `var(X)`, for a reference to a variable `X`, and `let(X,Exp1,Exp2)`, for a `let` expression that evaluates `Exp2` in an environment where the variable `X` is bound to the value of `Exp1`. So the AST for the expression above would be

```
let(y,const(3),times(var(y),var(y)))
```

An Interpreter

For Language One, a predicate `val1(AST,Value)` was written that took an `AST` and computed its `Value`. For Language Two, something more powerful is needed. The value of an AST node for an Language Two expression can depend on the context of variable definitions in which the expression is evaluated. To interpret Language Two, a predicate `val2(AST,Context,Value)` will be written that computes the `Value` of a given `AST` in a given `Context`.

Before getting to the implementation of `val2`, there has to be a way to represent contexts. The Prolog term `bind(X,V)` will represent the binding of a variable `X` to a value `V`. For example, the binding of the variable `y` to the value 3 that is needed for the example above will be represented as `bind(y,3)`. Notice that these `bind` terms are not AST nodes; they are created by the interpreter while evaluating an AST. A list of zero or more `bind` terms will represent a whole context. The empty list is the empty context—the context in which no variables are bound.

This predicate will look up the binding of a variable in a context:

```
lookup(Variable,[bind(Variable,Value)|_],Value).
lookup(VarX,[bind(VarY,_)|Rest],Value) :-
  VarX \= VarY,
  lookup(VarX,Rest,Value).
```

Notice that when a context contains more than one binding for the same variable, `lookup` finds only the first one. So when the interpreter is working on a `let` expression, it should build the new context by adding the new `bind` term to the head of the list. That way, the new definition will hide any previous definitions of the same name, which is the desired behavior.

Now let's define an interpreter for Language Two.

```
val2(plus(X,Y),Context,Value) :-
  val2(X,Context,XValue),
  val2(Y,Context,YValue),
  Value is XValue + YValue.
```

```
val2(times(X,Y),Context,Value) :-
  val2(X,Context,XValue),
  val2(Y,Context,YValue),
  Value is XValue * YValue.

val2(const(X),_,X).

val2(var(X),Context,Value) :-
  lookup(X,Context,Value).

val2(let(X,Exp1,Exp2),Context,Value2) :-
  val2(Exp1,Context,Value1),
  val2(Exp2,[bind(X,Value1)|Context],Value2).
```

This `val2` predicate says how to evaluate Language Two expressions. Here, it evaluates the AST for `let val y = 3 in y*y end`:

```
?- val2(let(y,const(3),times(var(y),var(y))),[],X).

X = 9

Yes
```

Here is a Language Two program with nested `let` expressions:

```
let val y = 3 in
  let val x = y * y in
    x * x
  end
end
```

`val2` evaluates the AST for that program:

```
?- val2(let(y,const(3),
|          let(x,times(var(y),var(y)),
|           times(var(x),var(x)))),
|         [],X).

X = 81

Yes
```

This next example shows that the program is implementing the classic block scope rule, with inner definitions hiding outer definitions of the same name. The expression is `let val y = 1 in let val y = 2 in y end end`.

```
?- val2(let(y,const(1),let(y,const(2),var(y))),[],X).

X = 2

Yes
```

This final example shows that the program can still evaluate expressions in the Language One subset. The expression here is `1+2*3`.

```
?- val2(plus(const(1),times(const(2),const(3))),[],X).

X = 7

Yes
```

A Natural Semantics

The ideas in the `val2` implementation also appear directly in a natural semantics for Language Two. As with Language One, a relation will be defined that captures how ASTs are evaluated. The same symbol will be used as before, →, but the → relation for Language Two is not the same as for Language One. The things that appear on the left-hand side of the new → relation are not just ASTs, they are pairs containing an AST and the context in which to evaluate it. $\langle E,C\rangle \to v$ will be written to mean that the evaluation of the AST *E* in the context *C* produces the final value *v*. Here are the rules defining this relation:

$$\frac{\langle E_1,C\rangle \to v_1 \quad \langle E_2,C\rangle \to v_2}{\langle \texttt{plus}(E_1,E_2),C\rangle \to v_1+v_2}$$

$$\frac{\langle E_1,C\rangle \to v_1 \quad \langle E_2,C\rangle \to v_2}{\langle \texttt{times}(E_1,E_2),C\rangle \to v_1 \times v_2}$$

$$\langle \texttt{const}(n),C\rangle \to eval(n)$$

$$\langle \texttt{var}(v),C\rangle \to lookup(C,v)$$

$$\frac{\langle E_1,C\rangle \to v_1 \quad \langle E_2,bind(x,v_1)::C\rangle \to v_2}{\langle \texttt{let}(x,E_1,E_2),C\rangle \to v_2}$$

These five rules correspond closely to the five Prolog clauses for `val2`. To be complete, this semantics needs definitions for the low-level functions (+, ×, and *eval*), the new functions *bind* and *lookup*, and the cons operation (::).

About Errors

Language One is so simple that any syntactically correct program runs without errors. This it not the case with Language Two. In particular, a program can contain a reference to a variable that is not in the scope of any definition for that variable. The `val2` interpreter has a clear behavior in that case: it fails, indicating that no value is defined for such an expression.

```
?- val2(let(a,const(1),var(b)),[],X).

No
```

Similarly, the → relation does not associate such an erroneous program with any final value.

Ordinarily, language systems perform various error checks after parsing, but before running the program. These include checking that all variables are defined and (in statically type checked languages) that there is a consistent way to assign a type to everything in the program. This part of a language definition is sometimes called the *static semantics*: parts of the definition that are neither part of the formal syntax, nor yet part of the runtime behavior. The runtime semantics we have been specifying is called the *dynamic semantics*.

One way to handle errors in a formal semantics is to specify the static semantics and the dynamic semantics separately. We could specify what it means for a Language Two program to be legal (with every reference to a variable in the scope of some definition for that variable), then allow the dynamic part of the specification to assume that the running program is legal. This takes care of all the errors that can occur in Language Two.

In full-size languages, however, there are other kinds of errors that cannot be handled so easily. The runtime behavior of exception handling must be specified in the dynamic part of the semantics. This can be done with a natural semantics. One approach is for the → relation to have a set of final outcomes that includes both normal and abrupt termination. For example, if a `divide` node in the AST causes an exception for division by zero, → might be defined to handle both outcomes.

<`divide(const(6),const(3))`,*C*>→<*normal*,2>

<`divide(const(6),const(0))`,*C*>→<*abrupt*,*zerodivide*>

This book will not look at the problem of error semantics any further; it is quite challenging enough merely to give a dynamic semantics for correct programs.

23.4 Language Three—Adding Functions

Let's now extend Language Two by adding ML-style function values and function calls. (Don't be alarmed, it is not as difficult as it first appears!) The new tokens `fn` and `=>` will be added, and the grammar will be modifed to permit `fn` expressions and function application. Here is the syntax for Language Three:

```
<exp> ::= fn <variable> => <exp> | <addexp>
<addexp> ::= <addexp> + <mulexp> | <mulexp>
<mulexp> ::= <mulexp> * <funexp> | <funexp>
<funexp> ::= <funexp> <rootexp> | <rootexp>
<rootexp> ::= let val <variable> = <exp> in <exp> end
            | (<exp>) | <variable> | <constant>
```

As in ML, function application has higher precedence than addition or multiplication. This program in Language Three makes use of the new constructs:

```
(fn x => x * x) 3
```

(The parentheses are necessary in Language Three as in ML, because `fn` expressions have lowest precedence.) Two new types of AST nodes need to be defined for programs in Language Three. A node of the form `apply(Function,Actual)` will represent the application of the `Function` to the `Actual` parameter. A node of the form `fn(Formal,Body)` will represent the `fn` expression with the given `Formal` parameter and `Body`. So the AST for the example above is

```
apply(fn(x,times(var(x),var(x))),const(3))
```

An Interpreter

To build a predicate `val3` that interprets Language Three, start by reusing all the clauses for `val2`. All the previous constructs, including the `let`, still work the same way:

```
val3(plus(X,Y),Context,Value) :-
  val3(X,Context,XValue),
  val3(Y,Context,YValue),
  Value is XValue + YValue.

val3(times(X,Y),Context,Value) :-
  val3(X,Context,XValue),
  val3(Y,Context,YValue),
  Value is XValue * YValue.
```

```
val3(const(X),_,X).

val3(var(X),Context,Value) :-
  lookup(X,Context,Value).

val3(let(X,Exp1,Exp2),Context,Value2) :-
  val3(Exp1,Context,Value1),
  val3(Exp2,[bind(X,Value1)|Context],Value2).
```

Additional `val3` clauses need to be added to handle the two new AST nodes. A `fn` node evaluates to a function value, which simply contains the formal parameter and the (unevaluated) function body:

```
val3(fn(Formal,Body),_,fval(Formal,Body)).
```

In this clause, note that the `fn` term is part of the AST, while the `fval` term is not—it is one of those terms the interpreter creates while evaluating an AST, like the `bind` terms you have already seen. The rule above makes an `fval` term that contains exactly the same information as the `fn` term from the AST: the formal parameter (a variable name from the program) and the function body (an unevaluated subtree of the AST, which will be evaluated only when the function is called with an actual parameter). You might wonder, why bother with the `fval` term at all—why not just have the `fn` term evaluate to itself? There is a reason for using two different kinds of terms, even though at the moment they contain the same information, as you will see shortly.

An `apply` node is evaluated by evaluating the function (remember, it evaluates to an `fval` term), evaluating the actual parameter, and then evaluating the function body in an environment in which the formal parameter is bound to the value of the actual parameter.

```
val3(apply(Function,Actual),Context,Value) :-
  val3(Function,Context,fval(Formal,Body)),
  val3(Actual,Context,ParamValue),
  val3(Body,[bind(Formal,ParamValue)|Context],Value).
```

That's all it takes. The new predicate `val3` now interprets the function call and the function definition. Here it evaluates the expression `(fn x => x * x) 3`:

```
?-  val3(apply(fn(x,times(var(x),var(x))),
|          const(3)),
|         [],X).
```

```
X = 9

Yes
```

Chapter 10 looked at the difference between static and dynamic scoping techniques. Consider the following Language Three code. What should the value of this expression be?

```
let val x = 1 in
  let val f = fn n => n + x in
    let val x = 2 in
      f 0
    end
  end
end
```

The answer depends on whether Language Three is using static or dynamic scoping. With static scoping, the binding for `x` in the body of function `f` will be governed by the definition `val x = 1`, so the expression will have the value 1. With dynamic scoping, the binding for `x` in the body of function `f` will be governed by the definition `val x = 2`, so the expression will have the value 2. Here is what Language Three does, according to the semantics:

```
?- val3(let(x,const(1),
|           let(f,fn(n,plus(var(n),var(x))),
|            let(x,const(2),
|             apply(var(f),const(0))))),
|          [],X).

X = 2

Yes
```

It seems we have a dynamic-scoping semantics! That is probably not a good idea. Chapter 10 showed some of the drawbacks of dynamic scoping and that almost all languages (including ML) implement static scoping instead.

Let's look again at the `val3` interpreter to see what produced this behavior. If you think about it, it is evident from this single clause of `val3` that static scoping will be impossible:

```
val3(fn(Formal,Body),_,fval(Formal,Body)).
```

The second parameter to `val3`, the context, is ignored in this clause. So a function value does not keep track of the context within which it was constructed. That means that when it runs it will have no way to look up variables in that context.

Instead, when running the function, `val3` uses the caller's context, as underlined below:

```
val3(apply(Function,Actual),Context,Value) :-
  val3(Function,Context,fval(Formal,Body)),
  val3(Actual,Context,ParamValue),
  val3(Body,[bind(Formal,ParamValue)|Context],Value).
```

In the last condition of that clause, the body of the function is evaluated in a new context that adds a binding for the formal parameter to the caller's own `Context`. That is dynamic scoping.

To get static scoping instead, both of those offending clauses will have to be redefined. A function value must include the context within which to run it. Remember the nesting-link idea from Chapter 12? A function's implementation and its nesting link are kept together to form a function value. That is what `val3` needs to do when it evaluates an `fn` node:

```
val3(fn(Formal,Body),Context,fval(Formal,Body,Context)).
```

The `fval` term is used by the interpreter to keep the implementation and the static context together. (That is why an `fn` node does not evaluate to itself.) Now the clause for `apply` nodes just needs to be modified to use the recorded context when evaluating the function body.

```
val3(apply(Function,Actual),Context,Value) :-
  val3(Function,Context,fval(Formal,Body,Nesting)),
  val3(Actual,Context,ParamValue),
  val3(Body,[bind(Formal,ParamValue)|Nesting],Value).
```

These changes result in a static-scoping semantics. The same example that gave the dynamic-scoping result before, now gives the static-scoping result, which is the same answer ML produces:

```
?- val3(let(x,const(1),
|          let(f,fn(n,plus(var(n),var(x))),
|           let(x,const(2),
|            apply(var(f),const(0))))),
|         [],X).

X = 1

Yes
```

Even ML-style, higher-order functions can be written in Language Three. This one, for example, makes use of static scoping:

```
let
  val f = fn x =>
    let val g = fn y => y + x in
      g
    end
in
  f 1 2
end
```

The function `f` takes a parameter `x` and returns another function that knows how to add `x` to its parameter. In other words, `f` is a curried function that adds two numbers. Recall from Chapter 12 that the activation record for `f` cannot be deallocated when `f` returns. In this interpreter, contexts represented with `bind` terms take the place of activation records. The function `g` makes use of its nesting context after `f` (which created the context) has returned.

```
?-  val3(let(f,fn(x,let(g,fn(y,plus(var(y),var(x))),
|                    var(g))),
|          apply(apply(var(f),const(1)),const(2))),
|         [],X).

X = 3

Yes
```

A Natural Semantics

The ideas in the `val3` implementation also appear directly in a natural semantics for Language Three. The same symbol will be used as before, →, but with a new definition for Language Three. As with Language Two, $<E,C>\to v$ will mean that the evaluation of the AST E in the context C produces the final value v. Here are the rules defining this relation. First, for a dynamic-scoping semantics:

$$\frac{<E_1,C>\to v_1 \quad <E_2,C>\to v_2}{<\texttt{plus}(E_1,E_2),C>\to v_1+v_2}$$

$$\frac{<E_1,C>\to v_1 \quad <E_2,C>\to v_2}{<\texttt{times}(E_1,E_2),C>\to v_1\times v_2}$$

$$<\texttt{const}(n),C>\to eval(n)$$

$$<\texttt{var}(v),C>\to lookup(\mathrm{C},v)$$

$$\frac{\langle E_1,C\rangle \to (v_1) \quad \langle E_2,bind(x,v_1)::C\rangle \to v_2}{\langle \texttt{let}(x,E_1,E_2),C\rangle \to v_2}$$

$$\langle \texttt{fn}(x,E),C\rangle \to (x,E)$$

$$\frac{\langle E_1,C\rangle \to (x,E_3) \quad \langle E_2,C\rangle \to v_1 \quad \langle E_3,bind(x,v_1)::C\rangle \to v_2}{\langle \texttt{apply}(E_1,E_2),C\rangle \to v_2}$$

In this natural semantics, function values are represented as pairs containing the formal parameter and the function body. To get the static-scoping semantics, the last two rules are changed like this:

$$\langle \texttt{fn}(x,E),C\rangle \to (x,E,C)$$

$$\frac{\langle E_1,C\rangle \to (x,E_3,C') \quad \langle E_2,C\rangle \to v_1 \quad \langle E_3,bind(x,v_1)::C'\rangle \to v_2}{\langle \texttt{apply}(E_1,E_2),C\rangle \to v_2}$$

Now function values are represented as triples containing the formal parameter, the function body, and the static evaluation context.

About Errors

Language Three is susceptible to type errors, unlike Language Two. In particular, it has function values and integer values, and it is easy to write a program in Language Three that uses functions as integers or integers as functions; `1 1`, for example. As you saw with Language Two, the interpreter fails on such programs, indicating that no result is defined for them in the language.

```
?- val3(apply(const(1),const(1)),[],X).

No
```

Similarly, the $\to$ relation does not associate such an erroneous program with any final value.

A complete semantics for Language Three would have to deal with this in one of two ways. First, Language Three might be dynamically type checked. In that case the dynamic semantics would have to be expanded to explain what happens at runtime when type errors occur. Second, Language Three might be statically type checked. In that case it could be assumed in the dynamic part of the semantics that type errors do not occur, but a formal static semantics would have to be given for type checking and type inference. Either case ventures further into formal semantics than this chapter should go.

In Language Three, using the dynamic-scoping semantics, it is possible to have recursive functions. This is such a program:

```
let val f = fn x => f x in f 1 end
```

This is not legal under the static-scoping semantics, because the scope of the definition of `f` does not include the function body. But with dynamic scoping, the undefined `f` is found in the caller's context. Of course, this program does not terminate. What does the semantics say about that?

The `val3` interpreter simply interprets. Since the program never terminates, `val3` never terminates. It does not find a value for the expression, nor does it just say No as in the case of type errors. The natural semantics, on the other hand, is not an interpreter. It is just a mathematical definition of a relation, the $\rightarrow$ relation. The $\rightarrow$ relation does not associate a non-terminating program with any final value. Thus it does not distinguish between the case of an erroneous program and the case of a non-terminating program. This is typical of natural semantics.

About the Order of Evaluation

This is a good time to mention a semantic issue ignored so far: the order of evaluation. When an expression `(f 1)+(g 1)` is evaluated, which gets called first, `f` or `g`? The `val3` interpreter evaluates a `plus` node in the AST by first evaluating the left operand, then evaluating the right one, and then adding the results. But the natural semantics does not specify the order of evaluation. The rule for a `plus` node says that if the first operand evaluates to v_1 and the second operand evaluates to v_2, the whole node evaluates to $v_1 + v_2$; but it does not mention the order of evaluation at all. In fact, according to the natural semantics, the whole question is meaningless. There are no side effects and (assuming a proper semantics for static type checking) no runtime errors, so the order of evaluation is unobservable.

That will not do for a language with side effects or runtime errors, because such features make the order of evaluation observable. For example, if `f` assigns 1 to a global variable `x` and `g` assigns 2 to `x`, then the value of `x` after evaluation of the expression `(f 1)+(g 1)` depends on the order of evaluation. For such languages a formal semantics must specify the legal order of evaluation—or all the legal orders of evaluation, if the actual order is implementation dependent.

Here is a simple Java example for which the outcome depends on the order of evaluation:

```
x=1;
x+=(x=2);
```

That second statement can be thought of as being performed in three separate steps, but in what order do they occur? The AST for the statement does not answer the question. It is up to the definition of the semantics of the language. Three possibilities are

```
x=2;
oldx=x;
x=oldx+2;
```

```
oldx=x;
x=2;
x=oldx+2;
```

```
oldx=x;
x=oldx+2;
x=2;
```

These three different orders produce three different final values for `x` (4, 3, and 2, respectively). The definition of Java semantics specifies the second order above; the only permissible outcome is the final value 3. The same syntax is also legal in C, but with a different semantics. It is implementation dependent, and all the outcomes are permissible.

A formal semantics for a language with side effects or runtime errors has to cope with many order-of-evaluation issues. Luckily, such issues did not arise for Language Three.

23.5 Other Kinds of Formal Semantics

Natural semantics is only one of many ways of defining the formal semantics of programming languages. There are three major approaches: operational semantics, axiomatic semantics, and denotational semantics. Natural semantics is an example of the first of these approaches.

Operational Semantics

An *operational semantics* specifies, step by step, what happens when a program executes. It sounds like an interpreter, doesn't it? But an operational semantics defines the "steps" in the execution of a program abstractly. An operational semantics provides a mathematical model of an interpreter for the language. There are several different varieties of operational semantics, and they differ in how abstractly they model interpretation.

A *natural semantics* is the most abstract. It defines a relation between programs and their final outcomes—outcomes like final values (for functional programs) or final machine states (for imperative programs). In effect, a natural semantics defines interpretation as one big step, which is justified by a lengthy proof. A natural semantics is sometimes called a *big-step operational semantics*. It can be very useful, because the final outcome is sometimes the only thing of interest about a computation. For example, an optimizing compiler can change the intermediate steps of a computation, but must preserve the final outcome. On the other hand, a natural semantics is not very useful for studying what happens during a computation. It says nothing about infinite computations, except that they produce no final value.

To reason about the intermediate steps of a computation, a less abstract form of operational semantics can be used. A *structural operational semantics* (or SOS), also called a *small-step operational semantics*, specifies a computation as a series of smaller steps. There are still rules, much like a natural semantics, but the relation those rules define is the relation between one state of the computation and the next. A structural operational semantics specifies an infinite sequence of states for infinite computations.

If the steps are small enough, and the conditions for each step simple enough, a structural operational semantics can begin to look more and more like an implementation of an interpreter. It interprets a program by applying rules to transform each state to the next until a final state is reached. The states are still rather abstract, however. The interpreter is for an *abstract machine* designed to simplify interpretation, rather than for a machine designed to make execution efficient.

An operational semantics is especially useful for guiding the development of real interpreters and compilers and for proving them correct.

Axiomatic Semantics

A common programming technique is the use of assertions. At key points in the code, the programmer places statements about things that he or she expects to be true. For example, here is the `remove` method from the `Stack` class of Chapter 15:

```
public String remove() {
  Node n = top;
  top = n.getLink();
  return n.getData();
}
```

This method only works if there is something on the stack when it is called, so an assertion like this might be added:

```
public String remove() {
  assert(top != null);
  Node n = top;
  top = n.getLink();
  return n.getData();
}
```

The `assert` method might do something like print an error message or throw an exception if the assertion being tested turns out to be false. Even if `assert` does nothing, however, the assertion still has value as documentation. Such assertions might even be used to document some other important properties of the method:

```
public String remove() {
  // P: length X of list starting from top is > 0
  Node n = top;
  top = n.getLink();
  return n.getData();
  // Q: length of list starting from top = X - 1
}
```

How can you prove that the assertions in a method are correct? This is just another way of asking that critical question: how can you prove that a method is correct with respect to its specification? How can you prove that a sort really sorts, that a search really finds, that an autopilot really pilots? To reason about assertions, you need to understand how each statement affects them. For example, when you know an assertion P holds before statement S, what is the strongest assertion you can make after statement S? This is really a question about the semantics of S. An *axiomatic semantics* defines the semantics of a language in a way that is useful for reasoning about assertions.

An axiomatic semantics might define an assertion transformer for each statement S. One way is to give a function $sp(P,S)$ that computes the *strongest postcondition*, the strongest assertion you can make after statement S given that assertion P is true before S. An alternative, and often more useful, formulation is to ask the question in the opposite direction: given some assertion Q that is desired to hold after statement S, what is the weakest assertion that must hold before S to guarantee it? An axiomatic semantics might define a function $wp(S,Q)$ that computes the *weakest precondition*, the minimum assertion the programmer must establish before executing statement S so that assertion Q will be true after S.

An axiomatic semantics might express the properties of a statement S in terms of *Hoare triples*, which look like this:

$$\{P\}\ S\ \{Q\}$$

This says that if the assertion P, the *precondition*, is true before the statement S is executed, then the assertion Q, the *postcondition*, is true afterwards. (Some forms work with *partial correctness*. The reading then is that if P is true before, and if S completes, then Q is true afterwards.) An axiomatic semantics might give rules of inference for Hoare triples, like this one for an `if` statement:

$$\frac{\{E_1 \wedge P\} S_1 \{Q\} \quad \{\neg E_1 \wedge P\} S_2 \{Q\}}{\{P\}\ \texttt{if}\ E_1\ \texttt{then}\ S_1\ \texttt{else}\ S_2\ \{Q\}}$$

An axiomatic semantics must work with a specific vocabulary of assertions. This is rarely intended to be a vocabulary that can capture every detail of program execution, and an axiomatic semantics is rarely intended to be a complete specification of the language. That is part of what makes it useful for reasoning about assertions and correctness. An operational semantics is, ideally, a complete specification of the language. You could use it to reason about assertions, but it just isn't the right tool for that job. It is too detailed, too low-level; proofs of program correctness in terms of operational semantics are too long and detailed to be convincing. For reasoning about program assertions and correctness, an axiomatic semantics is more appropriate.

An axiomatic semantics can be useful not only for reasoning about the correctness of programs after they are written, but also for guiding the development of correct programs. There is a school of thought about programming that says that programs and proofs of correctness should be developed simultaneously, with the proof ideas helping to guide the programming. That requires the programmer to have a working knowledge of an axiomatic semantics for the language.

Denotational Semantics

The most mathematically elegant kind of semantics is a *denotational semantics*. A denotational semantics has two key properties.

First, according to a denotational semantics, each phrase of a program *denotes* some element of a mathematical domain. The word *domain* here has a formal meaning, which won't be elaborated here; essentially it is just a set, but one that satisfies certain mathematical properties. The denoted domains might be a domain of integers, a domain of arrays of integers, or a domain of functions. This last is most common, and most of the interesting domains are domains of functions. A denotational semantics maps each piece of a program to an element of some such domain.

The second key property of a denotational semantics is that it defines the meaning of larger phrases of a program *compositionally*, by combining the meanings of its component phrases. An operational semantics might be said to have the first of the two key properties, since the $\rightarrow$ relation is usually a function. But an operational semantics defines this function operationally, as the end result of a potentially non-terminating sequence of computational steps. A denotational semantics constructs its denotations merely by combining simpler denotations, without ever resorting to interpretation at all.

For example, a denotational semantics might say that an integer constant denotes some element of a domain of integers, like this:

$$D[[\texttt{const}(c)]] = eval(c)$$

Then it might say that a sum is the sum of its components, like this:

$$D[[\texttt{plus}(E_1,E_2)]] = D[[E_1]] + D[[E_2]]$$

Notice the compositionality—it defines the meaning of the sum in terms of the meanings of its parts. That's easy enough for addition without side effects, but harder for other programming-language constructs. For a language with assignment, for instance, it might be said that the denotation of an assignment statement is a function that takes a current environment and produces a new environment:

$$D[[\texttt{assign}(v,E)]](\sigma) = \sigma[v \mapsto D[[E_2]]]$$

The denotation $D[[\texttt{assign}(v,E)]]$ is a function that takes a current environment σ and produces a new environment in which the binding of the variable v has been replaced by the denotation of expression E.

The hard part comes when you try to give denotations for constructs that, through looping or recursion, may not terminate. For example, in an imperative language, the denotation of a while loop, $D[[\texttt{while}(E,S)]]$, might need to be defined. The denotation of a while loop, like the denotation of an assignment statement, might be a function from environments to environments. In this case it would be the function mapping the initial environment at the beginning of the loop to the final environment when the loop terminates (or some other value to indicate non-termination). It is an interesting exercise to define this compositionally, in terms of the denotations of expression E and statement S, without reverting to an operational description that describes the steps to be carried out. Unfortunately, it requires more mathematics than this book ventures into: the mathematics of lattices, partial orders, and fixpoints. The interested reader should refer to the Further Reading section at the end of this chapter.

23.6 Conclusion

This chapter has shown three different kinds of formal semantics: operational, axiomatic, and denotational. Each is useful for certain kinds of things. An operational semantics is especially useful for language implementation. An axiomatic semantics is especially useful for proving assertions in programs written in the language and for guiding the construction of correct programs. A denotational semantics is especially useful for proving general program properties, such as the equivalence of two programs or program fragments.

Beyond these specific applications, all the different kinds of formal semantics are valuable for a reason that you have no doubt observed: *they are very hard to read.*

Why is that valuable? Most definitions of programming language semantics do not use formal methods at all, but describe the language informally. The trouble with informal descriptions is that they always seem plausible. They are too easy to read. We nod and smile and fool ourselves into thinking that the language is well defined, even when the definition is riddled with errors, contradictions, and ambiguities. Perhaps it is the difficulty of the subject, or perhaps it is just human nature to believe anything we read. For whatever reason, informal language definitions are almost impossible to read critically.

The Nobel physicist Richard Feynman said, "Science is a way of trying not to fool yourself." Formal semantics is scientific in just that sense. Working with a formal semantics is an exercise that forces us to think with (sometimes agonizing) clarity and precision about the definition of a programming language. It helps us to not fool ourselves about the languages we create.

Exercises

Exercise 1 In Language Three, for any variable x and any expressions E_1 and E_2 and in any context, the expression `let val` x `=` E_1 `in` E_2 `end` is equivalent to the expression `((fn` x `=>` E_2`)` E_1`)`.

a. Using the dynamic-binding version of the natural semantics for Language Three, show that the assertion above is true. *Hint:* Show that the conditions in the natural semantics for $\langle$`apply(fn(`x,E_2`),`E_1`)`$,C\rangle \rightarrow v$ are equivalent to the conditions for $\langle$`let(`x,E_2,E_2`)`$C\rangle \rightarrow v$.

b. Show it using the static-binding version of the natural semantics.

The previous results show that it is possible to implement `let` in terms of function definition and application. With that, the `let` AST node could have been dispensed with in Language Three, and the Prolog interpreter and the natural semantics could have been simpified correspondingly.

Exercise 2 In this exercise you will define Language Four, an extension of Language Three. Here is a sample program in Language Four, showing all the new constructs:

```
let
  val fact = fn x => if x<2 then x else x * fact (x-1)
in
  fact 5
end
```

As you can see, Language Four extends Language Three with three new constructs: the < operator for comparison, the - operator for subtraction, and the conditional (`if-then-else`) expression. The sample program above defines a recursive factorial function and uses it to compute the factorial of 5.

a. Define the syntax of Language Four by extending the syntax of Language Three with the three additional constructs required. Show your new BNF. Make sure it is unambiguous.
b. Define the three new kinds of AST nodes you need to match your extended syntax. Extend the Prolog implementation of Language Three to handle them. (You will need to start with the dynamic-scoping implementation, since the static-scoping one cannot handle recursive definitions. For this reason, the sample program above is not legal in ML.) Verify that your implementation evaluates the sample program correctly—the factorial of 5 is 120.
c. Give a natural semantics for Language Four.

Exercise 3 Recursive functions are not legal under the static-scoping semantics for Language Three, because the scope of the definition of a variable does not include the function body. ML works the same way. The scope of the definition of `f` produced by `fun f...` includes the function body being defined, but the scope of the definition of `f` produced by `val f = fn...` does not. So in ML, only the `fun` definitions can be recursive.

a. Extend the syntax of Language Four from Exercise 2 to allow simple definitions with `fun`, so that, for example, this program is legal:

```
let fun f x = x + 1 in f 1 end
```

b. Define the new kinds of AST nodes you need to match your extended syntax. Extend the Prolog implementation of Language Four to handle them. Use a static-scoping implementation for both kinds of function definitions (`fun f...` and `val f = fn...`). Allow functions defined with `fun` to be recursive. *Hint:* The static-scoping `val3` used an `fval` term to represent function values created with `fn`. Use a different term to represent function values created with `fun` definitions—one that records the name of the function—and a different clause for `apply` to handle it. Try your implementation on a recursive factorial function defined with `fun`.

c. Give a natural semantics for your extended language.

Exercise 4 Both the static-scoping and the dynamic-scoping semantics for Language Three specify by-value parameter passing. They evaluate each parameter before calling the function.

a. Implement a Prolog interpreter for Language Three that uses static scoping with by-name parameter passing. (Although it is difficult to test this in the absence of side effects, you should at least be able to verify experimentally that your interpreter does not evaluate an actual parameter if the corresponding formal parameter is never used.)

b. Give a natural semantics for the language.

Exercise 5 In this exercise, define the semantics for a language called After. Here is a BNF grammar for After:

```
<exp> ::= <exp> > <difexp> | <difexp>
<difexp> ::= <difexp> - <mulexp> | <mulexp>
<mulexp> ::= <mulexp> * <rootexp> | <rootexp>
<rootexp> ::= after <stmt> get <exp> end
            | (<exp>) | <variable> | <constant>
<stmt> ::= <compound-stmt> | <while-stmt> | <assignment-stmt>
<compound-stmt> ::= { <stmt-sequence> }
<stmt-sequence> ::= <stmt-sequence> <stmt>| <stmt>
<while-stmt> ::= while ( <exp> ) <stmt>
<assignment-stmt> ::= <variable> := <exp> ;
```

The start symbol for this grammar is *<exp>*, so a program is an expression to be evaluated. Informally, After works like this:

- All values manipulated by the program are integers.
- The value of $a > b$ is 1 if a is greater than b, 0 otherwise.
- The value of a - b is the difference, a minus b.
- The value of a * b is the product, a times b.
- The value of `after` *s* `get` *e* `end` is the value of the expression *e*, evaluated in the final environment that results after executing statement `s` in the current environment. Changes made by `s` to the current environment are not visible outside of the `after` expression.
- Within a compound statement, changes to the environment are cumulative. Each statement in the compound sees any changes to the environment left by the statement before.
- The statement `while (`*e*`)` *s* evaluates the guard expression *e*. If the guard is 0, nothing else happens. If the guard is not 0, the body statement *s* is executed and the whole action repeats.
- An assignment statement *v* := *e* changes the value of the variable *v* in the current environment (or introduces a value for *v*, if this is the first assignment to *v* in this environment).

For example, the following After expression computes the factorial of 5:

```
after {
  n = 5;
  sofar = 1;
  while (n > 0) {
    sofar = sofar * n;
    n = n - 1;
  }
} get sofar end
```

a. Define the kinds of AST nodes you need for this syntax. *Hint:* For compound statements try using a node `seq(X,Y)` for the sequence of two statements, `X` followed by `Y`. Longer compounds can be represented in terms of this `seq`; for example, `seq(X,seq(Y,Z))`. Implement a Prolog interpreter for After. Show your representation of the program above as an AST, and show your Prolog interpreter's output for that AST.

b. Give a natural semantics for After.

Further Reading

There is no way to study formal semantics, even at an introductory level, without a fair amount of mathematics. This is an excellent book that has no more mathematics than necessary and introduces all the unusual mathematics it uses:

> Nielson, Hanne Riis, and Flemming Nielson. *Semantics with Applications: A Formal Introduction.* New York: John Wiley & Sons, 1992.

In 1999 the authors made a new edition of the book available on the Web. Interested readers should check on its current status.

Readers who are especially interested in axiomatic semantics might want to check out this classic:

> Gries, David. *The Science of Programming.* New York: Springer-Verlag, 1981.

The book presents a technique for using axiomatic semantics to guide the development of provably correct programs. The axiomatic approach to programming is hard—too hard for most programmers, perhaps, since it has not won many converts. But like formal semantics itself, the difficulty of the technique is part of its merit. It helps you to not fool yourself about the correctness of the programs you write.

Chapter 24 The History of Programming Languages

24.1 Introduction

A history of programming languages is in the place of honor, the last chapter of this book. It is last rather than first because it cannot be read without some understanding of the concepts of programming languages.

In one short chapter it is not possible to do justice to the whole history of programming languages. Instead, only a selection of its many interesting stories are presented, chronologically arranged. If these stories capture your interest, the "Further Reading" section at the end of this chapter suggests where to go for more.

24.2 The Prehistory of Programming

The story of programming languages begins long before the invention of programmable computers. In this section are three stories from this prehistory of programming languages.

The Story of the Programmers of Babylon

On the Euphrates river near present-day Baghdad stood the ancient city of Babylon. It was the seat of the Babylonian empire, founded by Hammurabi around 1790 B.C. In the Babylonian empire a *cuneiform* script was used. Cuneiform simply means "wedge-shaped," the script being formed from wedge-shaped marks. A number of clay tablets with this writing have been recovered by archeologists. Though the language the tablets record is no longer used, they have been translated, and they tell an interesting story.

The Babylonian empire was a prosperous center of art, commerce, agriculture, religion, and science. Our interest here, of course, is in the science: the Babylonians had a well-developed mathematics. They used a base-60 number system, vestiges of which can still be seen in our units of time (60 minutes in an hour) and angle (360 degrees in a circle). They used a floating-point notation that did not explicitly represent the exponent; for example, the written number 1,10 might represent $1 \times 60^1 + 10 \times 60^0 = 70$, $1 \times 60^0 + 10 \times 60^{-1} = 1\frac{1}{6}$, or, in general, $1 \times 60^{i-1} + 10 \times 60^i$ for any i. Presumably, the Babylonian mathematicians kept the correct exponent in mind while they worked—not usually hard to do, since they had to estimate the result only to within a power of 60. The idea of doing floating-point computation without an explicit exponent appears in several more modern examples: slide rules worked that way (in base 10) and many of the earliest digital computers worked that way.

A number of the cuneiform tablets that have been recovered record instructions for computation—algorithms, in fact. Here is part of a translation of one:

> A cistern.
> The length equals the height.
> A certain volume of dirt has been excavated.
> The cross-sectional area plus this volume comes to 1,10.
> The length is 30. What is the width?
> You should multiply the length, 30, by . . .

The instructions go on to describe how to compute the width. The idea of variables as symbolic placeholders for values does not seem to occur. Nevertheless, the description is an algorithm and not just a trace of a particular computation. The numbers 1,10 and 30 are given as examples for the general computational procedure being described. The instructions even use a standard syntax; for example, they always close with the statement, "This is the procedure."

No one knows when the Babylonians (or perhaps the earlier Sumerians, also using cuneiform) first started writing down algorithms this way, and no one knows how far they advanced. The cuneiform tablets that have been recovered seem to be only a small fraction, a few pages from the library of their accomplishments. One thing is clear from the story of the Babylonian programmers: programming is among the earliest uses to which written language was put.[1]

The Story of Mohammed Al-Khorezmi

Near that same ancient city of Babylon stands the modern city of Baghdad. The city was founded around 762 and became one of the great cities of Islam, a renowned center of scholarship, art, and poetry. Not long after the founding of the city, between 780 and 850, a court mathematician named Mohammed Al-Khorezmi lived and wrote.

Two of his books were remarkably influential. One is called *Kitâ al-jabr wa'l-muqabâla*—the calculations of reduction and confrontation. The word *algebra* stems from its title. The work was translated into Latin and made its way into Europe, which was behind the rest of the world scientifically in those days. It served as a mathematics text throughout Europe for 800 years.

The original Arabic text of his other major work is now lost. It too was translated into Latin and strongly influenced the course of medieval European mathematics. Its Latin title is *Algorthmi de numero Indorum*. The word *Algorithmi* is a Latinized version of Al-Khorezmi's name, and the source of our word *algorithm.* The book gives algorithms for working with the positional number system we use today: a base-10 positional number system including a symbol for zero. (Many people call the symbols of this number system Arabic numerals, but Al-Khorezmi called them Hindu numerals. They seem to have originated in India.)

Al-Khorezmi's books introduced into Europe a fundamental kind of technology: a data structure (the new number system) with its associated algorithms. The mathematics of Europe was bogged down in Roman numerals, a completely inadequate technology for computation. Today, when we think of advances in technology, we think of machines; but the impact of the algorithms that Al-Khorezmi's books taught was as great as that of any machine.

---

1. Programming languages have now multiplied so extensively that they call to mind another achievement of the Babylonians, which may have been started in the time of Hammurabi: the construction of the temple tower referred to in the Bible as the Tower of Babel.

The Story of Augusta Ada, Countess of Lovelace

George Gordon, Lord Byron, was an English poet who lived and wrote in the early 1800s. He was a handsome man of high social rank, a talented poet and satirist, a defier of social conventions, a worldly traveler, a melancholy philosopher, and a tempestuous lover—such, at least, was his public, romanticized image. His wife knew him more immediately as an abusive drunk. The two were separated shortly after the birth of their daughter, Augusta Ada. Though Ada never saw her father afterwards, his notoriety kept her in the public eye throughout her life.

At that time in England (as elsewhere) women were denied higher education. Math and science, in particular, were considered unsuitable studies for a woman, and women were not permitted to receive university degrees. But Ada's mother had some mathematical interests (Byron called her his Princess of Parallelograms) and insisted on a sound scientific education for her daughter—in part as an antidote to the emotional excesses it was feared Ada had inherited from her father. Ada married at age 19 and had three children. Her husband, who became the first Earl of Lovelace, supported her unconventional interests. Ada, now Lady Lovelace, managed to continue to study mathematics with a private tutor.

The English mathematician Charles Babbage was, at this time, working on his lifelong project—the design and construction of computational machines. His Difference Engine was a mechanical device for performing computations automatically; we would now call it a printing calculator. Its development was for a time financed by the government, but construction of it was not completed.[2] His Analytical Engine was something more: a completely mechanical, yet conceptually modern, computer. It had a processing unit and a memory (the Mill and the Store, as he called them). It was programmable, using punched cards. It supported iteration and conditional branching. It had some aspects of what we would now call pipelining. There were designs for many input and output devices. It was a brilliant design, though never built.

Babbage was a friend of the Lovelace family, and Lady Lovelace studied the designs for his Engines. In 1842, an Italian engineer, Luigi Menabrea, wrote a paper describing Babbage's Analytical Engine, which appeared in a Swiss journal. Lady Lovelace translated the paper into English, and quadrupled its length with her own explanatory notes. She published the paper, "Sketch of the Analytical Engine," in a scientific journal in 1843. The author of the notes is identified only as A.A.L.—authorship by a woman would not have been considered proper.

---

2. Not completed in his lifetime, that is. In 1991 a Difference Engine, implementing one of his designs with careful historical accuracy, was completed at the Science Museum in London, celebrating the two-hundredth anniversary of his birth.

The notes contain a detailed account of a program for computing a well-known mathematical sequence, the Bernoulli numbers. For this reason Lady Lovelace is sometimes called the first programmer—an exaggeration, almost certainly, since Babbage originated the programs in the paper, though she documented and debugged them. Regardless of the authorship of the programs, however, the paper has a good claim as the first use of a programming language. Prior written algorithms, going back to the Babylonians, were presented in natural language augmented with mathematics. They were meant to be executed by people. In the "Sketch of the Analytical Engine" programs are, for the first time, written in a programming language—the machine language of punched cards for controlling the Analytical Engine. The program for the Bernoulli numbers consists of 25 cards for controlling the Mill (the Operation-cards); about 75 additional cards (the Variable-cards), three for each operation, would have been used to specify the operand sources and write targets in the Store.

Babbage's Analytical Engine, like early electronic computers 100 years later, was focused on numerical computation. Babbage showed little interest in non-numerical applications for it. Lady Lovelace understood that automatic computation could be thought of as symbolic manipulation and was not limited to the purely numerical. She speculated that such a machine might someday compose music and produce graphics. She wrote,

> The bounds of *arithmetic* were however outstepped the moment the idea of applying the cards had occurred; and the Analytical Engine does not occupy common ground with mere "calculating machines." It holds a position wholly its own; and the considerations it suggests are most interesting in their nature. In enabling mechanism to combine together general symbols in successions of unlimited variety and extent, a uniting link is established between the operations of matter and the abstract mental processes of the most abstract branch of mathematical science.

The modern programming language Ada is named in her honor.

24.3 Early Programming Languages

Now for some important early programming languages of more recent vintage: those invented after the first programmable digital computers.

The Story of the Plankalkül

Konrad Zuse was a German engineer and inventor. In 1936, at the age of 26, he built a computer in his parents' living room in Berlin. This machine, later named the Z1, was a mechanical computer using a clever arrangement of metal strips and pins, very different from the wheelwork of Babbage's designs.[3] Zuse was unaware of Babbage's work at the time—which was probably just as well, since an imitation of the Analytical Engine would not have been as successful as Zuse's original design. The Z1 could be hand-cranked or driven by an electric motor. The Z1 was groundbreaking in many ways. It was a programmable computer, reading its program from punched tapes, which Zuse made from the discarded film of old movies. It worked in binary, like modern computers. It used floating-point numbers with an explicit exponent. Zuse's second design, the Z2, used telephone relays for the arithmetic unit, but still used a mechanical memory. The Z3, completed in 1941, was built entirely with relay technology. In the early 1940s, Zuse was working in Berlin on the Z4, which he envisioned as a commercial product.

Then war got in the way. Berlin came under heavy daily bombardment, and Zuse fled the city with his Z4 prototype and his pregnant wife. They eventually made their way to Hinterstein, a small Bavarian village, where the Z4 was hidden in a barn. Zuse was an artist as well as an inventor, and to earn money he made woodblock prints of the local scenery and sold them to the American soldiers.

He also completed, in 1946, a design he had been working on for a programming language: the Plankalkül, the Plan Calculus. It is a high-level programming language, in the sense that it describes algorithms not in terms of instructions for a particular computing machine, but in terms of machine-independent operations. The Plankalkül includes many features found in today's high-level languages. In particular,

- It has assignment statements with expressions. The language of expressions includes subexpressions and parentheses. Array references can have subscripts, which can be variables. The syntax used by Zuse is difficult for eyes conditioned by modern languages to read. Each statement is arranged on up to four lines. A variable is a letter followed by a number, with the number appearing on the line directly *below* the letter. Below that is the subscript, if any, and below that an optional comment line noting the type.
- It has constructed types. The only primitive-type values are individual bits—*Ja-Nein-Werte*. From these, composite types can be built, such as

3. The machines were originally named V1, V2, and so on. Zuse changed the names later to avoid any association with the rockets used by Germany in the Second World War.

integers, floating-point numbers, complex numbers, records including nested records, arrays including higher-dimensional arrays, and variable-length lists.

- It has control constructs: conditional execution, loops, and subroutines.
- It has assertions. Assertions like those of an axiomatic semantics are made within the language, not merely as comments. First-order logic is used operationally as well; there is, for example, a simple way to refer to the first element of an array satisfying a given predicate.

Zuse developed a large collection of example programs using his Plankalkül, everything from sorting an array to playing chess.

There was no implementation of the Plankalkül, nor would any implementation have been possible. Language systems were still more than 10 years beyond the state of the art in software or hardware. The Z4's memory consisted of 64 words of 32 bits each, and it executed its programs directly from punched tape, not wasting any of the 64 words on mere instructions. Indeed, most of Zuse's example programs for the Plankalkül were also beyond the capacities of his own hardware. It is clear that Zuse understood some of the potential of his invention. He understood that future hardware would be far more capable, and that future software would be complex enough to require a high-level language.

Zuse returned to the commercial design and construction of computers after the war. Many of his early designs and prototypes were destroyed in the war, and his achievements went unrecognized for many years. Many of his ideas appear in modern languages—so many that it might appear that the Plankalkül was very influential. In fact, it was unpublished until 1972, and few people knew of it. Zuse's language ideas were invented again by others. But although it had little direct influence on the course of programming-language evolution, the Plankalkül stands as the first high-level language.

The Story of Fortran

Computer programming requires every degree of cunning—that's part of what makes it so much fun. In the early days of large-scale digital computers, however, it was also labor intensive in a way that modern programmers can only dimly appreciate. Coding for the first large-scale digital computer, the Harvard Mark I, was done in machine language—in octal, using the numerals 0 through 7 to represent groups of three bits. In the U.S. Navy, Lieutenant Dr. Grace Murray Hopper (later Rear Admiral) was one of the first coders working on the first large-scale digital computer, the Harvard Mark I, in 1944. This was part of her keynote address at the first conference on the history of programming languages:

> In the early years of programming languages, the most frequent phrase we heard was that the only way to program a computer was in octal. Of course a few years later a few people admitted that maybe you could use assembly language. . . . I have here a copy of the manual for Mark I. I think most of you would be totally flabbergasted if you were faced with programming a computer, using a Mark I manual. All it gives you are the codes. From there on you're on your own to write a program. We were not programmers in those days. The word had not yet come over from England. We were "coders."

The Mark I and other early machines lacked architectural features that make even machine-level coding easier today. They represented real numbers without an explicit exponent (Babylonian-style, but in base 2). They had little support for array indexing. They used absolute addresses, so that even though the coders collected their own handwritten libraries of commonly used subroutines, the codes for these had to be altered by hand to reflect the addresses at which they were loaded in memory.

Coders began to develop tools to help speed up the process. Assemblers were developed in the early 1950s. These substituted mnemonics like ADD and MUL for octal codes and substituted symbolic addresses for hand-computed absolute addresses. More ambitious tools also appeared. Some, like Grace Hopper's A-0 and A-2, were like subroutine libraries invoked by macro expansion. (Her later system B-0, known as FLOWMATIC, was the first business data-processing language and was one of the major influences on Cobol—but that's another story.) Other early coding tools, like John Mauchly's Short Code in 1949 and John Backus's Speedcoding in 1954, were more like intermediate-code interpreters. Using these systems, the coder could write in a more powerful virtual machine language—one with proper floating-point numbers, indexing, and relative addressing. The intermediate code was then interpreted. Although the resulting programs ran five or ten times slower than equivalent programs coded directly in the physical machine language, the savings in programmer time often made up for it.

Saving programmer time—people began to see the importance of that. Computers were getting faster and more powerful, while people were not, so the time spent on coding was taking a bigger and bigger fraction of the total cost of a project. In late 1953, John Backus wrote a memo to his boss at IBM, proposing the creation of a language to make programming easier for IBM's mainframe computer, the 704. Management went for the idea, and by late 1954 Backus had organized a research group at IBM and produced an interesting document: "Preliminary Report: Specifications for the IBM Mathematical FORmula TRANslating System, FORTRAN." The world's first popular high-level programming language was about to be born.

The Fortran project focused pragmatically on compiler construction. The problem, as Backus and his team saw it, was to compile Fortran programs into efficient machine code for the 704. Backus wrote,

> As far as we were aware, we simply made up the language as we went along. We did not regard language design as a difficult problem, merely a simple prelude to the real problem: designing a compiler which could produce efficient programs.

Starting from some basic design decisions—the assignment statement, the array subscripting notation, and the `DO` loop for iteration—the Fortran team developed the language by a process of adding things that seemed necessary for programming and omitting things that would interfere with the compilation of efficient programs. Some of Fortran's early design decisions, such as the lack of recursion, the use of by-reference parameter passing, the limitation of array dimensions to three, and the placement of the `DO` loop test at the end of the loop, should be read in this light. They were driven by implementation concerns. If the Plankalkül was designed but never implemented, it is only a minor exaggeration to say that Fortran was implemented but never designed.

The Fortran team had to overcome a great deal of skepticism. Most people did not believe it was possible for compiler-generated code to be competitive with code written by hand. The team began development of the compiler in 1955 and released the first version to IBM customers in 1957. They had succeeded in their goal: the Fortran compiler amazed programmers with the clever code it generated. In spite of the initial skepticism, it was adopted quickly and was in heavy use by IBM customers by late 1958.

Fortran succeeded in eliminating many of the low-level chores that had been plaguing programmers since the early days of the Mark I. No doubt this improvement is what the designers of Fortran had in mind when they wrote, in the 1954 report, that Fortran would "virtually eliminate coding and debugging." Of course, as modern programmers understand those terms, they have not been eliminated or even reduced. Programmers continue to work at the limits of their cunning. But Fortran moved those limits up, so that programmers could focus their coding and debugging efforts on higher-level challenges.

One defect in the language was that it did not support separate compilation. As customers began to write larger and larger Fortran programs, they ran into this problem. Changing a program of more than a few hundred lines took too long because all of it had to be recompiled simultaneously. Separately compiled subroutines had been part of the original plan, but were not implemented in the first release. They were included in Fortran II, which was released in 1958. Many subsequent versions of Fortran followed, and implementations for many machines other than the IBM 704. (Early Fortran dialects were very IBM 704–specific, with statements like `SENSE LIGHT`, `PAUSE`, `STOP`, `PUNCH`, and `READ DRUM`.) Modern dialects of Fortran are still widely used, especially for high-performance numerical computation.

Today, undergraduates majoring in computer science often take a course in compiler construction. The initial phases of a compiler, the scanner, and the parser, can be written automatically by tools that take formal definitions of the syntax of the language as input. Using such tools and applying other compiler-writing techniques, a student can complete a simple compiler in a semester. But when John Backus and his team developed the first Fortran compiler, they were exploring an uncharted territory of compiler-development techniques. They pioneered many techniques of scanning, parsing, register allocation, code generation, and optimization.

John Backus went on to make a number of other major contributions to programming languages. For example, he contributed to the designs of the first two Algol languages, and he developed the BNF (Backus-Naur Form) grammar, which this book has used for defining programming-language syntax. His most unusual accomplishment is that, unlike many inventors, he did not fall in love with his invention. Although he enjoyed the Fortran project immensely and was proud of the results, he came to believe that imperative languages were too low-level, too limiting, too difficult to reason about. He developed a purely functional language, FP, and argued for the importance of new, more declarative approaches to computer programming. In 1978 he wrote,

> My point is this: while it was perhaps natural and inevitable that languages like FORTRAN and its successors should have developed out of the concept of the von Neumann computer as they did, the fact that such languages have dominated our thinking for twenty years is unfortunate. It is unfortunate because their long-standing familiarity will make it hard for us to understand and adopt new programming styles which one day will offer far greater intellectual and computation power.

The Story of Lisp

About the same time that John Backus and his team were working to complete the first implementation of Fortran, Professor John McCarthy of Dartmouth College was organizing a conference: the Dartmouth Summer Research Project on Artificial Intelligence. The Dartmouth conference, held in the summer of 1956, marked the birth of a new field. It was the first organized workshop on artificial intelligence; in fact, it was the first use of the term *artificial intelligence*. It was also the first meeting of many of the future leaders of the field, including John McCarthy, Marvin Minsky, Alan Newell, and Herbert Simon.

At the Dartmouth conference, Alan Newell, J. C. Shaw, and Herbert Simon had the most impressive demonstration. They had implemented a system called Logic Theorist that could automatically prove theorems of propositional logic. Logic Theorist was written in a language called IPL, which had support for processing linked lists. The use of linked lists was novel and caught the attention of McCarthy.[4] McCarthy wanted a language for his AI projects. He was working with sentences and formulas, and he realized that list-processing capabilities would be useful. He also realized that IPL was not the answer. IPL was a very low-level language closely tied to the architecture of the JOHNNIAC computer. McCarthy had read about the Fortran project and wanted to work in a high-level language.

In fact, the first language McCarthy worked with was an extension of Fortran. A group at IBM was inspired to work on an AI problem by the Dartmouth conference. Their problem involved proofs in plane geometry. To support it they extended Fortran with list-processing capabilities. McCarthy was a consultant on the project, and the resulting language was called FLPL, Fortran List Processing Language. But FLPL did not satisfy McCarthy. By writing some AI applications, including systems for playing chess and for doing symbolic differential calculus, McCarthy discovered some missing features that he wanted.

For one thing, he wanted a conditional expression. Fortran had a three-way conditional branch statement, which jumped to one of three labeled targets depending on whether a numeric expression was negative, zero, or positive:

```
IF (A-B) 5,6,7
```

But what McCarthy found he needed was a conditional *expression*, like those now used in ML and Java: a short-circuiting expression `if` *a* `then` *b* `else` *c*, whose value is the value of either *b* or *c*. One important application for a conditional expression,

---

4. In papers from this period, you will sometimes see the phrase *NSS memory*. The *NSS* is Newell, Shaw, and Simon, and *NSS memory* refers to linked lists. The idea of a linked list seems simple and obvious today, hardly worth an eponymous acronym, but it was revelatory when it was new.

as you saw back in Chapter 5, is to control recursion—another feature McCarthy found he really wanted in a language. (A program to do symbolic differentiation works out much more neatly if it can be written recursively, since the derivative of an expression can be defined in terms of the derivatives of its subexpressions.) That is part of the reason McCarthy needed the conditional expression to be short-circuiting; he wanted to be able to write, in effect, `if` *done* `then` *base-case* `else` *recursive-case* and not end up evaluating both cases.

McCarthy also wanted higher-order functions. In particular, he found that a function like ML's `map` function, to apply another function to every element of a list and collect the results in a new list, would be really useful. This led to a need for anonymous functions (like those created by `fn` expressions in ML). One final thing on McCarthy's wish list was garbage collection. Although IPL had primitives for list processing, list elements had to be explicitly deallocated by the program. McCarthy did not want to clutter his systems up with a lot of explicit deallocations for list elements.

McCarthy's wish list was too big for IBM. They did not want to make the radical changes to the Fortran system that would have been necessary to add all these things to FLPL. In late 1958 he started the MIT Artificial Intelligence Project and began development of a new language: Lisp.

The most eye-catching feature of Lisp is its unusual syntax. Lisp programs not only manipulate lists, they *are* lists. The ML expression `a+b*c` is written in Lisp this way:

```
(+ a (* b c))
```

This is, as you can see, a representation of the abstract syntax tree for `a+b*c`. A Lisp program is a direct representation of an AST in list form. Oddly enough, this syntax was unintentional. McCarthy's group developed the language by an experimental process that involved hand-translating example programs into assembly language. On paper, the programs they experimented with were written in a Fortran-like notation. At first they planned to compile from this language. But in 1960 McCarthy published a paper arguing for the simplicity and power of recursive functions as a tool for computation. The paper included an example of a function named `eval`, a Lisp interpreter written in Lisp. To keep this interpreter simple, he wanted to avoid all the mechanics of parsing, so he wrote an interpreter that took as input the AST of the program to be interpreted—just as in Chapter 23.[5] One of McCarthy's

---

5. Another parallel with Chapter 23 is that the original Lisp `eval` used dynamic scope instead of static scope. As you saw in Chapter 23, this is an easy behavior to get by accident. In fact, McCarthy viewed it as a bug. It persisted widely in Lisp for years and is still found in a few dialects, though most have now adopted static scope.

graduate students observed that taking McCarthy's `eval` from the paper and hand-translating it into assembly language would result in a working Lisp interpreter, assuming that Lisp programs were entered as ASTs in list form and not using the Fortran-like syntax. The modern Lisp syntax was born.

The group never gave up the idea of compiling Lisp from a Fortran-like syntax, but they never got around to doing it either. In later years, people often designed some Fortran-like or Algol-like syntax for Lisp and wrote parsers to convert it into the list representation, but none of them caught on. Most Lisp programmers preferred to use the list notation. There are advantages to having programs and data use the same syntax, as you saw with Prolog. It is easy to write a Lisp program that transforms another Lisp program, and it is easy (using `eval`) to execute the transformed code. Modern macro facilities in Lisp systems also make it easy to add any syntax the programmer cares to use. Lisp programmers often view a programming problem as a kind of language-design problem. They work by adding syntax and function definitions to the language until they have a language in which the solution to their original programming problem is trivial. This can make Lisp programs difficult to read, as they often appear to be written in a custom language; but it certainly makes them fun to write.

Lisp was implemented on many different systems. It quickly became, and remains, the most popular language for AI projects. Lisp language systems are usually easy to modify, often being written largely in Lisp itself. It was natural for different AI groups to evolve their own Lisp dialects and tools. By the late 1960s there were many different dialects. Throughout the 1970s there was another Lisp phenomenon: the development of commercial Lisp machines. These machines, by Lisp Machine, Inc.; Symbolics; Texas Instruments; and others, offered improved support for Lisp, with large address spaces, and hardware support for Lisp's dynamic type checking and garbage collection. Each commercial machine had its own dialect. In the late 1980s a modest reduction began in the number of dialects in use. One cause was the demise of the Lisp-machine companies, once improved general-purpose workstations and improved Lisp compilers were able to provide competitive Lisp performance. Another cause was a reduction in commercial and government funding for AI research. Also, Lisp standards developed. There is a standard for a Lisp dialect called Common Lisp, which is a large language with a very large API. There is also a standard for Scheme, which is a considerably smaller and simpler Lisp dialect.

Lisp is the second-oldest, general-purpose programming language still in widespread use. Some of its ideas, like the conditional expression and support for recursion, were adopted by Algol and so made their way into many other imperative languages. Other ideas, like the function-oriented Lisp programming style, influenced modern functional languages like ML.

The Story of Algol

Algol was intended to be *the* language: the one universal, international, machine-independent language for expressing scientific algorithms.

Development of Algol began in Europe. There had been a number of designs for high-level programming languages, not widely known in America: Zuse's Plankalkül in Germany in 1946, Heinz Rutishauser's in Switzerland in 1951, Corrado Böhm's in Switzerland in 1954, and several others. Although these languages were not implemented, there were enough of them, and enough similarities among them, to trigger the natural response: the feeling that it would be better to get together and design one universal algorithmic language. In 1955, a European working group was organized for that purpose. In America, a profusion of manufacturer-specific implementations of programming languages arose at about the same time as Fortran. Again, the natural response was to attempt to unify the languages and stop their multiplication. In 1957, an American working group was organized for that purpose. In 1958 the two working groups met and cooperated on a design.

That was the beginning of Algol. Eventually, there were three major designs: Algol 58 (originally called IAL, International Algorithmic Language), Algol 60, and Algol 68. Each version was developed by an international committee—the later versions by increasingly large international committees. It is difficult to make an interesting narrative out of the long and often rancorous political process by which the Algol committees arrived at their designs, so let's move past the design process and examine only the results.

The results are impressive. Virtually all languages invented after 1958 used ideas that were pioneered by the Algol languages. Algol 58, for example, introduced the idea of the compound statement, bracketed by the keywords `begin` and `end`. Algol 60 introduced the idea of local variables with block scope. It also introduced the idea of an array whose size is not known until runtime, making it one of the first languages for which memory allocation could not be completely static. Algol 68 introduced the idea of an array whose size can be changed at runtime, without static bounds. The Algol languages used a free-format lexical structure, unlike the card-oriented, fixed-format lexical structure of most other early languages. They supported recursion. They had static typing, which got stronger as Algol evolved.

The flow of control in early Fortran dialects was specified using numeric statement labels; for example, a program could execute an unconditional branch to the statement numbered 27 using the statement `GO TO 27`. Similarly, the `IF` and `DO` statements jumped conditionally or unconditionally to targets specified by labels. Other early languages, like Cobol and Basic, also used label-oriented control. The Algol languages had `GO TO` constructs, but used them much more rarely, because the languages included modern-style, phrase-level control constructs, like the `if` and `while` constructs of Java, along with a number of others: `switch`, `for`, `until`, and so on. In fact, starting in the early 1960s, a number of people began to observe that algorithms expressed using phrase-level control were often easier to write, read, and maintain than the same algorithms expressed using `go to` constructs. A debate began to heat up about the proper place for label-directed control, a debate that burst into flame in 1968 when Edsger Dijkstra published his famous letter, "Go to statement considered harmful." In the letter Dijkstra stated his opinion that the `go to` statement should be completely eliminated from all high-level languages. There was a great deal of argument about it, and many programmers found it difficult at first to do without `go to` and to think in terms of phrase-level control. The debate has long since died down. Here is the judgment of history on the issue: the `go to` has quietly perished from many modern languages, including Java, and quietly persisted in others, like C++; but all modern languages include enough flexibility in phrase-level control structures that it is rarely used even when permitted. Programmers no longer complain about the inconvenience of having to think in terms of phrase-level control instead of label-directed control; it just seems natural. This revolution in programming practice and programming-language design is part of what people used to call *structured programming*. The phrase is seldom heard now since the revolution has been quite complete and unstructured programming is no longer practiced. The structured programming revolution was triggered, or at least significantly fueled, by the Algol designs.

The Algol designs reflect a strong and growing desire to avoid special cases. The choice of a free-format lexical structure is one expression of this. It eliminates a bunch of special cases about column numbers. Another expression of this desire is that the languages avoid arbitrary limits, such as the early Fortran limits on the number of characters in a name (six) or the number of dimensions in an array (three). More profoundly, Algol 60 and Algol 68 attempted to avoid the special forbidden combinations that other languages were (and are) often riddled with. Suppose, for example, that the kinds of things manipulated by a language include integers, arrays, and procedures, while the kinds of operations include passing as a parameter, storing in a variable, storing in an array, and returning from a procedure. The possible combinations can be pictured as a grid:

	Integers	**Arrays**	**Procedures**
Passing as a parameter			
Storing in a variable			
Storing in an array			
Returning from a procedure			

Each combination, each position in the grid, that is *not* permitted by the language amounts to a special case that the programmer must remember. To avoid special cases, a language design should permit every combination. This is a design principle called *orthogonality*, that every meaningful combination of primitive concepts in the language should be legal. Orthogonality is just another way of avoiding special cases. The Algol languages avoided special cases more thoroughly than any of their contemporaries. By Algol 68, every position in the grid above is legal, and that is only a small sample of its orthogonality.

The Algol languages also pioneered many of the techniques of language definition and implementation and much of the terminology used today for describing languages. BNF grammars were first used in the definition of Algol 60. An operational semantics was part of the definition of Algol 68. Terms such as *block, identifier, declaration, coercion,* and *activation record* were first used in their modern sense in descriptions of the Algol languages.

In spite of all these wonderful qualities, Algol was never dominant among implemented language systems. IBM began an implementation of Algol 58, but eventually decided to concentrate on Fortran instead. Several languages were implemented that were extensions of Algol 58. (Jovial was one of these, the official scientific programming language of the U.S. Air Force for many years.) Implementations of Algol 60 were used occasionally in America and more widely in Europe. But even in Europe, Algol 60 did not become the dominant language for scientific programming or drive Fortran out of its niche. Algol 68 had only a few full implementations and was never widely used. The most important direct use of the Algol languages was not for person-to-machine communication, but for person-to-person: Algol 60 was the standard language for scholarly publication of algorithms for 20 years.

If the Algols were so much more advanced than their contemporaries, why were they not more widely used? There are many possible reasons. For one thing, the Algol languages lacked some of the machine-specific features that programmers wanted, such as support for I/O. Another reason is that the Algol languages included some awkward inventions, such as by-name parameter passing. Another possible reason is that the Algol designs led the way from too far out in front. The ideas were new and strange to programmers and a considerable challenge for the implementers of language systems. Still another reason is that, unlike Fortran, the Algol languages did not have the weight of a major corporation behind them.

Whatever the reason, Algol never succeeded in becoming *the* language for scientific computation. That goal, as it turns out, was unattainable. Perhaps one day language evolution will slow and converge, but it shows no immediate signs of doing so. The dream of creating a universal language is one that seems to grip people, and especially organizations, at regular intervals. There are some similarities with the development of PL/I, for example, and Ada. At present, however, it does not appear possible to create a single language that will be used by a majority of people for a majority of their applications. The time for a universal language, even within a single application area such as scientific computation, has not yet come. It may never come.

The real success of the Algol designs is their influence on later programming languages and on the whole field of programming-language design and implementation. Virtually all modern languages and language systems use ideas that were pioneered in Algol. Many, including Pascal, the Modula languages, and Ada, are Algol's direct descendants.

The Story of Smalltalk

Among Algol 60's important descendants are the Simula languages, Simula I and Simula 67. These were developed by Kristen Nygaard and Ole-Johan Dahl at the Norwegian Computing Center, starting in 1961. The Simula languages are the ancestors of all modern object-oriented programming languages.

Simula I is a language for describing simulations: airplanes landing and taking off at an airport, customers arriving and being served at a bank, or any other kind of dynamic process that can be modeled as a collection of passive components (*customers*) moving through a collection of active components (*stations*) in a sequence of discrete events. Simula I was implemented as a modification of an Algol 60 compiler and runtime system. In particular, it required a modification of Algol 60's memory-management routines to support heap storage.

Simula I showed the beginnings of object orientation. There was a definition like a class definition for each kind of customer. Each customer had its own variables, like instance variables, and any number of customers could be instantiated at runtime. Each station had a *queue part* and a *service part*, the service part being a bit like a collection of methods. But each station was statically declared, not instantiated at runtime. Customers did not have methods. There was no inheritance or polymorphism.

Later, Nygaard and Dahl began to feel that a modified version of Simula could be used as a general-purpose language and not just for programming simulations. Their new dialect, Simula 67, eliminated some of the simulation-specific terminology of Simula I. Instead, they introduced the terms *class* and *object* and an organized scheme for inheritance. (Simulation was still a principal application for the language, but most of the simulation-specific things were moved to class libraries.) One thing that Simula 67 lacks, from the point of view of modern object-oriented languages, is the idea of a method. In Simula 67, a class looks much like a single Algol 60 procedure, and an instance of a class is an activation of the procedure. Using *detach* statement, these procedures can transfer control back to the caller without deallocating the activation record, leaving the caller with a reference to the object. Later, using the *resume* statement, control can be returned to the activation.[6]

Simula I and Simula 67 never had large user communities, but implementations of both dialects made their way to many sites. One such site was the University of Utah.

The University of Utah was the home of a strong research program in computer graphics. A interactive drawing system call Sketchpad was developed there. Although not written in an object-oriented language, Sketchpad illustrated some object-oriented ideas about graphics. There were, for example, master drawings that could have instances. All the new graduate students in the department had to learn about the Sketchpad project. When a young man named Alan Kay arrived in the department in 1966, after learning about the Sketchpad project, he was given his first programming chore: to figure out some mysterious new software that the department had received. He writes,

> The documentation was incomprehensible. Supposedly, this was the Case-Western Reserve 1107 ALGOL—but it had been doctored to make a language called Simula; the documentation read like Norwegian transliterated into English, which in fact it was. There were uses of words like *activity* and *process* that did not seem to coincide with normal English usage.
>
> Finally, another graduate student and I unrolled the program listing 80 feet down the hall and crawled over it yelling discov-

6. Procedures that pass control back and forth without a stack-ordered call/return discipline are called *coroutines*. Coroutines are useful for occasional programming problems, like some of those that arise when programming simulations, but most high-level languages, unlike the Simula languages, do not support them. Simula 67 objects are activations of procedures, which can transfer control to each other as coroutines.

> eries to each other. The weirdest part was the storage allocator, which did not obey a stack discipline as was usual for ALGOL. A few days later, that provided the clue. What Simula was allocating were structures very much like instances of Sketchpad. There were descriptions that acted like masters and they could create instances, each of which was an independent entity. What Sketchpad called masters and instances, Simula called activities and processes. Moreover, Simula was a procedural language for controlling Sketchpad-like objects. . . .
>
> This was the big hit, and I have not been the same since.

Kay was interested in computing for children. He saw the computer as a medium for learning by doing and was intrigued by Seymour Papert's work with the Logo system—a language and graphical environment in which children could learn and do programming. In 1968, Kay began to design a computer system he called the Dynabook, a graphical notebook computer for children. Such a thing is easier to imagine now, but in 1968 almost all computers were gigantic, expensive engineering tools used exclusively by adults. Kay's Ph.D. work, completed in 1969, involved an object-oriented language in a graphical computer for non-computing professionals. This FLEX system was a pioneering personal computer—if a computer that still weighs more than a person can be called *personal*!

Kay took his Dynabook vision with him to Xerox, where he was one of the founders of the Xerox Palo Alto Research Center in 1970. Xerox PARC in the 1970s was a wonderfully productive research center, where many of the ideas of the modern personal computer were invented or significantly advanced, including bitmapped displays, modern graphical user interfaces, the mouse, the Ethernet, the laser printer, and the client-server architecture. At Xerox PARC, Kay led a group that developed the Smalltalk language. An early version they developed in 1971 looked quite a bit like Logo; Kay planned to develop it into a visual, iconic language for his Dynabook. In the event, however, the language evolved in a very different direction.

Smalltalk is an object-oriented language. In fact, it was Kay who coined the term *object oriented*. Smalltalk is far more object oriented than its recent and more popular descendants. In Smalltalk, *everything is an object*: variables, constants, activation records, classes, everything. There is no static typing. All computation is performed by objects sending and receiving messages. The expression `1+2*3` is evaluated by treating the constant `1` as an object and sending it the message `+` with parameter `2`; the result is an object which is sent the message `*` with parameter `3`. Smalltalk has a very small and elegant, but not at all obvious, core design. Kay's 1972 design, which he refers to as the first real Smalltalk, was implemented by Dan Ingalls in just a few days.

Smalltalk and Lisp are very different languages, but they share a design philosophy. In both cases, the language designers tried to find the most elegant language they could, starting from a small set of basic elements. In Lisp's case, the basic elements include lists, recursion, and `eval`. Given these, the rest of Lisp follows quite naturally. In his presentation at ACM's first History of Programming Languages Conference, McCarthy said,

> Because Lisp forms a kind of neat whole, one might think that it was planned that way, but it really wasn't. It sort of grew and then, one might say, snapped into some kind of local maximum, or maybe a local minimum, in the space of programming languages.

The design of Smalltalk also seems to have snapped into a local maximum. In Smalltalk's case, the basic elements included objects and message passing. Smalltalk is a language, one might say *the* language, that follows from a strong commitment to these basic elements. Like Lisp, Smalltalk language systems are often fairly easy to modify; like Lisp, it is a good language for rapid prototyping and exploratory programming; like Lisp, it supports a style of programming that often feels like designing a custom language to make the solution of your original problem easier.

Development of Smalltalk continued at Xerox PARC throughout the 1970s, but it remained an in-house system during that time. A platform-independent version of the language, Smalltalk-80, proliferated widely after its general release in 1983. Its ideas have inspired a generation of newer object-oriented languages and object-oriented design techniques. Though not quite as popular as its more recent (and less object-oriented) descendants, Smalltalk remains in widespread use.

24.4 This Book's Languages

This chapter on programming language history concludes with the three main languages from this book: Prolog, ML, and Java.

The Story of Prolog

As you might expect, Prolog arose from work on automated theorem proving. In 1965, Alan Robinson published a paper introducing the idea of theorem proving based on resolution. Resolution, as you will recall, is the foundation of Prolog; it is the same basic inference step Chapter 20 gave a variation of. But Prolog did not arise immediately after the publication of Robinson's paper or follow easily from Robinson's results. There is a whole family of possible algorithms for automated inference based on resolution, with widely varying degrees of power and efficiency. Robinson's paper was followed by a great deal of work around the world on resolution-based theorem proving. Several researchers saw the connection between automated inference and general computation and observed that the behavior of theorem provers could parallel the behavior of programming-language interpreters. But most of the research focused on getting theorem provers to prove impressively difficult things—not on getting them to do the simple computation tasks that Fortran and Lisp could already do.

In 1971, a group led by Alain Colmerauer at the Université d'Aix Marseilles was working on an AI project: a system to answer questions about natural-language texts. The system they were building required automated deduction; for example, if the text said that Jerry is a mouse and that mice eat cheese, the system needed to be able to answer the question, does Jerry eat cheese? For the automated deduction part of the system, the group was using a resolution-based technique. They invited Robert Kowalski of the University of Edinburgh to visit, and he explained his resolution-based theorem prover. Kowalski called his technique *SL-resolution.* Philippe Roussel implemented a simplified version of SL-resolution for the first Prolog system in 1972.

The name Prolog was suggested by Roussel's wife, as a derivation of *programmation en logique.* Colmerauer and Roussel found that the system could be used for their entire application, not just for the deductive part. It was a general-purpose programming language. The first design for Prolog used a variety of different punctuation marks at the ends of clauses—`..`, `.;`, `;.`, and `;;`—each with a different effect on backtracking. These were dropped in the 1973 version of the language, and the modern cut operation was introduced in their place. The occurs check was also dropped, and the 1973 version looked much like modern Prolog.

Early implementations of Prolog were interpreted systems and were extremely slow and memory intensive. In 1977, David Warren at Edinburgh developed the first Prolog compiler. In 1983 he developed an important compilation technique for Prolog: the Warren Abstract Machine, an intermediate-code target for Prolog compilation which is still used in some form by many Prolog compilers (including SWI-Prolog). The availability of compiled implementations, and the commercial success of various expert systems implemented in Prolog, helped Prolog find a wider audience in the 1980s. It remains an important language for artificial intelligence development.

Like Lisp and Smalltalk, Prolog is a language that follows naturally from a small set of basic elements—in Prolog's case, resolution-based inference. Colmerauer and Roussel wrote,

> Prolog is so simple that one has the sense that sooner or later someone had to discover it.

Certainly, the connection between theorem proving and programming occurred to several researchers before Prolog was born. It was in the air, one might say, and seemed to suggest itself to the prepared mind. But the success of Prolog is due to an important insight about how to make that connection practical. Anyone who has experimented with resolution-based theorem proving knows how easy it is to come up with a correct but useless variant: a theorem prover that wanders around proving exponentially many true things, but none to the point. The difficult thing is to find an algorithm for theorem proving that is general enough to be the basis of a programming language, and yet can be implemented efficiently enough to be useful in practice. Of all the logic languages that have attempted this balancing act since, Prolog is still the most successful.

The Story of ML

Like Prolog, ML began as part of a project involving automated theorem proving. It was to be used for developing the LCF system, a tool for machine-assisted construction of formal logical proofs. The initial design and implementation in 1974 was the product of a group led by Robin Milner of the University of Edinburgh. The original version had ML's trademark strong typing, parametric polymorphism, and type inference. The language remained closely tied to research on the LCF system for several years, but around 1980 Luca Cardelli implemented a version for the VAX computer. This was the first compiled ML language system. Of this implementation, *The Definition of Standard ML* says,

> By providing a reasonably efficient implementation, this work enabled the language to be taught to students; this, in turn, prompted the idea that it could become a useful general purpose language.

In 1983, Milner wrote the first draft of a standard for ML. Several iterations of a standard for ML were published, implemented, and discussed by many contributors, and the language acquired several new features. Pattern matching was added, drawn from the functional language Hope. In addition, there were new features such as named records, modules, an improved exception-handling mechanism, and I/O using streams (which was beyond the scope of this book).

A major part of Milner's design goal for ML was to construct a full formal semantics for the language, not tacked on as afterthought to the implementation, but developed concurrently with the design. The resulting formal semantics for ML is a natural semantics, similar to the ones introduced in the last chapter, though much deeper and more intricate. This insistence on a solid semantic foundation is a natural product of the original requirements of the LCF project; to believe the formal logical proofs produced by LCF, one must start by believing in the correctness of the language in which LCF is implemented.

In addition to standard ML (SML), the language has several other important dialects, including Lazy ML, Caml, and Objective Caml. Lazy ML uses lazy evaluation of function parameters, like the language Haskell. Caml is a dialect that diverged from standard ML before modules were added. Objective Caml, sometimes written and pronounced as "OCaml," adds modules and constructs to support object-oriented programming.

The Story of Java

Java is a relatively new language with a biblically long lineage; Algol 60 begat CPL, CPL begat BCPL, BCPL begat B, B begat C, C begat C++, and C++ begat Java.

You have already met Algol 60. It was intended to be a universal language, but only within the domain of scientific programming. It was recognized that the language would not be ideal for other application areas like process control (where Apt was used) and business data processing (where Cobol was used). The language CPL was influenced by Algol, but was considerably bigger, because it included features for business data processing. CPL was a joint project of the University of Cambridge and the University of London. One of its principal designers was Christopher Strachey, who (with Dana Scott) also developed the ideas of denotational semantics. About CPL, Strachey commented,

> From about 1962 until 1966 [I] was engaged with several collaborators at Cambridge and London on the design of a general purpose programming language which came to be known as CPL (an acronym which stood for so many different titles in the course of its existence that it finally acquired a life of its own). During the course of this design work a rather large number of concepts became clear, including many of those concerned with

> the store such as the distinctions between L- and R- modes of evaluation. . . . CPL was never satisfactorily implemented and only inadequately publicized; the most complete document concerning it was only circulated privately (although quite widely).[7]

One of Strachey's students, Martin Richards, devised a simplified version of CPL called BCPL (Basic CPL). "Simplified" is perhaps a bit of an understatement here; the language has only one data type, the machine word, which is treated in different ways by different operators, with neither static nor dynamic type checking. BCPL introduces the idea of treating arrays as memory addresses, so that a reference to the `i`th element of an array `A`, written as `A!i`, was equivalent to a reference to the contents of the memory word at address `A+i`. (C and C++ still handle arrays in much the same way. Java is the only language in the lineage to eliminate this interpretation.) Richards implemented BCPL while visiting MIT in 1967. The language was used for a number of systems programming projects in the 1970s, including some of the work at Xerox PARC. It was also ported to the computers being used by the systems research group at Bell Telephone Laboratories. There, a group led by Ken Thompson was beginning to write (in assembly language) the first Unix operating system.

Thompson wanted to use a high-level language for Unix systems programming and liked the look of BCPL. The Unix project had very limited resources at first, and Thompson needed the language system to run on very small computers. He simplified BCPL even further. The new language, first used around 1969, was called B. B included compound assignment operators (like the `a+=b` of Java), which came from Algol 68. B is the simplest language in the Java lineage.

Starting in 1971, Dennis Ritchie at Bell Labs began extending the B language. Once the Unix group had more resources (in particular, a PDP-11 computer to work with) some of the weakness of B began to show up. Its single data type was inadequate for working with the characters and floating-point numbers supported by the PDP-11, and Ritchie added a type system. The new language was originally called NB (New B) but was renamed C. By 1973 it had most of the characteristics of modern C—the type system, the macro preprocessor, the standard I/O library—and the Unix kernel was rewritten in C. Throughout the 1980s, Unix and the C language spread together, and of course they remain extremely popular today.

---

7. The mellifluous CPL acronym still has legs. For Strachey's language it was often taken as standing for Combined Programming Language. More recent and unrelated uses of the same acronym include Conceptual Prototyping Language, Call Processing Language, and Computer Pidgin Language.

The next link in the chain to Java is the language C++, designed by Bjarne Stroustrup. Stroustrup had two critical experiences while he was a graduate student at Cambridge in 1979. His work required programming a simulation of distributed software. At first he used—critical experience number one—Simula. But although he admired the language, the language system he was using was inadequate for a simulation of the size he needed, and he had to rewrite the whole thing in—critical experience number two—BCPL. *That* he considered to be a miserable language for the job, but at least the BCPL language system was small enough and fast enough to handle his project. Stroustrup took these experiences with him when he went to work for Bell Labs. In 1979 he developed a C preprocessor that added Simula-style classes to C. The language accepted by the preprocessor was called simply "C with Classes." It added classes, inheritance, and access control to C. It did not have dynamic dispatch. In 1984, Stroustrup used the name C++ for the evolving language. His 1984 version added optional dynamic dispatch (so-called *virtual functions*), overloadable operators, and overloadable function names. Later versions added multiple inheritance, parametric polymorphism (using templates), and exception handling (using a `try/catch` construct). The user community for C++ grew with unprecedented speed. The language achieved enormous popularity organically, with almost no marketing effort on the part of Bell Labs and with no sponsorship from a government agency or other organization. C++ remains one of the most widely used languages today.

Which brings us, at last, to Java. In 1990, Sun Microsystems gave a small team of people within the company the chance to do whatever they wanted. Sun's main business strength was as a manufacturer of higher-end workstations. It did not compete in the low-end desktop marketplace. But the Sun team had a vision of an even lower-end market. They pictured a future with computers as ubiquitous but largely invisible components in consumer technology—in cars, in appliances, in televisions, in automated homes—all networked with each other. They wanted to build something for this vision of the future of computing.

One of the original members of the project was James Gosling. The project began to focus on embedded computers for consumer electronics, and Gosling felt that C++ was not the right language for the job. He had been working on a language that would be smaller, more strongly typed, and more platform independent. His first version, completed in 1991, was called Oak, after the tree outside his office window. The idea of networked consumer electronics did not take off at the time, and the language languished for a few years. In 1994, however, Oak finally found the application it had been waiting for: programming for Web pages. The Internet was a network of different platforms, much like the networks of consumer devices the Sun team had been planning for, and the rising popularity of Web browsers was bringing it into many homes. In 1995 the Oak language was renamed Java, and the team retargeted it for the Web. With its virtual machine incorporated into Web browsers, Java could be used to add platform-independent active content to Web pages. Java was released to the public in 1995, and quickly rose to its present height of popularity. The language may yet achieve success with the designers' original vision—it is being implemented inside consumer electronics such as cell phones and smart credit cards—but at present it owes much of its popularity to its suitability for Web programming.

This has been the story of Java told linearly, through a sequence of languages starting with Algol 60. However, Java's design shows the influence of other languages as well. Java has garbage collection, which was introduced in Lisp and is not present in any other language in Java's line. Java's model of concurrency comes from a language called Mesa. Java *packages* are also new to the line and were inspired by the Modula languages. Although Java has been successful in a unique way, nothing in Java is really new. As *The Java Language Specification* says,

> Java is related to C and C++ but is organized rather differently, with a number of aspects of C and C++ omitted and a few ideas from other languages included. Java is intended to be a production language, not a research language, and so, as C. A. R. Hoare suggested in his classic paper on language design, the design of Java has avoided including new and untested features.

24.5 Conclusion

There are, of course, many more stories to tell. But this is not an encyclopedia; this chapter's goal has been to relate enough of the history to catch the reader's interest, but not so much as to lose it again! The Further Reading section, below, has some pointers into the literature for the interested reader.

The Turing Award, given annually by the ACM, is the most prestigious prize in computer science. Since it was first awarded in 1966, many of the winners have been (at least in part) programming-language pioneers. These include Alan Perlis, John McCarthy, Edsger Dijkstra, Donald Knuth, Dana Scott, John Backus, Robert Floyd, Kenneth Iverson, C. A. R. Hoare, Dennis Ritchie, Niklaus Wirth, John Cocke, Robin Milner, Kristen Nygaard, and Ole-Johan Dahl. One striking thing about the history of programming languages is how hard these very bright people have had to work on things that now seem easy. Take the idea of local variables with block scope, for example. Most beginning students have no trouble understanding this idea: an example or two, perhaps some brief explanation, and they have it. Or take the idea of using phrase-level control structures instead of `go to` statements; most beginning students immediately concede that this is almost always a good idea. But these ideas emerged only from the concentrated effort of great minds, and in some cases after long debate. Before becoming perfectly obvious to everyone, they were unknown and unguessed.

Within any branch of science it is always tempting to speculate that history is over. Perhaps all that will be discovered and invented, has been; perhaps no new history books will need to be written. The history of physics, for example, is full of such speculations. People routinely declare that physics is closed, only to have some new observation break it open again. What is next for the history of programming languages? It is possible that all the great discoveries have already been made—that research and development will now converge on one or several relatively stable languages. However, it seems likely that we will have the pleasure of seeing new ideas in programming languages, now unknown and unguessed, become perfectly obvious to everyone. The future development of programming languages will be fascinating to watch, whatever happens. Enjoy!

Further Reading

The quotation from a Babylonian algorithm is from a translation by Donald Knuth. It and others are found in his excellent paper on the Babylonian programmers:

> Knuth, Donald E. "Ancient Babylonian algorithms." *Communications of the ACM* 15, no. 7 (July 1972): 671–677.
>
> —"Errata." *Communications of the ACM* 19, no. 2 (February 1976): 108.

On the history of Charles Babbage and the Difference Engine, see

> Swade, Doron. *The Difference Engine: Charles Babbage and the Quest to Build the First Computer*. New York: Viking Press, 2001.

The history of Augusta Ada, Lady Lovelace, has been treated very differently by different historians. Her life was a strange and tragically short one. The extent of her mathematical knowledge and her technical contributions to Babbage's projects have been hotly debated. This book is a recent treatment of her life and times:

Woolley, Benjamin. *The Bride of Science: Romance, Reason, and Byron's Daughter*. New York: McGraw-Hill, 2000.

Konrad Zuse's autobiography is interesting and very readable:

Zuse, Konrad. *The Computer—My Life*. New York: Springer-Verlag, 1993.

Konrad Zuse's son Horst Zuse maintains a home page with many links to additional information about Konrad Zuse. His recent book, *Konrad Zuse, Der Vater des Computers*, had not yet been translated into English as of this writing.

The conference proceedings of the two ACM SIGPLAN History of Programming Languages conferences are highly detailed resources for the history of Fortran, Lisp, Algol, Simula, Smalltalk, Prolog, C, C++, and many other major programming languages:

Wexelblat, Richard, ed. *History of Programming Languages*. Burlington, MA: Academic Press, 1981.

Bergin, Thomas, and Richard Gibson, eds. *History of Programming Languages*. New York: ACM Press Books, 1996.

The quotations from Hopper, Backus, McCarthy, Kay, and Colmerauer and Roussel are taken from these sources.

This article is a fascinating look at the structured programming revolution:

Knuth, Donald E. "Structured programming with `go to` statements." *Computing Surveys* 6, no. 4 (December 1974).

It contains an interesting review of the `go to` debate. It is also interesting as a 1974 snapshot of Knuth's thinking on the future of programming languages.

The quotation from Christopher Strachey is from this source:

Stoy, Joseph E. *Denotational Semantics: The Scott-Strachey Approach to Programming Language Theory*. Cambridge, MA: The MIT Press, 1977.

The book is a technical account of denotational semantics, but it contains an interesting biographical sketch of Strachey in a foreword written by Dana Scott.

A number of articles on the history of Java are available online at the **http://java.sun.com** site.

The history of ML is outlined in Appendix E of this reference work:

> Milner, Robin, Mads Tofte, and Robert Harper. *The Definition of Standard ML*. Cambridge, MA: MIT Press, 1990.

The book is a complete technical definition of Standard ML, including the full natural semantics.

Finally, this book contains enjoyable nontechnical biographical sketches of Backus, McCarthy, Kay, Dijkstra, and other pioneers of computer science:

> Shasha, Dennis, and Cathy Lazere. *Out of Their Minds*.
> New York: Springer-Verlag, 1995.

Postscript

Let Us Go Down and Confuse Their Speech

It starts with isolation. After all,
If I could know your mind and feel your pain,
And undergo the workings of your brain—
It happens by induction. When you fall
You say the word. I hear and I recall
How falling felt. The meaning seems quite plain.
You sing, I soar; I thirst, you pray for rain.
But that prayer echoes from the temple wall
And, mumbled from mouth to mouth, develops fine
Distinctions, many meanings, low and high,
Some true, some false, all different, each one fits.
I say: I hope you'll have your God assign
His language its semantics. You reply:
And I, you, yours, His, its.

Index

Symbols

D

E

F

K

L

R

V

W

X

Z

Other Titles

from Franklin, Beedle & Associates

To order these books and find out more about Franklin, Beedle & Associates, visit us online at **www.fbeedle.com**.

Computer Science

ASP: Learning by Example (isbn 1-887902-68-6)
Basic Java Programming: A Laboratory Approach (isbn 1-887902-67-8)
Computing Fundamentals with C++: Object-Oriented Programming & Design: Second Edition (isbn 1-887902-36-8)
Computing Fundamentals with Java (isbn 1-887902-47-3)
Data Structures with Java: A Laboratory Approach (isbn 1-887902-70-8)
DHTML: Learning by Example (isbn 1-887902-83-X)—*Upcoming*
Fundamentals of Secure Computing Systems (isbn 1-887902-66-X)—*Upcoming*
Guide to Persuasive Programming (isbn 1-887902-65-1)
Prelude to Patterns in Computer Science Using Java: Beta Edition (isbn 1-887902-55-4)
XML: Learning by Example (isbn 1-887902-80-5)

Operating Systems

Linux eTudes (isbn 1-887902-62-7)
Linux User's Guide: Using the Command Line & Red Hat Linux with Gnome (isbn 1-887902-50-3)
Understanding Practical Unix (isbn 1-887902-53-8)
Windows 95: Concepts & Examples (isbn 1-887902-00-7)
Windows 98: Concepts & Examples (isbn 1-887902-37-6)
Windows 2000 Professional Command Line (isbn 1-887902-79-1)
Windows 2000 Professional: Concepts & Examples (isbn 1-887902-51-1)

Windows Millennium Edition: Concepts & Examples (isbn 1-887902-49-X)
Windows User's Guide to DOS: Using the Command Line in Windows 95/98 (isbn 1-887902-42-2)
Windows User's Guide to DOS: Using the Command Line in Windows 2000 Professional (isbn 1-887902-72-4)
Windows User's Guide to DOS: Using the Command Line in Windows Millennium Edition (isbn 1-887902-64-3)
Windows XP Command Line (isbn 1-887902-82-1)
Windows XP: Concepts & Examples (isbn 1-887902-81-3)

The Internet & the World Wide Web

Internet & Web Essentials: What You Need to Know (isbn 1-887902-40-6)
JavaScript Concepts & Techniques (isbn 1-887902-69-4)—*Upcoming*
Learning to Use the Internet & the World Wide Web (isbn 1-887902-78-3)
Searching & Researching on the Internet & the World Wide Web: Third Edition (isbn 1-887902-71-6)
Web Design & Development Using XHTML (isbn 1-887902-57-0)
The Web Page Workbook: Second Edition (isbn 1-887902-45-7)

Software Applications

Access 97 for Windows: Concepts & Examples (isbn 1-887902-29-5)
Excel 97 for Windows: Concepts & Examples (isbn 1-887902-25-2)
Microsoft Office 97 Professional: A Mastery Approach (isbn 1-887902-24-4)

Professional Reference & Technology in Education

The Dictionary of Computing & Digital Media Terms & Acronyms (isbn 1-887902-38-4)
The Dictionary of Multimedia (isbn 1-887902-14-7)
Technology Tools in the Social Studies Curriculum (isbn 1-887902-06-6)